New Media Influence on Social and Political Change in Africa

Anthony A. Olorunnisola
Pennsylvania State University, USA

Aziz Douai
University of Ontario Institute of Technology, Canada

A volume in the Advances in Human and
Social Aspects of Technology Book Series
(AHSAT)

An Imprint of IGI Global

Managing Director:	Lindsay Johnston
Editorial Director:	Joel Gamon
Production Manager:	Jennifer Yoder
Publishing Systems Analyst:	Adrienne Freeland
Development Editor:	Austin DeMarco
Assistant Acquisitions Editor:	Kayla Wolfe
Typesetter:	Christina Henning
Cover Design:	Jason Mull

Published in the United States of America by
Information Science Reference (an imprint of IGI Global)
701 E. Chocolate Avenue
Hershey PA 17033
Tel: 717-533-8845
Fax: 717-533-8661
E-mail: cust@igi-global.com
Web site: http://www.igi-global.com

Library of Congress Cataloging-in-Publication Data

New media influence on social and political change in Africa / Anthony A. Olorunnisola and Aziz Douai, editors.
    pages cm
  Includes bibliographical references and index.
  Summary: "This book addresses the development of new mass media and communication tools and its influence on social and political change, analyzing democratic transitions and cultures with a theoretical perspective"--Provided by publisher.
  ISBN 978-1-4666-4197-6 (hardcover) -- ISBN 978-1-4666-4198-3 (ebook) -- ISBN 978-1-4666-4199-0 (print & perpetual access) 1. Social media--Africa. 2. Mass media--Africa. 3. Social change--Africa. 4. Africa--Politics and government--21st century. I. Olorunnisola, Anthony A. II. Douai, Aziz, 1973-
  HM1206.N49 2013
  302.23'1--dc23
                                    2013009727

This book is published in the IGI Global book series Advances in Human and Social Aspects of Technology Book Series (AHSAT) (ISSN: Pending; eISSN: Pending)

British Cataloguing in Publication Data
A Cataloguing in Publication record for this book is available from the British Library.

All work contributed to this book is new, previously-unpublished material. The views expressed in this book are those of the authors, but not necessarily of the publisher.

Advances in Human and Social Aspects of Technology Book Series (AHSAT)

Ashish Dwivedi
The University of Hull, UK

ISSN: Pending
EISSN: pending

MISSION

In recent years, the societal impact of technology has been noted as we become increasingly more connected and are presented with more digital tools and devices. With the popularity of digital devices such as cell phones and tablets, it is crucial to consider the implications of our digital dependence and the presence of technology in our everyday lives.

The **Advances in Human and Social Aspects of Technology (AHSAT) Book Series** seeks to explore the ways in which society and human beings have been affected by technology and how the technological revolution has changed the way we conduct our lives as well as our behavior. The AHSAT book series aims to publish the most cutting-edge research on human behavior and interaction with technology and the ways in which the digital age is changing society.

COVERAGE

- Activism & ICTs
- Computer-Mediated Communication
- Cultural Influence of ICTs
- Cyber Behavior
- End-User Computing
- Gender & Technology
- Human-Computer Interaction
- Information Ethics
- Public Access to ICTs
- Technoself

IGI Global is currently accepting manuscripts for publication within this series. To submit a proposal for a volume in this series, please contact our Acquisition Editors at Acquisitions@igi-global.com or visit: http://www.igi-global.com/publish/.

Titles in this Series

For a list of additional titles in this series, please visit: www.igi-global.com

New Media Influence on Social and Political Change in Africa
Anthony A. Olorunnisola (Pennsylvania State University, USA) and Aziz Douai (University of Ontario Institute of Technology, Canada)
Information Science Reference ● copyright 2013 ● 373pp ● H/C (ISBN: 9781466641976) ● US $175.00 (our price)

Cases on Usability Engineering Design and Development of Digital Products
Miguel A. Garcia-Ruiz (Algoma University, Canada)
Information Science Reference ● copyright 2013 ● 362pp ● H/C (ISBN: 9781466640467) ● US $175.00 (our price)

Human Rights and Information Communication Technologies Trends and Consequences of Use
John Lannon (University of Limerick, Ireland) and Edward Halpin (Leeds Metropolitan University, UK)
Information Science Reference ● copyright 2013 ● 324pp ● H/C (ISBN: 9781466619180) ● US $175.00 (our price)

Collaboration and the Semantic Web Social Networks, Knowledge Networks, and Knowledge Resources
Stefan Brüggemann (Astrium Space Transportation, Germany) and Claudia d'Amato (University of Bari, Italy)
Information Science Reference ● copyright 2012 ● 387pp ● H/C (ISBN: 9781466608948) ● US $175.00 (our price)

Human Rights and Risks in the Digital Era Globalization and the Effects of Information Technologies
Christina M. Akrivopoulou (Democritus University of Thrace, Greece) and Nicolaos Garipidis (Aristotle University of Thessaloniki, Greece)
Information Science Reference ● copyright 2012 ● 363pp ● H/C (ISBN: 9781466608917) ● US $180.00 (our price)

Technology for Creativity and Innovation Tools, Techniques and Applications
Anabela Mesquita (ISCAP/IPP and Algoritmi Centre, University of Minho, Portugal)
Information Science Reference ● copyright 2011 ● 426pp ● H/C (ISBN: 9781609605193) ● US $180.00 (our price)

Social Computing Theory and Practice Interdisciplinary Approaches
Panagiota Papadopoulou (University of Athens, Greece) Panagiotis Kanellis (University of Athens, Greece) and Drakoulis Martakos (University of Athens, Greece)
Information Science Reference ● copyright 2011 ● 382pp ● H/C (ISBN: 9781616929046) ● US $180.00 (our price)

Law and Order in Virtual Worlds Exploring Avatars, Their Ownership and Rights
Angela Adrian (University of Bournemouth, UK)
Information Science Reference ● copyright 2010 ● 238pp ● H/C (ISBN: 9781615207954) ● US $180.00 (our price)

www.igi-global.com

701 E. Chocolate Ave., Hershey, PA 17033
Order online at www.igi-global.com or call 717-533-8845 x100
To place a standing order for titles released in this series, contact: cust@igi-global.com
Mon-Fri 8:00 am - 5:00 pm (est) or fax 24 hours a day 717-533-8661

Editorial Advisory Board

Table of Contents

Detailed Table of Contents

Section 1
The Politics of Change: Traditional Media, New Journalism and the Struggle for Reform

This introductory chapter maps out the trajectory of democratization in Africa and how old and new forms of mass media remain embedded in these efforts. Drawing on decades of media and political science research, the authors argue that no genuine democracy may exist without a vibrant media environment. Democracy thrives on "transparency" and "difference," and the media offer the platforms most suitable to ensure their existence and proliferation. The authors provide a theoretical grounding in order to further delineate the democracy media nexus, and review recent approaches to a systematic study of how communication technologies further or reverse the cause of social and political change. The authors conclude with a synoptic look at the important contributions published in this volume.

A core assumption of much of the literature on media in developing countries is that a more independent press with greater freedom will make a positive contribution to political change. In Morocco, a democratic transition started in 1997, when the opposition socialist party came to power and led the government. The new government's mission was to enact political reforms that aimed at promoting human rights, civil liberties, an open and pluralist media, and at establishing the rule of law. This paper examines the interplay between media policy, media institutions, and the government. To evaluate the nature of the political role of media in democratic transitions requires close scrutiny of three major factors: the legal, the economic, and the political environments. One important outcome of this research is that it will help determine whether Morocco's democratic reforms are meaningful reforms, or just empty attempts to pacify domestic and international public opinion.

Chapter 3

Terje S. Skjerdal, NLA University College, Norway

This chapter discusses recent developments in Ethiopian media governance. The developments point in two directions: Formally speaking, media policy is liberalized, exemplified by improved media legislation, better access to public information, and issuing of private broadcasting licences. However, informally speaking, Ethiopian media governance shows signs of coercion. This is seen for example in increased government control with the official news agency, use of anti-terrorism legislation against journalists, and obstruction of political websites. The chapter suggests that the paradoxes in Ethiopian media governance may be explained as a case of selective liberalization, implying that liberalization is primarily found in areas where the risk of losing control with the flow of information is less for the government. Alongside selective liberalization, there is an undercurrent of unofficial policy in Ethiopia that may represent a return to informal coercion towards the media industry.

Chapter 4

Heather Gilberds, Carleton University, Canada

The adoption of western models of journalism is a hallmark of media democratization movements in post-conflict, transitional or developing nations. However, media strengthening programs have received wide criticism from critical development scholars. This chapter interrogates the assumptions that underlie media development projects in Africa, which work to establish or reform journalism practices, by drawing on a case study of media strengthening in Rwanda. Drawing on discourse theory, it maps the discursive field that forms the basis for international assistance to build media capacity in developing and post-conflict regions. It also highlights the ways dominant development models are resisted in and through discourse, thereby drawing attention to the fluid and contingent operations of power that manifest in such institutionalized sites of knowledge production.

Chapter 5

Timothy W. Kituri, Royal Roads University, Canada

Democracy depends on a free and independent media to survive. As a democratic country, Kenya enjoys a media that is relatively free. This includes radio stations that broadcast in local languages and which provide the majority of Kenyans with access to news and entertainment. These local language radio stations have been singled out as a catalyst to the post-election violence that rocked Kenya in December 2007. Tribal messages that propagated hate and fear, based on political and historic events, were broadcast- -thus inciting violence. Critical Discourse Analysis is used in this study to explicate the ideologies of power through systemic investigation of the messages created and transmitted over the local language radio stations. This study contributes to the body of work done on media and democratization in Africa by showing how a gap regulatory and journalistic monitoring can jeopardize the watchdog function of media. The author recommends further research in these areas as a means of strengthening the role of media in building democracy in Africa.

Chapter 6

Ufuoma Akpojivi, North West University, South Africa

Media freedom is pivotal to the sustenance and consolidation of democracy, as the quality of democracy in any society depends on the level of freedom accorded the media and the plurality of views entertained (Diamond, 2008). The ability of the mass media to carry out their traditional functions of educating, entertaining and enlightening the public about their democratic rights, and holding governments accountable, will subsequently lead to the establishment of a strong democratic institution. Hence there is need to protect media freedom in any democratic society (Baker, 2007; Norris, 2008). The Nigerian media environment, however, is characterised by a series of laws such as sedition law, official secret act, amongst others, which have directly and indirectly hindered the freedom of the mass media and their responsibility of promoting and advancing democracy. This is made worse by the incomprehensive nature of the 1999 Constitution. Using interviews and policy analysis, this chapter critically examines the policy framework of media freedom in Nigeria and its impact on the operation of the mass media. The ability of the media to live up to their responsibility of promoting and advancing the democratisation process in Nigeria within the available framework is also examined.

Chapter 7

Twange Kasoma, Radford Univeristy, USA

Given their unparalleled histories and the dichotomous media regulatory frameworks that Zambia and Ghana have, the two countries make for an interesting pedagogical coupling for examining press freedom and the role of the media in African society. That is what this chapter strives to do. Methodologically, a textual analysis of pertinent documents as well as in-depth interviews with journalists is conducted. Some similarities and distinct differences are noted in the two countries' media regulatory landscapes. For example, both countries continue to lapse where passage of Freedom of Information legislation is concerned. Ghana, however, exhibits more progress than Zambia. The enabling laws Ghana has instituted in the past decade are telling. Ghana's progress is also evident in how journalists perceive their role in society in comparison to their Zambian counterparts. The former puts more emphasis on the media's agenda setting role than the latter.

Chapter 8

Ullamaija Kivikuru, University of Helsinki, Finland

The 1990s brought radical changes to Sub-Saharan Africa. In the rhetoric, the ownership mode appeared as a crucial marker of freedom. However, neither the access to the media nor the media content has changed much. The media mode, inherited from previous phases of social history, seems to change slowly. Old modes reproduce themselves in new media titles disregarding ownership mode. In this chapter, empirical evidence is sought from Namibia and Tanzania. The empirical evidence is based on two sets of one-week samples (2007, 2010) of all four papers. In this material, a government paper and a private paper from one particular country resemble each other more than when ownership modes are compared. Bearers of the journalistic culture seem to be to a certain extent media professionals moving from one editorial office to another, but the more decisive factors are the ideals set for journalism. The "first definition of journalism" reflects old times.

Brilliant Mhlanga, University of Hertfordshire, UK

This chapter focuses on the mediation of cultural pluralism by the South African Broadcasting Corporation's three ethnic minority radio stations: Munghana Lonene FM, Phalaphala FM, and X-K FM. By discussing these radio stations as case studies, the focus will be on their contribution to democratic ideation, and as forms of political disjunctures and continuities in radio broadcasting policy. On disjunctures, the chapter provides a microscopic perspective of the disengagement with the apartheid period as part of a throwback and as a way of charting a new path for a democratic South Africa. Its aim is to show the structural arrangements created and enacted into law by apartheid that had to be repealed and discontinued after 1994. During apartheid, radio broadcasting had been organised along ethnic lines, beginning with two broadcasting schedules in 1937; one for English speakers, known as service A; and service B for Afrikaans speakers. The 1960s in the South African broadcasting landscape marked the establishment of 'Bantu radio stations', which broadcasted mainly in indigenous ethnic languages. This stencil encouraged the creation of more ethnic focused radio stations in the '80s, which were later embraced by the post-apartheid leaders as a way of engendering cultural pluralism aimed at fostering democratic ideation and social transformation.

Irina Turner, Bayreuth University, Germany

The colonization of discourses (Chilton & Schäffner, 2002) is a wide-spread phenomenon of globalization and naturally affects politics. The power of business-speak over politics and the media seems to be steadily increasing. Most vulnerable to that development, which the author calls businification, seem to be countries in transition that have to assert themselves rhetorically on a global scale while keeping traditional voters content at home. In an application of critical discourse analysis, the chapter seeks to trace this businification by comparing three presidential state-of-the-nation-addresses (SoNA) of three South African presidents after one year in office (1995, 2000, and 2010). Through contextualizing these texts with their media reception from a corpus of 15 newspaper articles reporting on the speeches, the outer influences on the core text become transparent. The findings suggest a parallelism between a growing professionalism in politics and the businification of political rhetoric whose development cannot be viewed as exclusively negative.

Section 2
Technologies of Change: Understanding Africa's New Media Landscape

Sahar Khamis, University of Maryland, USA

This chapter analyzes the role of new media, especially Internet-based communication, in accelerating the process of political transformation and democratization in Egypt. It analyzes the Egyptian media landscape before, during and after the 2011 revolution which toppled the regime of President Hosni Mubarak. In the pre-revolutionary phase, the eclectic and paradoxical political and communication landscapes in Egypt, and the role that new media played in paving the way for the revolution, is discussed. During the 2011 revolution, the role of new media, especially social media, such as Facebook, Twitter, and YouTube, is highlighted in terms of the multiple roles they play as catalysts for change, avenues for civic engagement, and platforms for citizen journalism. In the post-revolutionary phase, the multiple changes and challenges exhibiting themselves after the revolution are analyzed, especially the divisiveness between different players in the Egyptian political arena and how it is reflected in the communication landscape.

Chapter 12

Aziz Douai, University of Ontario Institute of Technology, Canada
Mohamed Ben Moussa, McGill University, Canada

This chapter reports preliminary findings from a larger investigation of the role of social media and communication technologies in the "Arab Democracy Spring." The goal of the study is to analyze how Egyptian activists used Twitter during the 2011 protests. This stage of the project specifically outlines ways of identifying and classifying some of the most influential Egyptian Twitter users during these events. In addition to profiling the "influentials," this study applies a framing perspective to understanding Twitter's use among Egyptian activists.

Chapter 13

Mohamed Ben Moussa, McGill University, Canada

This chapter explores the role of the Internet in collective action in Morocco, and examines the extent to which the medium has empowered civil society and social movements in the North African country. Drawing on in-depth interviews conducted with activists belonging to key social movement organizations, the article analyzes how the appropriation of the Internet in activism is mediated through the socioeconomic and political structures proper to Morocco as a semi-authoritarian and developing country. In so doing, it sheds light on various intersections between technology diffusion, social movements' organizational structures, and multiple forms of power relationships among social and political actors. The article argues that the Internet has certainly transformed collective action repertoire deployed by Moroccan social movements; nevertheless, it also demonstrates that the impact of the Internet is conditioned by multiple forms of digital divides that are significantly shaping its implications for social and political change in the country.

Chapter 14

Duncan Omanga, Bayreuth University, Germany
Pamela Chepngetich-Omanga, Bayreuth University, Germany

Before the close of 2011, Kenya launched its own local version of a 'war on terror' following persistent border incursions by the al-Qaida affiliated al-Shabaab militant group. In a conflict that was seen by many to be fought largely through modern military hardware, the emergence and effective use of social media as yet another site of this warfare reflected the growing influence of new media in mobilizing, debating and circulating issues of public interest. Specifically, this chapter reveals the particular frames that were used in Twitter to keep members of the public informed on the front line developments of the

Operation Linda Nchi. Secondly, the study also investigates how the entrance of al-Shabaab into Twitter shaped the media framing of a war previously dominated by the more 'legitimate' Kenya Defence Force Twitter account. Finally, in a situation where the Twitter discourse was perceived and defined by the KDF as the official account of the war, this paper shows how the new and the old media converged in news reports in Kenya's main newspapers and the resultant frames from this convergence.

Chapter 15

Brandie L. Martin, The Pennsylvania State University, USA
Anthony A. Olorunnisola, The Pennsylvania State University, USA

Participants in varying but recent citizen-led social movements in Kenya, Iran, Tunisia, and Egypt have found new voices by employing new ICTs. In some cases, new ICTs were used to mobilize citizens to join and/or to encourage use of violence against other ethnicities. In nearly all cases, the combined use of new ICTs kept the world informed of developments as ensuing protests progressed. In most cases, the use of new ICTs as alternative media motivated international actors' intervention in averting or resolving ensuing crises. Foregoing engagements have also induced state actions such as appropriation of Internet and mobile phone SMS for counter-protest message dissemination and/or termination of citizens' access. Against the background of the sociology and politics of social movements and a focus on the protests in Kenya and Egypt, this chapter broaches critical questions about recent social movements and processes: to what extent have the uses of new ICTs served as alternative platforms for positive citizens' communication? When is use of new ICTs convertible into "weapons of mass destruction"? When does state repression or take-over of ICTs constitute security measures, and when is such action censorship? In the process, the chapter appraises the roles of local and international third parties to the engagement while underscoring conceptual definitions whose usage in studies of this kind should be conscientiously employed. Authors offer suggestions for future investigations.

Chapter 16

Auma Churchill Moses Otieno, Nation Media Group, Kenya
Lusike Lynete Mukhongo, Moi University, Kenya

The youth in Kenya are by far the majority age-group, yet their role in politics is hampered by their inability to access mainstream political information. The objective of the study is to determine whether there is any relationship between the level of youth engagement on social media and their level of interest in politics. The study uses the post-test quasi experiment to compare political interest between a naturally occurring group of Facebook users and a naturally occurring group of non-Facebook users. The findings of the study reveal that Facebook has provided the youth with a platform where they can access political information in formats that are appealing to them. Consequently, young people have been able to mobilise themselves online and push for a political agenda. There is, therefore, need to open up online exchanges in order to create a place for young people in mainstream political discourse in Kenya.

Chapter 17

R. Bennett Furlow, Arizona State University

Somalia has been plagued by political instability and ongoing conflict for over two decades. Yet, that does not mean Somalia has been completely isolated from modern technologies and new media. The construction of cell phone towers and other means of communication is a popular and profitable business in Somalia. One of the more recent additions to Somali new media is the use of microblogging. On

December 7, 2011, Somalia's al-Shabaab began a Twitter feed in both English and Arabic. In its first two months of tweeting, al-Shabaab promoted its successes on the ground, condemned what they see as unjustified acts of violence perpetrated against them, and engaged in a Twitter war with the Kenyan Defense Forces. This chapter seeks to analyze these first few months of al-Shabaab's Twitter activity. What are the main goals of al-Shabaab's use of Twitter? How effective have they been? How does their use of microblogging compare to other extremists' (such as the Taliban) use of Twitter? As Somalia is largely considered a failed state and internet penetration is not particularly dense, who is the intended audience?

Chapter 18

During the Benin presidential election of March 2011, a new communication tool (Internet) was added to the traditional tools of electoral campaign: meetings, electoral promotion gimmicks, political songs, broadcast and print media, and posters. Indeed, the three main candidates to the presidential elections integrated Internet in their comprehensive strategy, recruiting staff to take care of a Website, several user profiles on famous social networks. Meanwhile, the Internet is used by only 2.2% of the population. This chapter analyzes the Websites of the three candidates, paying particular attention to graphic design, uploaded available information, frequency of updating, and interaction with the audience. It also scrutinizes the use of various profiles on social networks. The chapter then interrogates why there was such an important investment on the Internet during this campaign, whereas data show that very few potential voters are actually connected to the Internet in Benin. This chapter identifies the role of Internet campaigning and the place that the Internet has taken in the electoral communication strategies, and tries to understand the real purpose behind this use.

Chapter 19

The purpose of this chapter is to evaluate the effect and potentials of social media as a tool for social, political, and economic change in Africa. This chapter argues that social media has become so entrenched in various facets of society that it has become a mechanism impacting social, political, and economic life in Africa. This chapter looks at the 2011 Nigerian elections and the worldwide Kony Movement against Kony the Ugandan warlord, as tools/examples of analysis. These are some of the developments that have driven the debate about the ability of social media in bringing about social, economic, and political change and participation in the African continent. The research method adopted in this chapter involves an analysis of a growing scholarship addressing the various arguments proffered on this topic. The chapter concludes by establishing the impact of social media on social, economic, and political life in Africa as well as identifying challenges posed by this development and making recommendations for the regulatory framework required to effectively harness these potentials in Africa.

Chapter 20

As popular movements of citizens of countries in the Middle East and North African (MENA) region progressed, and in their aftermath, pundits in Nigeria and the Diaspora wondered if there would be a bandwagon effect in Africa's largest democracy. Yet, despite offline and online mobilizations, a growing national insecurity and the "Occupy Nigeria Movement" that sprang up against fuel price hikes in Nigeria, protests and revolts in Nigeria remained short-lived and aimed at piecemeal policy reforms rather than becoming a revolution to unseat the current government. Relying on a human development factors chart, the authors suggest that Nigerians' discontent appears to be motivated by yearnings for what citizens of some MENA countries already have and vice versa. As such, neither democracy nor autocracy—as systems of governance—has delivered the aspirations of African citizens.

Chapter 21

Kennedy Javuru, Journalist & Independent Scholar, UK

This chapter gives an exploratory overview of the emergence and growth of new media in Uganda and how the alternative nature of new media is scaffolding the notion of citizenship and deliberative democracy. The chapter also suggests that despite the new found vigour, it is too early to say whether the Ugandan new media landscape have so far become a true alternative or complementary participatory space or a genuine platform for the distribution of uncensored information. It concludes that Ugandans use new media more for social interaction and dissemination of information (in a limited way) than as an alternative political public sphere. However, there are signs that online media is emerging and the anecdotes presented in this chapter indicate the potential of this media to be a place of participation and deliberation and reducing the authoritarian control of the communicative space.

Chapter 22

Tendai Chari, University of Venda, South Africa

Online publications have become critical sites for the expression of views alternative to those of the state. This is true in Zimbabwe as in many developing states where the mainstream media operate under onerous legislative frameworks. However, the real impact of these 'new public spheres' on the country's democratization agenda is subject to contestation. This chapter examines the impact of online publications run by exiled Zimbabwean journalists on the country's democratization process. The chapter evaluates the extent to which these online publications constitute genuine alternative spaces for the mediation of national discourses. Data is elicited through focus group interviews, in-depth interviews, and textual analysis. The chapter argues that a combination of technical, social, and economic factors which limit Internet access and professional shortcomings conspire against online publications becoming genuine alternative public spheres, thus minimizing their role in the democratization of the Zimbabwean state.

Chapter 23

Nhamo Anthony Mhiripiri, Midlands State University, Zimbabwe
Bruce Mutsvairo, University of Twente, The Netherlands

Social media in its various forms drew international attention to Zimbabwe during the most intense period of the Zimbabwe crisis up to 2008. It is arguable that social media activism was contributory to the current dispensation of Government of National Unity between ZANU PF and the former opposition Movement for Democratic Change. Social media induced revolution and mass rejection of the status quo of the magnitude seen in the Arab Spring might be difficult to replicate in Zimbabwe. A similar revolution with different magnitude but critical results unfolds in Zimbabwe, especially since the disputed 2008 presidential elections and the mayhem that followed. The use of new communication technologies helped publicize extra-legal activities and human rights abuses often blamed on ZANU PF affiliated militia groups and the security forces. International attention has led to diplomatic intervention.

This summative chapter synthesizes a few of the 26 contributors' solo and interconnected presentations
and lays out the ideas and propositions therein in a way that a single author of a book would have done.
To achieve these objectives the chapter draws readers' attention to the conceptual and practical evidences
that scholars—whose joint efforts have helped us put this book together—employed in their treatment
of a hydra-headed issue with multi-dimensional questions. The intent is to present readers with some, of
many possible dimensions, from which to appraise the chapters in this book. To this end, thematic categories
are employed and efforts made to underscore consistencies and inconsistencies between authors'
propositions. The chapter also includes suggestions of areas needing further inquiries as those pointers
may help scholars sustain an ongoing conversation about the evolving issues addressed in this volume.

Preface

Though the terms are independent and often conjoined, the media in Africa have always played an important role in democratic and non-democratic states. African countries under autocratic dispensations have witnessed media collaborations with civil society to resist and oppose as well as to confirm prevailing public and political views on issues of the day. As well, media in African nations transiting from autocracy to democracy have focused on politicians, diplomats, activists, and members of civil society who worked toward completion of political transformations. As institutions, the mass media have also been objects of scrutiny, particularly when they are controlled by government and/or are run by major businesses and when their editorial policies are either influenced by partisanship or by profit margins; both of which stir controversies. Communication researchers, in particular those whose publications focus on the media and political institutions in Africa, have extensively treated foregoing issues using competing paradigms and different methodological approaches.

This book steps into that tradition but offers new insights into the ways in which old and new media and communication technologies have influenced Africa's struggles for social and political change in the 21st Century. While the "Arab Spring" events have rekindled scholars' interests in the new/media's role in democratic shifts worldwide, little attention has been paid to the way in which these winds of change are affecting countries on the African continent. The easy but deceptive answer could be that most African countries have been immune from these political upheavals because of the intransigence of political regimes, failed democratic transitions, and/or stultifying political cultures in most of the continent. A closer analysis of African realities and developments, however, would reveal an alternative portrait of several fundamental changes that are constantly transforming the political and cultural landscapes. This book documents these transformations by focusing on how traditional mass media and new information and communication tools are spawning digital cultures that contribute to the continent's long struggle for democracy. Contributing authors–twenty-six in all based on four continents--offer theoretical depth, a broad set of cases and national experiences for consideration by (new) media and democracy scholars as well as practitioners in government, inter-governmental and non-governmental organizations and activists in civil society–all of whom are concerned with the focus of this volume.

Contributors analyze national cases in which both traditional and new media have been deeply involved in Africa's struggle for social and political change. Several reasons explain the editors' decision to devote roughly a quarter of the book to "traditional" media. One of the reasons is our strong conviction that the terms "old" and "new" might be simplistic and misleading in suggesting a neat and rigid distinction between traditional mass media and digital media. In reality, however, the boundaries between "old" and "new" media are more fluid and fuzzy as traditional media increasingly move toward digitization–bearing in mind as well that segments of the media now categorized as "old" were at a stage in media-technology development considered "new." Radio was "new" and posed challenges to "old" newspapers; when TV was "new" it posed challenges to "old" radio and so on. In today's world of convergence all those media forms remain in coexistence. For instance, African newspapers, as an example of traditional or "old" media, have been moving to digitize their contents in order to make them available online to local and diaspora audiences. Newspapers' incorporation of "new" media goes beyond the online availability of their content to include adaptation of "new" media formats, such as blogging, in reporting the news. The boundaries become even fuzzier and muddled when some well-established newspapers in the West, such as *The Christian Science Monitor*, cease their print edition and decide to exclusively publish their news reports online. The nature of the medium aside, media professionals in African countries are working in outfits that combine both traditional media and "new media" environments. Today's reporters are expected to post their stories online, be proficient in the use of social media, as well as possess "traditional" media skills, such as reporting and writing. In addition, the legal and regulatory environments in which "old" and "new" media operate are largely similar, if not the same, in many countries. Many governments of African states have found ways to impose restrictions on new media–including those whose operations are in remote places (e.g., African Diasporas). To this end, many contributors' chapters straddle both "old" and "new" media references, though some chapters weigh heavily on one than the other.

The book's thematic organization brings "traditional" and "new" media together to address two overarching and interrelated questions: How have new information and communication technologies informed traditional media's struggle for political and social reforms in Africa? And how might "new" media be called upon in the fight for political reform? Section I, "The Politics of Change: Traditional Media, New Journalism and the Struggle for Reform," includes contributions that analyze several African nations' struggles to enact credible reforms and enhance sustainable democratic institutions. In Section II of the book, "Technologies of Change: Understanding Africa's New Media Landscape," the contributors switch gears and critically assess the "new" media debates in Africa, presenting actual cases in which new media played, or were called upon to play, a central role in the fight for social and political reforms. Within these two sections of the book, the chapters are organized geographically: We begin each section from North Africa, move to East, West, Central African nations and end with contributions focused on Southern African nations.

This book does not sugarcoat strides that have been made in several African nations nor does it cover transgressions involving stakeholders across government, media (old and new), and citizens as the struggle for the administrative souls of represented African countries continue. On the contrary, contributing authors unabashedly assess the successes and challenges that have accompanied attempts to install democratic governance in African countries. Authors responded to Editors' call for chapters that question received answers and problematize the consistencies and inconsistencies between principles and institutions informing western democracy vis-à-vis African political cultures. Many authors identified autocratic symptoms in the form of stringent media regulations including cases where newly installed media reforms have been reversed. Simply put, and as readers will find, the implementation of democratic reforms in Africa's political systems have had mixed outcomes and influences on personal and institutional freedoms to engage in social and political discourse. This book volume takes stock of these developments.

From the editors' initial call for chapters, the ambition driving this book project was abundantly clear. We wanted to publish a volume that would connect scholarship from both the global North and South in the analysis of Africa's complex social, cultural and political landscapes. The original vision was to have a volume that would transcend the traditional biases of geography and politics by providing a broad and deep coverage of African democratic experiences. Showcasing seasoned and upcoming scholars from four continents, we are pleased and grateful that this crop of contributors has assisted us to achieve these lofty goals. We thank all the contributors for their time and effort, and we would like to express our deep gratitude to the scholars who assisted us in peer-reviewing more than 60 initial submissions. Their rigorous assessments made this work possible. We are grateful to Dean Douglas Anderson and Associate Dean Marie Hardin–both of the College of Communications at the Pennsylvania State University–for their generous donation of funds with which we employed editorial assistants. We appreciate the assistance of Dr. Ralph B. Ojebuyi of the Department of Communication and Language Arts at the University of Ibadan. Though removed by many nautical miles, he assisted with proofreading under a stringent deadline but with diligence. To IGI's editorial staff, thank you for your dedication and indispensable assistance through stages of the publication process. We dedicate this work to our families whose sacrifice and tolerance have made this book possible. In the final analysis the main actors, heroes and heroines in our analyses of the trajectories of democratic governance in Africa are its peoples–Africans of all ethnic and racial backgrounds who have gone through decades of struggle in search of "good governance." We doff our hats to their courage over the years and continuing resilience.

Aziz Douai
University of Ontario Institute of Technology, Canada

Anthony Olorunnisola
Pennsylvania State University, USA

Section 1
The Politics of Change:
Traditional Media, New Journalism and the Struggle for Reform

Chapter 1
New Media and the Question of African Democracy

Aziz Douai
University of Ontario Institute of Technology, Canada

Anthony Olorunnisola
Pennsylvania State University, USA

ABSTRACT

This introductory chapter maps out the trajectory of democratization in Africa and how old and new forms of mass media remain embedded in these efforts. Drawing on decades of media and political science research, the authors argue that no genuine democracy may exist without a vibrant media environment. Democracy thrives on "transparency" and "difference," and the media offer the platforms most suitable to ensure their existence and proliferation. The authors provide a theoretical grounding in order to further delineate the democracy media nexus, and review recent approaches to a systematic study of how communication technologies further or reverse the cause of social and political change. The authors conclude with a synoptic look at the important contributions published in this volume.

GENERAL INTRODUCTION

The Internet is the first truly post-colonial medium for the simple reason that its popularity has taken root in a world that is largely decolonized. That has not prevented it from becoming a pivotal tool in peoples' struggle for democratic governance across the globe, from Ukraine's "Orange Revolution" to "Occupy Wall Street" In New York.

Scrutinize the context of the "Arab Spring," and it will be impossible to escape the mesmerizing talk of the possibilities the Internet and new media have opened for social and political action in the contemporary world. Indeed, the "Arab Spring" has decimated authoritarian regimes in the Middle East and North Africa, including those of Tunisia's Zine El Abidine Ben Ali, Egypt's Hosni Mubarak, and Libya's Muammar Gaddafi. Like their name-

DOI: 10.4018/978-1-4666-4197-6.ch001

sake, the "Prague Spring" of 1968, these historical developments reminded the world that the peoples residing in this strategic part of the globe are tired of being denied their basic freedoms, participation in democratic governance and absence of the rule of the law. However, the analogy between the two "springs" might end there because the "Arab Spring" was unprecedented in the way it catapulted scholarly and layman discussions of social media's potential effects on social and political change. The technological tinge of these debates can be directly gleaned from news headlines that dubbed Egypt's uprising against authoritarianism a "Twitter Revolution," or described Tunisia's sacking of its dictator as the first "WikiLeaks Revolution." If Twitter and Facebook largely testify to our wired and interconnected "global public sphere" (Sparks, 2001), WikiLeaks and its founder, Julian Assange, speak for an ethos that defends the transparent and free-flow of information. Information and the means of acquiring and spreading it globally have underpinned how the "Arab Spring" was covered in local and global media (Stepanova, 2011), how non-Arab audiences arguably perceived it (Shelley, 2011), and how new media have been mobilized in the struggle for social and political change worldwide.

This introductory chapter maps out the trajectory of democratization in Africa and how old and new forms of mass media remain embedded in these efforts. Drawing on decades of media and political science research, we argue that no genuine democracy may exist without a vibrant media environment. Democracy thrives on "transparency" and "difference," and the media offer the platforms most suitable to ensure their existence and proliferation. We provide a theoretical grounding in order to further delineate the democracy media nexus, and review recent approaches to a systematic study of how communication technologies further or reverse the cause of social and political change. We conclude with a synoptic look at the important contributions published in this volume.

THE DEMOCRACY/MEDIA NEXUS: AFRICA'S "LOST" DECADES

The advent of mass media has coincided with the growing legitimacy of modern democracy as a form of governance. Since liberal democracy is predicated on the rule of law, free elections, press freedom and civil society (Henze, 1998), a brief look at how it functions would reveal a symbiotic relationship between the democracy and media. Democracy involves the peaceful competition among political actors and parties to implement their social and economic vision in a society. Instead of resorting to arms and guns to settle ideological disputes, these political actors resort to the ballot box through which voters voice their support for or rejection of a political platform or a leader. Democracy involves "checks and balances," the institutional constraints placed on those who gain voter support, what is usually known as the executive branch of government. A third condition or aspect of democracy is ensuring that all citizens have the right to express their opinions and enjoy their civil liberties without fear of reprisal. In all these steps of the democratic ladder, the news media enhance the democratic process. The news media offer a platform to these political actors to air and share their visions with voters and the rest of society. The media's coverage of elections not only seek to hold political candidates to task, but they guarantee most citizens and voters sufficient information to make informed judgments about the merits of each election's platforms. Finally, the media strengthen those "checks and balances" in their "watchdog" functions on those who wield political power. Article 19 of the Universal Declaration of Human Rights captures this link between these two fundamental freedoms:

Everyone has the right to freedom of opinion and expression; this right includes freedom to hold opinions without interference and to seek, receive and impart information and ideas through any media and regardless of frontiers.

No wonder that all modern democratic experiments could not survive without the existence of a free press (as any review of the history of democracy would demonstrate).

Political scientists, democracy analysts and policy researchers have confronted a serious question: What factors lead authoritarian countries to democratize? A large body of research has tackled the question of democratization, the process by which countries transition from authoritarian rule to a democratic political system. Rummel (1996) observes that while very little consensus exists about the pathways to democracy, "incremental development" of democratic institutions seems to be the favorite means of achieving democracy. Great Britain's enduring democratic system came to being because of the people's gradual and incessant demands for more political rights and curtailment of the monarchy's powers. A second path to democracy lies through revolutions, like the American or French revolutions, although this path

can be uncertain. During the 20th century, foreign powers "midwifed" democracy through defeating authoritarian regimes, as the examples of Japan and Germany showed, or "incubated" democratic institutions during colonization eras (Rummel, 1996). In general, contemporary democratization can be viewed as the outcome of both "external" and/or "internal" forces that push authoritarian regimes to reform their approaches to governance, or relinquish their powers to democratically elected representatives (See Figure 1).

The "external" forces refer to "exogenous" parties that persuade a state to adopt democracy, including but not limited to foreign powers, international donors, and international organizations (governmental and non-governmental). "Internal" forces refer to "endogenous" parties from within the country whose clamor for more rights and reforms eventually establishes a democratic system. The "internal" forces include but are not limited to local elites, social movements, labor

Figure 1. Media and Democracy interactions

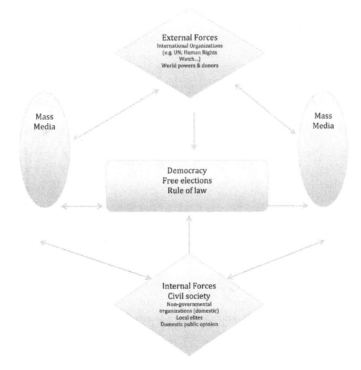

and student unions, political oppositions, and other members of civil society. Sometimes, these "external" and "internal" forces have to merge and coordinate their efforts to compel recalcitrant regimes to adopt, and in some cases not to "backslide" from, democracy. Moreover, the mass media as institutions play mediating roles that enable these "external" and "internal" forces to make their cases for democracy.

Democratic governance has continued to develop in fits and starts, expanding and receding throughout the globe. Democracy scholars have described the expansion of democracy worldwide in terms of three long "waves," three broad eras in which democracy has become prevalent in contemporary nation states (Huntington, 1991; Diamond, 1996). The first "long" wave of democratization corresponds with the period between 1802 and the 1920s. Political rights, holding regular elections, and safeguarding other civil liberties became part of the democratic institu-

tions in the U.S., Canada, and some European countries. The "second wave" of democratization began roughly after 1944 with the triumph of the Allies over Nazi Germany. During this period, many former colonies in Africa, Asia, and Latin America experimented with democratic governance. Many countries, however, pursued the path of socialism and communism with one party rule during the Cold War (1944-1989). The collapse of Portugal's dictatorship in 1974 and of Franco's dictatorship in Spain in 1975 ushered the "third wave" (1974-present) of democratization. Along this path, democratic reversals, "reverse waves," and backsliding have frequently halted the expansion of democratic governance, with many new democracies failing to consolidate their gains and reversing to authoritarianisms. The Polity Project (2012) has coded the characteristics of authority in world states, and captured the historically uneven path of democratic governance featured in Figure 2. This visual representation reveals how the late

Figure 2. Global trends in governance (courtesy of University of Colorado and University of Maryland's Polity IV Project: Political Regime Characteristics and Transitions, 1800-2010; see http://www.systemicpeace.org/polity/polity4.htm)

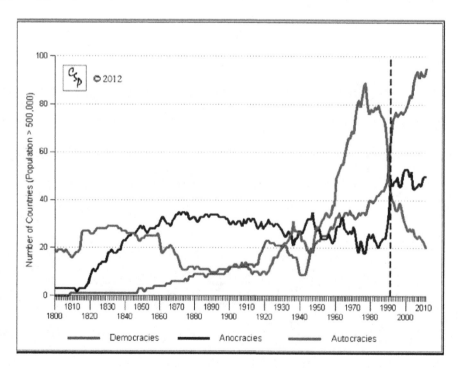

1990s showed a clean break for democracy, as the number of democratic states exceeded the number of authoritarian regimes for the first time in history.

What did this democratization wave mean for Africa and how did it work? First, several factors converged to push some African countries to democratize during this "third wave," chiefly authoritarian regimes' loss of legitimacy and world powers' shifting policies towards their "client" states. The end of the Cold War and the collapse of the Berlin Wall indicated that the receding bipolar international system was no longer there to prop up corrupt authoritarian regimes in order to score "ideological" goals. No longer was it possible for African strongmen to use the crutch of decolonization and anti-imperialism to establish their post-colonial legitimacy. Second, economic expansion and liberal economic policies were increasingly associated with this latest democratization wave (Huntington, 1991). The liberalization wave of the 1990s meant that international institutions like the International Monetary Fund (IMF) and the World Bank linked their financial and economic assistance in Africa to the promotion of democratic governance. African countries were required to conduct regular elections, open their markets to outside competition, privatize state-owned enterprises, and establish competitive and transparent economic policies. Although he was not very optimistic about the future of democratization in Africa, Huntington (1991) asserted that "(e)conomic development makes democracy possible; political leadership makes it real" (p. 35). In other terms, economic and political forces jointly decide the fate of democratic experiments.

Africa had not been immune to the post-Cold War democratization "third wave" as multiparty elections, constitutional reforms, and political transitions from autocratic rule frequently dotted the continent in the 1990s. From Nigeria, Niger, and Mali to Benin, Senegal, and Ghana, democratization trends were unmistakable albeit uneven (Young, 1996). Take the example of Ethiopia's

democratic transition in the 1990s. As soon as the communist regime of Mengistu Haile Maryam was overthrown, the Ethiopian People's Democratic Revolutionary Front (EPRDF) opened up the political landscape by encouraging a multi-party system in an "ethnic federal" state. Paul B. Henze, a close observer of Ethiopian politics, commented on the democratic stalemate in the country and lauded its press environment that ensured the democratic transition as a net gain for democracy. He described foregoing scenario as follows:

One encouraging development has been the emergence since the mid-1990s of more responsible and informative, independent newspapers that are not connected to political parties. Several appear two or three times a week, offering readers objective news and well-researched reports on important economic and social issues, as well as intelligent editorial comment. They do not hesitate to challenge government spokesmen and to encourage responsible public debate. Their competence and professionalism has (sic) won them the respect of government officials. At the same time, more polemical publications, some supported by exiles via facsimile and electronic mail, continue to spread misinformation (Henze, 1998, n.p.).

The 1990s' slow move toward democracy screeched to a halt as President Meles Zenawi and his party decimated political opposition in the decade following 2000. The latter was unfortunately a common experience in several African nations.

In Morocco, for instance, King Mohamed VI ascended the throne and initiated political transition and democratic reform that fostered a free and independent press (Douai, 2009). It took only a few years to quash a fragile press freedom as journalists were routinely harassed or jailed in the country (Reporters Without Borders, 2010).

Nigeria's return to post-militaristic democracy has stabilized since 1999 when the last military autocracy handed over to a democratically-elected government. The return to partisan politics produced many parties with regional bases reminiscent of Nigeria's first and second republics. All through ongoing fourth republic, the People's Democratic Party (PDP) has emerged as the only party with a national clout. Though attempts have been made multiple times, regional opposition parties have exhibited minimal abilities to mount strong opposition at the national level to the PDP which has won all presidential elections to date and continues to dominates the lower and upper houses of the national assembly.

Given its checkered history of democratic incursions, the media in Nigeria have enjoyed wider margins of freedom than media in other African countries. Among newsworthy developments during the fourth republic is the adoption of the Freedom of Information Act in May 2011. The development followed a decade or longer of consistent advocacy for transparency by stakeholders in the civil society. President Goodluck Jonathan signed the "right to information" law soon after his inauguration in order to expand citizens' and media practitioners' access to government information. In the words of Fatou Jagne-Senghore of Article 19 West Africa, the "new Freedom of Information Act will consolidate the existing legal arsenal established over the years to curb corruption and create an accountable government. It will contribute to empowering Nigerian citizens to exert some degree of control over the actions of their leaders and monitor the use of public resources," (Article 19, 2011).

However, the extent to which the media in Nigeria can capitalize on the provisions of this law to expand the space of transparency in governance remains to be seen. Observers have noted the inability of practitioners in the old (print, especially newspapers and news magazines) media to continue under democratic dispensation the investigative and journalistic incisiveness with which they fought against colonial and military rulers. More recent evidence of investigative journalism has migrated to online locations where citizens' media–with operators located outside

of Nigeria–have led efforts to hold the extant democratic government accountable. As Farooq Kperogi (2012, p. 452) noted:

Government's response has ranged from "blackmail, arrests, detention of bloggers, attempts to block diasporan citizens media sites from being viewed in Nigeria, web counter-offensives, hacking of the diasporan citizen media, and cooptation of oppositional bloggers, to the initiation of expensive libel suits against particularly radical online media like Sahara Reporters and Elendu Reports (before it lost credibility due to its infiltration by the same corrupt politicians it had exposed in its earlier form.

It is now more common for practitioners in the local media to report scoops that originate in citizens' media located online, perhaps as a way of deflecting reprisals from government to citizens that are geographically out-of-reach until they make attempts to visit Nigeria and are arrested at the airports. The ability of practitioners in the old media to find a way to hold Nigeria's democratic government accountable is the challenge of contemporary times.

The post-Apartheid South Africa represented the most sustained democratic experiment in the continent. South Africa has since the commencement of multi-racial democracy in 1994 stabilized government by the majority. The country's post-apartheid journey is against all odds at the precipice of a third decade. On December 17, 2012, President Zuma won re-election as leader of ANC, South Africa's ruling party. By default and going by the comparative powerlessness of parties in opposition to ANC, he will win a second term in office. However, events leading to and during the party's Congress in Bloemfontain underscore location of South African democratic governance under the ANC. Criticized for weak leadership and his inability to unify factions of the party among other administrative problems, President Zuma defended the ANC's ability to lead the rainbow nation's economic recovery program. "We want to dismiss the perceptions that our country is falling apart because of the downgrades," he said. "We continue to do our development work, we continue to plan for a recovery," he added (Herskovitz & Govender, 2012). The downgrades–from "BBB+" to "BBB-"–to which Zuma referred were handed down by international rating agencies, including Fitch, which cited policy uncertainty, absence of progress on education and labor reforms as well as insufficient job growth to stem a 25% unemployment rate among others.

Challenges to the democratic space in South Africa during President Zuma's first five-year term have not been limited to the inability of his political party to sustain a political economy able to sustain South Africans' economic empowerment to the satisfaction of all stakeholders. A number of policy changes also threatened to limit the power of the media. A good example is the Protection of State Information Bill (POIB) which remained controversial as stakeholders debated its contributions to state secrecy and the dangers that it posed to investigative journalism. The ANC offered to remove a clause that would diminish provisions of a pre-existent Promotion of Access to Information Bill and a second provision that would impose tough sentences on those who reveal information classified by the State Security Agency. Zwelinzima Vavi, the general secretary of the Congress of South African Trade Unions (COSATU), and a strident critic of POIB opined that the iteration of the bill that passed before the National Assembly in 2011 would return South Africa "to the police state we left in 1994 ... (e) verything marked confidential and everybody seeing something marked confidential suddenly fearing 15- to 25-year imprisonment" (Hlongwane, 2012).

While democracy literature does not explicitly describe it as such, there is no escaping the fact that all democratic transitions have to involve some level of media reform, or media "transitions." The "third wave" of democratization in many African nations spawned a raft of such press laws and media reforms with the explicit intention of supporting new and fragile democratic institutions and the rule of law. Many African states concurred with The Windhoek Declaration signed in Namibia on May 3, 1991. Following a UNESCO sponsored seminar on freedom of the press, this Declaration reiterated the principle that information is a fundamental human right, and thus reaffirming the international principles and laws regarding these issues. Article 1 of The Windhoek Declaration makes these linkages absolutely clear:

Consistent with article 19 of the Universal Declaration of Human Rights, the establishment, maintenance and fostering of an independent, pluralistic and free press is essential to the development and maintenance of democracy in a nation, and for economic development.

Following the declaration, Gabon's Ordinance No. 07/93 (1 October 1993) laid out the legal framework for the operation of the media and guarantees journalists' freedom to gather and use information. The Central African Republic's 1995 constitution recognized these freedoms by unequivocally stating that "the freedom to inform, and to air one's views through speech, writing and pictures, subject to the right of the other person shall be guaranteed" (Cited in Lingo & Lober, 2001). Audio-visual/broadcast laws were revamped in Cameroon with the passage of a governmental Decree (April 3, 2000). Access to information and other freedom of information laws were ensconced in constitutional reforms. Further, Ethiopia's 1992 press law affirmed that the press "have the right to seek, obtain and report news and information from any government source of news and information" and that they "have the right to disseminate news, information and other products of press in their possession" (Proclamation No 34/1992; Berger, 2007).

Independent regulatory agencies and bodies sprang in Senegal, Cameron, and Morocco, among others. Morocco's Haute Autorité de la Communication Audiovisuelle (HACA), for instance, was charged with ensuring "the freedom of audiovisual communication, and the freedom of audiovisual enterprise, in the respect of universal principles of pluralism and information objectivity, as well as the values of Moroccan civilization." More importantly, it signaled the country's stated intention to liberalize and privatize the broadcasting sector. Professional journalists' associations seeking to uphold and establish professional ethics sprang in many countries such as the "Journalistes en danger" (Journalists in danger). While The Windhoek Declaration went on to inspire the UN General Assembly to declare May 3 as World Press Freedom Day, 53 African states sought to incorporate these press rights and recommendations in the Constitutive Act of the African Union by promising to promote "human and peoples' rights in accordance with the African Charter on Human and Peoples' Rights and other relevant human rights instruments" (Berger, 2007).

Our book's contribution to Africa's democratization debate underscores how "new" media appear to resuscitate the hope for social and political change across the continent. We revisit several democratic experiences to specifically address our first central question: How have new information and communication technologies informed traditional media's struggle for political and social reforms in Africa? In Part I, "The Politics of Change: Traditional Media, New Journalism and the Struggle for Reform," the first 10 chapters of the volume tackle this question and present findings that highlight the problematic and challenging quest for democracy. In Chapter 2, for instance, Bouziane Zaid reviews Morocco's media landscape and concludes that "[s]ocial media triggered a revival of the watchdog function of the media and paved the way for it to act as a fourth estate in controlling the misconduct of the political regime" (p. 15). Terje Skjerdal examines the question from the vantage points of "media

reforms" in Ethiopia's "emerging democracy," as he convincingly argues that "the paradoxes in Ethiopian media governance may be explained as a case of *selective liberalization*" (Chapter 3, p. 32). Heather Gilberds' Chapter 4 focuses on how international media development work is implicated in the project of media reform. She presents this thorough interrogation of "the assumptions that underlie media development projects in Africa, which work to establish or reform journalism practices, by drawing on a case study of media strengthening in Rwanda" (p. 51). In Chapter 5, Timothy Kituri's discursive analysis of local radio broadcasts finds out that radio messages still play an important role in "fanning the flames" of hate, inciting ethnic violence after a contested election in Kenya.

Ufuoma Akpojivi's critical policy analysis of media freedom in Nigeria concludes that democratic consolidation hinges upon the country's "media laws and policies governing the media sphere must be re-examined and reviewed" (Chapter 6, p. 84). In Chapter 7, Twange Kasoma further supports such call as her comparison of Ghana's and Zambia's reasserts the primacy of constitutional and legal reforms in ensuring media freedom. Chapter 8 offers a different take on the issue of media freedom in the continent, specifically the journalistic culture in Tanzania and Namibia. Ullamaija Kivikuru concludes that "Far more important than the ownership mode and even media laws in Africa is to learn to discuss and reflect with the people, not to the people" (p. 118). Democratic consolidation should not neglect the importance of cultural pluralism in the media's landscape, as Brilliant Mhlanga's analysis of South African Broadcasting Corporation's three ethnic minority radio stations reveals. Irina Turner's Chapter 10 brings this discussion back to how business discourse dominated media discourse covering South African politics. She warns that "(t)he particular danger in the naturalization of business language in the political and media discourse lies in the condensation of meaning that disguises complex implications known to experts from the business world, but unknown to the general public" (p.).

A NEW MEDIA LANDSCAPE: IS IT AFRICA'S PROMISED "FOURTH WAVE"?

The proliferation of new information and communication technologies (ICTs) might be said to coincide with, if not usher, a "fourth wave" of democratization, not unlike the grunt work involved in updating regulatory press regimes that happened largely during the "third wave" of democratic transitions in the late 1990s. While the continent as a whole lags behind in terms of Internet penetration and adoption of ICTs, recent data from the United Nations (UN ICT Task Force, 2005) demonstrate a viable growth in the ICTs sector. At the end of the 20th century, the number of African mobile phone users was on track to exceed traditional landline phone users according to statistics compiled by the International Telecommunication Union (ITU). Impressive growth in the sector continued as total African telecoms market was projected to grow by more than US$40 billion in 2013. The linkages between ICTs and economic development are strong for the simple reason that ICTs have become central to the way business thrives at the level of product innovation and services delivery (Tcheng et al., 2007). Some studies have suggested that ICTs' penetration in Africa have led to greater financial inclusion of underprivileged citizens (IMF, 2010). The exponential growth of social media and Internet-based communication indicate that the continent will be integrated into the global information economy. What effects do these new media-driven integration processes have on African societies and politics? The following theoretical "entry" explores the potential social and political effects of new media.

"New" media as a term might engender strong conjectures about, if not biases towards, the technical aspects of these technologies such as wiring and devices. We prefer to refer to "new" media and ICTs as "infrastructures with three components: the *artefacts or devices* used to communicate or convey information; the *activities and practices* in which people engage to communicate or share information; and the *social arrangements or organizational forms* that develop around those devices and practices" (Lievrouw & Livingstone, 2006, p. 2). This book's overwhelming focus is on two components: the "*activities and practices*" and the "*social arrangements or organizational forms*" involved in how people use ICTs in Africa. The understanding that new media are embedded in a web of social contexts that could differ from one national experience to another should still encourage scholars to hone their theoretical approaches to study the socio-political implications of these new communication tools. It is useful–even in an edited volume--to succinctly review some of the most relevant conceptual frameworks to emerge from communications research regarding the socio-political implications of the mass media, in general, and of new media in particular. Such a review aims at contextualizing the intellectual conversation in which our contributors engage the book's readers.

The Public Sphere: In its liberal pluralist application, democratic governance is conditioned upon the development of a vibrant media system to enable public debate. In theorizing this complex relationship between democratic deliberation and the media, Habermas was interested in answering a simple yet fundamental question: What social conditions facilitate public debate of issues among citizens regardless of social status (Calhoun, 1992)? Habermas labelled the space in which this rational deliberation takes place as the "public sphere," a communicative infrastructure that is free of government intervention in which citizens reach "consensus" about how to run their society (Habermas, 1989;1991). While the concept has been subjected to much critique and modulation (Fraser, 1990; Kellner, 2000), its main thrust about the public deliberation of issues offers an ideal vision about how an inclusive and pluralist democracy ought to run. The reality is that all citizens (including those of Western and developed nations) do not have equal access to the media and communication technologies. As discussed earlier, the traditional mass media landscape has been largely dominated by intrusive and authoritarian states and a "development" media paradigm (Bourgault, 1995). Despite a relative opening during the "third wave" of democratization (Young, 1996), African citizens' literacy rates and states' backsliding continued to hamper a genuine media reform that can foster the mass media's formidable democratic role.

New media, however, offered alternative communication tools that could conceivably be the harbingers of an *online public sphere.* By online public sphere, we refer to a virtual sphere (Pappacharissi, 2002) in which "new, previously excluded, discussants" (Poor, 2005, n.p.) engage in political and social debates facilitated by new media technological convergence (Jenkins, 2004). To understand the "online public sphere" involves tracing how new media have transformed the traditional public sphere in at least three levels--structural, representational, and interactional (Dahlgren, 2005). At the structural level, new media enable users to circumvent the problems that hamper traditional media, specifically the dominance of corporate or state control. If traditional mass media's democratic potential has been severely curtailed by authoritarianism, ideological purity, and economic imperatives, the World Wide Web's porous nature offers reporters, activists, and citizens multiple and accessible ways of disseminating information without fear of official retaliation. At the representational level, the Internet's "massification" (Dalhgren, 2005) makes it a viable mass medium to reach a whole nation. At the same time, it is easy to reach subgroups whether they are based on ethnic, social class, regional or political identities. Having the full social spectrum, as well as the variety of political voices heard and represented in the online public sphere appears to be a net gain of using the Net. The "interaction dimension" of the online public sphere lies in how citizens react to, make sense of, and use online content, as well as citizens' interactions with other citizens. Dalhgren correctly emphasizes that the Internet blurs the "representation" and "interaction" dimensions of the public sphere.

We must acknowledge, however, the difficulties associated with applying "Western-centered" concepts to the African experience with democracy. What Dahlgren (2002) describes as "democracy's communication space," this Web-enabled public sphere that permits "civil society" to deliberate, remains a murky construct at best. Not only does the lack of a democratic tradition, but Colonial legacies, decolonization projects, and (long strains of) ethnicity-driven and authoritarian political regimes necessitate a rethinking of how scholars approach and study democracy in the continent (Berger, 2002). In the words of Berger (2002):

A final and compelling reason why we need to go beyond the taxonomic and analytical approaches associated with liberal pluralism is because these assume, inextricably, a modernist environment characterized by many competing elite interest groups and a dense media environment. This is not the case in much of Africa (p. 23).

Moreover, Berger cautions that while the concepts of "civil society" and "public sphere" might be problematic, they can be useful if we don't lose sight of the fact that the "media are not free- floating, autonomous social actors" (p. 37). Berger's, as well as other scholars' wariness and critique of the blind application of Western concepts of democracy and civil society to Africa are legitimate. Yet, concurring with such critique should not derail us from a critical assessment of (what is taking place) the realities of democratic experiments in the continent. Given new media's ascendancy in the continent, we pose the following question: to what extent has Africa's ICTs development journey created a participatory, inclusive and democratic online "public sphere"?

ICTs Diffusion & "Leapfrogging": Despite the contentious application of the public sphere to Africa's experiences with democracy, ICTs' "positive" contributions have invaded dominant discourses about new communication technologies' impact on social and political change. This proselytizing technological discourse pervades neo-liberal economic policies underwritten by the World Bank (Mansell, 2012). African countries have been encouraged to embrace ICTs because these tools provide the fastest path to post-industrial development and economic prosperity without having to undergo full industrialization (Singh, 1999). This "leapfrogging" process was motivated by a widely shared belief that joining the global information "superhighway" and closing the "digital divide" ensures that the continent will not be marginalized during this global information revolution. However, some scholars have critiqued this developmental paradigm in which social and political "progress" is assumed to be a linear trajectory propelled by a "deterministic" view of ICTs and new media technologies (Mudhai, Tettey, & Banda, 2009). For instance, Alzouma (2005)'s critical review of this dominant ICTs discourse raises legitimate questions about how issues of access, language, culture, and democratic governance hamper the overtly "utopian" vision. As digital iniquities persist *within* African societies and *across* the continent, the belief in the "magical" power of technology to solve the intractable problems of literacy, health, and poverty will be misguided (Alzouma, 2005).

Our book seeks to flesh out these "new" media debates in Africa and how "new" media might be called upon in the fight for political reform. Some glimpses of this struggle are offered in Part II of the book, "Technologies of Change: Understanding Africa's New Media Landscape," in which we

address the book's second main question: How have new media transformed Africa's social and political landscape? The question's intentional generalization invites a wide range of views to account for the continent's diverse experiences. The first chapter in Part II explores the ways in which new media functions shifted before, during, and after the Egyptian revolution (Chapter 11). In this sobering examination of the "Arab Spring," Sahar Khamis cautions scholars about "the limitations of cyberactivism efforts in bringing about the desired results in terms of actual political change on the ground, which always requires the physical presence of large numbers of people out on the street who are willing to face the high risk of personal injury, arrest, or even death" (p. 188). Field research data about the role of the Internet in empowering Morocco's grassroots movements lead to qualified assertions about how new media contribute to social change. While recognizing that the Internet has empowered various social movements through "building networks of solidarity," Mohamed Ben Moussa argues in Chapter 13 that "the political impact of the Internet cannot be attributed to intrinsic qualities of the technology alone; neither can it be reduced to one online platform" (p. 218). In Chapter 12, Aziz Douai and Mohamed Ben Moussa analyze how Egyptian activists harnessed social, particularly Twitter, during the 2011 protests. Their chapter offers some empirical taxonomies of the most influential Egyptian Twitter users during the uprising. In addition to profiling the "influentials," this study applies a framing perspective to understanding Twitter's use among Egyptian activists and social movements in general.

New media's influence should not be limited to political advocacy as the rest of the chapters in the second section demonstrate. Duncan Omanga and Pamela Chepngetich analyze how social media became central at the forefront of international conflict seeking to frame and define the legitimacy and the goals of war during Kenya's with Somali-based al-Shabaab fighters (Chapter 14).

Moreover, instead of the totalizing discourse about the empowering nature of ICTs, Brandie Martin and Anthony Olorunnisola argue that ICTs can be tools for state-repression and internecine ethnic conflict in Chapter 15. Social media's penetration in Africa may be uncovering generational divides. For instance, Facebook users are predominantly young people who turn to social media for political activism and civic engagement, as Auma Churchill Otieno's and Lusike Lynete Mukhongo's Kenyan youth research discovers (Chapter 16). The generational divide might explain the paradox that al-Shabaab, Somalia's Al-Qaeda affiliated group, exhibits in adopting new media technologies, such as Twitter and other social media, while rejecting other forms of western culture (see Bennett Furlow in Chapter 17). The realm of politics can be another battleground to scrutinize how new media are harnessed effectively to win votes. In Chapter 18, Bellarminus Gildas Kakpovi examines how Benin's political elites are increasingly embracing new media in their campaigns to mobilize and communicate the electorate. The impressive influence and growth of social media in the continent faces a regulatory vacuum that Oluwabukola Adelaja warns against in Chapter 19.

How do new media contribute to the public sphere and what are the prospects of a Democracy Spring in the rest of the continent? In Chapter 20, Anthony Olorunnisola and Ayo Ojebode begin a provocative discussion of the political limitations of ICTs and how the "Arab Spring stopped in the desert." Kennedy Javuru's analysis of Uganda's online mediascape offers guarded optimism, particularly how online discussion forums and bulletin boards provide alternative information lacking in traditional media, as well as facilitate the inclusion of more voices in the public sphere (Chapter 21). The inclusive nature of the emerging online public sphere is further supported by how African immigrants in the diaspora contribute to the homelands' political discourse. In Zimbabwe,

Tendai Chari explores the challenges facing online publications based outside the country, established by Zimbabweans in the Diaspora (Chapter 22). Nhamo Anthony Mhiripiri and Bruce Mutsvairo elaborate on the Zimbabwean experience, pointing out that social media's lack of success in instigating mass uprisings should not obscure how they effectively influenced international opinion despite the regime's oppressive attacks (Chapter 23). The concluding chapter of the volume synthesizes the contributors' main findings and teases out some answers to the book's guiding questions (Olorunnisola, Chapter 24).

The passionate debate between "technological determinists" and "social determinists" might be perennial and long-standing, but it should not obscure our quest to empirically analyze how new media technologies might affect African societies. Our quest is based on a view best described as the "social shaping of technologies," with which we underscore the "dialectical" relationship between new media and society: ICTs and their social environments exert mutual influence on (shaping and in turn being shaped by) each other. For the editors of this book, we find it too naïve to subscribe to the utopian vision about the way in which the diffusion of technologies can transform the continent from an authoritarian quagmire into a democratic oasis overnight. Likewise, we find it too pessimistic and unrealistic to join the opposing narrative that the introduction of ICTs in Africa will have little to no impact on its peoples and societies. The only common ground these opposing narratives appear to create is that more empirical and case-based research are required from communication and political science scholars (among others) to assess how new information and communication technologies have been shaped by, as well as how they have affected African societies and politics. This edited volume contributes to this urgent task.

REFERENCES

Alzouma, G. (2005). Myths of digital technology in Africa Leapfrogging development? *Global Media and Communication*, *1*(3), 339–356. doi:10.1177/1742766505058128.

Article 19 (June 7, 2011). Nigeria: Freedom of Information Act - A ray of hope for democracy. Retrieved from http://www.typepad.com/services/trackback/6a00d83451e0be69e201538f04b3c8970b

Berger, G. (2002). Theorizing the media-democracy relationship in Southern Africa. *International Communication Gazette*, *64*(1), 21–45. doi:10.1177/17480485020640010201.

Berger, G. (2007). *Media legislation in Africa: A comparative legal survey*. Grahamstown, South Africa: UNESCO.

Bourgault, L. M. (1995). *Mass media in sub-Saharan Africa*. Bloomington, IN: Indiana University Press.

Calhoun, C. (1992). Introduction: Habermas and the public sphere. *Habermas and the Public Sphere*, 1-48.

Dahlgren, P. (2005). The Internet, public spheres, and political communication: Dispersion and deliberation. *Political Communication*, *22*(2), 147–162. doi:10.1080/10584600590933160.

Diamond, L. J. (1996). Is the third wave over? *Journal of Democracy*, *7*(3), 20–37. doi:10.1353/jod.1996.0047.

Douai, A. (2009). In democracy's shadow: The 'new' independent press and the limits of media reform in Morocco. *Westminster Papers in Communication and Culture*, *6*(1), 7–26.

Fitch Ratings. (2012). South Africa mine violence highlights structural challenges. Retrieved on August 24, 2012, from www.fitchratings.com

Fraser, N. (1990). Rethinking the public sphere: A contribution to the critique of actually existing democracy. *Social Text*, (25/26): 56–80. doi:10.2307/466240.

Habermas, J. (1989). *The structural transformation of the public sphere: An inquiry into a category of bourgeois society*. Cambridge, MA: MIT Press.

Henze, P. B. (1998). A political success story. *Journal of Democracy*, *9*(4), 40–54. doi:10.1353/jod.1998.0062.

Herskovitz, J., & Govender, P. (2012). *South Africa is not falling apart: Zuma*. Retrieved from http://www.msnbc.msn.com/id/50215912/ns/world_news-africa/t/south-africa-not-falling-apart-zuma/

Hlongwane, S. (2012). *South Africa: ANC backtracks on key clauses, but the secrecy bill battle is far from won*. Retrieved from http://allafrica.com/stories/201208300390.html

Huntington, S. P. (1991). Democracy's third wave. *Journal of Democracy*, *2*(2), 12–34. doi:10.1353/jod.1991.0016.

Jenkins, H. (2004). The cultural logic of media convergence. *International Journal of Cultural Studies*, *7*(1), 33–43. doi:10.1177/1367877904040603.

Kellner, D. (2000). Habermas, the public sphere, and democracy: A critical intervention. In Hahn, L. E. (Ed.), *Perspectives on Habermas* (pp. 259–288). IL, Peru: Open Court.

Kperogi, F. A. (2012). The evolution and challenges of online journalism in Nigeria. In Siapera, E., & Veglis, A. (Eds.), *The handbook of global online journalism*. Malden, MA: Wiley-Blackwell. doi:10.1002/9781118313978.ch24.

Lievrouw, L., & Livingstone, S. (2006) Introduction to the updated student Ed. In L. Lievrouw, & S. Livingstone (Eds.), *Handbook of new media: Social shaping and social consequences* (pp. 1-14). London: Sage. Retrieved from http://eprints.lse.ac.uk/21502/1/Introduction_to_the_updated_student_Ed._(LSERO).pdf

Mansell, R. (2012). ICTs, discourse and knowledge societies: Implications for policy and practice. In D. Frau-Meigs J. Nicey, M. Palmer, & P. Tupper (Eds.), NWICO to WSIS: 30 years of communication geopolitics: actors and flows, structures and divides. Bristol, UK: ECREA series.

Mudhai, O. F., Tettey, W. J., & Banda, F. (Eds.). (2009). *African media and the digital public sphere*. Basingstoke, UK: Palgrave Macmillan. doi:10.1057/9780230621756.

Papacharissi, Z. (2002). The virtual sphere: The Internet as a public sphere. *New Media & Society*, *4*(1), 9–27. doi:10.1177/14614440222226244.

Poor, N. (2006). Mechanisms of an online public sphere: The website Slashdot. *Journal of Computer-Mediated Communication, 10*(2), 00-00.

Rummel, R. J. (1996). Democratization. In Vogele, W., & Powers, R. (Eds.), *Protest, power, and change: An encyclopedia of nonviolence action from act-up to women's suffrage*. Hamden, CT: Garland Publishing. Retrieved from.http://www.hawaii.edu/powerkills/DEMOC.HTM#

Shelley, F. M. (2011). Orientalism, idealism, and realism: The United States and the Arab Spring. *The Arab World Geographer*, *14*(2), 169–173.

Singh, J. P. (1999). *Leapfrogging development: The political economy of telecommunications restructuring*. Albany, NY: SUNY.

Sparks, C. (2001). The Internet and the global public sphere. In Bennett, W. L., & Entman, R. M. (Eds.), *Mediated politics: Communication in the future of democracy* (pp. 75–95). Cambridge, MA: Cambridge University Press.

Stepanova, E. (2011). The role of information communication technologies in the Arab Spring. *Implications beyond the region*. PONARS Eurasia Policy Memo no. 159. Washington, DC: George Washington University.

UN ICT Task Force. (2005). Measuring ICT: The global status of ICT indicators. Retrieved from https://www.itu.int/ITU-D/ict/partnership/material/05-42742%20GLOBAL%20ICT.pdf

Young, C. (1996). Africa: An interim balance sheet. *Journal of Democracy*, *7*(3), 53–68. doi:10.1353/jod.1996.0053.

Chapter 2
Moroccan Media in Democratic Transition

Bouziane Zaid
Al Akhawayn University, Morocco

ABSTRACT

A core assumption of much of the literature on media in developing countries is that a more independent press with greater freedom will make a positive contribution to political change. In Morocco, a democratic transition started in 1997, when the opposition socialist party came to power and led the government. The new government's mission was to enact political reforms that aimed at promoting human rights, civil liberties, an open and pluralist media, and at establishing the rule of law. This paper examines the interplay between media policy, media institutions, and the government. To evaluate the nature of the political role of media in democratic transitions requires close scrutiny of three major factors: the legal, the economic, and the political environments. One important outcome of this research is that it will help determine whether Morocco's democratic reforms are meaningful reforms, or just empty attempts to pacify domestic and international public opinion.

1. INTRODUCTION

The relationship between media and democracy has been widely researched. Classical liberal theorists from Milton through Locke and Madison to John Stuart Mill have argued that free and independent media can play a critical role in the process of democratization. Edmund Burke's concept of the 'fourth estate' has traditionally been regarded as one of the most efficient mechanisms of checks and balances. In the Arab world, this interplay among mass media, politics and society did not lead to political change. It is a common belief among communication scholars that Arab mass media were inefficient in promoting democratization in the Arab societies in which they operated (Rugh, 1987). Rather, mass media functioned as a support system for the authoritarian regimes. Arab

DOI: 10.4018/978-1-4666-4197-6.ch002

regimes used mass media mostly for propaganda and entertainment purposes at the expense of other functions and services (Ayish, 2003). The effects of mass media on democracy, politics, and society were at best minimal.

Since the late 1990s, some Arab governments have taken steps towards the democratization of their political systems. In Morocco, a democratic transition started in 1997, when the opposition socialist party came to power and led the government. The new government's mission was to enact political reforms that aimed at promoting human rights, civil liberties, an open and a pluralist media, and at establishing the rule of law. The new government led a campaign to formulate a new press law that promised to enhance press freedom.

A core assumption of much of the literature on media in developing countries is that a more independent press with greater freedom will make a positive contribution to political change. According to the literature, the media performs one of three specific political roles in a given society: an agent of stability by helping preserve social and political order (developmental press), an agent of restraint by denouncing government corruption (social responsibility), and an agent of change by helping oust authoritarian regimes (revolutionary press) (Hatchen, 1993). One of the shortcomings of this conceptualization of the relationship between media and society is that it tends to focus on the relationship between media and political systems (authoritarian, libertarian, communist, etc.) and it tends to ignore the relationship among media policy, media economics, and issues of access to media contents.

This paper provides a historical analysis of the major developments in Moroccan media since the country's independence in 1956. To evaluate the nature of the political role of media in democratic transitions requires close scrutiny of three major factors: the legal, the economic, and the political environments.[1] The paper examines the media policy as enacted in the Press Code, the Audiovisual Communication Law, and the *Haut Autorité*

de la Communication Audiovisuelle HACA (High Commission for Audiovisual Communication), and it explores the potential for further policy reforms. The paper also provides a careful and detailed examination of the economic and political environments and addresses the degree of political control over the contents of news media and the government's tendency to use media policy to limit the ability of media to operate. Finally, the paper addresses the issues of access to media contents, and it argues that the potential of Moroccan media to have a positive impact on the democratic transition does not depend only on the existence of an independent and free media. The media are only efficient for democracy if all sectors of society, especially those which are most disadvantaged or marginalized, can access media content to gain information and make informed decisions that affect their lives. The paper will first provide a brief historical analysis of the major developments in Moroccan media. It includes print, broadcasting, and the Internet.

2. HISTORY OF MOROCCAN MEDIA

2.1 Print Media

Early newspapers were issued by foreign colonial rulers, namely French and Spanish. By 1911, there were 17 foreign publications and all served as instruments of colonialism. The root of Moroccan press lies in their reactions to these papers (Alami, 1985, p. 25). Moroccan nationalists used the print press to mobilize people against colonialism. By 1956, there were a dozen publications issued by Moroccan nationalists. Print press remained a tool in the struggle for liberation and independence. Under the imperative of security, the French colonial powers introduced a number of press laws to regulate the nationalist press and contain its influence. For instance, in the 1950s, as the struggle for independence intensified, all Arabic papers were banned (Jaidi, 1999).

After the independence in March 1956, print media became a site of political tensions between the opposition political parties and the monarchy (Ashour, 1992). The print press was mostly owned by political parties. Opposition leaders used newspapers in particular as chief weapons of political agitation because they had no alternative for articulating their challenges against the regime, given the fact that TV and Radio were government-owned and controlled. If we consider the high rates of illiteracy among Moroccans, estimated in the 1960s at 86%, it remains to be seen what kind of effect, if any, newspapers may have had.

The relationship between the regime and the print media took a radically different turn when the opposition and socialist party led government in 1997. Government restrictions on the press have eased. Today, Morocco is home to a large number of print publications, many of them owned by political parties, and a growing number is owned by private persons. The independent print press opened new spaces where journalists are not tied to the strict and highly politicized editorial policies of their employers.

As of December 2005, there were 20 political party newspapers, six private newspapers, 19 of which were in Arabic and seven in French. The total circulation was of 350,000 per day, one of the lowest circulation rates in the Arab world; less than 1% of the population read a newspaper every day. The largest daily newspaper was *Al Massae* with a daily circulation of 120,000 copies. The second was *Essabah* with a circulation of approximately 60,000. The third and fourth were *Al-Ahdath Al-Maghribiya* and *Le Matin du Sahara* with a circulation of approximately 30,000 each. The circulation of other newspapers was less than 20,000 each.[2]

The new political environment also prompted diversity in the magazines industry. Major Moroccan magazines target different kinds of audiences and specialized topics such as women, health, sports, films and businesses. The democratiza-tion process gave these papers a circulation boost. Rapid growth occurred in both the number and in the circulation of independent magazines.

Since 1987, the Moroccan government has followed the policy of giving a fixed subsidy to newspapers and magazines that support its official versions of political reality. In 2006, the government subsidized 50 print media organizations (18 dailies, 27 weeklies, and five monthlies). The total amount was $US4 million.[3] The government realized the effectiveness of this subtle maneuver of controlling the print media; it decided to increase the amount of subsidies granted to the print media as part of its mechanisms of political control. Given the percentage of illiteracy,[4] there are large numbers of non-literate or marginally literate individuals who live out their lives in print-scarce environments with few or no reading materials in their homes but have easy and regular access to radio and television.

2.2 Radio

The French colonial rulers were the first to start broadcasting in Morocco in February 1928, when radio signals were sent from the city of Rabat. The French Resident General[5] was positioned to appoint the director of the station and to supervise news programs contents (Alami, 1985). The Moroccan resistance sought the use of radio in their fight for independence. Nationalist leaders used clandestine radio stations based in Spain and Italy to voice their ideas for liberation (Alami, 1985). The colonial powers issued a royal decree in 1929 to define the scope of the monopolization to include all signal transmissions, whether they were radio, telephony or telegraphy (Ibahrine, 2007). This restriction was designed mainly to prevent Moroccans from using radio transmissions. The *Voice of Cairo,*[6] the Egyptian pan-Arab radio station established by Egyptian president and Arab revolutionary figure Gamaal Abdel Nasser, was the new platform for Moroccan nationalists and allowed them to communicate their political messages in their fight for independence (Alami, 1985, p. 22).

In March 1962, the government established the county's broadcasting system offering radio and television services by the name of *Al-Idaa WaTalfaza Al-Maghribiya* (Moroccan Radio-diffusion and Television; French: *Radiodiffusion et Télévision Marocaine*, RTM). The Moroccan government either took over or bought the existing infrastructure in Rabat, Tangier, Tetouan and other major cities (Ibahrine, 2007). RTM provided one Arabic Language and one French Language radio services and was under the control and administration of the Ministry of Information[7]. As the central mouthpiece of the government, extending radio services to reach all Moroccan citizens especially in isolated areas has been a top political priority for RTM since the 1960s (Ibahrine, 2007).

Moroccan radio's golden age happened during the 1970s. A 1973 study found that 92.1% of the urban population and 75.2% of the rural population listened to radio on a regular basis (Ibahrine, 2007). The advent of TV and satellite broadcasting, however, dramatically affected radio. The number of radio listeners declined substantially in the late 1990s.

Medi 1, the first private radio, was launched in 1980 as part of a Moroccan-French partnership comprising associates from banks and major enterprises of the two countries. Medi 1 is a bilingual radio station (French and Arabic) of international news and entertainment. In 1987, Casablanca Radio, a regional and private radio station, went on the air. The station provided mostly music (70%), but it also aired news and cultural programs. The broadcasts were mainly for the Casablanca area. In 2003, Radio Sawa began broadcasting in Moroccan soil. Sawa is a service of U.S. International Broadcasting and is publicly funded by the U.S. Congress. It is a 24-hour, seven-day-a-week Arabic-language station. Radio Sawa received an

exceptional authorization from the government to broadcast in Morocco. There was at the time no legal framework for such authorization.

In August 2002, The *Haut Autorité de la Communication Audiovisuelle* (HACA), the High Commission for Audiovisual Communication, was created by royal decree to establish the legal framework for the liberalization of the audio-visual sector. Until the creation of HACA, the broadcasting sector functioned in a legal void. TV and radio stations were established via the use of royal decrees. In September 2002, HACA promulgated a decree[8] that ended the government's monopoly of the national broadcasting system and allowed the licensing of new private television and radio stations. The Moroccan parliament adopted the reform law on November 25, 2004. By virtue of this Audiovisual Communication Law, the number of radio stations increased from 6 stations in 2006 to 24 in 2008. Of these radio stations, 18 are new private stations,[9] 8 are regional, and the others are national. The number of TV channels also increased from 3 stations in 2004 to 8 in 2010.[10]

The new private radio stations reinvigorated the audiovisual sector especially through their live debate programs and news programs. They introduced the impetus and space to create possibilities for national debates on a variety of issues. In a country as diverse as Morocco, there are a multitude of voices vying for a share of the national conversation. Unlike public radio and TV, private radio news programs tend to focus on local, regional, and national events. They tend to use a language that is accessible to their listeners, somewhere between modern standard Arabic and *Darija*.[11]

2.3 Television

In 1951, the first TV license was issued for a French private television company, TELMA. It began broadcasting in 1952 and was considered the first Arab and African private television (Bertrand, 1966). It operated for three years and had to stop in May 1955 due to severe financial hardships and to the tense political situation at the time in Morocco. The arrival of radio and television in the post-independence period was part of Morocco's efforts to modernize.

RTM was launched in March 1962. Although self-proclaimed as a public service television, RTM was the mouthpiece of the government and the palace. In terms of newsworthiness, coverage of the royal family and government activities took priority over all other criteria. RTM's role was to promote nationalism, reinforce the sacredness of the monarchy, and discredit communist and anti-monarchy/republican ideologies.

Color television transmission began in 1972. By 1973, television only covered 33% of the national territory. Until the late 1970's, the price of a television set was too expensive for the overwhelming majority of Moroccans (Ashour, 1992). There were an estimated 3.1 million TV receivers in 1997. Today, virtually every urban Moroccan home has a television set (*Ministry of Communication Report*, 2006).

RTM remained the only TV channel till the creation of 2M in 1989.The station—2M— was Arab world's first terrestrial pay-TV channel. It began transmission from Casablanca. The channel's self-proclaimed function was to entertain. The news bulletins were short in form of news briefs. French Language was predominant with 80% of the programs in French. It was subscription based and needed a decoder to get clear signals till January 1997, when it turned public and its signals only needed a regular aerial antenna to be received. The TV station (2M) was going through financial difficulties due to the fact that an increasing number of its subscribers cancelled their subscriptions in favor of free and often more interesting programs on various satellite television channels.

The takeover by the government was carried out in the name of preserving the freedom of speech that 2M came to symbolize. Politicians from different ideological streams supported the move since 2M was seen as the only national channel open to political debates. The TV channel (2M) brought in a breath of fresh air for most Moroccans who were unsatisfied with the programs of RTM. The station broke some old taboos and tackled controversial issues. The first taboo it broke was manifested in the format of its news bulletin. Contrary to RTM, the format was rather compact and its content was not necessarily focused on the daily engagements of the king or the government. It addressed these issues with brevity and more objectivity than RTM. It also featured programs on what was considered then controversial issues such as poverty, corruption, and government ineffectiveness.

In September 2002, HACA promulgated a decree[12] that assigned public service obligations to the two major television stations in Morocco (RTM and 2M). The law also put an end to the Government's monopoly in terms of broadcasting management by transforming Moroccan Radio and Television (RTM) from a subsidiary of the Ministry of Communication into an independent and self-governing body, the *Société Nationale de Radiodiffusion et de Télévision*, SNRT (National Radio and Television Company). The SNRT is a public company that manages both television stations but is no longer subject to the financial control and supervision of the Ministry of Communication. RTM[13] was renamed *Al Oula* (meaning "the first" in Arabic).

Al Oula and 2M are the most important sources for news and information. This is due to the low cost, ability of TV to move beyond issues of illiteracy, and universal access. According to the report of Marocmétrie, the official Moroccan TV audience ratings firm,[14] Al Oula and 2M have a share of the audience in March 2010 of 40.3%, 27.3% for 2M and 13.0% for Al Oula.

The new TV stations are: *Arriyadia* (sports), *Assadissa* (religion), *Arrabia* (education and culture), *Aflam TV* (fiction) and *AmazighTV*. The other stations are *Laayoun* station and *Medi 1 Sat,* which are, respectively, a regional station in the southern province of Morocco and a satellite news channel.

2.4 Internet

Since the early 1990s, research universities led the development of the Internet. In 1993, Mohammadia's School of Engineers in Rabat established the first national Internet connection. The general public started having access to Internet services in November 1995. Students and researchers were the first to use it. The diffusion of the Internet in Morocco was slow due primarily to the high cost of computers and poor infrastructure.

Internet access has considerably improved and widened. The number of internet users grew by an estimated 60% from 2005 to 2010.[15] In 2009, the number of subscribers to the Internet had reached 1.2 million, 4.51% of Morocco's population.[16] Of these internet users, 54% use 3G, more than 566,000 customers, 1.8% of Morocco's population. In 2005, internet users reached 3.5 million. The number of cybercafes had reached 8,950. According to the Network Information Centre,[17] the centre in charge of managing the domain "ma," there are 36,024 registered domain names with the extension .ma in 2010.

For a long period of time, reporting was the reserved monopolized domain of professional journalists. Internet users demonstrated intensive use of social media to aggregate and collect user-generated reports of riots and police violence against students, labor unions, and other activists. Posting online videos on websites has contributed to the quality of news and information. The use of mobile cameras made many Moroccans deserve the label of mobile iReporters. These grassroots journalists have on many occasions broken the news of many incidents to Moroccan mainstream

media. A case in point that illustrates the contribution of digital media in the quality of reporting is a scandal that involved the Minister of Communication and the spokesperson of the government, Mr. Khalid Naciri. The minister was caught "on tape" while using his status as minister to release his son from police custody. The event was filmed with a mobile phone and posted on YouTube and other websites. The video reached 300,000 hits. Many newspapers reported this event in their hard copies and their websites with links to YouTube.

3. LEGAL ENVIRONMENT

In order to evaluate the nature of the political role of media in democratic transitions, the paper will analyze three major environments: the legal, the economic, and the political environments. The legal environment includes a discussion of the media policy as enacted in the Press Code, the Audiovisual Communication Law, and the regulator, *Haut Autorité de la Communication Audiovisuelle* HACA (High Commission for Audiovisual Communication). The paper also explores the potential for further policy reforms.

3.1 Media Policy

Morocco perpetuated a French concept of the freedom of the press that emerged from the authoritarian regimes of the nineteenth century (El Kobbi, 1992). Generally, the Moroccan government accepts mild forms of political criticism but does not tolerate attacks on the monarchy, Islam, or the Western Sahara.[18] Media professionals are considered patriotic citizens who must be mindful of their social responsibility to the public.

3.1.1 Press Code[19]

King Mohammed V (1956-1961) instituted the first national Press Code in 1959 on the basis of the French legal framework that had been in force under the French protectorate between 1912 and 1956. King Hassan II (1961-1999) strengthened this repressive press law by instituting the Press Codes of 1963 and 1973. According to these press codes, and in the name of guaranteeing public order and insuring national security, newspapers can be fined, suspended, or banned, and journalists' freedom can be threatened (Hidass, 1992). The regime hardened its position vis-à-vis print media because the latter were too critical of the monarch's actions. The regime stated that a completely free press would undermine the country's security (Hidass, 1992).

Since Mohammed VI's accession to the throne in 1999, and following the reform of the Press Code in 2002, there had been hope that radical reforms of Moroccan press laws would take place, but such aspirations have not been fully realized. Article I states that citizens have the right to information and that freedom to publish is guaranteed by law. These freedoms are practiced in conformity with the constitutional rights. However, the new press code still maintains prison sentences for journalists and gives the government the right to shut down any publication "prejudicial to Islam, the monarchy, territorial integrity, or public order."

For instance, Article 41 states that anybody who offends the king and the royal princes and princesses in any way (i.e., in writing, print, audio, video, poster, or speech) will be imprisoned for three to five years and must pay a fine of 10,000 to 100,000 MAD (roughly US$800 to US$8000). The same sentence applies to anybody who attacks Islam, the monarchy, and the territorial integrity. The publication can be suspended for up to three months or can be permanently banned.

3.1.2 High Authority for Audio-Visual Communication (HACA) and the 2004 Audiovisual Communication Law

HACA was established in August 31, 2002 as an independent administrative body in charge of regulating the audio-visual communication sec-

tor. However, a closer look at this organization sheds doubt on its self-proclaimed independence from government. HACA consists of the Higher Council of the Audio-Visual Communication; it is a nine-member council, five of whom are appointed by the King, including the President. The Prime Minister appoints two members, and the last two members are named by the presidents of the two Chambers of the Parliament. The council has three major missions:

- **Advice:** To the King, the Prime minister and government, and both chambers of the parliament on issues related to audio-visual sector.
- **Regulation:** Authorizes the creation of audio-visual companies, and grants licenses and the use of radio frequencies.
- **Control:** Monitors the compliance to the laws and regulations applicable to audio-visual sector, compliance to the pluralism (in particular in the matter of political parties access), and compliance to advertising legislation and regulation.

HACA also consists of the General Directorate of Audio-Visual Communication (*Direction Général de la Communication Audiovisuelle--DGCA*). DGCA is run by the HACA's general director, and it represents the HACA's administrative and technical services. The DGCA includes the following services: research and development, program monitoring, technical infrastructure, and the legal department.

HACA receives many bids from private individuals or companies seeking new licenses. HACA overseas the compliance of all TV and radio stations to their Licensing Obligation documents (*Cahier des Charges*). The *Cahier des Charges* constitutes a written agreement between the HACA and broadcast media outlet and the HACA, through its mechanism of monitoring and surveillance, makes sure the media outlets comply with their own obligations.

In the preamble of the Audio-Visual Communication Law, it is stated that the general philosophy is founded on the kingdom's constitutional principles of Islam, monarchy, national unity, and the universal human rights. The objectives of this law are summarized as follows: to reinforce freedom of expression and opinion; to promote democratic ideals and the respect of human rights and pluralism; to contribute to the socio-economic and cultural development of the nation; to promote public service broadcasting; to enhance audio-visual communication production; to encourage national production and to preserve the national cultural heritage.

3.2 Discussion

An examination of the legal environment shows that the principles of freedom of expression, diversity and pluralism underlie all the laws and policies. However, the Press Code still maintains prison sentences for journalists and gives the government the right to shut down any publication. Besides, the Moroccan government controls the licensing, production and distribution of broadcast media, considered as the most powerful and influential of all existing media. Given the high rate of illiteracy in Morocco, TV and radio are the main sources of news and information for most Moroccans, and they are considered as the most powerful of all existing media.

HACA granted the first TV and radio licenses exclusively to government-owned TV and radio stations. The second wave of licenses granted by HACA on February 23, 2009 proved to be a disappointment for many observers in terms of enhancing pluralism in broadcast media.[20] Five TV license applications were denied by the HACA. The decision was based on "the deteriorating situation in the advertising market."[21] The government abused the powers of the regulator and managed to secure licenses for their broadcasters to remain in control of this sector. HACA granted licenses to only four new radio stations that were regional and thematic; bids for news radios and privately owned TV stations were not granted licenses.

News delivery on the Internet and mobile platforms is not yet regulated. The Law that is currently applied to online journalists is the 2002 Press Code. No authorization or licenses are required from an organization or an individual to launch a website. But the legal censorship mechanism applied to all media activities has been extended to cover materials in the Internet. As long as the Internet was not directly challenging the government's hegemony, the use of the Internet was generally tolerated.

It is important to note, however, that Internet access in Morocco is, "for the most part, open and unrestricted," according to Open Net Initiative (ONI).[22] ONI testing shows that Morocco no longer blocks a majority of sites that support the independence of the Western Sahara, which is one of the three taboo subjects in Moroccan media. The report states, however, that Morocco occasionally blocks access to a small number of blogging platforms and anonymizers. The regime of filtration is not comprehensive, which means that access to similar content can be found on other Web sites. Yet, there are instances of prosecution of Internet users and bloggers because of their writing and online activities.

4. POLITICAL AND ECONOMIC ENVIRONMENT

This section provides a careful and detailed examination of the political and economic environments. It addresses the issues of ownership and degree of political control over the contents of news media and the government's tendency to use the laws and legal institutions to limit the media's ability to operate. The first part addresses the political and economic environments during the "Years of Lead," a metaphor that democracy activists use to describe the oppressive political regime during the period from the independence in 1956 to 1999. The second part addresses the political and economic environments from 1999, the year when King Mohamed V became king, and 2010.

4.1 The Years of Lead 1956-1999

4.1.1 The Political Environment

It is important to discuss the role of Driss Basri, a former chief of police, who in 1979 was nominated by late King Hassan II as the Minister of Interior and Minister of Information.[23]Driss Basri was late King Hassan II's notorious minister in charge of domestic security and political repression. Basri is the embodiment of the despotism and the rampant corruption of King Hassan II's era. Basri was known as the "King's Policeman" during his time as Interior Minister under Hassan II. The same man was in charge of the media and the police force, a contradiction that only an authoritarian regime can enforce. In 1999, Basri was removed by King Mohamed VI, a sign that Morocco was heading towards democratic reforms.

Under Basri's media regime, all media outlets were subject to the same censorship. It did not matter whether the media outlet was owned by the government or by private persons. Basri used the 1973 press code fully. It gave the Minister of Interior the power to seize and censor any publication. These measures evoked numerous protests and press strikes but to no avail.

The struggle between the regime and opposition continued through the 1980's. There were few moments of relative openness, but mostly repression in the name of preserving national security was the rule. For instance, *Kalima* was a newsmagazine that lasted for two years, from 1986to1987. In April of 1987, the magazine published a report on prostitution in Morocco's tourism cities of Marrakech and Agadir. Two weeks later, it published another report on homosexuality. Basri ordered the magazine to be seized from the newsstands and ordered its editor to shut down

the publication. One may wonder how prostitution and homosexuality, as social phenomena, can be threats to national security.

In 1962, the year RTM was launched, late King Hassan II oversaw the writing of the first constitution which defined the role of the king, giving him broad powers, including the power to appoint ministers, governors, judges; the power to dissolve the parliament, declare a state of emergency, and revise the constitution.

Since its inception, and although self-proclaimed as a public service television, RTM has promoted nationalism, reinforced the sacredness of the monarchy, and discredited socialist and anti-monarchy and republican ideologies. The national prime time news consisted of news related to the king and government activities. The striking things about RTM news bulletin were the countless stories about royal engagements and ministers' activities. The "holiness" of such stories in the running order remains unchallenged till today.

During the time when the Ministry of Interior and the Ministry of Information were under the supervision of Basri, it was difficult to determine whether television cameras were used for journalistic purposes or for policing purposes. When TV cameras attended public demonstrations, it was not clear whether the footage would end up in an editing room at the TV station or at the secret service offices. The line between providing information to audiences and providing information to police services was blurred for thirty years.

The period from 1956 to 1999 was authoritarian. Media professionals lived in fear. At the time of Driss Basri, RTM journalists, management, and staff considered themselves salaried employees of the ministry of Interior. In an interview with Mr. Mohamed Moudden, a senior news editor and presenter and currently news director, he said that the journalists were assigned to report on specific events and were told the editorial line to follow. Most of the work at RTM and its radio affiliates consisted of writing government press releases.

The journalists did not have the right to report, interpret, or investigate news events (Interview, March 10, 2008).

4.1.2 Economic Environment

The regime owned and controlled directly and indirectly all audiovisual media. One private radio station (Medi 1) and one private TV station (2M) were launched respectively in 1980 and 1989; they were both initiated by King Hassan II (Lamnadi, 1999). Medi 1 was launched as part of a Moroccan-French partnership comprising associates from banks and major enterprises of the two countries. The radio was an initiative of King Hassan II and French President Valéry Giscard d'Estaing. The private TV station, 2M, was a creation of the Royal Palace and the *Omnium Nord Afrique* (ONA), Morocco's largest economic conglomerate (Lamnadi, 1999).

Print media were owned by the leading political parties and a few private persons. Print publications of Political parties managed to survive thanks to self-censorship. A political party newspaper (*Al Moharir*) and private magazines such as *Kalima* (1986-1987) and *Lam Alif* (1966-1988) were shut down by the government because they dared discuss issues deemed sensitive.

The next section will cover the main developments in the political and economic environments in Morocco from 1999 to 2010. This period witnessed important improvements in terms of human rights and media ownership policies.

4.2 The Political and Economic Environment 1999 – 2010

4.2.1 Political Environment

The major improvements that occurred in Morocco are due to the democratic transition initiated by King Mohammed VI. After he succeeded his father Hassan II in July 1999, Mohammed VI instantly became a symbol of hope for a more democratic and free Morocco. Unlike his father, whose 38-year rule was stained by human rights violations, corruption and a discredited political system, Mohammed VI—famed in the Moroccan and foreign media as the "king of the poor"—embodied modesty, social justice and moderation (Maghraoui, 2001). He made the promotion of human rights a priority.

One of the first major pro-human rights measures under his reign was the creation of the Forum for Equity and Reconciliation[24] in 2003 that investigated the human rights violations of the past. Besides establishing the truth about the past violation, the Commission organized public forums in 2004 to allow victims to voice their pains and sufferings under the old regime. These forums were broadcast live on TV, which constituted a very important moment in Moroccan television history. The goal of the Commission was to facilitate the reconciliation of Moroccans with their recent past.

Another major initiative was the new Family Status Law or *Moudawana*. It was decreed in 2003 to protect women's rights. The lived experience of Moroccan women does not go hand in hand with their constitutional rights and civil status. Since the Independence in 1956, women have been given the right to vote, the right to own businesses, the right to run for public office, but their status in marital relationships such as divorce, custody of children, inheritance and alimony was far from being equal to men. This has been the focus of continued advocacy and awareness-raising efforts of women's rights activists. A Freedom House's study[25] (2004) on women in Morocco, *Women's Freedom in Focus: Morocco*, praised this initiative and noted the improvements of the status of women and their rights.

Mohamed VI also created the *Institut Royal de la Culture Amazigh* IRCAM (the Royal Institute of Amazigh Culture).[26] The role of the Institute is to safeguard and promote Amazigh Language and culture. Amazigh people are the majority ethnic group in Morocco, yet Amazigh culture was undermined for many years. For political reasons, the Hassan II regime identified with Arabism, hence the predominance of the Arabic culture and identity. Amazigh activists have been calling for more equitable representation in the media and more recognition of their contribution in Moroccan history and culture. IRCAM was a response to these calls.

4.2.2 Economic Environment

The Moroccan government is the only monopoly in terms of media ownership. It has control over radio and television and their online platforms. It also exercises significant influence on newspapers owned by political parties and has a legal arsenal to control and manage the competition. Article 21 of the 2004 Audiovisual Communication law stipulates that any broadcasting company or a shareholder in a broadcasting company can own or control another broadcasting company as long as he/she/it does not exceed 30% of the shares of the new company. In other words, only the government can own and control more than one media outlet. The government clearly abused the powers of the regulator (HACA) and managed to secure licenses for their broadcasters to remain in control of this sector.

Morocco's current media system consists of a mix of public and private ownership. The liberalization of the audiovisual sector allowed new private radio stations and new TV stations to emerge. The print press also became considerably diversified and relatively competitive, and they are gradually developing into a professional press. The newspapers with the highest circulation are private newspapers. Morocco's national papers were predominantly political parties' newspapers, and they lacked aggressiveness in putting forward their political opinions. Unlike the new independent and private newspapers, political parties' newspapers reflect the political views and ideas of their particular parties. The independent press targets a middle class mass market, filling the void left by the party press.

The new political environment also prompted diversity in the magazines industry. The new magazines target different kinds of audiences and specialized topics such as women, health, sports, films, and business. The democratization process gave these magazines a circulation boost.

4.3 Discussion

The political environment is certainly more open and conducive to more freedom than it was during the years of lead. The Mohamed VI era is more democratic in form and substance. Many taboos are broken, from reporting on the king's salary to reporting on the arrest of high officials close to the palace. Journalists denounce corruption, and some have called for the resignation of many powerful government and army personalities, something that was inconceivable during the reign of Hassan II. The last decade witnessed an unprecedented opening of the political system in Morocco.

Ahmed Benchemsi, the director of *Telquel* magazine, critiqued in one of his editorials the communication skills of King Mohamed VI. In one of his reports in December 2004, he also published the salary and expenses of the king. None of these acts triggered an official reaction from the government. In 2006, many newspapers, magazines and even the public TVs and radios published reports on the arrest of the chief of security of the royal palaces about his alleged connections to a drug lord. No journalist could ever dream or imagine publishing such sensitive information during the reign of Hassan II. However, the government still interferes with the content of the media in ways that do not serve the country's democratic transition and its image abroad.

Instances of government censorship are recurring events in Moroccan journalism. What are more important are instances of auto-censorship. Journalists avoid the three taboo areas: the monarchy, Islam and territorial integrity (southern Sahara provinces). According to the *Reporters Without Borders* (RWB) 2009 report,[27] Morocco ranks 127 out of 177 countries in terms of media freedom. The report states that there are encouraging developments but press freedom seems to have lost its hard-won ground in the past few years. The number of titles has increased in recent years, an indication of a higher degree of pluralism, and the broadcasting liberalization has given way to new audiovisual content providers. However, in the first seven months of 2009, the Moroccan government favored the use of financial penalties, instead of prison terms to keep the most outspoken journalists in line. Excessive fines led to the shutting down of *Le Journal Hebdomadaire*, one of the most courageous magazines in Morocco, and one that came to symbolize the opening that began under the reign of Mohamed VI. The government tolerates mild forms of criticism but does not allow anyone to cross the "red lines": Islam, Monarchy, and Sahara. The RWB report cites Mohammed Erraji who was sentenced to prison in September 2009 for critiquing the social policy of king Mohamed VI. He posted an article on his blog and on Hespress. com entitled: "The king encourages dependency on handouts." He was later acquitted on appeal. The report also cites Driss Chahtane, editor of *Al Michaal* newspaper who was sentenced to one year in prison in October 2009. The report stated that the Moroccan authorities also ban foreign publications deemed unpleasant. *Le Monde* was banned on 4 August 2009 because it carried an opinion poll on the Mohamed VI's ten years reign. *Telquel* and *Nichane*, two Moroccan magazines, were the initiators of this opinion poll but they were denied authorization to publish the results.

In terms of digital activism, the Internet has created a dynamic and networked public space where lively debates can take place on many issues considered "off-limits" to mainstream media. It is also a space where support and solidarity can be expressed with regard to each case of imprisonment of journalists or censorship of the press online and offline. The government knows well the reach it has especially among Western audiences and the impact it has on international public opinion in particular Western human rights associations.

Social media triggered a revival of the watchdog function of the media and paved the way for it to act as fourth estate in controlling the misconduct of the political regime (p.30) . In the summer of 2008, Targuist Sniper video, a case in point for online video advocacy, was widely circulated on YouTube. An amateur cameraman filmed traffic police while taking bribes from drivers. This video resulted in a police investigation that led to the arrest of the some police officers. With these videos, cyberactivism against daily and mundane corruption entered a new phase by setting a model for followers in other Moroccan cities. Despite the fact that the Youtubization of corruption resulted in the arrests of some police officers, it remained short-termed and limited even if the Moroccan government did not block the access to the video-sharing site—YouTube.

The Moroccan political regime does not tolerate all online activities. Fouad Mourtada, a young engineer, was sentenced to jail for allegedly stealing the identity of Prince Moulay Rachid, the king's younger brother, on the social networking website, Facebook. The alleged Facebook royal impostor was sentenced to three years in prison and a fine of US$1,350 for allegedly showing disrespect to the royal family, considered a sacred domain. After one month in custody, Mourtada was released by a royal pardon.

In September 2008, Mohammed Erraji was arrested for criticizing on his blog King Mohammed VI's charitable activities, which he labeled as a source of laziness and fatalist culture. He was given a two-year prison sentence and fined US$630. This stirred protests from Internet users around the world and marred Morocco's international image. Like Mourtada, Erraji was released by a royal pardon.

In 2009, Hassan Barhoun, a journalist and blogger, was sentenced to six months jail-time and a US$600 fine for publishing a memo signed by 60 political and human rights activists and intellectuals. He was known for his investigative reporting and for condemning corruption in Morocco. He also led a press initiative entitled "Journalists without Limits" on YouTube.

Since the relative rise to prominence of the social media in Morocco, the reactions of the government to these new technologies have reflected its political culture of oppressing freedom of speech. The government has not yet learned how to deal with bloggers in a democratic way. The use of the Press Code to sanction and oppress freedom of expression is an indication that the government is committed to keeping this space from becoming a nucleus for new political progressive discourse.

5. MEDIA, DEMOCRACY AND ACCESS TO MEDIA CONTENT

Another important dimension of the function of media in democracy is the extent to which audiences have access to media contents. Norris (2002) argues that an independent media with a watchdog function is a necessary but not sufficient means of strengthening good governance. An independent media is only efficient for democracy if all sectors of society, especially those who are most disadvantaged or marginalized, can access media contents to function as an educated citizenry and contribute constructively to civic discourse.

A 2010 study[28] was conducted to examine the manifest contents of Al Oula and 2M programming, being Moroccans' major sources of news and information. The quantitative content analysis addressed the issues of access to and participation in public service television. Access and participation refer to, among other things, the gender of the TV hosts and guests of the television shows and the languages used. The sample consisted of all locally produced shows in both public stations over the span of one year, from January 2007 to January 2008.

With regard to gender, the results indicate that women are misrepresented in Moroccan public service television. The television shows of both stations featured more men than women, with 70.7 per cent of men and 29.3 per cent of women. For Al Oula, the percentage of female participants is 23.3% compared to 76.6% for male participants. For 2M, the percentage of female participants is relatively higher with 33.4% compared to 66.7% for male participants. Though women make up more than half of Morocco's population *(Haut Commissariat au Plan*--Moroccan Census Bureau's statistics of 2004), less than one third of the hosts and guests featured on television are women.

With regard to language, the results indicate that 33.3% of the shows use Arabic or French and only 15.4% use *Darija*. The use of a mix of *Darija* and Arabic has the highest percentage with 35% and 10.3% use a mix of *Darija* and French. What is even more striking is that the number of shows that use French alone is higher than the number of shows that use *Darija* alone or Arabic alone. Seven shows use French, while six use Arabic and only two use *Darija* alone.

The study concluded that the choice of language restricts access to and participation in public television for a large portion of Moroccan society. The choice of language allows access for only the wealthy and highly educated classes of Morocco. Moroccans speak *Darija* in their everyday life, but both public service television stations mainly use formal Arabic and French. In 2004, 43% of the Moroccan population aged ten and above were illiterate. Half the literate population, 28.5% of the Moroccan population aged ten and above, knew how to read Arabic and French. About 19% or one-third of the literate population knew how to read and write Arabic alone.[29]

Using Arabic and French projects an undemocratic social order in the sense that it limits the possibilities of access to the media for participation in public discourse. The question of access and the relationship it entails between contents and audiences show that the potential of Moroccan media to have any positive impact on the democratic transition does not depend only on the existence of an independent and free media.

6. CONCLUSION

Western understandings of the media's roles as agents of change, restraint, and stability do not translate well to the media's function in Morocco's democratic transition. These assumptions overlook the plural and diverse character of media and the internal cultural dynamics of the country. Based on the findings of this study, it is obvious that the Moroccan government either does not possess a clear vision for the role of media in democratic society, or lacks the willpower to make such use possible. Government interference has eased during the democratic transition, but it is still there. It is still unpredictable and inconsistent.

The nation's democratic transition does not depend only on the existence of an independent and free media but also on the extent to which its media policies promote pluralism and diversity, and the extent to which its media offer the possibilities of access to the majority of Moroccan audiences. Understanding the political role of Moroccan media in the country's democratic transitions requires a nuanced approach, based on uncovering multiple layers of ambiguity that address the legal, economic, and political environments as well as the relationship between content and audiences.

The ubiquity of Facebook, Twitter, blogs and news websites in the unfolding of the Arab Spring makes the study of Arab media in general and of digital media in particular crucially important. On February 20, 2011, a group of online Moroccan activists, inspired by the revolutions in Tunisia and Egypt, swayed tens of thousands of their countrymen and women to take to the streets to call for democracy, dignity, and political reforms. Many banners carried slogans castigating state media and demanding freedom of the press. In response, King Mohammed VI gave an historical address to the nation on March 9, vowing to relinquish parts of his executive prerogatives and to propose a new constitution that guarantees more individual liberties and media freedom.

REFERENCES

Agence National de Réglementation des Télécommunications. (2010). *Tableau de bord trimestriel du marché Internet.* Retrieved June 2, 2010, from http://www.anrt.ma/fr/admin/download/upload/file_fr1891.pdf

Agence National de Réglementation des Télécommunications. (2010). *Tableau de bord trimestriel du marché Internet.* Retrieved June 2, 2010, from http://www.anrt.ma/fr/admin/download/upload/file_fr1874.pdf

Agence National de Réglementation des Télécommunications. (2010). *Tableau de bord trimestriel du marché Mobile.* Retrieved June 10, 2010, from http://www.anrt.net.ma/fr/admin/download/upload/file_fr1888.pdf

Asante, C. E. (1997). *Press freedom and development: A research guide and selected bibliography.* Westport, CT: Greenwood Press.

Ayish, M. (2003). *Arab world television in the world of globalization.* Hamburg, Germany: Ubersee Institute.

Ben Ashour, A. (1992). *Mass media in Morocco.* Unpublished Master's thesis. Institut Supérieur de Journalisme.

El Kobbi, M. (1992). *L'Etat et la Presse au Maroc.* Paris: L'auteur.

Faquihi, F. (23 April 2010). 2M Capte plus de téléspectateur qu'Al Oula. *L'Economiste*, p. 12.

HACA. (2009). *Rapport sur l'Attribution de Nouvelles Licences.* Retrieved June 9, 2010, from http://www.haca.ma/pdf/Rapport%20G2%20 MEP.pdf

Hatchen, W. (1993). *The growth of media in the Third World.* Ames, IA: Iowa State University Press.

Haut Autorité de la Communication Audiovisuelle. (2004). *Loi Relative à la Communication Audiovisuelle.* Retrieved April 15, 2010, from http://www.haca.ma/pdf/commaudiovisuelle.pdf

Haut Commissariat au Plan. (2004). *Recensement Général de la Population et de l'Habitat.* Retrieved May 20, 2010, from http://www.hcp. ma/pubData/Demographie/RGPH/RGPH_Rapport_National.pdf

Hidass, A. (1992). *Liberté et Communication au Maroc. L'Information au Maghreb.* Tunis, Tunisia: Ceres Production.

Human Development Reports. (2005). *Fifty Years of Human Development & Perspectives to 2025.* Retrieved January 10, 2008, from http://hdr. undp.org/en/reports/nationalreports/arabstates/ morocco/name,3380,en.html

Ibahrine, M. (2007). *The Internet and politics in Morocco: The political use of the Internet by Islam oriented political movements.* Berlin, Germany: VDM Verlag.

Katulis, B. (2004). *Women's freedom in focus: Morocco.* Retrieved June 6, 2010, from http://www. freedomhouse.org/uploads/special_report/32.pdf

Lamnadi, A. (1999). *Communication policy making and electronic media in Morocco: The introduction of private television.* Unpublished Dissertation, Ohio University, OH.

Leveau, R. (1985). *Le Fellah Marocain Défenseur du Trône.* Paris: Presses de Sciences Po.

Maghraoui, A. (2001). Morocco in transition: Political authority in crisis. *Middle East Report.* Retrieved June 15, 2007, from http://www.merip. org/mer/mer218/218_mghraoui.html

Mindshare. (2008). *Media scene in Morocco.* Unpublished Document.

Ministry of Communication. (2003). *Le Domaine de la Communication au Maroc.* Rabat, Morocco: Al Anbaa.

Ministry of Communication. (2006). *Rapport Annuel sur l'Etat de la Presse Ecrite et la Communication Audiovisuelle Publique.* Retrieved May 15, 2010, from http://www.mincom.gov.ma/NR/ rdonlyres/319E32BD 570D-4490-834D-319FB-5344BE5/0/RapportdelapresseVF2006.pdf

Network Information Centre. (2010). *Statistiques, nic.ma.* Retrieved June 4, 2010, from http://www. nic.ma/statistiques.asp

Norris, P. (2002). *Democratic phoenix: Political activism worldwide.* Cambridge, MA: Cambridge University Press. doi:10.1017/ CBO9780511610073.

Open Net Initiative. (2009). *Internet filtering in Morocco.* Retrieved June 10, 2010, from http:// opennet.net/sites/opennet.net/files/ONI_Morocco_2009.pdf

Reporters Without Frontiers. (2009). *2009 Country Report.* Retrieved June 8, 2010, from http:// en.rsf.org/report-morocco,160.html

Rugh, W. (1979). *The Arab press: News media and political process in the Arab World.* Syracuse, NY: Syracuse University Press.

Rugh, W. (2004). *Arab mass media: Newspapers, radio, and television in Arab politics.* Westport, CT: Praeger Publishers.

UNESCO Institute for Statistics. (2003). Retrieved July 8, from http://www.uis.unesco.org/ev.php?URL_ID= *3754&URL_DO=DO_TOPIC&URL_SECTION=201*

Waterbury, J. (1970). *The commander of the Faithful: The Moroccan political elite: A study of segmented politics.* New York: Columbia University Press.

World Bank. (2006). *Annual Report.* Retrieved January 8, 2006, from http://treasury.worldbank.org/web/AnnualReport 2006.pdf

Zaid, B. (2010). *Public service television policy and national development in Morocco: Contents, production, and audiences.* Saarbrück, Germany: VDM Verlag.

ENDNOTES

[1] I borrow these three concepts from Freedom House, a non-profit organization that promotes democracy and freedom around the world.

[2] Mindshare. *Media Scene in Morocco 2008.* Unpublished Document.

[3] Ministry of Communication. *Rapport annuel sur l'état de la presse écrite et la communication audiovisuelle publique 2006.* http://www.mincom.gov.ma/NR/rdonlyres/319E32BD-570D-4490-834D-319FB5344BE5/0/Rapportdelapresse VF2006.pdf (accessed 1 June 2010).

[4] In 2004, 43 per cent of the Moroccan population aged ten and above are illiterate. The illiteracy rate is at 60.5 per cent in rural areas and 29.4 in urban areas, 54.7 per cent among women and 30.8 per cent among men.

[5] The official representative and head of the French colonial power in Morocco.

[6] Based in Cairo, Egypt, this station was an international service, which in the 1950's and 1960's became the pulpit of revolution across the Arab world.

[7] Called Ministry of Communication since February 1995.

[8] Haut Autorité de la Communication Audiovisuelle. *Loi relative à la communication audiovisuelle.*
Dahir n° 1-04-257, Loi n° 77-03. Retrieved April 15, 2010 from http://www.haca.ma/pdf/commaudiovisuelle.pdf.

[9] HACA. List of private radio stations. Retrieved May 12, 2010 from http://www.haca.ma/indexFr.jsp?id=65.

[10] HACA. List of TV stations. Retrieved May 12, 2010 from http://www.haca.ma/indexFr.jsp?id=64.

[11] *Darija* is the spoken language of Moroccans. It is a variation of Arabic; it refers to the dialect spoken in Morocco, Algeria and Tunisia. The official languages are modern standard Arabic and French.

[12] HACA. *Loi relative à la communication audiovisuelle* (Audiovisual Communication Law).
Dahir n° 1-04-257, Loi n° 77-03, available online at http://www.haca.ma/pdf/commaudiovisuelle.pdf

[13] The nomination "Al Oula" will be henceforth used to refer to this television channel.

[14] Faiçal Faquihi. « 2M Capte plus de téléspectateur qu'Al Oula. » *L'Economiste*, 23 April 2010. p. 12.

[15] Agence National de Réglementation des Télécommunications (ANRT). *Tableau de bord trimestriel du marché Internet Mars 2010.* 4 May 2010. Retrieved June 2, 2010 from http://www.anrt.ma/fr/admin/download/upload/file_fr1891.pdf.

[16] ANRT. *Tableau de bord trimestriel du marché Internet Décembre 2009.* 25 February 2010. Retrieved June 2, 2010 from http://www.anrt.ma/fr/admin/download/upload/file_fr1874.pdf.

[17] Network Information Centre. *Statistiques.* Retrieved June 4, 2010 from http://www.nic.ma/statistiques.asp.

18 The Western Sahara refers to the southern province in Morocco. The legal status of the territory and the question of its sovereignty remain unresolved; the territory is contested between Morocco, Algeria and the Polisario.

19 A Code suggests self-regulation, but this is a legal instrument imposed on the press as a law.

20 Reporters Without Frontiers. *Country Report Morocco.* 2009. Retrieved June 15, 2010 from http://en.rsf.org/report-morocco,160. html.

21 HACA *Rapport sur l'attribution de nouvelles licences d'exploitation de services radiophoniques FM et sur les extensions de couverture des radios à de nouveaux bassins d'audience.*2009. Retrieved June 9, 2010 from http://www.haca.ma/pdf/Rapport%20 G2%20MEP.pdf.

22 Open Net Initiative. *Internet Filtering in Morocco.* 2009. Retrieved June 10, 2010 from http://opennet.net/sites/opennet.net/ files/ONI_Morocco_2009.pdf.

23 The Ministry of Information became Ministry of Communication in February 1995.

24 Instance Equité et Réconciliation. Retrieved June 6, 2010 from http://www.ier. ma/?lang=en

25 B. Katulis. *Women's Freedom in Focus: Morocco.* Freedom House. 5 March 2004 Retrieved June 6, 2010 from http://www. freedomhouse.org/uploads/special_report/32.pdf.

26 L'Institut Royal de la Culture Amazighe. http://www.ircam.ma/ (accessed 6 June 2010).

27 Reporters Without Frontiers. *2009 Country Report.* Retrieved June 8, 2010 from http://en.rsf.org/report-morocco,160.html.

28 B. Zaid. *Public Service Television Policy and National Development in Morocco: Contents, Production, and Audiences.* 2010. Saarbrücken, Germany: VDM Verlag.

29 Haut Commissariat au Plan. *Recensement Général de la Population et de l'Habitat.* 2004. Retrieved May 20, 2010 from http:// www.hcp.ma/pubData/Demographie/ RGPH/RGPH_Rapport_National.pdf.

Chapter 3
Selective Liberalization:
An Analysis of Media Reform in an Emerging Democracy

Terje S. Skjerdal
NLAUniversity College, Norway

ABSTRACT

This chapter discusses recent developments in Ethiopian media governance. The developments point in two directions: Formally speaking, media policy is liberalized, exemplified by improved media legislation, better access to public information, and issuing of private broadcasting licences. However, informally speaking, Ethiopian media governance shows signs of coercion. This is seen for example in increased government control with the official news agency, use of anti-terrorism legislation against journalists, and obstruction of political websites. The chapter suggests that the paradoxes in Ethiopian media governance may be explained as a case of selective liberalization, implying that liberalization is primarily found in areas where the risk of losing control with the flow of information is less for the government. Alongside selective liberalization, there is an undercurrent of unofficial policy in Ethiopia that may represent a return to informal coercion towards the media industry.

INTRODUCTION

There are, generally speaking, two competing accounts as regards current media reform on the African continent: one emphasizing a drive towards liberalization and the other emphasizing increased state control. Indeed, the latter appears to be the most foregrounded story concerning media democratization in Africa recently. Despite prescribed democratic progress, recent years have—in the view of many—been paved with disappointments. Promises of media liberalization have not been kept, newspapers have been forced to close down, airwaves remain largely under government control, and the average citizen has very limited access to the public arena. What I

DOI: 10.4018/978-1-4666-4197-6.ch003

intend to do in this contribution, nonetheless, is to discuss whether the apparently growing pessimism towards media policy in Africa is indeed a fair representation of long-term media reform on the continent. I will challenge this portrayal by suggesting that there is a need to distinguish between formal media policy, which is spelled out in laws and regulations, and media governance as a whole, which includes informal means of control as well (Puppis, 2010). Clearly, there are many examples of attempts at reintroducing restrictive clauses in African media regulation, but even so, I shall suggest that the long-term development in formal media policy still points towards liberalization and professionalization. However, the important lesson is that coercion remains a problem at informal level, and–perhaps–increasingly so. As formal regulation improves, media coercion assumes new forms and eventually threatens professional media activity. In theoretical terms, these developments in African media governance may be described as *selective liberalization*. Governments push liberalization in areas where the risk of losing control with communication is miniscule, but they retain control in areas where media communication could seriously challenge the power of the incumbent.

The concept of selective liberalization is exemplified by recent developments in media governance in the second-largest African country–Ethiopia. An emerging democracy on the Horn of Africa, Ethiopia broadly resembles other African nations in terms of media regulation and development. Like several other regimes on the continent, Ethiopia came out of an authoritarian situation and introduced multiparty democracy in the early 1990s. One of the first issues on the agenda for the new-born government was to allow private media outlets. In reality, however, the state retained control with the airwaves, and media pluralism was only allowed in the less important print media market. As the new private publications increasingly infuriated the Ethiopian government in the 1990s, the authorities began to use various types of restraints to control journalistic activity. However, as the present analysis will show, formal media policy in the country has simultaneously shown clear signs of improvement during the last two decades. The developments in Ethiopian media governance are, therefore, not unidirectional, but are subject to seemingly contradictory trajectories–as is the case for many other African nations. These contradictions in media governance will thus be explained within the framework of selective liberalization. Before turning to a closer analysis of the media situation in Ethiopia, it is therefore necessary to do an overview of the seemingly contradictory tendencies in African media policy over the past few decades.

DEVELOPMENTS TOWARDS LIBERALIZATION IN AFRICAN MEDIA POLICY

It is generally assumed that there is some sort of correlation between democratization and media liberalization, even though the relations are complex and unique to each national context. The paradox on the African continent, nonetheless, is that decolonization and national independence in the immediate decades after the 1950s did not bring with it larger media freedom—quite the contrary, actually, in many cases. The new African leaders—with hardly any exception–regarded the media as a convenient instrument for their political project. Kwame Nkrumah, the father of African nationalism, thus advocated a close partnership between political and journalistic forces when declaring that "our revolutionary African press must carry our revolutionary purposes" (cited in Bond, 1997, p. 30). To varying degrees, the media became mouthpieces of nationalism in the newly independent states. Many outlets, both private and official ones, began to censor themselves in order to tune in with official political ideas. They resembled "muffled drums" (Hachten, 1971) and the radio in particular became an instrument of political propaganda (Hydén & Okigbo, 2002). The situation turned even worse in military regimes such as Ethiopia, Somalia, Uganda and Guinea, where there was no room for independent voices at all.

It is towards this backdrop Hydén and Okigbo (2002) see a significant change in the African media landscape around 1990, when the second wave of democracy washed over the continent[1]. The second wave marked the diversification of media markets. New publications flourished and the independent media grew "like the savannah grass after prolific rainfalls" (Karikari, 2010, p. 23). Governments turned out to be more reluctant in bringing into fruition the liberal principles in the broadcasting sector, in contrast to the print sector (Van der Veur, 2002), yet independent radio stations were increasingly allowed and began to assume the role of a democratizing institution in society (Balancing Act, 2008). In the view of Hydén and Okigbo (2002), the democratizing potential of the media became particularly important during the second wave of democracy because the media partly replaced the role that social movements had played in the first wave. The precondition for the new role of the media was changes in constitutional provisions in the new multiparty democracies recognizing freedom of expression as a key principle (Ogbondah, 1997; 2002), though rightly there has been slowness in translating the clauses into political action as will be discussed later. The liberal-minded national constitutions of the 1990s have been backed by various pan-African agreements concerning media rights. For example, the African Charter on Human and People's Rights (OAU, 1981) stipulated the right of citizens to seek information and express opinions, and more specifically in relation to media operations, the Windhoek Declaration (UNESCO, 1991) pronounces fundamental principles for an independent and pluralistic press for all African societies. The Windhoek Declaration was later succeeded by an equivalent African Charter on Broadcasting (UNESCO, 2001). Also worthy of mention is the Table Mountain Declaration of

June 2007, calling for the conclusive abolishment of insult and criminal defamation laws in Africa.

According to Blankson (2007), there are numerous examples that the fundamental ideas of free speech as enshrined in constitutions and pan-African charters have been followed up in subsidiary laws. Criminal penalties were abolished in countries like the Central African Republic, Senegal and the Democratic Republic of Congo. The responsibility to ensure media freedom has been handed over to the courts and other non-government bodies, for example in Kenya, Ghana and Togo. Blankson further notes that local advocacy organizations such as the Media Institute of Southern Africa (MISA) serve to safeguard media rights, and media businesses themselves have started to collaborate on activities, capital and audiences, as illustrated by the media markets in Kenya, Tanzania and Uganda. All these developments point to a strengthened African media landscape and a "revival of democratic optimism across the African continent", in the words of Blankson (2007, p. 15; Ogbondah, 2004). As of late, African parliaments have also begun to pass access to information laws which intend to ease journalists' rights to documents in the public administration. Ethiopia, Uganda, Liberia, Nigeria, Angola and South Africa[2] were among the first countries to pass such laws, and Ghana, Mozambique and Rwanda are nearby–to name a few (Callamard, 2010). Adding to the broad picture of improvement of the African media situation is increased focus on professionalization as demonstrated by the opening of new journalism training programmes all over the continent (De Beer, 2007; Berger, 2007a). Despite some recent setbacks for the human rights record in Africa, Agnès Callamard, executive director of Article 19, concludes that "since the 1990s, the trend as far as free expression, transparency and accountability goes is a positive one and progress has been real" (2010, p. 1237).

Improvements in African media policy may not only be attributed to local dynamics but are a result of international impulsion as well. The international state-supported donor community has increasingly declared public transparency and freedom of expression a motivating force and a precondition for state-to-state support. Direct support to media development is often linked to the overall foreign policy (Nelson, 2011). The flow of direct media assistance alone, excluding the U.S., is estimated to be US$1 billion a year, much of which goes to African countries (Becker & Tudor, 2005). Thus, expectations of Western donors on advancements in governance and democratic rule have been a compelling force for the liberalization of African media policy.

To sum up, since the early 1990s, there has been a development towards liberalization of African media policy in at least five areas: Constitutional reforms embracing freedom of expression principles; demotion of criminal libel laws and related restrictions; introduction of private media outlets; increased access to public information; and the planning and setting up of self-regulatory systems for the media. The critical issue, however, is to what extent the regulatory principles are followed up in actual practice. A number of analysts remain sceptical concerning the developments in years, as will be discussed in the next section.

COUNTER-READINGS: SIGNS OF INCREASED STATE CONTROL

Despite the prospects for freer media markets after the introduction of multiparty democracy in the 1990s, some commentators claim to see a recent relapse back to increased state control with the African media. In connection with Kenya's private newspaper *Daily Nation*'s 50th anniversary in March 2010, veteran Ugandan journalist Charles Onyango-Obbo pinpoints this argument when claiming that press freedom is becoming a "sectarian right" in Africa (Onyango-Obbo, 2010). He maintains that governments have made it virtually impossible to criticize the rulers. He further gives evidence of newly introduced media

legislation in various countries which provides effective protection for the government and its supporters. In the view of Onyango-Obbo, the birth of the nationalist media in the 1960s (such as Kenya's *Daily Nation*) would be inconceivable today because the cause of nation-building has lost to tribal and sectarian interests. The renowned editor claims that the freest period for the Africa media was between 1990 and 2005, after which the situation has reverted to increased repression.

Critical views of recent developments in the African media situation focus on three main issues: first and foremost–changes in media legislation; secondly, and on a more informal level–intimidation of journalistic activity; thirdly, and largely underestimated–greater sophistication of government communication strategies. All three areas have been subject to notable changes over the past few years, and one could arguably read into this a change in the direction of overall media governance.

First, changes in media legislation are often taken as the most concrete sign of a new direction in the government's approach to the media. In this regard, there is a remarkable similarity in the policy development of various African governments. Certain legal clauses have been dismissed as anachronistic while others are protected because they are deemed still important. Sections in the laws that forbade private media outlets and legalized official censorship were largely done away with in the early 1990s, as were most provisions that gave the President a position above the law and exempted him[3] from criticism. Recently, however, a number of African states have attempted to reintroduce laws that strengthen national security and heighten control with media businesses and media workers. For example, anti-terrorism acts which restrict media activity have been introduced or proposed in countries such as Uganda[4] (Mwenda, 2007; Tabaire, 2007), Swaziland[5] (Motsa, 2009) and Ghana[6] (Berger, 2007b). Regulation which delimits the reporting of ethnic hatred has recently been passed in, for example, Chad[7] and Kenya[8].[9]

Furthermore, generally well reputed media societies like Kenya and Uganda have reintroduced registration (in the case of Kenya) or licensing (in the case of Uganda) of media outlets and journalists. A system of registration and licensing "lends itself to chilling effect" and serves to reinforce self-censorship problems in African journalism, warns Guy Berger (2009, p. 282). Somewhat less controversial from a press freedom perspective, though still a sign of increased state regulation of the media, are measures which limit foreign and cross-ownership of the media. Mozambique, Nigeria, Ghana and Mali are but a few examples of countries which have implemented ownership regulations lately. The introduction of media councils is another means to exert media policy and has increasingly come into focus by media organizations. Initially intended to enhance media self-regulation, independent media councils have turned out to be hounded by authorities, or are infiltrated by government bodies (Tettey, 2006). The Botswana government, for example, practically outlawed the media's own press council by introducing a parallel statutory media council through the new Media Practitioners Act in 2009 (Krüger, 2009; Taylor, 2009)., However, the recent supplements in South African media legislation have received more attention than any of these changes in media regulation. In 2010, the ANC (African National Congress) government proposed a Media Appeals Tribunal and a Protection of Information Bill with the intention to prevent the media from abusing their freedoms and harming the dignity of people. The media environment and human rights groups, however, perceived the proposed legislation as nothing but measures to hamper with free speech and restrict critical reporting on the government itself. The fact that these legislative moves took place in South Africa, the beacon of liberal democracy on the African continent, was taken as a worrying sign of the overall direction of media regulation in this part of the world (Berger, 2010).

Second, the African media situation is marked by frequent infringements of journalistic activity.

These are more difficult to measure, but they include harassment of journalists and other staff members, threats of fines and punishments, legal action, physical insecurity for media workers, and the general indisposition of public officials to assist journalists in their daily work. It is difficult to determine whether such intimidation has become stronger or weaker in African media practice lately, but press freedom groups maintain that promises of increased media freedom have not at all materialized in enhanced attitudes towards the media and journalists. The safety record is not getting much better either. According to statistics by Committee to Protect Journalists (CPJ), 11 African journalists were killed between 2001 and 2005 (averaging 2.2 a year), while the number increased to 36 in between 2006 and 2010 (averaging 7.2 a year). One should be cautious when drawing general lessons regarding developments in press freedom on the basis of the number of journalists killed (much of the increase in recent years is due to military unrest in Somalia), but the statistics nevertheless serve to illustrate that the safety situation for many media workers has deteriorated. On the basis of numerous accounts of intimidation, the International Federation of Journalists (IFJ) concludes that "press freedom is still in danger in Africa despite 20 years of democratisation" (IFJ Africa Press Freedom Report 2009[10]). This has resulted in a rapid increase in the number of journalists going into exile, particularly from the Horn of Africa and Zimbabwe, according to CPJ (Salazar-Ferro, 2010).

Third, developments in media governance are also observable through the government's communication strategy. In this context, "communication strategy" does not point to policy guidelines as defined in formal media legislation, but to the actual means through which the government communicates with its citizens and the world community, where use of mass media plays a key role. This remains an under-researched area in studies of African media policy. Priorities in national budgets, nonetheless, indicate that authorities are increasingly channelling resources into a conscious communication and Public Relations (PR) strategy. A forerunner in this area was the replacement of the South African Communication Service (SACS) by the Government Communication Information System (GCIS) in 1998, marking a new era in the professionalization of government communications in Africa. GCIS aims to play a facilitating and strategizing role for all government communication in South Africa. It also promotes the government and the country internationally. GCIS has become a model for the restructuring of government communication services elsewhere in Africa, for example in Ethiopia, as will be discussed later. The remodelling of government communication in African nations signifies a significant break with various types of propaganda offices that existed earlier, but the professionalized services have also come under criticism, inter alia, for their alleged lack of independence from political actors in the government structure (e.g. Butler, 2000).

All these developments regarding media legislation, intimidation of journalism activity and sophistication of government communication arguably signal overall tighter control with the African media. Explanations of the root causes of these unsolicited developments in the African media situation differ. Jimmy Ocitti (1999) mainly puts the blame on powerful governments, which, in his view, pretend to go by democratic constitutional principles, but in reality continue to pass bills and directives that are utterly hostile to any type of critical media activity. Katrin Voltmer (2008) turns the issue around and argues that for new democracies in Africa, "the problem is not so much an all-powerful state, but a state that is too weak to generate the necessary policies" (p. 16). Similarly, a weak economic system has an effect on the media situation. The weak economy impacts on the relative strength of media organizations and implies that organizations fail to attract investors and an educated work force. This leaves media businesses susceptible to corruption, both organized and lesser-scale, for example in the case of bribery and acceptance of so-called brown envelopes among journalists (Skjerdal, 2010b). In turn, lack of professionalism within the media industry itself becomes a reason for governments to restrain liberalization in media regulation and similarly justifies restrictions on reporting activity. Along these lines, Francis Kasoma (1997), in a forward-looking perspective, and Francis Nyamnjoh (2005), looking back on recent developments, put great emphasis on the media's own responsibility when explaining the lack of progress in African media operations. "The independent press in Africa's multiparty states of the 1990s has developed a confrontational relationship with governments, which is largely being brought about by the press's own unprofessional behaviour," writes Kasoma (1997, p. 295), while Nyamnjoh contends that "contrary to some optimistic accounts (Hydén et al., 2002), media that have facilitated genuine democratisation may appear rare in Africa" (2005, p. 272).

In an attempt to synthesize the various theories of continuing media suppression in Africa, Yusuf Kalyango and Petya Eckler (2010) use agenda-building theory to explain how governments retain and strengthen control mechanisms. An examination of the conditions that affect media behaviour, agenda-building theory as employed by Kalyango and Eckler in the evaluation of the East African media situation suggests that the governments are central players in weak democracies, controlling the media through restrictive legislation, intimidation and state patronage from media ownership. The result is that the media, both private and state-owned, "unconsciously propagate the government agendas" (Kalyango and Eckler, 2010, p. 382). The experiences from Ethiopia, to be explicated in the following, however reveal a paradox in media governance: Legislation and various provisions are indeed liberalized, but the media themselves experience increasing control.

AN OVERVIEW OF THE ETHIOPIAN MEDIA SITUATION SINCE 1991

Before discussing important developments in Ethiopian media governance, a brief overview of the changes in the country's media landscape since 1991 helps to situate the analysis in the particular socio-political context. The year 1991 is chosen because this was the year when the military Dergue regime (r. 1974–91) was overthrown by revolutionary groups that later formed the coalition government of EPRDF (Ethiopian People's Revolutionary Democratic Front) which remains in office until today. Led by TPLF (Tigrayan People's Liberation Front), the resistance movement in the 1980s used clandestine radio broadcasts as one of its methods to gather the revolutionaries against the Dergue and to communicate with different groups in the opposition. All types of private or government-independent media were strictly forbidden during the military regime (Janas, 1991). It thus became one of the central issues for the EPRDF coalition to eradicate the propaganda regime of the Dergue and open up for pluralized media markets when it came to power in 1991. The press law of 1992 (Proclamation no. 34/1992, A Proclamation to Provide for the Freedom of the Press) subsequently forbade censorship and allowed private media outlets. The result, similar to other media societies that came out of a repressive situation around the same time–for example Somalia (Höhne, 2008), Mongolia (Nielsen, 2009) and the Baltic countries (Harro-Loit, 2005)–was a flourishing of new publications. However, many of the publications were sensationalist rather than serious and folded after a brief period on the market–either by choice as a result of disinterested audiences or by force as a result of government pressure (Shimelis, 2002; Skjerdal & Hallelujah, 2009). The late-'90s subsequently marked the beginning of Ethiopian journalists going into exile after experiencing intimidation by government-affiliated actors. The latest "wave" of journalists fleeing the country came after the 2005 national elections, which ended in violent clashes between protesters and security forces followed by detention of 14 editors and publishers together with a number of opposition members. In less than a year, the number of newspapers dropped from 85 to 51 (Mekuria, 2005; Kibnesh, 2006). According to recent statistics, there are now approximately 25 newspapers in Ethiopia (Ethiopian Broadcasting Authority, January 2013), 17 of which concentrate primarily on politics and current affairs. A majority of these are private weeklies; four are government-run; and, interestingly enough, the vast majority of print publications in Ethiopia are in local languages (mainly Amharic), contrasting the situation in most other African countries where newspapers generally use European languages (Salawu, 2006). The Ethiopian media situation is as such characterized by a local media tradition in contrast to the foreign news language dominance in many other media markets in Africa.

The Ethiopian broadcasting sector remains more state-controlled than the print sector. All national radio and television services are owned by the state and controlled by the government. In principle, the 1992 press law opened up for private broadcasting organizations, but the first radio licences were only awarded in 2006. However, on the air since 1985, the TPLF revolutionary outlet Radio Fana has always retained a position on the outskirts of official media regulation. For many years the station was neither categorized as a commercial radio, nor as a state-owned radio, although it has strong links to the ruling coalition EPRDF. Today, it is formally licensed as a commercial radio together with three other private radio stations which broadcast in the capital city Addis Ababa. This puzzling escape from formal regulation illustrates some of the characteristics of Ethiopian media governance. It is an applied policy which tends to favour government-friendly media initiatives (to be discussed later). In the area of television, no commercial or independent licence has been awarded yet. Officially, this is because it would not be economically viable to establish new analogue television stations while awaiting a new digital broadcasting network (Desta Tesfaw, deputy director general of Ethiopian Broadcasting Authority, personal interview, 6 August 2009).

Audience figures are highly uncertain for all sections of the Ethiopian media. Television broadcasting covers approximately 51% of the country, while for radio the official scheme is to reach full coverage for all parts of the country by 2014 (information provided by Ethiopian Broadcasting Authority/EBA). The print media are scarcely distributed outside of Addis Ababa. No more than 1% of the 85-million strong population read newspapers on a regular basis. Internet access is on the rise, but still only available to approximately 960,000 citizens (Internet World Stats, 2012). Only Sierra Leone is noted to have less Internet penetration in Africa than Ethiopia, largely explaining why online media are not much pursued by the local media businesses. Diaspora Internet channels, however, represent a significant alternative to the local media market in Ethiopia. These and other media initiatives may be interpreted as a reaction to official media policy in mainland Ethiopia, in line with the argument next.

IMPROVEMENTS IN ETHIOPIAN MEDIA LEGISLATION

Contrary to the impression conveyed by various press freedom groups, formal Ethiopian media legislation has shown notable signs of liberalization during the two decades of EPRDF rule. This is evident both in the abrogation of the 1992 press law and in the developments in broadcasting regulation from 1999 to 2007.

In 2008, the 1992 press law was replaced by a wider media law entitled "The Freedom of the Mass Media and Access to Information Proclamation" (Proclamation no. 590/2008). Despite eradicating state censorship and opening up for private media outlets, the 1992 proclamation had a number of drawbacks from a press freedom perspective. The major restrictive clauses can be grouped into four types: compulsory licensing of media outlets; banning of material that could threaten the safety of the state; prohibition of defamation and false accusations (resulting in a penalty of ETB 10,000-50,000 [US$1,000-5,000 in 2005 currency] or 1-3 years in prison); and the opening for the authorities to confiscate in advance any press product that they believe could instigate illegal actions. These clauses, particularly the last one which implied a value judgment on behalf of the authorities, resulted in verdicts against a number of editors and publishers throughout the 1990s and early 2000s. As a consequence, Prime Minister Meles Zenawi came on the worldwide record of "press freedom predators" when the list was first released by Reporters Without Borders (RSF) in 2001. The Ethiopian press law became a major target for human rights organizations, with the result that the government eventually drafted a new press law in 2002. International press freedom organizations noted that there were some improvements in the draft proclamation, but overall it was condemned as yet another draconian bill (Barker & Mendel, 2003; Alemayehu, 2003). Certain revisions had followed before the eventual promulgation of the final media law on 4 December 2008, but press freedom groups remained largely critical to the new law. Nevertheless, the argument here is that the 2008 law represents a significant improvement since the 1992 law, particularly in five areas.

Firstly, the 2008 proclamation is significantly different from the 1992 proclamation in that it contains a weighty section securing access to public information. Public offices are instructed to serve the media and shall provide requested information as speedily as possible, no later than 30 days after the request is posted. Once a year, every public office is obliged to report thoroughly on transparency to the Ombudsman, including how many requests there have been for information and how many have been accepted and rejected. The public transparency section makes Ethiopia the third country in Africa to adopt an access to information regulation after South Africa and

Uganda, according to Friedrich-Ebert-Stiftung[11]. At the same time, it must be added that the proclamation gives public officials a range of reasons to reject impartment of information, for instance if the information could damage Ethiopia's international relations. The second significant change in the 2008 proclamation is that it abolishes the licensing of print publications and news agencies, in contrast to the developments in Ugandan media regulation, for example. According to the new proclamation it is now sufficient to notify the Ethiopian Broadcasting Authority (EBA) of the opening of a new publication, and in the case of no response from EBA within 30 days, the publication is deemed registered by default. There is no longer a fee attached to the registration. The defunct licensing process is often falsely recorded by rights groups as a formal obstacle for newspaper publishing in Ethiopia[12].

Thirdly, broadcasting activities are inherently part of the freedoms granted in the 2008 proclamation, contrasting the 1992 proclamation where the focus was practically only on the print media. The new proclamation acknowledges that private broadcasting is in the shaping in Ethiopia, although matters of licensing and programming are dealt with in a separate broadcasting law (Proclamation no. 533/2007). Fourthly, the 2008 media law explicitly grants journalists the right to form professional organizations. Article 5.2 reads, "Journalists have a right to organize themselves into professional associations of their choice." Though this might seem like a redundant clause, in Ethiopia, professional journalism associations have been subject to harassment by authorities and the right to formally establish such groups is deemed important by media workers themselves. Fifthly, and importantly in light of previous misuse of law enforcement, the new media proclamation prohibits the use of pre-trial detention of journalists.

The 2008 media proclamation, therefore, represents significant steps forward from the 1992 press proclamation. At the same time, it should

be noted that important protective clauses have survived in the new law. What has perhaps received most attention is the opening for harsh penalties for defamation and false accusations (Ross, 2010). The compensation for such damage amounts to up to ETB 100,000 (US$6,000)[13], up from ETB 50,000 in the 1992 proclamation[14]. Also, the authorities can lawfully confiscate press products if such are believed to represent a serious threat to national security (article 42). On the basis of this, the U.S.-based organization, Freedom House, concludes that the new law provides a "reinforced legal basis for government oversight and control[15]."

Parallel to the advancements in the general media proclamation, there have also been improvements in broadcasting regulation. This is detectable in the Broadcasting Service Proclamation No. 533/2007, which replaced the previous Broadcasting Proclamation No. 178/1999. The main intention of the law is to regulate radio and television service by means of licences, of which the latest proclamation defines three types: public, commercial and community broadcasting licences. The most interesting development since the 1999 proclamation in this regard is that the state broadcasters, responsible for public broadcasting, are now under equal jurisdiction with private broadcasters. This is significant because in Ethiopian media regulation, like elsewhere in Africa, state media traditionally operate within an extra-legal sphere, privileged by their strong linkages to the overall state apparatus structure. The 2007 broadcasting proclamation represents a shift in this thinking when assuming the same regulation for state broadcasters as for private broadcasters. Concurrently, the legislation introduces the term "public broadcaster" instead of "state broadcaster," thus drawing on the European public service broadcasting terminology. The duty of a public broadcaster, according to the legislation, is to:

- Enhance the participation of the public through the presentation of government policies and strategies as well as activities related to development, democracy and good governance.

- Present programs which inform, educate and entertain the public.
- Present programs which reflect unity of peoples based on equality.
- Promote and enhance the cultures and artistic values of the public.
- Serve political parties operating in accordance with the Constitution and the electoral laws of the country on the basis of fair and just treatment. (Ethiopian Broadcasting Service Proclamation No. 533/2007, article 16.2).

The policy thus resembles that of a classic European public service broadcaster, with the exception of the first sub-article, which gives the public broadcaster a special mandate to communicate government policies. The emphasis on close linkages between the government and the media in promoting social development is in line with the government's pronounced development journalism policy as explicated in a separate policy document (Ethiopian Press Agency, 2008). What the amendments in broadcasting regulation suggest is a transition from old-style state broadcasting to modern public broadcasting, but the transition is not comprehensive; the government still has special access to using the national broadcaster for certain purposes. At the same time, the government is aware of the potential short-comings of government-affiliated public media outlets and duly warns in its development journalism policy document against the public media "being a tool for propaganda" for the government and instead calls for the media to adhere to "strengthening investigative journalism and adopting appropriate liberal media practices" (Ethiopian Press Agency, 2008, clause 4.2.3.4).

To manage licensing and control with broadcasters, the new broadcasting proclamation announces the establishment of Ethiopian Broad-

casting Authority; EBA (replacing Ethiopian Broadcasting Agency of the previous proclamation). The office subsequently came into operation in February 2009. Although the formal duties of EBA appear to be similar to those of the previous agency, EBA has obtained more genuine authority in accordance with its status as an "autonomous federal agency having its own legal personality" (article 4.1). Later in 2009, EBA also took over the duty to register print media publications, which previously was the responsibility of the Ministry of Information. Organizationally speaking, it, therefore, appears that the licensing, registration and control with media organizations, both public and private, have taken a step away from the formerly close association with the ministerial wings of the government.

RESTRUCTURING OF THE STATE MEDIA

Changes in Ethiopian media policy can also be seen in the reorganizing of the state media institutions. Indeed, these organizations have undergone substantial restructuring since 2007, and the reforms largely point in the direction of media professionalization. The restructuring began with the implementation of a Business Process Reengineering (BPR) Programme, which the entire state administration was subject to starting in 2007. The BPR programme aimed to improve the state edifice in cost, quality, speed and service. For the state media, this was eventually articulated in three main goals: exercising transparency, serving the public better, and ensuring quality coverage. Various international media organizations were benchmarked in the process. On the broadcasting side, the main models were the South African Broadcasting Corporation (SABC), All India Radio, and the British Broadcasting Corporation (BBC). The idea was not to duplicate successes of other institutions, but to draw from their experiences and adjust the models for an Ethiopian context. The BPR process in the state media was headed by the government's spokesperson himself, Bereket Simon. The outcome came to be different for the different media institutions. Two institutions that went in diverse directions will be discussed here as they represent seemingly opposing trends in Ethiopian media policy: Ethiopian Television and Radio Agency (ERTA) and Ethiopian News Agency (ENA).

For Ethiopian Television (ETV) and Ethiopian Radio, the BPR process ended with a full merger into one organization: Ethiopian Radio and Television Agency (ERTA). In the process, employees in the media organizations were organized in committees that came up with recommendations for a reformed organization. The practical recommendations from ETV included: more simplicity in retrieving information; reducing unnecessary steps in reporting events; improving the editorial policy in terms of ethical standards; creating more self-reliance; pursuing journalistic ideas instead of just following events; and striving for more merit-based appointments in the higher levels of the organization (member of BPR steering committee, personal interview, 29 November 2008). The leadership responded by relocating the radio and television divisions in one company instead of the formerly two. In 2009, Ethiopian Radio, which previously had offices on the outskirts of the city, moved in with ETV in downtown Addis Ababa. In practical terms for the journalists, this meant for instance covering the same event for both television and radio when going out for reporting. According to one editor in ETV, journalists are generally happy with the merger, "The journalistic style has not changed, but we produce content for both media" (personal interview, 18 November 2009). However, the new organizational model has demonstrated that the radio medium is subordinate to television in journalistic priorities. Journalistic coverage is still determined by government interests, according to the reporters. During the restructuring process, it was also seriously considered on management level to rename the

organization as "Ethiopian Broadcasting Corporation" so as to resemble a full-blown public service broadcaster. Although the name ERTA was kept, "public media" became the new official term for the state media. By and large, the directions of the developments in ERTA, at least in the intention, appear to signal a more journalistically-minded and publically-oriented institution.

In light of the route chosen for ERTA, it is perhaps surprising that the BPR process resulted in the opposite move for Ethiopian News Agency (ENA), the country's official news bureau. It was decided that ENA, instead of having a (semi-)autonomous board like in the past, would be directly organized under the Ministry of Information. For the 125 journalists in ENA, this indicated that news from now on had to be reported in a style that was more government-friendly. Dissatisfaction started to unfold in the newsroom. "We are not satisfied. I only work here to get bread," imparts one journalist who has been with ENA for many years (personal interview, 17 November 2009). He further complains that recently employed journalists are government stalwarts. "There are so many cadres. Most journalists now are party-affiliated," he contends. In contrast to the situation in television and radio, where the restructuring signalled increased professionalism, ENA was drawn closer to the Ministry of Information and became an important component in the government's communication strategy. How should this be interpreted in the overall media governance strategy?

A NEW COMMUNICATION STRATEGY FOR THE GOVERNMENT

The relocation of ENA directly under the government is arguably part of an intentional strategy to strengthen Ethiopian government communications in general. Soon after the decision to place ENA under the Ministry of Information, in October 2008, Prime Minster Meles Zenawi announced that the ministry was about to be dismantled altogether. In place of the ministry, but with different duties and in a different geographical location, an Office for Government Communication Affairs (OGCA) was set up and began operation in February 2009. To head the office, Meles Zenawi picked his personal advisor and right hand, Bereket Simon, who had also served as the Minister of Information 2001–2005. The model for OGCA was the equivalent office in South Africa, the Government Communication and Information System (GCIS). Akin to the model in South Africa, OGCA's main duty is to serve as a communication office for the state and the government and assist the various media outlets— privately-run and state-run, domestic and foreign.

One of the first initiatives of OGCA was the introduction of weekly press briefings for the media (began April 2009), as well as bi-monthly press conferences with the prime minister–which indeed represent a rare case of open access to the nation's leadership in African regimes. Notably, the press conferences are open to all sections of the media, both private and official outlets; contrasting the situation in earlier years when the rule of thumb was that only the state media were invited to events arranged by government offices.

The recent restructuring of government communications in Ethiopia may be interpreted in two seemingly contradictory ways. On the one hand, the government exhibits a need for more control with media content through its take-over of the official news agency, which is an important source of information for state media outlets in particular. On the other hand, the dismantlement of the Ministry of Information and the subsequent erection of OGCA signify a desire to serve all parts of the media better and to cater for increased transparency in the government's activities. One should of course be open for the possibility that both of these interpretations are reasonable.

OTHER TENDENCIES IN ETHIOPIAN MEDIA GOVERNANCE

In addition to the changes in media policy discussed previously, there are certain other moves that indicate the direction of Ethiopian media governance directly or indirectly. The first issue relates to the Ethiopian take on media councils alongside the previous discussion of African media governance, where it was noted that authorities are increasingly eager to control such councils. The Ethiopian situation contrasts these developments. In the first draft of the new press law dating back to 2002, a media council with government representation was indeed proposed, but the idea was scrapped after criticism from advocacy organizations. Instead, the government challenged the media themselves to set up a self-governing media council. An organizing committee for the council was formed in July 2010 with the aim to advance media accountability and self-governance. The committee consisted of members from both the private and the state media, though the main proportion rests with the private media. It remains of course to be seen how strong the media council will be in the context of self-accountability and to what extend it will stay independent of government interests—and whether the council will at all materialize, of course.

More critical in the name of press freedom, however, and more in line with the developments elsewhere in Africa, is the introduction of Ethiopian anti-terrorism legislation. The law was deemed necessary by the government following several bomb attacks on Ethiopians by insurgent groups on the Horn of Africa in recent years. Passed by the parliament on July 7, 2009, the anti-terrorism proclamation provides, in the view of Human Rights Watch, "an extremely broad and ambiguous definition of terrorism that could be used to criminalize non-violent political dissent and various other activities that should not be deemed as terrorism" (p. 3; cf. Article 19, 2010). Specifically, in relation to free speech concerns, the proclamation provides for up to 20 years imprisonment for anyone who "publishes or causes the publication of a statement that is likely to be understood by some or all of the members of the public [...] as a direct or indirect encouragement [...] to the commission or preparation or instigation of an act of terrorism" (article 6). The broad definition of terrorism and involvement in supporting activities will arguably have a chilling effect on journalism work, as seen elsewhere (McNamara, 2009; Okumu, 2007). A case in point is that accusations of terrorism links led to the closing of the critical weekly *Addis Neger* in November 2009 and its editors subsequently going into exile (Mesfin, 2010).

Moreover, the Ethiopian parliament in January 2009 adopted a proclamation that significantly limits the operations of international NGO work in the country. The Charities and Societies Proclamation, popularly referred to as the NGO law, prohibits any civil society group that receives more than 10% of its income from international sources from engaging in human rights work in Ethiopia. Though not specifically addressing the media, the law indirectly affects the conditions for the media because media rights groups are cut back and critical voices in the civil society are fewer than they used to be (McLure, 2010). A parallel to this provision in the NGO law may be found in the 2007 broadcasting law and the 2008 media law, which prohibit foreign ownership of media outlets. However, limitation of foreign ownership in the media may be justified as a means of securing local industry and content (Berger, 2007b), but in the case of NGOs, the plain issue is that many local organizations are simply not able to function on internal support alone. This law thus strongly indicates a government eager to use coercion to control civil society and dissident voices.

CONCLUDING DISCUSSION

Ethiopian media governance is not unidirectional. It is neither a one-way development towards increased suppression, as rights groups argue, nor could the media policy said to be "on par with the best in the world," as the late Prime Minister proclaimed in an interview with Newsweek (McLure, 2008). In order to understand the ambivalent situation, a distinction between formal and informal media governance is needed. On the formal level, amendments in Ethiopian media legislation since 2007 do indeed denote significant steps forward towards increased liberalization. Suppressive clauses have been scrapped, licences are no longer required for print publications, journalists are allowed to form professional associations – and the associations prosper like never before. Not only that; the media have been given formal rights to access public information, government press conferences are arranged on a regular basis, private radio licences have been awarded, the state media have started on their route towards becoming public media outlets, journalism education is blossoming (Skjerdal & Ngugi, 2007; Skjerdal, 2011), the Ethiopian Prime Minister no longer appears on RSF's list of press freedom predators, and the media have begun to fortify self-governance through the establishment of an independent media council. These changes notwithstanding, the informal side of Ethiopian media governance remains a concern, perhaps increasingly so. Legislation adjacent to media regulation has a controlling effect on media activity, as in the example of the anti-terrorism proclamation. The official news agency has been drawn closer to the government, possibly with the intention of controlling the flow of information. Websites and radio channels run by Ethiopians in the diaspora are readily blocked by Ethiopian authorities. In-depth interviews with journalists show that they operate with lesser or larger degree of fear for reactions from outsiders and public officials, causing both private and state media outlets to execute self-censorship and shun critical reporting (Skjerdal, 2008; 2010a).

In theoretical terms, the paradoxes in Ethiopian media governance may be explained as a case of *selective liberalization*. Liberalization is found to occur in formal regulation (where it is easily observed by outsiders), and in areas where the risk of losing control with the flow of information is less for the government. Like in Zambian broadcasting reform, which has been characterized by partial and reluctant liberalization (Moyo, 2010), Ethiopian media reform ensures that the state media remain a dominant voice while opening up for limited competition in the private media market. Importantly, however, the move towards liberalization is challenged by a strong undercurrent of unofficial policy which may represent a return to informal coercion towards the media industry. There are several indications of such informal pressure in Ethiopia, though much more difficult to verify than developments in official media policy. For example, strategic appointments in both the state media and regulatory units such as EBA are mainly of political nature. Broadcasting licences are similarly assumed to be awarded merely to groups close to the government; at least not to groups that directly oppose the ruling interests (Amare, 2009). Publications critical of the authorities experience informal threats, as in the case of *Addis Neger*. As a strategy of survival, journalists and media businesses choose the safe route and engage in critical reporting only in small portions every so often. Formal media regulation is improved, but suppression prevails through the media's own self-imposed mechanisms.

On a concluding note, the paradox between formal liberalization and informal coercion has implications for research strategies into African media governance. If the theory presented here is valid, studies of media legislation alone will fall short and may even give a false image of media improvement in semi-democratic states in spite of renewed oppression. Certain relapses in media legislation notwithstanding, the overall trend does indeed signal liberalization of African media policy if one scrutinizes media laws in isolation. A new form of media coercion, however, calls for a broader research approach. Policy studies and document analyses are still needed, but more importantly, and more demanding, researchers must enter the newsrooms and investigate how media governance is operationalized and negotiated on the professional and organizational levels.

ACRONYMS

- **ANC:** African National Congress
- **BBC:** British Broadcasting Corporation
- **BPR:** Business Process Reengineering
- **CPJ:** Committee to Protect Journalists
- **EBA:** Ethiopian Broadcasting Authority
- **ENA:** Ethiopian News Agency
- **EPRDF:** Ethiopian People's Revolutionary Democratic Front
- **ERTA:** Ethiopian Radio and Television Agency
- **ETB:** Ethiopian Birr
- **ETV:** Ethiopian Television
- **GCIS:** Government Communication and Information System (South Africa)
- **IFJ:** International Federation of Journalists
- **MISA:** Media Institute of Southern Africa
- **OAU:** Organization of African Unity
- **OGCA:** Office for Government Communication Affairs (Ethiopia)
- **RSF:** Reporters sans frontières/Reporters Without Borders
- **SABC:** South African Broadcasting Corporation
- **TPLF:** Tigray People's Liberation Front
- **UNESCO:** United Nations Educational, Scientific and Cultural Organization
- **USD:** US Dollar

REFERENCES

Alemayehu G. M. (2003). A discourse on the draft Ethiopian press law. *International Journal of Ethiopian Studies, 1*(1), 103–120.

Amare A. (2009). Democracy and press freedom. In Müller-Schöll, U. (Ed.), *Democracy and the social question. Some contributions to a dialogue in Ethiopia* (pp. 26–34). Addis Ababa, Ethiopia: Falcon Printing Enterprise.

Article 19. (2010, March). Comment on anti-terrorism proclamation, 2009, of Ethiopia. Report.

Balancing Act. (2008). *African broadcast and film markets.*

Barker, J., & Mendel, T. (2003). *The legal framework for freedom of expression in Ethiopia.* Retrieved January 9, 2012, from www.article19.org/pdfs/publications/ethiopia-legal-framework-for-foe.pdf

Becker, L. B., & Tudor, V. (2005). *Non-U.S. funders of media assistance projects. Report, James M.* Cox Center for International Mass Communication Training and Research.

Berger, G. (2007a). In search of journalism education excellence in Africa: Summary of the 2006 Unesco project. *Ecquid Novi: African Journalism Studies, 28*(1–2), 149–155. doi:10.3368/ajs.28.1-2.149.

Berger, G. (2007b). *Media legislation in Africa: A comparative legal survey.* Grahamstown, South Africa: Rhodes University/Unesco.

Berger, G. (2010). The struggle for press self-regulation in contemporary South Africa: Charting a course between an industry charade and a government doormat. *Communicatio, 36*(3), 289–308. doi:10.1080/02500167.2010.518783.

Berger, (2009). How to improve standards of journalism education. *African Communication Research, 2*(2), 271–90.

Blankson, I. A. (2007). Media independence and pluralism in Africa. Opportunities of democratization and liberalization. In Blankson, I. A., & Murphy, P. D. (Eds.), *Negotiating democracy. Media transformations in emerging democracies* (pp. 15–34). Albany, NY: State University of New York Press.

Bond, S. (1997). *Neocolonialism and the Ghanaian media: An in-depth look at international news coverage in Ghanaian newspapers, television and radio.* Retrieved from http://digitalcollections.sit.edu/cgi/viewcontent.cgi?article=1058&context=african_diaspora_isp

Butler, A. (2000). Is South Africa heading towards authoritarian rule? Instability myths and expectations traps in a new democracy. *Politikon: South African Journal of Political Studies, 27*(2), 189–205. doi:10.1080/713692335.

Callamard, A. (2010). Accountability, transparency, and freedom of expression in Africa. *Social Research, 77*(4), 1211–1240.

Chiumbu, S., & Moyo, D. (2009). Media, politics and power: Re-gearing policy and propaganda in crisis Zimbabwe. In Skare Orgeret, K., & Rønning, H. (Eds.), *The power of communication. Changes and challenges in African media* (pp. 177–214). Oslo, Norway: Unipub.

Chuma, W. (2010). Reforming the media in Zimbabwe: Critical reflections. In Moyo, D., & Chuma, W. (Eds.), *Media policy in a changing Southern Africa. Critical reflections on media reforms in the global age* (pp. 90–109). Pretoria, South Africa: Unisa Press.

De Beer, A. (1997). *The state of journalism education in Africa – East, West and South: An overview for the World Conference on Journalism Education.* Institute for Media Analysis in South Africa.

Ethiopian Press Agency. (2008). Basis and directives for a developmental and democratic philosophy of our media operation. Draft policy document.

Frère, M.-S. (2009). After the hate media: Regulation in the DRC, Burundi and Rwanda. *Global Media and Communication, 5*(3), 327–352. doi:10.1177/1742766509348675.

Hachten, W. A. (1971). *Muffled drums: The news media in Africa.* Ames, IA: Iowa University Press.

Harro-Loit, H. (2005). The Baltic and Norwegian journalism market. In Bærug, R. (Ed.), *The Baltic media world* (pp. 90–120). Riga, Latvia: Flera Printing House.

Höhne, M. V. (2008). Newspapers in Hargeysa: Freedom of speech in post-conflict Somaliland. *Afrika Spectrum, 43*(1), 91–113.

Human Rights Watch. (2009, June 30). *An analysis of Ethiopia's draft anti-terrorism law. Report.*

Huntington, S. P. (1991). Democracy's third wave. *Journal of Democracy, 2*(2), 12–34. doi:10.1353/jod.1991.0016.

Hydén, G. Leslie. M. & Ogundimu, F.F. (Eds.) (2002). Media and democracy in Africa. New Brunswick, NJ: Transaction Publishers.

Hydén, G., & Okigbo, C. (2002). The media and the two waves of democracy. In Hydén, G., Leslie, M., & Ogundimu, F. F. (Eds.), *Media and democracy in Africa* (pp. 29–54). New Brunswick, NJ: Transaction Publishers.

Janas, J. (1991). *History of the mass media in Ethiopia.* Warsaw, Poland: Warsaw University Press.

Kalyango, Y. Jr, & Eckler, P. (2010). Media performance, agenda building, and democratization in East Africa. In Salmon, C. T. (Ed.), *Communication Yearbook, 34, 354–89.* New York: Routledge.

Karikari, K. (2010, August). African media breaks 'culture of silence'. *Africa Renewal*, pp. 23–25.

Kasoma, F. P. (1997). The independent press and politics in Africa. *Gazette, 59*(4–5), 295–310.

Kibnesh C. (2006). Use of Internet as a medium of disseminating information by Ethiopian newspapers. Unpublished MA thesis, Addis Ababa University, Addis Ababa, Ethiopia.

Krüger, F. (2009). *Media courts of honour. Self-regulatory councils in Southern Africa and elsewhere.* Windhoek, Namibia: Friedrich-Ebert-Stiftung.

Mbaine, A. E. (2010). *Concurrent state and self regulation: A unique challenge for journalism practice in Uganda.* Paper presented at World Journalism Education Congress. Grahamstown, South Africa.

McLure, J. (2008, April 10). Stuck in Somalia. *Newsweek.* Retrieved January 9, 2012, from http://www.newsweek.com/2008/04/10/stuck-in-somalia.html

McLure, J. (2010, May 14). Ethiopian rights groups forced to reduce work before elections. *Bloomberg Businessweek.* Retrieved April 19, 2011, from http://www.businessweek.com/news/2010-05-14/ethiopian-rights-groups-forced-to-reduce-work-before-elections.html

McNamara, L. (2009). Counter-terrorism laws: How they affect media freedom and news reporting. *Westminster Papers in Communication and Culture, 6*(1), 27–44.

Mekuria M. (2005). *The Ethiopian media landscape.* Ethiopian Mass Media Training Institute.

Mesfin N. (2010). Welcome to Addis. What it means being a journalist in Ethiopia. In F. Mdlongwa & M. Letlhaku (Eds.), *Harnessing Africa's digital future* (pp. 64–73). Johannesburg, South Africa: Konrad Adenauer Stiftung. Retrieved from http://www.spiml.co.za/uploads/1285226894.pdf

Motsa, M. (2009). *African Media Barometer 2009 – Swaziland*. Windhoek, Namibia: Media Institute of Southern Africa & Friedrich-Ebert-Stiftung.

Moyo, D. (2010). Zimbabwe and Zambia: Musical chairs and reluctant liberalisation. In Moyo, D., & Chuma, W. (Eds.), *Media policy in a changing Southern Africa. Critical reflections on media reforms in the global age* (pp. 169–200). Pretoria, South Africa: Unisa Press.

Mwenda, A. M. (2007). Personalizing power in Uganda. *Journal of Democracy*, *18*(3), 23–37. doi:10.1353/jod.2007.0048.

Nelson, A. (2011). *Funding free expression: Perceptions and reality in a changing landscape.* Center for International Media Assistance. Retrieved April 19, 2011, from http://cima.ned.org/sites/default/files/CIMA-Funding_Free_Expression_06-01-11.pdf

Nielsen, P. E. (2009). Media in post-communist Mongolia. Challenges and opportunities in the democratization process. *Nordicom Review*, *30*(2), 19–33.

Nkrumah, K. (1965). *The African journalist.* Dar es Salaam, Tanzania: Tanzanian Publishers.

Note: Ethiopian authors are listed according to the local name tradition (i.e. by first name). The father's name is added for clarification.

Nyamnjoh, F. (2005). *Africa's media. Democracy and the politics of belonging.* London: Zed Books.

Ocitti, J. (1999). *Media and democracy in Africa. Mutual political bedfellows or implacable arch-foes?* Cambridge, MA: Harvard University Retrieved from www.wcfia.harvard.edu/fellows/papers/1998-99/ocitti.pdf

Ogbondah, C. W. (1997). Communication and democratization in Africa: Constitutional changes, prospects and persistent problems for the media. *International Communication Gazette*, *59*(4–5), 271–294. doi:10.1177/0016549297059004003.

Ogbondah, C. W. (2002). Media laws in political transition. In Hydén, G., Leslie, M., & Ogundimu, F. F. (Eds.), *Media and democracy in Africa* (pp. 55–80). New Brunswick, NJ: Transaction Publishers.

Ogbondah, C. W. (2004). Democratization and the media in West Africa: An analysis of recent constitutional and legislative reforms for press freedom in Ghana and Nigeria. *West Africa Review, 6.* Retrieved from www.westafricareview.com/issue6/ogbondah.html

Okumu, W. (2007). Gaps and challenges in preventing and combating terrorism in East Africa. In Okumu, W., & Botha, A. (Eds.), *Understanding terrorism in Africa: Building bridges and overcoming gaps* (pp. 60–70). Pretoria, South Africa: Institute for Security Studies.

Onyango-Obbo, C. (2010, March 17). The death has occurred of Mrs Africa Media Freedom. *Daily Nation*. Retrieved January 9, 2012, from http://www.nation.co.ke/blogs/The%20death%20has%20occurred%20of%20Mrs%20Africa%20Media%20Freedom%20/-/445642/881294/-/view/asBlogPost/-/6pgorcz/-/index.html

Organization of African Unity (OAU). (1981, June 27). *African Charter on Human and Peoples' Rights*. Retrieved January 9, 2012, from http://www1.umn.edu/humanrts/instree/z1afchar.htm

Puppis, M. (2010). Media governance: A new concept for the analysis of media policy and regulation. *Communication, Culture & Critique*, *3*(2), 134–149. doi:10.1111/j.1753-9137.2010.01063.x.

Ross, T. J. (2010). A test of democracy: Ethiopia's Mass Media and Freedom of Information Proclamation. *Penn State Law Review*, *114*(3), 1047–1066.

Salawu, A. (2006). Indigenous language media: A veritable tool for African language learning. *Journal of Multicultural Discourses*, *1*(1), 86–95. doi:10.1080/10382040608668533.

Salazar-Ferro, M. (2010, June 17). *Journalists in exile 2010. An exodus from Iran, East Africa. CPJ special report*. Retrieved January 9, 2012, from http://cpj.org/reports/2010/06/journalists-exile-2010-iran-africa-exodus.php

Shimelis B. (2002). The state of the press in Ethiopia. In Bahru, Z., & Pausewang, S. (Eds.), *Ethiopia: The challenge from below* (pp. 184–200). Stockholm, Sweden: Nordiska Afrikainstitutet.

Skjerdal, T. S. (2008). Self-censorship among news journalists in the Ethiopian state media. *African Communication Research*, *1*(2), 185–206.

Skjerdal, T. S. (2010a). Justifying self-censorship. A perspective from Ethiopia. *Westminster Papers in Communication and Culture*, *7*(2), 98–121.

Skjerdal, T. S. (2010b). Research on brown envelope journalism in the African media. *African Communication Research*, *3*(3), 367–406.

Skjerdal, T. S. (2011). Teaching journalism or teaching African journalism? Experiences from foreign involvement in a journalism programme in Ethiopia. *Global Media Journal: African Edition*, *5*(1), 24-51.

Skjerdal, T. S., & Lule, H. (2009). Uneven performances by the private press in Ethiopia: An analysis of 18 years of press freedom. *Journal of Communication and Language Arts*, *3*(1), 44–59.

Skjerdal, T. S., & Ngugi, C. M. (2007). Institutional and governmental challenges for journalism education in East Africa. *Ecquid Novi – African. Journalism Studies*, *28*(1–2), 176–190.

Tabaire, B. (2007). The press and political repression in Uganda: Back to the future? *Journal of Eastern African Studies*, *1*(2), 193–211. doi:10.1080/17531050701452408.

Taylor, S. (2009). *African Media Barometer 2009 – Botswana*. Windhoek, Namibia: Media Institute of Southern Africa & Friedrich-Ebert-Stiftung.

Tettey, W. (2006). The politics of media accountability in Africa: An examination of mechanisms and institutions. *International Communication Gazette*, *68*(3), 229–248. doi:10.1177/1748048506063763.

UNESCO. (1991, May 3). *Windhoek declaration on promoting idependent and pluralistic media*. Retrieved from www.cpu.org.uk/userfiles/WINDHOEK%20DECLARATION.pdf

UNESCO. (2001, May 3). *African Charter on Broadcasting*. Retrieved from www.misa.org/broadcasting/brochure.pdf

Van der Veur, P. R. (2002). Broadcasting and political reform. In Hydén, G., Leslie, M., & Ogundimu, F. F. (Eds.), *Media and democracy in Africa* (pp. 81–106). New Brunswick, NJ: Transaction Publishers.

Voltmer, K. (2008). *Government performance, collective accountability, and the news media*. Paper presented at the Harvard-World Bank workshop The Role of the News Media in the Governance Reform. Cambridge, MA.

World Association of Newspapers. (2007). Declaration of Table Mountain. Retrieved from www.declarationoftablemountain.org

ENDNOTES

[1]   Hydén and Okigbo's (2002). 'second wave of democracy' in Africa coincides with Samuel P. Huntington's (1991) 'third wave of

democracy'. Hydén and Okigbo contend that Africa was not hit by the wave that Huntington describes as the first democratic wave in the 19th century. Huntington's second wave (and Hydén and Okibgo's first African wave) came in the period after the Second World War.

2 Despite the recently proposed 'counter' law, the Protection of Information Bill.

3 All African heads of states were males until Ellen Johnson Sirleaf became the first African female President in Liberia in 2006.

4 Anti-Terrorism Act, passed by Ugandan Parliament 2002; Interception of Communication Bill, passed by Ugandan Parliament 14 July 2010.

5 The Suppression of Terrorism Act, ratified in 2008.

6 Article 7 of Right to Information Bill, proposed in 2002, lied before Parliament in February 2010, not yet ratified.

7 Press law passed by Chadian national assembly 18 August 2010.

8 Code of Conduct for the Practice of Journalism, incorporated in the 2007 Kenyan Media Bill.

9 It should also be remarked that clauses to prevent the spread of ethnic hatred through the media have been recognized in professional ethical journalistic codes as well, for example in Liberia, Botswana and Benin (cf. Frère, 2009).

10 http://africa.ifj.org/en/pages/africa-press-freedom-report-2009

11 http://fesmedia.org/access-to-information. Zimbabwe has also had an access to information act since 2002, but the act is generally considered dysfunctional for the purpose of retrieving information (Chiumbu and Moyo, 2009; Chuma, 2010).

12 E.g. Global Integrity report 2010 (www.globalintegrity.org/report/Ethiopia/2010); Amnesty International report 2011 (www.amnesty.org/en/region/ethiopia/report-2011); Ross, 2010, p. 1062.

13 The law bulletin has in fact a printing error in the English translation, where it says ETB 1,000,000. The correct amount according to the authoritative Amharic text is ETB 100,000 (article 43.7).

14 Interestingly enough, due to the inflation, there is actually no increase in the fine levels if compared with foreign currency. ETB 100,000 in 2011 currency equal slightly less than USD 6,000, which is exactly the same amount as the exchange rate for ETB 50,000 in 2007, the year before the new media law was introduced.

15 www.freedomhouse.org (Freedom in the World 2009 report, Ethiopia).

Chapter 4

Articulations and Rearticulations:
Antagonisms of Media Reform in Africa

Heather Gilberds
Carleton University, Canada

ABSTRACT

The adoption of western models of journalism is a hallmark of media democratization movements in post-conflict, transitional or developing nations. However, media strengthening programs have received wide criticism from critical development scholars. This chapter interrogates the assumptions that underlie media development projects in Africa, which work to establish or reform journalism practices, by drawing on a case study of media strengthening in Rwanda. Drawing on discourse theory, it maps the discursive field that forms the basis for international assistance to build media capacity in developing and post-conflict regions. It also highlights the ways dominant development models are resisted in and through discourse, thereby drawing attention to the fluid and contingent operations of power that manifest in such institutionalized sites of knowledge production.

INTRODUCTION

The adoption of western models of journalism is a hallmark of media democratization movements in post-conflict, transitional or developing nations. In the summer of 2007, the United Nations Educational, Scientific and Cultural Organization (UNESCO) introduced its new *Model Curricula for Journalism Education for Developing Countries and Emerging Democracies* at the World Journalism Educators Congress (UNESCO, 2007a). The model curricula serve to provide a guide for implementing journalism education programs in economically impoverished or politically unstable regions. Such programs, which are often institutionalized in formal journalism and mass communications programs at the university level, are premised upon one of the fundamental assumptions underwriting western journalism: a vibrant media system is the key to a robust civil society

DOI: 10.4018/978-1-4666-4197-6.ch004

and is fundamental to wider political democratization. In so-called developing or transitional regions, the progression toward democratic forms of government is linked to the ability of the media to provide objective and credible information to the people who will then make informed choices on policies that affect public life. As such, building and reforming national media systems through the development of standards of journalistic practice and communications policies related to freedom of expression is considered a key component in wider efforts to build democratic capacity.

Media education and reform projects in Sub-Saharan Africa, many of which explicitly rely upon, or at least gain legitimacy from, UNESCO's recommendations, have received an array of criticisms. The most salient critiques derive from critical development theory (Escobar, 1995; Ferguson, 1994), which purports that such projects assert modernization perspectives of development, and related theories that question the applicability of normative media models derived from western socio-historical contexts to African countries (Kasoma, 1996; Shah, 1996; Banda, 2009; Murphy and Scotton, 1987). Another line of criticism, one that has gained less currency in the academic literature and is often marginalized by studies that focus on evaluating the potential feasibility of journalism reform projects in Africa, focuses on the epistemological and ontological underpinnings of such projects. This critique derives from discourse theory and attempts to articulate the following questions: What are the epistemes (Foucault, 1970) that form the basis for intervention in national media systems by external donors and international organizations? Which interpretations of the social world are privileged? What alternative interpretations are marginalized? Where is power located and, more importantly, how is it resisted or challenged?

This chapter will interrogate the assumptions that underlie media development projects in Africa, which work to establish or reform journalism practices, by drawing on a case study of media strengthening in Rwanda. It does not aim to provide an evaluation of the feasibility of such programs, or to determine whether is it appropriate for outside actors to contribute to reforming the media sector in countries where press freedom still faces great challenges. Rather, its purpose is to map the discursive field that forms the basis for international assistance to build media capacity in developing and post-conflict regions, and to outline the ways dominant development models are resisted, in order to draw attention to the fluid and contingent operations of power that manifest in such institutionalized sites of knowledge production.[1]. This chapter draws on critical discourse analysis and related theories that focus on the discursive production and reproduction of power and knowledge. Specifically, it relies on Laclau and Mouffe's (1985) "confrontational strategy" to examine the antagonistic relations between dominant or hegemonic discourses, such as the one UNESCO provides, and alternative or counter-hegemonic models to explicate the ways power is created and assured, as well as reformed and contested in socially mediated texts. The discourse theories of Laclau and Mouffe, Howarth, Fairclough and Foucault in combination with literature that focuses on media development, media democratization and alternative media (Downing, 2001; Rodriguez, 2005; Carroll and Hackett, 2006; Howley, 2009), are drawn upon to provide a close reading of the dominant media development models promoted by the UNESCO document and to contrast it with alternative media models and journalistic reform movements. While there are a number of alternative media models, including development/emancipatory journalism, the focus here is on the participatory-democratic model (Carpentier, 2001) advocated for in community or citizens media movements. The following analysis will put two different types of text into confrontation with one another–A *Rwanda Media Strengthening Program* (2009) request For applications, project proposal and work plan produced by the International Exchange and Research Board

(IREX) and funded by USAID, and declarations on media reform produced by organizations promoting alternative media development in Africa, such as The World Association of Community Radio Broadcasters (AMARC), Search for Common Ground (SFCG) and Communication Rights for the Information Society (CRIS). The comparison aims to lay bare the discursive field that surrounds media assistance programs in the developing world.

Before moving to an analysis of the documents, it is necessary first to establish the theoretical elements of discourse analysis that are useful for the confrontational strategy outlined previously. The analysis will articulate the following discursive elements that are evident and meaningful in media reform proposals: antagonistic nodal points, genre and intertextuality. "Nodal Points" (Laclau & Mouffe, 1985; Carpentier, 2005) are privileged signifiers that create stability for "orders of discourse" (Fairclough, 2001). Without delving extensively into the concept of hegemony, this chapter is resting on the assumption that development encounters are hegemonic projects that create knowledge forms based upon a distinctively western, liberal social ontology (Ferguson, 1994; Escobar, 1995; Freire, 1977; DeChaine, 2005). As such, it assumes that the objective of media capacity-building projects, in line with other development interventions, is "to construct and stabilize nodal points that are the basis of a social order" (Laclau as cited in Carpentier, 2005, p. 200), which together structure a field of intelligibility or "social imaginary" (ibid). More specifically, this project will examine the textual instances when nodal points come into confrontation with one another as divergent ideologies enter into conflict. However, contrary to many traditional approaches to ideology, the discourse theories relied on here do not assume that ideologies are necessarily negative or false. That is, not only dominant groups may have ideologies used to legitimate their power or to manufacture consent or consensus; dominated groups may also have ideologies that effectively organize the social

representations needed for resistance and change (Van Dijk, 1998). The analytical emphasis is placed on these "antagonisms" (Laclau & Mouffe, 1985; Howarth, 2002), or points of struggle, to highlight the articulations present in the dominant discourses and the ways counter-hegemonic or alternative models attempt to establish new articulations in their discursive attacks on the dominant nodal points. The reason for this choice is that, within this discursive interplay, the nodal points in particular are subject to contestation. One of the consequences of this confrontation is that this struggle makes these hegemonic signifiers and their counter-hegemonic opposites clearly visible and identifiable (Carpentier, 2005). In the construction of a social imaginary that privileges state-sanctioned media reform, the following nodal points–media professionalism and objectivity–are extrapolated from normative media theories and are central to the discursive terrain. These are useful signifiers to analyze, given that they are oft contested in participatory-democratic media movements.

In addition to nodal points, two other aspects of critical discourse analysis are utilized–genre and intertextuality. Another way to utilize a confrontational strategy is to explore the ways antagonisms manifest in the genre, or discourse type, of a text. Discourse types contain implicit assumptions and ground rules, which are often ideological in nature, that work to socially constrain processes of production and interpretation (Fairclough, 1992). Genre is important to look at in addition to the more substantive analysis of content given that "the most persuasive ideologies may seldom be expressed at all" (Van Dijk, 1998, p.142) and a series of theoretical steps is therefore required to elucidate the often indirectly ideological nature of discourse. Moreover, genre can be a site of resistance for social movements that aim to rearticulate the construction of dominant discourses. This typically happens in one of two ways: counter-hegemonic movements will either usurp the dominant genre in order to gain legitimacy, or subvert it by using an opposing form in order to draw attention to how the format of a text can obscure articulations of power and agency. In development projects, genre is often a crucial site of subject interpellation. By utilizing the concept of "inscription" (Latour, 1995), this analysis will examine the effects of discourse type in both dominant media development projects (i.e., project proposals and work plans) and alternative proposals (i.e., declarations or manifestos).

Intertextuality is "the property texts have of being full of snatches of other texts" (Fairclough, 1992, p. 84). Highlighting the ways discursive events carry traces of other texts is crucial to discuss in any discursive analysis as it draws attention to the fact that texts are socially constructed and historically contingent. The reference to other texts, whether explicit or implicit, or the deliberate omission of a reference, often brings to light the conditions which stabilize the hegemony of dominant discourses while rendering alternate interpretations invisible. An exploration of the intertextual features of an object of analysis draws attention to the power relations that are implicated in the production and transmission of communicative events (Van Dijk, 1998). Intertextuality is an important feature of discursive resistance and rearticulation in counter-hegemonic movements. Fairclough (1992) asserts that bringing a prior text into the present enables it to become a site for "transforming the past" (p. 85). With regard to journalism capacity-building in Africa, the intertextual and interdiscursive elements comprise a long history of contestation over western-led development interventions and media reform initiatives that inscribe a liberal and arguably neoliberal social imaginary.

BACKGROUND: THE MEDIA LANDSCAPE IN RWANDA

The Reporters Without Borders Press Freedom Index currently rates Rwanda 157th out of 175 countries. *Human Rights Watch, Amnesty Inter-national*, and many other groups have criticized Rwanda's lack of press freedom for over a decade.[2] As Nyamnjoh (2005) notes, restrictive media policies designed to suppress possible dissent date back to the colonial period when colonialists enacted "strict laws regulating the right of Africans to set up and operate newspapers, and aimed at stifling the spread of 'subversive' ideas" (p. 19). In many African countries, stringent control over media ownership and content extended into the postcolonial period, yet, unlike other countries in the region, Rwanda provides constitutional provision for freedom of expression (Armijo, 2009). Such freedom, however, is severely tempered in practice as officials work to ensure that media cannot be used as tools of sectarianism and hate as they were in the 1994 genocide.[3] Despite considerable growth in the private media sector since 1994, the Paul Kagame-led RPF government is frequently accused by human rights organizations and press freedom monitors of creating a media climate characterized by self-censorship and intimidation of journalists by government proxies (Thompson, n.d.). There are many indications of control over freedom of expression despite constitutional axioms. The Ministry of Information is highly critical of the correspondents of outside outlets such as Voice of America and the BBC, who have aired stories regarding unfavorable country reports by international human rights organizations. In 2009, the BBC Kinyarwanda service was temporarily suspended for allegedly referencing genocidal ideology (Muganwa, 2007). At this year's World Press Freedom Day celebration in Kigali, information minister Louise Mushikiwabo expelled journalists deemed to be critical of the government (ibid). Moreover, many journalists critical of the government have left the country fearing persecution (Thompson, n.d.). Prior to the passage of the 2002 Press Law, the Rwanda Independent Media Group (RIMG) reported that ten journalists had fled the country and four were arrested or harassed as a result of writing stories critical of the ruling party (Armijo, 2009).

The government's Penal Code and 2002 Press Law both subject Rwandan journalists to a host of criminal penalties for a variety of offenses. The law mandates criminal punishment for defamation, publications that endanger public law and order threaten, public decency, or contempt for the President, as well as recording, transmitting or recounting words uttered privately (Armijo, 2009). The most serious crime a journalist or media outlet can be accused of in Rwanda under either statute, however, is divisionism, a broadly defined charge that in essence equates any discussion of Rwandans in terms of Hutus and Tutsis with the separatist ideology that caused the genocide (Armijo, 2009, p. 40). Rwanda's Press Law also regulates participation in the media sector. It defines a "journalist" as someone who has studied and is experienced in the subject, and who holds a press card issued by the High Council of the Press, the body that regulates the Rwandan media. Although the RIMG has stated that there have been no detentions of journalists since 2004, the relationship between the government and the Kinyarwandan-language newspapers is contentious. In public press conferences, President Kagame has chastised the private media for its reporting methods, and private journalists have complained of lack of access to information. (Armijo, 2009). Many journalists report that they self-censor and are worried about harassment or economic punishments (i.e., losing employment if editors and managers feel that a story could incite rebuke from the state) if they criticize the government. Other articles undermine advancements in recent press legislation reform, such as provisions that guarantee access to public information. For instance, the same recent press law draft that favors access to information bars criticism of the President or the army and forces journalists to reveal their sources in court, a measure that is considered to be "a death sentence for journalism" (*Umuvugizi* editor Gasasira as quoted in EurAC, 2009). Government controls on journalistic freedom operate in a number of more covert ways as well, such as economic benefits

for news sources that are pro-government. [4]Public ministries are the largest ad-buyers in the country and purchase space in government friendly newspapers such at the New Times, while opposition newspapers receive little advertising revenue. Also, opposition papers are not allowed to use government printing presses and must print their issues on presses rented in Uganda. Contention surrounding criticism of the state is often framed in the language of normative journalism standards where critical reporting is considered non-factual and unobjective, and is deemed sensationalistic or tarred as "hate speech" (EurAC, 2009).

INTERNATIONAL MEDIA ASSISTANCE IN RWANDA

In comparison with other forms of international aids, media assistance by international donors is fairly limited in Rwanda (Kayumba & Kimonyo, 2006). Kayumba and Kimonyo identify five different types of international assistance that formed the media development sector from 1993-2002: (1) Financial assistance for the establishment of "alternative" media to counteract hate media, to support internally displaced persons and refugees, and to facilitate reconciliation and national development[5]; (2) Assistance to national and international media outlets; (3) Training of journalists and media professionals; (4) Support to reform the regulatory framework; and (5) Political support for media freedom. This project specifically focuses on the third category—training of journalists and media professionals—given that a lack of professional journalistic standards is considered endemic to Rwanda's contemporary media landscape and, as such, is implicated in the other categories of assistance. Prior to the genocide in 1994, there were no formal journalism education programs (Thompson, n.d.). Journalists were trained outside the country or on the job. The School of Journalism and Communication at the National University of Rwanda was established in 1996 with major support from UNESCO (Kayumba and Kimonyo, 2006). It is important to note that this was the same year that UNESCO began to draft its original curricula for journalism education: *Communications Training in Africa: Model Curricula*. The present-day program emphasizes practical skill development and aims to raise the professional standards of journalism in the country. Various international educational institutions, including the University of Lille in France and the Rwanda Initiative at Carleton University in Canada, have formed relationships with the school to help build its capacity and have provided financial resources, equipment, instructors and exchange opportunities.

MEDIA STRENGTHENING IN RWANDA - IREX, USAID AND UNESCO

Launched in July 2009, the Rwanda media strengthening project is a two-year long capacity-building initiative funded by USAID and implemented by the International Research and Exchange Board (IREX). It is designed "to increase the sustainability and professionalism of the Rwandan media, enabling the sector to more effectively provide the kind of news and information important to Rwandan citizens" (USAID project website). The project aims to redress some of the challenges facing the Rwandan media sector, which are listed as: a limited number of skilled journalists with sufficient training and knowledge of the profession; a lack of profitability and sustainability among private sector media houses; and a distrust of the media due to its role in the genocide (ibid). Two key program objectives are defined by USAID: (1) (To) Increase the sustainability of Rwandan media outlets and the professionalism of Rwandan journalists, media owners, managers, and editors; and (2) (To) Increase the capacity of media associations to provide appropriate services to their

members and to effectively engage with government in the interest of their members (IREX, 2009). Although this analysis is specifically focused on the training and education of journalists and media professionals, there are other stated objectives, including strengthening business and management practices of private media outlets, increasing the capacity of media associations to provide professional support, developing media literacy programs, and building two community radio stations to provide local news and information. The media-strengthening project as a whole is an interesting case study of an ambitious assistance program that aims to reform an entire media landscape and is a fruitful place to explore the social ontology of media assistance on a broad level. However, these additional objectives are outside the scope of this project, which will explicitly focus on components related to institutionalized education and training of journalists. The decision to focus on this element is strategic because it is often at the level of media professionalism that antagonisms between normative media models and participatory-democratic ones come into conflict. The following IREX objectives will be considered in relation to UNESCO's efforts at journalism education, and include plans to "Deliver Quality Journalism Instruction through Continuation and Expansion of Rwanda Initiative Visiting Lecturers Program"; and provide "Curriculum Review and Development for NUR/School of Journalism and Communication and Great Lakes Media Center." Although this is a small component of the overall work plan and project proposal, it provides an opportunity to write large the epistemological implications of western-led journalism reform projects and to place them in confrontation with alternative models that advocate for grassroots reform of the media sector. Specifically, it enables an exploration of the ways that the ontology of the "media professional" (Carpentier, 2005) is created through development interventions, thereby opening space to explore how such an ontology is contested through a re-articulation of the fundamental assumptions underwriting media professionalism.

INTERTEXTUALITY

If discourses are constructed by linking different elements into a discursive structure, then an important aspect to consider is how chains of discourse work to solidify specific social imaginaries. According to Fairclough (1992), this element of analysis posits that "texts always draw upon and transform other contemporary and historically prior texts" (p. 39) and places investigation on the structuring of discursive formations in relation to one another within a particular institutional order of discourse. As stated earlier, the IREX project proposal and work plan, as a text that works to create one particular kind of social world while marginalizing others, emerges from a long history of conflict and contestation over media assistance by international donors who arguably promote western values and ideals. Although not explicitly, the principles that form the basis for the media strengthening project in Rwanda, which center on journalism professionalism as the *sine qua non* of media capacity building, are based upon UNESCO's (2007) one-size-fits-all *Model Curricula for Journalism Education for Developing Countries & Emerging Democracies*. Designers of the model curricula promote it as a vehicle to improve journalism education worldwide and it assumes that a generic model is widely—even universally—applicable in diverse national, social, economic, political, and cultural contexts. The text wholly avoids discussion or identification of anticipated country-specific or region-specific impediments to implementation. The UNESCO report "presumes a Western media model that is adapted from the scientific method, based on the notion of objectivity and adherence to universally accepted news values, professional ethical standards, and collection and reporting of facts and

information in an impartial manner" (Freedman & Shafer, 2008, p. 10). What the UNESCO report fails to discuss, perhaps, are the insurmountable obstacles and problems that will invariably arise when poor countries, authoritarian countries, and countries with strong cultural and religious constraints on "democratic journalism" go about the process of implementing the model, in whole or in part.

Journalism reform projects cannot be adequately analyzed without placing them within the UNESCO-inspired New World Information and Communication Order (NWICO) debates of the 1980s and the related MacBride Commission report, *Many Voices, One World* (UNESCO, 1980). The commission report explicitly asserts that the diversity of world cultures and existence of varied patterns of social, economic, and cultural life prohibit the application of universal communication models (ibid). The philosophical foundation of the 2007 UNESCO curricula is, in reality, the type of universally applicable model the commission warns against. It is predominantly North American and Western European in its content, pedagogical and professional approach and operational standards. It assumes market-based financial support for the media and loose government controls. Despite the defeat of a NWICO, strong sentiments persisted that Western principles of press independence and media professionalism were not adaptable to conditions in developing or transitional regions. The failure of the 2007 model to reflect on past disputes between northern and southern nations over the role of mass media in the development process may be an oversight or an intentional omission. Either way, many earlier problems related to dominant media development models remain unresolved. Freedman and Shafer (2008) argue that "past accusations that UNESCO is complicit in fostering Western press ideologies and conventions at the expense of alternative models that may be more appropriate for lesser developed societies might also be leveled at the organization today" (p. 9).

The 2007 curricula is not UNESCO's first venture into journalism education. In 2002, it released *Communication Training in Africa: Model Curricula*. This emerged from a project launched in 1996 to improve media education in Africa. In contrast to the 2007 UNESCO model, the 1996 document confesses its dominant, and perhaps problematic, theoretical and historical origins thus anticipating potential criticisms. For instance, it acknowledges the problematic and potentially contentious reliance on western tools and ideological frameworks:

Communication education in Africa, like modern mass communication on the continent, is an import from West Europe and North America. The source of inspiration of teachers, curricula and textbooks is Western. Teachers are mostly Western educated, curricula are drawn from Western models and most textbooks are authored and published in the West and North America. Under these circumstances, communication training in Africa can hardly be said to be culturally relevant, although cultural inculcation was usually the main justification for its introduction and sustainability (UNESCO, 2002, p. 1).

Although the 2007 model advocates traditional Western news values, and promotes the "democratic" journalism traditions, values and practices that have informed the world's dominant media systems and were the targets of NWICO debates about western media hegemony, such reflexivity has fallen by the wayside. The new model seems to make a conscious effort not to resurrect those debates or to raise any related issues that impassioned media policy makers, academics, students and national development experts three decades ago (Freedman & Shafer, 2008). The absence of indicators that predict criticism in the 2007 model points to an order of discourse that has greater stability that it did in the late 1990s and suggests that the principles it establishes were entirely consensual. Where the 1996 curricula

indicates that there were a plurality of voices determining the central tenets of the model, the 2007 document masks the polyvalence of interests and interpretations that exist both at the site of production and the site of reception. The USAID/IREX media-strengthening project is another link in this discursive chain. Although there is a provision for the development of community radio in the project, it remains overwhelmingly focused on state-sanctioned media reform rather than on unofficial or oppositional media. Emphasis is on a paradigm of journalism that has been subjected to numerous critiques for its potential complicity with elite domination of public discourse (Hackett & Zhao, 1998).

ARTICULATION AND REARTICULATION: NODAL POINTS AND ANTAGONISMS

As stated earlier, the analytical component of this chapter primarily draws on Laclau and Mouffe's (1985) discourse theory, specifically the notion of nodal points and antagonisms in the confrontation between normative and alternative models for media reform. Although there are a variety of different models that have developed in resistance to interventions based upon western ideologies, this chapter is focusing upon the participatory-democratic conception of journalism promoted by community media scholars and advocates.[6] A confrontational strategy is useful for such an analysis because, as Carpentier, Lie and Servaes (2001) argue, "antagonism plays a crucial role in the identity of community media" (p. 2). In their wide-ranging analyses of alternative media in various countries and historical periods, Downing et al. (2001) argue that radical media have often had an under-recognized but critical role in vast historical transformations, especially when they operate in conjunction with popular movements. Some of their most notable examples are taken precisely from the transitional societies that are the focus of media reform. From this theoretical viewpoint, community media can be seen as the attempt to offer alternatives to a wide range of hegemonic discourses on journalism, media, organizational structures, politics and democracy.

The nodal points that are central to the discursive terrain underlying media reform projects in developing regions are primarily extrapolated from normative media theories (i.e., Siebert et al.'s *Four Theories of the Press*), but modernization theories of development, which posit that conflict and development obstacles result from forces internal to a nation's boundaries, are also implicated. This perspective obscures critical and Marxist-influenced development theories, which argue that "underdevelopment results primarily from external factors, particularly a nation's disadvantaged position in a capitalist world economic system dominated by a few wealthy and powerful countries that benefited from the rest of the world's enforced state of political and economic powerlessness" (Freedman & Shafer, 2008, p. 8). For media reform advocates, practitioners and theorists aligning with either of these conflicting development perspectives, the debate centers on whether to argue for government-supported development projects to professionalize the media sector, or to argue that the media should advocate social change, both by empowering local grassroots movements and civil society to challenge oppressive state policies, and to counter international media expansion objectives that suppress indigenous media development (ibid.). Alternative models of media reform contest the epistemic-ontological roots that form the basis of the dominant discourse, which emphasizes the professionalization of journalists, the ethos of public service, and "objectivity." By rearticulating the dominant nodal points, such approaches call into question reform measures that take the Western media as an unquestioned democratic benchmark for the performance of media in transitional societies (Hackett, 2003). Two nodal points are central to the confrontation of these opposing discourses: media professionalism and objectivity.

In both the UNESCO curricula and the USAID/IREX project, media professionalization is considered to be at the forefront of building a healthy democracy. The UNESCO curricula focus solely on building the capacity of media professionals. The model comprises three axes: (1) the norms, values, tools, standards, and practices of journalism; (2) the social, cultural, political, economic, legal and ethical aspects of journalism practice; and (3) knowledge of the world and journalism's intellectual challenges (UNESCO, 2007). It aims to "form journalists who are in command of the complex skills marking the craft and are also in command of the knowledge and thought to support the reporting and analysis called for in a beat" (ibid, p. 9). Similarly, the USAID/IREX project views a lack of media professionalism as the essential component of a media system that has historically failed to bring peace and democracy. In discussing the 1994 genocide, the project states that the successful use of hate media was due, in part, to a "lack of professionalism and ethics" (p. 23). The report goes on to claim that the contemporary media sector faces a number of challenges that have resulted from the nation's historical tragedy, including "a limited number of skilled journalists with sufficient training and knowledge of the profession; a lack of profitability and sustainability among private sector media houses; and a distrust of the media due to its role in the genocide" (ibid). The project nonetheless expresses encouragement over the Government of Rwanda's commitment to media reform and feels that state support has created an environment conducive to intervention:

The GOR has committed itself to protecting and advancing civil rights and liberties in Rwanda by creating an enabling legal environment for media freedom, and building its professional capacity to act responsibly in this environment. The GOR believes that this can be achieved if media practitioners adhere to the basic tenets of professional conduct and ethics in an environment of enhanced media freedom (USAID/IREX, 2009, p. 23).

The Government of Rwanda's most recent draft press law further entrenches this commitment by imposing institutional accreditation for all practising journalists.

There are two normative theories of journalism's role in society that underlie assertions to professionalize the media sector. Carpentier (2005) defines "the liberal model (as) one of the classic normative media theories that has played a crucial role in the hegemonic articulation of the media professional's identity" (p. 204). According to this model, media organizations are seen as purely private organizations that function within a market economy. The second model–which aims to correct the deficiencies of liberal approaches–is "the model of social responsibility" (ibid). According to this approach, media organizations remain private enterprises but are viewed as stewards who carry public responsibility. In both models, media organizations are deemed to be crucial in the distribution of information, which enables citizens to act as a watchdog or fourth estate. Within these models, media professionals are part of professional elite, which not only comprise technical competences but also possess an ethics of service. In alternative models, which explicitly foreground participation, this hegemonic articulation is heavily critiqued. Community media movements are founded upon an anti-elitist discourse, and claim that journalistic tasks must not (and should not) be taken on exclusively by media professionals, but by members of the community (Girard, 1992; McQuail, 1994). Furthermore, community media movements stress horizontal organization, and reject the hierarchically structured organization that defines a professional media sector (Carpentier, Lie, & Servaes, 2001; Downing, 2001; Girard, 1992; Rodriguez, 2005; Howley, 2009).

The antagonism between these two discourses is illustrated when reference is made to processes of media reform promoted by the dominant paradigm alongside those advocated by participatory-democratic proponents. The IREX work plan outlines the following aspects of capacity building for media professionals: The transfer of skills and knowledge to journalists, publishers, media owners, managers, and editors shall result in increased knowledge and capacity in the following areas:

- Media business management necessary to establish and/or sustain for-profit private media organizations (developing media advertising, financial management, low-cost audience research, how to expand newspaper circulation, etc.).
- The rights, responsibilities, and ethics of the practice of journalism: Ways to build an effective dialogue between media owners and government about issues impacting the media.
- The importance of promoting an independent, professional media to a democratic society.
- Research techniques for journalists in the investigation of government activities of public and national interest, with a particular focus on media coverage of local public affairs.
- Long-term, in-depth, research techniques that result in high-quality stories characterized by objectivity and accuracy (USAID, 2009, p. 25).

Other components include reporting grants for journalists, pitch labs and technology access provisions in addition to providing professional business and editorial management grants and training to private media owners (IREX, 2009, Sub-component 1.2a, p. 6). Management training includes workshops on audience research, advertising, strategies for consolidation, and governmental legislation regulating ownership. According to this model, media reform is primarily about liberalization–"the regularization of media laws and individual (and corporate) rights of expression" (Hackett, 2003)–marketization, and the commodification of information and audiences.

In contrast, community or alternative media reform models emphasize participation in media programming and policies and popular representation (Howley, 2009). Hackett (2003) makes a distinction between democratization *of* media institutions, which often focuses on autonomy from the State, and democratization *through* the media, which is mainly a process of grassroots movements colonizing the site of media production to tell their stories and mobilize support for social change. An example of the re-articulation of media professionalism as a nodal is found in the World Association of Community Radio Broadcasters (AMARC)'s *International Charter of Community Radios*. According to AMARC, media strengthening initiatives in transitional or underdeveloped regions should aim to:

- Express the aspirations of civil society, especially those excluded from decision making, by age, gender and from the economic arena.
- Promote socio-cultural and linguistic heritage, independent from commercial and governmental interests, partisan political and religious proselytize.
- Represent the interests of all communities.
- Assist them to define themselves as non-profit civic organizations and to seek sufficient diversity in their financing, to prevent the compromise of their objectives.
- Offer quality programming services that are informative, educational, entertaining and are subject to community participation and evaluation.
- Operate as a platform for citizen's participation, where their voices and perspectives can be heard and where diversity is encouraged (AMARC, 2003).

The recommendations by AMARC are explicitly non-elitist and resist discourses that stress the role of political elite. Other grassroots organizations establish similar frameworks to carry out media reform efforts. For instance, Search for Common Ground (SFCG) is a media development non-governmental organization that also works to provide media training in transitional or post-conflict regions. While it too recognizes the need for "fair and accurate journalism and media content that builds confidence and counteracts misperceptions" (Melone, Terzis, & Beleli, 2002, p. 1), it rearticulates the professionalization of media systems and the deontological identity of media professionals by expanding the definition of the media. SFGC argues that the media refers "not only to journalism itself" but also to "a whole host of communication types...ranging from drama and documentary to discussions, using a host of technologies such as radio, television, print media, and the Internet" (ibid, p.2). As such, it enables a space for community members as well as professional journalists to access sites of media production. Both models rearticulate the dominant discourse of authority and leadership to support a more dialogical view of democratic participation. Furthermore, they establish alternative ways of producing content that is not solely the reserve of professionals with a specific set of technical competencies.

Another nodal point that forms the cornerstone of media reform discourse is "objectivity." Objectivity is one of the fundamental lessons taught in journalism education programs; arguably, it is the nodal point that has the greatest stability in the articulation of professional journalism. Professional journalists claim access to the representation of factuality, journalistic ethics and ritualistic procedures that guarantee their integrity and reliability as "authorized truth-tellers" (McNair, 1998, p. 65). The majority of the more formal attempts to rearticulate the hegemonic journalistic identity focus on the problem of objectivity. These critiques can be summarized in the proposition that "some say that journalism is not objective, others say that journalism cannot be objective and still others say that journalism should not be objective" (Lichtenberg, as quoted in Carpentier,

2005, p. 206). In particular, this last critique–that journalism should not be objective–is important in this regard, since most of the alternative media models acknowledge this position. A reliance on the politico-normative commitment to objectivity as a crucial aspect of media reform is evident in both UNESCO's curricula and the USAID/IREX Rwanda Media Strengthening project. UNESCO's curricula place emphasis on teaching journalism ethics that promote:

A critical examination of key ethical issues and values related principally to truth-telling, such as journalistic autonomy (including conflicts of interest); evidence, fact-checking, and corroboration; sources, named and anonymous; clarity, fairness and bias; photo and digital manipulation and misrepresentation; invention; speculation, rumors and gossip; cheque-book journalism; the Internet; quotations; plagiarism; "objectivity" and stenographic journalism; sustained coverage of stories; corrections; etc. (UNESCO, 2007, p. 22).

According to this model, objectivity is a skill that is developed when a journalist learns to "distinguish relevant from irrelevant information, to assess evidence and argument, to detect bias, and to think independently, courageously and creatively, questioning deeply, challenging common assumptions, making interdisciplinary connections, and comparing perspectives, interpretations and theories" (ibid, p. 30). The USAID/IREX project relies on a similar assumption: it is only by ensuring that "media practitioners adhere to the basic tenets of professional conduct" that they can be trusted to "act responsibly...in an environment of enhanced media freedom" (USAID 2008, p. 23). Institutionalized standards of objectivity are assumed necessary to prevent the partisan and xenophobic journalism that has historically plagued the Rwandan media sector.

Although objectivity is a laudatory goal, it has historically been critiqued on a number of levels. Turnstall (1977) attacks what he calls

American-dominated media standards, which promote a type of professionalism which assumes that journalists are independent and autonomous enough from political and commercial influence to make such professional decisions. Media advocates and scholars that promote a development journalism paradigm have long argued that western principles of objectivity and autonomy are not suitable for developing contexts (Freedman & Shafer, 2008). Alternative or community media paradigms similarly reject objectivity as the foundational assumption and primary goal of media reform. These participatory-democratic approaches stress advocacy over impartiality and narrative over truth-telling. In the Kathmandu Declaration (2003), AMARC stresses that developing nations should strive to develop community-based media that will "operate as a platform for citizens' participation, where their voices and aspirations can be heard and where diversity is encouraged," "represent the interests of all communities," and "express the interests of civil society, especially those excluded from decision making." Search for Common Ground similarly rejects adherence to a standard of objectivity, claiming:

The media cannot be neutral towards peace...the perception that journalists need to be neutral ought to be overcome. Simply by being there and reporting on a conflict, the media alter the communication environment and are thus inherently involved in the conflict and non-neutral (Melone, Terzis, & Beleli, 2002, p. 6).

The focus on factuality and impartiality is rearticulated by an emphasis on subjectivity, where the journalist is a participant or a character in the story (Carpentier, 2001). Undermining objectivity is often a specific goal of participatory media models, which aim to signify the constructedness of the concept. In this way, they draw attention to the ways objectivity often acts as a force to marginalize the perspectives of those farthest removed from centers of power.

GENRE

One final aspect of a confrontational discursive analysis that deserves a brief analysis has to do with genre. Given that media reform projects are planned, recorded and archived in text via project proposals, work plans and progress reports, the form the text takes is a central aspect of its hegemonic or counter-hegemonic force. Based on Latour's (1995) notion of inscription, each model of journalism reform inscribes reality through the use of different and often opposing genres. Fairclough (1992) describes genres as "different means of production of a specifically textual sort, different resources for texturing" (p. 12). Both the UNESCO model curricula and the USAID/IREX document utilize an institutionalized genre–that is, they are based upon an empirical view of the world where elements of social life can be determined, parsed, and measured according to a specific set of tools, and within a designated and pre-determined time frame. Both could be classified as formal styles based upon a descriptive rhetorical mode (Fairclough, 1992) that echoes technical or scientific discourse, and as teleological in nature, based on outcomes that are assumed to be readily discernible and coherent. The use of clinical language and tools of inscription that translate complex social problems into programs of intervention read as factual, commonsensical and objective. As such, they obscure the political dimensions and resulting epistemological tensions that are inherent to western-led development efforts in transitional regions. Alternative or oppositional paradigms, on the other hand, tend to utilize declarations and manifestos. AMARC's *Kathmandu Declaration* is a case in point–it utilizes a genre and rhetorical mode that is explicitly political. Where the dominant discourse obscures political motivation, participatory-democratic approaches are overtly political, often using the word "We." This genre expresses a revolutionary tone where subject interpellation is not masked by the language of objectivity, but is promoted as an explicit goal–subjects are hailed to join the movement.

However, it is important to note that this distinction is not universally the case. Many grassroots media organizations develop project proposals that utilize genres similar to the dominant development paradigm. At times, this is done to establish legitimacy in order to gain entry into a discursive field. In other cases, it reflects the fact that hegemonic and resistant discourses are not fixed in binary opposition but are always shifting in dialectical relation to one another. In this sense, a social imaginary is something that is inherently unstable; and dominant and resistant discourses are forces within it that are in continual tension between difference and equivalence.

CONCLUSION

Social antagonisms are "evidence of the frontier of a social formation" (Howarth, 2002, p. 11). Antagonisms rupture the social order by showing the point where meaning is no longer fixed thereby identifying the space where the discourses that constitute social reality can be contested (Howarth, 2002). A discursive analysis focused on antagonisms enables the analysis of several confrontations: between meaning and resistance, between hegemony and subversion, and between a movement's promise and its inherent limits. The presence of a number of rupture points, or places of antagonism, in the discursive field surrounding media reform points to a social imaginary whose hegemonic dominance is contingent as social subjects struggle to achieve their respective identities within it (Laclau & Mouffe, 1995). This confrontational approach, one that is adopted not only by alternative media but also by a whole host of resistant social movements, highlights "the real nature of political frontiers and the forms of exclusion that they entail" (Mouffe, 2000, p. 12) thereby making room for dissent.

In dominant media reform projects, which rely on normative theories of the media's role in society and emphasize the professionalization of journalists as the foundation of a healthy media system and a vibrant democracy, there is an egregious silence about the more serious democratic deficits of Western media, which include inequality of access to media and the effect of political power, which results from media systems that are highly commercialized and marketized (Hackett, 2003, n.p.). Other related themes that are likewise absent are the continued dominance of international communication flows by Northern-based transnational media corporations; the integration of media with the political project of global corporatization; and the possibility that global media, marketized economies, and authoritarian regimes actively reinforce each other (ibid). The assertion of alternative models of reform that rearticulate the dominant nodal points—professionalization and objectivity being the most salient, but there are surely others—expresses the contingency of a social reality that has historically entrenched relations of domination and created media systems where a few voices serve to represent a wide diversity of interests, aspirations and identities.

REFERENCES

AMARC. (2003). *The Kathmandu declaration.* Kathmandu, Nepal: AMARC. Retrieved from http://www.amarc.org/index.php?p=The_Kathmandu_Declaration

Armijo, E. (2009). Building open societies: Freedom of the press in Jordan and Rwanda. *International Journal of Communications Law and Policy, 13,* 26–48.

Banda, F. (2009). *Towards an Africana agenda for journalism education. Introductory address at WJEC Africa-Regional preparatory colloquium.* Grahamstown, South Africa: Rhodes University.

Carpentier, N. (2005). Identity, contingency and rigidity: The (counter-) hegemonic constructions of the identity of the media professional. *Journalism, 6*(2), 199–219. doi:10.1177/1464884905051008.

Carpentier, N., Lie, R., & Servaes, J. (2001). *Community media: Muting the democratic media discourse?* Paper presented at Social theory and Discourse: The International Social Theory Consortium Second Annual conference. Brighton, UK.

Carroll, W. K., & Hackett, R. A. (2006). Democratic media activism through the lens of social movement theory. *Media Culture & Society, 28*(1), 83–104. doi:10.1177/0163443706059289.

Downing, J. D. (2001). *Radical media: Rebellious communication and social movements.* Thousand Oaks, CA: Sage.

Eur, A. C. (2009). *Report 2009 on press freedom: Rwanda.* Retrieved April 19, 2011, from http://www.eurac-network.org/web/

Fairclough, N. (1992). *Discourse and social change.* Cambridge, UK: Polity Press.

Foucault, M. (1970). *The order of things: An archaeology of the human sciences.* New York: Pantheon Books.

Freedman, E., & Shafer, R. (2008). *Ambitious in theory but unlikely in practice: A critique of UNESCO's Model Curricula for Journalism Education for Developing Countries and Emerging Democracies.* Paper presented at the International Association for Media and Communication Research. Stockholm, Sweden.

Girard, B. (1992). *A passion for radio: Radio waves and community.* Montreal, Canada: Black Rose Books.

Hackett, R. Media reform: Democratizing the media, democratizing the state [Review of the book]. *Canadian Journal of Communication, 28*(3). Retrieved April 19, 2011, from http://www.cjconline.ca/index.php/journal/article/view/1380/1457

Hackett, R., & Zhao, Y. (1998). *Sustaining democracy? Journalism and the Politics of Objectivity.* Toronto: Garamond Press.

Howarth, D. R. (2000). *Discourse.* Philadelphia, PA: Open University Press.

Howley, K. (2009). *Understanding community media.* Thousand Oaks, CA: Sage.

International Research and Exchange Board (IREX). (2009). *Media strengthening in Rwanda program: Cooperative agreement and work plan narrative for July 2009-June 2011.* Washington, DC: IREX.

Kasoma, F. P. (1996). The foundations of African ethics (Afriethics) and the professional practice of journalism: The case of society-centered media morality. *Africa Media Review, 10*(3), 93–116.

Kayumba, C., & Kimonyo, J. P. (2006). Media assistance to post-genocide Rwanda. In Zeeuw, J., & Kumar, K. (Eds.), *Promoting democracy in post-conflict societies* (pp. 211–236). Boulder, CO: Lynne Reinner Publishers.

Laclau, E., & Mouffe, C. (1985). *Hegemony and socialist strategy: Towards a radical democratic politics.* London: Verso.

Latour, B. (2005). Reassembling the social: An introduction to actor network theory. New York: Oxford.

McNair, B. (1998). *The sociology of journalism.* London, New York, Sydney, Auckland: Arnold.

McQuail, D. (1994). *Mass communication theory. An introduction.* London: Sage.

Melone, S., Terzis, G., & Beleli, O. (2002). *Using the media for conflict transformation: A common ground experience.* Berlin: Berghof Research Center for Constructive Conflict Management. Retrieved from http://www.radiopeaceafrica.org/assets/texts/pdf/Common_Ground_Experience_en.pdf

Mouffe, C. (2000). Politics and passions: The stakes of democracy. *Ethical Perspectives, 17,* 143–150.

Muganwa, G. (2007). *The enigma of press freedom in Rwanda.* Kigali, Rwanda: The Tizianoproject. Retrieved April 19, 2011, from http://tizianoproject.org/features/the_enigma_of_press_frededom_i/

Murphy, S. M., & Scotton, J. F. (1987). Dependency and Journalism Education in Africa: Are There Alternative Models? *Africa Media Review, 1*(3), 11–35.

Nyamnjoh, F. (2005). *Africa's media: Democracy and the politics of belonging. London, New York.* Pretoria: Zed Books & UNISA Press.

Ram, N. (2007). A response to the journalism education curricula. A Speech at the World Journalism Education Congress. Singapore.

Rodriguez, C. (2001). *Fissures in the mediascape: An international study of citizens' media.* Cresskill, NJ: Hampton Press, Inc..

Shah, H. (1996). Modernization, marginalization, and emancipation: Toward a normative model of journalism and national development. *Communication Theory, 6*(2), 143–166. doi:10.1111/j.1468-2885.1996.tb00124.x.

Siebert, F., Peterson, T., & Schramm, W. (1956). *Four theories of the press.* Urbana, IL: University of Illinois Press.

Thompson, A. (n.d.). *Journalism training and media freedom in Rwanda*. Retrieved April 19, 2011, from http://www.waccglobal.org/en/20074-communicating-peace/476-Journalism-training-%09and-media-freedom-in-Rwanda.html

Tunstall, J. (1977). *The media are American*. New York: Columbia University Press.

United Nations Educational, Scientific, and Cultural Organization. (2007a). *Model Curricula for Journalism Education for Developing Countries & Emerging Democracies*. Retrieved April 19, 2011, from http://unesdoc.unesco.org/images/0015/001512/151209E.pdf.United Nations

United Nations Educational, Social, and Cultural Organization. (2002). *Communications Training in Africa: Model Curricula*. Retrieved April 19, 2011, from http://portal.unesco.org/ci/en/files/24219/11731978671com_training_en.pdf/com _25 training_en.pdf

United Nations Educational, Social, and Cultural Organization. (1980). *Many Voices, One World*. Paris: UNESCO.

USAID. (2008). *Rwanda media strengthening program: Request for applications*. Washington, DC: USAID.

Van Dijk, T. A. (1998a). *Critical discourse analysis*. Retrieved April 19, 2011, from http://www.hum.uva.nl/teun/cda.htm

ENDNOTES

[1] Assistance is not only provided through capital, but also comprises knowledge transfer and symbolic resources such as induction into the "international community".

[2] See reports by Human Rights Watch. Available from http://hrw.org/englishwr2k7/docs/2007/01/11/rwanda14782.htm. Amnesty International: http://thereport.amnesty.org/eng/Regions/Africa/Rwanda. Reporters without Borders: http://www.rsf.org/country-36.php3?id_mot=203

[3] The most well-known examples of this were two Hutu power propaganda media outlets – the Kinyarwandan- and French-Language newspaper *Kangura*, and the private radio station Radio-*Television Libre des Milles Collines*, or RTLM. Both are widely considered to be instigators of genocidal actions. On December 3, 2003, the International Criminal Tribunal of Rwanda found RTLM directors Ferdinand Nahimana and Jean-Bosco Barayawiza, and *Kangura* editor Hassan Ngeze guilty of public incitement to commit genocide, conspiracy to commit genocide, and crimes against humanity for the roles their respective outlets played in the events of April 1994, (Armijo, 2009, p.40).

[4] Public ministries are the largest ad-buyers in the country and purchase space in government friendly newspapers such at the *New Times*, while opposition newspapers receive little advertising revenue. Also, opposition papers are not allowed to use government printing presses and must print their issues on presses rented in Uganda (Armijo, 2009).

[5] This is primarily assistance for radio and includes the creation of content from organizations such as Search for Common Ground and Radio LaBenevolencija and the establishment of Radio Salus – an independent campus station affiliated with the National University of Rwanda's School of Journalism and Communication.

[6] There is a robust and extensive corpus of literature that asserts a specifically African ethics in journalism, i.e. Kasoma, as well as a body of literature that is focused on the development/emancipatory potential of media in Africa.

Chapter 5

Fanning the Flames of Fear:
A Critical Analysis of Local Language Radio as a Catalyst to the Post Election Violence in Kenya

Timothy W. Kituri
Royal Roads University, Canada

ABSTRACT

Democracy depends on a free and independent media to survive. As a democratic country, Kenya enjoys a media that is relatively free. This includes radio stations that broadcast in local languages and which provide the majority of Kenyans with access to news and entertainment. These local language radio stations have been singled out as a catalyst to the post-election violence that rocked Kenya in December 2007. Tribal messages that propagated hate and fear, based on political and historic events, were broadcast--thus inciting violence. Critical Discourse Analysis is used in this study to explicate the ideologies of power through systemic investigation of the messages created and transmitted over the local language radio stations. This study contributes to the body of work done on media and democratization in Africa by showing how a gap regulatory and journalistic monitoring can jeopardize the watchdog function of media. The author recommends further research in these areas as a means of strengthening the role of media in building democracy in Africa.

INTRODUCTION

Within hours of the announcement by the Chairman of the Electoral Commission of Kenya, Mr. Samuel Kivuitu, that incumbent President Mwai Kibaki was the winner of the presidential elections held on December 27, 2007, reports of violence began to trickle in from different parts of the country. The fighting intensified and soon took on an ethnic dimension resulting in two months of violence and turmoil, the deaths of over 1,000 people, and the displacement of hundreds of thousands from their homes. The international community, led by former UN Secretary General

DOI: 10.4018/978-1-4666-4197-6.ch005

Kofi Annan, stepped in to support efforts towards finding a political solution to the crisis. The ultimate solution took the form of a 50-50 power sharing agreement between President Mwai Kibaki and Raila Odinga, leader of the official opposition and closest opponent in the presidential race. The post-election violence is believed to have its roots in political, social, and ethnic inequalities that can be traced back to colonial times. It is also believed that the media played a catalyzing role in the violence by failing to uphold journalistic ethics.

Democracy in Kenya, and of course in Africa, has been measured by, among other indicators, the continued independence, liberalization, and the proliferation of independent media (Ismail & Deane, 2008, p. 320). As a result, and mainly due to market-driven factors geared towards increasing advertising revenue, numerous local language radio stations have sprung up. The radio stations have capitalized on ethnicity to provide a stable audience and thus guarantee advertising revenues. For example, Inooro FM, which broadcasts in Kikuyu (language of the Bantu family spoken primarily by the Kikuyu people of Kenya) is believed to have a 54% audience share in the Central Province (Maina, 2006, p. 22). These stations have also given the once marginalized ethnic population a voice in their local dialects. However, these local language radio stations have been heavily criticized for their role in catalyzing the violence after the 2007 general elections; they have been accused of spreading fear among the different tribes. Through local language radio call-in talk shows, the general public, and sometimes politicians, were able to encode messages of fear aimed at undermining the credibility, on tribal grounds, of opposing candidates. This ideology of fear stemming from historic events inevitably acted as a catalyst to the post-election violence.

Critical discourse analysis (CDA) will be employed to expose the instances of fear of tribal oppression and powerlessness rooted in the divide-and-conquer strategies used during colonial times. CDA is relevant in studying the relationship between discourse, power, dominance and social inequality, and the position the analyst takes in such a relationship. CDA is a multidisciplinary method used to uncover how discourse structures and strategies (re)produce dominance and power in society (Van Dijk, 1993, p. 249; Hay, 2002). The messages encoded in the call-in talk shows hosted by the local language radio stations, and the lack of well-trained, ethically conscious journalists and moderators, acted as catalysts to the violence by feeding on the historic fear of tribal domination. The research conducts a systematic investigation of the historical context of the messages propagated by the local language radio stations as documented in academic journals and transcripts from the commission of inquiry set up to investigate the violence.

It could be argued that the independent media did not foster democracy, but instead eroded it largely through unprofessional journalism. The role played by the local language radio stations in the post election violence threatens the notion that democracy is fundamentally reliant on the existence of an independent media (Kasoma, 1995). This research paper will contribute to the ongoing discussions as to the role of, and need for, free and independent media in the creation and maintenance of democracy in Africa.

THEORETICAL FRAMEWORK: LIBERAL THEORY OF PRESS FREEDOM

The media in Africa and in Kenya have, as a direct result of colonial rule followed by one-party rule, had the tendency to evolve into an authoritarian press system of direct government control (Nyamnjoh, 2005; Odhiambo, 2002). In order to survive, African journalists allowed their governments to use them and the media as propaganda tools rather than serve as watchdogs to inform the public. African leaders have long been aware of the influence electronic media has in their countries and considered it unwise to allow radio and television free to challenge their rules. Consequently, radio and television stations had, until very recently, remained in control of the government in order to ensure political stability, promote national unity and development, and minimize foreign cultural influence (Heath, 1988, p. 96). This mentality has had to change with the rise of democracy in Africa.

Critics of the authoritarian press system argue that this form of media does not and cannot promote democracy, viewed here "…as the realization of individual rights and civil liberties" (Kivikuru, 2006, p. 8), and that it is only through a free press, one which is removed from government control, that a true democracy can arise (Kasoma,1995; Kasoma,1997; Ogbondah, 1997; Tettey, 2001; Berger, 2002; Nyamnjoh, 2005). A free and independent media is therefore a crucial ingredient for democracy and society at large.

In contrast to an authoritarian system is the liberal theory of press freedom which highlights the independent role of media in society. One of the arguments for freedom of the press is based on the idea that, "The smooth operation of the political system depended on the free expression of public opinion. It was [is] necessary for good governance" (Williams, 2003, p. 39). This theory is centered on utilitarianism, a principle that recognizes the good of the majority. Therefore, proliferation of local language stations in Kenya is a direct result of the liberalization of the press in Kenya, which should have resulted in democracy.

A democratic system of government includes three conditions, "competition among individuals and groups for positions in government, political participation through regular and fair elections and civil liberties—including freedom of expression, freedom of the press and freedom of association" (Pitts, 2000, p. 271). Given the power of the press, it is no doubt that, "… media freedom resides in a legal and political netherworld where it is precariously exposed to political machinations and predatory practices of capitalist competi-

tion" (Odhiambo, 2002, p. 295). The potential for the media to influence and generate revenue has meant that it has, and will always have, to balance this responsibly through upholding the utmost of journalistic ethics, in order to successfully campaign for democracy.

As with the rest of Africa, the media in Kenya has played a crucial role in ushering in democracy, and increasing freedom of the media demonstrates the country's resolve to maintain that democracy:

…The media has been seen nationally and internationally as a principal indicator of the democratic validity of Kenya. The media has been at the forefront of moves to transform Kenya from a one-party state to a multiparty democracy. It has gained a reputation for exposing corruption and acting as a vigorous forum for public debate, and it is seen as a guardian of public interest against state power (Ismail & Deane, 2008, p. 320).

It is with this role of media in mind that the magnitude of the accusations made against them can be fully realized. It is ironic however that increasing media freedom has resulted in the increased number of local language radio stations, which catalyzed the post-election violence and thus eroded democracy in Kenya.

The liberalization of the press and media resulted in the creation of numerous local language radio stations. Radio is the most popular medium in Africa south of the Sahara, as it is widely accessible to the vast majority who live in rural areas (Straus, 2007; Tettey, 2001, p. 9; Ugboajah, 1985, p. 158). Almost half of the population listens to public radio stations regularly (Kivikuru, 2006, p. 8). Radio is, therefore, the best medium to reach the vast majority of citizens, and local language radio stations means that even more people have access to the discussions shaping their lives.

The watchdog role played by the media is crucial in a democracy. In this role, the media are charged with actively, "…exposing activities within the state that would otherwise have been unknown to the citizenry…what we see, therefore, is a certain measure of accountability on the part of these officials which they did not have to worry about in the past" (Tettey, 2001, p. 10). This role as watchdog to the government reflects the importance of the media in the creation and maintainance of democracy. The watchdog function is best acvhieved when many independent radio stations are operating and the use of local language means that even those who do not understand English, at least 50% of the population, still have access to relevant information. However, the high standards of journalistic ethics need to be maintained in order to ensure democracy.

Democracy is the preferred neoliberal system of government as it disperses power to the people in society. In a democracy, every citizen has a voice and every voice is valuable. "The essence of democracy is that the citizens rule" (Mueller, 2003, p. 12). Other authors view democacy as, "the realization of individual rights and civil liberties" (Kivikuru, 2006, p. 8). Hence the dependance on the media in ensuring that the electorate is fully knowledgable in matters of policy.

Ironically, the neoliberal policies of the International Monetary Fund (IMF) are severe deterrents to democracy as they erode the economic freedom of the people through Structural Adjustment Programs (SAPS) and other instruments of economic control. A true democracy cannot stand in the absence of total freedom because the most important characteristic of a democracy is freedom (Pitts, 2000, p. 271).

The erosion of economic freedoms in a democratic state, especially in a relatively young country such as Kenya, can lead to catastrophic consequences. The neoliberal policies of the IMF work very well in quashing the economic freedom. "By insisting that national leaders place the interests of the international financial investors above the needs of the citizens, the IMF "…have short circuited the accountability at the heart of self-governance, thereby corrupting the democratic process" (Exchange, 2001, p. 2). The inabliity to change or affect economic policies to meet the needs of the population forces politicians in Africa to campaign on ethnic and tribal grounds when seeking office.

Ethnicity and belonging are common in Africa's discourse on democracy and both have been partially blamed for the failure by Africans to institutionalize liberal democracy. The political elite in Africa, and Kenya specifically, have been charged with mobilizing ethnic ideology and a tribal sense of belonging to either seek or defend power. There are many explanations given for this trend and some scholars contend that the fact that the politicians in Africa are unable to, "articulate any original or critical view" on economic policy because of the heavy commitment on World Bank (and IMF) policies, means that there is very little to choose from in ideological terms among rival politicians and parties. Therefore, politicians are hard pressed to find any social or economic interest groups or issues that have not been fairly represented in the past, and all they have to fall back on is the ethnic divide (Nyamnjoh, 2005, p. 34). This tendency to fall back on ethnicity coupled with the fact that most Africans, and Kenyans in particular, are living in poverty, means that the liberal democratic process is hard pressed to gain any ground in Africa, and Kenya specifically.

The economic status of a particular country plays a crucial role in the nature and success of her democracy. Many scholars have found evidence that there is a direct correlation between the level of economic stability in a country and the success of the democratic process. Przeworski (n.d.) states in a paper written for the United Nations Development program that, "even if democracies do spring up in poor countries, they are extremely fragile when facing poverty while in wealthy countries they [democracies] are impregnable" (Przeworski, n.d., p. 20). He also asserts that there is a link between the level of poverty in a country and the probability of violence breaking out, "… poverty means that people… are more likely to suffer from collective violence" (Przeworski, n.d., p. 20). Given the alarming state of poverty in Kenya, it is no wonder that the democratic process is sensitive. The frustration coming from poverty has resulted in individuals blaming each other based on historic tribal grounds for their poverty and liability to progress. This blame is based on historic events which originated in colonial times and was the key to the fear messages aired on the local language radio call-in talk shows.

HISTORY OF POST COLONIAL KENYA

The post-election violence of 2007 is widely believed to have been rooted in ethnic, social and political inequalities which can be traced back to colonial times. As we review the history of Kenya, the sources of the ideology of fear is seen in the "divide and conquer" strategies employed, first by the colonial government and later, by post-colonial governments. This ideology of fear, coupled with economic and social inequalities, was the underlying theme of the messages broadcast in the local language, which subsequently catalyzed the post-election violence.

Kenya's political history, as it played out over the decades, brought about another theme in the ideology of fear. Regionalism or *Majimboism* has been part of the country's political discourse and has, as in elections past, always elicited the fear of the unequal distribution of natural resources crucial for survival (Anderson, 2005).The fears, which fed the *majimboist* cause, were the direct product of colonial rule. After independence, the mobilization of the smaller ethnic groups within the Kenya African Democratic Union (KADU) established a barricade against the dominance of the larger, wealthier and better educated Luo and Gikuyu, groups that had taken earlier and lasting advantage of the opportunities of colonialism. KADU's promotion of *majimboism* was a logical and potentially effective means to disarm the overwhelming political and economic power represented by this Luo-Gikuyu axis within the Kenyan African National Union (KANU). The demonizing of the Gikuyu in the colonial propaganda

campaign against the Mau Mau between 1952 and 1960 had done wonders in fostering distrust for all Gikuyu politicians, but the deeper history of Gikuyu colonization of Kenya's Rift Valley and Western Highlands over more than 50 years of colonial rule gave the fear of Gikuyu domination a sharper edge (Anderson, 2005, p. 552).

The fear of economic domination and political exclusion still lives in the minds of Kenyans today and was the core reason which sparked the post-election violence. The deep fear of the Gikuyu from the history of *majimboism*, aggravated further by harsh economic conditions meant that Kenya was vulnerable to the slightest spark.

For more than 30 years, the history of Kenyan politics has been under the shadow of nationalism. KANU was the main narrator of this history— the victor of the independence election of 1963. This version of history has purposely avoided the uncomfortable Mau Mau period (1952-60), and avoided those who held regionalism (*Majimboism*) as an alternative to Kenya's political future (Anderson, 2005, p. 547).

Majimboism was the centre-piece of the KADU, KANU's rival party, and was initially promoted in pre-independence negotiations as the basis for, "a devolved constitutional arrangement that would protect smaller "minority" communities from the dominance of larger communities (p. 547). Talks of *Majimboism* have been the historic cause of division among tribes based on political affiliations, especially between the Kalenjin, Kikuyu and Luo.

Since the early 1990s, *majimboism* has been revisited in Kenya many times by some of the same politicians who began their careers in KADU over 40 years ago. In fact, "ethnic violence in the election campaigns of 1992 and 1997 was stimulated by cries of *majimboism*...the *majimboist* alternative...refuses to die" (p. 547).

As a direct result of her colonial past, Kenya has been segregated into tribal and ethnic factions who have been at loggerheads over land and power. After independence, the ancestral land of the Luo and Kalenjin, which British colonial farmers had acquired, were sold to wealthy Kikuyu individuals (Perry & Blue, 2008). At the individual level of analysis, this can be considered from a territorial imperative perspective, put forward by Robert Ardrey, which states that, "…humans, like animals, are compelled by instinct to possess and defend territory they believe belongs exclusively to them" (Levingstone, 1999). What this means is that the Luo and Kalenjin instinctively had cause to defend the title to their land with immense resolve against the perceived intruders, in this case the Kikuyu.

At the state level the country has been under the rule of presidents who have taken advantage of this ugly phenomenon, and manipulated this basic need and made policy decisions that have resulted in the 1992 and 2007 election crisis (Kegley, 2007). It was widely documented that the Moi Government used the fear of land loss to incite violence in the 1992 elections between the Kalenjin and the Gikuyu (Nowrogee & Manby, 1993). Prior to independence, the Mau Mau rebellions led the British to demonize the Gikuyu and spread propaganda which resulted in distrust towards the Gikuyu by all other tribes, especially those in the central highlands (Anderson, 2005). Distrust and fear of domination in an environment of unending poverty lives on today.

These factors have contributed to the long standing sense of fear and distrust the Kenyan public has had for the government, coupled with a track record riddled with accusations of greed. This is a political history that has spawned the current government accused of impunity (KNCHR, 2007, p. 7). Amidst this turbulent history one sees a great improvement in the development of democracy in Kenya, marked by liberal press.

LIBERAL MEDIA'S ROLE IN DEMOCRACY

Many scholars have successfully demonstrated that there is a causal relationship between liberal media and democracy. These scholars contend that democracy cannot be sustained without a free

media (Kasoma, 1997; Nyamnjoh, 2005). Democracy has several definitions across many academic fields. The underlying requirements for democracy are the "realization of individual rights and civil liberties" (Kivikuru, 2006, p. 8). The realization of these individual rights and civil liberties can only be realized when the electorate, and public at large, have a thorough knowledge of political and social issues in order to make informed decisions (Kasoma, 1995). This knowledge is facilitated by the media and in particular an independent media.

In essence, independent media are co-requisites for democracy as one cannot exist without the other. The free choice in democracy means knowledge of the options to choose from made possible through the free flow of information (Kasoma, 1995). The notion of a free, independent media in this context is taken from the Declaration of Windhoek which states that, "By an independent press, we mean a press independent from governmental, political, or economic control or from control of materials and infrastructure essential for the production and dissemination of newspapers, magazines and periodicals" (UNESCO, 1991). Free media "is independent of big business and/or government control or domination" (Nyamnjoh, 2005, p. 267). That said there may be numerous circumstances in which the press cannot be said to be truly independent (Kasoma, 1997)

Most contentious are the circumstances surrounding economic and market factors. It is widely postulated that market forces can and do sometimes influence what is covered by the media. For example, there have been cases where the media have succumbed to the whims of advertisers in order to guarantee advertising revenues. This is normally at the expense of their role in democracy (Berger, 2002). As a popular theory, "Political Economy sees the content, style and form of media products such as newspaper [radio] stories, computer games as shaped by structural features such as ownership advertising and audience spending" (Williams, 2003, p. 56). This means that, arguably, the media is enslaved to the profit maximizing commercial interests of its owners and shareholders, and is, therefore, not truly free and independent. The growth in numbers of independent radio stations in Kenya was motivated primarily by commercial interests. The main incentive was profit as these stations were created principally as entertainment vehicles (Abdi & Deane, 2008). The potential to earn increasing advertising revenues through increasing listenership prompted the proliferation of local language radio stations.

What started as a commercial endeavour quickly turned political in nature. The local language radio stations in a bid to keep their listenership moved to hosting call-in talk shows. The content of the call-in shows turned political in the heat of the campaigning prior to the 2007 general elections. The controversial political scene, coupled with the fact that the disk jockeys moderating the shows had no journalistic training, resulted in a discourse of fear, grounded in historic inter-tribal conflict, dominating the airwaves (Abdi & Deane, 2008; Mäkinen & Kuira, 2008). The ideology of fear was the main ingredient in the catalytic effect the local language radio stations had on the post election violence. The fear of tribal domination through economic and political exclusion originated during colonial rule and has been regularly used as political leverage. Federalism also referred to here as regionalism or *Majimboism* has been the recurring theme in all previous elections, and is continually the dividing factor (Anderson, 2005). The callers on the local language talk shows fuelled the fear that their particular tribe was being dominated, and incited violent action as a means to right the injustice against them (Ismail & Deane, 2008; Perry &Blue, 2008). Though never explicit, the inciting was done using local languages which were only understood on tribal lines, and rooted in historic cultural and contextual parameters.

METHOD

The main objective behind this study is to contribute to the discussion around press freedom and democracy. Authoritarian governments can use the crisis in Kenya as an argument towards more government involvement in the media. This paper will explore data from a variety of sources. The main source will be peer reviewed articles which discuss in detail the role of social media in the post election crisis (Mäkinen & Kuira, 2008), and the role of local language radio in the violence following the 2007 general elections in Kenya (Abdi & Deane, 2008; Ismail & Deane, 2008). As well, testimony taken as part of the Commission of Inquiry into the Post-Election Violence (CIPEV) published in a report released in September 2008 will be factored into the analysis (CIPEV, 2008). These sources will provide the data for analysis in the form of particular phrases translated from local languages into English which were used on air by three radio stations, Kass FM, Lake Victoria, and Inooro FM.

This study would have been better conducted had there been actual transcripts from the offending stations available. Unfortunately, transcripts have not been available, as most of the stations were not required to keep records. This data will be analyzed because it is the closest to the actual transcripts in that, the persons interviewed under oath in the CIPEV had all listened to the various radio stations in the local language. The peer-reviewed writings are useful in providing a contextual reference, which is crucial in the analysis and the subsequent affects of those phrases. It has to be emphasized that the lack of transcripts is not a hindrance to this study. It was revealed through the various investigations carried out for the CIPEV that the radio stations in question were able to solicit true feelings the callers held about rival tribes because since the conversations were not being recorded, the callers would not be held accountable for their utterances (CIPEV, 2008).

This paper will explore this data by using critical discourse analysis and specifically by analyzing the data by applying a three dimensional analytical approach developed by Norman Fairclough (Fairclough, 1992), which brings together text analysis, the production process of the text and the impact that particular text has on society.

Each phrase selected will be analyzed in light of these three dimensions. All of this was conducted in order to contribute to the literature on the role of the media in the process of democracy, and in particular how that applies to Africa.

CRITICAL DISCOURSE ANALYSIS

Critical discourse analysis is the method of choice because it has a main agenda to demystify ideologies and power through systematic investigation of semiotic data, be they written, spoken or visual (Wodak, 2004). As well, the purpose of critical discourse analysis is in the analysis of "opaque as well as transparent structural relationships of dominance, discrimination, power and control as manifested in language (Blommaert & Bulcaen, 2000, p. 361). This is a crucial element because the messages used over the local language radio stations were never explicit but rather, coded (Abdi & Deane, 2008), and only understood in the social context they were presented in.

A discourse can be defined as:

a systematically organized set of statements that give expression to the meanings and values of an institution. It describes, delimits and defines what it is possible to say and to do and not possible to say and to do with respect to an area of concern of that institution. A discourse provides a set of possible statements about a given area, and organizes and gives structure to the manner in which a particular topic, object, process is to be talked about. And as a result it provides descriptions, rules, permissions and prohibitions of social and individual actions (Williams, 2003, p. 160).

This definition is important because it is held here that the data, in the form of the statements being analyzed, was deliberately and systematically organized for the explicit purpose to spread ethnic stereotypes and in so doing perpetuate the ideologies of fear and consequently incite the violence post election.

Norman Fairclough (Fairclough, 1992), developed the methodology, contributed to the theory, and created toolkits to facilitate the greater use of CDA in the social sciences. His three-tiered framework for conducting CDA involves first focusing on the actual text of a discourse and employing all the tools of a textual analysis. He notes that each element of a text is the result of a choice, and every choice is analyzed against other possible choices. The second level goes on to analyze the implications of extraneous factors to the text, such as how it was and is produced, and even more importantly, how it is consumed in society. Because meaning is encoded in a particular context, the decoding of this meaning can be done more effectively if this context is fully appreciated. The same can be said about the audience reception of a text as this takes place in a social context which determines the nature of the decoding. The third level involves examining the text in relation to the broader society in which it is produced. This level of analysis focuses on the ideological or hegemonic effects of the text, and particularly how it participates in society today. This is the framework I will use to analyze the data observed. The first level will look at the actual wording in the messages used. The implicit coding took the form of metaphors and idioms which were spoken in local languages. There is significance in the choice of wording used as will be shown in the discussion. The second level will look at how the text was produced. In this instance, all the messages were produced for the local language radio through call-in talk shows. The significance here is the medium which is a radio station set up exclusively for a particular tribal base, and broadcasting in a language and context only members of that particular tribe could understand. Ideologies of language as presented here are never straight forward and never about language alone but, "are always socially situated and tied to questions of identity and power in societies… [ideologies of language] are positioned in, and subject to, their social, political and historical contexts" (Blackledge, 2005, p. 32). Therefore, broadcasting in their local languages had the influence of rallying Kenyans on a tribal basis and thereby perpetuating the ideologies of fear. Radio as the medium, had the capacity to give power and currency to the views being aired (Abdi & Deane, 2008), and dehumanized the victims, in this case other tribes, as was the case in Rwanda (Straus, 2007). The third level, which looks at the text in relation to society, will focus on the ideology of fear as perpetuated by the text, with the aim to reveal that the text did indeed capitalize on the historical context in conjuring the ideology of fear. Ideology is important here because it is developed by dominant groups in order to reproduce and legitimate their dominance (van Dijk, 1997). Therefore, CDA is the ideal method of analysis because of its ability to expose ideologies perpetuated in discourse.

Given that CDA seeks to expose and counteract the inconsistencies that are produced by the effects of texts on society (Fairclough, 1989), the discourse-historical approach may be the best in this context to extrapolate the role of political and national history in the creation of the ideologies of fear. The discourse-historical method' attempts to systematically integrate all available background information in the analysis and interpretation of a multitude of layers in text (Fairclough & Wodak, 1997). Once again, the historic context within which the messages were crated is crucial in understanding and uncovering the link between the discourse and the post-election violence.

FINDINGS AND IMPLICATIONS

As per the CIPEV report and a plethora of academic writing (Abdi & Deane, 2008; CIPEV, 2008; Mäkinen & Kuira, 2008), it is irrefutable that there were implicit messages perpetuating prejudices and ethnic stereotypes with the aim of inciting violence. Through incompetent journalism, these messages were allowed to be aired on several local language call-in talk shows. In this section, examples from three of the major offending FM

stations are presented, and analyzed analyze using Fairclough's three tiered framework and the discourse-historic framework.

Kass FM

Kass FM, which broadcasts in the Kalenjin Language, was singled out in many reports as one of the worst offenders as "having contributed to the climate of hate, negative ethnicity, and having incited violence in the Rift Valley (CIPEV, 2008). On Kass FM, there were references to the need for "people of the milk" to "cut grass". On other occasions, there were complaints that the mongoose has come and "stolen our [Kalenjin] chicken" (Kenya: Spreading the Word of Hate, 2008; Nyagudi, 2008;). The Kalenjin refer to themselves as the people of the milk because of their traditional pastoralist roots. The call to "cut grass" was an implicit call for ethnic Kalenjins to remove ethnic Kikuyus from traditional Kalenjin homelands in the Rift Valley Province (Ryu, 2008). The reference to the Kikuyus living in the Rift Valley as mongoose that came to steal Kalenjin chicken leaves very little to the imagination. Both these references were made repeatedly in the period leading up to the elections in December and shortly after. The main gist was for the Kalenjin to liberate themselves from Kikuyu dominance (Vernacular Radio Fuelled Ethnic Clashes, 2008).

Level One

There is an active choice in the language and choice of wording. Kass FM exclusively broadcasts in the Kalenjin language and is, therefore, only understood by the native speakers. The words and phrases chosen are based on tribal or ethnic myths which were highly idiomitic but the meaning was clear to the audience, in this case, Kalinjin speakers. For example, to "cut the grass" has the explicit meaning to cut weeds from farmland. Impicitly, the reference is to remove Kikuyus, who like weeds, are unwanted and need to be removed (Eyes on Kenya, 2008). The wording was chosen to evoke specific emotions and action in the listerners, which in this case is the ilberalization of land from the Kikuyu. These messages were calls to reclaim land and birthright from the Kikuyu specifically by eviccting them (Eyes on Kenya, 2008). The choice in the wording was implicit enough that a direct translation from Kalenjin to Engllish or Swahili for that matter, would not expose the real and intended meaning.

Level Two

Here we are concerned with the extraneous factors to the text, more specifically, the discursive practices behind how the text is produced and consumed in society. Majority of people living in the Rift Valley have access to the radio and listen to Kass FM (Odhiambo, 2002; CIPEV, 2008; Maina, 2006). The Kalenjin have historically been at loggerheads with the Kikuyu over land, and they blamed the Kikuyu for their economic oppression stemming from the policies of Kenyatta, the first Kenyan President and a Kikuyu (McGreal, 2008). Messages sent over the radio confirming this fear of Kikuyu dominatin simply galvanized the fear of the Kikuyu taking an even stronger hold on the Kalenjin politically (Abdi & Deane, 2008). The call to "cut the grass" catalyzed the violence post election by drawing on the historical context of oppression by the Gikuyu (Anderson, 2005). Linking of texts to context can be done through "manifest intertextuality," which refers to, overtly drawing from other texts" (Blommaert & Bulcaen, 2000, p. 449). The texts to draw from here are those that called for *Majimboism* because these texts were also created out of the fear of Kikuyu domination (Anderson, 2005).

Level Three

The third level looks at the ideological and hegemonic effects. The hegemonic effects are clearly evident in the mass call by Kalenjins in the Rift Valley to evict Kikiuy by use of deadly force. There are numerous reports from areas in the Rift Valley of Kikuyus being evicted by mobs of kalenjins. Mugo, a second generation Kikuyu living in Rift Valley on land given to his grandfather during Kenyatta's era, was forcefully evicted from that land. The people who burned him out were his Kalenjin neighbours who claimed he never belonged there in the first place (McGreal, 2008). The entire Kalenjin community believed and were convinced that they had been wronged and the only way to make it right was to forcefully evict the Kikuyu from the Rift Valley (McGreal, 2008). The ethnic Kalenjin viewed the Rift Valley as their ancestral land, and viewed ethnic Kikuyus as outsiders. Kalenjins were determined to evict all ethnic Kikuyus from the Rift Valley, in a bid to right the wrongs made against them in the Kenyatta era (Ryu, 2008a). The hegemonic effect of the messages is fear of continued donimation of the Kalenjin by the Kikuyu.

Lake Victoria FM

Lake Victoria FM, a Luo language radio station in its morning talk show, "just say it" had, in addition callers supporting the Orange Democratic Movement (ODM) candidates, played Luo-language songs some with reference to "the leadership of Baboons" (Nyagudi, 2008; Vernacular Radio Fuelled Ethnic Clashes, 2008). The veiled reference here is in relation to the leadership by the ethnic Kikuyu President and his Kikuyu dominated cabinet (Ryu, 2008). This reference was later repeated by callers and perpetuated the hate and distrust for the Kikuyu.

Level One

Once again at this level we are concerned by the choice of wording used. The songs and calls depict Kikuyu leadership as that of baboons. In this case as with the others, the message is in

Luo, and only understood by that tribe and language group. The choice of wording is implicitly undermining and vilifying the Kikuyu power in Kibaki's leadership, but not explicit so as to be understood that way when directly translated from the Luo language into English. The reference to baboons is strategic and purposeful with the aim to discredit and dehumanize the Kikuyu in the eyes of the Luo. The Luo contend that since they have never been in power in Kenya, this election was their best chance through the opposition leader Raila Odinga (Kenya: Spreading the Word of Hate, 2008). Once again, although implicit, the meaning in these phrases was clear to all those listening. Therefore, analyzing the word choice, in this case refereing to the leadriship by Kikuyus similar to that of baboons, is crucial in uncovering the level of distrust that exists between the Luo and Kikuyu.

Level Two

The text utilized is very similar to the Kalenjin stations. The difference is in the choice of words and the language used, but the medium remains the same in radio. Once again, the majority of Luos had access to the radio and this access helped them to know how the election results were unfolding (CIPEV, 2008; Odhiambo, 2002). It was genrally believed by Luos that the government of President Mwai Kibaki, rigged the December 27th elections in order to prevent their leader, Raila Odinga from taking over the presicency (Swain, 2008). The Luo context is heavily dependent on the fact that no one from that tribe has been president, and thus they have not had the opportunity to build their political and economic base as have the Kikiuy and Kalenjin (Anderson, 2005). There were reports of statments made by Luos to the effect that, "if he [Kibaki] stays it will mean civil war." Nearly all Luos want Mr. Kibaki forced from office (Ethnic cleansing in Luoland, 2008). This election provided the closest opportunity for the Luo, and they felt marginalized, both politically and economically

by the Kikuyu who have been in leadership twice through Kenyatta, and recently Kibaki (Wafula, 2008). An example of this is in statements made by Luos, as a part of the marginalized minority, saying that it is "our turn to eat" referencing that it is their turn to be in power and for once, control the distribution of resources in their favor (Aluoka, 2008). The reference to baboons therefore, draws on the context of marginilization which also stems from historic and political sources. Refriencing Kikuyus in this manner over the radio galvanizes the idea that Kikuyus are to blame for the systmatic marginalization of the Luo, both politically and economically (Abdi & Deane, 2008). CDA claims that actual language products can be formative for larger social porocess and structures (Blommaert & Bulcaen, 2000). In this case, the choice of wording shapes how the Luo view the Kikuyu as being responsible for their economic and political marginalization.

Level Three

At this level, we see the hegemonic impact of the message in the mobilization of the Luo against the Kikuyu. Hegemony concerns power which is achieved through integrating classes and groups through consent (Blommaert & Bulcaen, 2000). Hegemony here is observed in the general consent by the Luo listeners of Lake Victoria FM, and in rejecting the dominance of the Kikuyu. The rejection of Kikuyu dominance was manifested by the evictions of Kikuyu from parts of Luo dominated Kisumu town immediately after the election results (Ethnic cleansing in Luoland, 2008). Once again, the use of violence was the only way the Luo felt united in the struggle against the domination by the Kikuyu.

Inooro FM

The Kikuyu stations were not entirely innocent here either. Just like Lake Victoria FM, there were several reports of songs in the Kikuyu language chastising Raila Odinga and his Orange Democratic Movement (ODM). The songs talked negatively about "beasts from the west" a veiled reference to Raila. The songs went on to describe Mr. Odinga and Luos in general, as murderers, power hungry people, who cared only about their tribe, the Luo, at the expense of all other tribes. An example is the song by Miuga Njoroge, broadcast on Inooro which was believed to have been sponsored by the governing Party of National Unity. This song echoed the statements prior that Raila Odinga, the leader of the opposition and a Luo is a power hungry murderer (IRIN, 2008). The songs continue to reference the Luo as lazy hooligans who do not work and do not pay rent (Abdi & Deane, 2008; Vernacular Radio Fuelled Ethnic Clashes, 2008; Wafula, 2008) These words were specifically chosen to instill fear in the Kikuyu listeers of the consequences of Luo leadership as revealed by the three-tiered analytical framework.

Level One

The analysis of this text, similarly to the previous two cases, begins with the fact that this text was created in the Kikuyu language with the aim of mobilizing other Kikuyus to shared feelings of negativity against the Luo. The choice of wording and metaphors is deliberate with the intention to incite fear in Luo leadership. Reference to the Luo as power hungry murderers in the Kikuyu language was made implicitly (Abdi & Deane, 2008). Like the other cases, this means that the message of hate and distrust against the Luo would not have been understood outside the Kikuyu language and context. The songs did not talk about the Luo, or Raila Odinga, but instead referred to the "beasts from the west" which infers to the western origins of the Luo (IRIN, 2008). The idea behind this was to deter voters from casting a vote for Luo leadership in Raila Odinga and his ODM party. We therefore see a concrete instance of discourse in the choice of text used

on this particular radio station. The text choice was made with the intention to galvanize Kikuyu ideas of superiority to the Luo.

Level Two

The context of this message to the Kikuyu community is also based on the historic and political circumstances surrounding the two tribes. The Kikuyu fear that having the Luo in power will result in Kikuyu marginalization, as was the case in the Moi presidency (McGreal, 2008). The context of this fear goes back to the days of the *majimbo* movement, and texts produced during the onset of this movement are very similar to those used in the Kikuyu songs (Anderson, 2005). For example, the "beast from the west" reference was coined after the ideological fallout between Jomo Kenyatta, a Kikuyu, and Jaramogi Oginga Odinga, then Vice President and a Luo. The fallout was the result of Odinga advocating for the immediate equitable sharing of the countries resources among the 42 tribes. The Kenyatta regime needed to discredit this movement and began vilifying the Luo (Koyugi, 2008). The context here is the fear of economic and political domination which was the same fear that lead the Kikuyu to resist calls for federalism. The discursive practice is in the perpetuation of the Kikuyu fear of Luo domination if Kibaki, the incumbent president, lost to Raila the Luo opposition leader. Hence the specific use of terms like "power hungry" and "murderer" in the songs played on Inooro FM.

Level Three

The hegemonic impact of these messages is clear in the mass action that Kikuyus took against their fellow countrymen and women, especially the Luo and Kalenjin. The mobilization of a Kikuyu militia, the *mungiki*, charged with the protection of Kikuyu rights was the most blatant sign of Kikuyu resolve (CIPEV, 2008). It was through the messages in the songs played on Inooro FM that integrated group concent and hegemony was achieved. The concent was that the Kikuyu were indeed vulnerable to marginalization under Luo leadership, and that all should be done to prevent this from happening (McGreal, 2008; Swain, 2008).

DISCUSSION

As the most dominant medium in Kenya, radio covers about 97 per cent of the population in the country (Odhiambo, 2002). Vernacular radio has offered a large majority of Kenyans, typically the poorest and most politically marginalized, access to a media which is not controlled by a distrusted government (Abdi & Deane, 2008). That the messages presented before were not only transmitted in vernacular languages, but also broadcast over the radio gave them credibility. The ideology of fear existed in the fact that people had ideas and opinions as to which communities were to blame for their problems. These opinions were not discussed in face to face meetings, but when broadcast over the radio; such views gained power and currency and thus galvanized people into action (Abdi & Deane, 2008).

Once again, the availability of transcripts would greatly aid this analysis, but it is also important to note that the stations mentioned previously were not monitored and thus, callers had even more incentive to speak their minds knowing that there would be no evidence collected (Abdi & Deane, 2008; CIPEV, 2008). The context in which the messages were coded was one of fear and distrust stemming from the political and national history. According to Fairclough, liking of text to its context can be done through "manifest intertextuality," which refers to "overtly drawing from other texts" (Blommaert & Bulcaen, 2000, p. 449). In this study, it is clear that the texts mentioned prior were drawn from the historic struggle for *majimboism*. It is clear that the "...*majimboist* ambitions were

defensive in character and born out of fear—for Moi and the other belligerent Kalenjin this meant fear of the Gikuyu colonization of the Rift Valley" (Anderson, 2005, p. 255). It is evident that the utterances in the Kalenjin stations drew from utterances made about Majimboism, and thus evoked the same ideology of fear.

The discourse-historic method is applicable as well. The history here is the national and political history on which the ideology of fear is based. Outside this context, the text in the messages broadcast over air through the local language radio stations ceases to have any impact.

CONCLUSION

The local language radio stations played a big role in the violence following the 2007 general elections. They acted as a catalyst by allowing, through incompetent journalism, messages of tribal hatred which evoked fears based on historic events to fill the airwaves. In an atmosphere of economic desperation and a general distrust for the government, Kenyans were looking for changes and were emotionally invested in the election process. As a fairly young democratic country, Kenya needs media which will act as watchdogs and ensure that the government and all elected officials are held accountable. It is only with a free and independent press that democracy can thrive (Kasoma, 1995; Kasoma, 1997; Nyamnjoh, 2005). Therefore, the local language radio stations are a crucial part of the independent media system as they allow the larger majority in rural Kenya access to political debates which affect them. The onus is on the journalists and reporters to maintain professional standards and act as watchdogs for society. Had the journalists working in the stations previously mentioned been professional, they would not have allowed such messages of hate to air unchecked.

It is very reassuring that the journalists have accepted their role in the post election violence and are striving to remedy their situation through training. It is also reassuring that the government has refrained from stepping in and monitoring the media as this would mean that the media would cease to be independent of government control which would jeopardize democracy in Kenya.

It is noted that the avalability of transcripts would have benefited this study and the official investigation into the post election violence. It is the lack of monitoring that allowed the radio stations to broadcast messages they knew would generate tribal hatred. It is, therefore, recommended that stricter policies be enforced by the Kenya Media Council requiring all radio stations to maintain records of broadcast. As well, miminum journalistic training should be mandatory for all broadcasters and presenters. This way, the faith in the media will be restored, thus allowing them to carry out their role in sustaining democracy.

RECOMMENDATIONS FOR FUTURE RESEARCH

The media play a crucial role in the democratic process and it is, therefore, of fundamental importance to understand how this relationship functions. Research is particularly needed in the area of local language media. The cultural disparity among the various language speakers means that how they interact with the media is equally disparate. Further research is therefore required in investigating how local language media can be used as a tool to foster democracy.

The lack of transcripts posed a big challenge in this study and other studies into the post-election violence. Further research is necessary on best practices around media monitoring, especially by the media themselves. The danger of this monitoring role falling on the government and thus stifling media freedom is real and can be avoided by research into best practices. This is especially important in a climate where numerous local language media operate. Research into monitoring best practices should also address how the law will support the media monitoring bodies by providing legal basis upon which action can be taken against offending stations (Nderitu, 2008).

Finally, research needs to be done on best practices around journalism ethics and its importance in a climate where local language reporting is the order of the day. Research into what minimum competencies journalists working in local language media require in order to ensure that they succeed as watchdogs is necessary. It is no doubt that Local language media is necessary in the democratic process (Abdi & Deane, 2008). However, they have to be cognizant of the damage, as seen in the post-election violence, that they can cause to the entire process, if they fail to uphold the highest form of journalistic ethics.

REFERENCES

Abdi, J., & Deane, J. (2008). *The Kenyan 2007 elections and their aftermath: The role of media and communication.* London: BBC World Service Trust.

Aluoka, O. (2008.). Kenya's Post-Election Violence. Retrieved November 21, 2008, from http://www.tokyofoundation.org/en/sylff/voices-from-the-sylff-community/kenya2019s-post-election-violence

Anderson, D. M. (2005). Yours in struggle for Majimbo: Nationalism and the Party Politics of Decolonization in Kenya, 1955-64. *Journal of Contemporary History, 3*(40), 547–564. doi:10.1177/0022009405054571.

Berger, G. (2002). Theorizing the media-democracy relationship in South Africa. *International Communication Gazette, 64*(1), 21–45. doi:10.1177/17480485020640010201.

Blackledge, A. (2005). Discourse and power in a multilingual world. *Journal of Language and Politics*, 1-263.

Blommaert, J., & Bulcaen, C. (2000). Critical discourse analysis. *Annual Review of Anthropology*, 447–466. doi:10.1146/annurev.anthro.29.1.447.

CIPEV. (2008). *Report of the Commission of Inquiry into Post-Election Violence*. Nairobi, Kenya: Commission of Inquiry into Post-Election Violence.

Economist. (2008, February 7). *Ethnic cleansing in Luoland*. Retrieved November 21, 2008, from http://www.economist.com/world/mideast-africa/displaystory.cfm?story_id=10653938

Eyes on Kenya. (2008, February 7). *Eyes on the media in Kenya: Kenya's wolf in sheep skin or her redemption?* Retrieved December 21, 2008, from http://eyesonkenya.org/blog/?p=55

Fairclough, N. (1989). *Language and power*. London: Logman.

Fairclough, N. (1992). *Discourse and social change*. Cambridge, UK: Polity.

Fairclough, N., & Wodak, R. (1997). Critical discourse analysis. In van Dijk, T. A. (Ed.), *Discourse as social interaction. Discourse studies: A multidiciplinary introduction* (pp. 258–284). London: Sage.

Hay, C. (2002). *Political analysis: A critical introduction*. New York: Palgrave.

Heath, C. W. (1988). Private sector partcipation in public service broadcasting: The case of Kenya. *The Journal of Communication*, *3*, 96–108. doi:10.1111/j.1460-2466.1988.tb02062.x.

IMF/World Bank. (2001). How the International Monetary Fund and the World Bank undermine democracy and erode human rights: Five case studies. *Global Exchange*, 1-16.

IRIN. (2008, January 22). *Kenya: Spreading the word of hate*. Retrieved November 12, 2008, from http://www.irinnews.org/printreport.aspx?reportid=76346

Ismail, J. A., & Deane, J. (2008). The 2007 General election in Kenya and its aftermath: The role of local language media. *The International Journal of Press/Politics*, *3*(13), 319–327. doi:10.1177/1940161208319510.

Kasoma, F. P. (1995). The role of the independent media in Africa's change to democracy. *Media Culture & Society*, 537–555. doi:10.1177/016344395017004002.

Kasoma, F. P. (1997). The independent press and politics in Africa. *International Communication Gazette*, *59*, 295–310. doi:10.1177/0016549297059004004.

Kegley, C. W. (2007). *World politics: Trend and transformation*. Toronto: Thomson Nelson.

Kivikuru, U. (2006). Top-down or bottom-Up?: Radio in the service of democracy: Experiences from South Africa and Namibia. *International Communication Gazette*, *68*(1), 5–31. doi:10.1177/1748048506060113.

KNCHR. (2007). *Still Behaving Badly*. Nairobi, Kenya: Kenya National Commission on Human Rights.

Koyugi, J. (2008, January 20). *Kenya will never be the same*. Retrieved January 1, 2009, from http://kenyaburning.wordpress.com/2008/01/20/kenya-will-never-be-the-same/

Levingstone, S. (1999, April 14). Does territoriallity drive human aggression? *International Herald Tribune*.

Maina, L. W. (2006). *African media development initiative: Kenya research findings and conclusion*. London: BBC World Service Trust.

Mäkinen, M., & Kuira, M. W. (2008). Social media and postelection crisis in Kenya. *The International Journal of Press/Politics*, *13*(3), 328–335. doi:10.1177/1940161208319409.

McGreal, C. (2008, February 7). *'Who's to blame? It depends where you begin the story'*. Retrieved December 10, 2008, from http://www.guardian.co.uk/world/2008/feb/07/kenya.chrismcgreal

Mueller, D. C. (2003). *Capitalism and democracy: Challenges and responses in an increasingly interdependent world*. Northampton, MA: Edward Elgar Publishing.

Murphy, C. (2003). *Violence in Kenya*. Denver, CO: University of Denver.

Nderitu, T. (2008). When radio spreads violence: Free speech questioned in Kenya. Retrieved January 5, 2009, from http://towardfreedom.com/home/content/view/1268/63/

Nowrogee, B., & Manby, B. (1993). *Divide and rule: State-sponsored ethnic violence in Kenya*. New York: Human Rights Watch.

Nyagudi, L. (2008, January 24). *Kenya: Spreading the words of hate*. Retrieved November 4, 2008, from http://mfoa.africanews.com/site/list_messages/15067

Nyamnjoh, F. B. (2005). *Africa's media: Democracy & the politics of belonging*. New York: Zed Books Ltd..

Odhiambo, L. O. (2002). The media environment in Kenya Since 1990. *African Studies, 61*(2), 295–318. doi:10.1080/00020180822000032965.

Ogbondah, C. W. (1997). Communication and democratication in Africa: Constitutional changes, prospects and persistant problems for the media. *International Communication Gazzette*, 271-294.

Perry, A., & Blue, L. (2008). The Demons That Still Haunt Africa. *Time*, 32–35.

Pitts, G. (2000). Democracy and press freedom in Zambia: Attitudes of members of parliament towards media and media regulations. *Communication Law and Policy, 5*(2), 269–294. doi:10.1207/S15326926CLP0502_5.

Przeworski, A. (n.d.). Democracy and economic development. *Political Science and Public Interest*, 1-27.

Relief Web. (2008). *Kenya: Spreading the Word of Hate*. Retrieved November 9, 2008, from http://www.reliefweb.int/rw/RWB.NSF/db900SID/AMMF-7B4DL3?OpenDocument

Ryu, A. (2008, January 30). *Radio broadcasts incite Kenya's ethnic violence*. Retrieved September 4, 2008, from http://www.voanews.com/english/archive/2008-01/2008-01-30-voa38.cfm

Ryu, A. (2008, March 19a). Despite power-sharing accord, ethnic division in Kenya runs deep. Retrieved December 20, 2008, from http://www.voanews.com/english/archive/2008-03/2008-03-19-kenyaland.cfm

Straus, S. (2007). What is the relationship between hate radio and violence? Rethinking Rwanda's "Radio Machete". *Politics & Society, 35*, 609–637. doi:10.1177/0032329207308181.

Swain, J. (2008, February 3). Kenya violence: 'We waited, now we'll chop them to bits'. Retrieved November 21, 2008, from http://www.timesonline.co.uk/tol/news/world/africa/article3295501.ece

Tettey, W. J. (2001). The media and democratization in Africa: Contributions, constraints and concerns of the private press. *Media Culture & Society, 23*, 5–31. doi:10.1177/016344301023001001.

Ugboajah, F. O. (1985). Media habits of rural and semi-rural (slum) Kenya. *International Communication Gazette, 36*, 155–174. doi:10.1177/001654928503600301.

UNESCO. (1991). *Final Report: Seminar on promoting an independent and pluralistic African Press*. Windhoek, Namibia: UNESCO.

van Dijk, T. A. (1993). Principles of critical discourse analysis. *Discourse & Society, 4*(2), 249–283. doi:10.1177/0957926593004002006.

van Dijk, T. A. (1997). Discourse as interaction in society. In van Dijk, T. A. (Ed.), *Discourse as Social Interaction: Discourse Studies: A Multidiciplinary Indtoruction* (*Vol. 2*, pp. 1–37). London: Sage. doi:10.4135/9781446221884.n1.

van Noppen, J.-P. (2004). CDA: A discipline come of age. *Journal of Sociolinguistics*, *8*(1), 107–126. doi:10.1111/j.1467-9841.2004.00253.x.

Vernacular Radio Fuelled Ethnic Clashes. (2008). *The Nairobi Chronicle*. Retrieved November 22, 2008, from http://nairobichronicle.wordpress.com/2008/08/04/vernacular-radio-fuelled-ethnic-clashes/

Wadhmas, N. (2008). World Spotlignt: Kenya in Crisis. *Time*, 7.

Wafula, E. (2008, May 6). *Africa Brief*. Retrieved November 9, 2008, from http://africabrief.blogspot.com/2008_05_04_archive.html

Williams, K. (2003). *Understanding media theory*. New York: Oxford University Press.

Wodak, R. (1999). Critical discourse analysis at the end of the 20th century. *Research on Language and Social Interaction*, *32*(1&3), 185–193.

Wodak, R. (2004). Critical discourse analysis. *Qualitative Research Practice*, 185-201.

Chapter 6
Looking Beyond Elections:
An Examination of Media Freedom in the Re-Democratisation of Nigeria

Ufuoma Akpojivi
North West University, South Africa

ABSTRACT

Media freedom is pivotal to the sustenance and consolidation of democracy, as the quality of democracy in any society depends on the level of freedom accorded the media and the plurality of views entertained (Diamond, 2008). The ability of the mass media to carry out their traditional functions of educating, entertaining and enlightening the public about their democratic rights, and holding governments accountable, will subsequently lead to the establishment of a strong democratic institution. Hence there is need to protect media freedom in any democratic society (Baker, 2007; Norris, 2008). The Nigerian media environment, however, is characterised by a series of laws such as sedition law, official secret act, amongst others, which have directly and indirectly hindered the freedom of the mass media and their responsibility of promoting and advancing democracy. This is made worse by the incomprehensive nature of the 1999 Constitution. Using interviews and policy analysis, this chapter critically examines the policy framework of media freedom in Nigeria and its impact on the operation of the mass media. The ability of the media to live up to their responsibility of promoting and advancing the democratisation process in Nigeria within the available framework is also examined.

DOI: 10.4018/978-1-4666-4197-6.ch006

INTRODUCTION: THE INTERWOVEN RELATIONSHIP OF MEDIA FREEDOM AND DEMOCRACY

Democracy is an ambiguous concept with no universal definition as it can be seen from different perspectives. According to Rozumilowicz (2002, p. 9), any definition of democracy is "contentious" and subject to huge debate. Nonetheless, two principal elements of competition and participation must be recognised in every definition of democracy (ibid, p. 11). These two elements are the underlying objectives of democracy in any society (i.e., promoting a competitive political sphere and encouraging active participation of the public in the political and civil spheres of society (Akpojivi, 2012).

The media system and democratic process of any society are affected when these elements are lacking. Blankson (2007, p. 16) argues that the level of any democratic process lies in the ability of the media to encourage active political competition and citizens' participation. Hence the sustenance and consolidation of democracy depend on the freedom of the media to provide the public with "adequate information to make decisions, as well as ensure a forum for the development of ideas and opinions" (Rozumilowicz, 2002, p. 13). Moyer (2008, n.p.), while summing the interwoven relationship between media freedom and democracy, argues that the "250 year old experiment in self government (of the United States) will not make it, as journalism goes, so goes democracy." In order to enhance societal development, there is need to maintain plurality of views through the free flow of information within society (Ake, 1991).

THE CONCEPTUALISATION OF MEDIA FREEDOM

Media freedom is a complex and ambiguous concept. Scholars discuss media freedom from two perspectives: the philosophical and political perspectives (Barendt, 1985). These perspectives of media freedom have been influenced by the arguments of "truth, self fulfilment, and democracy" which surround the media freedom debate.

The philosophical perspective of media freedom is rooted in John Mill's work, "On Liberty", that sets out to address salient questions affecting the mass media in democratic societies. This included questions like, what role the should media play in enhancing democracy; who regulates the mass media; and what kind of regulation will support the mass media in fulfilling their goals and roles in the society? These questions form the central argument of Mill's "On Liberty" as he examines the "nature and limits of power which society can legitimately exercise over the individual and the need to protect the public from the tyranny of the state" (Mill, 1974 p. 8; Levi, 1966).

According to Mill (1974), everyone has the right to freely express opinion, as the interference and restriction to free exchange of information will cause public damage to the society since diversity of views is a public utility. The information disclosed can nourish government with diverse views whether dissent or not, which will in turn aid the government in policy formulation (Holmes, 1990). Kant also stated that denying the public the right to free speech means "withholding from the rulers all the knowledge of those matters which if he knew about them he would himself rectify" (Holmes, 1990 p. 29).

However, this right to free speech for citizens has necessitated regulation of the media since society could be exposed to the danger or the excesses of freedom (Lichtenberg, 1990). Mill buttresses this danger by arguing that the only freedom from restraint is that which does not affect others (Riley, 1998; Mill, 1974), and this is impossible to achieve since man is evil by nature and cannot make an informed judgement (Hegel, 1896). Thus the state needs to regulate freedom of speech in order to secure the interest or welfare of others (Mill, 1974). The rationale behind government regulation of the media (both content and structural) is to protect the security of the nation, hence the exclusion of certain information from both the media and public domain (Lichtenberg, 1990). Holmes (1990) and McQuail (1992) argue that if these regulations are not in place, society will be at the mercy of the media and the private interest of a selected few will suppress the views of the public.

On the other hand, classical liberal theorists like Milton, Spinoza, Tocqueville and Locke have criticized the idea of regulation as they see freedom as a catalyst to democracy and development (Curran, 1979; Ocitti, 1991; Ambrose, 1995). These political theorists believe that democracy gives every citizen the right to air their views, and that it is morally wrong to deprive the public of this right (Ambrose, 1995). In addition, they argue that government hide under the complex nature of "public interest" and "national interest" to regulate the media by "overestimating" the threat of the media to society and democracy (Scanlon, 1990). Both national interest and public interest used by the government to regulate the media are simple but complex contested concepts in contemporary democratic societies (McQuail, 2003). This complexity has given room to the various controversies surrounding media freedom debate.

A new dimension of free speech has been added to the philosophical debate of media freedom. This argument, associated with Madison, holds that society has to protect the inalienable human right of speech from being hijacked by the "abusive censorship of political debate" in order to safeguard the democratic process (Richard, 1999, p. 18-19). Proponents of this view argue that speeches (dissent or not) should be tolerated by society whether public or government, and this call of tolerance "extends the protection of free speech as broadly as the underlying right to conscience and threats thereto" (Richard, 1999, p. 26). Although the concept of tolerance is utopian and its application unrealistic (Marcuse, 1969), it has been generally recognised as most countries have drafted constitutions to protect this right of free speech from certain forms of state control (Richard, 1999). This has also formed the basis by which media freedom is measured politically.

Moreover, the state of freedom accorded to the media and citizens within a society determines how democratic the society is politically (Tom, 2004; Lindberg, 2006). This is because the level of freedom given to the citizens to access diverse sources of information, participate in media debate and actively participate in the electoral process will strengthen and increase the democratic quality (Lindberg, 2006; Diamond, 2008b). This position is equally reflected in the reports of media watch-dog organizations like *Freedom House, Article 19* amongst others who adjudge the level of freedom within countries based on this.

These different arguments have influenced the various definitions of media freedom, as it is commonly referred to as the ability of the mass media to engage in their activities without fear or favour (Humphreys, 1996; Tettey, 2006). However, for the purpose of this paper, media freedom is defined as the ability of the mass media to carry out their constituted functions of information, education, and entertainment without interference from government or media owners to the editorial position of the media (William 1979). This definition recognises that there is no absolute freedom as already discussed but that there are common standards which extend to media freedom. These standards include the ability of the media to engage in their functions without interference (Righter, 1978), and provide a platform for public participation in media debates. According to Linz & Stepan (1996, pp. 7-10), the ability of emerging democracies to allow freedom within the state will encourage participation of the public in political and civil spheres which is essential in the consolidation of democracy.

THE TRANSITION PROCESS AND POLITICS: HOW DID WE GET HERE?

Nigeria gained independence from Great Britain in 1960. With a population of over 140 million (according to the 2006 census figures from National Population Commission (NPC)), it is regarded as the most populated country in Africa. The mass media played a significant role in the struggle for independence in Nigeria which was gained without violence unlike in other African countries (Bourgault, 1995). Thus, many scholars believe that the struggle for independence was fought and won within the media sphere (Nyamnjoh, 2005). According to Bourgault (1995), early nationalists made use of their chains of newspapers to advance the cause of independence. Nnamdi Azikiwe and Obafemi Awolowo used the *West African Pilot*, and the *Nigerian Tribune* and *Western Nigerian Television* respectively to propagate the ideology of freedom (Bourgault 1995). However, since the attainment of independence, the democratization process of Nigeria has remained fragile and unstable (Qadir, Clapham, & Gill, 1993). This is largely attributed to the social and political antecedents of the country (Jeffrey, 2000).

The current drive to democratisation started in 1999 after 29 years of military rule which suppressed media freedom and the principles and values of democracy, and underdeveloped the country (Ojo, 2003; Ogbondah, 2004; Nyamnjoh, 2005). Ake argues that the underdevelopment witnessed during the period of military rule was worse off than in the period of colonisation (Ifidon, 2002). The start of this re-democratization process in 1999 was born out of pressure and the need to overcome perennial problems of economic undergrowth, political instability, and international boycott confronting the nation (Boadi, 2004; Tettey, 2001). Thus the concept of democracy and its principles of free and fair elections, media freedom and civil rights are relatively new in Nigeria even though the struggle for independence and institution of democracy dates back to the colonial era (Nyong'O, cited in Joseph, 1991).

Since the institution of democracy in 1999, some success has been achieved. There has been successful transition from one democratically elected government to another. However, the electioneering process in Nigeria is widely criticised both home and abroad due to electoral malpractices and uneven playing field for all

political candidates. This phenomenon has created the challenge on how the democratisation process can be consolidated. According to Boadi (2004), this makes one less optimistic about the democratisation process, since within the African standards of judging democracy, a lot still needs to be done to reposition the country to be like other successful democratic countries like South Africa and Ghana.

Attempts by the Nigerian state to consolidate its democracy through the conduct of frequent elections have been widely criticized by international communities, civil societies, labour movements and political organizations like the Conference for Nigerian Political Parties (CNPP) and Save Nigeria Group (SNG) for the wide spread electoral frauds that have characterized almost every election in the country (especially the 2003, 2007 electioneering period), despite the renewed presence of competitive political parties across the states (Diamond, 2008a). In the electioneering periods of 2003, 2007, and 2011, incumbent politicians used state apparatus and resources to hold onto power. Calingaert (2006), while giving typical examples of events that characterize elections in Nigeria, holds that ballot boxes are stuffed with fake voters cards, names of eligible voters are missing from the election registers, registers are filled with names of deceased persons and even children, and thugs hijack ballot boxes into undisclosed locations where election results are prepared. Consequently, the results from these elections have been challenged in the courts, and the elections subsequently cancelled (as witnessed in states such as Ondo, Anambra, and Edo, where the opposition parties were declared the winners), or rerun (e.g., in Ekiti state).

Such practices have made a mockery of the democratisation process, and so made Nigeria's electoral process less credible and lacking the necessary recognition it deserves (Joseph, 2008). Scholars argue that Nigeria cannot be regarded as a democratic society as the level of freedom of her citizens to choose their government and of the mass media to facilitate the democratic consolidation has not improved over the years despite the periodic elections conducted (Tom, 2004; Lindberg, 2006). Diamond (2002) opines that Nigeria is becoming an electoral authoritarian as it is repeatedly conducting elections which promote a one party state and lack credibility (Calingaert, 2006; Lindberg, 2006).

Nonetheless, Calingaert (2006) stated that the mass media are a significant tool that can help establish a transparent electoral process that will aid democratic consolidation. According to him, the ability of the media to engage in their rudimentary watchdog functions will help create a transparent electoral process, expose electoral frauds, and securitize politicians because the media have the potential of determining the political significance of a society. In addition, Joseph (2008) argues that it is only when the electoral process and other relevant institutions are transparent that democracy can be consolidated. Therefore, there is need to look beyond just conducting elections in Nigeria and reviewing the freedom accorded the mass media to bring about democratic consolidation since the media are pivotal to any democracy. There is also need to ascertain if the Nigerian media, regarded as the most vibrant in Africa (Oyeleye, 2004; Uko, 2004), are to be blamed for the imbalances in the electoral process due to their failure to live up to their responsibility as argued by Schedler (2002), or if institutional structure (whether ownership or regulatory) has affected the media's ability to promote transparent, free and fair elections.

POLICY FRAMEWORK AND THE MEDIA ENVIRONMENT

The Nigerian media environment is governed by a number of laws and policies that provide a framework for the operation of the media. These policies determine and influence the activities of the media and the ability to carry out their watchdog role essential for the consolidation of democracy. For the purpose of this paper, the following policies

which form the dominant documents that govern the media landscape were reviewed. These include the national mass communication policy 1987, the sedition law, the 1999 constitution of the federal republic of Nigeria, the Freedom of Information (FOI) act 2011, and the Nigeria broadcasting code. Next are the synopses of each policy and the rationale of the policies.

The National Mass Communication Policy, 1987

This policy document was formulated during the military regimes of General Babangida, who was under constant pressure to reform the media (Anyanwu, 1992). This is currently the only policy document in Nigeria that states the role of the media in the socio-political and economic development of Nigeria (Akpojivi, 2012). Apart from classifying the media into three groups (i.e., print, electronic, and communication technology), the central objective of the policy is that all media should assist in nation building and development (*National Mass Communication Policy,* 1987).

The Sedition Law

This is one of the laws Nigeria inherited from the colonial masters (Great Britain). This law, according to Tom (2004), is based on the ideology that the King or Queen of England cannot be wrong. This idea is vividly reflected in Sections 50 and 51 of the Nigerian Criminal Code 1990 that seeks to protect Nigerian leaders (see Akpojivi, 2012). According to Akinfeleye (2003), this law is mainly used to prevent the media from carrying out their watchdog role, and subsequently protect the private interest of the leaders.

The 1999 Constitution of the Federal Republic of Nigeria

The 1999 constitution was formulated without public consultation by the military regime of General Abdulsalaam Abubakar prior to the institution of a democratic government (Aguda cited in Akpojivi, 2012). Although the constitution was formulated along the 1960 and 1970 constitutions and the universal ideas of bill of rights, like that of other African countries, it failed to provide for the freedom of the media to carry out their functions.

The Nigeria Broadcasting Code, 2006

The Nigeria Broadcasting Code was formulated by the *National Broadcasting Commission* (NBC) in accordance with Decree No 38 of 1992 now amended and known as NBC Act No 55 of 1999, which requires them to regulate the broadcasting industry. The broadcasting code stipulates the guidelines for the operation of the media. The central objective of the code is that all media contents should be fair, equitable and promote national interest (Akpojivi, 2012).

The FOI Act, 2011

The FOI bill was passed into law on May 28, 2011 after 12 years of deliberation. The passage of the bill was facilitated by pressure from both national and international organisations like Article 19, Media Right Agenda and the Newspapers Proprietors Association of Nigeria (NPAN) (Akpojivi, 2011). It is believed that the FOI Act will strengthen the democratic process due to its framework of making information accessible by the public. Conversely, the restrictive clauses contained in the Act and other administrative mechanisms will affect the media's ability to access information (Akpojivi, 2011).

THE MASS MEDIA AND DEMOCRATIC CONSOLIDATION IN NIGERIA: A DISCUSSION

As earlier stated, the mass media are central to the democratisation process of Nigeria as they have played significant roles from the colonial,

to the military and the post independence era. It is, therefore, germane to ensure the freedom of the media from both economic and political factors in order to safeguard democracy. Diamond (2008a) argues that the quality of any democracy is dependent on the freedom accorded to the media and the plurality of views entertained and allowed; as such plurality will allow democracy to flourish. Thus, the ability of the media to exercise their functions of informing, educating and persuading the public and holding government accountable will subsequently lead to the establishment of stronger democratic institutions (Baker, 2007; LeDuc, Niemi & Norris, 2008).

The concept of media freedom has generated huge debates and controversy within the Nigerian media sphere. These debates stem from the belief that the level of liberty accorded the media and individuals determines the level of freedom and democracy in a country (Tom, 2004). There is also a debate on what the precise functions of the mass media in new democratic societies like Nigeria should be: should the mass media speak softly or act boldly in order to sustain the fragile democracy (Kuper & Kuper, 2001)?

Constitutionally, the watchdog function is ascribed to the mass media. Section 22 of the Nigerian 1999 constitution states that:

The press, radio, television and other agencies of the mass media shall at all times be free to uphold the fundamental objectives contained in this chapter and upholding the responsibility and accountability of the government to the people.

According to the foregoing provision, the ability of the mass media to monitor, hold government accountable and responsible is dependent on the media's ability to inform, educate and enlighten the public (Lasswell, 1948), and the realization of these functions will lead to democratic consolidation. As a senior policymaker puts it "what better freedom does the media in Nigeria requires other than to have the responsibility of promoting transparency, responsibility and accountability in government which is a major bane in Nigeria" (Interview, 24 July 2010). However, the ability of the media to exercise the functions stated in Section 22 of the constitution is dependent on their freedom to unrestricted access to information and the freedom to publish such information without restraint or fear of being sanctioned (*Media Right Agenda*, 2002). According to Calingaert (2006), when there is a free exchange of information and citizens can participate in political debates within the media sphere, accountability and transparency within government can be achieved and democracy consolidated, since the beginning of any electioneering malpractice starts with the suppression of the media freedom and their ability to ensure transparency.

There is limitation to the ability of the media to promote transparency and accountability in government. Normatively, the media derive their freedom to exercise Section 22 of the 1999 constitution from the fundamental human rights of speech contained in Section 39(1) and (2). There is no clear cut provision for media freedom in the constitution as contained in the constitutions of other African countries (e.g. Article 162 of the 1992 constitution of Ghana is an explicit provision for media freedom separate from fundamental human rights).

Section 39, Sub section 1 and 2 of the Nigerian 1999 constitution holds that:

Every person shall be entitled to freedom of expression, including freedom to hold opinions and to receive and impact ideas and information without interference. (2). without prejudice to the generality of subsection (1) of this section, every person shall be entitled to own, establish and operate any medium for the dissemination of information, ideas and opinions.

This provision which serves as the framework within which the mass media operates is problematic. According to a senior media practitioner,

"Section 39 of the 1999 constitution has nothing to do with media freedom, but the freedom of individuals to own mass media. The ability of the media to live up to Section 22 (i.e., promoting accountability and transparency) is limited because there is no framework to guarantee that" (Interview, 26 July, 2010). Another media practitioner added that:

The conceptualisation of media freedom in Nigeria should revolve around the freedom and absolute right of the media to engage in their constituted functions without interference which is the basic ideology shared by all practicing journalists. However, the 1999 constitution does not promote this idea but responsibility of the media to the public, the realisation of media freedom has been problematic...where is the freedom needed to perform the responsibility? (Interview, 3 November, 2010).

The previous assertions reveal the complexities associated with the media living up to their responsibilities, as freedom of the media to carry out their democratic functions stipulated in the constitution is not explicitly guaranteed within the legal framework. Nevertheless, the provision in Section 39 of the constitution coupled with the deregulation of the broadcast media in 1992 has facilitated the proliferation of the mass media as it allows for private ownership, participation and expansion of the media sphere. Over 50 licences were granted to private individuals and corporations (Jibo & Okoosi, 2003; Ojo, 2003). If we go by these arguments, there is tendency for media practitioners to think that the media are relatively free to carry out their democratic mandate as contained in Section 22 of the constitution without interference from relevant authorities (Eribo 1997). For instance, a senior media practitioner stated that "...since the embrace of democracy in 1999, there has been an expansion of the media space with greater opportunities for media practitioners to do their work" (Interview, 27 July, 2010). The previous assertion is worrisome because the freedom and independence of the media from interference are not guaranteed within the policy framework (Media Sustainability Index Report, 2006/2007).

To McQuail (1992, p. 69), freedom of the media goes beyond the "absence of a legal imposing licence and legislative provisions" but extends to the "degree of independence." This independence is essential in a democratic society since it will aid the media in promoting accountability and responsibility which are pertinent in the survival of democracy (Pye, 1963). The independence of the media to access information without restraint and exchange the information accessed without undue pressure or interference has been questioned by scholars and media watchdog organizations like *Article 19* and *Freedom House,* as most times government and private owners interfere in media activities by harassing and intimidating them. Such acts of interference indicate that "the official rhetoric of prevailing democracy, freedom of expression as an essential ingredient of democratic practice is lacking" (Ocitti, 1991). This is because "the true colour of democracy resides in the power and wish to communicate with one another via press reports" (Salazar, 2000, p. 60) and this is not adequately covered by the constitution.

More so, the freedom of the media to access and exchange information is withdrawn in Sub section 3a and b, Section 39, of the constitution on the pretext of national interest and public interest. This provision states that

....*(3) nothing in this section shall invalidate any law that is reasonably justifiable in a democratic society (a) for the purpose of preventing the disclosure of information received in confidence, maintain the authority and independence of court or regulating telephony, wireless broadcasting, television or the exhibition of cinematograph film (1999 Constitution).*

Although this provision is necessary in every democratic society since there is no absolute freedom (Andsager, Wyatt, & Martin, 2004), the concepts of national or public interest are vague in nature in this context. This explains the indiscriminate use of both words by the government to suppress media that are critical of them (Tettey, 2001; Akinfeleye, 2003). A media practitioner also opines that "the controversy surrounding Section 39 (3a) borders on interpretation (i.e., translating it from mere words to action), and in most cases because of the African culture, it is interpreted based on the leader's perspective" (Interview, 20 August, 2010). An example of the misuse of the concepts of national interest can be seen in the incident on April 5, 2000, when "Nigerian government security agents invaded the office of *Thisday Newspaper* for publishing information that exposed the involvement of some government officials in questionable business transactions" because the publication was considered a threat to national security by the government (*Vanguard,* cited by Ogbondah, 2004, p. 19). Likewise in December 2008, *Channels Television* and *News Agency of Nigeria* were shut down for their coverage on the health state of late president Yar' Adua. In the previous examples, the concept of national or public interest is questionable as it is the responsibility of the media to monitor and promote good governance.

Again, there are also controversies with the FOI Act passed in 2011. No doubt the passage of the FOI bill into law in May 28, 2011, will change the media sphere as Section 3 (1) and (5) of the Act require public institutions to keep all records and make it available upon request within 7 days. Scholars like Ogbondah (2004, p. 9) have also argued that formulation and implementation of freedom of information (FOI) act will help make information accessible to the public and expound the media freedom. And although, the framework of this act has received both national and international commendation, according to a senior media practitioner, "the framework of the act is sufficient for the practice of journalism in Nigeria" (Interview, 27 July, 2010), the Act contains restrictive clauses in Sections 12, 13, 15, 16, 17, 18 and 20 which prevent the disclosure of security matters, law enforcement investigation, trade secret, third party information, personal information, conduct of international affairs, and technical, commercial and scientific information (FOI Act, 2011). Based on the prior classifications, the media are made redundant as no information will be readily available to the media since most issues covered by the media fall under the prohibitive disclosure of information classification, thus making the Act an opportunity to disclose administrative information and not information needed to advance democracy (Akpojivi, 2011).

Wilkes (1986) argues that information is central in any democratic society as it affords the public the opportunity to critically evaluate and discuss government actions, thus strengthening democracy (Baker, 2007). Ishiekwene Azubuike, the Executive Director of *The Punch* Newspaper asserts that the inability of the Nigerian media to access information is a major challenge confronting the media which has invariable influenced the media's role in the society (cited in *World Association of Newspapers*, 2007). This lack of information is further compounded by the unwillingness of public officials to disclose information due to the high level of secrecy within government establishments. Most government officials are made to undertake an oath of secrecy as was done to the principal staff of the presidency during President Yar'Adua's administration. This culture of secrecy is further strengthened by Sections 1 and 2 of the Official Secret Act of 1999 which forbid the disclosure of information classified as secret by the government and prescribe 2 years imprisonment for the discloser and receiver of information. This raises the question of who determines which information is secret and why.

Also, scholars like Ziegler & Asante (1992), Baker (2007) and media practitioners like Ray Ekpu (1990) have argued that the ownership structure have influenced the ability of the mass media to carry out their watchdog functions. Nigeria operates a national broadcasting system where the mass media are predominantly owned by both the Federal government and the State governments, with only a few private media which are linked to those in political power (Jibo & Okoosi, 2003). According to Oyeleye (2004), the Federal Government owns 32 televisions and 10 radio stations which operate the network broadcast system, the State governments own 30 television stations and 52 radio stations while the private sector owns 9 television stations and 8 radio stations. The private media are mostly owned by individuals with vested economic and political interests. A media practitioner wondered; "who owns these media that are operational in Nigeria? Have the mass media been able to rise above the primordial levels of ownership interest?" (Interview, 31 August, 2010). Similarly, a media owner and practitioner while commenting on the interplay of owners' influence on media freedom asserted that "the owners of these private media are Nigerians who have political and economic interests; they have friends in government and in the business world. So the media know how far they can go in holding government accountable to the people, because if they go too far the political and business interests of their owners could be affected" (Interview, 27 July, 2010). This scenario is not healthy for the media industry, as the media are hindered from performing their constitutional duties of promoting accountability and transparency. More so, their dependence on political and economic factors for survival will influence their content and independence.

One factor that has contributed to the maintenance of this ownership structure is Section 39 (2) of the 1999 constitution which states:

...provided that no person, other than the government of the federation or of a state or any other person or body authorized by the president on the fulfilment of conditions laid down by an Act of the National Assembly, shall own, establish or operate a television or wireless broadcast station for any purpose whatever.

The previous provision requires the approval of applications by the President before the establishment of any broadcast media. Such a clause is a prerequisite for obtaining licences in any country with a functional democracy. However, given the antecedent of Nigeria, where the relationship between government and the media has not been rosy, such a provision is questionable. According to Tom (2004), the provision does not make it mandatory for the President to sign every application. He is to use his discretionary powers to grant approval and his decision to decline any application cannot be questioned. As such, the President can decline any application he perceives to belong to the opposition or organisations critical of his government. This to a large extent coupled with the high cost of setting up a media house is responsible for poor private participation in the media sphere that could actively reinvigorate the political domain.

NATIONAL BROADCASTING COMMISSION (NBC) FAIRNESS CLAUSE, THE MEDIA FREEDOM AND DEMOCRATIZATION

The possibility of a free and fair election is centred on transparency during electioneering period. However, the ability of the Nigerian mass media to ensure this transparency is endangered by the NBC fairness doctrine. The NBC was established in 1992 by General Ibrahim Babangida to regulate the broadcasting industry. NBC's other functions include licensing, monitoring and regulating the broadcasting industry, upholding the principles of fairness and equity in broadcasting and formulating policies that will aid the effective management of the broadcasting industry (NBC, Act 38 of 1992). The NBC in turn formulated the Nigerian Broadcasting Code 2006 which serves as the policy framework for regulating the broadcasting industry. The Commission, however, has been criticized for its lack of autonomy which has invariably affected its ability to regulate the industry objectively.

According to NBC Act no. 55 of 1999, the Commission (NBC) is directly under the Ministry of Communication which is headed by a minister and depends on the government for funding of its operations. In addition, the President is to appoint the board members of the commission. This structure has made the Commission vulnerable to government interference and pressure which will consequently affect their policy formulation and implementation, and their ability to effectively regulate the broadcasting industry without any bias. The management structure of the regulatory body also contravenes the African Charter on Broadcasting 2001 that calls for both the independence of the mass media and regulatory agency, as an un-autonomous regulatory agency cannot ensure an independent media.

In addition, the Nigerian Broadcasting Code 2006 currently used by the NBC to regulate the media industry has generated huge controversies. One of such controversies is the equity and fairness clause within the code which is capable of hindering the mass media from promoting free, fair, and transparent electioneering processes during electioneering periods. Firstly, Section 3.3.3 of the code states that: "any issue of public interest shall be equitably presented to ensure fairness."

Likewise, Section 4.6 known as the fairness doctrine states that:

- No individual or organization shall be treated in an unjust or unfair manner in any programme.

- Broadcaster shall always ensure that all parties to a programme are offered the chance to contribute so as to achieve fairness.
- When the views of a person or organization that is not participating in a programme are being represented, they shall be done in a fair and just manner.
- In a phone-in programme, unsolicited prank-style calls and set-ups shall not be exploited (NBC, Broadcasting Code, 2006).

In general, the provisions in the fairness doctrine as presented prior are adequate in a democratic society; however, salient issues are ignored in the doctrine. These issues include questions like what constitute fairness, how is fairness determined and measured, and who determines what is fair or unfair in media coverage. Another concern is the ability of the media to discern between an honest and an "unsolicited prank call" during phone-in programmes. The inability of the code to address these issues within its framework shows that the power to determine the previous issues lie on the NBC. A senior officer with the NBC opines that "there is only one meaning to fairness and equity, as what is fair is fair, and equity is as clear as it is; the idea is to try to make all sides of the story clear...this is how we determine fairness, and equitable coverage" (Interview, 27 September, 2010). Determining fairness and equitable coverage is more complex than as is it portrayed in the previous statement, as what is fair to a person might not be to another. Another senior media practitioner buttresses this in his statement; "I can present both sides of an issue which to me is balanced but the NBC may think otherwise. Their interpretation of fairness and equitable coverage might be affected by many intangible factors like government influence and pressure" (Interview, 26 July, 2010).

The application of this fairness clause within the periphery of the political broadcast clause further reveals the complexity of the fairness clause. Section 5.2 of the broadcasting code known as political broadcast clause states that all media contents during electioneering shall fulfil certain criteria:

- Political broadcast shall be in decent language.
- It is the responsibility of every station to produce and broadcast activities in the political arena and such production shall be objective, fair and balanced.
- Stations shall in using politics as a ready material for news, avoid taking inflammatory and divisive matter in its provocative form.

A critical review of the fairness clause within the context of political broadcast shows that the clause pays more emphasis to the choice of words and content of each media broadcast. Media freedom is, therefore, limited as media organizations are sensitive to the provision. Lindberg (2006, p. 148) substantiates this fact by arguing that "during election periods, media entrepreneurs are likely to stretch and redefine the boundaries of what may be said or written," as failure to do so will pose great challenge or difficulty on the media. In this present re-democratization era, many media organizations have fallen victims of this clause and have even challenged its applicability within the provision of Section 39 of the 1999 constitution. For instance, *Adaba Radio* which covers mainly the south-west region was shut down over its coverage of the elections in Ekiti and Ondo State. NBC alleged that the radio station violated the fairness clause in its coverage as the language used in its political debate and programme could excite violence and threaten national security. The station was fined a sum of N500000.00 by the commission and subsequently shut down by security operatives (NBC, 2009). Contrary to the claim of NBC, political analysts and observers argued that *Adaba Radio* always gave a balanced view on their political debate programmes and that

NBC's action against Adaba Radio was to please members of the ruling Party (Peoples Democratic Party [PDP]) who saw the station as a threat to their political relevance in the south-west region (Ayodele, 2009).

Similarly, in 2006, *Freedom Radio* located in Kano State was shut down by NBC who claimed that the station violated the political code on broadcasting because they were incapable of managing the views expressed by callers during live phone-in programmes. According to the commission, the views expressed by callers could "heat up the polity" which could lead to break down of law and order, thus the station got a fine of N200000.00 and was shut down (NBC, 2006). Here, NBC's actions are questionable within the framework of the constitution, as Section 39 of the constitution entitles everyone to the fundamental human right of free speech and expression. And so the radio station is duty bound to hear all views {whether dissent or not} of the public. Moreover, democracy thrives within the plurality of views and opinions. According to Findahl (1999), the mass media are required to act as a platform for rational debates where government policies and activities can be critically examined. Nonetheless, under these provisions, the media are rendered ineffective and incapable of fulfilling their constituted responsibilities of meeting the public interest.

In the same vein, during the build-up to the 2007 elections, the NBC prevented *The Africa Independent Television* (AIT) from broadcasting a documentary critical of President Obasanjo and the People's Democratic Party (PDP). Likewise, the NBC stopped the *Raypower FM* station from broadcasting contents about opposition parties, with the threat of being shut down if the station did not comply with the order. The commission argued that broadcasting such materials could threaten the stability of the country (Article 19, 2007). Such interference from the regulatory agency has made the media less critical in their debates and cautious of what to say and how to say it. For instance, on December 22, 2009, a caller

asked Kunle Adewale, a presenter with *The Africa Independent Television* (AIT) on "Focus Nigeria Programme" why AIT no longer featured critical panellists in their programme. The presenter's response was that "it is their responsibility to moderate all views to ensure that democracy survives in Nigeria." In other words, media practitioners have to practise self-censorship in order to avoid being sanctioned by the government through the regulatory agency.

CONCLUSION AND RECOMMENDATIONS

Many questions about the sustenance of Nigeria's democratization process have been raised following the recent celebration of 12 years of democratic institution (since May, 1999) and her 50th independence anniversary. According to Shilgba (2010), issues like the mediocrity in governance and the lack of power of the electorate to decide their leaders due to the massive electoral fraud question the relevance of such celebrations and threaten the political stability of the country. He believes that this is largely due to the politics of "do or die" as coined by former President Olusegun Obasanjo. This has shown that democratic consolidation goes beyond the regular conduct of elections which are flawed with irregularities. It focuses on the establishment of stronger democratic institutions like a free and vibrant mass media that will produce a transparent electoral process which is clearly lacking in Nigeria.

The establishment of transparency within the electoral process can only be achieved when the mass media are accorded the necessary freedom that will enable them disseminate information that will empower the public (by informing and educating them about the electoral process), thus ensuring integrity of the electoral process. The inclusion of everyone in the democratization process and all other important factors will lead to the fulfilment of democratic choice (Scheler,

2002). Thus, media freedom is germane in building transparent and stronger democratic institutions in new democratic societies like Nigeria whose electoral process has widely been criticized.

The process of consolidating Nigeria's democracy should start with the review of the 1999 constitution which is largely incomprehensive. Its present "give and take nature" (Tom, 2004, p. 96) has made the realisation of Section 22 of the constitution, which is germane in democratic sustenance, difficult. The constitution should be amended to accommodate the freedom of the mass media which should be separate from the fundamental human rights already provided for. It should also provide for the independence of the regulatory agency as advocated by the *African Charter of Broadcasting 2001*. This will enhance the cause of media freedom since only an independent regulatory agency can guarantee the freedom of the mass media. Furthermore, the autonomy of NBC can be guaranteed by restructuring its board members so that they cut across various groups in the society like Nigeria union of Journalists, Nigeria Bar Association, and the civil societies amongst others. These groups should appoint their representatives who should be accountable to the National Assembly in order to promote accountability and transparency within the commission. In addition, the funding of the commission should be from a special consolidated fund administered by the National Assembly (Akpojivi, 2012).

Besides, the FOI Act should be reviewed to exclude the clauses that seek to deliberately withdraw and hinder the freedom of the media to access relevant information as such information will promote accountability and transparency and encourage good governance (Akpojivi, 2011). Likewise, a whistle-blowers' act needs to be put in place. This will help to break the culture of secrecy within government ministries and private establishments that have made it difficult for public officials to disclose information to the mass media which may facilitate their watchdog function.

Furthermore, the fairness clause in the Nigeria Broadcasting Code should be well defined in line with the present democratic principle of free speech. This clause currently contradicts Section 39 of the Nigerian 1999 constitution that guarantees freedom of expression, and of opinion. It should be noted that in countries with similar fairness clauses where such clauses have questioned the principle of free speech or media freedom like in the United States, such clauses are examined within the framework of the constitution (Feintuck, 1999).

In conclusion, in order for Nigeria to advance democratically, the media laws and policies governing the media sphere must be re-examined and reviewed. The mass media must be accorded the necessary freedom to effectively carry out their functions. Without such freedom that will guarantee a stronger and transparent electoral process, Nigeria will continue to conduct elections fraught with electoral frauds, and widely criticized. This situation will invariably stall the consolidation of her democracy.

REFERENCES

African Charter on Broadcasting. (2001). *Final Report Ten Years On: Assessment, Challenges and Prospects*. Retrieved January, 12, 2001, from http://portal.unesco.org/ci/en

Ake, C. (1991). Rethinking African Democracy. *Journal of Democracy*, 2(1), 32–44. doi:10.1353/jod.1991.0003.

Akinfeleye, R. (2003). *Fourth estate of the realm or fourth estate of the wreck: Imperative of social responsibility of the press*. Lagos, Nigeria: University of Lagos Press.

Akpojivi, U. (2011, June 27). The FOI Act: Beyond the euphoria. *Guardian Newspaper*. Retrieved from http://www.ngrguardiannews.com/index.php?option

Akpojivi, U. (2012). *Media freedom and media policy in new democracies: An analysis of the nexus between policy formation and normative conceptions in Ghana and Nigeria*. PhD Thesis. Leeds, UK: University of Leeds.

Ambrose, B. (1995). *Democratization and the protection of human rights in Africa: Problems and prospects*. London: Praeger.

Andsager, J., Wyatt, R., & Martin, E. (2004). *Free expression and five democratic publics support for individual and media rights*. Cresskill, NJ: Hampton Press Inc..

Anyanwu, J. (1992). President Babangida's structural adjustment programme and inflation in Nigeria. *Journal of Social Development in Africa*, *7*(1), 5–24.

Article 19. (2007). Nigeria's 2007 elections and media coverage January 2007. Retrieved May 12, 2008, from http://www.article19.org

Ayodele, L. (2009). *Court restrains NBC from shutting Adaba FM-PM News Lagos*. Retrieved May 12, 2009, from http://www.saharareporters.com

Baker, E. (2007). *Media concentration and democracy: Why ownership matters*. Cambridge, UK: Cambridge University Press.

Barendt, E. (1985). *Freedom of speech*. Oxford, UK: Clarendon Press.

Blankson, I. (2007). Media independence and pluralism in Africa opportunities and challenges of democratisation and liberalisation. In Blankson, I., & Murphy, P. (Eds.), *Negotiating democracy media transformations in emerging democracies* (pp. 15–34). Albany, NY: State University of New York.

Boadi, G. (2004). Africa: The Quality of Political Reform. In Boadi, G. (Ed.), *Democratic Reform in Africa the Quality of Progress* (pp. 5–28). Boulder, CO: Lynne Rienner Publishers Inc..

Bourgault, L. (1995). *Mass Media in Sub-Saharan Africa*. Bloomington, IN: Indiana University Press.

Calingaert, D. (2006). Election Rigging and How to Fight it. *Journal of Democracy*, *17*, 138–151. doi:10.1353/jod.2006.0043.

Curran, J. (1979). Press Freedom as a Property Right: The Crisis of Press Legitimacy. *Media Culture & Society*, *1*, 59–82. doi:10.1177/016344377900100106.

Diamond, L. (2002). Elections Without Democracy Thinking about Hybrid Regimes. *Journal of Democracy*, *13*, 21–35. doi:10.1353/jod.2002.0025.

Diamond, L. (2008a). Consolidating Democracy. In Leduc, L., Norris, P., & Niemi, R. (Eds.), *Comparing Democracies 2 New Challenges in the Study of Elections and Voting* (pp. 210–227). London: Sage Publications.

Diamond, L. (2008b). Progress and Retreat in Africa the Rule of Law vs. the Big man. *Journal of Democracy*, *19*, 138–149. doi:10.1353/jod.2008.0029.

Ekpu, R. (1990). Nigeria's Embattled Fourth Estate. *Journal of Democracy*, *1*, 107–116. doi:10.1353/jod.1990.0025.

Emerson, T. (1982). The First Amendment in the Year 2000. In Halpern, S. (Ed.), *The Future of our Liberties: Perspectives on the Bill of Rights* (pp. 57–73). Westport, CT: Greenwood.

Federal Government of Nigeria. (1987). *Nigeria Mass Communication Policy*. Lagos, Nigeria: Federal Government Press.

Federal Government of Nigeria. (1990). *Official Secret Act*. Lagos, Nigeria: Federal Government Press.

Federal Government of Nigeria. (1992). *National Broadcasting Commission Act No. 38*. Lagos, Nigeria: Federal Government Press.

Federal Government of Nigeria. (1999). *National Broadcasting Commission Act No. 55*. Lagos, Nigeria: Federal Government Press.

Federal Government of Nigeria. (1999). *Nigeria Criminal Code*. Lagos, Nigeria: Federal Government Press.

Federal Government of Nigeria. (2011). *Freedom of Information Act*. Lagos, Nigeria: Federal Government Press.

Federal Republic of Nigeria. (1999). *1999 Constitution of the Federal Republic of Nigeria*. Lagos, Nigeria: Federal Government Press.

Feintuck, M. (1999). *Media Regulation, Public Interest and the Law*. Edinburgh, Scotland: Edinburgh University Press.

Findahl, O. (1999). Public Service Broadcasting–A fragile, yet durable Construction. *Nordicom Review*, *20*, 13–19.

Hegel (1896). *Hegel's Philosophy of Right*. Translated by S. W. Dyde. London: George Bell and Sons.

Herbst, J. (2000). Understanding Ambiguity during Democratization in Africa. In Hollified, J., & Jillson, C. (Eds.), *Pathways to Democracy: The Political Economy of Democratic Transition* (pp. 275–289). London: Routledge.

Holmes, S. (1990). Liberal Constraints on Private Power?: Reflections on the Origins and Rationale of Access Regulation. In Lichtenberg, J. (Ed.), *Democracy and the Mass Media* (pp. 21–65). Cambridge, UK: Cambridge University Press. doi:10.1017/CBO9781139172271.003.

Humphreys, P. (1996). *Mass Media and Media Policy in Western Europe*. Manchester, UK: Manchester University Press.

Ifidon, E. (2003). Transitions from Democracy in Nigeria: Toward a Pre-emptive Analysis. *American Journal of Political Science*, *7*(1), 109–128.

Jeffrey, H. (2000). Understanding Ambiguity during Democratization in Africa. In Hollified, J., & Jillson, C. (Eds.), *Pathways to Democracy: The Political Economy of Democratic Transition* (pp. 245–258). London: Routledge.

Jibo, M., & Okoosi, A. (2003). The Nigerian Media: An Assessment of its Role in Achieving Transparent and Accountable Government in the Fourth Republic. *Nordic Journal of African Studies*, *12*(2), 180–195.

Joseph, R. (1991). Africa: The Rebirth of Political Freedom. *Journal of Democracy*, *2*, 20–24. doi:10.1353/jod.1991.0055.

Joseph, R. (2008). Progress and Retreat in Africa Challenges of a Frontier Region. *Journal of Democracy*, *19*, 94–108. doi:10.1353/jod.2008.0028.

Kunle, A. (2010). *Focus Nigeria*. [Television series].

Kuper, A., & Kuper, J. (2001). Serving a New Democracy: Must the Media Speak Softly? Learning from South Africa. *International Journal of Public Opinion Research*, *13*(4), 355–376. doi:10.1093/ijpor/13.4.355.

LeDuc, L., Niemi, R. G., & Norris, P. (2008). Introduction: Comparing Democratic Elections. In Leduc, L., Niemi, R., & Norris, P. (Eds.), *Comparing Democracies 2 New Challenges in the Study of Elections and Voting* (pp. 1–39). London: Sage Publications.

Levi, A. (1966). The Value of Freedom: Mill's Liberty (1859-1959). In Radcliff, P. (Ed.), *Limits of Liberty: Studies of Mill's On Liberty* (pp. 6–17). Belmont, CA: Wadsworth Publishing.

Levitsky, S., & Way, A. (2010). Why Democracy needs a Level Playing Field. *Journal of Democracy*, *21*, 55–68.

Lichtenberg, J. (1990). Introduction. In Lichtenberg, J. (Ed.), *Democracy and the Mass Media* (pp. 1–20). Cambridge, UK: Cambridge University Press. doi:10.1017/CBO9781139172271.002.

Lichtenberg, J. (1990). Foundations and Limits of Freedom of the Press. In Lichtenberg, J. (Ed.), *Democracy and the Mass Media* (pp. 102–135). Cambridge, UK: Cambridge University Press. doi:10.1017/CBO9781139172271.005.

Lindberg, S. (2006). The Surprising Significance of African Elections. *Journal of Democracy, 17,* 139–151. doi:10.1353/jod.2006.0011.

Linz, J., & Stepan, A. (1996). *Problems of Democratic Transition and Consolidation.* Baltimore, MD: The Johns Hopkins University Press.

Marcuse, H. (1969). Repressive Tolerance. In Wolff, R., & Marcuse, H. (Eds.), *A Critique of Pure Tolerance* (pp. 95–137). London: Beacon Press.

McQuail, D. (1992). *Media Performance Mass Communication and the Public Interest.* London: Sage Publication.

McQuail, D. (2003). *Media Accountability and Freedom of Publication.* Oxford, UK: Oxford University Press.

Media Rights Agenda. (2002). *Airwaves Monitor Report 2002.* Nigeria: Lagos.

Media sustainability Index. *Africa 2006-2007 Nigeria.* Lagos, Nigeria.

Mill, S. J. (1869). *On Liberty* (4th ed.). London: Longman.

Mill, S. J. (1974). *On Liberty.* London: Penguin Group.

Moyer, B. (2008). Is the Fourth Estate a Fifth Column?: Corporate Media Colludes with Democracy's Demise.Retrieved on September 10, 2008, from.http://www.inthesetimes.com/article/3790/is_the_fourth_estate_a_fifth_column/

National Broadcasting Commission. (2006). *Nigeria Broadcasting Code* (4th ed.). Lagos, Nigeria: Regent.

National Broadcasting Commission. (2006). *Quick News Update.* Retrieved January 12, 2010, from http://www.nbc.gov.ng

National Broadcasting Commission. (2009). *NBC Suspends Radio Adaba Licence.* Retrieved December 23, 2008, from http://www.nbc.gov.ng

Nyamnjoh, F. (2005). *Africa's Media Democracy and the Politics of Belonging.* London: Zed Books.

Ocitti, J. (1999). *Media and Democracy in Africa Mutual Political Bedfellows Or Implacable Arch-Foes.* Cambridge, UK: Weatherhead Center for International Affairs.

Ogbondah, C. (2004). Democratization and the Media in West Africa: An Analysis of Recent Constitutional and Legislative Reforms for Press Freedom in Ghana and Nigeria. *West Africa Review, 6,* 1–36.

Ojo, E. (2003). The Mass Media and the Challenges of Sustainable Democratic Values in Nigeria: Possibilities and Limitations. *Media Culture & Society, 25,* 821–840. doi:10.1177/0163443703256006.

Oyeleye, A. (2004). The Mediation of Politicians and the Political Process in Nigeria. *Parliamentary Affairs, 57,* 157–168. doi:10.1093/pa/gsh013.

Pye, L. (1963). *Communications and Political Development.* Princeton, NJ: Princeton University Press.

Qadir, S., Clapham, C., & Gill, B. (1993). Sustainable Democracy: Formalism vs. Substance. *Third World Quarterly, 14*(3), 415–422. doi:10.1080/01436599308420334.

Republic of Ghana. (1992). *The 1992 Constitution of the Federal Republic of Ghana.* Accra, Ghana: Government Printers.

Richards, D. (1999). *Free Speech and the Politics of Identity.* Oxford, UK: Oxford University Press.

Righter, R. (1978). *Whose News? Politics, the Press and the Third World*. New York: Times Books.

Riley, J. (1998). *Routledge Philosophy Guidebook to Mill On Liberty*. London: Routledge.

Rozumilowicz, B. (2002). Democratic Change: A Theoretical Perspective. In Price, M., Rozumilowicz, B., & Verhulst, S. (Eds.), *Media Reform Democratising the Media, Democratising the State* (pp. 9–26). London: Routledge.

Salazar, P. (2000). Press Freedom and Citizen Agency in South Africa: A Rhetorical Approach. *The Public*, 7(4), 55–68.

Scanlon, T. (1990). Content Regulation Reconsidered. In Lichtenberg, J. (Ed.), *Democracy and the Mass Media* (pp. 331–354). Cambridge, UK: Cambridge University Press. doi:10.1017/CBO9781139172271.013.

Schedler, A. (2002). Elections without Democracy the Manipulation. *Journal of Democracy*, 13, 36–50. doi:10.1353/jod.2002.0031.

Shilgba, L. K. (2010). On President Jonathan and His Political Party. Retrieved June 19, 2010, from http://www.saharareporters.com

Tettey, W. (2001). The Media and Democratization in Africa: Contributions, Constraints and Concerns of the Private Press. *Media Culture & Society*, 23(1), 5–31. doi:10.1177/016344301023001001.

Tettey, W. (2006). The Politics of Media Accountability in Africa: An Examination of Mechanisms and Institutions. *International Communication Gazette*, 68, 229–248. doi:10.1177/1748048506063763.

Tom, D. (2004). The Watchdog inside a Cage: The Nigerian Press and Censorship Laws. *Ethiope Research Abraka Journal of the Arts. Law and Social Science*, 1, 91–118.

Uko, N. (2004). *Romancing the Gun: The Press as a Promoter of Military Rule*. Trenton, NJ: Africa World Press Inc..

Wasserman, H., & Boloka, M. (2004). Privacy, the Press and the Public Interest in Post-Apartheid South Africa. *Parliamentary Affairs*, 57, 185–195. doi:10.1093/pa/gsh015.

Wilkes, A. (1986). Freedom of Information. In Curran, J., Ecclestone, J., Oakley, G., & Richardson, A. (Eds.), *Bending Reality the State of the Media* (pp. 229–235). London: Pluto Press.

Williams, R. (1979). Institutions of the Technology. In Mattelart, A., & Siegelaub, S. (Eds.), *Communication and Class Struggle: Capitalism, Imperialism* (pp. 265–268). New York: International General.

World Association of Newspapers. (2007). Press Freedom in Africa: the Key to Good Governance and Development 2007. Retrieved February 24, 2009, from http://www.wanpress.org/print.php3?id_article

Ziegler, D., & Asante, M. (1992). *Thunder and Silence the Mass Media in Africa*. Trenton, NJ: Africa World Press Inc..

ENDNOTES:

- A total of 12 interviews were conducted with media practitioners, policymakers, and NGOs'. However, for ethical reasons, their identities are not revealed.
- *Transparency Declaration:* Some aspects of this paper were findings from my PhD thesis titled "Media Freedom and Media Policy in New Democracies: An analysis of the Nexus between Policy Formation and Normative Conceptions in Ghana and Nigeria."

Chapter 7
Press Freedom, Media Regulation, and Journalists' Perceptions of their Roles in Society:
A Case of Zambia and Ghana

Twange Kasoma
Radford University, USA

ABSTRACT

Given their unparalleled histories and the dichotomous media regulatory frameworks that Zambia and Ghana have, the two countries make for an interesting pedagogical coupling for examining press freedom and the role of the media in African society. That is what this chapter strives to do. Methodologically, a textual analysis of pertinent documents as well as in-depth interviews with journalists was conducted. Some similarities and distinct differences are noted in the two countries' media regulatory landscapes. For example, both countries continue to lapse where passage of Freedom of Information legislation is concerned. Ghana, however, exhibits more progress than Zambia. The enabling laws Ghana has instituted in the past decade are telling. Ghana's progress is also evident in how journalists perceive their role in society in comparison to their Zambian counterparts. The former puts more emphasis on the media's agenda setting role than the latter.

INTRODUCTION

One of the residual effects of the democratic tide that swept across sub-Saharan Africa in the early 1990s has been the philosophical shift in the media environment. Many African governments traditionally renowned for stifling press freedom and excessively controlling the media loosened their grip albeit in varying degrees at the outset of democracy. Zambia and Ghana present an interesting pedagogical coupling for studying this phenomenon because of their dichotomous

DOI: 10.4018/978-1-4666-4197-6.ch007

political backgrounds. Given the fact that Ghana oscillated between military juntas and Zambia largely maintained a one-party autocratic regime, one would expect the latter to have a more favorable media environment today. But conversely, as will be discussed later, the over-sweeping constitutional changes Ghana made in 1992 to liberalize the media and defend press freedom have been unmatched; making Ghanaian media "one of the most unfettered in Africa" (Media Foundation for West Africa, MFWA, 2010, p. 48).

A commonality in the current media environment of the two countries is the proliferation of privately-owned media that resulted from the liberalization policies embarked on in the 1990s. A legacy that these independent media are increasingly being known for is exposing corruption in government. The first democratic governments of Jerry Rawlings in Ghana and Frederick Chiluba in Zambia were not spared in this regard. The two administrations were exposed for misdirecting donor funds, electorate bribery, vote rigging, and so forth, and as such reportage increased it had profound impact on donors, most of whom started conditioning their balance-of-payments support on good governance. This prompted the new governments to start interfering in the media in an effort to mute them. For example, Rawlings repeatedly denounced the private media as irresponsible and selfishly motivated by profit and denied them access to Osu Castle where he frequently held presidential press briefings.

STATEMENT OF PURPOSE AND METHODOLOGY

Although the independent media have been perceived as a causal factor in democratization and attainment of good governance in Africa (Hyden, Leslie, & Ogundimu, 2002), the processes from the 1990s to date that led to their current disposition have been understudied. This is particularly so at a comparative level, and to help fill that

void the purpose of this article is to examine the prevailing press freedom and media regulatory framework in Zambia and Ghana. Additionally, journalists' perceptions of their roles in the newly found democratic dispensations are also analyzed. Methodologically, both qualitative (entailing a textual analysis of pertinent articles and documents; and interviews) and quantitative (a survey) techniques were employed.

POLITICAL OVERVIEW: 1990s TO DATE

Civil society—comprising non-governmental organizations (NGOs), civic and lay organizations and the labor movement, among others—was the centripetal force that drove the transition to democracy in 1991 in Zambia and 1992 in Ghana. In Zambia, it was the Zambia Congress of Trade Unions (ZCTU) that was responsible for securing Frederick Chiluba—a trade unionist by profession—his presidential win (Buhlungu & Adler, 1997; Rakner, 2003). Prior to the elections, ZCTU had mobilized its members to strike as a last resort in demanding better wages and living conditions. In June 1990 the country was engulfed in nationwide riots, which culminated in a short-lived coup a month later. Some media analysts have argued that the riots provided the last straw for the then president Kenneth Kaunda to heed peoples' wishes for change. Therefore, on December 4, 1990, Article 4 of the 1973 Constitution, which stipulated that United National Independence Party (UNIP) would be the sole legal party in Zambia, was abrogated, paving the way for multiparty politics. Shortly afterwards, the Movement for Multiparty Democracy (MMD) was registered and the new party held its seminal national convention in February 1991. It was at this convention that Chiluba emerged as MMD's presidential candidate, eventually beating Kaunda in the November 1991 elections.

In Ghana, on the other hand, change was initiated and sustained by the Movement for Freedom and Justice (MFJ). MFJ, which was formed in August 1990 comprised various social and political groupings and had the mandate of restoring multiparty democracy and civilian rule in Ghana (Abdulai, 2009; Gyimah-Boadi, 1997). President Rawlings, who had assumed power through a military coup, responded to MFJ's call for change by creating the National Commission on Democracy (NCD) to investigate Ghana's transition to multiparty democracy. The elaborate report, which NCD submitted to Rawlings' ruling Provisional National Defense Council (PNDC) upon completion of its mandate, was unanimously adopted via a national referendum thereby paving way for multiparty democracy. Rawlings then formed the National Democratic Congress (NDC), which superseded PNDC, to contest in the multiparty elections and stood as its presidential candidate. Although Rawlings and NDC emerged victorious in the presidential elections, the opposition parties complained of electoral fraud and boycotted the December 1992 parliamentary elections, giving NDC a monopoly in Parliament (Abdulai, 2009).

The democratic governments in Zambia and Ghana were sworn in at a time when economic woes, exasperated by high food prices, shortages of daily necessities in shops, dilapidated infrastructure, mal-functional health and educational systems, and so forth, were at an all time high. As President Chiluba pointed out in his maiden speech to the National Assembly, his government had inherited "an economy in ruins." Adding that his predecessor had "contracted external indebtedness to the point where we owe something like one thousand United States dollars to the rest of the world for every Zambian. Our economy is in ruins and even the ruins are in danger" (Frederick Chiluba's Opening Speech to the National Assembly, November 29, 1991). To resuscitate their ailing economies, Chiluba and Rawlings instituted IMF/World Bank-sponsored structural reforms, which were detested by civil society because of the stringent conditions attached (Carbone, 2009; Rakner, 2003; Abdulai, 2009). One of those conditions was the speedy privatization of state-owned companies and this generally resulted in high levels of unemployment.

A surveillance function provided by the media into the speedy privatization of state-owned companies in the two countries soon showed that the process was embroiled in corruption and untransparency (Arkosah-Sarpong, 2008; Rakner, 2003). In Zambia, for instance, some of the pioneering members of the MMD such as Baldwin Nkumbula and Akashabatwa Lewanika resigned from the Party citing disgust with the high levels of corruption as the reason. These resignations climaxed by November 1993 and by-elections had to be held to replace 11 MMD Members of Parliament. Simutanyi (2002), in a national survey, found that even the citizenry had become cynical of the MMD government because of corruption. The majority of citizens surveyed (51%) said that "almost all" or "most" officials in government were involved in corruption.

Notwithstanding the corruption allegations, Chiluba's government managed to secure another term of office in the November 18, 1996 elections. The opposition challenged the legitimacy of the election results pointing out that a contentious voter register was used (Foundation for Democratic Process, FODEP, 1996). In fact, a situation similar to what had happened in Ghana in 1992 where the opposition boycotted the parliamentary elections transpired. The biggest opposition then, which was Kaunda's UNIP, boycotted the elections complaining that the procedures adopted were discriminatory and arbitrary. Like Rawlings' NDC in 1992, MMD now enjoyed a parliamentary majority and took advantage of this position to include a parentage clause in the Constitution that would permanently bar Kaunda from ever standing for president. Article 34(b) of the Constitution read: "A person shall be qualified to stand as a candidate for elections as president if both his parents are Zambian by birth or by descent."

Almost a year into his second and last term of office, Chiluba survived a coup attempt by Captain Stephen Lungu (alias Captain Solo) on October 28, 1997. Ironically, this did not deter him from campaigning for a drop of the two-term cap for president in the Constitution to allow him another term. To win favor with the electorate, Chiluba ensured that there was a presidential discretionary fund of K12 billion (US$5 million) set aside in the 1998 budget that he used to make generous donations to civic organizations of his choice. Furthermore, in 1999, Chiluba established the Presidential Housing Initiative meant to help people realize dreams of home ownership. Despite these measures, however, Chiluba failed to secure the third term that he wanted and handpicked his successor Levy Mwanawasa who was fielded as MMD's presidential candidate for the 2001 elections. Chiluba's pick incensed MMD's influential National Secretary Michael Sata who was one of those in the forefront of Chiluba's "third-term" campaign (Rakner, 2003). Sata quit MMD and formed his own party called Patriotic Front (PF) in accordance with a notable legacy of the second republic, which Rakner (2003) describes as a phenomenon where many politicians like to conceive of themselves as the president of a political party. They envisage being the next republican president and treat their parties as personal vehicles to that end.

Although Mwanawasa won the December 27, 2001 elections, it was a close call. Results published by the Electoral Commission of Zambia showed that Mwanawasa only beat his main rival Anderson Mazoka of United Party for National Development (UPND) by 1.9% of the votes cast. This gave Mwanawasa the weakest electoral mandate ever recorded by a Zambian president, and as if this was not enough, the opposition challenged the results (FODEP, 2002). But Mwanawasa was determined to prove his critics who had written him off as Chiluba's puppet wrong. He put up a fierce fight against corruption, ensuring that Chiluba and others were tried for corruptly amassing

wealth while in power. Unfortunately Mwanawasa did not live long enough to see the conclusion of the trials he had instigated as he died in office in 2008 after suffering a stroke. His Vice President, Rupiah Banda, succeeded him. Banda's presidential stint was short-lived. After completing what was left of Mwanawasa's term he was defeated by PF's Sata in the fifth multiparty elections held in September 2011. During the election campaigns PF operated under the slogan: *donchi kubeba* (literally translated--"don't tell them"). *Donchi kubeba* was a mockery of the MMD government, which had been rumored to be dishing out cash and other incentives to entice people to vote MMD. In essence, *donchi kubeba* was a subtle hint to the electorate to accept the freebies the MMD government was offering and give a false hope that they would vote MMD when in actual fact their vote would be contrary.

Based on the ensuing discussion, some similarities can be drawn between Zambia and Ghana. Like the Zambian case under Chiluba, the Rawlings administration also won another term of office in the 1996 elections despite the corruption allegations. Unlike Chiluba, however, Rawlings made no attempt to redress the two-term clause in the 1992 Constitution, probably because he had already ruled the country for 19 years factoring in his military regimes. Rawlings nonetheless handpicked his successor, Professor John Evans Atta Mills, just as Chiluba had done following his failed third term bid. According to Sangaparee (2011) cadres who opposed Mills' selection as presidential candidate for NDC protested Rawlings' decision and several ended up incarcerated without charges proffered against them. However, unlike the Zambian situation with Mwanawasa, Rawlings' handpicked successor lost, and his opponent John Kufuor of the New Patriotic Party (NPP) won. Not too long after the new government settled in, Rawlings went on the offensive accusing it of massive corruption, prompting a former Senior Minister J.H. Mensah to respond thus: "Rawlings has no moral right to accuse the

NPP government of corruption when he and the PNDC government did worse things... If the former President [wa]s not corrupt, then how come a whooping sum of US$7 million went missing under his supervision...Rawlings owes Ghanaians an explanation ..." (Arkosah-Sarpong, 2008).

Despite the corruption accusations, NPP retained power in the 2004 elections. The battle between NDC and NPP resumed in 2008 when President Kufuor completed his two terms. In a bid to prevent NDC from bouncing back to power, NPP reminded the electorate that NDC's presidential candidate, Professor Mills, was Rawlings' pick in the 2000 elections and that if he won he would be easily manipulated by Rawlings. NPP's strategy backfired and Mills ascended to presidency in 2008. Much like the Mwanawasa/Chiluba case in Zambia, as President Mills' first term in office was coming to a close, some commentators declared that he had proven to be independent of Rawlings. However, like Rawlings, the independent media were also critical of Mills. As stated in a *Statesman (*May 25, 2011) editorial: "Since President Mills took over from January 7, 2009, he has made no discernable policy advancement towards the quest for integration. Considering the conducive democratic continental environment, Mills is proving to be the worst Ghanaian leader ... there is a serious leadership paralysis." Mills suffered the same fate as Mwanawasa. He was the first president to die in office. He died on July 24, 2012, a few months shy of re-contesting his presidency in elections that were held on December 7, 2012. John Dramani Mahama, who catapulted from vice president to president following Mills' untimely death, carried victory in the December 2012 elections. At the time of this writing, the losing candidate, NPP's Nana Akufo-Addo, had filed a petition at the Supreme Court challenging the election results.

PRESS FREEDOM

A starting point in analyzing a country's commitment to press freedom is the biggest law of the land—the Constitution. In Zambia, the Constitution explicitly guarantees freedom of expression: "... no person shall be hindered in the enjoyment of his freedom of expression, that is to say, freedom to hold opinions without interference, freedom to communicate ideas and information without interference ..." (Article 20), which is operationalized to cover press freedom. Conversely, Chapter 12 of the 1992 Constitution of Ghana explicitly guarantees freedom of the press, with a host of other protective clauses. As Gadzekpo (2005) submitted:

The coming into effect of Ghana's 1992 Republican Constitution significantly changed the media landscape and created a conducive environment for the growth of pluralistic media. Constitutional provisions on the media are captured in Chapter 12 of the Constitution and are considered one of the most liberal provisions on media on the continent. Comprising 12 Acts (162-173), the media provisions guarantee the freedom and independence of the media (162:1); prohibit licensing of media (162:3); prohibit media censorship (162.2) and seek to insulate state media from governmental control (167c). The Constitution enjoins the media to act responsibly, to publish rejoinders (162:6), and to promote good governance (162: 5).

Beyond the constitutional safeguards, Ghana also introduced other enabling laws. For example, the Ghanaian Parliament passed the Whistleblowers Act in 2003 meant to counteract the "culture of silence" that characterized the country prior to 1995 (Blankson, 2002). Moreover, in fulfillment of a campaign promise by President Kufuor's administration, Ghana expunged criminal libel law, which was arbitrarily used to jail journalists (Gadzekpo, 2006). In Zambia, on the other hand, criminal libel law still exists. Section 69 of the Penal Code makes defamation of the President a criminal offense punishable by three years imprisonment without the option of a fine. The MMD government invoked this law in 2005 when the managing editor of *The Post*, Fred M'membe, was arrested for defaming President Mwanawasa in an editorial. The editorial, commenting on the feud between President Mwanawasa and former President Kaunda, read in part:

The foolishness, stupidity and lack of humility exhibited by President Mwanawasa on Saturday in Livingstone can never be imagined to come out of the mouth of a President of the country. Only a stupid fool can react to humble advice in that way. To suggest that the mistakes Dr. Kaunda made should disqualify him from commenting on national issues is really being foolish, stupid and shortsighted. Even being President of Zambia has not helped him... (The Post, November 10, 2005).

While on one level the editorial illustrated some level of press freedom, even advocators of the abolishment of criminal libel heavily criticized it. For instance, the defunct self-regulatory body, Media Council of Zambia (MECOZ), which will be discussed in a subsequent section, admonished *The Post* for its derogatory language. A mass communication lecturer at the University of Zambia who also weighed in noted that: "I think that journalists can do their job without being opinionated and adding adjectives in their writing about the President ..." (F.Muzyamba, personal communication, September 6, 2006). Yet another notorious law is seditious libel. Anthony Mukwita, then a reporter for Radio Phoenix, who is now deputy managing director of the *Zambia Daily Mail*, was threatened with this law in 2006 after he read a fax critical of the MMD government during his talk show (Freedom House, 2010). Due to mounting pressure from the government Mukwita was later fired. The information minister under the MMD regime, Ronnie Shikapwasha, was also infamous for arbitrarily threatening radio

stations in the country to control the content of their live phone-in programs failure to which he would revoke their licenses. In fact, he delivered on his threat when he revoked the license of Radio Lyambai in the Western Province. Shikapwasha's actions illustrate the stranglehold that the MMD government had maintained on the regulation of broadcast media, much to the detriment of press freedom. This partly explains why Ghana, as will be discussed in the next section, where the communications minister cannot arbitrarily revoke radio licenses, outscores Zambia on the Freedom House (2010) press freedom index. Freedom House has consistently ranked Zambia in the mid-60s and Ghana in the mid-20s on a 100-point scale where 0 to 30 is regarded as "Free" media environment; 31 to 60 as "Partly Free"; and 61 to 100 as "Not Free". Similarly, data collected by African Media Barometer (2009) showed that using a 5-point Likert-type scale where 1 was "country does not meet indicator" and 5 was "country meets all aspects of the indicator and has been doing so over time," Ghana performed better than Zambia on a number of press freedom indicators. As shown in Figure 1, the difference between the two countries is particularly pronounced on Indicator 3, whose emphasis is on having no laws that unreasonably interfere with the responsibilities of the media. This discrepancy can be attributed to the lip-service approach adopted by Zambia versus Ghana's actual-implementation. While NDC and NPP in Ghana actually implemented the campaign promises made with regard to press freedom, the MMD government in Zambia failed to fulfill a number of its promises. Instead, the MMD government, during its 20 years in power, continually set up media task forces to investigate and recommend the best way to institute media reforms. Yet, as Matibini (2006) explains, when it came to implementing the recommendations, the MMD government hid under the guise of making further consultations.

Figure 1.

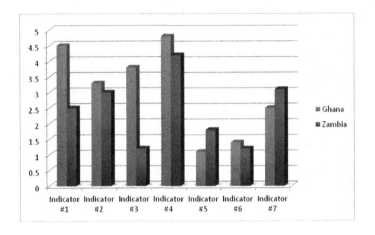

Indicator 1: Freedom of expression, including freedom of the media, is guaranteed in the Constitution and supported by other pieces of legislation.

Indicator 2: The right to freedom of expression is practiced and citizens, including journalists, are asserting their rights without fear.

Indicator 3: There are no laws restricting freedom of expression such as excessive official secret or libel acts, or laws that unreasonably interfere with the responsibilities of the media.

Indicator 4: Entry into and practice of the journalistic profession is legally unrestricted.

Indicator 5: Confidential sources of information are protected by law and/or the courts.

Indicator 6: Public information is easily accessible, guaranteed by law, to all citizens.

Indicator 7: Civil society in general and media lobby groups actively advance the cause of media freedom.

An impediment to press freedom that the two countries have in common is stalling on the passage of freedom of information legislation, which would grant journalists access to information held by public authorities. In Ghana, the administration of former President Kufuor failed to pass the Freedom of Information Bill (FOIB) despite repeated promises to do so. Under President Mills, progress was made when cabinet approved the Right to Information Bill in November 2009 (Freedom House, 2010). However, although advocacy groups swiftly called on Parliament to move quickly and pass the bill into law this had not come to fruition by the time of President Mills' death. One of the reasons advanced for the stalemate was fear that given Ghana's background with coups passing FOIB into law would incite journalists by giving them too much power. Some journalists have however found a way around this by engaging in a highly unprofessional technique of collecting information called "flashing out." "Flashing out" is a discomforting convention in which an unverified, deliberately exaggerated version of a story is published to provoke reaction from officialdom. Some Ghanaian journalists feel that "by putting out a version of the story, no matter how inaccurate, public officials would be compelled to come out to set the record straight" (Gadzekpo, 2006). The MMD government in Zambia had also been equally reluctant to enact FOIB into law citing the 9/11 terrorist attacks in the U.S. as an example of what would happen if there was too much access to information (K. Kaunda, personal communication, September 9, 2006). The MMD government had opined that it was exercising caution because "if not handled properly, the bill might pose danger to the peace and security of the nation" (ZNBC, June 3, 2011).

Following the pronouncements that the PF government had made during its first 90 days in power about the process towards the enactment of FOIB being underway, the Zambian media fraternity was cautiously optimistic. Heightening this optimism was the PF government's promise to do away with undue restrictions in the granting of broadcasting licenses. The government also showed support and gave encouragement to the media fraternity to launch a self-regulatory body called Zambia Media Council (ZAMEC), which will be discussed subsequently. A major and perhaps surprising shift from previous governments that the PF government made was the re-arrangement of the ministry of information and broadcasting services. Immediately after assuming power the PF government experimented with combining the information and broadcasting ministry with tourism and named Given Lubinda as the minister in-charge. A few months later, the ministry of information and broadcasting services was yet again re-structured. This time, it was combined with labor, and the tourism portfolio was moved to the ministry of foreign affairs. The new minister of Information, Broadcasting and Labor was Fackson Shamenda, a former longtime ZCTU president. A few months into the new arrangement, a third restructuring occurred. Labor was separated from the ministry of information and broadcasting services and given to Shamenda to preside over. Meanwhile, a new minister of information and broadcasting services, Kennedy Sakeni, was named. Although it is too soon to provide a holistic assessment of the PF government's impact on press freedom, the constant changes at the ministry of information and broadcasting services do not inspire a lot of confidence.

Regulatory Framework

Research has consistently shown that given the wide reach and efficacy of broadcast media in Africa, most governments, including the Zambian and Ghanaian, have maintained a stranglehold on regulation of broadcast media. Compared to print media, government interference, which ranges from being directly involved in the selection of boards of directors for broadcast regulatory bodies, to literally handpicking them, is excessive. In Zambia and Ghana, the two bodies in charge of regulating broadcast media are the Independent Broadcasting Authority (IBA) and the National Communications Authority (NCA), respectively.

NCA and IBA

Following the democratic reforms of the 1990s, the new governments of Zambia and Ghana, in illustrating their commitment to the democratization process, decided to re-organize and decentralize regulation of the broadcast industry. Ghana led the way with the National Communications Authority Act 524 of 1996, which established NCA, and Zambia followed suit six years later when IBA was enacted via Act Number 17 of December 31, 2002. The mandate of the two bodies was to issue, renew, suspend and cancel broadcasting licenses. NCA and IBA were also tasked with providing tariff rules and guidelines, and advising the information or communications minister on policy formulation and development strategies. In reality, however, the mandate of the two bodies has not panned out as envisioned. IBA, in particular, presents a unique scenario. Its existence to date has merely been on paper.

Act Number 17 of December 31, 2002, stipulated that the media fraternity was to submit names of IBA board members to the information minister who would in turn present them to Parliament for ratification. But upon receiving the names, the minister refused to submit them to Parliament. This decision really baffled the media fraternity, which decided to seek judicial interpretation on the issue (K. Kaunda, personal communication, September 9, 2006). On December 23, 2004, the Lusaka High Court ruled in favor of the media fraternity. Displeased with the ruling, the minister appealed and on March 14, 2007, the Supreme

Court overturned the High Court's decision. The Supreme Court argued that there was nothing illegal about the minister vetting certain names. By the commencement of 2013, a functional IBA board was yet to be constituted. Sakeni, the minister of information and broadcasting services, gave reassurance that the IBA board would be appointed in the first quarter of 2013, together with the ZNBC board once parliament ratified the nominees (QFM, 2013).

Unlike IBA, NCA has a functional board composed of seven members appointed by the President in consultation with the Council of State. Although the Minister of Communications serves as chairman of NCA, the President reserves the right to dissolve the Board at any time; a situation that some media analysts have deemed contentious. For instance, Haggarty, Sharley and Wallsten (2002) argue that granting that much power to the President compromises NCA's independence. And building on this argument, the National Media Commission (NMC), discussed next, asserts that its composition as an independent constitutional body makes it the most appropriate authority to preside over frequency allocation. NCA, it has been observed, "is best suited to deal with the technical aspects of spectrum and frequency management" (Gadzekpo, 2006).

NMC

NMC was established by the National Media Commission Act of July 7, 1993 and is covered under Article 166 of the Constitution: "There shall be established by Act of Parliament […] a National Media Commission which shall consist of fifteen members…" Unlike NCA, NMC is composed of several representative bodies which include: Ghana Journalists Association, Ghana Independent Broadcasters Association, the President's Office, Parliament, Trade Unions, Christian Council of Ghana, Ghana Bar Association, Advertisers and Publishers Association of Ghana, and Institute of Public Relations. NMC's responsibilities are:

1. Promoting and ensuring freedom and independence of the media.
2. Promoting and ensuring high journalistic standards.
3. Investigating, mediating and settling complaints made against or by the media.
4. Insulating state-owned media from government control.
5. Regulating the registration of newspapers and other publications.
6. Appointing members to the Boards of Directors of the state media.

However, by not having the purview of frequency allocation, NMC's job of monitoring content where broadcast media are concerned has been negatively impacted. Since NMC has no power to grant or withdraw licenses, or fine or subpoena erring journalists/media institutions, all it can do is issue reprimanding press statements and rely on the goodwill of erring parties to apologize (McKenzie, 2006). Therefore, it is not uncommon for NMC's reprimands to go unheeded. Former editor of the *Daily Graphic* observed that erring broadcast stations would be more wary of refusing to respond to NMC if the Commission was in charge of allocating frequencies (Y. Boadu-Ayeboafoh, personal communication, July 30, 2006). This "lame duck" nature of NMC has brought it into ridicule from certain sectors of the media that feel that the Commission needs to be empowered to do more than just issue press statements. Empathizing with NMC's power woes, the *Daily Graphic*, in an editorial of August 6, 2006, noted that NMC must be empowered legally, financially and in human resource terms to meet the needs and aspirations for a free but responsible media. On its part, NMC sought legal redress of its mandate asking the courts to give it powers over frequency allocation and powers to subpoena erring journalists/media institutions. Unfortunately, the courts decided otherwise, and despite its power limitations NMC wages on as a journalistic "Court of Honor." In Zambia, on the other hand, the concept of a "Court of Honor," which was first experimented with through the now defunct self-regulatory body, MECOZ, has been elusive. However, as will be discussed later, progress is being made to rectify this.

MECOZ

MECOZ was established on November 29, 2002, after the media fraternity won a court case against the government challenging the Media Council of Zambia Bill that the government had passed on January 17, 1997 to regulate the media (Matibini, 2006). Unlike NMC, which is constitutionally protected, MECOZ was not. MECOZ's stated objectives, which are comparable to those of NMC, were:

1. To promote professionalism by enforcing journalism ethics.
2. To promote freedom of the press.
3. To promote understanding between the media and the public.
4. To arbitrate complaints between the public and the media.
5. To promote gender equity in media practice.
6. To do such things as may be in the interest of the media and the public.

In terms of composition, MECOZ comprised a Board of Directors (refer to Figure 2) chaired by a retired High Court Judge and nine part-time members of which five were public representatives and four media representatives. One-third of the Board members had to be women. When it came to arbitration powers, MECOZ suffered a worse off fate than NMC. The situation was aggravated by the rift that existed between journalists that worked for the state-owned media and those that worked for the privately-owned media. While on average the state-owned media were more receptive to MECOZ's reprimands, the privately-owned *The Post* newspaper was publicly dismissive.

Figure 2. Map of MECOZ (Courtesy of Executive Secretary, Beenwell Mwale)

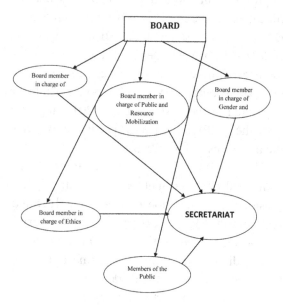

A typical response by *The Post's* managing editor, Fred M'membe, when MECOZ reprimanded his newspaper for use of strong language following a complaint from a minister was: "I have read Mr. David Kashweka's stupid complaint to you. Let him take his complaint to court because we are not part of MECOZ" (cited in Kruger, 2009). *The Post* was also scornful of MECOZ's leaders calling them "empty heads" and established its own internal regulatory body called the Press Freedom Committee funded by deductions from journalists' salaries. *The Post's* actions not only contributed to MECOZ's demise, but also went to show how disregarded the concept of a "Court of Honor" was in Zambia. The president of the Press Association of Zambia cautioned Zambian journalists that: "I'll be more ashamed if my fellow professionals regard me as a useless guy than if the high court decided that I acted unprofessional. I don't care about the high court. I care about my professionals because I won't be able to hold my head high among my peers ... MECOZ is a 'Court of Honor'" (A. Sakala, personal communication, September 10, 2006). As noted earlier, it is the reverence for the concept of a 'Court of Honor' that has made MECOZ's Ghanaian counterpart, NMC, and the Media Council of Tanzania (MCT), which provided a baseline for MECOZ during its formative years, stand the test of time. It is important to note that MCT took its reliance on the "goodwill" of offending news organizations to a whole new level. It instituted a practice of imposing a form of compensation awards called solatium. Solatium is paid by an offending news organization to a complainant and the amounts involved tend to be smaller than those awarded in court cases (Kruger, 2009).

Following MECOZ's demise the media fraternity made a number of attempts under the MMD government at launching another self-regulatory body known as ZAMEC, which was alluded to earlier. ZAMEC's initial launch, which was slated for May 3, 2010, failed because of, among other reasons, a technicality on whether membership would be voluntary or compulsory. A second launch date, which followed further consultations, was set for August 26, 2010, but ended up being postponed indefinitely. This time around, the MMD government was disgruntled that: "ZAMEC was based on the South African media self-regulatory model which [had] been found wanting and [was] now a subject of review and revision in that country" (*Times of Zambia*, August 12, 2010). The then information minister, Shikapwasha, warned that (if not revised) all government-owned media organizations would not be members of ZAMEC.

The MMD government had been pushing for the adoption of the Kenyan model, which according to the Media Institute of Southern Africa (MISA) Regional Secretariat Program Specialist for Freedom of Information and Media Law, Sampa Kangwa-Wilkie, had its shortcomings:

The conditions that led to the statutory media council in Kenya in 2007 are well documented and ironically reminiscent of the current situation in Zambia, that of a government having difficulties

with a watchful, assertive and forceful media. Statutory regulation in all its forms should have no place in a democratic nation like Zambia (The Post, May 3, 2010).

ZAMEC finally launched on July 6, 2012, under the PF government. What Zambia went through with the demise of one self-regulatory body and the struggle to start over mirrors what happened in Malawi. The initial self-regulatory body, the Media Council of Malawi (MCM), which was established in 1996, ceased to exist in 2001. Its premature death was attributed to, among other factors, lack of statutory backing and perceived lack of authority (Kruger, 2009). MCM was, however, reincarnated as a non-statutory body yet again in 2007 and seems to be going strong. Similar to the Ghanaian and Tanzanian cases there seems to be more solidarity among journalists and sensitization on the importance of a "Court of Honor." Finally, to situate the regulatory discussion into a bigger framework, it is imperative to discuss how regulation impacts the role of the media in society, and by extension how journalists perceive their roles.

ROLES OF THE MEDIA IN A DEMOCRACY: THEORETICAL FRAMEWORK

It goes without saying that in undemocratic countries, where the media are excessively controlled and regulated by the government, journalists fail to fulfill crucial roles such as being a window, mirror, interpreter, and interlocutor of events (McQuail, 2000). Moreover, in such states the concept of the media as an independent trustee of the public is anathema because the government puts strict filters on the media rendering them lapdogs rather than watchdogs. In the young democratic states of Zambia and Ghana the importance of the media in serving as the public sphere—an enlightening space of critical debate among citizens (Habermas, 1989)—is crucial. For this to happen, however, democratic theory posits that the media ought to be independent of the government. Therefore, as Zambia and Ghana progress towards "mature democracies" there is need to educate politicians on the importance of a free, independent and non-partisan editorial space for the media to operate (White, 2008, p. 309). Such independence would give the media impetus to provide the public with information necessary to critically evaluate governance and make informed decisions. Zambia and Ghana have made some progress in this regard given the evolution the media in the two countries have undergone since independence.

During the independence era, the media in both countries served as tools for political consolidation, nation-building and development (Hachten, 1981). But in the 1970s, this situation largely changed when the two countries evolved into autocratic, neo-patrimonial states. The role of the media then shifted to serving as tools for suppressing dissent (Wilcox, 1975) with the governments adopting the authoritarian theory of the press (Siebert et al., 1956). Currently, Zambia and Ghana are progressing towards a semblance of democratic theory marked by the proliferation of privately-owned media which are deemed to be independent of the government. The vigilant watchdog role that these new media have played, especially where reporting on corruption is concerned, is testimony of this. In Zambia, the cauldron of corruption stories included exposés on how the now deceased former president Chiluba and his top aides had corruptly amassed wealth. The media also avidly covered Chiluba's trial from 2002 until his controversial acquittal in 2009. Then there was the exposure of the missing millions of dollars at the Ministry of Health (Freedom House, 2010) that shook donors to the core. Similarly in Ghana, the media exposed the diversion of public funds by state officials (embezzlement, licensing fraud, tax evasion, election rigging, and divestiture kickbacks) while detailing the conspicuously lavish lifestyles of several ministers. Furthermore, the *Chronicle* reported that President Kufuor had diverted public funds

and used the money to refurbish his private house and lawns (Hasty, 2005).

Beyond corruption the media, particularly the church-owned in Ghana and Zambia, also covered other vices. For example, the *Catholic Standard* in Ghana pointed out the violation of human rights during Rawlings' reign (Asante, 1996, p. 108), while the *National Mirror* in Zambia clarified the illegal and anti-constitutional procedures of the Chiluba government in seeking a third term of office (Kasoma, 1997, p. 142). This watchdog role of the media was coupled with serving as important sources of political education and mobilization especially during elections. In Ghana, for instance, Joy FM broadcast phone calls from people reporting in the 2000 elections that soldiers were destroying ballot boxes and the people in the audience reacted by coming to chase away the soldiers (Blankson & Murphy, 2007). Another role the media have played through radio has been that of advocacy. As Kasoma (1997) reports, in the case of Zambia, the effectiveness of a program, which invited government ministers and even the president to take any phone-in questions from the audience cannot be underestimated.

Performing the previously-stated roles has not been an easy undertaking for the private media as they have faced resistance from government. Starting with Ghana, during Rawlings' regime when state officials were exposed for corruption by the private press; they retaliated with libel suits that prevented journalists from commenting on the cases once in the court system. In Zambia, on the other hand, some media analysts have argued that economic threats from the MMD government through tax-harassment and the increasing costs of libel suits have had a negative impact on investigative reporting. Additionally in Zambia, which does not enjoy the same level of press freedom as Ghana, the private media have been slapped with all sorts of charges. For example, a former editor at *The Post,* Chansa Kabwela, was charged under the MMD government for sending pictures of a woman giving birth unattended to the vice president, health minister, and other officials during a crippling strike by health workers which government was mute about. Although the charges against Kabwela were dismissed, the newspaper's editor-in-chief, M'membe, faced a contempt charge after publishing an editorial by a U.S.-based professor, Muna Ndulo, criticizing the case (Freedom House, 2010). Given these limitations faced by the media, and notwithstanding the progress made thus far, journalists' perceptions of their role in the two societies are examined next.

ZAMBIAN AND GHANAIAN JOURNALISTS' PERCEPTIONS OF THEIR ROLES IN SOCIETY

With data that was collected in 2006 (Kasoma, 2007) through a survey instrument adapted from Johnstone, Slawski and Bowman (1976) and Weaver and Wilhoit (1991), 107 Zambian and 108 Ghanaian journalists were compared on how they perceived their role in society. The results, presented in Table 1, show that overall the two groups of journalists were comparable in many respects. As expected of democratic societies, the majority of journalists perceived their role as investigating claims and statements made by the government (98.1% Ghanaian and 96.3% Zambian), and reporting on corruption and making leaders accountable to the people (i.e., the watchdog function (99.1% Ghanaian and 96.3% Zambian)).

The two groups of journalists also submitted to providing analysis and interpretation of complex societal problems (94.4% Ghanaian and 95.3% Zambian), and giving ordinary people a chance to express themselves (96.3% Ghanaian and 96.3% Zambian). A rather confusing finding was that when the watchdog function was juxtaposed with that of the media being an adversary of public officials by being constantly skeptical of their actions, few journalists from both camps agreed with the latter. Only 33.6% of Zambian journalists and 22.2% of Ghanaian journalists agreed. Drawing from an earlier discussion on the stalemate

on Freedom of Information legislation in the two countries, it is insurmountable for the media to play the investigative role without being an adversary of government. Zambian and Ghanaian journalists also held the agenda-setting role in lower esteem than the watchdog function. Only 82.4% of Ghanaian journalists and an even lower percentage (73.8%) of Zambian journalists perceived the role of setting the public agenda as important. The discrepancy between the two camps here can probably be explained by the milestone that Ghana has made in ensuring press freedom that has obviously given the media more impetus.

Other factors that were noteworthy included (1) the role of the media as a source of entertainment and relaxation, and (2) the media staying away from stories where factual content cannot be verified. More Zambian journalists agreed with the former statement (85% compared to 79.6%) and more Ghanaian journalists agreed with the latter (71.3% compared to 69.2%). The second finding was surprising given the existence of the concept of "flashing out" in Ghana, which was discussed earlier. Furthermore, there were more Zambian journalists (89.7%) compared to Ghanaian (82.4%) who agreed that it was important for the media to discuss national policy while it was still being developed. Finally, and perhaps not surprising, there was a statistically significant difference on how important the two groups of journalists felt promoting solidarity and nation-building was (chi-square(5) = 20.85, p < .01). One hundred percent of Ghanaian journalists reported this as important compared to 90.7% in Zambia. Ghana's checkered political history of one military junta after another explains the overwhelming appreciation of the importance of using the media to promote solidarity and nation-building among Ghanaian journalists.

Table 1. Journalists' perceptions of their roles

	Number/percentage "agreeing"	
Country/Media roles	**Zambia (N = 107)**	**Ghana (N = 108)**
It is very important for the media to investigate claims and statements made by the government.	103 (96.3%)	106 (98.1%)
It is very important for the media to get information to the public quickly.	98 (91.6%)	97 (89.8%)
It is very important for the media to provide analysis and interpretation of complex societal problems.	102 (95.3%)	102 (94.4%)
It is very important for the media to discuss national policy while it is still being developed.	96 (89.7%)	89 (82.4%)
It is very important for the media to stay away from stories where factual content cannot be verified.	74 (69.2%)	77 (71.3%)
It is very important for the media to concentrate on news that is of interest to the widest possible public.	91 (85%)	87 (80.6%)
It is very important for the media to develop intellectual and cultural interests of the public.	98 (91.6%)	97 (89.8%)
It is very important for the media to be an adversary of public officials by being constantly skeptical of their actions.	36 (33.6%)	24 (22.2%)
It is very important for the media to provide entertainment and relaxation.	91 (85%)	86 (79.6%)
It is very important for the media to provide functional education in literacy, disease prevention, new farming techniques, etc. for people at the grassroots.	94 (87.9%)	102 (94.4%)
It is very important for the media to give ordinary people a chance to express themselves.	103 (96.3%)	104 (96.3%)
It is very important for the media to report corruption in government and make leaders accountable to the people i.e. the watchdog function.	103 (96.3%)	107 (99.1%)
It is very important for the media to set the public agenda.	79 (73.8%)	89 (82.4%)
It is very important for the media to promote solidarity and nation building.	97 (90.7%)	108 (100%)

CONCLUSION

The vigor that accompanied Africa's entry into the democratic era in the 1990s is waning. As Rakner (2003) has observed, most of the new democracies have now entered a "grey zone." With emphasis on the media, specifically in Zambia and Ghana, this trend has been heightened by two factors. Firstly, the reluctance by the two governments to pass Freedom of Information legislation, which would give journalists access to information held by public officials, has had an adverse impact on good governance. Al Cross, director of the Institute for Rural Journalism and Community Issues at the University of Kentucky notes that: "Without laws that give the press access to government records, the press is like a watchdog that is placed on a short leash. And a watchdog on a short leash can't do a very good job ..." (*The Post,* May 27, 2010). The second factor is the state of the regulation of broadcast media. The fact that the Ghanaian and Zambian governments excessively interfere in the composition and operations of the two regulatory bodies NCA and IBA contradicts the purview of democratic theory. Whereas with NCA the contentious issue has been with having NMC, which is deemed more independent based on its composition, perform the function of frequency allocation and licensing, IBA continues to be at dire straits and only exists on paper. During its 20-year rule, the MMD government failed to actualize IBA's existence. The PF government, which assumed power in September 2011, has promised to actualize IBA during its tenure but only time will tell.

REFERENCES

Abdulai, A. (2009). *Political context study-Ghana*. Retrieved from http://www.polis.leeds.ac.uk/assets/files/research/research-projects/abdulai-ghana-political-context-study-jan09.pdf

African Media Barometer. (2009). *Ghana*. Windhoek, Namibia: Media Institute of Southern Africa.

African Media Barometer. (2009). *Zambia*. Windhoek, Namibia: Media Institute of Southern Africa.

Arkosah-Sarpong, K. (2008). *The corruption of Jerry Rawlings*. Retrieved from http://www.ghanaweb.com/GhanaHomePage/features/artikel.php?ID=150169

Asante, C. E. (1996). *The Press in Ghana: Problems and Prospects*. Lanham, MD: University Press of America, Inc..

Blankson, I. A. (2002). Re-examining civil society in emerging Sub-Sahara African democracies: The state, the media, and the public in Ghana. *Global Media Journal, 1*(1), Fall. Retrieved from http://lass.purduecal.edu/cca/gmj/fa02/gmj-fa02-blankson.htmgmj-fa02-blankson.htm

Blankson, I. A., & Murphy, P. (Eds.). (2007). *Negotiating democracy: Media transformations in emerging democracies*. Albany, NY: State University of New York Press.

Boafo, K. (1985). Utilizing development communication strategies in African societies: A critical perspective. *Gazette, 35*, 83–92.

Bratton, M., Mattes, R., & Gyimah-Boadi, E. (2005). *Public opinion, democracy, and market reform in Africa*. Cambridge, UK: Cambridge University Press.

Buhlungu, S., & Adler, G. (Eds.). (1997). Labour and liberalisation in Zambia. *South African Labour Bulletin, 21*(2), 48–64.

Carbone, G. (2009). *Does democratisation deliver social welfare? Political regimes and health policy in Ghana and Cameroon*. Retrieved from www.sisp.it/files/papers/2009/giovanni-carbone-425.pdf

Chanda, E. (2010, May 3). Statutory media regulation not an option for Zambia. *The Post*. Retrieved from http://www.postzambia.com

Foundation for Democratic Process. (FODEP, 1996). Zambia's 18 November 1996 Presidential and Parliamentary Elections: Final Election Monitoring Report. Lusaka, Zambia.

Foundation for Democratic Process. (FODEP, 2002). Zambia's 27 December 2001 Presidential and Parliamentary Elections: Final Election Monitoring Report. Lusaka, Zambia.

Freedom House. (2010). *Freedom of the Press*. Retrieved from http://www.freedomhouse.org/

Gadzekpo, A. (2005). *Ghana: Country Assessment Paper*. Legon, Ghana: University of Ghana.

Gadzekpo, A. (2006). *Guardians of Democracy: The Media and Good Governance. School of Communication Studies*. Legon, Ghana: University of Ghana.

Gyimah-Boadi, E. (1997). Civil Society in Africa: The Good, the Bad, the Ugly. *Journal for a Civil Society, 1*(1). Retrieved from http://civnet.org/journal/issue1/egboadi.htm

Gyimah-Boadi, E. (2004). *Democratic reform in Africa: The quality of progress*. Boulder, CO: Lynne Rienner.

Habermas, J. (1989). *The Structural Transformation of the Public Sphere: An Inquiry into a Category of Bourgeois Society*. Cambridge, MA: The MIT Press.

Hachten, W. A. (1981). *The World News Prism: Changing Media of International Communication* (3rd ed.). Ames, IA: Iowa State University Press.

Haggarty, L., Shirley, M. M., & Wallsten, S. (2002). *Telecommunication Reform in Ghana*. Retrieved from http://citeseerx.ist.psu.edu/viewdoc/download?doi=10.1.1.13.47&rep=rep1&type=pdf

Hasty, J. (2005). Sympathetic Magic/Contagious Corruption: Sociality, Democracy, and the Press. *Public Culture*, *17*, 339–370. doi:10.1215/08992363-17-3-339.

Hyden, G., Leslie, M., & Ogundimu, F. F. (2002). Preface. In Hyden, G., Leslie, M., & Ogundimu, F. F. (Eds.), *Media and democracy in Africa* (pp. vii–ix). New Brunswick, NJ: Transaction Publishers.

Johnstone, J. W. C., Slawski, E. J., & Bowman, W. W. (1976). *The news people: A sociological portrait of American journalist and their work*. Urbana, IL: University of Illinois Press.

Kasoma, F. (1997). Communication and press freedom in Zambia. In Eribo, F., & Jong-Ebot, W. (Eds.), *Press Freedom and Communication in Africa* (pp. 135–156). Asmara, Eritrea: Africa World Press.

Kasoma, T. (2007). *Brown envelope journalism and professionalism in development reporting: A comparison of Zambia and Ghana*. Unpublished PhD dissertation, University of Oregon, Oregon, USA.

Kruger, F. (2009). *Media Courts of Honour: Self-Regulation Councils in Southern Africa and Elsewhere*. Windhoek, Namibia: Friedrich Ebert Stiftung.

Matibini, P. (2006). *The Struggle for Media Law Reforms in Zambia*. Lusaka, Zambia: Media Institute of Southern Africa – Zambia Chapter.

McKenzie, R. (2006). *Comparing Media from around the World*. Boston, MA: Allyn & Bacon.

McQuail, D. (2000). *McQuail's Mass Communication Theory* (4th ed.). London: Sage Publications Ltd..

Media Foundation for West Africa. (2008). *Media Alert West Africa 2008: Annual State of the Media Report*. Ghana: MFWA.

Media Foundation for West Africa. (2010). *Ghana Freedom of Information coalition raises red flag over lack of transparency in the passage of the FOI*. Retrieved from http://www.mediafound.org/index.php?option=com_content&task=view&id=489&Itemid=45

Mukwasa, R. (2011, April 27). Ronnie threatens to close several radio stations. *The Post*. Retrieved from http://www.postzambia.com

Ogbondah, C. (2004). Democratization and the media in West Africa: An analysis of recent constitutional and legislative reforms for press freedom in Ghana and Nigeria. *West Africa Review*, (6), 1-36.

Press Reference. (n.d.). *Ghana*. Retrieved from http://www.pressreference.com/Fa-Gu/Ghana.html

QFM. (2012, November 23). *IBA to be operational in Jan 2013 – Sakeni*. Retrieved from http://www.qfmzambia.com/blog_details.php?idx=10450

Rakner, L. (2003). *Political and Economic Liberalisation in Zambia 1991–2001. The Nordic Africa Institute*. Sweden: Elanders Gotab.

Sangaparee, C. (2011, May 25). *Who Caused The Crisis In The NDC?* Retrieved from http://www.ghanaweb.com/GhanaHomePage/NewsArchive/artikel.php?ID=208870

Sangwa, J. (n.d.). Press freedom in Zambia. *Southern African Media Law Briefing*. Retrieved from http://www.fxi.org.za/pages/Publications/Medialaw/zambia.htm

Siebert, F., Peterson, T., & Schramm, W. (1956). *Four Theories of the Press*. Urbana, IL: University of Illinois Press.

Simutanyi, N. (2002). *Challenges To Democratic Consolidation In Zambia: Public Attitudes To Democracy and the Economy*. Afrobarometer Paper No. 17. Retrieved from www.afrobarometer.org/index.php?option=com_docman&task

The Press freedom Committee of The Post (2010, May 20). Al Cross Zambia FOI Speech. *The Post*. Retrieved from http://www.postzambia.com

Times of Zambia. (2010, August 12). *State opposed to ZAMEC launch*. Retrieved from http://www.times.co.zm/

Weaver, D. H., & Wilhoit, G. C. (1991). *The American journalist: A portrait of U.S. news people and their work*. Bloomington, IN: Indiana University Press.

White, R. A. (2008). The Role of the Media in Democratic Governance. *African Communication Research*, *1*(3), 269–328.

Wilcox, D. (1975). *Mass Media in Black Africa*. New York: Praeger.

Zambia National Broadcasting Corporation. (2011, June 3). *FOI to be presented when ready*. Retrieved from http://www.znbc.co.zm/

Chapter 8

When the History Turns Stronger than the Rhetoric:
The Journalistic Culture Drives over Democracy Ideals in Namibia and Tanzania

Ullamaija Kivikuru
University of Helsinki, Finland

ABSTRACT

The 1990s brought radical changes to Sub-Saharan Africa. In the rhetoric, the ownership mode appeared as a crucial marker of freedom. However, neither the access to the media nor the media content has changed much. The media mode, inherited from previous phases of social history, seems to change slowly. Old modes reproduce themselves in new media titles disregarding ownership mode. In this chapter, empirical evidence is sought from Namibia and Tanzania. The empirical evidence is based on two sets of one-week samples (2007, 2010) of all four papers. In this material, a government paper and a private paper from one particular country resemble each other more than when ownership modes are compared. Bearers of the journalistic culture seem to be to a certain extent media professionals moving from one editorial office to another, but the more decisive factors are the ideals set for journalism. The "first definition of journalism" reflects old times.

INTRODUCTION

The 1990s brought radical changes to Sub-Saharan African mediascapes. Countries governed by a one-party system with state-controlled media changed to a multi-party system, and the media started to expound a strong rhetoric of freedom. Private media emerged everywhere and easily found foreign support—radio stations and small-circulation publications most frequently called "independent" instead of "private" or "commercial" as they would have been called in Europe. The Windhoek Declaration (1991) became a symbol of a new era in Sub-Saharan Africa, placing democracy and freedom of expression entirely in the sphere of private "independent" media.

DOI: 10.4018/978-1-4666-4197-6.ch008

Today, the rhetoric of freedom has calmed down, but it still sells well, among both foreign donors and media professionals. Governments and media companies struggle to find a new balance among growing popular expectations, new legislation, media councils, and the status and educational standards of journalists (Ramaprasand, 2002).

As usual, legislation lags behind, although the field of broadcasting seems to have made more progress (Berger, 2007; Ndela, 2007). So far, governments have viewed legislation and policy actions as decisive tools for strengthening democracy, but seem to find it difficult to strike a balance between freedom and responsibility (Rioba, 2009; *So, This is Democracy*, 2009, p. 72).

Another area of struggle is the formation of media councils. Governments all over Sub-Saharan Africa frequently try to establish government-run media councils for "self-regulation" of the media. Most recently, Namibia attempted to establish a media council in April 2009 and Zambia tried in May 2009. So far, all such attempts have failed. In contrast to government-run councils, Namibia recently established a Press Ombudsman system that opens a path towards self-regulation and an independently-formed Media Council of Tanzania (MCT) has operated effectively for years in Tanzania.

Despite the changed rhetoric, the role of the media in African societies has not changed much. The number of newspapers and TV channels has multiplied, but circulation and viewers have not grown proportionately. The media still tend to concentrate in capital cities and major financial centres, while in several areas access to the media by rural populations has worsened significantly (Kivikuru, 2000, pp. 93-101).

Further, to a large extent the media are still in the hands of dominant political parties or big businesses; community-based media have succeeded properly only in South Africa (Teer-Tomaselli & Mjwacu, 2003; Kivikuru, 2006), Ghana and Mozambique (Jallov, 2011). There is much talk about web-based media, but so far their use is limited.

The journalistic culture of Sub-Saharan Africa has been merely an intervening factor in this twisted situation. In journalism, the initial news report defining a phenomenon is often decisive, because it tends to frame the succeeding reporting. On a systems level, the media mode inherited from previous phases of social history changes slowly. The old mode reproduces itself in new media titles, even though these titles claim to follow a different logic. Consequently, the form the media have taken while emerging in the media terrain can be decisive.

This claim is by no means new in the literature. In the 1970s, several researchers discussed the phenomenon, although from a somewhat different point of view:

A dependency relationship] refers to the process whereby the ownership, structure, distribution or content of the media in any country are singly or together subject to substantial external pressures from the media interest of any other country or countries without proportionate reciprocation of influence by the country so affected. (Boyd-Barrett, 1977, p. 117)

Boyd-Barrett and others (Golding, 1977; Hamelink, 1983; Senghaas, 1985) refer to dependency relationships, in which a lack of reciprocity is a crucial element. The end product is "mainstreaming" or "synchronisation": the dominant culture or a transnational company sets the dependent party's standards. Boyd-Barrett (1977) talks about how the communication vehicle in a dependent society easily adopts the mode of the communication vehicle in the dominant culture.

This research tradition does not necessarily deny space for peripheral autonomy, or as Senghaas (1985, p. 223-228) phrases it, "autocentric development," Senghaas points out that the most salient determinants for auto-centric development are the differentiated capacity for independent self-control and the freedom to self-steer one's politics, society, economy, and culture. Senghaas recommends having only selective contacts with the outside world. The idea of partial isolation sounds unrealistic in today's world, but the phenomenon of dependence in a nation's journalistic culture has not faded away. This is an important explanation for why it has been so difficult to establish diversity of journalistic modes in countries with a colonial past. Changes in legislation and ownership mode alone cannot bring multiplicity. According to Galtung (1971, p. 98-101), the convertibility of domination often takes the form of a "spillover" of culture; the domination does not need to be deliberate or planned.

Consonant with Senghaas, I do not claim that a change is impossible. My claim is that especially when cultural forms such as journalism are concerned, changes are slow, requiring time and reflection. This article tries to elaborate on the claim that an ownership mode is decisive in promoting a democratic mediascape.

The "public connection" (Couldry, Livingstone and Markhan 2007, p. 5-10) is a complex concept that resonates with theoretical considerations advocated by Dewey, Habermas and Arendt in numerous texts (e.g. Dewey, 1996; Habermas, 1996; Arendt, 1998), but it is also a far more concrete media practice. As Peter Dahlgren (2001, p. 85) has stated, the public connection deals with values, affinity, knowledge, practices, identities and discussion. A medium which has inherited such a complex journalistic mode at least partly reflects these firstborn rights, even under a different organisational rule. If the firstborn is a medium which has close contacts with the power elite, it is difficult to alter the course.

Most African mediascapes were established during colonial times. The form of the media vehicles there reflects this legacy even today; changes come slowly and are tied to the media history in a country. A nation's quest for development adds an interesting nuance. In principle, development aims at improving the standard of life for the majority in a society, but development has also become part of the power structure in societies dependent on

external funding for their developmental projects. Thus, equation marks cannot be made straight away between development and true democracy.

FIRSTBORN AND LASTBORN IN THE THIRTY YEARS' WAR

In the following section of this chapter, I analyse two sets of limited empirical evidence, leaving aside evidence from the entertainment media. Up to the 21st century, the media landscape in African societies was very serious; nation-building and development communication did not include any elements of entertainment. It is interesting that even today, the entertainment dimension has not been "allowed" in African multi-party mediascapes that is made possible financially by foreign donors.

The only "naturally born" form of development-related entertainment is the caricature, which is especially strong in Kenya and Tanzania (Gathara & Wanjau, 2009). In troubled Zimbabwe, political cartoons on the Internet have been one of the few channels for free expression of deviant views (Arntsen, 2009). As Appadurai (1996, p. 7) has stated, the cartoons are significant because they offer images of "irony, anger, humour and resistance" from the global, regional and local repertoires.

Further, the negative attitudes toward entertainment in many African societies have created tensions between the youth, who want access to mass entertainment, and the power elite and foreign donors, who have reservations about these "cultural" forms. Perhaps it would have been more justified to study African broadcasting instead of newspapers, which have been elite-oriented throughout history, but for practical reasons, it is impossible to study broadcasting genres. Let us turn, instead, to a study of newspapers.

At first, newspapers served the interests of colonisers; after that, they served the interests of various elite groups that either already had power or were striving to get power. The elite orientation of newspapers is exactly what makes this type of research relevant: how easy is it to turn the course of events by manipulating a medium so closely related to power?

Recently, some forms of tabloidization have emerged in the societies we are scrutinising: there are afternoon and free-of-charge papers in Namibia (e.g., *The Sun, Informanté*), and numerous Tanzanian private papers that have been nicknamed "rumour papers" by members of the public (e.g., *Alasiri, Dar Leo, Jambo Leo*). The nicknaming is evidence that the public has relegated these papers to the category of not-so-credible sources of information, so the following analysis ignores them.

There is no doubt that tabloids have a role in society. Martín-Barbéro (1997) has pointed out that entertainment-oriented media products teach people to "walk in the city," (i.e., to find one's function in an urban environment). However, this essay focuses on four of the most popular dailies, which upon analysis appear to differ only in their ownership. Two of the papers selected are publicly owned; the two others are private. All four are among the most popular papers in their country. These papers represent the media viewed by decision-makers and the middle class. Given the differences in ownership, we would expect that the content and orientation of these media would differ markedly: the government media are assumed to be non-critical advocates of their government's policies, while, according to the same assumption, "independent" media are far more open-minded.

The empirical analysis of newspapers usually requires a sample of 10-12 days, but recently, 2-3 day samples also have been accepted (Davies & Mosdell, 2006). The samples in this study include 15 issues in Namibia and 14 issues in Tanzania of two newspapers in each country, covering sample periods in 2006/2007 and 2010. The samples also include issues of all four papers on one day, April 27, 2009. No doubt, proper evidence would require a more extensive variety of material, but it is pos-

sible to draw conclusions based even on limited empirical material, because the formats are fixed. Analysis remains only an example, but an attempt is also made here to bring in more general frames of reference: production structures and modes, on the one hand, and the journalistic culture, standing for news criteria and style, on the other,

The Tanzanian and Namibian Mediascapes

Namibia and Tanzania represent two very different societies in Sub-Saharan Africa. These two countries represent the beginning and ending of what John Saul terms the "'thirty years' war for southern African liberation" (2008, p. 13-21). Saul views the period starting in the early 1960s and concluding in the 1990s as a specific and important "conjuncture" in African history, producing both decolonisation and recolonisation processes.

Tanzania, which became independent in 1961, paid considerable attention to media policies in the 1970s, but the government's official statements did not affect the local media landscape: the media remained weak. However, Tanzanian media provided an important base for the liberation movements in other countries of the region, giving media space to the African National Congress (ANC) and the Pan-Africanist Congress (PAC) in South Africa, and the South West African People's Organisation (SWAPO) in Namibia.

In 1990, Namibia became the last country in sub-Saharan Africa to reach independence. Given the intervening time, one could expect that by then the mediascape in long-independent Tanzania would be more settled and diversified than in Namibia. If our standard is only the number of present-day newspaper titles, Tanzania definitely outstrips Namibia, because Tanzania experienced a newspaper boom after the country entered the multi-party system in the early 1990s.

If, as claimed in this chapter, the standard should be the mediascape, then it is crucial to review the form in which the media was established originally. In Tanzania, the independence and decolonisation process which preceded it were relatively peaceful. In Namibia, on the other hand, the media participated in the independence struggle–not very profoundly, but definitely as actors in the process. The media in Namibia were forced to create an arena for debate and discussion during those years.

Before 1990, the 2.2 million population of Namibia had been long isolated from its Sub-Saharan neighbours, and the society was shaken by a dramatic change of political ideology after periods under several different colonial powers and a harsh struggle for independence. Today, Namibia seems to be moving toward a one-party system under the dominant SWAPO party, although small opposition parties have won a few seats in the Parliament.

In recent years, the political sphere in Namibia has become more tense as independence struggle veterans and "struggle kids"—Namibian youth born and raised abroad during the independence struggle—both demand more attention from the decision-makers. A totally new group emerged during the general elections in November 2009, the so-called young "born free" voters who carry no memories of the independence struggle, but nothing happened, since many of these young people seemed detached concerning politics.

The media landscape in Namibia has mixed public and private ownership for a long time. The freedom fighters and the apartheid system each used both kinds of media during the independence struggle.

After independence, a similar trend has continued. A national communications commission (NCC) officially allocates broadcasting frequencies, and the government occasionally takes a policy stand, for example, toward the publishing policies of the government-subsidised *Namibia Broadcasting Corporation* (NBC) as well as the private newspaper, *The Namibian*. The government has been reactive rather than proactive, taking *ad hoc* stands rather than exercising consistent me-

dia policies. The Parliament has discussed media matters, but has not passed any laws or issued any regulations concerning the media. Long having been isolated even from other African countries, Namibia has not been able to develop a regional scope for its media arena. Namibia is not among the poorest nations in Africa, but class differences in Namibia are greater than in Tanzania.

Tanzania (population 42 million) is an African country which has been fortunate to experience a steady development from a poor country with a mild colonial past followed by peaceful evolution into a nation-state. Tanzania started its independent existence as an African version of socialism under one party. It has later reoriented towards a market economy under a multi-party system, although the old dominant Chama Cha Mapinduzi (CCM) party still controls the political arena. The country has received enormous sums as development assistance during the past 35-40 years. This dependency on donors has left its mark on the Tanzanian society.

Compared to other African countries, the Namibian mediascape is well developed and diverse, although its sharp social differences are reflected in the availability of its media. For example, the print press publishes in three languages, which is a rarity in Africa, although multilingual broadcasting companies are common. In Tanzania, the media have been underdeveloped compared with neighbouring Uganda and Kenya. Today the media ownership is mixed in both countries. Government and private media operate side-by-side. The Namibian media operated under strong pressure during the South African apartheid regime, although there was no real media policy, while from the late 1960s, Tanzania has issued policy papers defining the role of the media in social development (Nordenstreng & Ngwanakilala, 1987).

The media systems in both countries still operate predominantly on the national level. Some local religious and commercial radio stations exist, but community media in the real sense (Howley, 2005, p. 19) have had difficulties getting established in both countries. Media in both countries operate in languages other than English: in Tanzania today some 85% of the media broadcast in Swahili, reflecting a change that took place in the 1990s. In Namibia, on the other hand, English has become even more dominant than before.

In Tanzania, the dominant print media form has been the publicly owned since the 1960s, while in Namibia the opposite has been the case: up through the early 1990s, the print media in Namibia were in owned privately. This historical difference has created an interesting contradiction in the outlook of the papers under examination. The government paper in Namibia, established in the early 1990s, sought credibility by distinctly repeating the format of the "firstborn" newspaper, *The Namibian[1]*. The layout and the reporting mode in *The New Era* and in *The Namibian*—long stories spreading over several pages—still closely resemble each other. Conversely, the *Guardian,* the private paper in Tanzania, was designed deliberately to be an opposite alternative to the government paper, the *Daily News.* The journalistic ideal for *The Guardian* can be traced back to private papers in Kenya. *The Guardian* in Tanzania was made different in order to create an impression of credibility, while the *New Era* in Namibia was made similar to the government publication in order to create the same impression of credibility. The professional status of *The Namibian* was strong, while the same could not be said about the *Daily News.*

The Tanzanian Mediascape

The early Tanzanian press was marked by colonial government and private ownership by missionaries and white settlers, but there was little tension between the two, given the similarity of their goals and audiences. The spread of the private press to the indigenous population in the 1940s and 1950s changed the picture. The private papers supported nationalist causes, while the colonial government struggled against them, but with independence, regional papers, particularly those supported by

religious groups, died out or were forbidden in the name of nation-building. The role of the press was clearly articulated in 1972 by President Julius Miserere in his message when he nationalised the press (Konde, 1984).

Until the mid-1980s, there were only three newspapers in Tanzania: *The Daily News* (government), *Uhuru* ("Freedom," CCM party) and *Mfanyakazi* ("Worker," a weekly trade union paper*).* The circulation of *The Daily News* exceeded 100,000 copies and *Uhuru* was slightly lower; of these, *Uhuru* in particular was distributed to the regions beyond the large cities, although the papers reached the villages only rarely.

The national radio reaches 80-85% of the population. On mainland Tanganyika, *Radio Tanzania Dar es Salaam (RTD)* had a monopoly over radio broadcasting. In the 1970s and 1980s, RTD had a strong educational orientation, with so-called radio fora: after an educational radio programme, villagers sat in a circle with an extension agent and "localized" the educational item reported during the programme (Ng'wanakilala, 1981). In the autonomous Zanzibar region, government-owned stations provided both radio and television. The mainland and Zanzibar still have separate media policies.

The transition to multipartyism started in 1993 and it came with a major growth in the number of media outlets. There are now 33 daily and 187 weekly registered newspapers (*So this is Democracy*, 2009) and as many as 54 private regional radio stations have emerged. A total of 27 private television channels started on the mainland in the 1990s, and public television (*Television Tanzania, TVT*) came on air in 2001.

Impressive as the figures sound, however, the total newspaper circulation barely exceeds the total circulation of *The Daily News* and *Uhuru* in the days before independence, and newspapers are distributed only in towns. The same characteristics apply to television and private radio stations. Less than 20% of the population is able to watch television, but some 88% of the population receive at least one radio station (*So this is democracy*, 2009). In sum, the media situation today in rural areas is roughly the same as it was before, if not worse (Kivikuru, 2000, p. 48-52), while in towns and semi-urban areas, television, commercial radio stations and newspapers printed in Swahili have found new audiences. Watching television together in homes, bars and restaurants is common (Ramaprasand, 2002; Mrutu, 2005). The media are part of Tanzanian urban life, and radio is slowly ceding its dominant position to television. This change is definitely new, and accompanies the hybridisation of culture, especially in cities (Edström, 2010).

The status of the Swahili language is very strong in Tanzania. It is therefore natural that the promotion of multi-party democracy demands that media employ the language used by the majority of the population. Today, some 85 per cent of the private newspaper companies publish in Swahili. Since 2006, the government's *Daily News* also has a Swahili-Language sister paper (*Habari Leo*).

In the early 1990s, Tanzania experienced a strong boom of sensationalism.The boom has calmed down now, and the Media Council—an institution running well—introduced new ethical codes. Today, the majority of the newspapers based in Dar es Salaam are tabloids, while the rest are broadsheets; *The Citizen*, the paper often assessed as the highest quality publication in Dar es Salaam circles, is a tabloid.

The Papers Studied

In the following portions of this article, news coverage by *The Daily News,* the oldest paper in the country and a government mouthpiece, and news coverage by *The Guardian*, the largest-circulation private paper, owned by the biggest media company in the country, the IPP Group, will be analyzed.

No official circulation figures are available, but it is said that *The Guardian* has a daily circulation of around 35,000 copies, while *The Daily News* prints barely 20,000 copies. Both papers are broadsheets that appear six days a week. On Sundays, the *Daily News* masthead reads, *The Sunday News*, and until 2010, *The Guardian* published as *The Sunday Observer* (starting in 2010, the name of the Sunday issue changed to *Guardian on Sunday* and that day's issue changed to a tabloid format). The Sunday issues are not included in the empirical analysis of this study. *The Daily News* was first published in 1930 under the name *The Standard*, and was owned by a British-origin transnational company. Over the past 15 years, the paper has lost its number-one status, but it still has authority, and it still collects considerable revenue from advertising. Since independence, the paper has focused its reporting on politics and public institutions and concentrated geographically on Dar es Salaam.

The IPP Group publishes 10 newspapers and owns a radio station, a television station and a news agency. Owned by local millionaire Reginald Mengi, the IPP Group was established immediately after the media liberalization in the early 1990s. *The Guardian* is better equipped than *The Daily News*, and the IPP Group commands considerable journalistic resources. *The Guardian* was deliberatively designed to distinguish it from *The Daily News*. During the 1990s, however, *The Daily News* altered its appearance and outlook toward the commercial papers in their market, including *The Guardian*.

The structure of both papers is similar. *The Guardian* includes a business and foreign section, a section for sports and entertainment, and a "basic" section of the paper that focuses on domestic news. *The Daily News* offers similar sections, but it adds a section called "African news" and the number of pages varies more from issue to issue. The average number of pages in *The Daily News* in 2006 and 2010 was 16-24 and 36 pages, respectively; the average number of pages for *The Guardian* during the same two years was 28-40 and 36, respectively. The differences in size between the papers have decreased during the three years intervening between the sample periods, and so have the differences in the number of stories.

More than eight out of ten (80%) of the stories in *The Daily News* during 2006 depended on only one source, while in *The Guardian,* the figure was slightly lower: three out of four (75%) of the stories used only one source. Most often this source was a person stating something as a fact or giving a speech. In this respect, there did not seem to be any change in 2010 (See Table 1).

What Happened, What was Covered

The sample week in December 2006 was fairly normal in the sense that there were a few significant news themes, but nothing that overshadowed all others. A scandal concerning unsuccessful power supply and disappearance of funds emerged; East African leaders signed an agreement on the East African Court of Appeal and a Great Lakes peace pact. The President, ministers and dignitaries opened seminars and arts exhibitions and visited various regions of their country.

In contrast, in 2010, Tanzania was preparing for the General elections in October 2010, and this fact strongly affected the media coverage. Above all, it seemed to expand the coverage given to the President, especially by the private paper. There was already considerable focus on the President in the 2006 sample, and that coverage doubled to 2010.

The question of cooperation among the nations of East African seemed to have grown in significance between 2006 and 2007. The figures from 2010 are probably higher than normal due to the World Cup competition in South Africa, which the Tanzanian papers followed and reported intently.

A Closer Look at the Coverage in 2006 and 2010

Both papers normally publish 3-4 stories on the front page, plus banners directing the reader to 3-4 headlines inside the paper. The headline style is dramatic in both papers, although in 2006, the government's *Daily News* tended to use more dramatic language and huge fonts. In 2010, *The Guardian* had larger headlines.

Most front-page stories dealt with domestic politics and the economy, with some occasional foreign stories: during the 2006 test period, *The Guardian* reported once on Russian politics, once on the Catholic Church, and once on Nigeria's ex-dictator. Both papers covered the East African economy, education and foreign assistance received. During the 2006 test period *The Daily News* also focused on Tanzanian troops readying to join the UN peacekeepers in Lebanon. A manslaughter case once ended up on the *Daily News'* front page; another time it was a story about the death of the UK's Princess Diana. In both samples, the front pages were clearly a combination of important and interesting news items, but the front pages focused on slightly different issues in 2006 and 2010. *The Daily News* was more formal, putting reports of seminars and speeches on the front page, while the *Guardian* concentrated on reporting corruption and crime

In 2006, both Tanzanian papers carried an editorial every day, and *The Guardian* also printed several columns and a caricature. The editorials mainly provided background descriptions for the news stories, with a mild concluding opinion.

Table 1. Focus of the stories in The Daily News and The Guardian (2006, 2009, and 2010)

	No of stories			Shared themes		
	2006/2007	**2009***	**2010**	**2006/2007****	**2009**	**2010****
Daily News	328	67	858	25%	35%	45%
Guardian	623	73	656	20%	30%	40%

*The one-day sample from April 27, 2009 is included in the table, but will be discussed separately in chapter 4.

* *The percentage refers to issues covered by both papers, measured by the space the stories occupied on the printed page The majority of shared themes are extensive texts and include pictures. Both papers prefer to place their own stories on the front page.

Frequently, both papers took a similar stand. To a large extent, both papers focused on the functioning of public institutions. In 2010, the volume of opinionated material grew: in addition to editorials, the papers published several expert columns or articles related to the news.

Stories about President Kikwete appeared on the front page of both papers three times in 2006. *The Daily News* referred to Kikwete's opinions and activities 16 times, *The Guardian,* 13 times. In addition, both papers reported twice about the First Lady's visits. *The Daily News* announced twice on its front page that the paper was going to run a supplement to mark the anniversary of President Kikwete's first year in office. In both papers, the stories about the President were neutral or positive.

In 2010, *The Guardian* clearly gave more space for the President than its competitor; the paper seemed willing to report on any detail about the President. *The Daily News* never reported anything negative about the President, but his activities did not get as prominent a position in the paper as they did in *The Guardian*. The charisma of the President seemed to have no bounds in *The Guardian*.

Both papers keenly followed the visits and statements by various ministers, and were, in general, strongly oriented to covering events and concerns in Dar es Salaam. They reported on the regions when a minister or other dignitary visited there, but at hardly any other time.

The public sphere was covered poorly by both papers in 2006. Both paid only limited attention to non-governmental organizations (NGOs) except when discussing the development projects they funded, although in donor circles these NGOs have been described as pioneers of democracy. Other areas getting regular coverage were HIV/AIDS and foreign assistance. HIV/AIDS received considerable attention in Tanzania. During the test periods in both 2006 and 2010, the development assistance aspect received regular attention in both Tanzanian papers. In 2006, when Denmark

announced a reduction in its assistance, both papers expressed alarm about the decision; there were no differences between the two papers in their coverage of this issue.

In 2006, *The Daily News* reported more about Zanzibar items than *The Guardian*, obviously due to the delicate political situation on the Isles. As an example, the government paper reported on student strikes in Zanzibar, but its reports concerning a water project there talked entirely about the scope of the project and did not mention the aspect that the private paper focused on: the dangers that tourism has created on Zanzibar's beaches. Let us compare the two following reports:

An ambitious water project, to be carried out by Konoike Contractors of Japan in Zanzibar's West-Urban Region, is scheduled to start next month at a cost of 10bn/-. The Principal Secretary in the Ministry of Water Construction, Land and Energy, Mr. Mwalimu A. Mwalimu, said here yesterday that the project was aimed at producing 10 million extra litres of water for the region. (The Daily News, December 14, 2006)

In a bid to control pollution of beaches and the Indian Ocean, authorities in Tanzania's semi-autonomous Island of Zanzibar issued an ultimatum on Monday to hotel owners and other investors to install sewage-treatment facilities on their premises or risk being barred from operating. (The Guardian, December 14, 2006)

There was a distinct difference in perspective in these stories. *The Daily News* exercised a ritualistic style, reporting what public officials told the media. In contrast, *The Guardian* aggressively went after a scoop of its own, but also used public sources, e.g. the Zanzibar Minister for Water, Energy and Lands. Interestingly enough, the crooks in the story were private entrepreneurs who failed to observe accepted regulations in order to save money. In this case, the private paper described a political figure as a representative of proper behaviour, while faulting private entrepreneurs for not valuing the common good.

In their foreign coverage during 2006, the papers reported on serious political processes and oddities side by side, plus long feature stories, mainly from other developing countries. East Africa was covered systematically, and there seemed to be a slight difference in the attitudes: *The Daily News* appeared hesitant about the re-emergence of the East African Union, while *The Guardian* was more positive, referring to business benefits of the affiliation.

The Guardian was somewhat better organized concerning its foreign coverage, but the difference was not great. *The Daily News* regularly followed events in the rest of Africa – with the exception of Darfur. That provinces problem came up once in *The Guardian* and twice in *The Daily News* during 2006, but these news-agency-based stories received scant coverage compared with, for example, the capture of a renegade general in Madagascar. The UN received very little attention from the leading papers in a country which had steadily supported the world organization.

In 2010, the number-one foreign theme in both papers was the World Cup competition in South Africa. *The Guardian* covered the World Cup more extensively and with an extra service, but South Africa also received other attention from both papers during 2006 and 2010. The regional superpower has been involved in the Tanzanian economy for quite a while. A "carefully-formulated distance" is perhaps the right phrase to describe the Tanzanian papers' attitude toward South Africa. Any distinct differences between the papers on this subject are difficult to discern.

In 2006, *The Guardian* provided its readers with some good background analyses in its business and foreign section. National interests were at stake, but the paper rarely looked at the issues from a citizen's perspective. A story in

2006 demonstrating this bias was *The Guardian*'s report on a one-day media stakeholders' seminar during which a new media bill suggested by the government was heavily criticized.

On December 14, 2006, *The Daily News* headline for its article reporting the seminar read, "Stakeholders reject Draft Media Bill"; *The Guardian*'s headline on the same date for the same report read, "Media stakeholders reject draft media freedom bill." *The Daily News* article was shorter, but it stated the basic arguments presented by the seminar participants. Their story was more diffuse than the story in *The Guardian*, because *The Daily News* did not report the arguments behind the rejection. The *Daily News* report was difficult for a reader to follow unless that reader had participated in the debate on the Bill. The reader learnt that there had been resistance to the suggested new Bill, but the reasons for the resistance remained unclear.

The government paper indirectly took the side of the government, but its story also included some aspects of the issue presented by representatives who resisted the Bill:

The provision in section 58(1), which stipulates functions of the new board, completely takes over the functions of the privately-established MCT. This must be rejected because it is against the struggle [not] to have a Fourth Estate that is independent of the government", said Dr. Sengolo Mvungi, who presented a paper after reviewing the Bill. (Daily News, December 14, 2006)

The private paper used rhetoric rather than analysis to report the same source:

By a single stroke, the whole struggle to have a fourth estate that is independent from government control is being put into jeopardy! This must be objected vigorously! Why is the government interested in controlling the media? Why should

Tanzania have a market economy on the one hand but dictatorship in terms of freedom of expression of the other? he (Mvungi) asked. (The Guardian, December 14, 2006)

In sum, both papers paid close attention to political debates and the agenda set by the government. The actors referred to on a daily basis were almost identical in the two papers.

On some issues, *The Guardian* represents a more up-to-date mode of journalism, but on some other issues, the paper appears merely to reflect the views of the political elite. Differences between it and the government paper are extremely small, and *The Daily News* seems slowly to be distancing itself from its publisher. Differences come up in cases which report either ideological interest— certain institutions, status of the media, but not often political figures or parties—or to fashionable slogans and keywords such as corruption or environment. But in cases dealing with HIV/AIDS or development assistance, the private paper clearly supports the official line. *The Daily News* style of reporting tended in 2006 to be somewhat more ritualistic, but according to the 2010 sample, that difference has disappeared.

The government paper seems to have set the framework of the established journalistic mode in the country. Papers using the Swahili language have obviously been more successful in resisting this mode, while a medium such as *The Guardian*, searching for both authority and a fairly large circulation, does not have space to depart radically from the mode it established in the 1930s.

THE NAMIBIAN MEDIASCAPE

As South African (SA) ruled Namibia, it used radio systematically as a propaganda medium, while the press remained an arena for struggle and debate. Although SA's control was tight, private ownership of the print media was accepted in principle

(Amupala, 1989). This contradictory history is still visible in Namibia today. The availability of newspapers per 1,000 inhabitants is highest on the whole continent of Africa, although the total number of newspaper copies remains around 80 000[2]. The population of 2.2 million is offered four daily newspapers – one in Afrikaans, one in German, two in English; in addition, there are three English-language weekly newspapers, one free-of-charge tabloid and a dozen magazines. Of the newspapers, all but *The New Era* are owned privately. The *Namibia Broadcasting Corporation* (*NBC*) has a monopoly over nationwide radio and television. It broadcasts in eight languages. The language services have a long tradition, because the policy of the apartheid rule was to approach each of the various language groups separately.

All the *NBC* radio services for years carried daily–in fact, twice daily and in all the languages used by the *NBC*–"Chat Show" programmes which have popularly been called the "People's Parliament" (Kivikuru, 2006). The Chat Show is comprised of phone-in questions, an answering service and an opportunity to criticise, debate and chat about politics.

These programmes have run since 1992; the basic idea was to motivate so-called ordinary citizens to participate in public debate. In May 2007, the Information and Broadcasting Ministry made the first attempt to muffle the programme. Protests against the limitation of citizens' right to speak were so strong that "Chat Show" was allowed to continue. In March 2009, however, the Ministry closed down all "Chat Show" programmes except the evening English broadcast, and in 2010 the programme disappeared completely.

Commentators interpreted closing down almost the entire "Chat Show" as trying to calm the media landscape before the elections in November 2009. Hard-line SWAPO members had been appointed to central positions on the Namibian Communications Commission, and the Ministry made attempts to establish a state-run media council. Further, the Ministry several times expressed its concern about the extremely popular daily short-message-service (SMS) pages in *The Namibian*. Often carrying messages similar in tone to discussions on the "Chat Show," the participants eagerly comment about politics and public institutions. All this indicates that Namibians are accustomed to discussing public matters in public. Notably, Namibian newspapers openly express their views in editorials and columns only once a week, on Fridays.

The well-to-do urban population subscribes to foreign satellite services, but they receive their national news predominantly via the *NBC*. The government owns *The New Era*, the news agency *Nampa* and the *NBC*. The dominant party SWAPO has its newspaper *Namibia Today* and is co-owner of a satellite service supplier, *MultiChoice*, which transmits entertainment channels. The government thus has a strong hold on the media system, and its grip is getting stronger. The government has frequently had conflicts with the media, especially with *The Namibian,* but also with the *NBC*.

Namibia thus has a tradition of a diverse mediascape, where the citizens are accustomed to discussion and debate. Today, the German-Language *Allgemeine Zeitung* concentrates on issues around the German language, tourism and commercial farming (von Nahmen, 2001); the Afrikaans-language *Republikein* is strongly business-oriented. These two papers are owned by the same publisher, who also distributes a tabloid called *The Sun*. The weekly *Windhoek Observer* is an interesting combination of sensationalism and hot political news.

In the following sections, two Namibian papers—one commercial and one government-owned—are scrutinised. *The Namibian* is a natural choice for the independent/commercial paper—it is the largest-circulation paper and a symbol of western-style journalism. *The New Era* is the only government paper available. It is a newcomer on the mediascape. My claim is that when the government paper emerged onto the mediascape

labelled with diversity, it had to adjust itself to the existing journalistic culture in an attempt to create relative editorial independence.

The Papers Studied

The Namibian started publishing in 1985. It was founded by a group of anti-apartheid liberals, whose figurehead, Gwen Lister, is still the editor. The paper was the stronghold for the Namibian independence struggle, including SWAPO.

When the country became independent, SWAPO found it difficult to tolerate the paper starting to criticise the party, now that it was a power-holder. The government has banned the paper since 2001; government institutions are not allowed to advertise in *The Namibian*, and the paper is not distributed in government offices. Today the paper publishes four pages daily in the Bantu dialect Oshiwambo. With circulation of around 20,000 copies,[3] the paper is the largest in the country. It comes out daily from Monday to Friday, with a large weekend supplement on Friday.

The New Era started as a weekly in 1992. Its publisher is a company owned by the Namibian government. The paper now comes out five times per week. No official circulation figures are available, but the number of copies printed is considerably less than that of *The Namibian*, perhaps 6,000-8,000. The paper devotes two pages to four indigenous languages, varying the language from day to day. The paper has bureaus in the regions outside Dar-es-Salaam. The leadership of *The New Era* has been turbulent, and the paper has changed its editor-in-chief several times.

Both papers are tabloids, but each issue of *The Namibian* is larger[4]. Both have 5-6 pages of advertisements every day. The majority of the advertisements cover public announcements, tenders, and job openings, but also consumer goods for sale. Many public institutions also place their advertisements and notices in *The Namibian*, although the government has officially banned the paper.[5]

Both papers have a similar structure and layout. *The Namibian* uses more pictures, and while the quality of its visual journalism is slightly higher, one could not claim that photojournalism is highly valued by either of the two papers. *The New Era* is quite formal in its photo policy—portraits of politicians and civil servants—but it also publishes a daily picture page portraying businessmen, entertainers, Miss Namibia contestants, and sports heroes. *The Namibian* constructs such a picture page only for its Friday editions. Both have a specific profile for the Friday issue: editorial, opinion columns, comments and letters-to-the-editor. Neither of the papers carries an editorial every day. The letters-to-the-editor texts are serious, often criticizing either politicians or public institutions. *The Namibian* started its popular daily SMS pages in 2008.

Both papers focus a considerable volume of text on foreign countries; more than half (53%) of all articles in *The Namibian* and more than one-third (40%) in the *New Era*. Articles about Africa, especially southern Africa, dominate foreign news coverage (*The New Era*: 45%; *The Namibian*: 37%). According to this study, the foreign coverage was almost identical in both papers. The main source was the national Namibia Press Agency (*NAMPA*), which is a client of the major international news agencies. Extremely few foreign news stories are written by local staff members. The main categories of stories about foreign affairs were political and economic news, plus reports on public administration (Simberg, 2011).

The entertainment material in both papers covers light features, mainly on American movie stars and musicians. Both also regularly publish humorous man-bites-the-dog human interest stories. The sports pages in both papers focus on football, rugby and boxing. The papers keenly follow what happens in the British football, rugby and cricket leagues. The *New Era* has a slightly stronger domestic orientation in its sports news. The national leagues are followed as well, but African sports

get far less attention than the British. Extensive reporting on The World Cup competition in South Africa (2010) was an exception.

It is important to remember in a study focusing on journalistic culture that some staff members of the government paper have worked previously at *The Namibian*. The country never experienced a merry-go-round in journalistic circles similar to that which roiled the Tanzanian mediascape when more-liberal winds started to blow, but there has been mobility between the various media, even surmounting language barriers. The *New Era* has also added staff from the national broadcaster and South Africa.

The newspapers that *The Namibian* and *The New Era* published during three periods—February 26-March 2, 2007; April 21–27, 2009; and August 16-20, 2010—have been studied. The sample covers altogether 15 days, because the papers are not published during the weekend. The homepages of both, especially *The New Era*, were considerably improved in 2009, and there were discussion-based elements added to them.

What was Covered?

The total number of stories indicates growth in *The Namibian,* but *The New Era* carries considerably longer stories than *The Namibian* does. The increase in numbers of stories published by both papers seems to have grown slightly more in *The Namibian* than in the *New Era* (See Table 2). The difference is limited and the theme areas they share appear to be the same in 2009 and 2010: domestic politics, African affairs, domestic events, sports, and economy, and especially on Friday entertainment. The scope of shared themes was slightly different: in 2007, African affairs, sports and domestic events dominated, while in 2009, the order was domestic politics, sports and domestic events. In 2010, the focus on African affairs was understandable because the Southern African Development Community (SADC) summit was

Table 2. Focus in The Namibian and The New Era (2007, 2009, 2010)

	Number of stories			Same themes		
	2007	**2009**	**2010**	**2007***	**2009***	**2010***
Namibian	235	305	577	10%	9%	15%
New Era	181	203	204	11%	15%	20%

* The number of stories refers to issues covered by both papers. The percentage refers to numbers of stories covered by both papers. Most joint texts are extensive and include pictures, but the papers try to keep the front page for their own scoops.

held in Windhoek during the sample period. Due to this exceptional event, the proportion of shared themes in this sample obviously was larger than normal.

It can be stated that the sphere of mainstream journalism is limited in Namibia. The different media still focus on different communities in the country, partly language-based[6], partly distinct for other reasons. *The New Era* serves more the state-administration and the middle-class public, while *The Namibian* caters to the urban middle- and upper-class public.

The media compete over how they cover themes, not over what themes to cover. The level of homogeneity is still quite low, but it indicates growth, and time disparities also offer an explanation. For example, both papers published reports from the 2009 floods in the north, but with almost a week's interval, while in this analysis compared only the issues published on the same day.

The considerably low level of mainstreaming also could be interpreted as an indication of weak news collection infrastructures. For foreign coverage, both papers depend primarily on the national *NAMPA* relaying material from the global news agencies, and as indicated in Simberg study (2011), the foreign news coverage was almost identical in both papers.

During the 2007 analysis period, the two main events reported broadly in both papers were the Zimbabwean President Robert Mugabe's official visit to Namibia and the Windhoek Magistrate Court's report on the death of a well-known Windhoek businessman. *The Namibian* carried a

total of 15 articles and features on Robert Mugabe and Zimbabwe, while *The New Era* carried 12 articles and features. The coverage on Robert Mugabe was more extensive than is usual during normal state visits, although official visits are an important part of politics and thus always well covered in Africa. Mugabe suggested to Namibian officials that Zimbabwe and Namibia cooperate in producing power to fulfil the growing electricity needs of Namibia's population. Mugabe's visit was also met with demonstrations. Both papers covered these stories, although the articles were placed differently within the issue.

A theme relevant for so-called ordinary people was the dairy industry's announcement concerning a drastic rise of milk prices on Monday February 26, 2007. Another theme that touched both politicians and ordinary people was electricity: EsKom, a power supplier in SA, threatened to stop selling electricity to Namibia that it needed to fulfil SA's own growing domestic needs. The shared themes in 2007 also included Parliament news, reports from the ministry and public institutions on unemployment, droughts, plus the usual run of accidents and crimes. *The New Era* gave more space for regional news, but both papers indicated a strong Windhoek focus in all the three samples.

The foreign news coverage in 2007 focused on southern Africa. In the *New Era*, the all-African focus was slightly stronger. More than two-thirds of the foreign articles came from southern Africa, Nigeria and Uganda. The second sample week (2009) was more "normal" in the sense that nothing special happened, despite the general elections approaching in November 2009. The country was recovering from dramatic floods in the northern parts of the country, the Parliament was discussing the budget, the International Monetary Fund gave its report, and SWAPO's 49th birthday led *The Daily News* to publish three extensive stories of the achievements of the country's leading party. Stories of this nature were totally absent from *The Namibian*. Both papers covered the South African elections extensively.

The foreign news sources were the same for both papers: the national news agency *NAMPA*, plus the international agencies is a client to, namely *Reuters, Agence France-Presse (AFP)* and *the Associated Press (AP)*. Even the headlines were often the same in both papers. Especially in reporting on economic matters, experts appeared to be quite an important source. The two papers did not use the same sources, but the themes were similar or the same. Opinion columns on Fridays (3-4 in each paper) had a personal tone, and the themes were distinctly not party-political. *The Namibian* has a slightly more outspoken style, but it still distinctly represented the same journalistic culture. The main mode of expressing opinions in these papers is undoubtedly indirect, that is, based on news transmission and on the selection of themes, sources and perspectives. In the case of *The Namibian*, the SMS page (2008) appeared to be an important arena for opinionated voices.

The sample week in 2010 was very exceptional, because the SADC Summit was organised then, and the president of the country celebrated his 75th birthday. Both papers carried an editorial on the SADC meeting on Friday August 20, 2010. The coverage of the SADC Summit was larger in *The New Era*, but perhaps surprisingly, *The Namibian* covered the president's birthday more in-depth. *The New Era* carried more than 20 pages of happy birthday- advertisements by various public institutions, but the paper's journalistic coverage was limited, while *The Namibian* had a supplement honouring the president.

The two most prevalent changes between 2007 and the more recent samples were, on the one hand, *The Namibian*'s daily SMS pages and on the other, the more active style of reporting in the *New Era*. In 2009, some two-thirds of the *Namibian*'s SMS reactions dealt with politics or the behaviour of public institutions—mainly failure to deliver services—while the rest were individual outbursts or criticism toward an individual. In 2010, the purely political content hardly reached to one-third, while for example, the president's birthday created a wave of greetings. Further, the delivery of goods, health services and pensions were on the agenda. The SMS pages are edited openly, with the newsroom guiding the discussion, but the policy seemed to be quite liberal. Although the paper is banned by SWAPO, most ministries give answers to direct questions posted on the SMS pages.

The political SMS comments dealt with party politics, and the majority were critical to the government or the leading party. The style in 2009 was quite arrogant, but seemed to have cooled down in most 2010 quotes as shown:

When a controversial statement is made by a Swapo member, it's freedom of speech, while by the opposition, it is insulting of the leaders. Who is fooling who now? (The Namibian, April 22, 2009)

What is the thing about the President appointing governors? How about democracy where people choose their leaders? Stop appointing wrong people into wrong places. (The Namibian, August 18, 2010)

The lively homepage of the *New Era* website is not the only sign of change in the government paper. Its journalistic standard has improved since 2007, but stories such as the SWAPO birthday report (2009) and Heroes' Day preparations (2010) show that the paper still frequently publishes documents straight from the bureaucracy sources, without polishing them much.

Especially in 2009—perhaps because of the elections year—both papers devoted more attention to the northern regions of the country. Further, both tried to reach out to the youth, but those attempts were not very well thought out: the papers seem to approach small school children and teenagers with the same type of material.

A third quality shared in 2009 was no doubt a reflection of the slightly changed mediascape in Windhoek: the appearance of tabloids has probably led these two papers to emphasise banal, insignificant details—129 penguins sent to South Africa to be washed after an oil spill (2009) collected almost as much attention as the oil spill itself, and an auction of zebras and rhinos by a game park (2009) was placed on the front page of both publications.

The situation seems to have calmed down slightly in the 2010 sample, but the news selection has become strongly personality-centred and favours sensational themes. Misuse of funds has been a popular theme on the front pages both in 2009 and 2010; on Friday August 20, 2010, *The Namibian* offered on its front pager a heavy scoop of misuse of funds in one of the country's central organs, the trade unions ("Pension scandal, BIG hot potatoes on NUNW [National Union of Namibian Workers] agenda"). The headline font in both papers is currently bigger than in 2007, but the headline style appeared more sensational in 2009:

Drug mule escapes from Magistrate's Court holding cells. (The Namibian, April 22, 2009)

One year in jail for breast groping. (The Namibian, August 20, 2010)

A Closer Look at the Coverage

During the 2007 period studied, the two papers had the same theme on the front page four times: Mugabe's visit, the Zimbabwean promise of a power plant, milk prices rising and the investigation about the death of a Windhoek businessman. In some cases, the placement of the article also indicated differing views. *The New Era* published a news item about Mugabe's programme on the front page and a news item about demonstrations against Mugabe on page 3, while *The Namibian* placed the demonstrations on the front page and skipped the formal report entirely. Instead, it carried on pages 2 and 3 two other stories tending to be critical of the government.

In the 2010 materials, the total proportion of shared themes was larger than before, but not once during the week did the papers have same themes on the front page. *The Namibian* muffled down the SADC meeting, placing its reports on the inside pages, while reporting on two days about the Windhoek police attempt to ban all demonstrations attached to the Summit. *The New Era's* front page was clearly that of a government paper. The business community's surprise party in the honour of the President also received attention on the front page. In 2010, both papers seemed to share their front pages between heavy news and interesting details like crime stories.

A considerable volume of the themes reported in both papers originate in press conferences, giving both papers the same sources. One-source reporting was marked in both papers in all the three samples. These stories were public reports, civil servants announcing something, police information and political speeches. Reports on political speeches were rare; far more often, the source was a public official or a representative of an NGO. Reports by organs such as SWAPO, UNESCO or the International Monetary Fund received a formal treatment. It was extremely rare for either paper to use ordinary people as sources.

Both Namibian papers had a strong national focus. There is a clear competition for news between the papers, perhaps less distinctly in 2009. Open opinions are rare–especially in *The New Era*–but the papers still discuss with each other. In the themes they cover, the focus is mainly on delivery, the politics behind the themes is discussed less. In 2009 *The Namibian* was slightly more ideological in the themes it reported about budget debates, but it also gave more space to reports about the opposition parties than the government paper. In 2009, both seemed concerned about the "struggle kids" and the "born free" youngsters who would first be entitled to vote in the following elections; these themes were described as elements able to shake the political boat.

Attitudes toward tribal differences (2007) and problems in adjusting the modern society and the traditional leaderships to each other (2009) were almost identical. Both were reserved in the issue of traditional leaders, challenging the need for double authorities and the credibility of an extensive traditional-leader component.

Both papers were also openly interested but reserved about the BIG (Basic Income Grant), a social policy pilot project aimed at balancing differences between the rich and the poor in the country through a "citizen salary" given to every person under 60 years of age. The reservations seemed to have weakened somewhat in 2010. The reporting style is similar in the two papers, *The Namibian* being slightly more outspoken. However, the difference in opinions is often distinct in editorials on the same theme:

NamPower-Zim Power Deal Needs Thorough Analysis. (The Namibian, Friday March 2, 2007)

Another Neighbour's Door Opens. (The New Era, March 2, 2007)

The Namibian suspected that Robert Mugabe tried to get financial support from Namibia for Zimbabwe's deteriorated power industries, while *The New Era*–acknowledging that the contract must be studied carefully–considered the Zimbabwean offer as a relief for Namibia from difficulties in power delivery after the eventual South African retreat. Therefore, the government paper expected that the information about the deal made by the government was valid, while the commercial paper suspected the deal. Examples are provided as follows:

Namibia's SADC test. (The Namibian, Friday August 20, 2010)

SADC pins hope for Pohamba. (The New Era, Friday August 20, 2010)

The Namibian stresses that the chairmanship of SADC, given to the Namibian President during the Summit, puts a great responsibility on the shoulders of Hifikepunye Pohamba. The SADC faces a number of accusations: the organisation has published declarations and recommendations; it has not had sufficient strength to oppose its member-state Zimbabwe; SADC set up a tribunal in Windhoek, but its operational policy remained vague; in other cases as well, the implementation of agreed policies has been delayed or totally forgotten. President Pohamba has a tough task ahead of him to accomplish all that has to be done in a timely manner, says the paper, concluding its editorial with almost a threat:

It is a fact that if he fails to act timeously, both history, and most particularly the people of Zimbabwe, will judge Pohamba harshly.

The first four paragraphs of *The New Era's* editorial focus on the importance of SADC as an organ for African cooperation, and the paper notes that SADC's implementation policies have improved enormously. Nonetheless, the editorial hints that behind closed doors, stormy discussions have been carried out, especially about Zimbabwe. *The New Era* emphasises that it is important to reach a consensus on these issues. The paper also declares that the regression of gender equality in SADC countries' parliaments should not be tolerated.

In fact, the substance of the two editorials is not contradictory. The themes selected are almost identical, but *The New Era* has adopted a declaratory style in its phrasing, making the strongest stand in an issue that is least controversial, namely the gender issue. *The Namibian* criticises SADC but confesses that the organisation is important. The paper's view about SADC's future is less optimistic than *The New Era*'s.

An area where the two papers clearly differed (2009) is media policy. *The New Era* did not show great interest in media matters, while *The Namibian* carried multiple stories about issues linked to media ("State media get more handouts from Govt," April 21, 2009; "MPs demand more TV time," April 23, 2009; "SWAPO hardliner on NCC board," April 24, 2009). Quite interestingly, neither of the papers discussed plans to establish a media council in the country, although a seminar on the matter had been arranged. In 2010, both papers published several news pieces on the proposed Information Bill in South Africa, which they interpreted as prohibiting press freedom. None of the papers took an open stand, but they were equally concerned, measured by the frequency of published news items on the subjects.

In sum, during the three periods studied, the performances of the two papers were surprisingly similar. In general, *The Namibian* seems to have slightly more resources and vigour, but the style of reporting, use of sources and selection of themes are similar. The standard story in both is a one-source report, based obviously upon a press conference. Both papers use quite critical tones, especially when the delivery of goods and services by public agents is concerned. The general image is discursive and inclined to debate. Quite interestingly, the layouts of their opinion pages strongly resemble each other.

The role given to the President of the country was modest in 2007 but considerably larger and more political in 2009 and 2010. President Hifikepunye Pohamba was shown as a ritualistic figure in 2007. In 2009 he was described as a counterforce to the former president Sam Nujoma, in *The Namibian* quite openly, and in *The New Era*, more implicitly. In 2010, the president was the central figure in the big events in the country. Quite interestingly, the private paper described his

personal history mildly but analytically, while the government paper's journalistic contribution came late and was far more superficial, even reserved.

The Mugabe case (2007) exposed a distinct difference: *The New Era* represented the power; *The Namibian* represented an opposition force, suspicious of the line selected by those in power. *The Namibian's* coverage was not strongly critical towards Robert Mugabe as a person—rather, the paper criticised his policies. African journalism respects other countries' leaders, and this reticence came up not only in the case of Robert Mugabe, but also in the reporting on the President of Malawi, who was accused of corruption. A similar stand was detected in the texts of both papers also in 2010. It was Zimbabwe more than Robert Mugabe that was criticized. In several SMS contributions in *The Namibian*, it was even emphasized that Mugabe has told the world the cruel history of colonialism.

In 2009, *The New Era* was more linked to governmental and parliamentary proceedings, especially around the annual budget, but it also had a fairly strong regional focus. In addition, the government paper collected some scoops (e.g., the new situation with the floods) distinctly a few days ahead of *The Namibian*. Both gave strong attention to the IMF report, although it did not make any special references to Namibia; international organs still receive considerable attention in the country.

What was new in 2009 what the fact that *The Namibian* devoted a full page to SMS messages following the style used the *NBC Chat Show*, forbidden only a month before. Roughly, one-third of the SMS page, consisting of some 30 messages per day, focused on political issues, the others mainly dealing with individual or event-based matters. In 2010, the SMS pages often expanded to two pages, but the content was clearly less political than it was the year before.

The use of other languages than English appeared as a very complicated one–it is commercially important because the majority of the population speaks a language other than English as their mother tongue. *The Namibia's* focus on only one dominant indigenous language, Oshiwambo, seems more solid than the policy exercised by *The New Era*, which changes the regional languages every day. In principle, such an approach appears as more democratic, but as a marketing tool, it might become counter-productive. In general, both papers seem to have a tendency to republish on their vernacular pages translations of news items which has come out 1-2 days before on the English-Language pages.

Despite efforts to reach to the regions, both papers are strongly oriented "inwards," to the urban middle-class audiences. They obviously assume that these audiences follow public issues keenly and thus it is unnecessary to provide background for the stories. During the sample weeks in 2009 and 2010, crime reports appeared on the front pages of the papers. The prominent place could not be explained without background information about the people involved—but neither of the papers offered such background. In this way, it can be said that both of the Namibian papers still represent a kind of small-circles reporting. Their communities are partly different, but they assume that their audiences have shared interests and are hungry to get more information about relevant themes they have experienced.

Especially, *The Namibian*'s crime reporting style is quite crude. The paper publishes the name of a woman who has passed out after heavy drinking and has been robbed (e.g., August 19, 2010). The paper also prints the names and pictures of people who have committed suicide. Some years ago, The *Windhoek Observer* sold well with its detailed descriptions—with pictures—of horrible murders of whites committed by members of the black community. The legacy of this type of journalism has its signs in present-day journalism, more strongly in *The Namibian* than in *The New Era*.

APRIL 27, 2009: TWO WORLDS

April 27, 2009 appeared in all four papers as a day strongly focusing on domestic issues. Some items were identical: the South African elections and pirates attacking ships close to Somalia. There were no news about Namibia in the Tanzanian papers and no news about Tanzania in the Namibian papers. More precisely, the African focus of the two Tanzanian papers was on East Africa, while the two Namibian papers, in addition to South African elections, reported about Angolan business and road conditions on the Zambian-Caprivi border. Thus, it can be claimed that the papers in the two countries seemed to live in two different Africas, where foreign news is concerned.

The two Tanzanian papers focused on a domestic ceremonial day (Union Day), while Namibian papers devoted space to South African elections. They stressed the uncertainty of the results for political developments in the neighbouring country. Quite interestingly, neither of the papers referred to Namibian elections, which were only a few months ahead. What was similar to all four papers was the interest in the political bigheads, presidents and ministers, even such as Robert Mugabe, whose policies were challenged. This general respect for authorities could be linked with state fragility, or rather the different composition of the state in Africa (Wuff Moe, 2010).

The two Tanzanian papers wrote considerably more about political issues, but mainly the agenda was set by the government and various ministries: issues around corruption and HIV/AIDS campaigns, plus developmental projects were popular. Contradictions were reported, but the actors were well established, well-known politicians and civil servants.

The relationship to politics was in fact quite interesting in all four papers. The Tanzanian papers published varying views on well-known facts and themes, but no real political discussion or debate was found in them on that particular day. Sometimes *The Citizen*–a small private quality paper–has brought the downslide of the dominant party into a discussion, but the two big papers rarely accept that kind of themes on their pages.

In Namibia, where political contradictions are considerably stronger than in Tanzania, political tensions are far less dominant in the papers, and so was it also on April 27, 2009. Some disagreements in the Parliament were published, predominantly with volumes reflecting the political power the MPs represented, but for example, the connection between politics and delivery was not made in critical stories about the road conditions. For example, before the elections of 2009, the dilemma of the "born free" generation was "discovered" by a social scientist, not by the media which eagerly joined the bandwagon.

SIMILARITIES AND DIFFERENCES

Compared to the Namibian papers, in 2006 both Tanzanian papers devoted considerably more space to political reporting. However, the most popular theme was the same as in Namibia: the delivery of services and malfunctions of public institutions. The basic policies were not challenged. In 2009, the party political emphasis seemed be cooling down in Tanzania and warming up in Namibia, but still, Tanzania appeared as considerably more politics-oriented. And the publicity around the Tanzanian president grew enormously by 2010. The Namibian president also received far more coverage in 2009 and 2010 than in 2007, due to his growing prominence as a representative of a particular political group within the SWAPO party. The same was repeated in 2010, when he was elected as SADC chair. However, his popularity was still more limited than that of his Tanzanian colleague.

Although the shared area was as limited in the Tanzanian papers and much more so in the Namibian ones, both Tanzanian papers included in their reporting several large articles which were in accordance with the basic ideology of the country: articles on agriculture, education, women's status, climate warning and malaria. The Namibian papers do not have as large a shared sphere, and development did not get a regular coverage.

In all four papers, two areas were shared: entertainment and sports. The volume of foreign news has been considerable, more than one-third of the total content. However, stories about Britney Spears, Madonna and Slumdog could perhaps be described as indications of good marketing by news and feature agencies. These wide–in *The Guardian* almost enormous– stories carry little relevance for any of the countries studied. The considerable volume of sports news from the UK and the U.S. could perhaps also be explained by its colonial past.

Genuine foreign news indicated differences. The two Tanzanian papers offered a wider scope of foreign news. They covered the rest of Africa to a considerably larger extent than the two Namibian papers. Namibian papers, perhaps due to the isolation the country experienced quite recently, did not feel a similar need to cover the outside world to the same extent. This became evident especially in the issues on April 27, 2009, included in the sample from both countries. The coverage of eastern Africa was broader and more consistent in the two Tanzanian papers, while the focus in the Namibian papers was almost entirely on South Africa. Quite interestingly, all four reported on the Somali pirates and the IMF, the Namibian papers far more extensively. In the case of the pirates, obviously traditional news values had their share: the pirates were oddities in the 21st century, and there was also a proximity aspect in the theme.

THE FIRST DEFINITION: SLOW TO CHANGE

On a very general level, Boyd-Barrett's idea of peripheral communication vehicles, adopting the modes dominant in the core societies, still carries relevance. The papers studied in Namibia and

Tanzania all attempt to fulfil the textbook ideals of a "free press". Private ownership stands for freedom and openness, public ownership stands for regulation, if not censorship. On the other hand, the dominant form of the existing media structures in the society provides a counterforce. As contradictory as it might sound, journalism in general tends to be quite conservative–no radical changes. The public is assumed to be accustomed to a particular form of reporting, and the new ideology is only gradually implemented properly in the journalistic praxis. On the level of rhetoric, the change takes part considerably faster.

The newspapers in Tanzania and especially in Namibia have quite a limited shared sphere, less than one-third of the total journalistic content. In Tanzania, shared values are expressed in both papers by publishing articles on areas generally accepted in the country. In Namibia, that dimension is not as well developed as in Tanzania. This contradiction is interesting: formally and by the basic orientation, the two Namibian papers resemble each other considerably more than do the two Tanzanian papers, but the shared sphere is larger in the Tanzanian papers. It can perhaps be claimed that thanks to its longer record of independence and its fairly smooth and stable development, the basic social values in Tanzania are better established than in Namibia, where the society is divided into a variety of interest groups separated by great economic differences.

Why are the journalistic cultures in the two countries so different, then? The answer calls upon peripheral autonomy. The historical past has been different in these countries, and this is why the media vehicles take different, nation-based forms. Since the early 1960s, Tanzania has been a source for various pan-African and especially eastern African unification policies, while Namibia has remained isolated as an outsider.

Diversity in the mediascape is an ideal in both worlds. Democracy requires a multiplicity of voices to be heard on the public arena; Senghaas' quest for regulated isolation does not fit in today's world. The present journalistic cultures in the countries are an interesting mix of the colonial heritage, the country's recent history and fringes of globalization culture. No doubt the dependences in communication modes are not deliberate or planned, but rather a spill over type phenomenon as Galtung (1971) claims.

Mainstreaming is modest in the papers in both countries: the core of reporting on a general level–mainly political reporting, focusing on the national level and taking part in the capital city–is found in both papers in both countries, but there is also considerable space for individual reporting on relevant (state machinery operating on various levels) as well as irrelevant topics (crime news, reporting on gossip, rumours and beliefs) rarely found in more industrial societies. In fact, compared with northern mediascapes, the two African newspaper spheres seem to have considerably more space for making a genuine journalistic profile of their own.

The results of the empirical analysis seem to support the significance of first definition in media vehicles. *The Namibian*, *The New Era*, *The Daily News* and *The Guardian*, resemble each other far more than *The New Era* and *Daily News*, or *The Namibian* and *The Guardian*. Ownership does not appear as a distinctive factor. The younger medium wants to offer a "new voice," but also to be accepted as a legitimate part of the journalism vehicle.

The layout and writing style in the Namibian and Tanzanian papers also resemble each other. This is natural from the standpoint that journalists move from one medium to another, and the mobility has primarily been from the older medium to the younger one. In Tanzania, there was a real merry-go-round in the early 1990s, when journalists from the publicly-owned media moved to better-paying private media positions. A similar change took place in Namibia, although much less dramatically. Several *New Era* editors-in-chief have worked at *The Namibian*. The professionals bring with them their professional ideals and knowledge. The situation is no doubt complex, because the new medium also wants to offer something new to the public, but it is bound to the existing journalistic culture, concerning both the presentation and news selection.

Herbert Gans (1980, p. 39-64) discusses the prevalence of Thomas Jefferson's "small-town pastoralism," the old moral order still offered by urban American media in the 1960s and 1970s. An equivalent to Gans' examples is the observation that all the four African papers still tend to focus in more detail on the countries with which their societies previously had a colonial-type relationship: British and South African sports, South African society and economy.

No doubt the strong reliance on global entertainment is explained largely as an attempt to please the youth. In both of the societies studied, there is a concern about how to reach to the younger generation. The Tanzanian society has had time to adjust to the fact that younger generations view the society differently than the generations who took part in the struggle for independence (Ekström, 2010, p. 248-253).

In these contradictions embedded in the journalistic culture, the public/private contradiction becomes if not trivial, at least less important. It does carry some significance, and no doubt the government and private media are treated in different ways by decision-makers when something exceptional occurs. It is easy to find examples of this, especially from Namibia, where political conflicts are more common than in Tanzania. But the Namibian examples also indicate that if a commercial medium is strong enough, as is *The Namibian*, the hands of decision-makers are partly tied: the power-holders cannot live without the biggest paper in the country, even if they dislike its editorial line. In Tanzania, the government paper, despite of its limited circulation, enjoys the firstborn rights, while in Namibia, the government paper, when trying to exercise liberties as does the private press, has had occasional difficulties with decision-makers.

It appears as if the press, government-owned as well as private, had been able to acquire more operational space for their functioning in Namibia, where political contradictions are sharper than they are in Tanzania. *The New Era* has been able to benefit from the struggle that *The Namibian* went through in the 1980s and 1990s. There is less rhetoric and more operational space–it might be misleading to call it freedom–than in Tanzania, where the political development has been smoother. In Tanzania, the press, public as well as private, has partly remained prisoners of *gazeti journalism* developed during colonialism: public information that the power-holders allow to be announced. One more contradiction is that the two Tanzanian papers appear to be far more party-political than the two Namibian papers, although the political situation in Namibia is More tense than it is in Tanzania.

All four papers reported somewhat on development campaigns, but in Tanzania, development seems to be far more "institutionalized" than it is in Namibia. It is reported on as a public activity like education, health, or traffic. Politicians and public institutions deal with development action, but it is rarely reported as a citizen activity. The evidence seems to support the claim by Amin Alhassan's (2004, p. 214) that "communication for development is re-articulated as communication for bureaucratic control." In short, the emphasis on development can be turned into a control mechanism, as well.

It was misleading to propose, based on the content analysis, that bureaucratic journalism does not have any space in Namibia. It does. In countries with limited or weak newsgathering systems, public institutions are "safe" providers of a continuous flow of information, and thus the media circle around them. The recent boom of public relations in both countries indicates that in the near future, government ministers and ministries are going to get rivals on the private side. Well-trained and well-paid PR officers provide the media with "ready-made" information packages and no doubt get access to the sphere of the media; there are already examples of this phenomenon. The distinction between public information and PR is not as clear in Africa as in Europe. Most journalism schools offer PR programmes, and they are more popular than journalism programmes.[7]

A remnant of legacies from history can be traced down in the foreign coverage of all four papers. The Namibian papers cover foreign items to a far less extent than the Tanzanian ones do, but the selection of material is haphazard in both. In sports, the papers follow the media of the former colonial powers. In entertainment, they select materials which have the support of the strongest marketing apparatus. In features, difficult problems found at home, as well, are projected to a far-off country. Concerning Africa, formalism has a strong position: the papers report on state visits, announcements of various public officials and the doings of the African Union or the SADC, but for example Darfur received very little coverage. In Tanzania, the East African region received attention, to a large extent as a reflection of growing political and economic interests. The linkage to power is easily found also in the fact that reporting from Burundi and Rwanda has grown considerably after these two countries were included in the East African Community and the East African Common Market Protocol.

Public Connection Missing

Based on the previous considerations, it is obvious that the public/private contradiction, in fact, is a fairly uninteresting detail in sub-Saharan mediascapes, brought there mainly via a rhetoric that originates from the so-called North. Instead, a real hindrance for the media to become supporters of citizenship is the fact that the media do not know how to operate with fragmented audiences and non-hierarchical management styles. The public connection that Couldry et. al (2007) refer to is still missing. Disregarding ownership mode, the Namibian and Tanzanian papers still talk to

privileged elite—this is perhaps why it has been so difficult for them to expand their circulations. Their attempts to reach out to the critical masses via entertainment and sports appear almost vulgar. Both Mark Deuze and Oliver Boyd-Barrett, while analysing a national journalistic skills audit carried out in South Africa (Deuze, 2002; Boyd-Barrett, 2002) talk about a need to extend practical skills of journalists to include cultural and critical reflexivity to be able to meet the critical masses:

Perhaps not enough is therefore said about how the very nature of journalism is defined and is changing, and how the respective struggle between 'commercial' and 'public sphere' functions of the media is playing out over time, and with what implications for the culture of the newsroom, how the new reporter sees the job and anticipates what is required of him or her. The movement towards 'lifestyle' reporting is one element of this: but does this also suggest that journalism is increasingly commercial, even becoming an adjunct to merchandising? How might this affect how young journalists regard their profession? In addition to asking how well journalists are doing their job, it is also reasonable to ask whether news institutions are defining the nature of the job in a suitably challenging and worthwhile way. (Boyd-Barrett, 2002, p. 95)

Boyd-Barrett talks about a mediascape distinctly more sophisticated than that of Namibia or Tanzania, but the concerns are the same. The contradiction between public and private might become a relevant and important topic for African mediascapes in the future, but before reaching that point, the media have to learn to talk with the citizens. So far the freedom rhetoric, especially strong in Tanzania, has focused on the freedom of the sender, this is the medium or the journalist (Rioba, 2009), while the rights of the receiver—that is, the citizen—have been put aside. Official institutions have become representatives of the "common good." Undoubtedly, the existence of political and social institutions is a signifier of "normality" of life that is not as self-evident as in the so-called North with its innumerable social safety-nets. It is comforting, when the media announce that there are institutions which have the responsibility to promote the well-being of the so-called ordinary citizens. All one-source stories are not worthless in that sense.

However, it is no doubt true that the newspapers in both countries still focus more on the elites in society, not the masses. The masses have had other means to express themselves, both via the traditional oral culture still very much alive in the two societies, in Tanzania and via the mass organisations during the CCM party monopoly period. But in a deeper analysis, both layers appear to be somewhat problematic. Although both societies have tried to plug the traditional culture and, for example, the paramount leaders, into the modern society, the success has not been complete. In the Namibian papers from 2009, this aspect was frequently discussed: the traditional leaders appeared to snatch a larger portion of public life and thus to construct a society with various layers. The same phenomenon has occasionally emerged in Tanzania. Mass organisations in Tanzania have died with the multiparty system. Though they were lead from above, grassroots activities allowed ordinary people, especially the youth and women, to express themselves in public matters. Such a dimension has now disappeared. It could be said that the public sphere which once was emerging has not taken off. It has never really reached the cities properly.

Somewhat surprisingly, the community media have not taken off in either country. Instead, in Namibia, representatives of the public, the so-called ordinary citizens, have learnt to express themselves in the modern media system better than citizens in Tanzania. The *People's Parliament* and *The Namibian's* SMS columns indicate clearly that ordinary people are prepared to express themselves too, mainly by asking about socially relevant issues, not proactively by bringing up new dimensions for discussion. It could perhaps

be claimed that social contradictions brew and gradually develop a public sphere, while a more peaceful development such as the case in Tanzania does not instigate new dimensions of social activity, when an ideological change takes place.

More lifestyle reporting and ordinary people's perspectives would no doubt be also financially profitable, increasing readership. The media could gradually move toward the people's media which Clemencia Rodriguez (2001) has talked about. More letters-to-the editor, more online discussions, more contact pages are needed. These forms of citizen participation are still framed by the sender, but the at least space is given to citizen voices, rare in the present circumstances. Of course, it is worth remembering what another study of African togetherness (Tynes, 2007) says of the substance of mediated communication in the troubled Sierra Leone:

If maintaining solidarity becomes too prevalent, then the listserv develops into a place for virtual friendships or a simple social-gathering oasis. It would lack a unifying purpose beyond sharing affect, would become more like a meet-and-greet online bar, where users might vent about the events of their day. If maintaining the signification of a nation significantly outweighs the other two dimensions (working on a political project, maintaining a solidarity), then a purely cultural commune, filled with aesthetic and philosophical text objects, will solidify. The nation would be discussed, however, the conversations might remain at the level of intellectual sparring or simple information exchange. [---] The list becomes a place to discuss politics only, which is closer to a state-based activity and further away from nation-imagining. (Tynes, 2007, p. 511)

The two mediascapes discussed here are far less dramatic than the one in Sierra Leone, which has been able to exist only in cyberspace. In Namibia and in Tanzania, the very fact that people-in-the-street or, rather, people-in-the-villages would have a chance to a "meet-and-greet media bar" would be quite a victory. It is perhaps wise not to count too much on new technology. James Ferguson's (2006, p. 113-154) description of the idealistic, short-lived Zambian internet magazine *Chrysalis* documents how the exercise actually became a battlefield for the elite. The Namibian "Chat Show" on radio became extremely popular because the ordinary people had previously not had an opportunity to say anything about public issues. In the "Chat Show," as well as on *The Namibian's* SMS pages, they have been able to do so, although the moderator frames the arrangement. The contacts with the citizens can be crucial in the future. As Thussu (2007) has elaborated about a television channel in India, the "Murdochization" of news might easily take the poorly resourced African media by surprise, and in such a process, the rhetoric of freedom might be crucial if it prevents professionals from seeing what is happening.

By "going native" [by using local journalists and by joint foreign/domestic ownership] and celebrating that process, a transnational corporation makes a gesture towards a given national culture and through assimilation transforms itself into an acceptable, even nationalist face of globalization. [---] (S)uch a transformation provides the transnational corporation with a greater degree of credibility and therefore with demographically desirable audiences for advertisers, on whose largesse the media edifice ultimately rests. (Thussu, 2007, p. 608)

Today, the Namibian and Tanzanian papers are sheltered because they are not assessed as interesting and profitable, neither by local elite nor by the Murdochs of the world. Television is by far more fascinating in the eyes of the political and financial elites. But with the new technology, the future might be different. National newspapers might give local credibility for transnational actors. So there is a possibility for the emergence of the brutal dependence forms which Boyd-Barrett talked about in the 1970s.

The answer is hardly Senghaas' demand for deliberate isolation, but no doubt our genuinely "own" journalistic voices and modes can construct a barrier against domination. In that sense community media and the multi-media centres (Teer-Tomaselli & Mjwacu, 2003; Dralega, 2008; Jallov, 2011) are more than just a favourite baby of northern donors. They offer a possibility for African journalism to find a voice of its own, but this does not mean that more conventional forms of journalism could be put aside. Community media are perhaps an equivalent to public journalism or civic journalism in the North–both are important as professional eye-openers, but they do not offer a mainstream path.

Increased credibility via locality and reflexivity in the sense Deuze and Boyd-Barrett (2002) talk about is not solved only with use of language. Local-language pages in Namibian papers and the vivid Swahili press in Tanzania point to the right direction, but the problem is deeper. The challenge is to address the masses. The problem is not easily solved in countries which colonialism left with centralized administrative structures and the independence struggle with a quest for nation-building. As long as the common person is only allowed a role as a victim or a target, the addressing does not hit the right chord.

There is a standard answer to this problem: development communication, communication for change. But this is a challenge which journalism in most African countries has lost. Development has either disappeared from the media agenda as it has done in Namibia, or it has been bureaucratised as in Tanzania. The coverage of development projects belongs to routine reporting, but the enthusiasm to change things–which labelled the large literacy and health campaigns in the 1970s and 1980s–is gone a long time ago. Journalism respects the money coming from outside and hence files reports on a new project or a campaign, but the enthusiasm has faded away.

This is hardly the case with globalisation. In India (Fürsich & Shrikhande, 2007), concerned voices have been heard about the fact that globalisation seems totally to engulf conventional development communication. New alternative models are needed to sustain the mandate of development in commercially-driven multichannel systems. Far more important than the ownership mode and even media laws in Africa is to the need to learn to discuss and reflect with the people, not to the people. This applies to the so-called North as well. Perhaps one very practical dimension is the fact Nick Couldry is referring to: to distinguish voices from talk (Couldry, 2010). By voices, Couldry understands people's practice of giving an account, implicitly or explicitly, of the world within which they act. This voice is not political, demanding for action and change—such accounts are placed under the concept of "speech" in the similar way as Aristotle does. Some 70-80% of the news stories in the papers studied had only one source, definitely a "speech."

Let the voices to emerge in the journalistic agenda!

REFERENCES

Alhassan, A. (2004). *Development Communication Policy and Economic Fundamentalism in Ghana*. Tampere, Finland: Acta Universitatis Tamperensis.

Amupala, J. (1989). Developmental *Radio Broadcasting in Namibia and Tanzania: A Comparative Study*. University of Tampere, Department of Journalism and Mass Communication. Report No 27.

Appadurai, A. (1996). *Modernity at Large: Cultural Dimensions of Globalization*. Minneapolis, MN: University of Minnesota Press.

Arendt, H. (1998). *Between Past and Future: Eight Exercises in Political Thought*. New York: Penguin.

Arntsen, H. (2009). *Drawings for Change? A view of the Zimbabwean 2008 General Elections as Interpreted by News Cartoons. Paper presented in the NordMedia09 Conference*. Sweden: Karlstad.

Berger, G. (2007). *Media Legislation in Africa: A Comparative Legal Survey*. Grahamstown, South Africa: Unesco & Rhodes University.

Boyd-Barrett, O. (1977). Media Imperialism: Towards an International Framework for the Analysis of Media Systems. In Curran, J., Gurewitch, M., & Woollacott, J. (Eds.), *Mass Communication and Society* (pp. 116–135). London: Arnold & Open University Press.

Boyd-Barrett, O. (2002). More research needed on changing nature of journalism re 'commercial' and 'public' spheres. *Ecquid Novi, 23*(1), 94–95.

Couldry, N. (2010). *Why Voice Matters: Culture and Politics after Neoliberalism*. London: Sage.

Couldry, N., Livingstone, S., & Markham, T. (2007). *Media Consumption and Public Engagement. Beyond the Presumption of Attention*. Basingdale, UK: Palgrave. doi:10.1057/9780230800823.

Dahlgren, P. (2001). The Transformation of Democracy? In Axford, B., & Huggins, R. (Eds.), *New Media and Politics* (pp. 64–68). London: Sage. doi:10.4135/9781446218846.n3.

Davies, M. M., & Mosdell, N. (2006). *Practical Research Methods for Media and Cultural Studies: Making People Count*. Edinburgh, UK: Edinburgh University Press.

Deuze, M. (2002). Global journalism education and Sanef audit: major issues to be taken seriously. *Ecquid Novi, 23*(1), 89–93.

Dewey, J. (1996). The Collected Works of John Dewey, 1882-1953. Charlottesville, VA: Intel ex. Corporation.

Dralega, C. A. (2008). *ICT Based Development of Marginal Communities: Participatory Approaches to Communication, Empowerment and Engagement in Rural Uganda*. Oslo, Norway: Faculty of Humanities.

Edström, Y. (2010). *"We are like Chameleons!" Changing mediascapes, Cultural Identities and City Sisters in Dar es Salaam*. Uppsala, Sweden: Acta Universitatis Upsaliensis.

Ferguson, J. (2006). *Global Shadows. Africa in the Neoliberal World Order*. Durham, NC: Duke University Press.

Fürsich, E., & Shrikhande, S. (2007). Development Broadcasting in India and Beyond: Redefining on Old Mandate in the Age of Media Globalization. *Journal of Broadcasting & Electronic Media, 51*(1), 110–128. doi:10.1080/08838150701308101.

Gans, H. J. (1980). *Deciding What's News: A Study of CBS Evening News, NBC Nightly News, Newsweek, and Time*. New York: Vintage Books.

Gathara, P., & Wanjau, M. K. (2009). Bringing change through laughter: Cartooning in Kenya. In N.J. Kimani & J.J. Middleton (Eds.), Media and Identity in Africa (275-286). Edinburgh, UK: Edinburgh University Press.

Golding, P. (1977). Media Professionalism in the Third World: The transfer of ideology. In Curran, J., Gurewitch, M., & Woollacott, J. (Eds.), *Mass Communication and Society* (pp. 291–308). London: Arnold & Open University Press.

Habermas, D. (1996). *Between Facts and Norms: Contributions to a Discourse of Law and Democracy*. Cambridge, UK: Polity Press.

Hamelink, C. (1983). *Cultural Autonomy in Global Communications. Planning National Information Policy*. New York, London: Longman.

Howley, K. (2003). *Community Media. People, Places, and Communication Technologies*. Cambridge, UK: Cambridge University Press.

Jallov, B. (2011). How Can the Internet and Social Media Contribute to Development Communication for Empowerment. In Braskov, R. S. (Ed.), *Social Media in Development Communication*. Roskilde, Denmark: Roskilde Universitets Trykkeri.

Kivikuru, U. (2000). *An Arm of Democracy for Promoting Human Rights or Simple Rhetoric? SSKH Medelanden 54*. Helsinki, Finland: University of Helsinki.

Kivikuru, U. (2006). Top-Down or Bottom-Up? Radio in the Service of Democracy: Experiences from South Africa and Namibia. *Gazette, 68*(1), 5–31.

Konde, H. (1984). *Press Freedom in Tanzania*. Arusha, Tanzania: East African Publications.

Mártin-Barbero, J. (1997). Cultural decentring and palimpsests of identity. *Media Development, 44*(1), 18–22.

Media Institute of Southern Africa. (2008). *So this is democracy? State of media freedom in Southern Africa*. Windhoek, Namibia: MISA.

Media Institute of Southern Africa. (2009). *So This is Democracy? State of media freedom in Southern Africa 2009*. Windhoek, Namibia: MISA.

Mrutu, E. (2008). *Community radio in Africa. Case study: Tanzania*. Unpublished Licentiate Thesis, University of Tampere, Tampere, Sweden.

Ndlela, N. (2007). Broadcasting Reforms in Southern Africa: Continuity and Change in the Era of Glocalisation. *Westminster Papers in Communication and Culture, 4*(3), 67–87.

Ngwanakilala, N. (1981). *Mass Communication and Development of Socialism in Tanzania*. Dar es Salaam, Tanzania: Tanzania Publishing House.

Nordenstreng, K., & Ngwanakilala, N. (1987). *Tanzania and the New Information Order. A Case Study of Africa's Second Struggle*. Dar es Salaam, Tanzania: Tanzania Publishing House.

Nyamnjoh, F. (2005). *Africa's Media, Democracy and the Politics of Belonging*. London: Zed Books.

Ramaprasand, J. (2002). Tanzanian Journalist Profile: Demographics, Work Background, Choice of Profession, and Assessment of Press Freedom. *International Communication Bulletin, 37*(1-2), 2–17.

Rioba, A. (2009). *Media in Tanzania's Transition to Multiparty Democracy. An Assessment of Policy and Ethical Issues*. Unpublished Licentiate thesis, University of Tampere, Tampere, Sweden.

Rodriguez, C. (2001). *Fissures in the Mediascape. An International Study of Citizens' Media*. Cresskill, NJ: Hampton Press.

Saul, J. S. (2008). *Decolonization and Empire. Contesting the Rhetoric and Reralitry of Resubordination in Southern Africa and Beyond*. Johannesburgh, South Africa: Wits University Press.

Senghaas, D. (1977). *Weltwirtschaftsordnung und Entwicklundspolitik*. Frankfurt, Germany: Plädoyer für Dissoziation.

Simberg, N. (2011). *African News Flow in Africa – New Patterns or Old Habits? African News Coverage in two Namibian and two Tanzanian Newspapers*. Unpublished Master's thesis. University of Helsinki, Helsinki, Finland.

Teer-Tomaselli, R., & Mjwacu, T. (2003). Developing the Communicative Competence: the Potentials and Limitations of Community Radio. In Malmelin, N. (Ed.), *The science of caring/transmitting. Communication perspectives to society, culture and citizenship* (pp. 24–43). Helsinki, Finland: University of Helsinki.

Thussu, D. K. (2007). The 'Murdochization' of news? The case of Star TV in India. *Media Culture & Society, 29*(4), 592–611. doi:10.1177/0163443707076191.

Tynes, R. (2007). Nation-building and the diaspora on Leonenet: A case of Sierra Leone in cyberspace. *New Media & Society, 9*(3), 407–518. doi:10.1177/1461444807076980.

von Nahmen, C. (2001). *Deutschsprähige Medien in Namibia. Vom Windhoeker Anzeiger zum Deutschen Hörfunkprogramm der Namibian Broadcasting Corporation. Geschichte, Bedeutung und Funktion der deutschsprachigen Medien in Namibia 1898-1998*. Windhoek, Namibia: Namibia Wissenschaftliche Gesellschaft.

Wiuff Moe, L. (2010). *Addressing state fragility in Africa. A need to challenge the established 'wisdom'?* The Finnish Institute of International Affairs Report No 22.

ENDNOTES

1   The government mimicked only the English-Language papers in the country. The Afrikaans paper *Republikein* and the German paper *Allgemeine Zeitung* are considerably older, and can also claim to be.

2   According to both WAN & UNESCO statistics, there are roughly 130 newspaper copies per 1,000 inhabitants in Namibia, while in South Africa, for example, the figure remains around 50 copies.

3   *The Namibian* is the only paper that has regularly participated in circulation check-ups by advertiser agencies. The reported figures have varied slightly under and above 20,000 copies in the recent years.

4   The average number of pages in an issue of *The Namibian* is 32 on Fridays and 28 for the other weekdays; the average number of pages in an issue of the *New Era* is 40 on Fridays and 20 for the other weekdays.

5   Several years ago *The Namibian* had a conflict with the government over its reporting critical of former President Sam Nujoma.

6   *Republikein* and *Allgemaine Zeitung*, although they share the same ownership, rarely share the same themes on their front pages, either.

7   For example, the main journalism education institution in Tanzania, The Institute of Journalism and Mass Communication at the University of Dar es Salaam, has a BA programme in PR, and in Namibia, the University of Namibia Institute of Communication and Media Studies also offers a specialisation in PR.

- **Tanzania:** Daily News & The Guardian, December 11-16, 2006, April 27, 2009, June 13-19, 2010
- **Namibia:** The Namibian & The New Era, February 28-March 4, 2007, April 22-27, 2009, August 16-20, 2010
- **"Firstborn":** The *Republikein* reflects models found earlier in the South African Afrikaans-language press, while *Allgemeine Zeitung* traces its journalistic ideals to early 20th-century Germany.

Chapter 9
Cultural Pluralism and Democratic Ideation– An African Story:
The Case Study of SABC's Three Ethnic Minority Radio Stations

Brilliant Mhlanga
University of Hertfordshire, UK

ABSTRACT

This chapter focuses on the mediation of cultural pluralism by the South African Broadcasting Corporation's three ethnic minority radio stations: Munghana Lonene FM, Phalaphala FM, and X-K FM.[1] By discussing these radio stations as case studies focus will be on their contribution to democratic ideation, and as forms of political disjunctures and continuities in radio broadcasting policy. On disjunctures, the chapter provides a microscopic perspective of the disengagement with the apartheid period as part of a throwback and as a way of charting a new path for a democratic South Africa. Its aim is to show the structural arrangements created and enacted into law by apartheid that had to be repealed and discontinued after 1994. During apartheid, radio broadcasting had been organised along ethnic lines, beginning with two broadcasting schedules in 1937; one for English speakers, known as service A; and service B for Afrikaans speakers. The 1960s in the South African broadcasting landscape marked the establishment of 'Bantu radio stations', which broadcasted mainly in indigenous ethnic languages. This stencil encouraged the creation of more ethnic focused radio stations in the '80s, which were later embraced by the post-apartheid leaders as a way of engendering cultural pluralism aimed at fostering democratic ideation and social transformation.

DOI: 10.4018/978-1-4666-4197-6.ch009

INTRODUCTION

The value of culture as an element of resistance to foreign domination lies in the fact that culture is the vigorous manifestation on the ideological or idealist plane of the physical and historical reality of the society that is dominated or to be dominated. Culture is simultaneously the fruit of a people's history and a determinant of history, by the positive or negative influence which it exerts on the evolution of relationships between man and his environment, among men or groups of men within a society, as well as among different societies (Cabral, 1974, p. 13).

This chapter presents the 'residual' and 'incremental policy models' as part of the structural continuities which the new democratic transformation process inherited, and as part of the emancipatory project continued with a view to usher a new era. It also seeks to contribute to a critical argument that has so far been largely ignored; the discourse on South Africa's eleven official languages and how the public radio under the auspices of SABC is offering them space as part of the social transformation's emancipatory project. The focus of this chapter, therefore, is to grapple with the postcolonial logic of continuing with ethnic minority media that had previously been created by apartheid to serve specific regions on ethnic lines. An emerging trend from this practice seems to project towards cultural pluralism and particularity. Further, in view of South Africa's changed political terrain and media landscape, theories of ethnic minority media will be engaged, in particular, Stephen Riggins' (1992) models.

In 1996, ethnic minority radio stations inherited form apartheid were renamed and remodelled, but still allowed to keep their original locations and to continue serving the same ethnic groups. However, this time, the radio stations had a new mandate: to serve as public service broadcasters and with a marked existential ethnic remit as opposed to state broadcasters. This move saw radio stations like *Munghana Lonene FM* and *Phalaphala FM*

gaining in stature and with a new mandate. For instance, Radio Venda, initially established in 1965, was transformed to *Phalaphala FM*. But as in the past, the radio station retained Pietersburg as its original, with Venda as the language of broadcasting. This move followed the 1996 crusade by the new South African government to transform the media; in particular, the broadcast landscape from state broadcasting to public broadcasting as part of its democratic ethos. These state policies began with name changes as seen previously in the case of *Phalaphala FM*, which refers to a traditional horn that was used in the village to announce a meeting, or used whenever there was a very important announcement to make.[1] As for *Munghana Lonene FM,* the station was originally established in 1965 as a station for the Tsonga people, and given the name *Radio Tsonga*. The station was also based in Pietersburg, and its first broadcasts were for less than five hours daily. The target listenership at that time was the rural community of the Tsonga or Shangaan speaking people. This policy by the new South African government to encourage the continuation and rise of ethnic hinged radio stations presents a healthy democratic practice within the communicative sphere. More so, it marks the opening of a democratic space and growth of other indigenous languages in the manner that accords them a linguistic profile that historically had been accorded only to English and Afrikaans.

As stated above, *Munghana Lonene FM* and *Phalaphala FM* continue to broadcast from their original location in Polokwane (formerly Pietersburg), Limpopo Province. And as part of the incrementalist policy model their broadcast spectrums have been expanded to cover Gauteng, North West and Mpumalanga Provinces. Further, they each have a transnational following, with *Phalaphala FM's* coverage stretching into Zimbabwe, while *Munghana Lonene FM's* extends to Mozambique and Swaziland. This move by the post apartheid government will further be presented as the 're-tribalisation' of the state but with a thrust towards a new pluralistic democratic dispensation.

As for *X-K FM*, the station was established in August 2000, in Platfontein, Kimberley as a development project under the auspices of SABC. The station broadcasts from 0600am to 2100pm, seven days a week. Its main languages of broadcasting are !Xûntali and Khwedam;[2] with Afrikaans as the language that bridges the ethnic divide. Its footprint covers a radius of between 30 and 50km, and it reaches around 4,500 !Xûntali and 2,000 Khwedam speakers (Mhlanga 2006; 2010). The station operates as a unique community radio station. First, its uniqueness lies in its quasi-self-determining arrangement, although this can be further challenged by the fact that the state, through SABC, devised control measures in a bid to ensure that such a community-centred project does not remain entirely in the hands of the community. Here we see a robust pre-emptive move by the government as part of a control and ownership strategy. It also emerged during research that these control measures are mainly through the management and ownership of the programme production process. Second, its uniqueness, as acknowledged by most of my respondents (some of them at the helm of Public Broadcasting Service (PBS) radio at SABC) is that the station serves two different ethnic communities: the !Xû and Khwe.[3] This radio station as part of South Africa's incrementalist policy model within the project of social transformation presents an example of a localised 'rainbow concept' given that the two communities are known for violent clashes. But by the time of my research in Platfontein my research respondents were eager to highlight the tremendous contribution made by *XK FM* in causing their two often conflicting ethnic groups to co-exist peacefully. In attempting to grapple with these developments as part of the democratic project this chapter seeks to make sense of the politics behind the existence of ethnic minority radio stations as a means of acknowledging and cementing the notion that South Africa is a 'Rainbow Nation'.

CONSTRUCTING A NEW PARADIGM OF CULTURAL PLURALISM AND DEMOCRATIC IDEATION

What is being witnessed in South Africa presents a generalised picture of cultural pluralism masking ethnic particularity. This development is in tandem with the new democratic ethos whose thrust is to be all embracing. As a result, the South African government has set forth a programme of social transformation in which eleven official languages are to enjoy access to a public radio station that broadcasts in their ethnic languages. This is presented as a major democratic imperative. It is also seen as operating in fulfilment of the two most basic tenets of democratic ideation: equality and liberty. Equality is presented as having equal access opportunities and resources (such as broadcasting) or processes that may influence decision-making. An example here is the perceived notion among most research respondents that they own and control the processes of programming and actual programmes for *Munghana Lonene FM, Phalaphala FM* and *XK FM*. Liberty on the other hand to Clifford Christians et al. (2009, p. 91) entails the 'right to mutual influence' such as 'freedom of communication' and expression. In the case of the South Africa's three ethnic minority radio stations, the view that these two tenets exist presents the notion of an existing democratic space in which the ethnic imperative plays a centre stage.

Furthermore, the mere existence of different ethnic radio stations as a whole and as part of the social transformation crusade presents an emancipatory project whose major thrust is also hinged on the object of accelerated public communication with radio broadcasting as a utility. It is this democratic imperative that this paper is interested in. This is coupled with the state-sanctioned ethnic particularity and spatial configurations of ethnic belonging—seen through the regional clustering of these ethnic focused radio stations as they attend to each ethnic group in a given territory or province of South Africa. In presenting the democratic imperative and a notch of social responsibility, this chapter also discusses the continuation of the old public service broadcasting Reithian model with the concept of 'public interest' providing a major spectacle; of course, with some changes in tandem with the changing global media flows. But the major structure and functioning of SABC as a corporation which is answerable to parliament through a body of appointed individuals like the British Broadcasting Corporation (BBC) remains unchanged.

While the project of transforming the SABC has continued within the constructed process of democratic ideation and punctuated by varying political episodes in the 'new' South Africa, very few scholars have set out to interrogate the arcane and, often, blurred nature of the notion of the 'public' in a public broadcaster. With SABC being answerable to parliament through an appointed board which is first subjected to parliamentary scrutiny before being finally appointed and sworn-in by the state president such a move is generally accepted as pointing to the functioning democratic wheels. However, that the whole process may itself be tainted and stage managed by politicians is not considered. The notion of democratic scrutiny herein finds acceptance through the belief that parliamentarians themselves are voted for by the public. However, the issues of cultural diversity and general configurations of public motivations and imaginations are issues worth considering. Often, it is assumed that legislators are the representatives of public will and also that everything they do is for the good of the 'public'. It is on this note that this chapter will interrogate the continuation of the apartheid stencil of ethnic minority radio as remodelled forms of democratic pluralism. This will further lead to the discussion of the attendant cultural ambivalence caused by

the possibilities of maintaining a new hegemonic arrangement within a managed democratic space.

REVISITING ETHNICITY IN SOUTH AFRICA: IN SEARCH OF PLURALISM

South Africa's social transformation process, in particular ethnic pluralism, presents an interesting case for analysis, especially when ethnicity and minority language issues are understood in relation to public radio broadcasting. Seen through the Salikoko Mufwene's (2002, p. 162) spectacles on the growth of a language, it can be argued that these ethnic language radio stations in South Africa act like 'anthropomorphic organisms with lives independent of their speakers and capable of negotiating on their own the terms of coexistence'. First, this is achieved through symbolism and the way they are configured. Second, the symbolism presented by the three ethnic minority radio stations creates a sociolinguistic context through the narration of memory in which different ethnic groups being served are encouraged to celebrate this constructed historicised notion of peoplehood. The symbolism contained therein is further enhanced by the ethnicised broader socio-cultural transformations as seen within South Africa's democratisation project.

Furthermore, its uniqueness lies in the provision of public broadcasting space to eleven official languages. This arrangement contributes to the democratic ideation process by further condensing political, historical and anthropological 'cleavages' into a cultural media spectacle with radio continuing to be the intrigue in most rural communities. In line with the pevious positions, the uniqueness of my case studies is hinged on the fact that nation-building in this case is not placed under the usual African postcolonial monolithic nationalistic lens. These monolithic lenses, as seen across Africa, have particularly been encouraged by the liberation ethos, whose mantra was that, 'for the nation to live, the tribe (ethnicity) must die'. In the case of South Africa, the new mindset seems to suggest that 'for the nation to live, everybody must be included'. As a result, South Africa stands as a typical critic of the monolithic presentation of an ideal nation-building process in Africa. Possibly, it can be further argued that this uniqueness was aggravated by the fact that South Africa's late entry into the postcolonial community. As a late decoloniser South Africa was able to assess the pitfalls of denying the existence of ethnicity in other African countries and set out to do things differently. By embracing every ethnic group--that is, allowing for the celebration of ethnic diversity, we see the creation of a PSB in which all ethnic groups are represented (Lekgoathi, 2009). Without seeking to dramatise South Africa's uniqueness, it must be emphasised that, unlike most Sub-Saharan states that settled for 'nativised' naming of the state, with the name of the state, usually taken from the major ethnic groups, South Africa opted for a mere geographical cardinal location; that is, the name 'South of Africa'.

Apart from the fact that ethnicity has often been considered anathema to the nationalist cause across Africa, South Africa's uniqueness is that by learning from other African countries, they instead decided to acknowledge ethnic identities, at the same time contradicting the ideals of the ANC Charter[4] on which the social transformation process was rooted. The 'charterist nationalism', which gave currency to the social transformation process, at first, denounced race-inclined nationalism in the same way it dismissed ethnic nationalism (Wesemüller, 2005). This could have been a deliberate move aimed at gradually coming back to a nativist form of African nationalism, which was later introduced by Thabo Mbeki. However, one response from my research at SABC provides a telling perspective of the new paradigm on ethnic minority radio stations in South Africa:

...if you want to build a strong nation, it has become clear now that you can only ignore ethnicity and minority languages at your own peril. In South Africa, we have the advantage as a new nation of being born when all nations were already born, so we learnt lessons from them. One major lesson is how to encourage ethnic diversity and yet still celebrate our nation and its ethos. We call that unity in diversity.[5]

It is also imperative to emphasize that 'ethnicity in Africa is more than a mere relic from the past. It is at the heart of the everyday realities of morality, accountability and representation and, as such, needs to form the bedrock of any realistic political theory of the continent' and cannot ignore that fact of life (Chabal 2009, p. 6). In view of Chabal's intervention it can be further suggested that media and politics are inextricably intertwined, particularly where nation building is at the centre and political elites are engaged in a ceaseless effort to unite races and ethnicities in a state like South Africa. In such a situation, media, especially public radio broadcasting, tends to be organised in a particular way to mediate the nation. SABC serves as an example, with its slogans 'Vuka Sizwe' (Re-awakening the Nation) and 'Broadcasting for Total Citizen Empowerment'.[6] In acknowledgement of this fact, Daya Thussu (2009, p. 2), quoting from Silverstone, acknowledges that media in society act as a contributor 'to our variable capacity to make sense of the world, to make and share its meanings'. In Thussu's view, it is in this ubiquity and complexity; its interlocking with the centrality of our everyday lives, that we must understand media with all their social, cultural and economic dimensions.

Furthermore, as this paper attempts to make a case for the centrality of radio broadcasting in post-apartheid South Africa; a country with 50% of its population living below the poverty line,[7] it is estimated that twice or triple 10 million people own radio gadgets so far. South Africa's rural poverty- stricken population is estimated at between 40-49% of the total, thus implying that radio, especially one that is ethnic inclined in its broadcasts; ethnic language stations provide the basic source of information. Given the unemployment rate of over 24%, it also becomes difficult for most of them to have access to other forms of media, like television and newspapers. This is further exacerbated by the remoteness of most rural areas. Similarly, Nkonko Kamwangamalu (2003, p. 233) and Last Moyo (2010, p. 427) add that radio broadcasting seems to have excelled as both a medium and platform for ethnic and linguistic minorities, especially in encouraging the celebration of their cultures, but the experience of television has been poor. Kamwangamalu emphasises that 'in spite of the change from apartheid to democracy, the indigenous African languages remain marginalised (by television and higher education), much as they were in the apartheid era' (2003, p. 233). For example, SABC television has continued to sideline ethnic minority languages, to the extent of prompting some sections of society to begin calling for ethnic minority television stations in the same way as there are ethnic minority radio stations.[8] This information provides a case for radio and is quite telling about the state of radio broadcasting in South Africa. It further compounds Louise Bourgault's (1995) and Fardon and Furniss' (2000) assertion that radio broadcasting continues to occupy a central position as the major medium of communication in Africa.

However, it is worth acknowledging that South Africa has made milestones in seeking to cause ethnic balancing and managing ethnic minority issues and rights. Even during the negotiations at the Convention for Democratic South Africa (CODESA), this issue became one major item on the transitional agenda. The basis of it being that South Africa during apartheid was under the tight grip of the Afrikaner ethnic minority group and, partly, other white ethnic minorities who converged on the use of English as their language of

communication, the CODESA era, as a watershed period of transition, found itself having to deal with the protection of ethnic minorities and, in particular, safeguarding their languages. Similarly, Moyo (2010, p. 426) trenchantly writes:

CODESA aimed to ensure that most of the democratic values, especially the respect for minority rights, became the hallmark of the new post-apartheid dispensation. This was done partly to allay the White minority fears of the retributive backlash from the Black majority who were the victims of the apartheid system...the agenda-setting in the negotiations was actually based on direct influence from the lobby groups that represented the economic, political and cultural interests of the Afrikaner and English people. As minorities they had more to lose if change was spontaneous, unnegotiated and revolutionary.

The suggestion above presents an interesting thesis on ethnic minority issues, especially that while the creation of a post-apartheid landing pad and constitutional safeguards were intended for Afrikaner and English people, its catchment area tended to indirectly benefit other ethnic minority groups. Leon (1998, p. 57) in his argument on the need to protect Afrikaans and other language rights, shares the same view by arguing that:

...A language does not become a living, breathing, growing thing merely because it is officially recognised. A language lives because it is used and respected.....if it is not used and respected it can die despite all the constitutional guarantees in the world, choked by the restrictions of practicality. The future of Afrikaans and other African languages in South Africa will not be determined by legal and philosophical debates about group or individual rights. It will be determined by the actions and decisions of the government, business and those who hold the language dear.

From the foregoing, it is clear that in a new dispensation, there was a need for constitutional safeguards for Afrikaans, as the language of the former coloniser and the colonised (Zegeye & Harris, 2003), especially the coloured communities. It must be highlighted that this forms a point of departure from the attitudes of most other African nation-states as they emerged from colonial rule. In the case of South Africa, however, a new challenge was obtaining whereby Afrikaans, a homegrown language, which is partly a dialect of Dutch, but has grown out of its mix with other African languages, could not be considered as the language for business. This new policy implied that Afrikaans, as both a language and an ethnic group, was being demoted. In view of this development, Mazrui and Mazrui (1998, p. 205) ask whether Afrikaans 'should be treated as just another 'native vernacular'? In response to that question one coloured presenter, who was interviewed at *RSG FM,* summed it up as follows:

Afrikaans is our language. We can claim ownership as Coloured people. We developed it and we are indigenous and natives of this land. When Whites came they only spoke Dutch, etc. Us [sic], their offspring, produced a mixture of these languages. An amalgamation of languages taken from our black mothers, who were either San, Khoe or from other Bantu languages fused with the Dutch to produce a brand of it commonly referred to as 'Fanikalo'. Out of 'Fanikalo', Afrikaans was born. But because White people are academic, they started to develop it at that level. They put the commas & full-stops, and then claimed it was theirs thereafter. The truth is; we are the original speakers of Afrikaans....

This is a well-intentioned and pertinent debate, but this study will not seek to partake in it further than this extent. The intention of raising it this far was to locate this study of ethnic minority radio stations within the matrix of South Africa's ethnic language policy and to tease out issues of ethnicity

and radio broadcasting within the official public broadcaster, SABC. However, if the thesis for this chapter is that other ethnic minority groups have benefitted from a policy motion that had initially been raised with the intention of offering Afrikaans a lifeline, then this study has an interesting issue to address.

MODELS OF ETHNIC MINORITY MEDIA

The discussion of ethnic minority media would not be complete if Stephen Riggins' five models were not presented here. The following are the models of ethnic minority media; the Integrationist model; the Economic model; the Divisive model; the Preemptive model, and the Proselytism model. It is also worth mentioning that there is no clear-cut model that neatly fits a radio station, instead these models tend to overlap. But a brief breakdown of these models is necessary:

- **Integrationist Model:** In this model state authorities tend to subsidise minority media with the assumption that such a move might better integrate minorities into national life. The underlying factor here is the presentation of the state as a 'benevolent institution' (Riggins, 1992). However, on the part of the state, the intention is to monitor minorities and to impede them from imagining political independence. The other aspect is to encourage 'functional bilingualism', as a way of gradually assimilating minorities into majority languages.
- **The Economic Model:** As encouraged by the state it pushes for the spread of a managed form of multiculturalism, which is groomed for the good of the state, usually in line with a managed literacy campaign, and targeted at enveloping minorities. Here the preservation of a language and culture

is not the concern of the state, rather the creation of a vibrant economy is. As a result Multiculturalism, in this case, is superficial, but may be publicly proclaimed as a façade, in the hope that it will not ultimately modify the core values of the State. This form of multiculturalism is usually shallow and not genuine (Riggins, 1992, p. 10).

- **The Divisive Model:** This model was common during colonialism, with the state encouraging ethnicity as a divisive means through which to further its agenda. The case of ethnic radio stations that broadcasted into Bantustans during apartheid provides a case in point.

- **The Pre-Emptive Model:** In this model the state usually encourages the establishment of minority radio stations that it will fund as a pre-emptive arrangement. Usually the intention is to ensure that minorities do not obtain funding from other sources. The case of *X-K FM,* for the !Xû and Khwe, presents a case in point. For example, according to William Heath,[9] when the Xû and Khwe communities organised themselves following the purchase of land at Platfontein, they set out to establish a community radio station. They approached *RSG FM*, as well as other local radio stations for assistance. The Government, through SABC, expressed a keen interest (Mhlanga 2006; 2009; 2010), thus leading to the establishment of *X-K FM* as a decentralised public broadcaster. From this explanation it emerged that the state's approach through SABC was a form of pre-emptive engagement with a view to repelling potential external sponsors. This argument holds in that South Africa now has more than a hundred community radio stations (Mhlanga 2006),[10] most of them with external funding.

- **The Proselytism Model:** Here the state, or any external organisation, tries to reach minorities by establishing a media in their language but the intention being to promote values through the use of a particular language. In some cases, it can be a faith-based organisation that sponsors the establishment of a media institution.

If we consider the discussion of the five models of ethnic minority media before, it can be gleaned that policies are most often formulated as a way of containing and managing ethnic minorities. While it may be acknowledged that during apartheid, the policy of containment was the major issue; pointers seem to suggest that even the new social transformation process had its policies anchored in the integrationist, economic and the pre-emptive models. Similarly, Comaroff (1997) adds that in as much as collective social identity always entails some form of communal self-definition; it is invariably founded on a marked opposition between 'we' and 'others'. As will be seen later, while the PSB theory allows for the conjuring up of the 'we' feeling, by providing a public realm for engagement, it also leads to the creation of boundaries between ethnic groups. This then implies that ethnicity, which is then translated into the collective identity of 'we' against 'them', becomes the new 'public' in PSB; thereby providing impetus to the ability to constantly arouse the consciousness of ethnic belonging using various social symbols and narrations of the past. While this may be progressive and positive, it can also lead to a backlash and chaos. However, in the case of South Africa, this challenge has been managed by allowing each ethnic group to have its own radio station as part of pluralism in a democracy.

Following the previous position it can be gleaned that ethnicity may be perpetuated by factors different from those that aroused it, in that, by continuing the ethnic radio stations inherited from apartheid, for example, the post-apartheid leadership has created a new ideology. This new ideology acts as a counter balance that progressively dismantles apartheid structures while also embracing the audience as rational agents who constantly negotiate their position in society. It is on this note that these five models of ethnic minority radio stations will be used.

RADIO BROADCASTING, PUBLIC CULTURAL TRUTHS AND COLLECTIVE CONSCIOUSNESS

Most African communities have been able to gain a form of attachment of sorts to a radio station based on the enigmatic instance of radio broadcasting; that is the fact of radio as a continuing intrigue in most societies. Apart from the fact that this scenario is a natural human element, whereby people identify with radio that communicates in their language, the imperative is to note that radio in Africa has continued to be pervasive. In South Africa, ethnic radio stations have encouraged ethnic consciousness and group identities. The major reason has been the continuation with the project of a bifurcated state (Mamdani, 1996; Young, 1997); using the inherited apartheid structures the state is demarcated along the old Bantustan lines, with the regional homelands remaining rural, traditional and having low literacy levels compared to the urban centres that continue to hold the niche for modernity and a progressive economy.

As stated before, *Munghana Lonene FM* and *Phalaphala FM* have a history that dates back to the 1960s, except *X-K FM,* a latter day development. According to information obtained from most research respondents at SABC, and confirmed by Lekgoathi (2009) and Tleane Duncan (2003), ethnic radio stations that existed before 1994 served the state by broadcasting into the Bantustan homelands and not to the audiences as the public, thus making them stand out as state broadcasters. Being aware of these realities, the government of Nelson Mandela decided to transform these radio stations into 'public' radio stations, with a new public mandate; to educate, inform and entertain, but still maintaining their

location within their original homelands. However, Tleane and Duncan argue that:

Given the country's past divisions that were based on the homeland or Bantustan system, which, as some argue, have been resurrected in the form of provinces, attempts to build a "provincial identity, culture and character' might be seen as further perpetuating the old divisions and, in fact, in direct opposition to attempts to build a nation (2003, p. 103).

The prior position is influenced by the monolithic position of nation-building in Africa whereby for nationalism to thrive ethnic allegiances must be discouraged. Its assumptions on nation-state formation as a continuous process were disputed by most of my respondents from these ethnic minority radio stations. 78% of them argued in favour of these ethnic inclined radio stations. They added that these radio stations had helped them to develop their sense of belonging in their different ethnicities. Further, they emphasized their allegiance to the state—South Africa. This, they argued, is because they were not coerced into it coming from their own ethnic groups. To them belonging to a state is not a product of coercion. But belonging to an ethnic group creates a sense of duty and responsibility in a democracy.

Given the previous position, it can be observed that while the project of encouraging different ethnic communities to celebrate their unique identities may be seen as divisive as Tleane and Duncan have argued, research actually shows that it can also have a cementing effect. But given the often absolutist monolithic engagement of this discourse as influenced by most nationalists it has become almost impossible to find any scholarly rendition that does not criminalise ethnicity. However, results from this research have shown how ethnic radio broadcasting has led to the creation of collective consciousness; not only within particular ethnic groups but with an outward form of engagement which encourages different ethnic groups to relate with the pride of belonging to the same state–South Africa. The latter forms a major part of what apartheid denied these ethnic communities–the notion of 'public cultural truth' as Christians et al. (2009, p. 85) would argue. This aspect is beyond the episteme of being overly ethnic conscious, but hinged on the notion of social justice and accordance of human dignity for an individual ethnic group. The notion of public cultural truth forms a major hallmark of any democratic society.

In this case, democratic public discourse is often influenced by the freedom enjoyed by members of different ethnic groups as they celebrate their cultural values. Christians et al. (2009) add that cultural truths are continually shifting together with their accorded meaning. In this case meaning can be located within a given ideology of the time but carried through symbolism. In South Africa ethnic radio stations such as *Munghana Lonene FM, Phalaphala FM* and *X-K FM* carry with them a 'anthropomorphic' symbol of cultural existence for their different ethnic communities. Collective consciousness for the different ethnic groups is then created within the ideology of social transformation as an emancipatory project that is seen as allowing for the cause of social justice and respect for human dignity.

At this juncture, it can be stated that radio, as a form of modern technology plays a role in the new form of transaction in which ethnic languages dialogue with the state in fulfilment of the cause of human agency, thus presenting a localised form of contra-flows, where radio feeds back into the ethos of South Africa's state formation process and the ideals of social transformation of celebrating 'unity in diversity'. The latter as a democratic normative paradigm is seen as performing an emancipatory role, thus leading to the celebration of cultural tourism (Comaroff & Comaroff, 2009). Cultural tourism, in this instance, uses modernised forms of communication to find an economic value for ethnicity as part of cultural tourism. The advantage of this approach, if assessed using Comaroff's (1997) proposition is that through radio ethnicity

is being perpetuated, this time, by a medium that is quite different from the one that would have caused its emergence.

From the previous statement, it can be further stated that when a message is communicated using a particular language it creates a 'we' feeling as part of ethnic belonging (Mhlanga, 2010), hence the view that language is the 'mother tongue' (Mazrui & Mazrui, 1998). In the case of South Africa, radio has taken advantage of this situation thereby presenting new lifeline to ethnicity. The three ethnic minority radio stations have captured the centrality of communicative action in ethnicity, by conjuring up a sense of ownership ('we' feeling) among their different ethnic communities. This has increased radio's popularity ahead of other types of media (especially newspapers, magazines and television).

Returning to the notion of the subliminal 'we' feeling that ethnic radio creates while at the same time encouraging the observance of the concept of the 'public' in a public broadcaster, it was also observed that radio seems to have substituted the role of traditional community elders. Further, an assessment of programme schedules showed that all the radio stations have programmes in which different issues relating to social groups and tastes are discussed; for example, for the girls among the Venda, Tsonga, !Xû and Khwe, their respective radio stations, now play the role of being 'aunts', having to deal with socially delicate issues, ranging from stages of growth to marriage (Mhlanga, 2010). It is, therefore, by being able to perform this function on the part of these ethnic minority radio stations that the 'we' feeling is concretised.

Furthermore, these minority radio stations, as decentralised versions of the public broadcaster, have been able to enhance ethnic diversity and to allow members of the communities to act it. If suggestions by various scholars, such as, Malešević (2004, p. 3) and Eriksen (1993, p. 10) are to be followed, especially Fredrik Barth's (1969) radical perspective that in order to understand ethnicity, the critical focus of investigation is the ethnic boundary that defines the group, not the cultural aspect that it encloses, it can be further argued that these ethnic minority radio stations encourage people to celebrate their ethnic identities by acknowledging the existence of other ethnic groups around them. Ethnicity, therefore, describes both a set of relations and also acts as a mode of consciousness (Comaroff, 1997, p. 72). It can be further gleaned using the case study of the three radio stations, that proximity is one major factor in the celebration of ethnic identities; that is, the closer these ethnic groups are to each other the more likely they are to experience ethnic hatred and rivalry. This can be extended to suggest that the closer in terms of proximity these ethnic groups are, the more likely they are to compete for resources in a democracy. This competition for resources plays the functionality of the awareness and celebration of one's ethnic identity and belonging.

Through these radio stations, ethnic groups do not only celebrate their ethnic identities, but also their social boundaries of group consciousness and collective entitlements. This sense of animosity caused by the existence of social boundaries and being in proximity is also evident among the Venda (*Phalaphala FM*), Tsonga (*Munghana Lonene FM*), and Pedi (*Thobela FM*). Due to their radio stations being located in one building, a story was told of how it was finally agreed that the names of each radio station had to be removed from the building housing the stations, as each group argued that they wanted the name of their radio station to be placed ahead of the others. While such a contest may be easily brushed aside as too weak, when deeply engaged what emerges is a story about the contest for space, visibility and public cultural communication for the different ethnic groups.

The building that houses these ethnic radio stations, as a resource, is seen as symbolic of the nature of phanerons held by society about each ethnic group; that is, the pecking order of being respected as an ethnic group. So, in their view, this meant that an ethnic group whose radio station

was listed below the others was also considered to be weak and insignificant. Following this crisis of naming it was finally agreed that the building would simply be named 'SABC'; that is, a neutral name to which no ethnic group can lay claim. A similar problem of ethnic rivalry was witnessed at *X-K FM*. It was stated that around 2003 ethnic clashes between the two ethnic groups, the !Xû and Khwe, were prevalent. Even the location of each ethnic group is clearly defined, with the radio station and the school acting as boundaries (Mhlanga, 2006; 2009). The Khwe are on one side of the school, while the !Xû are on the other. *X-K FM*, as a radio station, therefore plays the role of being a unifier.

However, this celebration of ethnic identities on one hand, and rivalry, on the other, presents a paradox in a state that boasts of ethnic diversity and of being a 'Rainbow Nation'. Charles Husband (2000, p. 200) further views this paradox as being based on 'instrumentalised citizenship'; that is, how these ethnic radio stations, in their quest to encourage national identity, as public entities enjoy the 'quasi-legal' status as 'para-statal' and are able to engrave their influence on the histories of each one of these social groups in order to extract from them the inner-core which can be exploited. It is from this state of extraction and construction of symbolic meaning that these radio stations act as 'anthropomorphic organisms' whose lives exist outside the scope of the original speakers of a language. History, Charles Husband further argues, 'carries within it deeply embedded notions of who are the 'real' members of the society', thus encouraging the creation of social boundaries, but radio, being the medium, which captures people's imaginations, has the ability to exploit these histories and create the 'we' feeling. Research findings from the three ethnic minority radio stations also suggest that the concept of the 'Rainbow-Nation' is predicated on this notion.

RECONCEPTUALISING 'PUBLIC' SERVICE BROADCASTING

In order to understand PSB as both a conceptual framework and policy process as part of democratic ideation, there is a need to further engage with the notion of the 'public' in a public broadcaster (Scannell, 1992; Curran & Seaton, 2003). In the case of South Africa's public radio broadcasting, the 'public' has two meanings. First, it is the conventional usage; that is, used loosely, by every politician who wishes to claim 'people-centred' ownership merely by deploying it for political correctness. Second; as a derivative of parliamentary politics with its conventions, whose usage denotes representation, thus implying that the legislators in parliament are representatives of the people and are mandated to act and behave on behalf of the ordinary citizens in the state (Curran & Seaton, 2003). These legislators gain their mandate through elections. Then, through the Legislature, each Member of Parliament (MP) is considered to represent the views of people from their constituencies. Using parliament – as both the institutionalisation of political democratic representation and space for political legitimacy they maintain control and regulation of public broadcasting through an act of parliament.[11]

To Downing (1992), the concept of the 'public' lies awkwardly next to the notion of collective signification. The latter entails ethnic consciousness; how it is raised as a catalyst for nation building, thus feeding into political legitimacy through parliamentary representation. Its fundamental sense entails openness or something common, whose antonym is 'private', 'secret', or 'restricted', Downing (1992, p. 260) adds. Then in South Africa, as in developed democracies, the concept of the 'public' has gained the status of a 'one size-fits-all' approach (Downing, 1992; Scannell, 1992) given its loose use and often deliberate vagueness disguised as a product of parliamentary representative democracy. John Downing in his attempt to provide a classical engagement with the concept, taken from Jürgen Habermas says:

The Basic laws guarantee: the spheres of public and private (the kernel of the latter being the sphere of intimate social relations); the institutions and instruments of the public on the one hand (press, parties) and the basis for private autonomy on the other (family and property); finally the functions of private people–political as citizens, economic as commodity-owners (Habermas, 1962, p. 96, cited in Downing 1992, p. 260).

Similarly, Scannell (2007, p. 234) says the notion of the 'public' has been granted normative value through an act of parliament. More so, this normative value goes with the expectations of a public broadcaster; for example that the SABC should be responsible and able to deliver to the citizens as part of the public cultural truth. SABC's current payoff line, 'Broadcasting for total citizen empowerment', spells it. Here the empowerment of citizens is further encouraged by decentralising the public broadcaster into ethnic regions; thereby embracing ethnic diversity as part of the post-apartheid nation-building ethos. However, while this normative value gains acceptance, citizens remain unable to influence programming, which is managed from SABC Headquarters. This form of command, while hinged on the normative acceptance of the role the government plays in the running of a public broadcaster, seems to thrive on the pragmatic side of control of the 'public'.

This pragmatic use of the 'public' element can be interpreted as an emphasis on the political nature of radio broadcasting as a major security area and a resource for control. In South Africa, the majority of citizens are found in their regions of ethnic belonging, so, radio broadcasting in different languages is always useful for the leaders when communicating with people in their ethnic regions. This assertion was further confirmed at *X-K FM,* with most respondents acknowledging that the station provides a means of communicating with the people on the ground (Mhlanga, 2010). Scannell (2007, p. 234) trenchantly puts it that; 'the rise of consumer capitalism and the mass-media combine with new forms of political management to suborn public life, which regresses to its earlier, pre-modern forms' He further sees this shift as hinged on the notion of morality, in which the state claims legal (normative) grounds for controlling these ethnic radio stations, yet the ultimate end is a pragmatic one which fulfils political ends. In this case 'it is a morality tale of the rise and fall of rational public opinion' which is emphasised (Scannell, 2007). Given this discussion, it can be understood that the three ethnic minority radio stations project a democratic imprint of being people–centred. It is here that the elusive concept of the 'public' gains conventional usage. In reality, the notion of the 'public', in the conceptualisation of a PSB, is political and tends to serve pragmatic ends (Habermas, 1989, p. 8; Scannell, 2007).

Furthermore, the state has a duty to manage and harness ethnicity before it becomes instrumentalised, as it has been elsewhere in Africa. This essentialisation of ethnicity has led to the state's management of the nation-building crusade by being able to register each ethnic group's interest. As a result, these ethnic groups claim to have collective rights within the state, and their ethnic minority radio stations stand as their ethnic symbols. By using ethnic radio stations as subsidiaries of the public broadcaster, South Africa has been able to retribalise the state and to mobilise ethnicity as a major national resource and an ingredient of state-formation (Comaroff & Comaroff, 2009). In such a retribalised state, ethnicity has become a major cultural resource for cultural tourism in furtherance of the state's neoliberal agenda. The three ethnic minority radio stations (*Munghana Lonene FM, Phalaphala FM,* and *X-K FM)* now have a duty, as decentralised public broadcasters, to parade their cultural artefacts in the service of the nation-state. They also work as conduits through which the state's nativist form of nationalism can

be communicated to its citizens. In view of such a development, Scannell (2007, p. 235) says:

The state begins to appear as a permanent public authority that increasingly intrudes upon the lives of the majority. Linked to these historic processes is the emergency of society.

While, according to Habermas (1989), the public has manifested itself through the literary works of print media and its marketable value, in this case radio, forms of 'public' and 'publicness' find expression in societal acceptance and through the languages of broadcasting, with their messages churned through these ethnic minority radio stations.

This approach has created a sense of social trust in these ethnic radio stations, as the media through which hopes and aspirations are communicated. The three radio stations demonstrate a special symbolic effect in the lives of the Tsonga, Venda, the !Xû and Khwe. Further, radio stations, for them, act as modernised technological systems that impart or herald messages, thus fulfilling their public utility role; for example, while, for the Venda, in the past important messages were communicated by blowing the horn, now it is through the radio as a form of 'Phalaphala', which performs a similar function. The station staff, management and presenters, consider themselves to be messengers; duty bound to blow the new modernised horn—the radio, for the Venda people. This has managed to create the feelings of group identity among the Venda people. Similarly, this can be said about other radio stations and their respective ethnic groups.

RELIVING THE BABELIAN EXPERIENCE: ETHNIC BELONGING AND LANGUAGE BROADCASTING

From the foregoing, it can be gleaned that the three ethnic minority radio stations were designed to use their different ethnic languages as subsidiaries to the public broadcaster and to serve the imaginary 'public'–the nation. This is because the nation cannot be pinned down to any physical location. Rather, it remains fixed into the inner recesses of people's imaginations as hope and aspiration. The ambivalence in this conception of a nation is that it is a group of people, as citizens, who clearly identify themselves as different ethnic groups that remain loyal citizens to the state. In such a scenario, ethnic nationalism among black South Africans, as Ali and Mazrui (1998, p. 205) see it, became a manifest destiny. This has created an interesting reincarnation of the biblical story of the 'Tower of Babel'[12], in which a unified effort of people who worked with one language as their medium of communication. From the legend of the 'Tower of Babel' a new concept emerges by ethnicity is understood, herein referred to as the 'Babelian motif'.

Using the 'Babelian motif', I contend that the creation of the structure of apartheid, which lasted more than four decades, had Afrikaans as its central language (the main language of communication), with English as the language of support, in particular, as the language of doing business. However, apartheid's negation gained through the encouragement of ethnic identities that had been contained within the Bantustan homelands. This encouragement of ethnic identities led to self-actualisation and the creation of a collective consciousness, as discussed before.[13] This position may be understood as an oxymoron and as a departure from the perspective, which views the retribalisation of the state as likely to lead to chaos. However, it strengthens the argument of the 'Babelian motif' by showing how the new leaders of independent South Africa, Nelson Mandela and Thabo Mbeki, were able to use these ethnic groups, in particular their languages, to dismantle apartheid and to usher a new type of state formation, based on the ideology of African nationalism (Mazrui & Mazrui, 1998).

This shift informed nativism as a new form of nationalism, derived from Thabo Mbeki's famous speech in 1996; 'I am an African'. The speech provided both an epistemological and ideological blueprint for the agenda of the new state. In it, the discourse of cultural pluralism as a hallmark of democratic transformation emerged. This was more in tune with the new conceptions of public cultural truths, as stated before in which citizens of a new state were charting a new constitutional dispensation and having to celebrate their cultural diversity as cultural and solidarity rights and as part of human dignity. Further, this form of cultural pluralism became the major rallying point for neo-liberalism, which Mazrui & Mazrui refer to as 'ethnic nationalism'. However, in order for it to be communicated to the masses, the transformed SABC, as a public broadcaster, was given a new mandate in which the old apartheid structures of the Bantu radio stations were continued, this time in the service of a new nation-state. Social transformation and the paradigm of a 'Rainbow Nation' then employed the slogans; 'Simunye'[14] and 'proudly South African'. The latter stands as South Africa's proprietary badge in a neoliberal market economy where cultural tourism is celebrated.

Following these ideological positions, the challenge of having to grapple with ethnic pluralism and, in particular, through ethnic minority radio stations that broadcast in different languages is quite enormous. However, it has emerged that the concept of cultural pluralism, which had earlier been encouraged by apartheid through Bantustans, also provided the platform on which to deconstruct the apartheid system. Research on the use of different ethnic languages has been able to confirm that dismantling process as the 'Babelian motif'.

CONCLUSION

This section as an epilogue to this discourse on ethnic pluralism and ethnic minority media in

South Africa's democratic ideation presents a summation of the foregoing arguments. The first observation is on hegemony. From the previous analysis of the three radio stations, three models of ethnic minority media interlock: the integrationist, the economic, and the pre-emptive models. It emerged that the new leadership embarked on a competitive mode, whereby policies are engineered in order to tacitly present an impression of a commitment towards recognising ethnic minority languages, while on the other hand the agenda is the economic front for the post-apartheid nationalist crusade and a policy of containment for these ethnic groups using radio. For example, *X-K FM* shows how the two communities are clearly divided along ethnic lines, with competing versions of histories and suppressed memories. This presents another model, herein referred to as the 'hegemonic model' of ethnic minority media. This model is in addition to the ones presented previously. The hegemonic model acknowledges the role played by politicians in any democratic process. It also takes into account their manipulative effort to want to control radio especially in situations that are like a melting pot in terms of ethnic and cultural diversity like South Africa. A need, therefore, arises to control and own the process of social construction of public cultural truths as meaning making process.

The challenge of ethnic minority radio stations as extensions of the main public broadcaster in South Africa, generally, lies on the one hand with appearing as 'community owned' stations a position that set the sites for a new hegemonic arrangement, while on the other hand we continue to see the state's fingers prints. This challenge fuels the ambivalent scenario of 'public' ownership as discussed before. The hermeneutical question being who the 'public' is in a public broadcaster presents us with an understanding of the notion of the 'public' seen as offering a service to a perceived community, whose existence is further linked to a particularised past as the basis (an ethnie); thus

giving it a sense of responsibility and 'ownership' (Smith, 1986).

It can be further argued that, *Munghana Lonene FM, Phalaphala FM and X-K FM* can largely be seen as fulfilling the tacit policy of containment and assimilation within the broader state project. Through these radio stations, the state has been able to encourage cultural tourism to enhance economic benefits. However, this form of cultural diversity is controlled. This was confirmed by most of my respondents at *X-K FM* who openly complained of being marginalised when it comes to taking national identity cards. Most of my respondents at *X-K FM* added that with these policies they still feel a close natal link with Namibia and Angola, from where they originally came.

However, the fact of 'community ownership', as a product of ethnic language broadcasting, which is constantly translated to mean 'public' ownership, further muddies the water. In this case, a line can be drawn to show how these ethnic radio stations indirectly feed into the government ownership of SABC through the Minister of Communications, a political appointee, thereby serving the ruling party (ANC). However, this paradox of 'public ownership' has gained currency through inculcating the impression that when a radio station broadcasts in a particular language, and is located within the community, coupled with the use of its naming and symbols, it is therefore a people's project. Also the engagement of cultural symbols, as payoffs for these ethnic radio stations, and the use of language as a major cultural tool of communication, seems to buttress the view of these ethnic radio stations as being 'community owned'.[15]

Furthermore, in a question to the station management and presenters on whether they considered their radio stations to be 'community radio stations', responses showed that 71% of the respondents saw these radio stations as community owned. Then another 29% acknowledged ethnic community belonging, but still felt that the stations were answerable to government through SABC, and thus not community owned. However, the 71% also presented a correlation between the radio station's languages of broadcasting, use of certain cultural symbols, such as the stations' crests and the fact that they, as radio station staff, actually came from the communities. This was despite the fact that this view contradicted the outcome of another question that was further raised; that is, whether there was any community involvement in programme production, and 92% of respondents had said there was no community involvement.

For these minority radio stations, when viewed from the perspective of the integrationist model, it can be argued that, by allowing the continuation of these radio stations the state sought to embark on a new form of 'assimilationism' (Riggins, 1992, p.9). As seen previously, when most respondents were asked what they saw as the objectives, purposes and reasons for the establishment of these radio stations during apartheid *(Munghana Lonene, and Phalaphala FM),* 71% cited state propaganda as the main reason for the establishment of the ethnic minority radio stations. When asked what they thought were the reasons for the continuation of these radio stations by the new government (Post-1994), responses from the station management and presenters showed that 63% believed these radio stations were established to cause ethnic empowerment, with another 12.24% citing nation-building. While these responses may have been projecting people's understanding of these policies, as narrated by the leaders, Riggins cautions that:

...because allocating money, time, or broadcast space to minorities reduces the available resources, it should not be assumed that technological and economic transfer are spontaneous gestures of goodwill. Instead, they would appear to be decisions made according to state objectives, which may not be fully articulated in public or necessarily identical with the objectives of minorities themselves (1992, p. 8).

The SABC, as a public broadcaster, has often found itself embroiled within the on-going élite struggles. Public radio as a mass communication project is often seen as likely to help those in power in terms of conjuring public opinion; thus confirming Habermas' (1989) concept of refeudalisation of society or, as Downing (1992) suggests, the colonisation of life-world. It is here that the existence of a public realm in a representative parliamentary democracy is acknowledged. However, it is seen as carrying with it both covert and overt powers. By being able to attract support from a wide section of the public, radio acts as political capital. Further, this notion finds currency through continued reference to the ideals of PSB, whose definition remains 'elusive'. For example, the argument that SABC serves to provide public cultural truths to ordinary citizens; giving them a voice, in particular, to act as a realm in which rational public discourse, debate and free discussion takes place requires critical engagement. However, as seen in the 92% who firmly stated that the public does not get involved in programme production, it is evident that political élites are able to use it in the formation of public opinion and the colonisation of life-worlds.

Further, these ethnic minority radio stations tend to create the 'we' feeling within their broadcasting communities by allowing them to broadcast in different languages. These radio stations had to be embraced for the symbolic meaning that they created in the communities. It can be further argued that while there is some modicum of community service in these ethnic minority radio stations, which undoubtedly can be gleaned, the major thrust was to concretise the new hegemonic arrangement. Following this perspective, it can be observed that the function of these ethnic minority radio stations is to gradually lead to the attainment of symbolic meaning through continued social construction of South Africa's social transformation process as a democratic project. This attainment of symbolic meaning also leads to the continued injection of ideas that are presented, on one hand, as being driven by the public, while; on the other hand, they represent the views of the élite. It is this primed acquiescence, which was displayed by the presenters and station managers, who proudly stated that these ethnic minority radio stations were symbols of their peoplehood. To Slavoj Zizek such a position:

…involves a paradoxical point at which the subject is ordered to embrace freely, as the result of his choice, what is anyway imposed on him (we must all love our country…).[16] This paradox of willingly (choosing freely) what is in any case necessary, of pretending (maintaining the appearance) that there is a free choice although in fact there isn't, is strictly co-dependent with the notion of an empty symbolic gesture… (Zizek, 2008, p. 36).

From the research findings, one can glean that the emergence of ethnic minority radio stations in South Africa becomes the battlefield for managed cultural pluralism (Riggins, 1992). By rebranding these ethnic minority radio stations, a new form of societal renegotiation was engineered; thus aligning them with the ideology of African nationalism (nativism) (Mazrui & Mazrui, 1998; Ndlovu-Gatsheni, 2009a) and neo-liberalism as the sod on which they travelled. This new ideology is alive to global economic trends and the need to enter the market with an 'exotic' agenda, this time hinged on the emergent cultural pluralism and the old ethnic identity, which is now being packaged as the end product of cultural tourism (Comaroff & Comaroff, 2009).

A closer analysis of the positioning of these ethnic minority radio stations presents the entire social transformation process as an ideology. Therborn (1980, p. 2) adds that ideology as a process 'forms part of that aspect of human condition under which human beings live their lives as conscious actors in a world that makes sense, or is made to make sense to them in varying degrees'. Ideology therefore becomes the medium (in the case of the three ethnic minority radio stations)

through which this consciousness and meaningfulness operates, also as part of the 'unconscious psychodynamic processes' (Therborn, 1980). The process of social transformation, with its nativist form of nationalism, has benefited from this 'psychodynamic' effect through various means by which memory is continuously reshaped, with stories being narrated and retold in the endless process of state-formation, hence the celebration of the 'proudly South African' moment and the elusive 'Rainbow Nation'. This consciousness of everyday life and general experiences informs my conception of ideology. However, the establishment of these ethnic groups can be seen as a way of easing the threat to the status quo for as long as these radio stations remain functioning as public broadcasters. Using Riggins' economic model it was observed how the state tends to shift the rules of the game slightly to suit its interests with the channelling of resources by the state usually tightly managed and closely guarded. A closer analysis of *X-K FM,* for example, using the pre-emptive model, shows that when the station was first mooted it was focused on being a community radio station, aimed at being owned and managed by the locals (!Xû and Khwe) and even its board would have been derived from the two communities. The same applies with *Munghana Lonene FM* and *Phalaphala FM* if the new government had decided to discontinue their existence, some of my respondents did highlight the possibility of continuing as ethnic radio stations independent of government. It therefore emerged that the government through the SABC came into the picture by way of capturing the actual processes of ownership and control of the radio station and placing them under the ambit of public broadcasting service. The major factor influencing this form of tacit state capture was the state's availability of limited resources; that is capital, broadcasting equipment, readiness to provide expertise in the establishment and managing a radio station.

In view of the prior suggestion, if one engages with the five models of ethnic minority media, it can be further suggested that while most responses cited ethnic empowerment and nation building, it should be considered that since these ethnic groups had become accustomed to having radio stations, which they considered to be theirs and which broadcast in their own languages, during apartheid, it follows that any attempt to dismantle them would have unsettled the process of social transformation as an emancipatory project. Furthermore, given this background and experience, these ethnic groups could have easily sourced external funding to establish their own ethnic radio stations had the post-apartheid leaders decided to abolish ethnic radio stations. In a bid to pre-empt such a possibility, the government decided to continue with them.

In line with this pre-emptive engagement, an economic and integrationist approach seems to show. An impression of a state, which while superficially committed to multiculturalism attempts to post a progressive streak given the challenges of social transformation. This process as shown previously presents a form of public cultural interest in which social justice and human dignity through the rights to freedom of expression and communication are accorded to each ethnic group. The notion of a 'Rainbow Nation', while remaining elusive, becomes one example of a new multi-culturalist discourse as part of the democratic society.

REFERENCES

Bailey, F. G. (2001). *Stratagems and spoils: A social anthropology of politics*. Oxford, UK: Westview Press.

Barth, F. (1969). *Ethnic groups and boundaries*. London: George Allen and Unwin.

Bhabha, H. K. (1994, 2002). The location of culture. London: Routledge.

Bourgault, L. M. (1995). *Mass media in Sub-Saharan Africa*. Bloomington, IN: Indiana University Press.

Cabral, A. (1974). National liberation and culture. *Transition*, *45*, 12–17. doi:10.2307/2935020.

Chabal, P. (2009). *Africa: The politics of suffering and smiling*. London: Zed Books.

Christians, C. G., Glasser, T. L., McQuail, D., Nordenstreng, K., & White, R. A. (2009). *Normative theories of the media: Journalism in democratic societies*. Urbana, IL: University of Illinois Press.

Comaroff, J. L. (1997). Of totemism and ethnicity: Consciousness, practice and the signs of inequality. In Grinker, R. R., & Steiner, C. B. (Eds.), *Perspectives on Africa: A reader in culture, history, and representation* (pp. 69–85). London: Blackwell Publishers.

Comaroff, J. L., & Comaroff, J. (2009). *Ethnicity. Inc*. Chicago: The University of Chicago Press. doi:10.7208/chicago/9780226114736.001.0001.

Downing, J. D. H. (1992). The alternative public realm: The organisation of the 1980s anti-nuclear press in West Germany and Britain. In Scannell, P., Schlesinger, P., & Sparks, C. (Eds.), *Culture and power: A media, culture and society reader* (pp. 259–277). London: Sage.

Eriksen, T. H. (1993, 2002). ethnicity and nationalism: Anthropological perspectives (2nd ed). London: Pluto Press.

Fardon, R., & Furniss, G. (2000). African broadcast cultures. In Fardon, R., & Furniss, G. (Eds.), *African broadcast cultures: Radio in transition* (pp. 1–20). Oxford, UK: James Currey.

Gramsci, A. (1971). *Selections from prison notebooks*. London: Lawrence and Wishart.

Habermas, J. (1989). *The structural transformation of the public sphere*. Cambridge, UK: Polity Press.

Husband, C. (2000). Media and the public sphere in multi-ethnic societies. In Cottle, S. (Ed.), *Issues in cultural and media studies: Ethnic minorities and the media*. Buckingham, UK: Open University Press.

Kamwangamalu, N. K. (2003). Social change and language shift: South Africa. *Annual Review of Applied Linguistics, 23*, 225–242. doi:10.1017/S0267190503000291.

Lekgoathi, S. P. (2009). You are listening to Radio Lebowa of the South African Broadcasting Corporation: Vernacular Radio, Bantustan Identity and Listenership, 1960 – 1994. *Journal of Southern African Studies, 35*(3), 575–594. doi:10.1080/03057070903101821.

Leon, T. (1998). *Hope and fear: Reflections of a Democrat*. Johannesburg, South Africa: Jonathan Ball Publishers.

Malešević, S. (2004). *The sociology of ethnicity*. London: Sage Publications.

Mamdani, M. (1996). *Citizen and subject: Contemporary Africa and the legacy of late colonialism*. Princeton, NJ: Princeton University Press.

Mazrui, A. A., & Mazrui, A. M. (1998). *The power of babel: Language and governance in the African experience*. Oxford, UK: James Currey.

Mhlanga, B. (2006a). *Community Radio as Dialogic and Participatory: A Critical Analysis of Governance, Control and Community Participation, A Case Study of XK FM Radio Station*. Unpublished Master's thesis.

Mhlanga, B. (2009). The community in community radio: A case study of XK FM, Interrogating Issues of Community Participation, Governance, and Control. *Ecquid Novi African Journalism Studies, 30*(1), 58–72. doi:10.3368/ajs.30.1.58.

Mhlanga, B. (2010). The ethnic imperative: Community radio as dialogic and participatory and the case study of XK FM. In Hyde-Clarke, N. (Ed.), *The citizen in communication: Revisiting traditional, new and community media practices in South Africa* (pp. 155–178). Claremont, CA: JUTA.

Moyo, L. (2010). Language, cultural and communication rights of ethnic minorities in South Africa: A human rights approach. *The International Communication Gazette, 1748-0485, 72*(4-5), 425-440.

Mufwene, S. (2002). Colonisation, globalisation and the future of languages in the twenty-first Century. *International Journal of Multilingual Societies, 4*(2), 162–193.

Ndlovu-Gatsheni, S., J. (2009a). Africa for Africans or Africa for natives only? new nationalism and nativism in Zimbabwe and South Africa. *Africa Spectrum, 1*, 61–78.

Scannell, P. (1992). Public service broadcasting and modern public life. In Scannell, P., Schlesinger, P., & Sparks, C. (Eds.), *Culture and power: A media, culture and society reader* (pp. 317–348). London: Sage.

Scannell, P. (2007). *Media and communication*. London: Sage.

Seaton, J. (2003). Broadcasting history. In Curran, J., & Seaton, J. (Eds.), *Power without responsibility: The press, broadcasting and new media in Britain* (pp. 109–236). London: Routledge.

Smith, A. D. (1986). *The ethnic origins of nations*. Oxford, UK: Blackwell.

Therborn, G. (1980). *The ideology of power and the power of ideology*. London: Verso.

Thussu, D. K. (2006). International Communication: Continuity and change (2ndEd). London. Arnold.

Thussu, D. K. (Ed.). (2009). *Internationalising media studies*. London: Routledge.

Tleane, C., & Duncan, J. (2003). *Public broadcasting in the era of cost recovery: A critique of the South African Broadcasting Corporation's crisis of accountability*. Johannesburg, South Africa: Freedom of Expression Institute.

Wallerstein, I. (1960). *Africa: The politics of independence, interpretation modern history*. New York: Vintage.

Wallerstein, I. (2001). *Unthinking social science: The limits of nineteenth-century paradigms* (2nd ed.). Philadelphia, PA: Temple University Press.

Wesemüller, E. (2005). *African nationalism from Apartheid to post-Apartheid South Africa: A critical analysis of ANC Party political discourse*. Stuttgart, Germany: Ibidem-Verlag.

Young, C. (1997). Democracy and the ethnic question in Africa. *Africa Insight, 27*(1), 4–14.

Zegeye, A., & Harris, R. L. (Eds.). (2003). *Media, identity and the public sphere in post-Apartheid South Africa*. Leiden, The Netherlands: Brill Publishers.

Žižek, S. (2008). *The plague of fantasies*. London: Verso.

ENDNOTES

[1] Brilliant Mhlanga holds a PhD from the University of Westminster. He is currently a member of the Mass Media and Communications Group & a Lecturer in Media Cultures at the University of Hertfordshire, and remains affiliated to the National University of Science & Technology (NUST), Zimbabwe. He is currently working on a number of topics, among them a book titled: *Bondage of Boundaries & the 'Toxic Other' in Postcolonial Africa: The Northern Problem & Identity Politics Today*, and another project provisionally titled: *On the Banality of Evil: Cultural Particularities & Genocide in Africa*. His research interests include: media and development communication, community radio, ethnic minority media, ethnicity, nationalism and postcolonial studies, media policies & political economy of the media. Email: b.mhlanga@herts.ac.uk

[2] The three selected radio stations serve different ethnic groups with the exception of X-K FM which while it is presented as a community radio station which also doubles as a decentralised public broadcaster, it serves to clearly distinct ethnic groups; the !Xû and the Khwe. As for Munghana Lonene FM and Phalaphala FM they serve the Tsonga and Venda, respectively.

[3] This information was obtained from one of my respondents, who also belongs to the management team at Phalaphala FM. He added that the station therefore occupies a very special role within the Venda community, since it symbolises their identity and peoplehood. More information will be discussed in the section of this thesis on the data presentation.

[4] !Xû is the name given to the speakers, the language they speak is !Xûntali, for the Khwe, the latter refers to the speakers, whereas the language is referred to as Khwedam.

[5] This acknowledgement was made by the Group Executive Officer, News and Current Affairs, Dr Snuki Zikalala.

[6] As espoused in the ANC People's Charter of 1955. The charter's preamble captures the spirit that influenced the social transformation.

[7] This statement was echoed by Zolisile Mapipa, one respondent with whom I enjoyed my encounter, in particular with his intellectual engagement with my research. Zolisile Mapipa is the Programme Strategist for Public Service Broadcasting Radio.

8   For more information on this slogan see the following website: http://www.sabc.co.za/ portal/site/sabc/menuitem.3eb4c4b520e08 a22f22fa121a24daeb9.

9   For more information please refer to: https://www.cia.gov/library/publications/ the-world-factbook/geos/sf.html.

10 This information was shared with me by two senior officers at SABC, one being the Head of Radio News and Current Affairs, the other being the Group Executive News and Current Affairs.

11 William Heath was one of my key respondents at *X-K FM*. He is the Manager of Radio Broadcasting Facility, a broadcasting section dealing with the management of technical aspects of broadcasting. Heath was very instrumental in the formation of *X-K FM*. He considers it to be his 'baby', as he put it during my face-to-face interview with him.

12 For more information on Community radio in South Africa see:
http://www.southafrica.info/about/media/ community-radio.htm.

13 For more information on this, please refer to the Broadcast Act of 1999, which was further amended in 2002 and finally had the President's assent on 4th February, 2003.

14 Legend has it that those who constructed the tower of Babel had reaching God as their sole purpose; but the tower miraculously collapsed. Following its collapse, people suddenly discovered that they now spoke in different languages.

15 Here I contend that the creation of the Bantustans with Afrikaans as the major language, coupled with Bantu radio stations (Lekgoathi 2009) was seen as a way by which the system entrenched itself. Contrary to this common position, I contend that that by creating these ethnic radio stations apartheid actually caused its own negation and ultimate demise as a structure.

16 This is the slogan that SABC uses on both radio and television. It means 'we are one.'

17 This view was captured as an answer to Question 16 in the Question Guidelines for Station Managers and Staff, please refer to the appendices.

18 My emphasis.

Chapter 10
The Changing State of the South African Nation:
Political Proximity to Business from a Rhetorical Perspective

Irina Turner
Bayreuth University, Germany

ABSTRACT

The colonization of discourses (Chilton & Schäffner, 2002) is a wide-spread phenomenon of globalization and naturally affects politics. The power of business-speak over politics and the media seems to be steadily increasing. Most vulnerable to that development, which the author calls businification, seem to be countries in transition that have to assert themselves rhetorically on a global scale while keeping traditional voters content at home. In an application of critical discourse analysis, the chapter seeks to trace this businification by comparing three presidential state-of-the-nation-addresses (SoNA) of three South African presidents after one year in office (1995, 2000, and 2010). Through contextualizing these texts with their media reception from a corpus of 15 newspaper articles reporting on the speeches, the outer influences on the core text become transparent. The findings suggest a parallelism between a growing professionalism in politics and the businification of political rhetoric whose development cannot be viewed as exclusively negative.

INTRODUCTION

During this year of action, let us work together to make local government everybody's business. (Zuma, 2010)[1]

In his 2010 state-of-the-nation address (SoNA), South African President Jacob Zuma emphasized the need for public involvement in decision-making. Implicitly, however, by employing business as a metaphor, Zuma revealed what he long had ingrained in his way of thinking, namely: com-

DOI: 10.4018/978-1-4666-4197-6.ch010

prehending government as a business enterprise that can be quantified, measured and optimized; and acting and speaking accordingly.

World-wide, from Great Britain to China, neoliberal business principles of commodification[2] sprawl into all spheres of society from education, arts, religion, to media and politics. In South Africa, pressures of globalization made the young democracy grow up fast and conform to Western expectations (Adam, van Zyl Slabbert, & Moodley, 1998, p. 2, p.140). South African post-apartheid presidents have to fulfill the schizophrenic task of appeasing the international (business) world, while at the same time giving hope to social upliftment back home.

The tendency to assess things according to their market value promotes a generally accepted naturalization of business principles within society via language and media frames (e.g., efficiency, branding, profit-, market-, and target-orientation) which—termed "professionalization"—grow into non-profit oriented spheres of life (Chilton & Schäffner, 2002, p.24); this development can be termed *businification*. The growing power that business principles gain within politics triggers feelings of uneasiness (Adam et al., 1998, p. 140). How far though, does this "colonization" (Chilton & Schäffner, 2002, p.17) really stretch?

Politicians' attitudes towards business are not only displayed in what presidents speak about, but also in how they speak about certain issues. The language itself contains a measure of business proximity through the use of typical terminology (Hundt, 1995; Thomas, 1997), and rhetorical gestures borrowed from business communication.

Based on the observation that presidential rhetoric moves South Africa from a people-centered democracy to an investor-oriented society, this chapter aims at examining traces of business discourse manifested in political and consequently media discourse. The rhetoric analysis (i.e., the focus on an intentional persuasive use of language) of three SoNA's, each held at the opening of parliament after one year in presidential office,

by Nelson Mandela (1995), Thabo Mbeki (2000) and Jacob Zuma (2010)[3] makes this assumption visible. They marked a reflection on past governing actions, and provided an outlook on future plans. Beyond that, the opening of parliament evolved into an emotional media event of pompous proportions comparable to royal weddings on a national level, as Tim Cohen remarked (1995, February 17).

A linguistically-oriented review of 15 exemplary newspaper articles reporting on the SoNA's, will show, how the speeches have been transmitted to the public. Linguistic analysis implies looking beyond content at discourse specific lexemes, semantic implications, framing patterns and genre specific text structure. Language is the common feature among the fields of politics, business, and the media. They are interdependent, because they impact on each other while at the same retaining their "own particular form of institutionalization" (Fairclough, 2002, p. 182).

The contemporary definition of politics as "the business of government" (www.etymonline.com) emphasizes the ever-changing morphology of views as well as the managerial and administrative aspects of government[4]. Politics is only tangible via language and creates reality through speaking (Peters, 2005, p. 754). SoNA fulfills three political functions: they declare the institutional framework for the political order (*polity*), identify action fields and strategies to tackle problem areas of society (*policy*), and lastly, enact and perform the speech to bring the party branding forward (*politics*) (Reisigl, 2008, pp. 244ff.). In this context, it will only be referred to as *politics* subsuming the two other dimensions. Politics regulates the economy[5] while business sustains it. The commercial aspect of *business* (e.g., "pertaining to trade" or "done for the sake of financial profit") only exists since the 18th century (www.etymonline.com; July 2010). Beyond that, *businification* furthermore refers to the continuous formalization of government. In postmodern society, business and politics seem to merge in certain aspects rather than further differentiate. Politics overlap with business in "managing" and "striving towards power" (see Schubert & Klein, 2001) and other features and processes, but the decisive difference remains the goal: Business' primary objective is profit; politics' primary objective is improving the life of its constituency (i.e., the voters).

How can a business discourse be identified? Hundt suggests instead of focusing on the mere lexemes, to rather consider functional features of business language which are triggered by a reference to a "market value" (1995, p. 21). That includes measuring, abstraction and quantification. The guiding maxim of efficiency is closely linked to the objectives of profit maximization and time-management. In modern Western society, time is perceived as a commodity, and therefore "saving time" is desirable (Lakoff, 1985, p. 8).

In a South African context, however, certain connotations differ from Western paradigms (Adam et al., 1998, p. 142). For most South Africans "growth" for instance, still means growing towards the access to basic human rights like clean water, health care, housing and food. The term is ambiguous in the context of a developing country with a staggering divide between rich and poor (Jacobs, 2003, p. 37), because it can simultaneously refer to growing out of poverty or growing market shares and investors' interests.

Another feature of business language is the aggregation of complex concepts and relations in one-word lexemes which are often consequently clarified to a non-expert audience through paraphrases (Hundt, 1995, p. 61ff.). As Thomas (1997) found to be true for annual reports, action-oriented verbs and active voice promote the idea of progress and aggression. Passive voice, non-human agents and forms of *to-be* are however "reserved for those occasions when the writer finds it advantageous to distance himself or herself from the message" (Thomas, 1997, p. 53). While this might not be business-specific, and generally valid for political rhetoric, it is noteworthy to observe how and when

the rhetor creates an aura of natural necessity and causality which shifts away personal responsibility (Thomas, 1997, p. 56).

Perhaps the character of business discourse reveals itself clearest in foreign terrain like So-NA's, since it sticks out by contrast. Presidential speeches are particularly interesting because they epitomize the pivotal point of power and claim to be the mouthpiece of society (Moriarty, 2003, p. 4). A speech is ideal for linguistic examination due to its strategically constructed body and its durable materiality, which is easier to deconstruct than a TV interview for instance (Reisigl, 2008, p. 243). SoNA's are commemorative in character because in terms of their rhetoric purpose, they aim at establishing an identification platform through "the commemoration of a past event considered relevant for the political present and future of an in-group" (Reisigl, 2008, p.254). The speeches simultaneously follow objectives which are deliberative ("asks the audience to judge a future action"), judicial ("a past action") and epideictic ("praise or blame of an individual action") (Moriarty, 2003, p. 8). Their field of action is the formation of public attitudes; their topic the state of the nation. Although one cannot expect aggressive advocating like in an election campaign, public anticipations towards the directive power of the speech are high and the undertone sets the political mood for the coming year.

METHODOLOGY

Rather than judging and criticizing political tendencies, this descriptive diachronic approach aims at showing how the historical shift towards neo-liberal politics in South Africa is reflected in the rhetorical gestures of her narrators; i.e., politicians and the media. Bearing in mind the complex interaction processes between contemporary politics, the media, and business, a "transdisciplinary politolinguistic approach" as advocated by Reisigl

(2008, p. 244) is applied by drawing from critical discourse analysis (Bloemmert, 2006), rhetoric analysis (Moriarty, 2003), and linguistic analysis (Hundt, 1995). The analysis focuses on written text and, therefore, context- related aspects of prosody, gesture, posture, and so forth, are not considered.

The *businification* tendency in political and media discourse is made visible through a two-step method. Firstly, the rhetoric structures of three SoNA's by Mandela (1995), Mbeki (2000) and Zuma (2010) are examined and compared in terms of framing content, rhetoric objectives, and stylistic and linguistic patterns according to a framework by Moriarty (2003). Moriarty analyzed the macro-structure of South African political speeches through the filter of reconciliation. He defined politics as a rhetorical conflict which functions as the motor of society (2003, p. 6) and proposed that first the political discourse in transitioning South Africa changed towards reconciliation, before the historical events realized the constructed reality of the speeches and hence, public speech enabled the end of apartheid (Moriarty, 2003, pp. 3ff.).

In a similar way, like South African politicians changed their rhetoric from struggle to reconciliation, post-apartheid rhetoric moved from a people-centered democracy to an investor-oriented society. The change in language effects a change in people's understanding. Therefore, Moriarty's schema "from struggle to reconciliation" helps to visualize the path "from people to business". Moriarty identified four key elements of rhetorical purpose in political speeches: 1. Creating an opposition, 2. Creating the "us," 3. Creating the current situation, and 4. potential future actions (2003, p. 3).

Secondly, several exemplary newspaper articles drawn from the major South African publishing houses *Independent News Media*[6], *M&G Media*[7] *and Avusa*[8] are reviewed. Emphasis is placed on including articles with an affinity to business (e.g., *Business Day*) as well as those from newspapers known to be critical towards business and government (e.g., *Mail & Guardian)*. The corpus furthermore represents three different genres (summary, reactions from public and experts, and commentary). The analysis of this corpus indicates how speeches have been received by the media during the past 15 years; which frames recurred (Scheufele, 2000) and what tendencies might evolve when analyzing a larger corpus.

SPEECH ANALYSIS

South Africa's first democratically elected president Nelson Mandela is the signifier of the "Rainbow Nation" concept[9], a marketing strategy favored by the ANC and taken on by the public media (Masenyama, 2006, p. 159; Salazar, 2002, p. 18). Shaped by his past as a lawyer, his rhetoric style is not overtly stylized and graphical, but rather "gentlemanly" and "implicit"(i.e., "it does not aspire to present itself as an exercise in the mastery of public speaking, because any such proclaimed command of rhetoric might seem redolent of the old regime […]") (Salazar, 2002, p. 19).

Since the apartheid regime left a legacy of "economic mess" (Sparks, 2003, p. 16), the government's first priority was budget consolidation. Mandela's presidency was known by the social democratic concept of RDP (Reconstruction and Development Programme), which focused on the upliftment of marginalized groups to the benefit of the greater economy. Mandela's 1995 speech was held in a context of great instability. There was the threat of a counter revolution and ongoing 'black-on-black' violence between the ANC and the IFP, which, according to annalist Allister Sparks, "much of the media portrayed as a grim indicator […] for the new South Africa" (2003, p. 4). Mainly through carefully directed discourse and "a series of extraordinary gestures of reconciliation" (Sparks, 2003, p. 5), Mandela managed to avert these threats via language (Salazar, 2002,

p. 27) and hence met the "paradoxical challenge of trying to build national unity while preserving cultural differences" (Sparks, 2003, p. 6; Salazar, 2002, p. 31).

Mandela's successor, Thabo Mbeki, as a former intellectual exile, did not possess the same degree of identification potential for the South African public. This might be one reason why his agenda focused on trans-national identity politics[10]. Rhetorically, Mbeki inherited a difficult legacy. Mandela as the founding father of the nation was able to merge public and private virtues in his speeches, i.e., attach his persona to his political message (Salazar, 2002, p. 40). A truly democratic sovereign, representing the voters as a collective, needs to step back behind the message. Mbeki's solution was to introduce a concept that moves from national to global: "The African Renaissance is a concerted effort to introduce a wide-ranging ideological coherence into the public deliberation [...]. Behind this effort is a belief and fear that once the first and founding phase of the democracy is removed, citizens may lose their direction and waste their efforts" (Salazar, 2002, p. 51). Under Mbeki, the rhetoric shifted from reconciliation to delivery and the tone against racism from within the society became more aggressive (Sparks 2003, p. 12). Mbeki's economic equivalent to the cultural framework of African Renaissance, was the GEAR-program (Growth, Employment, and Redistribution) which resulted on the one hand, in an establishment and recognition of South Africa on the global markets and economic consolidation, while on the other hand, rapidly accelerating the gap between poor and rich South Africans.

In 2008, after a dramatic political showdown around the Zuma Corruption Trial that tore the wings of the ANC apart, Mbeki had to step down as president of the country. Mbeki's successor, Jacob Zuma, promotes neo-conservative identity politics, which are dominated by his image of rising from grassroot level ("the Sheppard") to the top as the first Zulu President of South Africa. Zuma's economic politics seem to follow in Mbeki's footsteps. His relationship with the media is ambiguous. One the one hand, he tasks a personal legal battle against media critics and his government pursues efforts to cut freedom of the press[11], while on the other hand, masterfully understanding how to use the public arena to his advantage. Much like Mandela, he uses his personal life to receive airtime and headlines. Very much unlike Mandela, however, Zuma's appearances are not a reflection of virtue but scandalous at the best of times[12].

A good example for Zuma's media skills is the breach from conventions around the opening of parliament. The SoNA, formerly held on Friday mornings at the first joint sitting after the summer break, "marks the formal beginning of the parliamentary term" (Parliament of RSA 2004, p. 97). While Mandela and Mbeki kept with tradition and declared in an explicit speech act parliament to be open, Zuma broke with protocol by holding the address the night before, at TV prime time, so, as he said, "that the majority in our country, workers and schoolchildren, can be part of the occasion" (Zuma, 2010; Sapa, 2010). This adjustment indicates a growing mediatization of politics.

Although protocol for the outer framework of the speech is highly formalized (Parliament of RSA, 2004, p. 98[13]) and "address" as opposed to "speech" indicates a higher formality (Reisigl, 2008, p. 251), there are no official public guidelines about content and structure of the address itself. All the three presidents chose formal English as their addressing language[14]. Each president held his speech after one year in government, and the speech provided the opportunity to reflect on past achievements as well as to project to the year ahead. One indication of *businification* might be found in the lengths of the speeches which seem to condensate and be further truncated each year (Mandela: 6.645 words, Mbeki: 6.326 words, Zuma: 4.502 words) (Hundt, 1995, p. 61; Thomas, 1997, p. 61).

The Changing State of the South African Nation:

Although Zuma held the shortest address, his list of addressees was the longest and unlike Mandela and Mbeki, it included "the governor of the reserved bank" as well as "South African and foreign media" (Zuma 2010). All three addresses began and closed with an emotional appeal to the nation's ethos. The main middle part dealt with government's achievements, plans, priorities, programs and policies.

The first level audience was parliament and invited guests, the second level audience, who received the message via the media, was the South African nation. Rhetorically more emphasis seems to have lately been directed towards the third level audience: the international media, politics and the business world (Reisigl, 2008, p. 243).

Each president anchored his speech in a historical event and placed it under a distinct motto. While Mandela emphasized the importance of the year 1995, by mentioning the 50th anniversary of the end of the Second World War and the foundation of the United Nations, Mbeki used the decennial anniversary of the unbanning of the ANC as his anchor point. Zuma framed his speech within the 20th anniversary of Mandela's release from prison in 1990. Mandela projected the "construction of the people-centered society" (Mandela, 1995) and government as the servant of the people as his core message. Mbeki knitted the statement "never before have we been placed better than today" five times into his speech and in doing so established the year 2000 as a milestone in South African history. Zuma, in contrast, preferred an advertising style and proposed "2010, a year of action" as the leitmotif of his speech; referring mainly to the quality assurance measurements that he planned to implement into government administration.

According to Moriarty (drawing on deliberations of Burke, 1969), political activation of the audience is achieved by establishing a platform for identification. The author called this the "vision of the us" (Moriarty, 2003, p. 7). Political speeches aim to negotiate inclusion and exclusion in an interactive way (Reisigl, 2008, p. 251).

Pronouns are especially used to define in-groups and outsiders, take the president to the level of the people or refer to government as an elite (Chilton & Schäffner, 2002, pp. 30ff.). During the early years of the new dispensation, this vision of "nation building" in a highly riven society was vital. Mandela referred to the historical burden of apartheid as the unifying factor: "Coming as we do from *our own specific past*, it will be important that *we join* in the observance of these historic events"(1995)[15]. When he spoke to parliament as the representatives of "the people," he distanced himself as an individual from the vision but built on the institutional link: "[…] as individuals and as parties *we belong to the same government*. We therefore have a *collective responsibility* […]" (Mandela, 1995). Mbeki used the rhetoric device of "creating an us" rather sparingly, in his 2000 speech. He promoted identity rhetoric as a form of marketing when he said: "We are proud to be South African!" (2000)[16]. Zuma mixed languages and identities purposefully[17] in order to unify divides and to promote himself as the president of all South Africans[18]. These identity switches are important for creating an "us" in a highly diversified society (Chilton & Schäffner, 2002, pp. 31ff.).

In order to trigger a drift for change, conflict is created by formatting an "other", according to Moriarty. The speaker creates a negative image of an out-group to "discourage audience identification with it" (2003, p. 7). Although, the SoNA does not call for strong opposition building, like for instance an election speech would, a gradient or difference of level needs to be established to allow for dynamic rhetorical movement.

Mandela (1995) created a scenario of *the critics* (media and the outside world) against us—*the new South Africans*: "Whatever it is that *our critics* might have to say, *we can take pride* in the fact that […] we also ensured that they [houses of parliament] play their role in the government of *our* country." Typically for his simultaneously aloof and poetic style (Tomaselli & Teer-Tomaselli, 2008), Mbeki created the "other" as a metaphorical concept (e.g., when he referred to racism which "will continue to exist in our society unless all of us engage *this monster* consciously and systematically" [Mbeki 2000]). Employing a metaphor from theatre, Zuma (2010) used the economic situation as a threatening scenario against which the nation must unify when he said: "We are meeting *against the backdrop* of a *global economic* crisis [...]." This then allowed him to present economic growth as the savior of society.

Rather than to set yourself in a positive light through downplaying the opposition, the objective of a SoNA is to position and justify your course of actions within a continuum of party history and agenda through the legislative period. Positioning functions chronologically as well as ideologically. Mandela constructed a power hierarchy by placing government and himself below the constitution: "[...] not only did we succeed to establish our two houses of parliament, *as required by the Constitution,* [...]" (1995). This rhetorical move was well placed in an atmosphere of a young emerging democracy with still volatile power relationships and skepticism about the new order. Despite this typically humble approach, Mandela (1995) clearly positioned himself politically, where necessary: "*As South Africans,* [...] we must be extremely careful *not to reintroduce the McCarthyism* [...] *that sought the blood of* anybody who was labeled *a communist.*" He also established boundaries against imperialistic interventions during these times of political fragility when saying for instance, "we need *no educators*" (Mandela, 1995). Mbeki's strategy, on the contrary, was global inclusion instead of demarcation. He positioned South Africa historically and physically on the world map: "*Having ended our dark days* as a pariah country, [...] *the nations of our common universe* are confident that out of South Africa will emerge a thing of value [...]" (Mbeki, 2000). In an even more assertive way, Zuma (2010) positioned the country in relation to the rest of the world, when he said: "Let me [...] *extend* our heartfelt *condolences to* the Government and People of *Haiti* [...]. We are pleased that *our* rescue *teams* were able to go and

assist." Firstly, he established an emotive relationship with one of the first postcolonial countries worldwide, and secondly, he emphasized that South Africa's aid is needed in the world; claiming a former "first-world-towards-third-world" gesture. In this sense, the statement is directed towards the international audience.

Moriarty identified the establishment of the "current situation" as a rhetorical objective of political speeches (2003, pp. 7ff.). This is simultaneously a reflection on past achievements, because it poses the question of: where do we stand now? All three presidents referred to the same key issues (i.e., government's priorities, crime, HIV/Aids, racism, job creation, poverty, education, and public services) and what they have implemented to deal with it. The framing of their past achievements were, however, distinctly different. Regarding crime, Mandela employed metaphors from theatre and nature ("the judicial system *plays its proper role* [in] [...] reducing the levels of crime," "our country continues *to be engulfed by the crime wave*" 1995) and emphasized the voter's involvement, responsibility and voice in the fight against crime. Mbeki described racism as poison ("those who are forced to *swallow the bitter fruit* of racial inequality") but also used war metaphors ("*push back the frontiers* of racism," 2000). He abstracted the issue to a holistic "challenge" linked to poverty and to be solved by "commitment" and presented himself in charge and in control. His solutions to crime, HIV, and racism were a sufficiently formalized system, organizational bodies (e.g., *Partnerships Against AIDS*) and programs (e.g., *Tirisano Programme, National Congress against Racism*). Mbeki further shifted responsibility to the public and gave the impression that he had done his part. He set up a dialogue with himself to confirm the achievements of his past commitments. Zuma (2010) quantified problems and foregrounded managerial vocabulary. His solutions were identifying problems, efficient planning, and implementation. He employed business triggers like "*increase our productivity*," "*performance-oriented* state," "*measured by outcomes,*" and so forth. Zuma often also quantified people and put a monetary value on them (e.g., "the *cost* of hiring younger *workers*," "*invest* in our *youth*," "produce *additional engineers*," and so forth (Zuma 2010). When switching from manager to statesman, Zuma quoted certain key words established by his predecessors in a historicizing way: "As we *celebrate Madiba's_release* today, we recommit ourselves to *reconciliation*, national unity, *non-racialism* and *building a better future* together as South Africans, *black and white*" (Zuma, 2010).

Projection, the fourth category of rhetorical objectives, in Moriarty's terms "potential action"—where do we go from here?—is expressed by appeals "to logos (logic), pathos (emotions), and ethos (character/credibility of the rhetor)" (Moriarty 2003, p. 8). The use of appeals supports the interactive and dialogical nature of speeches (cf. Reisigl, 2008, p. 254). Mandela (1995) appealed to *logos*, addressing the nation, when he said:

[...] it is impossible to enter this next and critical stage of the dismantling of the system of apartheid until we have democratically elected structures of government [...] I would therefore like to [...] call on all our people [...] to take the forthcoming local government elections very seriously.

Notably, both Zuma and Mbeki referred to the Soccer World Cup in their closing section. Mbeki (2000), not having won the bid yet, appealed to the international audience both emotionally and ethically:

[...] it is clear that fairness and the development of soccer [...] demand that [...] the Soccer World Cup competition should take place in Africa. For these purposes, there can be no better venue than the land of human hope, that has all the necessary facilities, which our country is.

Mbeki clearly addressed international critics when he mentioned the infrastructure that South Africa can provide. By using non-human agents who "demand" action, he gave the impression that

there is no alternative. Zuma linked the Soccer World Cup to Mandela and thereby closed the narrative circle of his speech. He appealed to the nation's ethos:

President Mandela was central in assisting the country to win the rights to host this great event. We therefore have to make the World Cup a huge success in his honour. [...] Let us all buy tickets timeously to be able to attend the games (Zuma, 2010).

This frame commodifies the event through "buying tickets," whereby Zuma implied the financial benefits the world cup might have for the South African economy. The Soccer World Cup evolves through the speeches in a collaborative coherent effort into a symbol for international acknowledgement of African identity spearheaded by South Africa.

These content-related examples indicate a *businification* development on a rhetorical level which is furthered on a linguistic level (i.e., when looking at key terminology and metaphors). Quantification of this very corpus, ironically, makes the point visible[19]. The frequency of the key word *people* reveals a *businification* tendency and a shift away from a people-centered society. Mandela used the word 62 times (0.93%), Mbeki 31 times (0.47%) and Zuma referred to *people* only 14 times (0.31%) in his speech. A move towards business could also be detected by counting financial references. Mbeki, unexpectedly, leads in quoting financial figures (6 times) and percentages (12 times), followed by Zuma (financial figures 4 times; percentages 5 times). Mandela, notably, spoke about the state of nation without referring to either.

In the tradition of Lakoff (1985), who argued that all thinking happens in metaphorical categories and concepts and goes beyond comparison to existing analogue items, Hundt emphasized that the metaphorical use of domain-foreign metaphors increases semantic attributes and so opens new ways of understanding a concept (1995, pp. 43ff.).

The use of metaphors is, therefore, a constitutive part of communication. The reference fields indicate in which line of thinking each president operates when "recurrent source domains appear" (Chilton & Schäffner, 2002, p. 28). The metaphors are not necessarily business-related; however, a shift from organic and social reference fields (e.g., life, sickness/health, human body, nature, and play/game/sport) to fields of modernity (e.g., war, machines, business) can be detected.

All three presidents employed metaphors of WAR when describing future action: "*The battle against the forces* of anarchy and chaos has been joined" (Mandela, 1995); "Our common *national offensive* against all forms of inequality" (Mbeki, 2000); "We continue our efforts to *eradicate* corruption" (Zuma, 2010). When referring to the past, Mandela and Mbeki presented SOCIETY as a SICK or HEALING BODY (Mandela, 1995): "corruption in many forms has deeply *infected the fibre* of our society" (Mandela 1995); "problem created by some irresponsible *elements*" (Mbeki, 2010). Zuma (2010) framed the past in a solemn way drawing on metaphors of RELIGION: "They became a symbol of *the sacrifices* of many who *bore the brunt* of apartheid." When describing the current situation, stark contrasts in the reference fields appear between Mandela, who addressed the current challenges in the frame of PLAY/ GAME (e.g., theatre/sports): "It is always the case that the *spectators* are better than the *players* on the field" (1995) and Zuma, who presented the current state as an optimized manufacturing machine: "The work of departments will be *measured by outcomes*" (2010).

Collocations[20] become salient in discourse through repetitive use and triggers a range of familiar attributes connected to it (Chilton & Schäffner, 2002, p. 37). Meanings of metaphors, phrases and collocations have a certain half-life. The more often they are used, the less meaningful they become. In a South African context, terms like "comrades" (as reference to an in-group associated to the resistance movement), "black and white" (for all formerly racially classified people of South Africa), and collocations like "capacity building," "previously disadvantaged<" and "non-sexist" are transformed from being part of the struggle and transition discourse into branding tools. While mostly introduced by Mandela and his contemporaries and vital for the identity building of the post-apartheid society at the time, many of these expressions seem to have turned into clichés and therefore become devalued from their former ethical weight (Chilton & Schäffner, 2002, p. 28).

The balance between maintaining a historical trajectory and clearing the way for "a new way of doing things" (Zuma, 2010), is difficult to reach if you don't want to fall prey to employing hollow phrases for straining after effect. The shift from "people" to "investors" might be a result of new possibilities of distribution and recycling of content within the media, which have to be pre-considered in speech production and delivery (Reisigl. 2008, p. 259). Contemporary speeches need to fulfill a plethora of objectives; the dialogue partners are no more the voters alone but the international audience which results in a pixelated eclectic speech (Chilton & Schäffner, 2002, p.22). The presidency's influence on the message that reaches the public is however limited. Much of the content will be channeled and recontextualized through the media (Reisigl, 2008, p. 260). Due to the high level of professionalization, the individual president is no more the sole producer of the speech but reduced to being merely the "delivery boy," while the speeches are written by professional PR teams (Reisigl, 2008, p. 260). Hence, the process of speech production, delivery, and reception is highly complex and mutually interdependent (Fairclough, 2002, p. 198).

MEDIA RECEPTION ANALYSIS

Political discourse became a recycled media product that is endlessly repeated and multiply accessible. In order to assess how meaning is transported to the voters, the framing of the speeches by different newspapers should be considered: what they highlight and quote and what they omit. Is *businification* detected and critically assessed from a distance, or reiterated, reaffirmed and naturalized?

The framing process results in certain answers about causal relations, moral evaluation, and recommendations (Entman, 1993). It is the creation of a coherent narrative for presenting news. Framing can therefore be described as "patterns of interpretation through which people classify information in order to handle it efficiently" (Scheufele, 2004, p. 402). Since framing effects are evoked by "subtle nuances in wording and syntax" (Scheufele, 2000, p. 314), more often than not, they are unconscious and therefore not manipulative.

The following is a layout of work-in-progress research about tendencies in the South African newspaper landscape to frame these *businified* presidential speeches. Fifteen (15) exemplary articles about Mbeki's, Zuma's and Mandela's SoNAs have been sourced from the Internet and SA Media[21].

The majority of articles are summaries providing a clear cut structure that can conveniently be filled by "copying and pasting" from the written version of the speech. This genre is, therefore, a good example for the economization of text production which tends to eliminate critical complexity.

Typically for this newspaper, *The Citizen*[22] published, in its February 1995 issue, five articles featuring Mandela's SoNA each with a different focus (e.g., corruption, performance of government, economy) to fill the pages. Three of those can be classified as summaries striking through sloppy "cut and paste"- editing whereby it is not always possible to distinguish between direct and indirect quotes.

In summaries made up of quotes, framing appears either in the headline or through prioritizing, like in the article "Errors 'part of learning'" in *The Citizen* (Sapa, 1995). In the first paragraph a

surprise draws the reader's attention: the president admits errors. The second paragraph consolidates the reader's interest through quoting a metaphor: "Opening Parliament he [Mandela] said: "It is always the case that *the spectators are better than the players on the field*" (Sapa, 1995). Quoting of metaphors is a thankful tool for journalists as they make the article vivid, give it character and merge meanings; at the same time they are arbitrary. Interestingly, several articles from different newspapers quoted Mandela's metaphors of corruption "*infecting the fibre* of society" (Mandela, 1995) (e.g., *The Natal Witness* [Hartley, 1995]), or *The Citizen* (n.a. b, 1995). Another way to animate an article is to quote speech acts like warning, praising or threatening. Hartley Wyndham wrote in *The Natal Witness* for instance: "Mandela, […], in a tough message to those disrupting the country said 'let no one say they have not been warned'" (1995; n.a. d, 1995). If slogans like "building a better life for all South Africans" (n.a. c, 1995)) are quoted without commas, it is an indication that they have been naturalized into the media discourse. These marketing-like slogans have a certain half-life; if overused, they turn into empty cants.

Five years later, summary articles follow the same pattern. Through indirect unconsidered quoting, the article "An ABC guide to Mbeki's speech" on *IOL Online* reiterated Mbeki's institutional solutions to Aids: "South Africa will *host* the 13th International Aids *Conference* […], which *would help* to focus the country's attention on the challenge." (n.a., 2000Crime was framed as a success story only in reflection, i.e. without reference to future action: "Mr. Mbeki said the government *had followed through its commitment against crime* […]" (n.a., 2000).

Even when keeping a critical distance, journalists sometimes fall prey to naturalizing (*businified*) language. Karima Brown presented Zuma's speech in her *Business Day* article "Zuma sticks to state's five top priorities" as uninspired (2010). She suggested disguise: "He *claimed* a 97% victory on the 500000 job opportunities […]"; "On health, Zuma *vaguely mentioned* the government's commitment […]" (Brown, 2010). Despite her critical stance, the journalist later summarized and cited Zuma's business terms directly without reflection:

He said the government would provide detailed daily lesson plans and easy-to-use workbooks, he committed the government to a 'new way of doing things' and promised that the work of departments would be measured by outcomes. […]He said in December that the Cabinet approved a turnaround strategy […] (Brown, 2010).

The article presented most of its comments in the beginning and appeared to have been written in a rush as it turned into a summary mode made of indirect quotes.

While a dominance of direct and indirect quotes framed in an "objective" and uncritical manner might be expected in a summary report, the reiteration of *businified* political lingo seems less obvious in genres like *public and expert opinions and reactions*, because they seem to strive to reflect diversified and critical voices. *The Citizen* featured a rather impressionistic article titled "Address greeted by warm applause" sketching atmosphere and direct reactions at Parliament to Mandela's 1995 SoNA (n.a. a, 1995). The article almost poetically framed Mandela as a respected and loved father figure who had been affectionately received by the audience playing heavily on sentiment: "President Mandela received several rounds of *warm applause* […]. A buzz of *animated chatter reverberated* around the chamber […] before President Mandela entered […]. A *smiling* President shook hands with MPs […] he frequently paused to *wipe his eyes*, damaged […] during his long imprisonment" (n.a. a 1995).

Lynda Loxton commented on Mbeki's speech through assembling expert opinions; her framing happened through the selection of voices. The article "Mbeki put SA on course" in *Business Report* remained benignant throughout (2000). Tito Mboweni, governor of the reserved bank,

was quoted defending Mbeki's approach not to introduce a much expected "big bang" in economic policies. On the issue of strikes, Loxton quoted party opposition leaders Tony Leon (DP) and Marthinus van Schalkwyk (NNP) backing Mbeki's "hardline" stance (Loxton 2000). Overall, this is an article with positive connotations towards the SoNA and little criticism; a weak attempt of contrasting political voices.

Reporter Abbey Makoe (*The Sunday Independent*) collected public voices (2000). Her framing was apparently influenced by her personal experience. At first she did not find many potential interview partners watching the speech live on TV in Carlton Centre in downtown Johannesburg. This made her criticize the "*hordes of youths* […] apparently *oblivious* to the president's pronouncements" (Makoe, 2000). She eventually interviewed some critical viewers ('Job creation first, Mr. President, job creation!') (Makoe, 2000). Hence, the article framed the public as *not interested*, and *the president as detached from people's priorities*.

The article "Reactions to the State of the Nation Address" (Reuters, 2010) in *Business Report* framed Zuma's address through three elite *expert voices* from different sectors of society (public, private, and media). Firstly, business man Peter Attard Montalto (Emerging Market Economist, Nomura) was cited assessing Zuma's speech as "pretty unsurprising"(Reuters, 2010). The framing was negative and implied *empty promises* and *no new ideas*. Then, the article gave a more positive account ("Some excellent stuff" by political analyst Nic Borain (Reuters, 2010). Borain's statement framed Zuma's address as having *surpassed expectations*, but was also critical about the issue of job creation ("sounds like a *massaging of figures*" Reuters, 2010). Lastly the article quoted a negative opinion by law professor Shadrack Gutto (University of South Africa): "'It was *not inspiring*. It was more of a *regurgitation of policies* […] He really *tried to avoid* areas which are controversial'" (Reuters, 2010). This negative frame repeated the one given by Attard (*no new ideas; empty promises*) and implied a reproach of disguise. Although the article did not embed these "expert" comments any further, the structure of negative-positive-negative-negative comment and the repetition of the frames *uninspiring* and *no new ideas* left an overall negative impression; this is an example of framing by prioritizing.

The Sapa article "Disappointment follows Zuma's address" in *Business Report* (2010a), resembled Makoe's framing of 10 years before. A pro-business publisher notably created the illusion of being close to grassroot level: "President Jacob *Zuma failed* to deal with *job creation* [...], *said patrons* of a Germiston township tavern"(Sapa, 2010a). Again, frames of the *uninterested voter* ("Many left after the first 15 minutes, *saying they were bored*"), and *the president detached from people's priorities* ("'Zuma has virtually *ignored our plight* [...] [Mamazala Mqombothi, 49] said'") were employed (Sapa, 2010a). Zuma's reference to Mandela was critically framed, by quoting a man called Mpho Mashiloane who said: "He is now *riding on Mandela's* success" (Sapa, 2010a) . The statement suggested that the public is aware of government's strategic marketing gestures.

A higher degree of subjectivity and critical distance is expected from commentary. This genre can, however, also be used to bring a dead topic back into discourse, as the *Citizen* article "War on crime" (n.a., 1995d) demonstrated. The comment took Mandela's 1995 SoNA as a cause to debate on reintroducing the death penalty and was written like a letter establishing dichotomy between "the president" and "we" and encompassing in the author's voice "the public, facing a wave of criminal violence" (n.a., 1995d). While praising Mandela for speaking "with the measured tones of a true leader," the author argued that "words" don't go far enough in the "war on crime" but "action" is needed suggesting that the death penalty could be one solution. This article serves as a prime example for framing political discourse in a specific direction to embed a controversial issue and make it appear less threatening. In the light of Mandela's strong words against crime, the reader is left with the impression that government is just a stone throw away from reintroducing the death penalty.

A similar mechanism can be observed on the opposite end of the political scale. Self-constituted communist writer, Dale T. McKinley, argued in his article "The evolution of the ANC" in *Daily Mail & Guardian,* that the economic transformation proposed by the Mbeki government in the 2000 speech was neither new nor revolutionary (2000). There was no "big bang" commencing the "conversion from Marxist to "free" market ideology" (McKinley, 2000), but rather a maintaining of the ANC agenda since 1945[23]. McKinley zoomed in on Mbeki's statements pertaining to the economic strategies in government. In a sarcastic manner, he mentioned the nomination of the International Investment Council[24] as "who's who of big-time global capitalists" and continued to quote a business representative: "In the words of the *overjoyed* South African Chamber of Business (Sacob), 'we will be the first country guided by foreign-investor imperatives;'"(McKinley, 2000). Notably, McKinley referred to government's language; in this case finance minster Trevor Manuel's 2000 budget speech:

The neo-liberalspeak and endless statistics [...] merely confirms that the right mix is being proferred [sic]. [...] While the new, rationalising "free" market terminology might be more confusing than the well-known liberation slogans of the past, it cannot hide the fact that the practice remains [...] - removed from the masses (McKinley, 2000).

With his reference to Orwell's "1984," McKinley constructed the ANC's neo-liberal language and the attribution of its political implications as a threat and proved that the *businification* in political language had not gone unnoticed on the South African newspaper landscape.

From the business mouth, Gary van Staden, political analyst of SG Securities, lauded Mbeki's speech in his article "The Long View" in *Business Report* (2000). He also emphasized the rhetorical style of the speech: "[…], his address has *several clarity notches above* his usual tendency to understate and to *leave the audience to draw its own conclusions*. Mbeki […] was clear and *concise* […]" (van Staden, 2000). Van Staden's observation that Mbeki is known to leave much room for interpretation to the reader is noteworthy because it shows that media are indeed aware of rhetorical gestures and political avoidance strategies (Chilton & Schäffner, 2002, p. 12, 33; Thomas, 1997, p. 61).

When examining the media's methods in framing the Zuma speech, similarities to Mbeki's reception are evident. In her commentary summary article in *The Mail & Guardian* "In Madiba's shadow - Zuma stresses reconciliation but makes it clear there's little in state's kitty" (2010), Mandy Rossouw framed Zuma as a calculating business manager who made use of Mandela's rhetorical gestures for mere marketing purposes: "*His cashing in on the powerful public emotion around Mandela* made for an address that was strong on sentiment but weak on substance." About half the article consisted of direct quotes embedded negatively: "He did *not reflect much* on […]"; "promising remarks […] but *no details*"; "Zuma announced […] but "*declined to answer*"; "*refrained from setting* a target" (Rossouw, 2010). Rossouw criticized the emphasis on business rhetoric: "His *business-like approach* to government is echoed in the promise that 'government must work faster, harder and smarter' reminiscent of a *corporate slogan*" (Rossouw, 2010). This article both gave a detailed summary overview about Zuma's SoNA and kept a critical distance towards the content. Rossouw clearly detected Zuma's *businified* rhetorical style.

In publications like *The Mail and Guardian,* the *businification* trend in political language is critically reflected and commented. Three distinct genres in mediatized speech discourse on SoNA

in print media could be identified across publications: summary, account of oppositional and public voices, and commentary. As can be expected from a "fact-based"-genre, summaries tended to be less critical, however through the heavy use of direct–often formally sloppy–quoting, this genre lacked objective distance to the reported subject.

CONCLUSION

As early as in the 1995 articles, editing happened largely through omission and "copy and paste" rather than a distanced framing of certain issues. This suggests that there is no recent economization development of media discourse, but a long established procedural necessity of the profession which is under constant time pressure. Key *businified* terminology and rhetoric gestures from the source are reiterated, manifested and, therefore, naturalized. This kind of text commodification (i.e., growing formalization, gapping or elliptic structures) is not a new development but a general element of modernity (Hundt, 1995, p. 22). Stringency of text also increases the adaptability for cross-discourse use, because sentences become less discourse-specific due to brevity. Hence, discourses assimilate. One can observe a recycling and recontextualization process of frames between the discourses politics, media and business, which manifest cognitively in collective cultural memory (Chilton & Schäffner, 2002, p. 26). Politicians consume media frames and incorporate them into their way of thinking. Their utterances are edited, framed and published, and feed the discourse machinery anew. In this process, bits of an external discourse (e.g., business) could become transferred (Chilton & Schäffner, 2002, p.v17). Gestures (e.g., measuring), frames (e.g., quantifying), tools (e.g., marketing and branding) and key terminology (e.g., management language) are imported. The strategic purpose of this import is to appeal to a certain audience (e.g., the business world) and the portrayal of certain images (e.g., the president as the business manager).

Instead of recontextualization, one can also speak of "colonizing" a discourse (see Chilton & Schäffner, 2002) which highlights the implicit power relations assumed in this process. The particular danger in the naturalization of business language in the political and media discourse lies in the condensation of meaning that disguises complex implications known to experts from the business world, but unknown to the general public, as Thomas notes:

Many words originally and primarily used in terms of business practice are now common in everyday English, for example bottom line and priority […], and negotiate. A possible problem in the moderate familiarity of business practice is that it may seem more inclusionary than it is, and thus encourage interpretations that reflect desired expectations rather than less attractive realities. (Thomas, 1997, p. 61).

The naturalization of corporate values into the political field obscures other aspects of society which are vital for a democracy but non-profitable for economy. Business management largely follows modernistic principles like the top-down approach in goal-setting, assessment of the organization "in terms of economic contribution," the belief that dissent needs to be eradicated and that the world can be controlled through administrative procedures, as Holtzhausen (2003, p. 30) describes. Efficiency eliminates social irregularities and results in the "normalization" of society.

Businification in politics is nevertheless not necessarily and exclusively a negative development, since it also reflects growing professionalization and efficient handling of state's resources. A higher degree of governmental formalization does however not cause an improvement of living conditions of the voters per se (Jacobs, 2003; Adam et al., 1998). Jacobs argues that these pressing social issues are framed in the media as "policy questions to be corrected by laws and state intervention" (2003, p. 37) and the political focus remains fixed on legislative change.

It is, however, difficult to pinpoint a *businified* discourse beyond mere observation and description. Due to their fluidity and high degree of subjectivity, the structure of frames needs to remain "speculative, based on inference from the analysis of language and discourse" (Chilton & Schäffner, 2002, p. 26). The analysis of a larger corpus would reveal stable developments towards *businification* and allow for a more evident tracing of discourse-specific metaphors and collocations which evolve and wither while travelling through speeches and media reports.

REFERENCES

na. (2000, February 4). An ABC guide to Mbeki's speech. *IOL Online*. Retrieved January 17, 2013, from http://www.iol.co.za/news/politics/an-abc-guide-to-mbeki-s-speech-1.27209#.UPfQN6wx_9o

na. (2010, December 14). Zuma sues Zapiro, Avusa for R5m. *Mail & Guardian Online*. Retrieved January 17, 2013, from http://mg.co.za/article/2010-12-14-zuma-sues-zapiro-avusa-for-r5m

Adam, H., Van Zyl Slabbert, F., & Moodley, K. (1998). *Comrades in Business – Post-liberation politics in South Africa*. Cape Town, South Africa: Tafelberg Publishers.

Barrie, A. (2008). The "bring me my machine gun" campaign. *FoxNews*. Retrieved April 30, 2012, from http://www.foxnews.com/story/0,2933,321785,00.html

Blommaert, J. (2006). *Discourse: A critical introduction. Key topics in sociolinguistics*. Cambridge, UK: Cambridge University Press.

Brown, K. (2010, February 12). Zuma sticks to state's five top priorities. *Business Day*. Retrieved April 30, 2012, from http://www.businessday.co.za/Articles/Content.aspx?id=93571

Burke, K. (1969). *A rhetoric of motives*. Berkeley, CA: University of California Press.

Chilton, P., & Schäffner, C. (2002). Introduction: Themes and principles in the analysis of political discourse. In Chilton, P., & Schäffner, C. (Eds.), *Politics as Text and Talk. Analytic Approaches to Political Discourses* (pp. 1–44). Amsterdam, The Netherlands: John Benjamins Publishing.

Cohen, T. (1995, February 17). Visible shift required without a radical break – Mandela. *Business Day*, 0.

Davis, G. (2010, February 12). Zuma promises year of action. *Cape Times*. Retrieved April 30, 2012, from http://www.iol.co.za/index.php?set_id=1&click_id=13&art_id=vn20100212042130569C413199

Economy. *Online Etymology Dictionary*. Retrieved July 30, 2010, from http://etymonline.com/index.php?term=economy&allowed_in_frame=0

Entman, R. (1993). Framing: Toward a clarification of a fractured paradigm. *The Journal of Communication*, *43*(4), 51–58. doi:10.1111/j.1460-2466.1993.tb01304.x.

Fairclough, N. (2002). *Media Discourse (reprint)*. London: Arnold.

Flanagan, J. (2010, February 27). Jacob Zuma prepares for tea at Buckingham Palace. *Telegraph*. Retrieved April 30, 2012, from http://www.telegraph.co.uk/news/worldnews/africaandindianocean/southafrica/7333017/Jacob-Zuma-prepares-for-tea-at-Buckingham-Palace.html

Harper, D. (2001). Commodification. *Online Etymology Dictionary*. Retrieved July 30, 2010, from:http://etymonline.com/index.php?term=commodification&allowed_in_frame=0Politics. *Online Etymology Dictionary*. Retrieved July 30, 2010, from: http://etymonline.com/index.php?term=politics&allowed_in_frame=0

Hartley, W. (1995, February 18). It's time to get tough – Mandela. *The Natal Witness*, 1

Holtzhausen, D. (2002). A Postmodern Critique of Public Relations Theory and Practice. *Communicatio*, *28*(1), 29–38. doi:10.1080/02500160208537955.

Hundt, M. (1995). *Modellbildung in der Wirtschaftssprache: Zur Geschichte der Institutionen- und Theoriefachsprachen der Wirtschaft*. Tübingen, Germany: Niemeyer. doi:10.1515/9783110954685.

Independent Online. (1999). *About IOL and Independent Newspapers*. Retrieved January 17, 2013, from: http://www.iol.co.za/about-iol-1.458#id.d2yhp2g99e8

Jacobs, S. (2003). Reading Politics, Reading Media. In Jacobs, S., & Wassermann, H. (Eds.), *Shifting Selves- Post-Apartheid Essays on Mass Media, Culture and Identity* (pp. 29–53). Cape Town, South Africa: Kwela Books.

Lakoff, G., & Johnson, M. (1985). *Metaphors we live by*. Chicago, IL: University of Chicago Press. Retrieved April 30, 2012, from http://www.gbv.de/dms/bowker/toc/9780226468006.pdf

Loxton, L. (2000, February 5). Mbeki puts SA on course. *Business Report*. Retrieved from April 20, 2012, from http://www.busrep.co.za/index.php?fSectionId=561&fArticleId=74876

Mail & Guardian Online. (n.d.). *About Us*. Retrieved January 17, 2013, from http://mg.co.za/page/about-us/

Makoe, A. (2000, February 5). What we need are jobs, Mr. President! *The Sunday Independent*. Retrieved April 30, 2012, from http://www.iol.co.za/index.php?set_id=1&click_id=13&art_id=ct20000205175221108M126696

Mandela, N. (1995, February 18). Address of President Nelson Mandela on the occasion of the opening of the second session of the democratic parliament: Cape Town, South Africa. Retrieved April 30, 2012, from http://www.info.gov.za/speeches/1995/170595001.htm

Masenyama, K. (2006). The South African Broadcasting Corporation and Dilemmas of National Identity. In Alexander, P., Dawson, M. C., & Icharam, M. (Eds.), *Globalisation and New Identites- A View from the Middle* (pp. 157–171). Johannesburg, South Africa: Jacana Media.

Mbeki, T. (2000, February 4). *State of the Nation address of the president of South Africa, Thabo Mbeki, National Assembly Chamber.* Cape Town, South Africa. Retrieved April 30, 2012, from http://www.info.gov.za/speeches/2000/000204451p1001.htm

Mbembe, A. (2001). *On the Postcolony.* Berkeley, CA: University of California Press.

Mbembe, A. (2003). Necropolitics. *Public Culture, 15*(1), 11–40. doi:10.1215/08992363-15-1-11.

McKinley, D. T. (2000, March 1). The evolution of the ANC. *Daily Mail & Guardian.* Retrieved April 30, 2012, from www.hartford-hwp.com/37a/171.html

MDDA. (2009). Trends of ownership and control of media in South Africa. Version 3.3.[Research Report]. Media Development and Diversity Agency. Retrieved January 17, 2013, from http://www.mdda.org.za/trends of ownership and control of media in south Africa ver 3.3. final 20-june 202009.pdf

Moriarty, T. A. (2003). *Finding the words: a rhetorical history of South Africa's transition from apartheid to democracy.* Westport, CT: Praeger Publishers.

n.a. (1995a), February 18). Address greeted by warm applause. *The Citizen,* 11

n.a. (1995b, February 18). Corruption to be fought. *The Citizen,* 11

n.a. (1995c, February 18). Govt 'doesn't have money to meet demands'. *The Citizen,* 11

n.a. (1995d, February 18). War on crime. *The Citizen,* 6

Parliament of the Republic of South Africa. (2004). *National Assembly Guide to Procedure.* Creda, Cape Town. Retrieved April 30, 2012, from http://www.parliament.gov.za/content/GUIDE.pdf

Peters, H. (2005). Rede: England. In Ueding, G. (Ed.), *Historisches Wörterbuch der Rhetorik* (pp. 751–756). Tübingen, Germany: Niemeyer.

Ralphs, G. (2007). The Contribution of Achille Mbembe to the Multi-disciplinary Study of Africa. *Postamble, 3*(2), 18–29.

Reisigl, M. (2008). Rhetoric of political speeches. In Wodak, R., & Koller, V. (Eds.), *Handbook of Communication in the Public Sphere* (pp. 243–269). Berlin, New York: Mouton de Gruyer.

Reuters. (2010). Reactions to the State of the Nation Address. *Business Report.* Retrieved April 30, 2012, from http://www.busrep.co.za/index.php?fSectionId=552&fArticleId=5349000

Roodt, D. (2009, April 14). South Africa: Skins And Velskoene -- Why Zuma is Befriending Afrikaners. *Business Day,* 14. Retrieved August 30, 2010, from http://allafrica.com/stories/200904140038.html

Rossouw, M. (2010, February 12). In Madiba's shadow: Zuma stresses reconciliation but makes it clear there's little in state's kitty. Mail & Guardian, 4

Salazar, P. J. (2002). *An African Athens: Rhetoric and the shaping of democracy in South Africa. Rhetoric, knowledge and society.* Mahwah, NJ: Erlbaum.

Sapa. (1995, February 18): Errors 'part of learning'. *The Citizen,* 11

Sapa. (2010, February 11). Disappointment follows Zuma's address. *Business Report*. Retrieved April 30, 2012, from http://www.busrep.co.za/index.php?fSectionId=552&fArticleId=5348999

Sapa. (2010, February 11). Opposition critical of Zuma's speech. *IOL online*. Retrieved April 30, 2012, from http://www.iol.co.za/index.php?set_id=1&click_id=13&art_id=nw20100211211607751C657048

Sapa. (2010, February 18). Historic evening opening for Parliament. *Mail & Guardian Online*. Retrieved April 30, 2012, from

Scheufele, B. T. (2004). Framing-effects approach: A theoretical and methodological critique. *Communications*, *29*, 401–428. doi:10.1515/comm.2004.29.4.401.

Scheufele, D. (2000). Agenda-Setting, Priming, and Framing Revisited: Another Look at Cognitive Effects of Political Communication. *Mass Communication & Society*, *3*(2/3), 297–316. doi:10.1207/S15327825MCS0323_07.

Schubert, K., & Klein, M. (2001). *Das Politiklexikon*. Bonn, Germany: J.H.W. Dietz. Retrieved April 30, 2012, from http://kunstbewegung.info/cde/rlp-definitionen-lexika/4891-politik-definition.html.

Shaw, A. (2010, August 9). SA journalists fight proposed media laws. *Mail & Guardian Online*. Retrieved January 17, 2013, from http://www.mg.co.za/article/2010-08-09-sa-journalists-fight-proposed-media-laws

Sibeko, S. (2010, January 4). South Africa's President Zuma marries for fifth time. Retrieved July 24, 2010, from http://www.reuters.com/article/idUSTRE60325E20100104

Sparks, A. (2003). *Beyond the miracle*. Johannesburg, South Africa: Jonathan Ball.

The Proudly South African Campaign. (n.d.). *About Us*. Retrieved January 17, 2013, from http://www.proudlysa.co.za/consumer-site

Thomas, J. (1997). Discourse in the Marketplace: The Making of Meaning in Annual Reports. *Journal of Business Communication*, (34): 47–66. doi:10.1177/002194369703400103.

Times Media Group Limited. (n.d.). *Media Group Division*. Retrieved January 17, 2013, from http://www.timesmedia.co.za/businesses/media/

Tomaselli, K., & Teer-Tomaselli, R. (2008). Exogenous and Endogenous Democracy: South African Politics and Media. *The International Journal of Press/Politics*, (13), pp. 171–180. Retrieved April 30, 2012, from http://hij.sagepub.com/content/13/2/171

Van Staden, G. (2000, February 6). The Long View. *Business Report*. Retrieved April 30, 2012, from http://www.busrep.co.za/index.php?fSectionId=561&fArticleId=74876

Wonacott, P. (2010, February 8). Zuma Apologizes for Fathering Child Out of Wedlock. *The Wall Street Journal*. Retrieved January 17, 2013, from http://online.wsj.com/article/SB10001424052748704197104575051013852177470.html#

Zuma, J. (2010). *State of the Nation Address by his Excellency JG Zuma, President of the Republic of South Africa, at the Joint Sitting of Parliament*. Cape Town, South Africa. Retrieved April 30, 2012, from http://www.info.gov.za/speeches/2010/10021119051001.htm

KEY TERMS AND DEFINITIONS

ANC: African National Congress.

GEAR: Growth, Employment and Redistribution.

IFP: Inkatha Freedom Party.

RDP: Reconstruction and Development Programme.

SoNA: State-of-the-nation-address.

ENDNOTES

1 All speeches are available as online documents (www.gov.co.za). There are therefore no page numbers; reference is only made to time and speaker.

2 According to Marxist theory, "commodification" means the "assignment of a market value" (Harper w2001).

3 Thabo Mbeki's direct successor was acting president Kgalema Mothlante, who was inaugurated on 25 September 2008, after Mbeki was forced to step back due to allegations that he had been illegally involved in pursuing the Zuma corruption trial. Since Mothlante was not a president elected by the public, his interim presidency will not be part of this study.

4 US parliamentarian Fisher Ames (1758-1808): "Politicks is not a science so properly as a business. It cannot have fixed principles, from which a wise man would never swerve, unless the inconstancy of men's view of interest and the capriciousness of the tempers could be fixed" (Harper 2001).

5 "Economy (n.) c.1530, "household management," from L. oeconomia (…)" The sense of "wealth and resources of a country" (short for political economy) is from 1650s (Harper 2001).

6 The *Independent News Media* group is the largest newspaper publisher in South Africa (31%), owning 14 national newspapers and 13 community newspapers in Cape Town. The group's titles make 58% of the English language market (Independent Online 1999).

7 *M&G Online* belongs to M&G Media; 87,5% owned by Newtrust Company Botswana Limited, Trevor Ncube and 10% Guardian Newspapers Limited (*Mail & Guardian Online* n.d.).

8 BDFM Publishers (Pty) Ltd, publishes *Financial Mail, Business Day* and *Bignews*. It is owned by Avusa Limited (former Johnnic) and Pearson PLC (Times Media Group Limited n.d.).

9 This term is commonly known to be initially used by Archbishop Desmond Tutu to describe the unified existence of different identities living in South Africa.

10 Thabo Mbeki introduced the essentialist concept of African Renaissance as a guideline for African identity politics. It is an impulse for awareness building and the rediscovery of African achievements, values and African heritage beyond South Africa (see Masenyama 2006, p.160).

11 In December 2010, Jacob Zuma sued cartoonist Jonathan Shapiro for depicting him in a deprecatory way (n.a. 2010, December 14). Mid 2010, government proposed to introduce the so called "Protection of Information Bill" which was met by massive protests from media and academia (see e.g., Shaw 2013, August 9).

12 Around a month before the speech, Zuma has been in the international tabloids for marrying his 5th wife (cf. Sibeko 2010, January 4), and about a week before the speech in the national tabloids, for revealing another child born out of wedlock (e.g., Wonacott 2010, February 8).

13 "The presidential cavalcade arrives in the parliamentary precincts. The President alights, is welcomed by the presiding officers and their deputies, and proceeds to the Assembly Chamber. […] In the past a theme for the occasion has been selected, which is depicted in the form of music, dance and/or a tableau. There is a guard of honour, usually non-military. Broadcast and photographic opportunities are provided to the media" (Parliament of RSA 2004, p. 98).

14 Only Zuma wove in sentences in Zulu and Afrikaans. His speech is available online in all 11 official South African languages (see www.gov.za).

15 Underlining of lexemes is to emphasize the trigger words and cues; not in original text.

16 Later, this slogan became a brand for a "buy local"- campaign. It might have been introduced here by Mbeki for the first time (The Proudly South African Campaign n.d.).

17 He brands himself as the "Zulu boy" from the rural areas (see Barrie 2008, January 10) who drinks tea with the English queen at the same time (Flanagan 2010, February 27).

18 He spoke Afrikaans for example, the language of the former oppressor, but included himself by saying "ons" which means "we" (cf. Roodt 2009, April 14).

19 What postcolonial critic Achille Mbembe criticizes in scientific discourse, namely that African social experience tends to be framed under the premise of statistical abstraction, e.g., "growth percentages, GDP figures" (Ralphs 2007; p. 21), might also apply to the political and consequently media discourse. The quantification process implies "the subordination of everything to impersonal logic and to the reign of calculability and instrumental rationality" (Mbembe 2003, p.18).

20 Collocation is a short chain or arrangement of recurring words.

21 S.A. Media is a comprehensive newspaper clippings and periodical database provided by the University of the Free State. It contains over 3 million newspaper reports indexed since 1978.

22 The Citizen is Caxton's flagship paper with a circulation of 68,000 (ABC 2008) and readership of about 540,000 people (MDDA 2009, p. 51). During apartheid, the Gauteng-based tabloid had been the only English language newspaper favourable towards the apartheid regime.

23 "It was way back in 1945 that former ANC president AB Xuma captured its essence with an honesty that contemporary ANC leaders would, for obvious reasons, find politically unpalatable: 'It is of less importance to us whether capitalism is smashed or not. It is of greater importance to us that while capitalism exists, we must fight and struggle to get our full share and benefit from the system'" (McKinley 2000, March 1).

24 Mbeki introduced the Investment Council in his 2000 SoNA. It was built as an advisory board for South African economic policies.

Section 2
Technologies of Change:
Understanding Africa's New Media Landscape

Chapter 11
Revolution 2.0:
New Media and the Transformation of the Egyptian Political and Communication Landscapes

Sahar Khamis
University of Maryland, USA

ABSTRACT

This chapter analyzes the role of new media, especially Internet-based communication, in accelerating the process of political transformation and democratization in Egypt. It analyzes the Egyptian media landscape before, during and after the 2011 revolution which toppled the regime of President Hosni Mubarak. In the pre-revolutionary phase, the eclectic and paradoxical political and communication landscapes in Egypt, and the role that new media played in paving the way for the revolution, is discussed. During the 2011 revolution, the role of new media, especially social media, such as Facebook, Twitter, and YouTube, is highlighted in terms of the multiple roles they play as catalysts for change, avenues for civic engagement, and platforms for citizen journalism. In the post-revolutionary phase, the multiple changes and challenges exhibiting themselves after the revolution are analyzed, especially the divisiveness between different players in the Egyptian political arena and how it is reflected in the communication landscape.

INTRODUCTION

This chapter draws a picture of the rapidly shifting Egyptian political and communication landscapes, which are closely intertwined, and the role of new media, especially Internet-based communication, in accelerating the process of political transformation and the shift towards democratization.

It analyzes the Egyptian media scene during three important stages, namely: before, during and after the 2011 revolution which toppled the autocratic regime of President Hosni Mubarak. In the pre-revolutionary phase, the eclectic and paradoxical nature of the Egyptian political and communication landscapes, which witnessed limited freedom in the political domain coupled

DOI: 10.4018/978-1-4666-4197-6.ch011

with rising oppositional voices and diversity of opinions in the media domain, are be discussed. During the 2011 revolution, the role of new media, especially Internet-based communication platforms, such as *Facebook, Twitter*, and *YouTube*, will be highlighted in the context of the multiple roles they played as catalysts for change, avenues for civic engagement, and platforms for citizen journalism. In the post-revolutionary phase, the multiple changes and complex challenges exhibiting themselves one year after the eruption of the revolution are thoroughly analyzed, especially in relation to the divisiveness between different players in the political arena in Egypt and how it was reflected in communication practices, both online and offline. Finally, the most important findings about the transformative and interconnected Egyptian political and communication landscapes are summed up.

THE PARADOXICAL EGYPTIAN MEDIA LANDSCAPE PRIOR TO THE 2011 REVOLUTION

Before the 1952 revolution, Egypt was a monarchy under Ottoman rule, and it struggled against French and British occupations. This political context of fighting against Ottoman rule and foreign occupations gave birth to a general media atmosphere which was characterized by hot political debates, highly nationalistic sentiments, and patriotic struggles against foreign invasion and colonialism (Hamroush, 1989). This era was also rich in its cultural wealth and intellectual diversity, because the newspapers provided platforms for various writers, poets, and thinkers to display their literary contributions. It also witnessed the birth of a strong and dynamic partisan press and a highly politicized and vibrant media environment.

When a group of army officers toppled the monarchy and seized power, turning Egypt into a republic, the so-called 1952 revolution led to mostly tragic developments in the Egyptian media scene. The pluralistic and vibrant media scene that had prevailed before the 1952 revolution was replaced by a much more monolithic and restrictive media environment, after Egypt achieved her independence. In this new era, all media fell under strict governmental supervision, control, and ownership. Newspapers of the pre-1952 era started to disappear, as many were closed by the government, heavy financial fines were imposed on them, and many journalists were jailed (Abdel Rahman, 1985; 2002).

The era of President Gamal Abdel Nasser, in particular, was characterized by autocratic leadership, since he exercised an iron fist policy in dealing with his opponents. His policy led to a severe backlash in the margin of freedom enjoyed by various media, because he deliberately controlled mass media to mobilize people behind the government's policies and ideologies (Boyd, 1977; 1999). Most importantly, "Nasser's nationalization of the press marked the end of its freedom, professionalism, and excellence" (Nasser, 1990, p. 4) by curbing its diversity and plurality.

When Anwar Sadat came to power as president in 1970, after Nasser's death, he legitimized the birth of political parties and enabled them to publish their own newspapers. Although he started to ease off some of the harsh restrictions and limitations posed by Nasser on the media, the damage to the Egyptian media scene during the Nasser era was grave, and this remained for a long time. Under Sadat, "the press system changed several times, both towards and away from more diversity and freedom of expression. Sadat's attitude towards the press and toward freedom of speech generally was...ambivalent" (Rugh, 2004, p. 152). That was because he was torn between his desire to increase democracy and his fear of its exploitation. Therefore, his era, which started with the granting of a relatively wider margin of freedom and pluralization in both the political and media domains, ended with very strict and restrictive measures against his political opponents and their publications. Many of Sadat's political opponents were jailed, and the publications to which they contributed were shut down shortly before his assassination.

This ambivalent official attitude toward the media continued under President Hosni Mubarak, who assumed power after Sadat's assassination in 1981. Although he initially encouraged opposition parties to publish their own newspapers, the absence of true democratic practice and real political participation left these parties and their papers without a real base of popular support. Additionally, the high illiteracy rate in Egypt limited these newspapers' circulation, and the lack of trust in the political parties that published them limited their credibility in the eyes of the Egyptian people.

Moreover, Mubarak's ambivalent attitude toward the press was evident in that, although he allowed opposition parties and their publications to exist, "arrests and abuse of journalists—police assaults and raids, detentions, even torture—continued" (Rugh, 2004, p. 156). Although his era witnessed significant developments that affected the Egyptian media landscape, such as the emergence of media privatization, the introduction of private satellite television channels, the spread of privately owned opposition newspapers (both in print and online), and growing Internet accessibility, the continued enforcement of the emergency law, which grants the government unlimited power to suppress freedom of expression and to clamp down on opposition, posed a major obstacle to democracy and freedom.

Therefore, despite the major transformations brought about in the Egyptian media arena due to the introduction of satellite television channels (Sakr, 2001), as well as the widespread access to the Internet and the emerging concept of blogs (Abdulla, 2006; Atia, 2006; Iskandar, 2006) and other forms of online social media, such as Facebook and Twitter, which signified a shift from a monolithic to a more pluralistic media scene (Khamis, 2007; 2008), a number of important paradoxes characterized the Egyptian media landscape during Mubarak's era.

The first paradox was the complex, and often ambivalent, relationship between the press and the state in Egypt which meant that the margin of freedom allowed for the media often times oscillated between the poles of press freedom and government repression, at times stretching and at other times shrinking, depending on the general political atmosphere, the nature of the discussed topics, who the communicators were, and how tolerant the government was to their views. This governmental repression was demonstrated in different forms of direct and indirect state control, such as censorship, economic subsidies, media regulations, or governmental media ownership, especially over broadcast media and national daily newspapers (Al-Kallab, 2003), which were always under strict governmental control.

The second paradox was that the pace of change in the Egyptian media arena has been much faster than in the political arena, leading to an uneven development between press freedom and political freedom, whereby the accelerating rate of press freedom, despite its many handicaps, restrictions, and imperfections, was not equally matched by actual political reform or real democratic practice. This paradox could be referred to as a case of media schizophrenia (Iskandar, 2006) because of the wide gap between the very loud, critical, or even angry voices heard through opposition media avenues in Egypt at times, on one hand, and the absence of true democratic practice and actual political participation, on the other hand.

Therefore, it can be argued that the Egyptian media were largely acting as "safety valves" (Khamis, 2007; 2008) that allowed the public to vent anger and frustration at many political, economic, and social ills and injustices, especially given that people were not granted the chance to exercise real political rights or actual decision making, but without taking effective action on the ground.

This posed an interesting paradox, whereby new media substituted, rather than promoted, actual democratic practice and the exercise of real political rights (Seib, 2007). This trend was encouraged by the Egyptian government for the purpose of either absorbing the public's anger and frustration at major political, economic, or social grievances, or diverting the public's attention away from them (Khamis, 2007; 2008; Seib, 2007). In every case, the underlying assumption was that, if the public were offered some avenues through which to vent anger and frustration, more drastic actions, such as protesting or revolting, could be avoided or at least delayed.

The third paradox was that the Egyptian media scene witnessed a number of parallel, albeit contradictory, phenomena. The first was authoritarianism versus resistance. While governmental hegemony and control were widely exercised in the political domain without genuine political participation, many alternative, resistant voices were creating their own media as platforms to express their political thoughts and oppositional views (Zayani, 2008). One good example was the *kefaya* opposition movement; the name means "enough" in Arabic, and it was conveying a clear message to the Egyptian president who had been in office for several decades. This secular political group, like many others in Egypt, managed to have its views heard through Internet websites and blogging (Abdulla, 2006). Another example was the Muslim Brotherhood, or the *Ikhwan*, who, according to Radsch (2012), created some political alliances with their liberal counterparts, such as *kefaya* and April 6 movement, and, thus, became part of the general movement for change that swept through Egypt leading up to the revolution of 2011. Members of the Brotherhood participated actively in the protests and demonstrations that engulfed Egypt from 2004 to 2006, and adopted and adapted alternative media to their causes as they emerged (Radsch, 2012).

Other parallel, but contradictory, phenomena, that also exhibited themselves in the Egyptian media landscape included the coexistence of "state ownership" and "private ownership" or "governmental control" and "individual or party control," whether in the case of print or broadcast media, such as the existence of national televi-

sion in addition to private satellite channels and national daily newspapers in addition to opposition newspapers. There was also the coexistence of "old" and "new" forms of communication simultaneously, as exemplified in the reliance on new forms of communication, such as texting, chatting, skyping, or emailing, while at the same time relying on word of mouth and face-to-face communication, in addition to various types of folkloric and traditional arts.

Ironically, the Egyptian government under Mubarak played an active role in facilitating and accelerating the spread of the Internet, which afterwards became a very effective weapon used by protesters and political activists to topple the regime in 2011 (this will be discussed in the subsequent section of this chapter). Abdulla (2006) explains that "Although [the Internet was] off to a relatively slow start, in January 2002, the government started an ambitious plan to increase internet connectivity. Access to the network… became free for all users" (p. 94). This is in line with Khamis and Sisler's (2010) observation that although many Internet websites and blogs are used to defy and resist autocratic governments and dictatorial regimes in the Arab world, a number of these governments took steps to encourage Internet proliferation and accessibility, mainly in order to boost economic development. The Egyptian government under Mubarak was no exception.

The widespread access to the Internet and the emerging concept of the "blogs" (Atia, 2006; Iskandar, 2006), meant that a whole new arena became available to the public, in general, and to political activists, in particular, which didn't exist before, to express their views, ideas, and criticisms, to comment on everyday issues, and to discuss cultural, social, and religious topics.

However, it was not until the popular revolution of 2012 that media activism translated into some form of on the ground political activism in Egypt, through the vital and crucial role that social media, such as Facebook, Twitter, and YouTube, as well as new communication technologies, such as digital cameras and cell phones, played in accelerating political transformation, energizing civil society, and catalyzing public mobilization, as will be discussed later, thus creating the missing link between online and offline political activism in Egypt.

NEW MEDIA, CIVIC ENGAGEMENT, AND POLITICAL MOBILIZATION DURING THE 2011 REVOLUTION

The historical revolution which erupted in January 2011 forcing Mubarak out of office was characterized by a number of important features, namely: being a grassroots, popular, peaceful and across the board uprising, where youths and women played leading roles. It was also often described by many as a "leaderless revolution," due to its bottom-up nature, although the term "semi-leaderless" could provide a more accurate depiction of reality, due to the organized political efforts of many groups on the ground, such as *Kefaya*, April 6 movement, and the Muslim Brotherhood (*Ikhwan*), as mentioned prior.

Additionally, one of the most important features of this revolution was the instrumental and significant role that new media, such as Facebook, Twitter, and YouTube, in addition to text messaging through cell phones and photos via digital cameras, played in it. These new modes of communication enabled a form of cyberactivism, which is "the act of using the Internet to advance a political cause that is difficult to advance offline" (Howard, 2011, p. 145). This cyberactivism paved the way for political change and transformation through becoming a major trigger for street activism; energizing civil society and encouraging civic engagement, through aiding the mobilization and organization of protests and other forms of political expression; and promoting a new form of citizen journalism, which provides a platform for ordinary citizens to express themselves and to document their own versions of reality (Khamis & Vaughn, 2011).

The importance of citizen journalism stems from the fact that through social media citizen journalists who are dissatisfied with traditional media's version of events are telling their own stories, and that "these patterns of political expression and learning are key to developing democratic discourses" (Howard, 2011, p. 182). Most importantly, this pattern of reporting by ordinary citizens who are holding hand-held devices, such as cell phones and digital cameras, does not only reach a local or domestic audience, rather it has the capacity to reach a broad international audience, thanks to the amplifying effect of transnational satellite channels, such as *Al Jazeera* and *Al Arabiya*, which disseminate this type of media content globally by asking citizens to send their videos and to upload them online.

The value of this widespread coverage by citizen journalists is not only increasing awareness about the regime's brutality, corruption, excessive use of force against protesters and violations of human rights, but also encouraging hesitant or undecided citizens to come out and protest. As Freeland (2011) explains "opponents of a dictator need to feel that their views are widely shared and that enough of their fellow citizens are willing to join them." The marriage between satellite television channels and social networking sites made it easier to let each individual know that his/her views are shared by enough people to make protesting worthwhile and safe (Freeland, 2011).

An equally important role played by new media in this revolution was promoting civic engagement, as previously mentioned. The term civic engagement refers to the process through which civil society is invited to participate in ongoing political, economic and social efforts that are meant to bring about positive change in society (Khamis & Vaughn, 2011). This played an important function in terms of awakening the largely dormant, unengaged, and marginalized civil society in Egypt, thus, facilitating a shift in the role of new media from being "safety valves," as previously discussed, to becoming effective "mobilization tools." This took place through the ability of these new media to act as effective catalysts and accelerators for change in society, thus filling some of the most important gaps in the Egyptian political scene, namely: the gap between the vibrant media arena and the largely stagnant political life; the gap between online activism and on the ground organization; and the gap between the educated, middle class elites and the wider population.

One good example of this mobilization role of new media was exemplified in the "We Are All Khaled Said" Facebook page which was founded in June 2010 shortly after the death of Khaled Said, a young Alexandrian businessman who was dragged from an Internet café and beaten to death in the street by police in June 2010 for posting a video on the Internet exposing police corruption (Giglio, 2011, p. 15). This video, which was uploaded on YouTube, showed a group of Egyptian policemen allegedly sharing the confiscated drugs from a drug deal. This Facebook page was named after the murdered young man whose brutalized, deformed face became the face of the entire revolution's call for freedom, justice, and dignity (Khamis & Vaughn, 2011a).

The "iconic" value of Said's photo, according to Egyptian political activist and prominent blogger, Nawara Negm, stemmed from the fact that it was very easy for many middle-class people, including the young activists who were the driving force behind this revolution, to identify with this handsome, middle class, young man. "They felt that if this could happen to him, it can happen to me too," Negm explains. It was this process of "self-identification" with this victim, coupled with the wide circulation of his pre- and post-beating photos that have gone viral on the Internet, which made people extremely furious and outraged to the extent that they decided to take action against this brutality and to do something effective to put an end to it.

One important point to bear in mind was that each of the new media tools was best suited to play a different role in this revolution. For ex-

ample, Facebook was effective in finding others with similar political views and mobilizing and planning protests; *YouTube* was well suited for citizen journalism and encouraging engagement in activism; and SMS messaging and Twitter enabled on-the-move coordination and communication. Twitter has also been used for outreach to the international media and diasporic communities. Such widespread and easy access to these online communication tools posed new and threatening challenges to autocratic regimes and their censored media outlets, and offered new chances to counter their unlimited power. The combination and utilization of all of these different types of social media all at once, and in coordination with each other, created a very strong communication network, which became difficult to break (Khamis & Vaughn, 2011a).

However, it is important to bear in mind that social media were not causes of the revolution, but rather vehicles for empowerment. As Adel Iskandar, an adjunct faculty member in Georgetown University and an expert on Arab media, explains "Facebook amplified, magnified and expedited the process of revolt, through providing unique networking opportunities. The strategic use of new media helped the revolution to snowball, through using certain strategies, maneuvers, and tactics that turned small protests into a huge challenge to the regime that led to its ultimate demise." However, Adel Iskandar rightly adds that, "If it was not for the power and determination of the Egyptian people to act, organize, and mobilize on the streets, this revolution would have never succeeded."

Interestingly, it could be said that social media were not only "boosters" of the Egyptian revolution, but they themselves were "boosted" by this revolution. That's because in the year 2008, more than 6 million Egyptians had Internet access, and cell phones became ubiquitous, many of which were sold with the Facebook mobile web application (Nelson, 2008). By the year 2009, "five million Egyptians used Facebook, among

17 million people in the Arab region" (Ghannam, 2011). However, the number of Facebook users in Egypt jumped to over 7 million right after the 2011 revolution. This number increased to 9.4 million users in 2012, according to a report by the *Daily Trust* (Nurudeen, 2012). Also, according to a report by SBWire, the number of Internet users in Egypt is expected to double in 2012, as it became "one of the leading Internet markets in Africa, in terms of users, international bandwidth, and services offered."

ONE YEAR AFTER THE REVOLUTION: THE POLITICAL AND COMMUNICATION CHANGES AND CHALLENGES

One year after the eruption of this historical revolution, a lot of things have changed in both the Egyptian political and communication scenes. The new media, which played a significant role in mobilizing people and getting them out to the streets during the revolution, were less effective in aiding a smooth transition to democratization and reform through consensus building and bridging the differences between the various political actors. Divisiveness and separation, rather than unity and cohesion, started to characterize the new Egyptian political landscape; the army which was hailed by the Egyptian people for its courageous and noble role during the revolution, when it refused to open fire on unarmed civilians, came under fire for severe violations of human rights, abuses of power, and corruption. Women, who were highly respected because of their roles as activists and heroines during the revolution, were humiliated by being subjected to "virginity testing" and other acts of SCAF[1] brutality: they were attacked, beaten, assaulted, and insulted, not to speak of their marginalization in the political race. And, most importantly, the middle class, educated youth, who were the real heroes and the invisible leaders behind this revolution, failed to

achieve significant results at the voting polls in Egypt's first free parliamentary elections after the revolution, as they were eclipsed by members of Islamic groups, such as the Muslim Brotherhood, who have been active and well organized on the ground for years, despite official banning by successive governments.

All of these new realities necessitate revisiting the Egyptian political and communication landscapes one year after the revolution to shed light on the most significant changes and the pressing challenges that imposed themselves and what they mean in terms of the potentials and limitations of new media in paving the way for democratization.

In the months following Mubarak's ouster from office, social media assumed different roles and functions than those before and during the revolution. Their mission shifted to providing a forum for followers to discuss issues related to the future of Egypt, such as rethinking democratic practices in the country, promoting and encouraging developmental projects to support the economy, and proposing ways to improve the county's challenging social conditions, in addition to sharing news and views of political events in the broader Arab world, most notably Libya and Syria, on a constant basis.

In other words, the new role which these media assumed was providing online forums for practicing democracy-building, consensus-building, and nation-building, which are especially important in a country that is transitioning to popular participation. Additionally, they also served as the memory of the revolution through documenting its most important events and historical moments, provided a support mechanism for ongoing political activism on the ground, and increased local and international awareness of the political struggles in other Arab nations (Khamis & Vaughn, 2011a).

However, one of the main features of this new era on both the political and communication fronts was lack of consensus, which reflected the dynamics and mechanisms of the post-Mubarak era that was characterized by division, rather than unity, and plurality, rather than uniformity. "It is easy to oust a dictator from power, but it is harder to decide what to do next. Here lies the real challenge. Now there is more division of opinion among the various political groups as to how the country should be managed and how its affairs should be run. It is, therefore, harder to see the type of consensus that was reflected on some online pages during the revolution," Adel Iskandar explains.

Moreover, this divisiveness was reflected in the gap between the young online political activists, on one hand, and the broad offline Egyptian population, on the other hand. One of the explanations for this gap is that although the users of Facebook are very influential in Egyptian discourse and culture, they are still a small minority of the entire Egyptian population, because the medium requires Internet access, which can be expensive if you connect multiple times per day, and illiteracy is a persistent and serious problem in Egypt, which has more than 40% illiteracy rate.

This was clearly exemplified in the referendum on amending the constitution, which was carried out in March 2011. While the youth of the revolution, who were more active online, largely favored rejecting these amendments and strongly preferred drafting a new constitution altogether, the majority of voters, influenced by religiously-oriented groups, who were more active on the ground, voted in favor of these constitutional amendments. To illustrate this point, Elizabeth Iskander (2011) points out that the disappointing results of the constitutional referendum that took place in Egypt after Mubarak's ouster showed that "the views and discourses that dominate Egyptian Facebook spaces do not necessarily represent the political voice of the majority of Egyptians" (p. 1235).

Another even more visible example of this divisiveness between online and offline spaces was the inability of these young online political activists, who were the main inspirational force behind the revolution, to achieve any significant gains in the 2011 parliamentary elections, while

the Islamist groups, who had less online activism but much more on the ground organization, were able to win 70% of the new parliament's seats in the first free and fair election that has taken place in Egypt for a long time. This is another clear indication that the trickle-down effect of online discourses and virtual brainstorming on Facebook pages still needs to expand to reach a much broader and wider base in Egyptian society, before being able to meaningfully change existing public opinion trends or effectively shape the country's future.

This finding is supported by research evidence that indicates that online activity might not have much traction with public opinion. For example, a Gallup poll showed that only 8% of the Egyptian population got their news from Facebook or Twitter during the protests in January and February 2011, and only 17% of the protesters had Internet connections in their home; indeed, during the protests, 63% of Egyptians got their news of the protests from the satellite television channel *Al Jazeera* (Hellyer, 2012). However, after Mubarak's fall, in March and April 2011, 81% of Egyptians reported that they got their news about Egypt's political transition from the state television channel, and, furthermore, 59% of Egyptians polled in December 2011 reported that they perceived state media as accurate (Hellyer, 2012). The latter finding is particularly alarming because of SCAF's complete control over state media in the post-revolutionary phase.

According to Adel Iskandar (2012), SCAF's control over the media has steadily increased, beginning first with media silence during and after the military's violent expulsions of protesters from Tahrir Square on March 9, 2011, then active complicity in the following months, repeating the false evidence and counterclaims of SCAF after such incidents as the October 2011 incident in Maspero, where the military attacked Coptic Christian protesters, killing 29; in that case, state media reported that it was the protesters who attacked the military police, completely reversing the narrative. Adel Iskandar (2012) adds that state media again acted as a SCAF mouthpiece after two other incidents in 2011: in November when police killed 40 protesters near Tahrir and again in December when military forces attacked a sit-in at the Cabinet building, killing many protesters. When members of the state media do try to speak up or allow the other side of the story to be heard, Iskandar (2012) reports that they are "demoted, fired, or have had charges brought against them."

Moreover, a recent report makes more media control likely: the SCAF's leader, Field Marshal Hussein Tantawi, has called for a new "National Military Media Committee," comprised of generals, to counteract what it calls "biased" media coverage and provide the "military's account of any future events that take the media spotlight, particularly those that involve armed forces personnel" (El Badry, 2012).

Another distinguishing feature of this post-revolutionary media scene, at least in the few months' right after the revolution, was the remarkably shrinking role of the mobilization function on various online media forums, as well as the almost near absence of pinpointing the malpractices of SCAF and avoiding a confrontational approach in dealing with it.

However, as several incidents (such as the attacks on Coptic Christian demonstrators, which came to be known as the Maspero events; the violent clashes on Mohamed Mahmoud street, which left many dead and injured; and the shocking brutal attacks and assaults on female protesters) demonstrating SCAF's brutality, violation of human rights, and abuse of power, took place in later months, harsh attacks against SCAF started to flare on different online media forums, private satellite channels, and even through organized campaigns that took to the streets.

The most significant of these efforts was a campaign called "Askar Kazeboon" ("Lying Officers" or "Liars"), in which political activists used portable equipment to set up screens in public places such as squares, sidewalks, and even the outside wall of the Supreme Court in order to air video footage clearly showing military forces beating and shooting protesters, "interlaced with SCAF's denial of any wrongdoing" (Abdel Kouddous, 2012).

The main purpose of this counter-propaganda campaign was reaching citizens who watch only state-controlled television (Kirkpatrick, 2011). As part of this campaign, political activists projected the now-infamous video of a young female protester whose black *abaya* (long black dress) was pulled over her head, exposing her blue bra, as she was being beaten and stomped upon by soldiers (Kirkpatrick, 2011). The image of this woman was also disseminated in the form of spray-painted graffiti stencils, which appeared on walls and sidewalks along with stencils of other iconic victims of army violence (Mackey 2011a; 2011b). During one protest, a young man carried a sign saying "To the girl who stripped the men of Egypt: Will you marry me?" (Kirkpatrick, 2011a), ostensibly meaning that the young woman's honor had not been compromised, and that she instead had shamed the soldiers by exposing their brutality. SCAF attempted to justify the attack on the female protester by saying that she had "insulted the army" using a megaphone just prior to the brutal assault (Mackey, 2011).

The most interesting feature of this campaign is bridging the previously mentioned gap between online and offline activism, since it allowed online content to be widely shared and disseminated to broad offline audiences for the very first time, who represent the largest segments of the Egyptian population that may not have the privilege of Internet access and/or literacy, thus significantly increasing the level of exposure to this campaign and the public's awareness of it, in the hope of gaining their support and approval of its goals and objectives.

Interestingly, the mobilization function which became largely absent in online media forums in Egypt after the revolution was restored with full vigor in many forms and through different avenues, such as the Facebook page "January 25: Egypt's True Revolution," which started several online calls to gather electronic signatures from people in order to confirm their attendance at the large demonstration that political activists want to organize on the occasion of the first anniversary of the Egyptian revolution.

On the other hand, in response to these planned anti-SCAF demonstrations by activists on January 25, 2012, SCAF launched its own public relations campaign to "cement their place in their country's history as 'defenders' of the 18 days of revolution that began in Tahrir Square," planning fireworks displays, parades, and air force flyovers (Beaumont, 2012). Most significantly, they will drop prize certificates from planes in every province, a move activists allege was "designed to persuade poor Egyptians to stay in their neighborhoods rather than gather in the squares" (Beaumont, 2012).

Finally, the post-revolutionary phase in Egypt is characterized by heated "cyberwars" between the different political players, each of whom is trying to increase its visibility and to widen its base of popular support. Besides its online presence, Egypt's Muslim Brotherhood now publishes a daily newspaper for its Freedom and Justice party, and it has acquired its own satellite channel (El-Hennawy, 2011). The Supreme Council of the Armed Forces (SCAF), meanwhile, has been using a Facebook page since February 17, 2011, to disseminate official letters to the Egyptian people, totaling 93 as of the end of 2011 (Naguib, 2011). These letters, which were prolific at first, have since dropped off in number, but they continue to provide SCAF's viewpoints, which have become increasingly critical of the protesters and have begun to include conspiracy theories about foreign influence and interference in the revolution (Naguib, 2011).

Moreover, activists and political figures in Egypt have found their blogs and social media websites hacked, and, on the other side of the political divide, anti-revolutionary figures have also had their websites targeted, including attacks by a group calling itself the "Egyptian Knights" (El Gundy, 2012). In addition, political parties and other organizations have found their websites targeted. Examples are the Muslim Brotherhood, whose "Ikhwan Online" web forum was attacked by the "hacktivist" group Anonymous, and a Salafist party that had its Facebook page defaced with photos of scantily clad women (El Gundy, 2012). All these instances provide a clear evidence that the political struggle and the communication struggle have been, and still are, going hand in hand, whether before, during or after Egypt's revolution.

CONCLUDING REMARKS

This chapter offers a panoramic view of the Egyptian media and its changes and transformations during various phases, namely: before, during and after the historical Egyptian revolution of 2011. The underlying assumption throughout this chapter has been that answering the question of "why the media are the way they are?" (Hallin & Mancini, 2004) necessitates answering the equally pressing and interrelated question of "why the government-media relationship is the way it is?," since it is only through a careful and deep examination of the structure and dynamics of the government-media relationship that we can truly understand and analyze the nature of the media system in a certain country. Therefore, this chapter situates the complex government-media relationship in the transformative Egyptian media landscape within the overall political context and its complex and multifaceted realities during different phases.

It explores the shifting and changing functions that new media played before, during, and after the Egyptian revolution, showing how in the pre-revolutionary phase the media's functions were primarily increasing awareness and creating motivation, through disseminating news, pictures, and videos exposing police brutality and government corruption. During the revolution, the media played a central role in mobilizing political activists and coordinating protesters on the ground, as well as documenting arrests and abuses against the protesters, thus promoting political activism inside Egypt and boosting awareness on the international front. This role changed to engaging in nation-building, democracy-building, and consensus-building in the post-revolutionary phase, with a remarkable shrinking in the mobilization function, which prevailed during the revolution. However, when the first anniversary of the Egyptian revolution approached, a clear resurgence in this online mobilization function was witnessed via different Facebook pages, in addition to organized campaigns, both online and offline, which exposed the brutality and malpractices of SCAF.

New media, in general, and social media, in particular, acted as effective tools for supporting the capabilities of the democratic activists by allowing forums for free speech and political networking opportunities; providing a virtual space for assembly; supporting the capability of the protestors to plan, organize, and execute peaceful protests; and enabling ordinary citizens to document the protests and governmental brutality and to disseminate their own words and images to each other and to the outside world through foreign media, in order to gain support for the cause of human rights and political freedoms internationally (Khamis & Vaughn, 2011a).

However, we must also acknowledge the limitations of cyberactivism efforts in bringing about the desired results in terms of actual political change on the ground, which always requires the physical presence of large numbers of people out on the street who are willing to face the high risk of personal injury, arrest, or even death. In other words, it can be argued that the phenomenon of cyberactivism is a necessary, but not sufficient,

factor in bringing about actual political change and that social media could best act as "catalysts" and "accelerators" for political change, but they can't be "magical tools" that can bring about this type of change on their own.

This was clearly manifested in the limited role played by social media in the post-revolutionary phase in terms of bringing about the desired smooth shift towards democratization; aiding consensus-building; overcoming divisions between different political forces; or shaping public opinion trends in Egyptian society. This could be attributed to the existing gap between online and offline spheres, especially in a country like Egypt which has a struggling economy, limited Internet access, and high illiteracy rates. This meant that the online activists, despite their influential role during the revolution, remained a minority in Egyptian society, both numerically and politically, a fact which was clearly reflected in the parliamentary elections' results of 2011.

The previous discussion reminds us that new media, as in the case of Egypt, are only part of a complex and interrelated set of variables, and while, indeed, they may act as "boosters" or "stimulators" of change and reform, one should be careful not to assign too much power to them in the transition toward democratization (Seib, 2007). This is because "The complexity of democratization should be respected…and no single factor's impact should be overrated" (Seib, 2007, p. 2).

Therefore, it can be safely concluded that when it comes to the effort of reshaping a country's political future, rebuilding its economic capabilities, and restructuring its social underpinnings, online efforts alone can never suffice. It is indeed the interconnectedness between both online and offline efforts and activities that are well coordinated and carefully orchestrated by political actors, who may differ in their ideologies, agendas, and mechanisms, but who share the same fundamental goal of bettering their country, in a manner that can pave the way for freedom, dignity, and democracy.

REFERENCES

Abdel Kouddous, S. (2012). Egypt's new war of information. *Jadaliyya*. Retrieved January 12, 2013, from http://www.jadaliyya.com/pages/index/3960/egypts-new-war-of-information.

Abdel Rahman, A. (1985). *Studies in the contemporary Egyptian press*. Cairo, Egypt: Dar Al Fikr Al-Arabi.

Abdel Rahman, A. (2002). *Issues of the Arab press in the twenty-first century*. Cairo, Egypt: Al-Arabi lilnashr Wal Tawzi'.

Abdulla, R. A. (2006). An overview of media developments in Egypt: Does the Internet make a difference? [GMJ]. *Global Media Journal, 1,* 88–100.

Al-Kallab, S. (2003). The Arab satellites: The pros and cons. *Transnational Broadcasting Studies Journal (TBS), 10*. Retrieved January 21, 2013, from http://www.tbsjournal.com/Archives/Fall03/Salih_Kallab.html

Atia, T. (2006, July). Paradox of the free press in Egypt. USEF Expert Panel Discussion. Washington, DC.

Beaumont, P. (2012). Egypt: one year on, the young heroes of Tahrir Square feel a chill wind. *The Observer*. Retrieved January 12, 2013, from http://www.guardian.co.uk/world/2012/jan/15/tahrir-square-elbaradei-protesters

Boyd, D. (1977). Egyptian radio: Tool of political and national development. *Journalism Monographs (Austin, Tex.), 55,* 501–507, 539.

Boyd, D. (1999). *Broadcasting in the Arab world: A survey of the electronic media in the Middle East* (3rd ed.). Ames, IA: Iowa State University Press.

El Badry, Y. (2012). Military to form committee to provide 'true information' to the media (trans. from Al-Masry Al-Youm). *Egypt Independent*. Retrieved January 12, 2013, from http://www.almasryalyoum.com/en/node/604766

El Gundy, Z. (2012). Revolutionary activists take fight into cyberspace. *Ahram Online*. Retrieved January 12, 2013, from, http://english.ahram.org.eg/NewsContent/1/64/31488/Egypt/Politics-/Revolutionary-activists-take-fight-into-cyberspace.aspx

El-Hennawy, N. (2011). Looking to consolidate its influence, Brotherhood takes to the media. *Egypt Independent*. Retrieved January 12, 2013, from http://www.almasryalyoum.com/en/node/572181

Freeland, C. (2011). The Middle East and the groupon effect. *AFP*. Retrieved January 12, 2013, from http://blogs.reuters.com/chrystia-freeland/2011/02/18/the-middle-east-and-the-groupon-effect/

Ghannam, J. (2011). Social *media in the Arab world: Leading up to the uprisings of 2011. A report to the Center for International Media Assistance*. Retrieved January 12, 2013, from http://cima.ned.org/publications/social-media-arab-world-leading-uprisings-2011-0

Giglio, M. (2011, February 21). The Facebook freedom fighter. *Newsweek*.

Hallin, D. C., & Mancini, P. (2004). *Comparing media systems: Three models of media and politics*. New York: Cambridge University Press. doi:10.1017/CBO9780511790867.

Hamroush, A. (1989). *The story of journalism in Egypt*. Cairo, Egypt: Al Mostaqbal.

Hellyer, H. A. (2012). Violence and the Egyptian military. *Foreign Policy*. Retrieved January 12, 2013, from http://mideast.foreignpolicy. com/posts/2012/01/13/violence_and_the_egyptian_military

Howard, P. N. (2011). *The digital origins of dictatorship and democracy: Information technology and political Islam*. Oxford, UK: Oxford University Press. doi:10.1017/S1537592711004853.

Iskandar, A. (2006, July). *Paradox of the free press in Egypt*. USEF Expert Panel Discussion Notes. Washington, DC.

Iskandar, A. (2011, April 24). *Personal interview*. Washington, DC.

Iskandar, A. (2012). Egypt media flourish amid fears. *Huffington Post*. Retrieved January 12, 2013, from http://www.huffingtonpost.com/adel-iskandar/egypt-television_b_1195958.html

Iskander, E. (2011). Connecting the national and the virtual: Can Facebook activism remain relevant after Egypt's January 25 uprising? *International Journal of Communication, 5*, 1225–1237.

Khamis, S. (2007). The role of new Arab satellite channels in fostering intercultural dialogue: Can Al-Jazeera English bridge the gap? In Seib, P. (Ed.), *New Media and the New Middle East* (pp. 39–52). New York: Palgrave Macmillan.

Khamis, S. (2008). Modern Egyptian media: Transformations, paradoxes, debates and comparative perspectives. *Journal of Arab and Muslim Media Research*, *1*(3), 259–277. doi:10.1386/jammr.1.3.259_1.

Khamis, S., & Sisler, V. (2010). The new Arab 'cyberscape': Redefining boundaries and reconstructing public spheres. *Communication Yearbook*, *34*, 277–316.

Khamis, S., & Vaughn, K. (2011a). Cyberactivism in the Egyptian revolution: How civic engagement and citizen journalism tilted the balance. *Arab Media & Society, 13*(Summer), 2011. Retrieved January 12, 2013, from http://www.arabmediasociety.com/?article=769

Khamis, S., & Vaughn, K. (2011b). 'We Are All Khaled Said': The potentials and limitations of cyberactivism in triggering public mobilization and promoting political change. *Journal of Arab & Muslim Media Research*, *4*(2/3), 139–157.

Kirkpatrick, D. (2011). Egyptian premier, warning of economic dangers, pleads for peace. *New York Times*. Retrieved January 12, 2013, from http://www.nytimes.com/2011/12/23/world/middleeast/egypts-prime-minister-adds-more-blame-on-protesters.html

Kirkpatrick, D. (2011a). Tahrir Square, walled in. *The Lede. New York Times*. Retrieved January 12, 2013, from http://thelede.blogs.nytimes.com/2011/12/23/tahrir-square-walled-in/#more-150307

Mackey, R. (2011). Egyptian military adviser calls attack on woman justified. *The Lede. New York Times*. Retrieved January 12, 2013, from http://thelede.blogs.nytimes.com/2011/12/22/egyptian-military-adviser-calls-attack-on-woman-justified/

Mackey, R. (2011a). Observers confronted with anger, gunshots and a dead child in Syria. *The Lede. New York Times*. Retrieved January 12, 2013, from http://thelede.blogs.nytimes.com/

Naguib, R. (2011). A year in review: the SCAF rules in 93 letters. *Egypt Independent*. Retrieved January 12, 2013, from http://www.almasryalyoum.com/en/node/575366

Negm, N. (2011, August 20). *Personal interview* Cairo, Egypt.

Nelson, A. (2008). The web 2.0 revolution - extended version. *Carnegie Reporter.* Retrieved January 12, 2013, from http://carnegie.org/publications/carnegie-reporter/single/view/article/item/71/

Nurudeen, N. A. (2012, 16 January). Nigeria: Facebook users hit 4.3 million – Report. *Daily Trust.* Retrieved January 21, 2013, from http://allafrica.com/stories/201201161269.html

Radsch, C. (2012). *The revolution will be blogged: Cyberactivism in Egypt.* Unpublished doctoral dissertation. American University, Washington DC.

Rugh, W. (2004). *Arab mass media: Newspapers, radio, and television in Arab politics.* Westport, CT: Praeger.

Sakr, N. (2001). *Satellite realms: Transnational television, globalization and the Middle East.* London: I.B. Tauris.

SBWire. (2012). *Internet users in Egypt to get double by 2012.* Retrieved January 12, 2013, from http://www.sbwire.com/press-releases/sbwire-75087.htm

Seib, P. (2007). New media and prospects for democratization. In Seib, P. (Ed.), *New Media and the New Middle East* (pp. 1–18). New York: Palgrave Macmillan. doi:10.1057/9780230605602.

Zayani, M. (2008). The challenges and limits of universalist concepts: Problematizing public opinion and a mediated Arab public sphere. *Middle East Journal of Culture and Communication, 1,* 60–79. doi:10.1163/187398608X317423.

ENDNOTES

[1] SCAF is the commonly used abbreviation of the "The Supreme Council of the Armed Forces".

Chapter 12
Twitter Frames:
Finding Social Media's "Influentials" During the "Arab Spring"

Aziz Douai
University of Ontario Institute of Technology, Canada

Mohamed Ben Moussa
McGill University, Canada

ABSTRACT

This chapter reports preliminary findings from a larger investigation of the role of social media and communication technologies in the "Arab Democracy Spring." The goal of the study is to analyze how Egyptian activists used Twitter during the 2011 protests. This stage of the project specifically outlines ways of identifying and classifying some of the most influential Egyptian Twitter users during these events. In addition to profiling the "influentials," this study applies a framing perspective to understanding Twitter's use among Egyptian activists.

INTRODUCTION

The classic tension in the scholarship surrounding the primacy of communication technologies or human agency in social change was in full display during popular protests in the Arab world culminating in the overthrow of Egyptian and Tunisian regimes. In a fashion reminiscent of the Iranian post-election protests in 2009 (Grossman, 2009), western media's celebratory coverage of these popular uprisings may have exaggerated social media's power as a driving force behind these strong winds of change. Still, this article argues, emphasizing the human factor, agency and social movements in social change should not obscure a significant development in Arab

DOI: 10.4018/978-1-4666-4197-6.ch012

societies: young activists' demands for social change have found resonance and sustenance in social media. Cyber activists have become potent in demanding genuine political reforms from their autocratic governments.

Simply put, the "seeds of change" are both "human" and "technological." In other terms, Arab political protests have been fuelled by a potent convergence of these two forces, a convergence personified in the young Google executive, Wael Ghonim, who became a prominent global face of Egyptian protesters. Mr Ghonim had set up and managed a Facebook page, "We Are All Khalid Said," to protest the Mubarak regime's oppressive police tactics (Zetter, 2011). The Facebook page later announced a march on the "Friday of Anger," January 25, to demand political and social reforms in Egypt. Following the eruption of the protests, Egyptian authorities arrested Mr. Ghonim only to release him on February 7 after 12 days of incarceration (BBC News, 2011). Subsequent media profiles and emotional interviews with global media outlets such as CNN and Al Jazeera, have anointed Mr. Ghonim as the public face of a new Arab generation. More significant than the media attention, Mr. Ghonim's youthful character and his association with an international technological powerhouse perfectly illustrate how these protests have been an affair largely driven by technologically savvy young people. In this story, social media have seamlessly meshed with human agency.

The list of political revolutions in which communications media are professed to have constituted an influential factor is predictably illusive and contentious. From the *Samizdat* to fax machines, communications technologies were credited with speeding up the collapse of the Soviet Union (Downing, 2001). Modern social media, such as Twitter, are claimed to play a similar role (Gaffney, 2010). Twitter's renowned as a tool of dissent grew out of the disputed Iranian elections of 2009 and the clamp down on Mir Hossein Mousavi-led opposition. The U.S. State Department, media pundits and outlets declared Twitter to be a "liberation" technology encapsulated in Clay Shirky's claim that "this is it: The big one" (Gaffney, 2010). A few months before the Iranian protests, Molodova had witnessed another "color revolution" that was branded the first "Twitter revolution" (Mungiu-Pippidi & Munteanu, 2009).

As a social media platform, Twitter, a micro-blogging system, was launched in 2006 with the goal of allowing people to find "real-time" information to follow and take part in public discourse and "conversation."[1] Subscribers and users can tweet by posting short messages of 140 characters long that *Twitter* also describes as "small bursts of information." *Twitter* has marketed the length constraint of its tweets as one designed to instigate "creativity" and capture interest similar to a newspaper "headline." By September 14, 2010, Twitter has claimed 175 million registered users to author 95 million tweets per day from all parts of the world (Twitter, 2011). Twitter's international (i.e., non-U.S.) traffic stands at more than 65% of the system's overall activity (Fastenberg, 2010). Researchers found that people tweet for a variety of social reasons that include "keeping in touch" with friends, raising awareness about issues and topics of potential interest to one's social network, or emotional stress releasing valve (Zhao & Rosson, 2009).

The technical lexicon and conversational features of *Twitter* have been subjected to frequent analysis elsewhere (Boyd, Golder and Lotan 2010; Honeycutt & Herring, 2009). Twitter users have adopted the @user (e.g,. @WaelGhonim) and @ replies syntax to address and post replies to specific users. The hashtag (#) and a keyword indicate the tweeted topics, as well as unique short URL help hyper-link the social community to outside material. Twitter's unique brevity, the 140-long character cap on tweets, status updates features, and the network of followers extend users' social networks in "creative" ways (Gruzd, Wellman, &

Takhteyev, 2011; Boyd, Golder, & Lotan, 2010). Retweeting is a popular practice of forwarding other users' tweets that Twitter has adopted only years after it came into existence (Boyd, Golder, & Lotan, 2010).

Boyd, Golder, and Lotan (2010) conducted an observational study of these retweeting practices, describing retweeting as a multi-faceted "conversational activity" ranging from "retweeting for others," and "ego retweets," to "retweeting for social action" (n.p.). Some scholars (Huberman, Romero, & Wang, 2008; Gruzd, Wellman, &Takhteyev, 2011) have examined the architecture of the Twitter social networks focusing on the "friends" and "followers" that Twitter users develop. The number of "followers" and "followees" that Twitter users declare usually exceeds the number of "friends" (notwithstanding a "weak" or loose operationalization of the term) (Huberman, Romero, & Wang, 2008). The researchers go on to emphasize the role of "actual friends" in the Twitter social networks. Having successfully integrated blogging's technical features with those of social networking websites, Twitter has created "imagined communities" where "weak ties" are strengthened and "convey information and–connectivity- to and from other social circles" (Gruzd et al., 2011, p. 34).

This article grapples with the issue of social media influence during the Egyptian uprising and seeks to identify some "influential" Twitter users. The technical capabilities of Twitter and other social media aside, this article is grounded in a strong research tradition that views media technologies' influence as being facilitated by a certain group of "influentials" or "opinion leaders" who remain instrumental to the formation public opinion (Katz & Lazarsfeld, 1955). Thousands of research studies and papers have scrutinized these "influentials" describing them as early "adopters" who help in the "diffusion of innovations" and ideas. The "Two Step Flow of Communication," as the theory became formally known, provides a useful framework through which to examine the influence of Twitter during the Egyptian uprising by providing a preliminary portrait of these "influentials."

THE JANUARY 25 MOVEMENT AND SOCIAL MEDIA

Political contestation and advocacy have characterized Egyptian politics for decades and are rooted in the country's rich history as one of the first Arab countries to have NGOs and political parties. The January 25 movement, however, can be directly traced back and linked to two recent social movements: the Kifaya (meaning "enough" in Arabic) and April 6 movements. The Egyptian Movement for Change, commonly known as Kifaya, was launched in 2005 and one of its main objectives was to oppose the regime's plans to groom Hosni Mubarak's son, Gamal, to succeed his father as president, and also to extend Mubarak's presidency for another term. One of the movement's strength was its ability to unite diverse political groups under its banners; another was its efficient use of ICTs, particularly mobile SMS and the blogosphere (Oweidat et al., 2008). As to the April 6 movements, it was launched in support of textile workers in Mahalla who launched a strike on April 6, 2008 to protest against poor wages and high life costs. The movement's efficient use of Facebook for mobilization purposes signalled another step in Internet-mediated pro-democracy activism in the country. The mobilizing power of the social medium became apparent when activists were able to quickly attract some 60,000 followers in less than two weeks. The networking potential of Facebook clearly allowed dispersed groups of young activists to circumvent the repressive machine of Mubarak' regime and build a large group that police forces cannot easily disperse (Faris, 2008). Foreseeing the downfall of Mubarak regime, Faris succinctly pointed out that "April

6th was the day when organizing tool met political reality to create elements that were strong enough to form storm clouds on the regime's horizon" (Faris, 2008, p.2).

The recent movement that successfully led the popular uprising that toppled Mubrak's regime is widely known by the date—January 25, 2011— when the main demonstrations and civil disobedience acts started. The January 25 movement is a protest social movement that can be meaningfully understood only if situated in the context of Egyptian protest movements in the last decade, especially the Kifaya movement and the April 6 movement. It is the culmination of a long and bitter struggle marked by progressive and increasing appropriation of new technologies in political contestation. While middle class, young "Facebook" activists initiated the uprising, the movement quickly grew bigger to include groups from all ideological and social strands, including Islamists, workers, and marginalized social groups.

The January 25 movement falls within Diani's (2000) definition of social movements where networks and social networking form the backbone of structure of collective action: "A social movement is a network of informal interactions between a plurality of individuals, groups and/ or organizations, engaged in political or cultural conflict, on the basis of collective identity" (p. 165). The role of the Internet and social media particularly in the Egyptian case is a pivotal one since recent protest social movements have been built around online platforms that facilitated interaction between activists, coordination between geographically and ideologically distant groups and mobilizations around common objectives and offline action. According to Castells (2001), the Internet "fits with the basic features of the kind of social movements emerging in the Information Age .... The Internet is not simply a technology; it is a communication media, and it is the material infrastructure of a given organizational form: the network" (pp. 135–6). A major contribution of the Internet and social in particular to collective

action is through what social movement's theorist term "micromobilization" (i.e., "the collaborative work individuals do on behalf of a social movement or social movement organization to muster, ready, coordinate, use, and reproduce material resources, labor, and ideas for collective action" [Hunt & Benford, 2004, p. 483]). The concept of micromobilization allows is to link the appropriation of the Internet at the individual level to social movement's collective action.

Equally important, Stein (2009) summarizes existing literature on the impact of the Internet on social movements, pointing out six functions: (1) providing information; (2) assisting action and mobilization; (3) promoting interaction and dialog; (4) making lateral linkages; (5) serving as an outlet for creative expression; and (6) promoting fundraising and resource generation (p. 757).

Using this literature as a general guide, this research investigates the political uses of social media in Egyptian uprising, focusing Twitter as a case study. How did Egyptian activists use Twitter during these politically tumultuous times? How did the Jan25 movement draw on Twitter to achieve the main functions outlined prior?

RESEARCH RATIONALE AND QUESTIONS

Thus, a grounded understanding of how the January 25 movement appropriate social media's technical features to mobilize both the "real" and the "imagined community" remains the larger concern of the present research. Amidst the political turmoil, the Mubarak regime became intensely aware that its battle went beyond Tahrir Square to include social media and the Internet. The embattled regime's belated realization led it to take the drastic step of "turning off" the Internet switch that effectively cut off Egypt from the global communications network. For protesters and activists, the Internet represented a main vehicle to counter the Mubarak regime's attempt to demonize and discredit Tahrir Square's protesters. Mubarak's regime had used its muscular control of mainstream media to assert that foreign infiltrators were orchestrating street demonstrations. The claim was eerily echoed in Gaddafi's assertion that Libyan protesters were under the influence of hallucinating drugs or belong Al Qaeda operatives. But the Egyptian uprising also highlighted the limits and limitations of social media in collective action. Despite its mobilizing tool activists resorted to distributing leaflets asking "recipients to redistribute it by email and photocopy, but not to use social media such as Facebook and Twitter, which are being monitored by the security forces" (The Guardian, 2011, para. 4).

Among other goals of the current research is to gauge whether and how frequent tweets helped infuse the protesters with courage and enthusiasm, and amass global support for the cause of democracy in Egypt. By closely focusing on few "influential" Twitter users, this article provides a descriptive analysis and insights into the various mechanisms and tools this social networking website offered young activists in Egypt, Tunisia and elsewhere. Within this rationale, the study will address the following research question:

RQ 1: How influential was Twitter in covering the Egyptian revolution? Specifically, who are the "influentials" among Egyptian Twitter users?

RQ 2: How did Twitter contribute to the networking action of the Jan25 movement?

RQ 3: How did Twitter function as a mobilizing tool during the uprising?

With these larger questions in mind, the present project first profiles some of the most Egyptian "influential" Twitter users. Second, the study examines the tools that these top Twitter users from Egypt employ. Based on the literature review of studies about Twitter, this project will specifically analyze the number of Tweets, re-tweets, following and follower data.

RESEARCH METHOD: FINDING THE "INFLUENTIALS"

The breath-taking political developments that eventually culminated in the collapse of Ben Ali and Mubarak regimes in Tunisia and Egypt, respectively, constitute an attractive research topic and important social laboratory for media scholars. Focusing on the role of the media, particularly the Internet, in these developments poses several challenges for interested researchers and scholars, not least because of the evolving nature of the topic, but more because the Internet is almost a fast-moving research target. Due to this challenge, researching the role of the Internet, specifically how Egyptian activists employed Twitter in their political struggle, requires a higher degree of careful scrutiny beginning at the level of data gathering, data organization and analysis. For instance, typing the word "Egypt," "Egyptian revolution," or "Egyptian uprising" in Twitter's search bar is likely to yield millions of Tweets and postings. It is nearly impossible for researchers to verify the identity of all these Twitter users.

Deeply cognizant of these challenges, this researcher took several precautions to identify and study the most influential Twitter users during the Egyptian uprising. The first of those early precautions was to study only those Twitter users and activists who were based in Egypt. The second precaution was to select only "individual" users, and thus avoid "institutional" users and the Tweets of other organizations. After all, this research's primary concern is with how activists mobilize the Internet in their political cause. How to sift the most "influential" Twitter users from the least "influential" ones remains problematic and requires the "operationalization" of the concept of "influence." Twitter's architecture helpfully provides some "metrics" that can be used to operationalize the concept of "influence." Prominent among these "metrics" are number of "followers" and "followees" a Twitter user has, the number of tweets, and replies a tweet may receive. Imperfect as they may be, these tools provide some "objective" consistency and the researcher has decided to adopt these metrics to "order" the most influential Egyptian Twitter users.

While Internet related research could be challenging, the web offers some helpful tools for researchers as well. Because Twitter is notoriously difficult to research, several websites and search engines have sprung offering Twitter user directories and tweet archives. JustTweetIt.com, Twellow.com, and *Twitter*Packs.com, for instance, organize Twitter users by regions, professions, or topics. A user-generated directory of Twitter users, WeFollow.com is one of the main web resources that the researcher used to identify the most "influential" Twitter users from Egypt. Mashable, a digital technology news and culture website, this user-generated directory makes it "easy to find Twitter users with similar interests or in similar industries." Similar to the old phone directory or the Yellow Pages, Twitter users can add their user information by tweeting to "@wefollow hashtags that represent what categories they would like to be listed under. WeFollow sees these @replies and then organizes users based on those hashtags."[2]

Due to its voluntary and public availability, the researcher decided to use WeFollow.com as a directory to find some Egyptian-based microbloggers. A search of WeFollow.com's database using the keywords "Egypt" and "egypt" yielded 181 Twitter users. Similar search results were obtained after five search attempts conducted in five different and randomly selected days in March to check the reliability of the results as well as ensure that no users were excluded from the analysis. The latest search was conducted in March 19, 2011. Evidently, the list of Twitter users who had added their profiles to this directory is way below the number of Twitter users in Egypt whose Internet users exceed 20 million. The second step was to check the most "influential" users and use other credible sources to justify including them in the analysis. Selected Twitter users had to be clearly based in Egypt. Twitter users had to be "individuals," rather than "institutional,"

accounts. Organizing the list of Egyptian microbloggers in this way, the top five Twitter users who had the highest number of "followers" include the following Twitter users: @Sandmonkey, @waelabbas, @RamyRaoof, @3arabawy, and @alaa (See Table 1).

To the three most "influential" Egyptian Twitter users selected previously, the researcher added another user, @Ghonim, which belonged to Mr. Wael Ghonim who emerged as an "influential" voice and face of the Egyptian uprising during the protests. A young Google executive, Wael Ghonim has become a symbol of Egyptian youth tired of long autocratic rule in their country. He had set up and managed the Facebook page that called for demonstrations against the Mubarak regime known as the "Day of Rage." That Mubrak's security forces had arrested Wael Ghonim for a few days only sowed a sense of defiance, determination and invincibility among activists. Media interviews with Mr Ghonim sealed his reputation as the hopeful and dynamic face of this generation. For these reasons, the study considers that examining Ghonim's tweeting activities would provide a unique layer in understanding the role of social media in social change.

TWITTER'S INFORMATION SHARING

While Twitter supports only short messages (140 characters), a system that does not allow users to write long and complex ideas, this feature, none-

Table 1. Twitter users and locations

Twitter User Name	User's Real Name	Location
@Ghonim*	Wael Ghonim	Egypt/UAE
@Sandmonkey	Mahmoud Salem	Egypt
@waelabbas	Wael Abbas	Egypt
@RamyRaoof	Ramy Raoof	Egypt
@3arabawy	Hossam el-Hamalawy	Egypt
@alaa	Alaa Abd Al Fatah	Egypt

theless, distinguishes the platform from others such as blogs and websites. In fact, one of the biggest advantages of microblogging is that it allows messages and information to be shared on multiple platforms such as mobile phones, emails, IM, and websites (Jansen et al., 2009), maximizing, thus, their reach and impact. The ability to produce and disseminate alternative information and frames is crucial to the formation and success of social movements. According to Melucci (1994), conflicts now "tend to arise in those areas of the system that are most directly involved in the production of information and communicative resources but at the same time subjected to intense pressure of integration" (p. 101). This is the case of pro-democracy social movements in the last few years. According to Oweidat et al. (2008), one of the reasons explaining the failure of Kefaya movement in Egypt was its inability to counterbalance state propaganda. "Although Kefaya was adept in its use of electronic media, the more prevalent state-controlled media managed to overwhelm Kefaya's message" eventually (p.x). The advance of new social media such as Facebook and Twitter helped to readdress the asymmetrical power relationship between the state and the protest movements. In the words of Diani (2000), computer-mediated communication makes it easier "to transform sets of geographically dispersed aggrieved individuals into a densely connected aggrieved population, thus solving one key problem of mobilisation" (p. 388).

Information can be disseminated in various ways on Twitter. There are at least five ways: adding original messages, retweeting others' messages, replying to others' messages, providing links to information in other websites, sending private messages to individual users. The influence of users and their reach and impact as communicators is not equal.

This study relied on two types of crawlers or "Web-analytics" research tools to categorize Egyptian Twitter users and gauge their impact. First, backtweets.com was used to generate general information about the tweeting activity of the six users in the study. Results show that although original messages or updates constitute an important part of the tweets, replies and retweets form more than half of the tweeting activity of the studied users. This reflects highly interactive communication as well as heavy relaying action. In fact, a powerful feature of Twitter is the ability of users to retweets messages they receive to their followers, who, in turn can retweet them—an operation that enables messages to circulate beyond the networks directly affiliated with users. However, users, functioning as nodes in the networks, do not have equal impact. Users with more number of followers can see their original messages and retweets disseminated messages on a large scale (Table 2).

In order to measure users' impact, Twitter, a web crawler, was used. This tool classifies Twitter users in one of the following categories: "Everyday Users," "Reporters," "Social Butterflies," "Trendsetters," and "Thought Leaders." According to Twitter, "Everyday Users have a small circle of influence but great potential," while "Thought Leaders" represent "the voices people listen to most."[3] In addition to these categories, Twitter provides a metric called "Impact" for each Twitter user based on a combination of factors including followers, re/tweeting frequency metrics. The researcher used the "free" version of this software to construct a research portrait of the Egyptian Twitter sphere. Finally, in addition to

Table 2. Tweeting key functions' distribution

User	Updates	Retweets	Replies
@Ghonim	56%	17%	27%
@Sandmonkey	29%	20%	50%
@waelabbas	34%	18%	48%
@RamyRaoof	82%	9%	9%
@3arabawy	43%	36%	21%
@alaa	24%	25%	51%
Mean	44.6%	20.3%	34.3

these publicly available web metrics, the research verified Twitter users' accounts and included them in the upcoming analysis.

ANALYSIS: PROFILING THE "INFLUENTIALS"

The "Two Step Flow of Communication" theory considers the role of "influentials" central to the process of opinion formation and social influence. These "influentials" are opinion leaders, which Katz and Lazarsfeld (1955, p. 3) define as "the individuals who were likely to influence other persons in their immediate environment." Verifying the level of influence that these Twitter users possess remains beyond the purview of this article because it requires more complex and demanding resources. This article posits that publicly available data provide a potential list of "influential" Twitter users. With the exception of Wael Abbas, the social analytics website, Twitter, characterizes all these "influentials" as "Thought Leaders," that is, "the voices people listen to most."

The following section focuses on these Twitter users's own "self-presentation" to understand the context of Twitter use as a tool of political activism. The following portrait provides some significant insights into these Twitter users, and provides a tentative taxonomy of Twitter use in the Arab world. First, these selected microbloggers belong to a younger generation of Egyptians who have embraced technology as a way of political activism. Second, they represent a potent mix of political activists, human rights advocates, journalists, and cyber-activists that have embraced and wielded new media as a political mode of resistance. Their youthful face echoes the faces that dominated the Egyptian uprising. Roughly speaking, the "influentials" in the Egyptian Twitter sphere can be classified as "accidental influentials" or "veteran cyber-activists as described next."

1. **The Accidental "Influential":** This category of Twitter users refers to those who have not regularly been engaged in cyber activism. Marketing literature defines the "accidental influencers" as those who are not "instrumental in starting trends." There is usually a pre-existing social need receptive to arguments and trends that these "influencers" advocate or "sell." They may not be seriously engaged in the political process, but some incidents may constitute a "Tipping Point" (Gladwell, 2000) that induces them to be activists. Among the selected Twitter users, @ Ghonim became one of the "accidental influentials" because of a pre-existing desire for social and political change among Egyptians. Mr Wael Ghonim's story, his transformation from a well-heeled Google executive to a leading voice of Egyptian protesters, has become well known. His profile captures this mix in its briefness and mock irreverence. According to @Ghonim, this microblogger is "Constantly Changing, Serious Joker, Internet Addict, Love challenging status quo!"

As stated previously, Mr. Ghonim has galvanized young Egyptian protesters and upon his release after a 12-day incarceration, he never tired of emphasizing Egypt's young generation yearning for a reform. In emotional media appearances, he claimed that he had done nothing "heroic" and that the credit needed to be bestowed upon other young activists: "The heroes, they're the ones who were in the street, who took part in the demonstrations, sacrificed their lives, were beaten, arrested and exposed to danger." Ghonim's Facebook page, "We Are All Khaled Said," named after an Egyptian businessman tortured to death by Egyptian security forces, had played a central role in uniting the protesters around a concrete cause, namely stopping police abuse and torture of Egyptian citizens (BBC, 2011).

As @Ghonim captured the youthful face of Egyptian Twitter, his tweets became a regular feature in global media coverage of the uprising. For instance, *The New York Times*' news blog, "The Lede," was constantly citing Ghonim's Tweets in its live updates of the events. In its "Updates on Day 15 of Egypt Protests," The Lede republishes @Ghonim's pronouncements during a speech to protesters in the Tahrir Square, as Figure 1 illustrates (Mackey, 2011a).

The tweeting activity of this user category is best described as "irregular." As the January 25's "Day of Rage" approached, their tweets become more frequent and intense. Figure 1 illustrates this frequency and visually captures the intensity of @Ghonim's tweets. After January 25, @Ghonim's tweets spiked up. Understandably, this period was an important and decisive event in the Egyptian protests. There was a need to communicate with the outside world, providing constant updates about the movement and demands of the protesters. @Ghonim's tweet stats reveal that, in addition to providing updates, Twitter served as a means of broadcasting "Retweets," forwarding pronouncements and tweets. Figure 2 also shows that @Ghonim's Retweets more than doubled

Figure 1. Twitter updates

during after the protests erupted, although it is part of an overall increase in the user's tweeting activity.

2.   **The Veteran Cyber Activists:** This category consists of cyber activists who hope to engineer social and political change. Unlike the "accidental influentials," these veteran cyber activists have an established history, and their tweeting activity is part of an overall social media campaign they have been waging for quite some time. @Sandmonkey and @Alaa are two well known veteran cyber activists who have used Twitter in this manner. @Sandmonkey is the Twitter user name of an influential Egyptian blogger, Mahomoud Salem, while @Alaa belongs to Alaa Abd El Fattah, another influential blogger. As a blogger, Sandmonkey has been an object of attention among many researchers interested in the role of new media in political reform. For instance, Eskandar (2007) cites Sand Monkey's blog as one of those "sites of contentious news material about police brutality during opposition rallies and demonstrations as well as locales for political organization and mobilization" (p. 38).

Veteran cyber activists' tweeting patterns and frequency differ from the "accidental activists'" tweeting style. For instance, @Sandmonkey's frequent tweets are consciously making use of the medium's global audience and serve as a connector, or a bridge builder, for the protesters and the global community. Further, these "veteran" Twitters strategically exploit the interactive nature of Twitter by posting frequent replies to other tweets. As Figure 3 demonstrates, @Sandmonkey's @ replies comes second after his original Tweets. This is different from the tweeting behavior of @Ghonim, which emphasizes @Retweets, forwarding other people's tweets, rather than frequently responding to other postings.

Figure 2. January Tweeting activity of @Ghonim

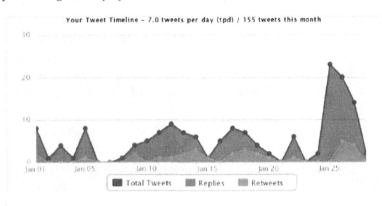

Figure 3. January Tweeting activity of @Sandmonkey

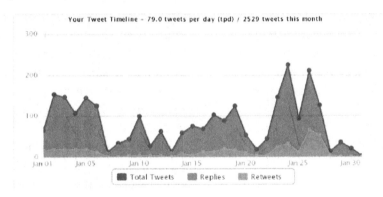

In their brand of "cyber activism," these veteran cyber activists blend cyber activism with old-fashioned campaigning and mobilization. For instance, Alaa Abd El Fattah has operated a blog, *Manal and Alaa's bit bucket,* which sought to united the fragmented Egyptian left (Isherwood, 2008). Under the umbrella of the oppositional political movement, Kefaya, these cyberactivists marched in protest against the Egyptian government's police abuse and torture. @waelabbas's tweets offer an additional platform through which the public shaming of the Egyptian regime conducted. Wael Abbas's blog regularly featured routine police abuse and torture of Egyptian citizens (Rifaat, 2008). In short, the unique influence that these cyber activists wield stems from marrying cyber activism to "old" fashioned political organizing and campaigning.

Which class of activists is more influential? According to Twitter's data, @Ghonim appears to be the most "influential" among Egyptian Twitter users with an "Impact Score" of 64.3%, followed by @3arabawy with an Impact Score of 55.3% (See Table 2). On their own, these metrics do not shed light on an important difference between these two classes of activists in the role they played during the uprising: the "accidental influentials" inspire protesters whereas "veteran cyber-activists" organize protesters. @Sandmonkey's tweets, as quoted by New York Times' "The Lede," drew attention to the perils of "lack of organization." In his Tweets, he opined that protesters should change tactics and devote more time to organizing themselves if their efforts were to succeed:

211

So here is my 2 cents: Instead of getting blankets, please get some foldable tables, chairs, papers, pens and a laptop.

Start registering the protesters, get their names, addresses & districts. Start organizing them into committees. & they elect leaders.

But the status quo won't due (sic). This lack of action and organization will be used against us in every way possible (Mackey, 2011b).

The "veteran cyber activists'" emphasis on organizing the people connects cyber-activism to traditional, bottom-up activism. The divergent strengths of both are complementary in the sense that they succeeded in mobilizing "net activists" and "traditional" political activists, which snowballed into a mass protest movement (Table 3).

HYPERLINKING FUNCTION OF TWEETING

The capacity to connect users fast and on large scale represents the major characteristic of social media. A key feature behind this function is their flexible design and structure to support and encourage easy hyperlinking. As Shih explains in the case of Facebook, for instance:

Table 3. Twitter users organized by number of followers*

	Followers	# Tweets	Impact Score
@Ghonim*	120,943	4572	64.3%
@Sandmonkey	30,204	19,829	49.5%
@waelabbas	30,141	50,617	35.1%
@RamyRaoof	21,727	9934	10.4%
@3arabawy	20,718	35,737	55.3%
@alaa	19,655	47, 516	45.9%

*Stats reflect data gathered and analyzed on 03/19/2011

The first social networks were just websites. Today they are software platforms, which means that, in addition to the web site Facebook creates and maintains, third-party software developers can build can build new applications that extend Facebook's functionality (2010, p. 23).

This also applies to Twitter since it is more than just an online platform but also a software that provides applications that can be downloaded to enable users, whether individuals, groups, or businesses, to share and distribute content as links via Twitter platform. Using backtweets.com, we tried to understand how Twitter was used as a hyperlinking hub to circulate information and frames from and into various online platforms during and in the aftermath of the Egyptian revolution. Results show that tweets providing link to external websites represent an important part (about a third) of all tweets generated by the six studied users (Table 4).

More importantly, social media platforms and software represent the third (32.14%) of the most popular websites that users connect to (Table 5). Sharing photos and videos about the revolution is crucial for mobilization and countering state propaganda. Blogs represents 17.5%; national and international newspapers (21.42%); NGOs and political institutions (21.42%).

MOBILIZATION ON TWITTER: A FRAMING ANALYSIS PERSPECTIVE

The notion of "mobilization" is central to social movements in so far the latter's reason-d'être is the employment of collective action to achieve societal change. From the perspective of social movement theory, mobilization refers to various processes in collective action, from access to material and non-material resources to the production of frames and symbols that delimit a movement's collective identity and field of action. Scholars have argued that the Internet favours a wide range

Table 4. Twitter users posted links

User	links
@Ghonim	19%
@Sandmonkey	9%
@waelabbas	12%
@RamyRaoof	63%
@3arabawy	47%
@alaa	15%
Mean	27.5%

Table 5. Most shared websites

Most shared sites	Type of website
Youtube.com	Social medium video sharing
Twitpic.com	Picture sharing
Google.com	Search engine
Facebook..com	Social media platform
Almasryalyoum.com	National newspaper
Shorouknews.com	National newspaper
Nytimes.com	International newspaper
Ahram.rog.eg	National newspaper
Yfrog.com	Picture sharing
Sanmonkey.org	Blog
Masrawy.com	Blog
English.ahram.org.eg	National newspaper
Thebobs.com	Blog award website
Paper.li	Social media software
Bambuser.com	Photo and video sharing platform
Hrw.org	International NGO
Eipr.org	National NGO
Egyptprotest-defense.blogspot.com	National NGO
Ebfhr.blogspot.com	Blog
Flickr.com	Photo sharing platform
Un.org	International institution
Dostor.org	National newspaper
Misrdigital.blogspirit.com	Blog
Arabwy.org	Blog
e-socialists.net	National NGO
alwafd.org	Political party website
purephoto.com	Photo sharing platform

of mobilization actions, such as disseminating information and symbols, coordinating action and building alliances and solidarity networks (Atton, 2004; Downey & Fenton, 2003; Downing, 2001). In addition to these functions, we add another one that has been largely ignored in this literature, namely collective action framing. The concept of framing is linked to Goffman's work (1974) where the term is used "to denote schemata of interpretation that enable individuals to locate, perceive, identify, and label occurrences within their life space and the world at large" (as cited in Snow, Rochford, & Worden, 1986, p. 464). A central epistemological basis for the concept and its relevance to social movements is the recognition that *meaning is constructed out of social and political interaction with supporters and opponents* [italic added] (Tarrow, 1998, p. 107).

In this article, we draw on Benford's and Snow's (2000) interpretation of the concept, particularly their identification of three core tasks of framing: "diagnostic framing," "prognostic framing," and "motivational framing" (pp. 615–7). Diagnostic framing deals primarily with "problem identification and attributions" (p. 615), wherein "injustice frames" (i.e., identifying victims and amplifying victimhood) constitute the main part of the framing process. Diagnostic framing also pinpoints the "sources of causality blame and culpable agents" (p. 616). Prognostic framing involves the "articulation of a proposed solution to the problem or at least a plan of attack and the strategies for carrying out the plan" (p. 617). As for motivational framing, it is a "call to arms" of sorts, or the "rationale for engaging in ameliorative collective action, including the construction of appropriate vocabularies and motive" (p. 617).

DIAGNOSTIC FRAMING

Commentators have maintained that recognizing peculiar situations as unjust precedes the collective action that strives to address the injustice (Mc-Adam, 1982, p. 51). Collective action frames are, indeed, built around "injustice frames," insomuch as movements facing oppression have to "develop a new diagnosis and remedy for existing forms of suffering, a diagnosis and remedy by which this suffering stands morally condemned" (Moore as cited in Tarrow, 1998, p. 111).

Analysis of users' tweets since the beginning of January 2011 shows very little evidence of frames focusing on injustice per-se. Just three weeks before the eruption of the street demonstrations on January 25, one would expect important efforts from activists towards building support for the movement by highlighting the injustices they want to address, and a discourse that clearly establish the difference between "us," the people of principles, cause, and rights, and "them," the regime and its networks. The quasi absence of "injustice" frames at this stage can be explained by a number of factors. First, the protest social movements, to which the January 25 movement is a continuation, have been going for a considerable time, and have developed over the last years into a mature stage. Activists in the movement, and those using Twitter in particular have reached a stage where they gone beyond the need of identifying injustice towards that of how to address it. Second, Twitter is used in parallel with other platforms, particularly Facebook, which has played a more central role, at least since 2008 when the April 6 movement was launched. Unlike Twitter, Facebook allows users to post threads of posts that include pictures, videos, text and link that add up to a page to form a coherent discourse necessary for identity building and effective persuasion. The page dedicated for Khaled Said on Facebook is a case in point. Posts on Twitter, on the other hand, sounds like a cacophony of sound bites, which can be sometimes difficult for new comers to follow.

PROGNOSTIC FRAMING

Compared to diagnostic framing, Twitter seems more suitable for prognostic and motivational frames, i.e. those dealing with identifying strate-

gies of change as well as for direct mobilization and action. We found more evidence about the use of Twitter for these two types of collective action frames. Thus, during the weeks preceding the revolution, a large number of tweets and threads dealt with the Tunisian revolution. The success of Tunisian people at ousting Ben Ali from power through peaceful popular demonstrations and the use of social media in it clearly caught the attention of Egyptian activists who seemed eager to apply it in their country. Writing about the success of Tunisian revolution, @Ghonim for instance posted on January 17:

A blogger who was arrested few days ago became the new secretary for youth & sport in Tunisia. Inspiring ☺*.*

While taking inspiration from the Tunisian model, Ghonim criticises the attempt to reproduce a copycat of it in Egypt, especially using self-immolation to ignite popular revolution:

Ghonim: An Egyptian man sets himself on fire while chanting slogans against Egyptian police. (Jan 17).

Ghonim: These people are ignorant. They don't know that the central police will organize excellent burnings that will take place in clam. (Jan 17).

Having decided to follow peaceful tactics, activists were also trying hard to keep demonstrations under control, and Twitter was used to remind others of the need to follow this strategy, even in the middle of action:

Ghonim: Now in Tahrir situation is out of control. Prevented 2 angry guys from throwing a huge metal on police cars top of the bridge (Jan 25).

In the same vein, Ramy Raoof (@Ramyraoof) puts emphasis on the need to keep the revolution peaceful in spite of state violence.

Jan 29: the regime is trying to picture the revolution as violence by spreading police thugs and attacking. Its peaceful assemblies #jan25 #Egypt

MOTIVATIONAL FRAMING

Examination of users' tweets before and throughout the January 25 uprising shows that motivational or action frames form the bulk of all tweeting activity. Motivational frames can serve various mobilization purposes. First, in addition their direct and instrumentalist function of disseminating alternative information and news about mobilization efforts being deployed, tweets focusing on action taken or in the process of being carried out serve also the purpose of pointing out to others the possibilities and opportunities available to take part in direct action. Explaining the role of communication about action in expanding collective action opportunities, Tarrow (1998) asserts that

by communicating information about what they do, once formed, movements create opportunities—for their own supporters, for others, for parties, and elites. They do this by diffusing collective action and displaying the possibility of coalitions, by creating political space for kindred movements and counter movements, and by producing incentives for elites and third parties to respond to. (p. 88)

Before becoming a mass popular uprising, the January 25 movement started with much smaller groups of hardcore of activists whose daring action and resistance against police brutality encouraged others to join the protests. Using his mobile phone to tweets updates about the unfolding action on January 25, Wael Ghonim, for instance, posted these two tweets:

We are heading to tahrir square now chanting bread, freedom and dignity #jan25

We are marching now in streets in downtown in hundreds after being beaten up by police and breaking siege #jan25

Everyone come to Tahrir now we are more than 20,000 no police #jan25

Jan25: Come to Harir please #jan25

Ghonim's last tweet signals, in fact, a turning point in the uprising when protestors were able to surmount police repression and regroup again. The use of Twitter appears crucial here since it allowed activists to remain connected even when broken into smaller groups and to regroup again. The ability of activists to use mobile phones to post tweets allowed them to address a major weakness in past direct action when dispersed demonstrators were unable to regroup fast again and start new protests in a different location. The use of the hashtag #jan25 facilitated mobilization since it allowed new users to follow and join the uprising on Twitter.

Motivation frames include also news about police brutality and sacrifices made by activists, which is meant to push others to join or at least show support for the uprising, as these examples illustrate:

@Ramyraoof: Jan28: several are injured from batons and tear gas. Demonstrations are also taking place in Maha, Manoura, Suez, Luxor, Qena. #Jan25 #egypt

Jan26: #picture showing signs of rubber bullets in the back of a demonstrator yesterday in Cairo [link] #Jan25 #Egypt

Despite the state's attempt to shut down the Internet and social media, Twitter was used to keep people mobilized over the three weeks of the uprising. This post illustrates such use:

@Ramyraoof: A call for the people of Egypt: a general strike tomorrow Jan 30

To Vodafone customers in #Egypt: change your message center number to +20105996713 and you will be able to send SMS. Please spread

FINAL REMARKS

The analysis of the "influentials" in the Egyptian Twitter sphere offers some insights about the most "influential" Twitter users during the Egyptian protests. While this research does not resolve the perennial debate about the role of social media in political change, it clarifies some of the ways in which that relationship plays out. The most crucial role that these social media technologies play is to disseminate and circulate information. @Ghonim's and @Sandmonkey's tweets became a regular feature in global media's coverage of the events. For instance, their tweets were frequently cited in *The New York Times, The Guardian, The BBC, and CNN,* to use some internationally well-known English speaking media outlets. Further, their political role is unquestioned. Activists used social media as "decentralized networks" to help fill the political gaps left by the decimation of strong and credible political opposition in Egypt and other authoritarian states.

Specifying how these "network activists" and armies use social media is definitely the first step in demarcating how social media impact politics. Twitter and social media may have encouraged protesters demanding the resignation of Hosni Mubarak. They may have provided some organizational tools to the activists. Another palpable influence is the fact that these "network armies" succeeded in galvanizing the global community and activists worldwide to support the cause of democracy and reform. The Egyptian uprising became more of a global revolution that strained the official diplomatic community. Like other world powers, the Obama administration's official diplomatic responses scrambled to play catch up with Egyptians' clamouring demands for home grown "regime change." Raising their simple slogan for weeks, "The People Want to Overthrow the Regime," Egyptian "smart mobs" made history in Tahrir Square forcing Mubarak to end his decades-long rule and resign on February 27, 2011.

REFERENCES

BOYD. D. M., Golder, S., & Lotan, G. (2010). Tweet, Tweet, Retweet: Conversational aspects of retweeting on Twitter. *HICSS43* (Vol. 0, pp. 1-10). Manoa, HI. IEEE. Retrieved January 13, 2013, from http://www.computer.org/portal/web/csdl/doi/10.1109/HICSS.2010.412

British Broadcasting Corporation [BBC] News. (2011). Profile: Egypt's Wael Ghonim. BBC News-Middle East. February 8, 2011. Retrieved January 13 2013 from http://www.bbc.co.uk/news/world-middle-east-12400529

Downing, J. (2001). *Radical media: Rebellious communication and social movements*. London: Sage.

Eskandar, A. (2007, May 7). Lines in the sand: Problematizing Arab media in the post-taxonomic era. *Arab Media & Society*. Retrieved from http://www.arabmediasociety.com/index.php?article=226&p=4

Fastenberg, D. (2010, October 20). Why is Twitter so popular in Brazil? *Time Magazine*. Retrieved January 13, 2013, from http://www.time.com/time/world/article/0,8599,2026442,00.html

Gaffney, D. (2010). iranElection: Quantifying online activism. In *Proceedings of the WebSci10: Extending the Frontiers of Society On-Line.* Raleigh, NC. Retrieved Janaury 13, 2013, from http://journal.webscience.org/295/2/websci10_submission_6.pdf

Gladwell, M. (2000). *The tipping point: How little things can make a big difference.* Boston, MA: Back Bay Books.

Grossman, L. (2009, June 17). Iran's protests: Why Twitter is the medium of the movement. *Time Magazine.* Retrieved January 13, 2013, from http://www.time.com/time/world/article/0,8599,1905125,00.html

Gruzd, A., Wellman, B., & Takhteyev, Y. (2011). Imagining Twitter as an Imagined Community. *American Behavioral Scientist Special issue on Imagined Communities.* Retrieved January 13, 2013, from http://homes.chass.utoronto.ca/~wellman/publications/imagining_twitter/Imagining%20Twitter_AG_Sep1_2010_final.pdf

Honeycutt, C., & Herring, S. C. (2009). Beyond Microblogging: Conversation and Collaboration via Twitter. In Proceedings of *HICSS 2009* (pp. 1-10). Manoa, HI: IEEE Press. Retrieved January 13, 2013, from http://doi.ieeecomputersociety.org/10.1109/HICSS.2009.89

Huberman, B. A., Romero, D. M., & Wu, F. (2008). Social networks that matter: Twitter under the microscope. *First Monday, 14*(1), 1-9. SSRN. Retrieved from http://arxiv.org/abs/0812.1045

Katz, E., & Lazarsfeld, P. F. (1955). *Personal Influence.* Glencoe, IL: Free Press.

Mackey, R. (2011, February 8). Updates on day 15 of Egypt protests. The Lede News Blog. *The New York Times.* Retrieved from http://thelede.blogs.nytimes.com/2011/02/08/latest-updates-on-day-15-of-egypt protests

Mackey, R. (2011, February 5). Updates on day 12 of Egypt protests. The Lede News Blog. *The New York Times.* Retrieved from http://thelede.blogs.nytimes.com/2011/02/05/latest-updates-on-day-12-of-egypt protests

Mungiu-Pippidi, A., & Munteanu, I. (2009). Moldova's 'Twitter revolution. *Journal of Democracy, 20*(3), 136–142. doi:10.1353/jod.0.0102.

Rifaat, Y. (2008). Blogging the body: The case of Egypt. *Surfacing: An Interdisciplinary Journal for Gender in the Global South, 1*(1). Retrieved January 13, 2013, from http://www.aucegypt.edu/GAPP/IGWS/GradCent/Documents/FrontPages.pdf

Zetter, K. (2011, March 5). TED 2011: Wael Ghonim—Voice of Egypt's revolution. *Wired.* Retrieved January 13, 2013, from http://www.wired.com/epicenter/2011/03/wael-ghonim-at-ted/

Zhao, D., & Rosson, M. B. (2009). How and why people Twitter: The role that micro-blogging plays in informal communication at work. *Human Factors*, 243-252. ACM. Retrieved January 13, 2013, from http://portal.acm.org/citation.cfm?id=1531710

ENDNOTES

[1] The site claims that "Twitter is the best way to discover what's new in your world" (Twitter, 2011). See http://twitter.com/about.

[2] That is how Mashable, a technology website, describes the launch of WeFollow.com. See http://mashable.com/2009/03/15/wefollow. See also WeFollow.com.

[3] For further information on these categories see the website: http://www.twitalyzer.com.

Chapter 13

A Grassroots Approach to the Democratic Role of the Internet in Developing Countries:
The Case of Morocco

Mohamed Ben Moussa
McGill University, Canada

ABSTRACT

This chapter explores the role of the Internet in collective action in Morocco, and examines the extent to which the medium has empowered civil society and social movements in the North African country. Drawing on in-depth interviews conducted with activists belonging to key social movement organizations, the article analyzes how the appropriation of the Internet in activism is mediated through the socio-economic and political structures proper to Morocco as a semi-authoritarian and developing country. In so doing, it sheds light on various intersections between technology diffusion, social movements' organizational structures, and multiple forms of power relationships among social and political actors. The article argues that the Internet has certainly transformed collective action repertoire deployed by Moroccan social movements; nevertheless, it also demonstrates that the impact of the Internet is conditioned by multiple forms of digital divides that are significantly shaping its implications for social and political change in the country.

INTRODUCTION

The potential of the Internet for democracy and politics is well researched. A considerable body of literature has developed since the mid 1990s, discussing various applications of the medium in political communication such as its contribution to building civil society and, providing good governance and good public services, encouraging direct democracy and deliberation, as well as supporting radical and agonistic public spheres. However, research studies addressing the political implications and applications of ICTs in developing countries have predominantly focused on how the new technologies can proote e-governance and e-government; they have all but ignored the use of

DOI: 10.4018/978-1-4666-4197-6.ch013

these technologies by grassroots advocacy groups, civil society and oppositional social movements. The limitations of this dominant paradigm have been clearly exposed in the last few months as the world's attention was captivated by the uprisings in the Arab world, particularly the North African part of it. The revolutions in Tunisia and Egypt that ended two of the most entrenched dictatorships in the region have demonstrated that radical forms of collective action empowered by new communication technologies can be effective in challenging these regimes when appropriate historical conjunctures arise. In other words, the structures and regimes of power and exclusion behind despotism in Africa and elsewhere in the developing world can be altered when challenged by oppositional democratic movements at the grassroots level.

Accordingly, this chapter explores the role of the Internet in enhancing the capacity of oppositional social movements in Morocco—a semi-autocratic North African country—to challenge hegemonic political, social, and cultural orders. It also examines the extent to which various social movements capitalize on the potential of the Internet in collective action, and how a group's organizational structure can shape its efficiency in using the Internet. In the process, the article analyzes how the diffusion and appropriation of the Internet is mediated through the socioeconomic and cultural structures particular to Morocco. In so doing, the chapter sheds light on the interplay of the various levels of intersection among technology, social and political structures, and human agency at the micro, meso, and macro levels. Such a task is highly urgent given the limited literature on the political role of ICTs in developing countries, and the numerous limitations characterizing the field, mainly its insufficient theorization and conceptual isolation, as well as the scarcity of evidence on grassroots appropriation of the technology in political advocacy.

From the perspective of social movement theory, the article argues that the Internet has certainly transformed collective action repertoire

deployed by Moroccan social movements, enhancing, consequently, their advocacy capabilities. Nevertheless, it also demonstrates that the impact of the Internet is better analyzed and understood as a dependent variable that is characterized by multiple forms of digital divides and constantly mediated through social, political and cultural processes proper to Morocco as a developing, North African country.

ICT-FOR-DEVELOPMENT: A CRITICAL PERSPECTIVE

The literature on the political role and democratic potential of ICTs and the Internet particularly is marked by what many commentators have termed a dichotomy between "utopian" and "dystopian" stances on technology (Saco, 2002; Dahlgren, 2005; Bentivegna, 2006; Dutton, Shepherd & de Gennaro, 2007;). A similar dichotomous theorization characterizes the scholarly examination of the role of ICTs in development insofar as two development paradigms are currently dominating the literature: on the one hand, there is the "modernization" development paradigm, and, on the other, the "social injustice" development one. While the modernization paradigm maintains that ICTs are crucial for development perceived to spread from the west to southern countries, the social injustice paradigm argues that ICTs exacerbate existing inequalities since they only benefit those who are "already dominant politically and economically" (Zembylas, 2009, pp. 18-19). Despite the polemics surrounding the issue, more evidence has emerged in the last few years as to the capacity of new technology to contribute to social and economic development, as the debate on the potential of ICTs has "shifted from whether but how ICT can benefit development" (Walsham, Robey, & Sahay, 2007, p. 317).

Compared to the large body of research on ICT4DEV, the implications of these technologies for and their impact on the political sphere and democracy in developing countries have received scant attention. Interestingly, the bulk of existing studies have focused on the role of ICTs in promoting e-government and governance in developing countries (Heeks, 2002; Ciborra, 2003; 2005; van der Graft & Sevensson, 2006; Chatfield & Alhujran, 2009; Navarra, 2010). Arguably, the ultimate objective of e-governance is to promote a more effective and transparent interaction between government and citizens (G2C), government and business (G2B), and inter-agency relationships (G2G) (Norris, 2001a). Whilst the objective of e-government projects is to effectively deliver and facilitate access to government services, e-governance involves a much broader process, since it seeks "to realize processes and structures for harnessing the potentialities of information and communication technologies … for the purpose of enhancing Good Governance" (Okto-Uma, as cited in Ciborra & Navarra, 2005, p. 144). The discourse on e-government conceives of governance and democracy development as projects to be planned and implemented by governments; consequently, it pays little attention to how the diffusion and appropriation of ICTs are shaped from later, that is at the level of grassroots civil society actors and groups.

In fact, underlying the research agenda on e-government is an understanding of the lack of democracy as underdevelopment that can be addressed by delivering better public services and providing good public management of resources. Such a view, however, overlooks the fact that absence of democracy in much of the developing world is rooted in despotism, hegemony and exclusion, to which local and global regimes of power contribute. Enhancing the efficiency of despotic government to deliver public services does not necessarily contribute to a democratic transformation; nor can it enhance real popular participation in governance. The UN 2010 e-government readiness survey, for instance, ranked Tunisia and Egypt first and third respectively among African countries (UN Department of Economic and Social Affairs, 2010). This survey, like numerous other reports issued by interna-

tional institutions that often applauded Tunisian "economic miracle" and Egypt "liberal" reforms, however, was used by Ben Ali and Mubarak to boost their international image, enhance internal legitimacy, and mask the repressive and mafia-like practices of their regimes. Indeed, the role of international institutions, experts and donors in promoting the agenda of e-government as a tool of development is by no means small. As Heeks (2002) observes, "the donors, providing a significant proportion of the income for government in many African countries, create powerful leverage for e-government" agenda in these countries. But it is an agenda that subscribes to the priorities and realities of established democracies in western countries, where ICTs are considered as tools to enhance established democratic institutions and practices. There is certainly an important role for ICTs to play in supporting sound and transparent governance in the developing world. However, the main priority in many of these countries is to end despotism and establish more representative, pluralistic public and political spheres.

Equally important, commentators pointed out various limitations in the research on ICT4Dev, in general. First, despite increasing attention to this issue, the literature remains scarce (Walsham, Robey & Sahay, 2007). This particularly applies to the African experience since there is a big need for research "that explores the potential of direct and indirect developmental benefits of ICT" in the continent" (Thompson & Welsham, 2010, p. 121). Furthermore, numerous commentators argued that theorization of ICT4DEV is insufficient and isolated from other disciplines (Heeks, 2002; 2007; b2010; Thompson, 2008). Thompson and Welsham (2010), for instance, contend that researchers in this domain will need to

Identify and engage with other research communities, their literatures, and theoretical constructs, while asking how some of the valuable insights developed within the information systems literature may complement some of these perspectives" (p.121).

In the same vein, Walsham and Sahay (2006) observe that the dominant development paradigms are incapable of grasping the complexities of such a topic as the implications of ICTs for social change in the developing world. Indeed, these "issues in developing countries are normally deeply intertwined with issues of power, politics, donor dependencies, institutional arrangements, and inequalities of all sorts," which calls for critical perspectives that can "open up the 'black box' as an aid to deeper understanding, and a stimulus to appropriate action" (p. 19).

The chapter aims precisely at contributing to opening up this black box by addressing some of the limitations pointed before, first, by focusing on bottom-up models of appropriation of the Internet in the political sphere, and, second, by opting for a conceptual perspective that enables the theorization of the political role of ICTs in developing countries from an original perspective. Such a perspective allows us, indeed, to account for multiple factors shaping this role in such a way as to reconcile divergent perspectives marking scholarly literature on this issue and bring human agency in our understanding of the interplay between technology and social and political structures and processes.

RE-CONCEPTUALIZING THE DEMOCRATIC ROLE OF ICTS IN DEVELOPING COUNTRIES

While the concept of civil society has gained much currency in the literature dealing with collective action in developing countries, it has also been criticized for being imprecise and for its inability to account for non-institutionalized forms of collective action. Social movement theory, indeed, offers an alternative perspective through which to analyze collective action and the role of ICTs, in general. First, and according to a large number of theorists (Touraine, 1981; 1985; Melucci, 1989; Tarrow, 1998; Diani, 2000a; ; Tilly & Tarrow,

2007), one of the distinctive features of social movements is that they are a form of contentious and oppositional collective action aimed at social, political, and/or cultural change. Such a characteristic is of particular relevance to the current project, as one of its main objectives is to assess the contributions of the Internet to changing, or at least affecting, power relations between the Moroccan state and oppositional groups. Moreover, the definition of social movements encompasses both institutionalized and non-institutionalized forms of advocacy, which helps account for highly decentralized and horizontal modes of communication characterizing many forms of online-based activism. In fact, social movements are constellations of organizations, groups, and individuals that are loosely connected, but that share collective identity and objectives.

One common feature shared by social movement theories is that they have been articulated mostly to analyze forms of collective action that emerged in industrial and postmodern societies. Shigetomi (2009) holds that "few researchers take the context of developing countries seriously in an attempt to identify the salient features of and approach to social movements" (p. 6). In the same vein, Ellis and Kessel (2009) point out several aspects distinguishing social movements and their environments within developing countries, particularly in Africa, compared to those in developed ones. The dependence of many social movements on foreign aid, the important role of diaspora in sustaining collective action in their countries of origin, and the weak status of central governments in many countries are some of the distinctive dimensions of African social movements and their contexts. This assessment lends credence to Stekelenburg and Klandermans (2009), who argue that studying collective action phenomena in developing countries should take into account specific national political and social contexts, as well as the supra-national institutions and structures that are increasingly shaping social movements in these countries.

Thus, in order to situate the study of social movements in the context of developing countries, the article links it to the notion of "digital divide." Indeed, the Internet's diffusion and its appropriation in collective action in the context of Morocco are marked by deep societal divisions and structural contradictions. For this reason, the article draws on van Dijk's (2005; 2006) model of digital divide. Dominant interpretations of the term 'digital divide' define it as differences between rich and poor countries and between people within the same country in terms of access to computers and Internet connection. Numerous commentators, however, have criticized the dichotomous interpretation of the term, pointing out various types of divide that operate at the societal and individual levels (Norris, 2001; Wilson, 2004; Van Dijk, 2005; 2006;). Accordingly, Van Dijk juxtaposes four levels of digital divide, namely:

1. **Motivational Access:** Motivation to use digital technology.
2. **Material or Physical Access:** Possession of computers and Internet connections or permissions to use them and their contents.
3. **Skill Access:** Possession of digital skills: operational, informational, and strategic.
4. **Usage Access:** Number and diversity of applications, and usage time.

The paper, thus, investigates how the appropriation of the Internet in collective action in Morocco is shaped by various types of divides, and what are the main implications of the latter on the political role and democratic potential of the medium in the context of the country.

THE CASE OF MOROCCO

The choice of Morocco is motivated by two main considerations. It is a country that is, although still not democratic, often described to have an active civil society and a relatively important experience with political pluralism. Notwithstanding its formidable economic and social problems, Morocco is also considered as "one of the telecommunications successes of Africa" (Sutherland, 2007, p. 8). Accordingly, the country offers an ideal context where to explore the implications of ICTs for advocacy, collective action and democratic change.

The development of the telecommunication sector in Morocco, in fact, spearheaded a very aggressive economic liberalization policy, under the supervision of international monetary institutions, which resulted in the privatization of key state-owned companies and sectors. According to the ITU, the number of Internet users in the country has jumped from 100,000 in 2000, to 10,442,500 million in 2010, representing almost 33% of the population (Internet World Stats, Internet Usage Stats for Africa, 2010). Though Internet penetration remains low—only 2.46% of the population—it is developing fast, as the country's digital subscriber line (DSL) access is one of the cheapest in Africa. Moreover, the rapid growth in Internet subscription in the last two years is linked to the entry into the market of 3G mobile Internet that now represents around 35.4% of total subscriptions.

Equally important, until the beginning of the Arab Spring in December 2010, Morocco's stood out in the region as witnessing serious, though hitherto unsuccessful, attempts to move towards real democratization (Bendourou, 1996; Desrues & Moyano, 2001; Cavatorta, 2005; 2006). According to the last United Nations Development Programme's (UNDP) report on the region, Morocco is "considered to have gone farther than any other Arab state along the path of political emancipation" (Leveau, 1997, p. 28). However, despite this rich political culture and experience, democratic transition has hitherto failed to materialize and the process is stagnating, at best. Summarizing the contradictions that distinguish Moroccan politics, Leveau (1997) points out that Morocco is neither a democracy nor a dictatorship insofar as its political system is based on "authoritarian pluralism" (p. 95). Kausch (2008) identifies four sets of barriers facing Moroccan civil society: (1) difficulties related to association registration; (2) access to the public sphere and public media; (3) infringement upon liberties and rights; and (4) lack of an independent judiciary system capable of guaranteeing fundamental liberties.

METHODOLOGY

Semi-structured in-depth interviewing was used as a methodology, a choice dictated by the subject of the paper and its objectives. The study is premised on the belief that the Internet is a socially embedded artefact that is equally based on hardware and software, as much as it is rooted in social practices, public policies, and power relations. Likewise, social movements are rooted too in social networks, practices and cultural modes of expression that are not usually easily visible. In-depth interviewing is thus a methodology that is appropriate for the type of investigation in which the researcher has to dig under the surface of social and cultural manifestations to discover "what is usually hidden from ordinary view or reflection or to penetrate to more reflective understandings about the nature of that experience" (Johnson, 2002, p. 107).

Blee and Taylor (2002) outline a number of benefits for applying in-depth interviewing to the study of social movements. First, it provides an insight into the "motivations and perspectives of a broader and more diverse group of social movement participants than would be represented in most documentary sources" (Blee & Taylor, p. 94). Moreover, it allows the researcher to grasp the way activists understand their participation and their social world, thus giving access "to such nuanced understandings of social movement outcomes as the construction of collective and individual identities" (p. 95). Finally, it is a

method that "brings human agency to the centre of movement analysis" (p. 96), while allowing the researcher to examine the ways in which the messages of social movements are received by actual and potential constituents (p. 96).

A combination of sampling methods was used to identify and locate respondents. In the first stage, purposive and representative samplings were used to identify a preliminary list of respondents. Participants were recruited from major social movements and SMOs that are active in the country at the national level, in addition to those following oppositional agendas and collective action tactics. Sampling for the study also sought to reflect the multiplicity characterizing Moroccan civil society in terms of ideological background, structure and gender. In the second stage, snowball sampling was used to find other suitable respondents who are connected to those interviewed initially.

In total, 37 respondents were interviewed[1]. The majority were members in seven key Moroccan social movements: (1) Islamic movement, (2) human rights movement, (3) feminist movement, (4) alter-globalization movement, (5) radical left movement (6) Amazigh cultural movement, and (7) the unemployed. These movements represent the major ideological paradigms and collective action-oriented groups constituting Moroccan civil society (Kausch, 2008; Sater, 2007; Sidi Hida, 2007), especially those that follow oppositional agenda, and aim at achieving social and political change in the country.

The interviews were conducted face-to-face in various Moroccan cities. To code and analyze the data, a qualitative method was employed, namely open coding. According to this method, "events/actions/interactions are compared with others for similarities and differences. They are also given conceptual labels. In this way, conceptually similar events/actions/interactions are grouped together to form categories and subcategories" (Corbin & Strauss, 1990, p.12).

ANALYSIS AND DISCUSSION

A New Resource of Mobilization

Commentators have argued that the success of collective action in mobilizing support and countering hegemonic discourses and orders depends largely on the size and the type of resources that groups can mobilize at various levels. According to this view, mobilization itself can be defined as "the process by which a group secures collective control over the resources needed for collective action" (Jenkins, 2008, p. 121). In Morocco, however, oppositional social movements have little access to public funds, media, and other resources. In the neo-patrimonial regime of the country, the state uses the patronage system whereby it tries to keep all political actors inside its patron-client networks. In addition to creating its own set of associations to counter the weight of "independent" civil society and recruit elites into its sphere, the state also tries to use its material resources and coercive power to neutralize groups and SMOs that may challenge its hegemony. Mohamed Lakjiri, an activist in the Amazigh cultural movement (ACM) and the webmaster of the collective Amazigh blog "Ageddim," argues:

There is a dialectic relationship between the [Amazigh] movement and its use of the media. [The movement] relies on voluntary work and self-funding, since it does not receive any type of support, especially from the state. It suffers from scarcity of material and human resources; there are only a few [Amazigh] print publications and only three in print that work in very harsh conditions.... It is a very difficult situation.

The majority of respondents pointed out that the Internet's key contribution to collective action is its providing a far cheaper and more efficient tool of mobilization and information dissemination. Abderrezak Idrissi, the webmaster and editor of the Moroccan Association of Human Rights' (AMDH) website and print newspaper, explains

how this medium radically transformed the way AMDH activists share information nationally and internationally:

The Internet is economical, it is fast, it enables you to do comprehensive coverage, and it is easy to use. Before, we used to write a statement and send it by post, which would take 15 days to reach its destination. Then came the fax. It was marvelous...but it was very costly at all levels. With the Internet, you send a message with one click on [e-mail] and it is received by some 4,000 members that include journalists and politicians in Morocco and outside it, in the countryside and in cities. We could not imagine that we could do something like that.

These testimonies confirm various commentators' claims that the principal impact of ICTs on developing countries is the empowerment of people to reproduce and communicate information "at virtually zero cost" (Heeks, 2010a, p. 24).

Networks of Solidarity and Action

The interlinking potential of the Internet is often described as the most defining characteristic of the medium, since it is inscribed into how the technology was built and is used. This potential has immense implications for collective action because it can enable individuals and groups to build alliances that are crucial to the success and effectiveness of mobilization, resistance, and contestation. The regional and international networking potential of the Internet is transforming the nature of collective action itself, by multiplying the capacity of SMOs to disseminate information and mobilize support. According to Castells (2001), the Internet "fits with the basic features of the kind of social movements emerging in the Information Age (...). The Internet is not simply a technology: it is a communication media, and it is the material infrastructure of a given organizational form: the network" (pp. 135–6).

Moroccan social movements have become more sensible to this potential, as they have started to adapt collective action tactics to it. Journalist and activist Khaled Jamaï argues:

Civil society has progressed along the development of the strategy of struggle. It's no longer about writing an article. It's the system of the network, and it is functioning incredibly. We have relay points in Paris, London—everywhere. Any time we write something, it is redistributed by our activists, which gives it another dimension as a snowball.

Jamaï's remark draws attention to the dialectic between collective action and repertoires as they shape one another and define their mutual limits. As Tilly and Tarrow (2007) remark, "repertoires vary from place to place, time to time, and pair to pair. But on the whole, when people make collective claims, they innovate within limits set by the repertoire already established for their place, time, and pair" (p. 16). In enhancing the capacity of social movements to build networks of solidarity across geographical and political borders, the Internet has not only empowered them to act against injustices, but enlarged the scope of their claims and the essence of their collection strategies and tactics.

The Internet is increasingly used to build up regional alliances and networks that are enhancing the ability of Moroccan NGOs to pressurize and lobby the government to recognize and investigate human right violations and abuses. Samira Kinani, an activist of the Moroccan Association of Human rights (AMDH) explains, for instance, how she contributed as a militant and blogger to free political and protest prisoners:

We issued communiqués about political prisoners. I wrote an article about it in my blog. I wrote about their lives, their families and children. I didn't write as a militant but as a human being... For example, in the case of Bougrine, who was

73 years old, I went to visit him in prison and I came back telling people about him in my blog. When you visit him, you feel as if you were invited to his home; he was so welcoming and warm. I wrote about it. People admired him. You should know, bloggers led a campaign for the political prisoners in France, Belgium and Quebec because I have friends everywhere.

The liberalization of the Moroccan economy and its integration in the global capitalist one has made Moroccan state keener at projecting an image of modernity and stability, and, thus, more susceptible to the global flow of negative news on the country. Various social movement groups try to exploit this relative vulnerability by using the Internet to circulate pictures, videos and articles on human rights violations and social injustices that can mobilize international NGOs and associations for their causes. Invoking this strategy, Mohamed Saied, an activist from the Unemployed Graduates movement, explains:

One of the objectives of our blog is to communicate with human rights organizations to provide information about our case and to make known the human rights violations we are subjected to.... They read it and I have email contacts on it so they can send emails to them. We receive solidarity statements and letters .... Thanks to the blog, our movement has become known worldwide. ... Media pressure constitutes a pressure and embarrassment for the state.

Lending credit to him, Abderrezak Drissi explains how the role of international NGOs, along other international institutions is crucial to successfully pressuring the Moroccan State, even if this tactic is not always very effective:

As a human rights association, we cannot put pressure on the State without the support of international bodies, especially that State officials sometimes, and I say sometimes because it is not systematic, take into consideration Amnesty International or Human Rights Watch or some other body concerned with human rights, such as the European Union or the UN; you find that there is an effect.

The regional and international networking potential of the Internet is transforming the way social movements now understand collective action, and plan their strategies and mobilization tactics. Leading an asymmetrical struggle against a more resourceful state and its vast networks of client media and businesses, oppositional SMOs use online networks of alliances and solidarity to multiply their collective action capabilities.

The Organizational Role of the Internet

In addition to using e-mail to communicate and intranet networks to link databases and sections, social movement groups post information and action calendars online to keep militants—particularly those living in remote areas—informed and updated, which contributes to the cohesion and effectiveness of both organization and action. Furthermore, social movements' collective action alternates between short and ephemeral periods of high visibility, as they "become visible only where a field of public conflict arises," and long period of "latency" (Melucci, 1989, p. 71). The Internet can play a significant role in maintaining the continuation of mobilization and action through online communication and interaction. In some cases, the Internet, and website interfaces in particular, plays a big role in imparting a sense of unity, cohesion, and continuity to movements or groups that are threatened either by internal divisions or external repression. This applies specifically to groups that lack strong organizational structures, are geographically dispersed, and/or lack other media outlets, as Jawad Moustaqbal points out in the case of ATTAC–Maroc:

The website plays this role of internal communication between ATTAC militants from various countries and between sympathisers. It is the only platform that guarantees the continuation of information sharing at the level of ATTAC, because print edition and bulletins are not sufficient.... There are some moments when we are very active and we issue a lot of brochures ... and there are other moments where activity is low, when we don't do many things. The website does not cost us a lot and we can do the updating. You don't need to print things to do it. In fact, one of the reasons for the continuation of ATTAC in Morocco is the Internet. It has allowed us to stay in contact with one another, to have a tool of communication that link us with sympathisers even during the most difficult moments—because when we were not able to walk in the street, we were still able to post our ideas on the website. I am convinced that this is important [in regard to] all the organizational problems I talked about—the fact that there are two factions of ATTAC, the problems after the first congress: the continuity was the website.

The dialectic between the "visibility" and "latency" of social movements and their use of the Internet also has important implications for the visibility of the websites themselves, as the latter receive more attention during periods of crisis or high mobilization. In the words of Jawad Mostaqbal:

If you do nothing, what are you going to post on your website? When I said we receive 2,600 visits per day, it is not consistent. There are peak moments, like during the Rosamor[2] fires, for instance. We went there immediately when it happened; and in Morocco, there is a need for information, and there is [media] opacity of tragedies like these, so we had the chance to transmit the information via our website. Like in the case of Sidi Ifni [and] Rosamor—people searched for information and did not find it anywhere. In the case of Sidi Ifni, we sent a fact-finding committee to the scene and we [posted] a report with pictures, and this raised sharply the number of visitors to our website. We did not do it to augment the number of visitors on our website, but it was an opportunity where we could express our solidarity.

While social movements' websites receive less attention during "latency" periods, these platforms continue to play an important role for these groups and their core members, providing them with the resources needed to enhance their collective consciousness, and sustaining their readiness and potential for collective action until the next mobilization opportunity arises.

Many respondents indicated that the organizational value and effectiveness of the Internet is mostly evident during special events such as elections and conventions, when it is used to reduce costs and time, and to enhance the transparency of transactions and the distribution of tasks and benefits, as is the case with the Unemployed Graduates movement. Each group within the movement has a point system, whereby militants are ranked according to their contribution to and participation in protests and other forms of action. This system is used to identify a list of members who will be first to benefit from employment openings once opportunities arise through negotiation with the government and with regional state institutions. Explaining the role of the Internet in the functioning of the movement, Said Rahmouni, of the Unemployed Graduates movement, asserts:

We use e-mail and other means. The Internet is the means that provides members with new information, changes on some course of action, or paper contributions. We do it for the sake of credibility and transparency with regard to the unemployed graduates who elected us in the executive council. Before we launch anything, we post the new information online.... Before you can hold a general assembly, you need to provide people with the program and agenda so that you can have a constructive discussion and come out with conclusions.

Zakaria Sahnoun, a journalist supervising the online version of the newspaper "Attajdid" (Renewal), the mouthpiece of the SMO Unity and Reconstruction (U&R) and an activist in the Justice and Development Party (PJD, the political arm of the U&R), too stresses the value of websites in providing the necessary information and documents for members during elections and congresses. Discussing the last national congress of the Justice and Development Party (PJD), the political arm of the Unity and Reconstruction movement, he states:

Websites have two functions: communication and archiving. But there is also the financial factor, since running a website demands only one or two people.... I will give you a vivid example of this: the sixth National Congress of the party will be held on July 19th, and you are invited to attend the opening session or some other sessions to get an idea of the election campaign. In terms of what concerns the congress, all the documents have been posted online, so the members and the general public can access them.

By facilitating access to these documents, the Internet contributes to the enhancement of the quality of political participation and discussions, and to the development of transparency and accountability within SMOs.

Web 2.0 and Social Media

The majority of respondents, however, stated that their groups are facing problems with properly setting up or regularly updating conventional websites because both operations require significant material and human resources. In fact, a study of a large number of conventional or web 1.0 websites used by Moroccan social movements demonstrated that a key problem facing these online platforms is their lack of updating and poor design (Ben Moussa, 2011). Conventional websites require continuous maintenance and high level of IT skills that the majority of groups cannot afford.

In comparison, many groups rely increasingly on web 2.0 and social media platforms such as wikis, blogs, and e-lists, because they are free and easy to maintain and use. Indeed, through web 2.0, "users can present, intuitively contribute, and network their personalized worldviews without any necessity to know HTML or any other complicated procedures, which is a significant improvement over most Web 1.0 applications" (Hilbert, 2009, p. 93). While the use of Facebook and Twitter in collective action has only become widespread in Morocco after the Tunisian revolution started in December 2010, other social media tools, mainly e-mail lists, have been heavily used for many years by the majority of social movement groups interviewed in the study. Email-lists can be used for unlimited purposes since they can "facilitate discussions on a topic of interest, technical support, neighborhood gatherings and advocacy, workgroup interactions, internal communities of practice, and even the exchange of goods" (Hansen, Shneiderman, & Smith, 2011, p. 19).

There are two major e-lists used by leftist associations and groups, namely PAD-Maroc and Press-Maroc, both of which are based on Yahoo Group e-mail software and service thousands of subscribers. Any person can subscribe to the two lists, but approval of the automatic subscription is required from the lists' moderators. In my interview with Idrissi, who is also one of three moderators of the Press-Maroc e-list, he shared numerous insights into the potential and limits of e-lists to the civil groups using them:

Idrissi: [The list] is considered like a press agency, and a free one. It takes little of your time to organize things, to have an eye for important messages that you acquire through time, to sort out the messages that you won't read, those you will delete—these things are necessary.

Ben Moussa: Are you the only person supervising Press-Maroc?

Idrissi: No, four of us are doing it.

Ben Moussa: And they belong all to AMDH?

Idrissi: They belong to various associations and bodies, but they are all linked to AMDH in one way or another. One of them lives in a remote place near Tawnat, but in reality he does not work much on it; two of us are in Rabat and the other in Khmissat[3].... The moderators have the right to refuse any contribution and have the right to reconsider the posting of contributions—for instance, double postings.

As Idrissi contends prior, the use of e-lists not only allows for the horizontal networking of civil society groups, but also contributes to redressing the imbalance between big, central urban centres and marginal regions in the country. Indeed, because within a network, the "distance between nodes tends to be zero" (Castells, 2004, p. 4), the use of social network technologies like the e-list leads to the elimination, at least online, of the distance between centres and margins, thus sometimes permitting activists in remote places to take the initiative and be at the centre of a local and transnational collective action network. This observation is further confirmed in the following conversation with Abdelilah Mansouri, a teacher and member of the national committee of the Unified Socialist Party (PSU):

A militant from our party was the one to launch PAD-Maroc. [The list] is supervised by Mohamed Awni and Mohamed Khoya, both of whom are militants in the PSU, although they both live in remote parts far from the centers in Ouerzazate[4].... PAD played a principal role in communication between the political elites in our country, particularly those from the Left, and also in covering a large number of events. It has now become one of the main sources of news for Moroccan newspapers, and also for communicating with militants outside the country.... PAD played a very important role in many events and created problems for the state, either in Sefrou or Sidi Ifni, by mobilizing support and solidarity; an event that happens in Rabat will draw solidarity in remote places in marginalized Morocco. We can say that it has greater influence than many daily newspapers in Morocco and is a source of national and international news. It also presents coverage of national newspapers, Algerian newspapers, as well as Spanish and French ones.

In addition to these two national lists, many SMOs have their own internal lists. Because shared membership is a key characteristic of Moroccan civil society, many activists who are members in various groups end up receiving a huge number of e-mails that may have repetitive content. A key problem with e-lists that many participants have identified is that they significantly augment the workload because of the time needed to process the huge numbers of e-mail received. Consequently, SMOs try to exercise control over this tool by setting restrictions on the subscription to internal lists in order to maximize their utility and the quality of the discussion that takes place on them. Jawad Moustaqbal explains the case for ATTAC:

Our internal list functions well, but we limit the number of adherents—not everybody can join, which allows us to concentrate on our struggles and discussions and not get diverted by other issues.

This testimony reflects some of the limitations of social media and participatory communication. In theory, social media have the potential—more than other online tools—to sustain the development of a truly participative and egalitarian public sphere. However, open participation produces a lot of "noise" that affects the quality of discussion and communication because of the time and cognitive capabilities needed to process a huge number of messages.

From Medium to Media Convergence

While the bulk of the debate around the potential of the Internet for political and social change deal with the technology as one medium, our data confirm that the impact of the Internet can rarely be disassociated from other communication tools and networks including non-mediated ones. Moreover, contrary to studies and mainstream media reports that deal with specific online tools as independent variables, many respondents indicated that convergence between various media and platforms is a key practice in their groups' communication strategy.

Though the majority of interviewees stressed the centrality of the e-mail list as a tool of mobilization and information dissemination, many indicated that websites, blogs, possess greater potential for collective action. Email-lists are a fast and effective means of sharing and disseminating information; however, their diffusion is limited to their members, which limits their impact and reach. Besides, despite their effectiveness, e-mail-lists can reinforce the isolation of "radical ghettos" (Downey & Fenton, 2003, p. 190), leading to more fragmentation of the public sphere. In comparison, websites have the potential to reach actual and potential constituents, as well as the large public constituted of the "bystanders." A website helps situate a group in the national and international shared arena, providing it with social capital and recognition, as Bennaoui explains in the case of La Ligue démocratique pour les droits des femmes (LDDF):

We need a website so that many other people know about our experience. We don't want our experience to remain only for us, we want other associations to know about it and benefit from it, both inside and outside of Morocco. We want our publication to reach people and our experiences to reach people. More than that, OXFAM is undertaking a project to learn more about experiences like ours. Many associations that are in the project want to know the details of our work and to publish it so other associations can benefit from it.

Moreover, the LDDF engages in both lobbying and development activities, as the organization seeks to improve women's economic and social conditions through awareness and training campaigns. The organization uses multiple sets of media, such as print material, including brochures, books and pamphlets, CDs, and cassette tapes, in addition to collective visits (caravans) to remote villages in the country and to diasporic communities in Europe. In most cases, different platforms can be used simultaneously or consecutively, as Mohamed Lakjiri explains:

When I joined the Amazigh cultural movement, I was receiving a lot of e-mail that concerned issues and new events in the movement. Each day, I was receiving between 15 and 20 statements, communiqués, [or] ads concerning ACM. I wanted to make those e-mails public.... I received some through PAD–Maroc and Press–Maroc, but I also received e-mail through my personal address. I have a relationship with many activists in the ACM who send me their statements and communiqués. I wanted everybody to benefit from them. Through these e-mail messages, I received [information about] many issues I didn't find in local newspapers, Amazigh websites, or national ones. So, I thought of setting up a website for this purpose.

Lakjiri's media intervention sheds light on the confluence between mobilization processes at the micro and meso levels as the blog project draws on material borrowed from personal e-mail and collective e-lists, as well as on private connections and collective action networks The project further illustrates how Web-based platforms can provide a higher level of "publicity" that cannot be attained through other interfaces. Sharing the same data on various platforms serves a number of purposes beyond their immediate informative functions. While a statement shared through an e-mail list provides information for other activists upon which they can further act, its posting on a blog acquires an added value—namely, accessibility; at least theoretically, it is available to members and adversaries alike, contributing to building a dynamic public sphere where opposing frames and interpretations counterbalance and sometimes integrate one another.

Furthermore, as the case of the Unified Socialist Party illustrates, during events that require quick mobilization, some SMOs may use the Internet to post detailed information and action calendars. However, mobile phones are often more convenient, as they allow faster mobilization, especially because not all members and adherents have easy access to the Internet:

Manssouri: We use the Internet and we send faxes to the offices that have [fax machines]. We use [short message service] SMS [to mobilize] protest and marches. For instance, during events protesting some crime related to the war in Iraq or to Palestine, we were able to mobilize militants and the general public to protest in front of the American consulate here in Casablanca [and] the embassy in Rabat. The incident happened in the morning and we were able to mobilize the protest in the afternoon, in which hundreds of militants and the general public were able to participate.

Ben Moussa: How do you reach all these people at once?

Manssouri: We ask every militant to send the message to five or ten people he knows, and thus it spreads quickly. Sometimes SMS is quicker; and when there is something urgent, we send messages to militants here in Casablanca. And so SMS plays an important role in this domain.

Convergence between online platforms as well as between the internet in general and various ICTs is a major characteristic of social movements' appropriation of new media in collective action. These forms of synergy ensure wider diffusion of information, more efficient mobilization and capacity of content production. In addition to its potential for direct mobilization, networking, and dissemination of alternative information, the Internet also plays an important organizational role as many groups increasing rely on it to remain connected.

Online and Offline Networks

Integration between platforms and media is not the only major form of convergence marking the use of the Internet in collective action; such a use is equally marked by deep intertwinement between online and offline social networks. Whilst the Internet is a relatively cheap, flexible, and effective tool of communication, it is largely insufficient in a country where almost half of the population, most of which are women, are illiterate and live where access to the Internet is very limited. This is illustrated by the case of the Democratic League of Women's Rights (LDDF), whose members have to use, in addition to the Internet, different tools in their information and mobilization campaigns (especially for interpersonal communication), in order to reach the largest possible number of women. As Halima Bennaoui explains:

So our work developed greatly and we used the caravans as we moved to remote regions in Morocco in order to work in close contact, to listen to women, to know their problems and not be elitist women speaking just from our own perspectives. So this enabled us to develop other forms of work, but from the start we have always worked as a movement, and we act in various spaces.... We could not cover all of the country and so we had to cooperate with teachers in schools—so we co-

operated with the Ministry of National Education to provide training for teachers on these themes so that they, in turn, can teach them to others.

Though the feminist SMO has significantly benefited from the Internet, which is used to coordinate work, reduce communication costs, and create an accessible online database, the LDDF has to rely on interpersonal communication and offline social networks—namely schools and teachers—to deliver their messages and get through to women in remote or poor regions and neighborhoods. Preexisting social networks thus play a central role in mobilization and in securing the continuation of collective action over time, for "embeddedness in social networks not only matters for recruitment; it also works as an antidote to leaving, and as a support to continued participation" (Della Porta & Diani, 2006, p. 118). The experience of Youth Action (Action Jeunesse), an association supported by Alternative International concentrating on the empowerment of young people, best illustrates this idea. Ghassan Garmouni, a student and activist in the association, explains in the following exchange:

At the national level, we have been able to organize six regional forums since 2005, and one general forum. We were able to organize these forums through the assistance of local associations like 'Intilaqua', 'Ashoala', 'Amish', and the local chapters of the Moroccan Association of Human Rights. In these forums, militants of Youth Action were able to meet other young people, to explain our projects [and] provide analysis of the situation. And so we were able to mobilize other young people who are active in other regional and national associations, and who constituted regional chapters of Youth Action. So the first tool of communication is interpersonal contacts. Each member of Youth Action is a member in a network that he can try to mobilize. It is this informal level that plays an important role in our mobilization capacity. Then, there is a second level that is more formal; it is all our organizational communication made up of two forms: the semester bulletins we publish and our website. Our site is our façade and our window on the world.

For Carmouni, the use of the Youth Action's website is limited to a supporting role (i.e., communicating and sharing the outcome of a long process of mobilization that draws mainly on interpersonal communication and existing offline networks).

The embeddedness of online networks within those that are offline is manifest in the case of grassroots movements that rely on dense social networks and cultural bonds, such as the Islamic ones. Benefitting from a wide network of disciplined and dedicated members and sympathizers, the Justice and Charity SMO, for instance, combines the use of alternative media, particularly the Internet; small media, such as cassettes and CDs; and interpersonal communication to customize its discourse for various types of members and potential adherents, and to cover the remotest parts of the country. In the words of Hassan Bennajah:

There is something that we are disciplined about: the fact that everyone of us should be an individual, mobile medium of information. Every member in the movement has to become a media body in which there is communication, politics, exhortation, and everything…. This is the most widespread means, since everyone has a number of people with whom he meets on a daily and regular basis—his family, his neighbors—and so because the movement is present in most of the country's regions, and it can reach regions that even the state is unable to reach. We reach people in these regions that are forgotten and left out of state policies—and in many cases, you will find that they know news about J&C through these alternative tools.

Communication becomes, therefore, a religious duty as much as political activism. Moreover, the case of J&C shows that networks are the outcome of the participation and work occurring at the micro or individual level, before they are the result of interactions between individuals. To build efficient networks, movements need much more than technical and organizational infrastructure, for the motivation of individuals using/forming networks is a precondition to the networks themselves. Consequently, grassroots movements that are identity-oriented are better placed to form more solid and effective networks. This allows them to customize their communication tactics according to the category of audiences they target. Despite clear evidence demonstrating the empowering impact of the Internet on social movements, our data, however, provided ample proofs on the limitations in this role, particularly the existence of multiple forms of digital divide marking the diffusion of the Internet and its use in collective action.

The Multidimensional Aspect of Digital Divide

Dominant discourses on ICTs diffusion and innovation proclaim that digital divides will disappear overtime as a result of market dynamics. Though statistics on the growth of Internet use in Morocco confirm in part this hypothesis, the respondents' statements revealed that material access to computers and Internet connection are far from being the only forms of digital divide affecting the diffusion of the technology in society and, particularly, in collective action. Other forms of divides such as gender and motivational ones are deeply intertwined with socioeconomic inequalities and cultural orders that make them more persisting even when the material access divide is bridged.

Material access divide (i.e. disparities in accessing computers and internet connections) is the most highlighted type of divide in the literature on ICT4dev and the diffusion of the Internet worldwide. In Morocco, the vast majority of people are still excluded from the "information society" despite the spectacular growth in the number of internet users over the last five years. This is bound to be reflected in the way the medium is appropriated in collective action. In fact, social movements are not homogeneous because they often reflect the very contradictions and disparities prevalent in society. In addition to digital divides between big cities and centers and peripheral regions, there are disparities between headquarters and chapters in small towns and villages, as well as between activists themselves in terms of availability of hardware, training and access to the Internet.

This forces us to rethink the concept of "divide" from a "bipolar division between the haves and the have-nots, the connected and the disconnected" to an interpretation that sees it as a "continuum" split with many shade to it (Warschauer, 2003, p. 297). Digital cleavages at the micro (individual) and meso (organization) levels are underpinned by occupational and social inequalities between activists. Though access divide touches all SMOs, it affects them differently. In general, professional SMOs are more able to bridge existing divisions between activists and chapters. Indeed, their constituencies are not very large, the majority of their activists tend to be university educated and have stable jobs, and many of them receive funds from INGOs and development agencies to purchase ICT equipment. Abderezzak Idrissi, for instance, points out that despite existing disparities between AMDH's chapters, most of them are getting access to the Internet:

The material equipment is available not only to the headquarters, but also to the AMDH sections around Morocco. This includes computers and other hardware. But there are also discrepancies between regions. Some regions don't have an office, and others have offices and equipment, a fact that is linked to activities of the section.

On the other hand, access divide within grassroots social movements that recruit from among the poorest and marginalized segments of society remains large and harder to bridge as Zakaria Sahnoun, talking of Islamic movements experience, explains:

There is shortage [at the level of access to technology] and the use of the Internet by members reflects its [diffusion] in the country in general. If we take 140 members we will find only 50 of them using the technology since many of them are traders and craftsmen and this category of people seldom has access to the Internet. Students, too, they have to pay public access, so the users are among those civil servants, teachers and others … You know to subscribe to the internet, you have to pay at least 300 dirhams per month[5]. This is a real challenge to all society and not just to political parties and associations.

Unlike professional SMOs whose collective action tactics center on lobbying and pressurizing the state and government, grassroots movements such as the Islamic-oriented one target the entire society by seeking to transform or reinforce collective identity. Material digital divides in society, thus, impact more the collective action strategies of these groups and shape their choice and use of available media to mobilize potential and actual members.

Access divide is not the only major barrier preventing social movements from taking advantage of the Internet's potential in collective action. Many respondents have indicated that the major problem their SMOs encounter relates to lack of skills rather than to a shortage in hardware and Internet connection. When I visited the office of the Union of Feminine Action in Casablanca, I noticed that it was well equipped with computers, but many were unused. I asked Soad Lekhmas, the president of the NGO about it, and she answered:

We had the equipment since 1996, when we started, but we only started using the Internet in 2000....We do have equipment, but we lack human resources more. We don't have a professional person to work on this domain....We wanted to organize a march in November 24, and we wanted to do a website for the event to mobilize local associations, women associations, artists, young people, etc... But if you want a website, you need a full-time person taking charge of it; you need a person to update it, to respond to people.

Sometimes, SMOs try to recruit volunteers from outside their constituencies because their members lack training, but the results are not usually satisfying as Soufian Ladham from the Democratic Association of Moroccan Women (ADFM) explains:

The current website is the most recent one. Initially, we started with a trial version set up by a trainee student. We were disappointed because the final product was not satisfying. You have to work with professionals, and you need money to do that.

In order to overcome this problem, the majority of NGOs try to provide their members with basic training in the use of the Internet, mainly on how to browse the web and send e-mails. In the words of Jawad Mostaqbal:

The cleavage between members still exists but it has diminished because we provided training to militants. The minimum is that everyone should have an email account, and know how to use it. I think that those who can't do it, are illiterate and we should not remain illiterate. I think that 90% of militants master this at least. But we are elite [group]. Most of us have a university degree.

Like digital divide at the level of access to the Internet, divide at the level of skill and know-how is easier to bridge in the case of small and leftist SMOs whose constituencies are made up principally of individuals with higher education and stable jobs. Data showed, however, that bridging the divide is not that easy for some movements, especially feminist SMOs.

Whilst availability of computers and Internet access, skill and usage opportunities are preconditions for the appropriation of the Internet in collective action, they do not necessarily guarantee an optimal appropriation of the medium in collective action. In fact, people can have access to the Internet or the means to do so, but still prefer not to use it or refuse to invest money or time to acquire the necessary skills to use the technology (Van Dijk, 2006). This lack of motivation to use the technology can be linked to psychological, social and cultural preferences and needs of individuals and groups. According to the uses-and-gratifications paradigm, for instance, "people are motivated by a desire to fulfil certain needs. So rather than asking how media use influences users, a uses-and-gratifications perspective asks how users' basic needs influence users' media choices" (Cho et al., 2003, p. 48).

Our data confirmed that the decision to invest resources in the usage of the Internet is motivated by an amalgam of factors that cannot be reduced only to the potential of the medium for collective action. When I asked Abderrezak Drissi why AMDH's website looks unprofessional and lack updating, for instance, he was very reluctant to answer the question, and upon my insistence, he pointed out:

There isn't a great awareness about the issue. The website is a personal work. Not a professional. The website is hosted by Ittisalat[6] for free. To tell you the truth, there is no rationality in the whole issue. I was discussing this with my colleagues about organizing this work and we found that the costs will rise sharply. So to answer your question about updating the website, there is a big output from AMDH at the headquarter and chapters, and so there should be a group who takes charge of it, but we don't have it.

Though Drissi was, in fact, trying to avoid criticising directly his colleagues in AMDH, his answer shows that underlying the hesitation of the association not to invest more resources to improve the website, there are practical considerations of costs and benefits, but also a certain bias against the medium that he qualifies as lack of "awareness" and "rationality".

A number of respondents indicated that existing limitations in the use of the medium in collective action is also linked to reluctance on the part of older generation of activists to use the new medium. If younger generations are quick and natural adopters of the technology, older generations, who form the majority of activists within many SMOs, specifically leftist and feminist ones, are more conservative in the way they view and appropriate the technology. Similarly, upon a question about the limited exploitation of the web potential on the Unified Socialist Party's website, Abdelilah Mansouri, a young leader and activist in the party and other leftist NGOs, criticized the older generations in the party for being unable to adapt to the new technology:

The website is being used but not in an ideal way, not in its full capacity.... This is mainly due to our current mentality which is closer to a traditional mentality that has been incapable of exploiting all the capacities provided to us by the information and communication technologies.

A common characteristic of Moroccan civil society is the rigid hierarchical structure reigning in most SMOs where leaders, like the kings and presidents in the region, seek to remain in power for life. As result, there are wide chasms between an old generation of leaders, some of whom have been in their positions since Morocco's independence, and younger constituencies at the grassroots level, and between civil society as a whole and the rest of the people. These leaders are more accustomed and attached to print media, which were, until the early 1990s when satellite television appeared, the major source of alternative information in the country. Explaining her personal preference for print media over the Internet, Rachida Benmesaoud points out:

One has to know how to exploit this tool but also to be cautious about its negative side....I am talking about relationships that become fixed and daily rituals, like entering and talking to this or that person. This process exhausts me and puts more pressure on me. I prefer face-to-face contacts.... It is perhaps a cultural disposition; I feel more at ease with pens and papers and with face-to-face contacts. Perhaps, I don't have the patience to sit for a long time to talk to somebody whose general features I don't even know. There is this psychological factor.

The generation gap in the context of Morocco clearly challenges a linear and mechanic conceptualization of the digital divide whereby lack of access to the technology will necessarily result in social, political and economic exclusion (Cammaerts, Audenhove, Nulens, & Pauwels, 2003).

Though younger generations constitute the largest group and most adept users of the Internet in Morocco and within social movements, they are, besides women, the most disadvantaged demographic groups in society. In the last few months, and benefitting from the dynamics created by the Arab Spring, Moroccan youth, empowered by social media and the Internet, launched the February20 movement, a protest movement demanding profound democratic reforms and social justice in the country. The movement has so far compelled the conservative regime in the country to react and respond to some of the movement's demands. It is, however, still early to conclude that this movement, as it is the case with most Arab countries, will lead to genuine democracy. As the chapter has argued, such a happy outcome can be only the culmination of a long and difficult process to which ICTs and the Internet contribute, but do not determine.

CONCLUSION

To sum it up, the Internet has indeed contributed to the empowerment of Moroccan social movements at various levels, notably by bringing down communication costs, enhancing organizational efficiency, building networks of solidarity and speeding up direct mobilization. Moreover, the political impact of the Internet cannot be attributed to intrinsic qualities of the technology alone; neither can it be reduced to one online platform. The "effect" of the medium can rarely be disassociated from other media with which it is used concomitantly, or from the offline networks in which it is embedded. Besides, being usually mediated through social, political and cultural structures of its own context and that of users and social actors, the Internet can affect but not radically transform existing power relations.

Equally important, as the popular uprisings and revolutions are spreading from one country to another in North Africa and the Middle East, understanding the role of ICTs in the social and political transformations in the region, and throughout the developing world in general, has become a crucial task. On the basis of the present study, three areas come out as important in refocusing the research agenda on the political and democratic role of ICTs in developing countries. First, there is an urgent need to pay more attention to down-top models of political appropriation of ICTs in order to understand the extent to which

these media are reinventing political advocacy and collective action, as well as contributing to reshaping asymmetrical power relations in repressive societies and countries. Using interdisciplinary conceptual models drawn from multiple fields, such as sociology, political science and political communication can help achieve this task, particularly to transcend dichotomous interpretations of the democratic role of ICTs. Second, instead of concentrating on determining the effect of ICTs, as independent and isolated variables, on socio-political realities, research should focus more on how ICTs are integrated into existing media, both new and traditional, and how they are embedded in offline social networks. Finally, while dominant ICT-for-development discourse conceives of digital divide mainly in terms of inequalities in physical access to technology, more efforts should be deployed to explore other types of divides in the context of developing countries, mainly gender, motivational, generational, usage and skill divides.

REFERENCES

Avgerou, C. (2007). *Information Systems in Developing Countries: A Critical Research Review.* Working paper series. London: London School of Economics and Political Science.

Ben Moussa, M. (2011). *The use of the Internet by social movements in Morocco: Implications collective action and political change.* Unpublished PhD thesis, Concordia University, Portland, Oregon.

Bendourou, O. (1996). Power and opposition in Morocco. *Journal of Democracy, 7*(3), 108–122. doi:10.1353/jod.1996.0041.

Bentivegna, S. (2006). Rethinking politics in the world of ICTs. *European Journal of Communication, 21*(3), 331–343. doi:10.1177/0267323106066638.

Blee, K., & Taylor, V. (2002). The uses of semi-structured interviews in social movement research. In Klandermans, B., & Staggenborg, S. (Eds.), *Methods of Social Movement Research* (pp. 92–117). Minneapolis, MN: University of Minnesota Press.

Cammaerts, B., Audenhove, L. V., Nulens, G., & Pauwels, C. (2003). *Beyond the digital divide: Reducing exclusion, fostering inclusion.* Brussels, Belgium: VUB Brussels University Press.

Castells, M. (2001). *The Internet galaxy: Reflections on the Internet, business, and society.* Oxford, UK: Oxford University Press.

Cavatorta, F. (2005). The international context of Morocco's stalled democratization. *Democratization*, *12*(4), 548–566. doi:10.1080/13510340500226101.

Cavatorta, F. (2006). Civil society, Islamism, and democratisation: The case of Morocco. *Modern African Studies*, *44*(2), 203–222. doi:10.1017/S0022278X06001601.

Cborra, C., & Navarra, D. (2005). Good governance, development theory and aid policy: Risks and challenges of E-government in Jordan. *Journal of Information Technology for Development*, *11*(2), 141–159. doi:10.1002/itdj.20008.

Chatfield, A. T., & Alhujran, O. (2009). *A cross-country comparative analysis of e-government service delivery among Arab countries. Information Technology for Development, 15(3).* Indianapolis, IN: Wiley Periodicals.

Cho, J., De Zuniga, H. G., Rojas, H., & Shah, D. V. (2003). Beyond access: The digital divide and Internet uses and gratifications. *IT & Society*, *1*(4), 46–72.

Ciborra, C. (2003). Unveiling e-government and development: Governing at a distance in the new war. Working Paper Series. London: London School of Economics and Political Science.

Ciborra, C. (2005). Interpreting e-government and development: Efficiency, transparency or governance at a distance? *Information Technology & People*, *18*(3), 260–279. doi:10.1108/09593840510615879.

Corbin, J., & Strauss, A. L. (1990). Grounded theory research: Procedures, canons, and evaluative criteria. *Qualitative Sociology*, *13*(1), 3–21. doi:10.1007/BF00988593.

Dahlgren, P. (2005). The Internet, public spheres, and political communication: Dispersion and deliberation. *Political Communication*, *22*, 147–162. doi:10.1080/10584600590933160.

Della Porta, D., & Diani, M. (2006). *Social Movements: An Introduction.* Malden, MA: Blackwell Publishing.

Desrues, T., & Moyano, E. (2001). Social Change and Political Transition in Morocco. *Mediterranean Politics*, *6*(1), 21–47. doi:10.1080/713604490.

Diani, M. (2000). The Concept of Social Movement. In Nash, K. (Ed.), *Readings in Contemporary Political Sociology* (pp. 155–176). Malden, MA: Blackwell.

DiMaggio, P., Hagittai, W., & Neuman, R. (2001). Social Implications of the Internet. *Annual Review of Sociology*, *27*, 307–336. doi:10.1146/annurev.soc.27.1.307.

Dutton, W. H., Shepherd, A., & di Gennaro, C. (2007). Digital divides and choices reconfiguring access: National and cross-national patterns of Internet diffusion and use. In Anderson, B., Brynin, M., Gershuny, J., & Raban, Y. (Eds.), *Information and Communication Technologies in Society: E-living in a Digital Europe* (pp. 31–45). London: Routledge.

Eddouada, S. (2001). Feminism and Politics in Moroccan Feminist Non-Governmental Organisations. Retrieved January 13, 2013, from http://www.postcolonialweb.org/poldiscourse/casablanca/eddouada2.html

Ellis, S., & Kessel, I. (Eds.). (2009). Introduction: African social movements or social movements in Africa? In S. Ellis & I. van Kessel (Eds.), Movers and Shakers: Social Movements in Africa (pp. 1–16). Leiden, Netherlands: Brill.

Fraser, N. (1995). From Redistribution to Recognition: Dilemmas of Justice in a 'Post-Socialist' Age. *New Left Review, 212*, 68–93.

Goldsmith, J., & Wu, T. (2006). *Who Controls the Internet?: Illusions of a Borderless World.* New York: Oxford University Press.

Graft, P. V., & Svenson, J. (2006). Explaining eDemocracy development: A quantitative empirical study. *Information Polity, 11*, 123–134.

Hansen, D. Shneiderman, B., & Smith, M. (2011). Analyzing social media networks with NodeXL: Insights from a connected world. Burlington, MA: Morgan Kaufmann.

Heeks, R. (2002). E-Government in Africa: Promise and practice. *Information Polity, 7*, 97–114.

Heeks, R. (2007). Theorizing ICT4D research. *Information Technologies and International Development, 3*(3), 4. doi:10.1162/itid.2007.3.3.1.

Heeks, R. (2010a). Development 2.0: The IT-enabled Transformation of International Development. *Communications of the ACM, 53*(4), 22–24. doi:10.1145/1721654.1721665.

Heeks, R. (2010b). Do information and communication technologies (ICTs) contribute to development? *Journal of International Development, 22*(5), 625–640. doi:10.1002/jid.1716.

Hilbert, M. (2009). The Maturing Concept of E-Democracy: From E-Voting and Online Consultations to Democratic Value Out of Jumbled Online Chatter. *Journal of Information Technology & Politics, 6*, 87–110. doi:10.1080/19331680802715242.

Internet World Stats. (2010). Internet users and population statistics for Africa. Retrieved January 13, 2013, from http://www.internetworldstats.com/stats1.htm#africa

Jenkins, G. (2008). Resource Mobilisation Theory and the Study of Social Movements. In Ruggiero, V., & Montagna, N. (Eds.), *Social Movements: A reader* (pp. 118–127). London: Routledge.

Johnson, J. (2002). In-depth interviewing. In Gubrium, J., & Holstein, J. (Eds.), *Handbook of Interview Research: Context and Method* (pp. 83–103). Thousands Oaks, CA: Sage Publications.

Kausch, K. (2008). Morocco: Negotiating change with the Makhzen: Project on freedom of association in the Middle East and North Africa. *Fundación para las Relaciones Internacionales y el Diálogo Exterior* (FRIDE) (pp. 1-27). Retrieved January 13, 2013, from http://www.fride.org/publication/391/morocco:-negotiating-change-with-the-makhzen

Leveau, R. (1997). Morocco at the crossroads. *Mediterranean Politics, 2*(2), 95–113. doi:10.1080/13629399708414621.

Marwell, G., & Oliver, V. (2008). Resource Mobilisation Theory and the Study of Social Movements. In Ruggiero, V., & Montagna, N. (Eds.), *Social Movements: A Reader* (pp. 128–143). London: Routledge.

McAdam, D., McCarthy, J. D., & Zald, M. (1996). *Comparative Perspectives on Social Movements: Political Opportunities, Mobilizing Structures, and Cultural Framings.* New York: Cambridge University Press. doi:10.1017/CBO9780511803987.

McCarthy, J., & Zald, M. N. (2003). *Social movement in an organizational society: Collected essays.* New Brunswick, NJ: Transaction Publishers.

Melucci, A. (1989). *Nomads of the Present: Social Movements and Individual Needs in Contemporary Society.* Philadelphia, PA: Temple University Press.

Melucci, A. (1996). *Challenging codes: Collective action in the information age.* Cambridge, UK: Cambridge University Press. doi:10.1017/CBO9780511520891.

Navarra, D. (2010). The Architecture of Global ICT Programs: A Case Study of E-Governance in Jordan. *Information Technology for Development, 16*(2), 128–140. doi:10.1080/02681101003741681.

Norris, P. (2001). *Digital divide: Civic engagement, information poverty, and the Internet worldwide.* Cambridge, UK: Cambridge University Press. doi:10.1017/CBO9781139164887.

Ruggiero, V., & Montagna, N. (Eds.). (2008). *Social Movements: A Reader.* London: Routledge.

Saco, D. (2002). *Cyber Democracy: Public Space and the Internet.* Minneapolis, MN: University of Minnesota.

Sassen, S. (2004). Towards a technology of Information technology. In C. Avgerou, C. Ciborra., & F. Land (Eds.), The Social Study of Information and Communication Technology: Innovation, Actors and Contexts (pp. 77–103). Oxford, UK: Oxford University Press.

Sater, J. (2007). *Civil Society and Political Change in Morocco.* London: Routledge.

Shade, L. R. (2002). *Gender and Community in the Social Construction of the Internet.* New York: P. Lang.

Shigetomi, S. (2009). Rethinking theories on social movements and development. In Shigetomi, S., & Makino, K. (Eds.), *Protest and Social Movements in the Developing World* (pp. 1–16). Cheltenham, UK: Edward Elgar Publishing.

Sidi Hida, B. (2007). *Social movements and stakeholder. Development NGOs face of globalization and the state in Morocco.* Unpublished doctoral dissertation. Catholic University of Louvain. Université catholique de Louvain, Belgium.

Stekelenburg, S., & Klandermans, M. (Eds.). (2009). *Protest and Social Movement in the Developing World.* Cheltenham, UK: Edward Elgar Publishing.

Sutherland, E. (2007). Unbundling local loops: global experiences. Learning Information Networking and Knowledge Centre (LINK). Retrieved January 13, 2013, from http://link.wits.ac.za/papers/LINK.pdf

Tarrow, S. (1998). *Power in movement: Social movements and contentious politics.* Cambridge, MA: Cambridge University Press. doi:10.1017/CBO9780511813245.

The Initiative for an Open Arab Internet. (2009). *The second report of the Arabic Network for Human Rights Information (HR info).* Morocco. Retrieved January 13, 2013, from http://www.openarab.net/en/node/364

Thompson, M. (2008). ICT and development studies: Towards development 2.0. *Journal of International Development, 20*(6), 821–835. doi:10.1002/jid.1498.

Thomspon, M., & Walsham, G. (2010). ICT research in Africa: Need for a strategic developmental focus. *Information Technology for Development, 16*(2), 112–127. doi:10.1080/02681101003737390.

Tilly, C. (1984). *Big Structures, Large Processes, Huge Comparisons.* New York: Russell Sage Foundation.

Tilly, C., & Tarrow, S. (2007). *Contentious Politics.* Boulder, CO: Paradigm Publishers.

Touraine, A. (1981). *The Voice and the Eye: An Analysis of Social Movements.* Cambridge, MA: Cambridge University Press.

Touraine, A. (1985). An introduction to the study of social movements. *Social Research, 52,* 749–788.

UN Department of Economic and Social Affairs. (2010). *UN e-government 2010 survey.* Retrieved January 13, 2013, from http://kz.mofcom.gov.cn/accessory/201009/1284225105383.pdf

UN Human Development Programme [UNDP]. (2009). *Human Development Report: Morocco*. Retrieved January 13, 2013, from http://hdrstats.undp.org/en/countries/country_fact_sheets/cty_fs_MAR.html

van der Graft, P., & Sevensson, J. (2006). Explaining eDemocracy development: A quantitative empirical study. *Information Polity, 11*, 123–134.

Van Dijk, J. A. G. M. (2005). *The Deepening Divide: Inequality in the Information Society*. Thousand Oaks, CA: Sage Publications.

Van Dijk, J. A. G. M. (2006). *The Network Society: Social Aspects of New Media*. Thousand Oaks, CA: Sage Publications.

Walsham, G., Robey, F., & Sahay, S. (2007). Foreword: Special issue on information systems in developing countries. *Management Information Systems Quarterly, 31*(2), 317–326.

Walsham, G., & Sahay, S. (2006). Research on information systems in developing countries: Current landscape and future prospects. *Information Technology for Development, 12*(1), 7–24. doi:10.1002/itdj.20020.

Warschauer, M. (2003). Dissecting the Digital Divide: A Case Study in Egypt. *The Information Society, 19*(4), 297–304. doi:10.1080/01972240309490.

Wilson, E. (2004). *The information revolution and developing countries*. Cambridge, MA: MIT Press.

Zembylas, M. (2009). ICT for education, development, and social justice: Some theoretical issues. In Vrasidas, C., Zembylas, M., & Glass, G. V. (Eds.), *ICT for Education, Development, and Social Justice* (pp. 17–29). Charlotte, NC: Information Age.

ENDNOTES

[1]   The paper is based on a larger study; given the limited scope of this article, not all respondents are quoted in it.

[2]   Rosamor is the name of a factory in Casablanca where 55 workers died in a fire in 2007, because they were locked inside the factory in rooms that had no exists when the fire broke out. They all died as they could not escape.

[3]   A city in the Middle Atlas Mountains in Morocco.

[4]   A city in the south of Morocco.

[5]   Since 2008, the fee has decreased significantly reaching now 100 Dh (around 11 USD), for basic DSL connection.

[6]   The major telecommunication company and main provider of ISP in the country.

Chapter 14
Twitter and Africa's 'War on Terror':
News Framing and Convergence in Kenya's *Operation Linda Nchi*.[1]

Duncan Omanga
Bayreuth University, Germany

Pamela Chepngetich-Omanga
Bayreuth University, Germany

ABSTRACT

Before the close of 2011, Kenya launched its own local version of a 'war on terror' following persistent border incursions by the al-Qaida affiliated al-Shabaab militant group. In a conflict that was seen by many to be fought largely through modern military hardware, the emergence and effective use of social media as yet another site of this warfare reflected the growing influence of new media in mobilizing, debating and circulating issues of public interest. Specifically, this chapter reveals the particular frames that were used in Twitter to keep members of the public informed on the front line developments of the Operation Linda Nchi. Secondly, the study also investigates how the entrance of al-Shabaab into Twitter shaped the media framing of a war previously dominated by the more 'legitimate' Kenya Defence Force Twitter account. Finally, in a situation where the Twitter discourse was perceived and defined by the KDF as the official account of the war, this paper shows how the new and the old media converged in news reports in Kenya's main newspapers and the resultant frames from this convergence.

DOI: 10.4018/978-1-4666-4197-6.ch014

INTRODUCTION

KDF is not keen on Twitter war nor propaganda. The rains have stopped pounding. Watch out for KDF.[2]

The mass movements commonly known as the 'Arab Spring' that began in North Africa and swept through the Arab world brought to the fore the crucial role of the social media in mobilizing and shaping discourse. The protests that began in Tunisia have so far seen the overthrow of dictators, extensive reforms in government, and also continued civil unrest in several other countries. And while debate still rages on the extent to which the social media was at the centre of these protests, it was not for nothing that some of these uprisings acquired the label 'Facebook revolution' or 'Twitter revolution', a testimony to the coordinating influence social media has on issues of significance in the world today.

Following persistent border incursions and several abductions of tourists by suspected Al Shabaab militants from Somalia, Kenya decided to launch perhaps one of its most ambitious military operations in its 50 year history. In mid October of 2011, the Kenyan Defence forces (KDF) moved heavy military equipment and massive divisions into the Somali boarder. On the 16th of October the first troops had crossed into Somalia and the now months old offensive dubbed *operation linda nchi* (operation protect the country) began. As expected, the public was eager to follow the proceedings at the frontlines and several journalists were embedded with the soldiers and would regularly file news reports to Nairobi.[3] In addition, the military leadership set up a weekly news briefing in which the military spokesman gave a report on the proceedings of the war.

For a while, partly due to a recurring public discourse on patriotism and coupled with predictable sources of news for the local media, the hegemonic version of events from the military was published uncritically as the only report of

the war. This was equally reflected in opinion columns and other commentaries, with only the most cautious and sublime critique on the war. The threat to this hegemonic voice first came through tweets from humanitarian organizations working inside war torn Somalia. The instantaneity and convenience of Twitter on reporting the war became equally apparent to the KDF. In late October, the military spokesman Emmanuel Chirchir complemented the weekly briefings with almost daily tweets[4] from the frontlines. At the time of compiling this research he had made over 680 tweets, attached several pictures and videos through *Twitpic*[5] and other links, all of which on several occasions converged to produce the major headlines or news accounts in the press and the broadcast media.

With more action increasing and the security situation on the ground becoming increasingly difficult for most humanitarian organizations to operate, the KDF held sway on Twitter in fortifying their hegemonic voice insofar as media accounts of the war proceeded. However, in early December of 2011, the al-Shabaab militants also created their own Twitter account and began tweeting under the handle HSM Press Office - an acronym for *Harakat al-Shabab al-Mujahideen*, or Movement of Holy Warrior Youth. From the onset, it was clear that al-Shabaab had set sights on a wider audience by using the English language. From then on the war included not just physical combat but also a virtual war that revealed the increasing role that the new social media is playing not only as an embedded practice of daily life, but as a pivotal tool in framing news.

This is not the first time that militant and jihadi groups are taking advantage of popular social media to advance their objectives. According to The Investigative Project on Terrorism (IPT),[6] jihadi media organizations are creating Facebook pages to bypass restrictions on terrorist organizations, and to pass on videos, pictures, and documents to followers. The report goes on to argue that such platforms allow these organizations the capacity to organize, act and recruit. While concern in these reports is how the vast social media such Facebook, YouTube and Twitter are used to mobilize, indoctrinate and manage public profiles of militant groups, there is need to probe how these sites are capable of reaching and influencing public opinion on a wider scale. While this paper does not purport to do this, a good starting point involves investigating the extent to which particular frames from social media discourse manifest as news frames in more mainstream media. This paper seeks to do exactly that, and goes ahead to show how they compete with legitimate sources of information in seeking to influence public opinion. Following Gamson and Mogdigliani (1989), this study considers frames to be 'interpretive packages' that give meaning to an issue. At the core of this package is a central organizing idea, or frame, for making sense of relevant events, suggesting what is at issue' (1989, p. 3). London (1993) argues that to identify frames, the informational content is less important than the interpretive commentary that attends it. Additionally, frames are frequently drawn from, and reflective of, shared cultural discourses and resonate with the larger social themes to which journalists, newsmakers and news sources tend to be acutely sensitive. However, Entman views framing as a deliberate and conscious process in communication. 'To frame, argues Entman,

is to select some aspects of a perceived reality and make them more salient in a communication text, in such a way as to promote a particular problem definition, causal interpretation, moral evaluation, and/or treatment recommendation for the item described.' (1993, p. 52).

That is to say that frames *define a problem* by determining either explicitly or implicitly, what a causal agent is doing, and with what costs and benefits usually measured in terms of common cultural values. Secondly, frames *diagnose causes,*

by identifying the forces creating the problem; they also make *moral judgments*, through evaluating causal agents and their effects; and *suggest remedies*; manifest by offering and justifying specific or general treatments for the problems and predict their likely effects. While it is possible that not all these functions will be fulfilled in a single frame, at least one or more of these functions will manifest in the frame.

This chapter reveals the frames that defined this war, on cyber space and also how this converges with one of the mainstream/traditional media, in this case the newspaper. Although it has several definitions, Grant and Wilkinson (2009) view convergence as a coming together of different equipment and tools for producing and distributing news. However, this study takes on Jenkins (2006) idea of convergence as 'flow of content across multiple media platforms,' (p.3) suggesting that audiences today play a crucial role in creating and distributing content, and convergence therefore has to be examined in terms of social, and not just in technological changes within the society. According to Jenkins (2006) media convergence is a dynamic process but certainly not a displacement of the old media, but rather an interaction between different media forms and platforms. Focusing on Kenya's military operation in Somalia, this study shows how social media and old media in Kenya interact. Specifically, the chapter focuses on how Twitter became the source of news reports in the Kenyan press, and the nature of this convergence between the new and the old media in reportage of war. While the focus on two Kenyan newspapers in a war involving Kenya might be argued to be limiting the full understanding of the scope of convergence between the old and the new media[7], the purpose of this study was not necessarily to reveal the extent of slant in news framing but rather to show the nature and complexion of the convergence.

The chapter begins by a short account of the state of social media in the African continent, particularly Twitter, which is widely popular in Kenya. This section describes how Twitter functions and briefly reviews literature on Twitter. In the following section, a brief description of the methodology is discussed showing how insights from framing research provide a methodology that reveals the frames on both Twitter sphere and the news reports. And in the final section on findings, the paper discusses the quantitative findings by providing rich in depth examples that could not be captured quantitatively, in order to fortify the conclusions reached.

TWITTER, AFRICA, AND BEYOND: SELECTED LITERATURE REVIEW

Twitter is a free social networking service that has changed how people, institutions and communication systems in Africa and much of the world function. Twitter allows users to send 'updates' or 'tweets', which are text-based posts, up to 140 characters long to the Twitter website via short message service (e.g., on a cell phone), instant messaging, from their computer at home or work, or through a third-party application. It is considered a social media akin to Facebook and is built on forging and maintaining social networks. Like Facebook, it is structured through simply reporting 'status updates' to friends, sharing pictures, links and increasingly also used in the news industry especially in capturing evolving events. According to Junco & Loken (2011), Twitter is more amenable to an ongoing, public dialogue than Facebook because Twitter is primarily a microblogging platform (Ebner et al., 2010). Indeed, some have described Twitter as a blog that is restricted to 140 characters per post but that also includes the functionality of social networking (McFedries, 2007). The site imposed character limit allows users' updates, or tweets, to be sent to cellular phones and other mobile devices as a text message. Bruns & Burgess (2012) argue that Twitter contains

an inbuilt ease with which additional materials (links, photos, video, and audio) can also be shared[8]. This makes it convenient for both the dissemination of first-hand, user-generated material documenting unfolding events as directly experienced by the user, and the sharing of secondary material in the form of links. These additions extend Twitter's effectivity far beyond the 140 character limit, adding a rich media layer to the Tweets themselves.

Accordingly, Twitter is a good example of a recent shift in social media, which has witnessed the convergence of explicit networking practices ('friending', 'following', interpersonal communication) with original content ('broadcasting' of updates), and large-scale information sharing and propagation (Bruns & Burgess (2012). It is through the social network that news and information spreads: Twitter is both a social networking site and an ambient information stream. Today, Twitter has become an important addition to the toolboxes both to journalists and media researchers (Ahmad, 2010). In the media, Twitter is used for first-hand reporting of events as they occur, such as the protests following the Iranian Elections in 2009, or the Arab spring, which occurred in a socio political environment characterized by autocratic systems uneasy with a free and independent media. In Kenya, Twitter has equally been instrumental to the media in the reportage of unfolding events, normally tweeted as updates, be it a football match, a demonstration, or a court proceeding to local and global audiences.

Research on Twitter is only beginning to blossom, but predictably much of what is coming out seems to be from the global north. Some recent research has analyzed the social network in Twitter, for instance Java, Song, Finin, and Tseng (2007) look primarily at the network structure and geographic distribution of Twitter users, in which they found that relationships tend to be reciprocal, and according to them users tend to be primarily in the United States and

Europe, whose links tend to be with others on the same continent. The same team also found that people use Twitter to share information and report on their activities. Similarly, Romero, and Wu (2009) found that relationships among Twitter users were largely reciprocal and that communication between people on Twitter takes place even beyond the circle of online friends, followers, or follower's network. This broad array of Twitter research reflects its continued significance in the contemporary networked world. Recent research on Twitter include health research (Heaivilin, Gerbert, Page, & Gibbs, 2011; Signorini, Segre, & Polgreen, 2011), marketing (Jansen, Zhang, Sobel, & Chowdury, 2009), government information (Wigand, 2010), political predictions (Tumasjan, Sprenger, Sandner, & Welpe, 2010), and closely related to this study, shaping of news stories in other media (Abel, Gao, Houben, & Tao, 2011; Jackoway, Samet, & Sankaranarayanan, 2011; Phelan, McCarthy, & Smyth, 2009). While a growing body of research on convergence of Twitter and the mainstream media is available (Hamdy, 2009; Lasorsa et al., 2012; Khamis, 2011) there is still a yawning gap on how this manifests in Africa. This study seeks to fill this gap.

In Africa today, the use and impact of the social media is huge, to say the least. This has been bolstered by the increase in mobile telephony which has made access to the internet convenient and easy. According to a BBC report, the number of subscribers on the continent has grown almost 20% each year for the past five years, and it is expected that there are more than 735 million subscribers today in Africa.[9] Meanwhile, huge submarine cable infrastructure has seen an increased growth of internet access not only in Kenya but also in the entire continent. According to the latest statistics from the Communications Commissions of Kenya, mobile phone subscriptions stand at slightly over 29 million out of a population of about 40 million people. Additionally, over 14 million Kenyans have access or subscriptions to the internet and slightly more than half this number access the internet through their phones[10]. It is the mostly younger subscribers in this category that have facilitated the meteoric rise of the social media in Kenya and the rest of Africa. Today, the social media is an integral aspect in Kenya's social and political dynamics and has been effectively used in driving positive change, galvanizing and channeling public discontent, political mobilization, governance and civil awareness from 'below', apart from simply connecting friends.

Among the various social media, Twitter has become one of the most effective and popular social media in Kenya. Twitter has been a key central organizing medium in popular movements in Kenya such as a recent Doctors strike[11], and the teachers strike, among others. In 2011, Portland Communication analyzed more than 11.5m geo-located tweets. In their study, Twitter is dominated by South Africa, which sent twice as many tweets (5,030,226) as the next most active Kenya (2,476,800). Nigeria (1,646,212), Egypt (1,214,062) and Morocco (745,620) make up the remainder of the top five most active countries[12]. And as evidence of the convergence of the old and the new media platforms, 68% of those polled said that they use Twitter to monitor news. Demographically, African tweeters are between 20 and 29 years old, and almost 60% access Twitter through their mobile phones. As the data indicates, Twitter plays a big part of Kenya's informational and social space, to the extent of having more traffic than bigger countries such as Egypt and Nigeria, and others such as Tunisia, whose political complexion has been significantly influenced by the social media. This fact among others makes a study on Twitter use in Kenya a timely study.

METHOD

The researchers did a framing analysis to identify the frames that defined the tweets on one hand and the emergent news on the two main leading newspapers in the country. The two papers were chosen because they control a combined significant readership in Kenya[13]. The method was divided into two phases. The first phase involved a close reading of tweets from both the Kenya's department of defence spokesman, Major Emmanuel Chirchir and those from al-Shabaab's Twitter account (HSMpress, referred in the text simply as HSM)). Specifically, the study covers the period between 14th October 2011 to end of March, 2012 shortly after Kenya's Defence Forces (KDF) were integrated into the AMISOM (African Union Mission in Somalia) forces in Somalia. At the time, Major Chirchir (for KDF) had made 685 Tweets, with 24,035 followers. On their part, HSM had 12,494 followers and had made 547 Tweets. Worth noting, the KDF tweets began on October 27, 2011, about two weeks after the operation. The HSM tweets began weeks later on December 7, probably as a reaction to the KDF tweets following the latter's dominance as a source of frontline news in both local and international media. Only tweets directly sent by the two were analyzed; retweets and other comments from followers were ignored. Also, while the exercise involved a close analysis of all the tweets, not all of them were useful to the study. Specifically, tweets seeking and giving clarifications, or those focused on frivolous social or ideological[14] swops were ignored.

The second part involved doing a subsequent frame analysis involving news reports drawn from *The Daily Nation* and *The Standard* in the same period. A total of 82 articles tracing their sources directly to the Tweets were selected for the framing analysis. In both phases, frames were appropriated following close reading of the tweets and the articles. Careful attention was given not only to manifest framing devices, but also to those devices that are embedded in the culture and context of production. It is also important to note that in several articles, and occasionally a few tweets, there was more than one frame. Also, As Kenyans, the authors were well acquainted with the context before and during the operation which made it possible to capture the cultural impulses critical in revealing the frames. Finally, it is worth to note that in seeking to probe only those articles directly sourced from Twitter postings, it was relatively easier to make comments on the nature of convergence of the mainstream traditional press and the social media.

DISCUSSION AND FINDINGS

Two weeks after the offensive in Somalia, Major Chirchir, the military spokesman posted the first Tweet on October 27, 2011, declaring "good to be here to give you the right and official information".[15] This first Tweet that deliberately anchors claims of legitimacy and further claims of offering the 'right' information served several functions[16]. For starters, journalists were primed to be on the lookout for continuous and up to date information on the developments at the frontlines. While a few journalists were (and still are) embedded with the KDF forces in Somalia, the prospect of capturing the events as they dramatically unfolded directly from the KDF itself was welcome news to the various media houses. But even more crucially, it was meant to forestall the possibility of losing its role at reporting and shaping opinion of the war. Soon after, all media houses in Kenya worth their name began 'following' the KDF handle. The data from the study shows that this opening tweet became the first of what would later come to be part of a prominent frame; "our tweets are true, their tweets are propaganda". This frame was dominated by Tweets from both handles sending posts warning of tweets and broadcasts that were considered inaccurate. It also included those tweets that sought to 'substantiate and clarify' information already circulating in the public domain. This was especially the case when one side proclaimed and exaggerated figures on fatalities and casualties.

As the KDF gained legitimacy and became the key source of the unfolding events on the frontlines, the grim possibility of losing this exalted position began to emerge, seen when the KDF posted regular tweets that any information about the war from another source other than KDF should be treated as propaganda. As Table 1 shows, the KDF spokesperson posted several tweets (12.1%) cautioning the public of propaganda and misinformation from the al-Shabaab Twitter handle (HSMpress, hereafter referred to as HSM) and other media houses such as Al Jazeera and the Iranian based Press TV. On their part, the HSM only issued 9 tweets (4.9%) dismissing the KDF posts as propagandist.

While the KDF tweets were considered legitimate and accurate representations of the war and the HSM handle successfully delegitimized as propaganda, discourse on Twitter revealed that KDF's posts were equally propagandist. Between January 10-12, Major Chirchir caused a stir describing atrocities committed by the al-Shabaab including beheadings and extra judicial executions. Using *Twitpic,* he uploaded a photo accompanied by a chilling post: "It is a fact that a Kenyan was executed in Kismayu, two more are likely to be executed on Friday afternoon."[17] The photos were gory, showing a man being whipped while buried almost up to the neck. A subsequent photo shows the man dead and covered in blood, his body surrounded by huge stones. Major Chirchir added that the man was from Nairobi, and had been stoned to death the previous day in Kismayo, at the time an al-Shabaab stronghold. However, a quick search by both followers of HSM and KDF handles revealed that the photos belonged to the Associated Press and were earlier published in the *Daily Mail* on December 15, 2009. According to the Daily Mail story, the man was a Somali man accused of adultery.

Table 1. Table showing frames drawn from the KDF and the al-Shabaab Twitter handles

		Twitter **Frames**			
	Frames	**KDF (N=182)**	**%**	**al-Shabaab (N=215)**	**%**
1	We are liberators	6	3.3	7	3.2
2	Civilians are (not) dying	2	1.1	15	6.9
3	Al- Shabaab War setback	79	43.4	09	4.9
4	KDF War setback	17	9.4	40	18.5
5	Caution, we are attacking!	12	6.6	01	0.5
6	Ours Tweets are true their Tweets are propaganda	22	12.1	09	4.0
7	Our strategy, their debacle	37	20.3	32	14.8
8	Twitter spat	07	3.8	47	21.7
9	Picturing death and 'PoW'	-	00.0	55	25.5

Shortly after, the Major was put on the defensive even as the story ran in the Kenyan press from KDF's perspective[18]. 'This photo is simply for propaganda purpose, major. This guy was stoned in 2009, not in 2012,[19]' posted a follower. Al Shabaab swiftly responded saying the tweets '…seem unsophisticated, even in their propaganda campaign…a simple Google search would have saved them such an embarrassment[20].' The surging criticisms prompted Major Chirchir to finally bring closure to the debate by admitting that he posted old photos, but still insisted that a Kenyan man had been executed in Kismayo and that two more were in line for similar treatment[21]. 'We acknowledge the tweet upload error, its reprint in our local press and regret the embarrassment caused across all our publics,' said the Major, 'out of over 300 postings ... you can't write me off over one error. I take responsibility.[22]' With this tweet he veered debate to other operational issues.

Both the *al-Shabaab War setback* frame and the *KDF War setback* frame were prominent for obvious reasons. As shown in Table 2, they formed the bulk of the sources of most news reports in the Kenyan Dailies. These are the tweets that essentially communicated the progress on the frontlines. On Twitter, seen in Table 1, the KDF handle posted 79 (43.4%) of tweets that were part of the *al-Shabaab War Setback* frame. This frame was composed of tweets that focused on *al-Shabaab* military losses among them loss of equipment, loss of geographical space, and most importantly details of their dead. As will be shown later, such information provided the bulk of the news reports in the subsequent convergence seen in Kenyan dailies. Although the KDF acknowledged setback on their ranks (9.4%), these were ascribed to either an accident or luck (on the part of al-Shabaab's aimless shooting). Most of their setbacks were injuries or loss of equipment to

Table 2. Showing frames drawn from news reports directly drawn from Twitter

| | Frames | News reports based on Tweet Sources | | | |
		KDF *(N=115)	%	Shabaab* (11)	%
1	We are liberators	17	14.8	-	-
2	Civilians are (not) dying	5	4.3	1	09
3	Al Shabaab War setback	32	27.8	-	-
4	KDF War setback	7	6.1	4	37
5	Caution, we are attacking!	13	11.3	-	-
6	Ours Tweets are true their Tweets are propaganda	14	12.2	-	-
7	Our strategy, their debacle	26	22.6	3	27
8	Twitter spat	1	0.9	1	09
9	Picturing death and 'PoW'	-	-	2	18

IEDs (11 Tweets). The liberalizing and equalizing nature of the social media meant that the public had to contend with different figures issued by the militant group on KDF losses, 40 (18.5%) tweets, of which 15 alleged that there were fatalities and 25 posted loss of equipment and territory.

Knowing well their perceived status as 'terrorists' and their own claims at being al-Qaida affiliates, and that their tweets would easily be dismissed as propaganda and get little if any attention, HSM devised rhetorical and online strategies that sought to mitigate these handicaps. At the onset, the heavy servings of religious discourse were interspersed with diatribes and ridicule[23] particularly aimed at the combined KDF and the TFG[24] forces (Transitional Federal Government of Somalia) fighting al-Shabaab. This Islamist discourse was effectively used to conflate military loss to a kind or religious gain, for instance on December 7, a day after the handle was created, HSM posted that a 'martyrdom seeker (read suicide bomber) had infiltrated Mogadishu and killed 10 AMISOM troops[25]. Another claimed that *mujahidin* forces had raided a base claiming tens of enemy casualties while another offered that some TFG soldiers had surrendered and were 'welcomed after proclaiming repentance from apostasy'[26]. Through its handle, al-Shabaab reported loss within its ranks by giving names and birth place of their fighters to show the international face of its own fighters. Foreign fighters from Yemen, Britain and other countries were routinely eulogized. HSM sought to frame the conflict not as war on a militant outfit, but as a religious war on Islam. In all posting involving their gains or losses, the HSM referred to their fighters as 'the *mujahedeen, martyrs* or *Holy Warriors*. It is worth to note that despite launching its account three months after KDF's, HSM had more posts per day than the former. One of the reasons for this was that HSM's Twitter handle was very interactive, and appeared to address several audiences. It doubled up as a platform for both extremist preaching and of posting nonmilitary texts. It was also burdened by the need to respond to many players. Apart from KDF's military onslaught, the AMISOM troops, TFG troops and the Ethiopian Army were launching different but simultaneous operations against the al-Shabaab. Thus, the HSM felt compelled to issue regular posts to deflate opinion of an al-Shabaab under siege from all corners.

At some point, as the operation progressed, international aid and humanitarian organizations equally posted on Twitter the developments from the war front. As expected, their focus was on the humanitarian crisis produced by the war, especially following the shelling of particular targets by the KDF jets. These tweets became the subject of sustained media focus, especially in international media.[27] Perhaps realizing that focusing on civilian casualties gained media publicity and undermined the legitimacy of the war, HSM took to posting Twitter feeds that focused on the civilian causalities following military raids, this strategy, possibly meant to gain (mainstream) media attention and undercut the legitimacy of the KDF operation is captured in the *civilians are (not) dying frame*. Unlike the KDF handle that had only two[28] postings detailing (or denying) civilian deaths, al-Shabaab had 15 (6.9%) postings on civilian deaths. These posts mainly focused on a gendered victimhood which reported that women and children were on the receiving end of the airstrikes. Throughout the operation, the KDF tweets revealed a particular pattern of absenting civilian toll through a deliberate process of dissimulation in which most of the casualties were reportedly al-Shabaab militants. The HSM would soon exploit this information gap. On 8th December, the first of such tweets reported that Kenyan jets had bombed the city of Baardhere, in the Gedo region, and one civilian casualty, a girl, had been seriously wounded. This construction of victimhood and human suffering got more personalized when a follow up tweet declared that 'bombs dropped from Kenyan aircraft pulverized the home of poor 67 year old man and his family.

He died and his only daughter is severely injured.[29]' These counter posts were ignored by the media in Kenya and were simply reported as an attack on two al-Shabaab training camps that had killed several militants and destroyed their equipment.

The continued rise in civilian deaths prompted first denial from the KDF, but later, possibly as an admission of culpability, KDF began issuing warnings of impending military targets. The frame *caution we are attacking*[30] began around this time when on November 3, 2011, KDF tweeted that it had sunk a skiff in the Indian Ocean with 18 militants on board[31]. A follow up tweet warned that the Somalia border is closed and that any maritime operations in these areas are banned. This change of tact in Twitter discourse was possibly designed to convey a concern for civilian welfare on the part of KDF but since this information on Twitter could not be accessible to Kenyan Fishermen who fish along the border, a disaster was looming. The next day, on November 4, KDF announced the sinking of yet another boat suspected to be with 'militants' on board[32]. It later turned out they were Kenyan fishermen from the Lamu Island returning home. KDF simply reissued their earlier warning on maritime activity, this time warning 'any merchant ships operating along this sea lane of communication to be very cautious about transporting fighters.[33]' No apologies were issued on Twitter concerning this incident. The very fact that the mainstream media (both print and electronic) in and outside Kenya picked these Twitter posts and made them news items meant that offline audiences had the possibility of accessing these information which, as earlier shown by the skiff incident, formed the thin line between being dead or alive. On yet another occasion a Tweet warned that a host of Somalia towns including Baidoa will be under continuous attacks following the suspected arms airlifts from Eritrea. A follow up tweet urged those with friends and relatives in the listed cities to advise them accordingly[34]. Another interesting tweet equally directed at offline audiences urged them not to sell their donkeys to the militant group as these were now being used to ferry weapons in the wake of heavy rains in Somalia. Revealing an aggressive tone, a tweet cautioned that 'any large concentration and movement of loaded donkeys will be considered as al-Shabaab activity.'[35] As seen in Table 1, HSM only issued a single cautionary tweet of an impending attack.

Another tactic that the al-Shabaab used was simply to provoke the KDF into a virtual duel. For instance, the frame *Twitter Spat* in Table 1, a frame that captures those tweets that were strictly between KDF in HSM, was the creation of the latter and involved mainly flippant and mischievous posts devised to demoralize the KDF, TFG and AMISOM troops. The handle soon gained attention as a virtual equivalent of the ongoing actual war. Some of these posts came in the form of verbal ridicules designed to poke fun at their adversaries, for example one tweet joked that 'by the time the intoxicated TFG militia sober up from the excessive *qaat*[36] sessions, the scales of war would have turned rather significantly[37].' Another quipped 'the formidable Somali terrain has subdued the vicarious thrill KDF boys got from war movies; the bullets, they've realized, are real here![38] The torrent of salvos caught the attention of the KDF spokesman. Following a barrage of invocations of fighting on God's behalf, KDF could not resist taking an aim at HSM's grandstanding; 'Whatever the name, time is up for chopping inovative (sic) Somali hands[39]. HSM picked on the miss-pelt word 'innovative' and shot back; 'inovative (sp) Somali hands'? Quite perplexing! Care to explain?[40] KDF answered back, 'life has more meaning than denying women to wear bras...RT in support of Somalia women'[41]. Recalling the earlier KDF tweet urging residents not to sell their donkeys, and that large movements of donkeys will be considered enemy activity, HSM ridiculed these events saying 'Like bombing donkeys, you mean! Your eccentric battle strategy has got animal rights groups quite concerned, Major. It was clear that HSM were savouring their virtual spat with the KDF, in just

two months they had posted 47 (21.7%) tweets directly aimed at ridiculing KDF. Perhaps noticing that al-Shabaab was gaining visibility from the virtual spat, KDF stopped direct replies to the former after giving a 7 (3.8%) tweet duel.

A third and perhaps more effective strategy for the militant group insofar as reaching audiences that rely on other media platforms was the effective use of pictures uploaded through *Twitpic*. As the Table 1 shows, the frame *picturing death, and POW*[42] *(prisoner of Wars)* was a conspicuous frame unique to HSM. As a conventional force, KDF could not have any posting on this frame as it cannot treat prisoners or dead militants as war trophies. HSM exploited this frame by posting 55 (25.5%) tweets. These posts were a result of two major incidences. The first came when an al-Shabaab ambush on AMISOM troops left several Burundian soldiers dead, a report that was initially dismissed as part of a well-choreographed propaganda campaign against the AMISOM. A few days later the HSM Twitter account announced that 'in response to the requests from their families in Burundi, HSM (will) publish some of the Burundian soldiers killed in Somalia.[43]'And in a deliberate move meant to embarrass AMISOM, HSM tweeted to an imagined Burundian online audience, urging individuals (family members) to contact them directly for reports of their loved ones. This obviously rogue tweet attracted ten requests according to the HSM, and in 'keeping their word,' they went ahead and published ten identification details of AMISOM soldiers killed in battle[44]. The drama surrounding this event was so compelling that both local and international covered it, although with varying degrees of depth. The identification documents posted contained the soldiers' passport size photos, names, ranks and religious beliefs[45].

A second incident that fed the frame *picturing death, and POW* occurred on January 11 when the militant group launched a brazen raid in Wajir County on the Kenya-Somalia border and took captive two government official, a district officer and a government clerk, and labeled them Prisoners of War.[46]After several tweets appeared to relay conversations with the captured men, on January 18, HSM published the photos of the two government officials, a 30 year old District officer and a 56 year old registration clerk[47]. These posts made frontline news the next day, complete with the pictures of the two, facing the cameras directly in forlorn subdued looks. The Kenyan television stations picked the story, and even went further to interview close family members, whose plea to the government to seek their release was made. Unlike the Burundian story, the story of the two Kenyan captives had the right attributes to attract extensive media focus that lasted for days on end. It was personalized, especially when the photos of the captured men were juxtaposed with images of grieving relatives. It was unambiguous, evidenced by the photos available on the Twitter handle of the HSM press and more importantly, it hit closer home. These were Kenyans. The pressure it put on the government to secure their release ensured that the story maintained significance for days on end. HSM had finally succeeded in giving the impression of success, and at the same time rattled its way into the front pages of an elusive (Kenyan) media that had either given them a media blackout, or that had filed consistent news reports of their (HSM's) imminent capitulation.

The frame *our strategy, their strategy,* captured the instances where both Twitter handles posted tweets of their military operations in terms of long and short term strategy, conditions and state of arsenal, allies involved and also enemy strategy. Of the KDF 37 (20.5%) tweets that revealed their war strategies, 12 of the tweets were derisive of the al-Shabaab's war tactics of hit and run, planting IEDs, needless shooting in the air, use of mercenaries and foreign fighters, using donkey to carry military hardware, using child soldiers, and using civilians as shields. Indeed, HSM tweets that focus on their war strategy in inadvertently confirm this. Unlike KDF's tweets, almost all the

32 (14.8%) tweets made by HSM on this frame revealed a clear absence of war strategy. Tweets posted revealed a series of ambushes, roadside bombs, suicide bombing and hit and run tactics. On their part, KDF emphasized an allied approach and a predictable city after city march towards the port city of Kismayo. While KDF talked mostly of taking over a city, or driving the al-Shabaab out of town, only rarely did they consider themselves as liberators. However, as Table 2 reveals, when the same tweets formed the source of news reports in Kenyan newspapers, every captured city fed triumphant metaphors that portrayed Kenyan troops as liberators. Although only six Twitter frames from KDF referred to them as liberators of Somalia, the Kenyan newspapers had a total of 17 (14.8%) instances in which the KDF troops were framed as liberators. While the KDF generally viewed its mission as that of securing Somalia, the Kenyan media regularly framed their troops as liberators. Most KDF tweets that reported the fall and securing of towns were interpreted by the press as acts of liberation in which the Kenyan forces were out to free a bound people.

In framing the plight of civilians, while there were 5(4.3%) frames directly drawn from Twitter posts, three of these emphasized injuries as opposed to actual deaths. The convergence between the KDF postings and what appeared on Kenyan dailies were remarkable through their similarities. Worth noting, only rarely did Kenyan newspapers cite their sources from the al Shabaab tweets, the reason for this is obvious. The few times the HSMpress tweets were cited they were mostly juxtaposed with a rejoinder from a KDF tweet dismissing its contents. For instance, in a the frame *our strategy, their debacle,* in which Major Chirchir posted an incident involving Kenyan troops in the Somalia city of Afmadow, it was reported that a confrontation did occur which resulted in fatalities, an event immediately denied by the major.

...al-Shabaab...had killed 8 soldiers from the Kenya Defense forces and the Transitional Federal Government (TFG) and captured 3 others. This was immediately denied by major Chirchir, who reconfirmed that 12 militants had been killed.
-Daily Nation, 18.Nov.2011

While this exchange reveals the equalizing power of the social media, in which both the powerful and those without much influence have as much a chance to influence opinion, the structures of the old media which privilege 'official sources' as the more legitimate sources of information mean that ultimately, these asymmetrical relations of power are still reproduced in the new media platforms. The result of these convergences serves to only prove this. While a focus on the Kenyan press might not have been expected to show much incongruence between a perceived legitimate source of official information on Twitter and subsequent news reports, the reliance of both local and international media houses[48] on the KDF Twitter account to follow the war proves that old media habits will still be used to appropriate and circulate content from the new media. Looking at how the Kenyan media routinely ignored HSMpress Twitter posts in Table 2, it is likely previous tweets from KDF urging 'followers' to be wary of HSM's propaganda was taken seriously.

Still, the frame *Twitter Spat* on Twitter gained coverage in Kenya in headlines complete with a feature story of the online spat. *The Standard*[49] produced a full length feature story on this virtual war titled 'Kenya military, Shabaab Swap Twitter insults; physical war has degenerated into a virtual one, which is being fought on the internet.' This online banter also became the subject of an Al Jazeera news feature.[50] As expected in any conflict, each of the Twitter handles accused the other of being propagandist with both warning their followers to be wary of incorrect information being circulated by the other. However, as seen in Table 2, warnings from al Shabaab of KDF

posts being propagandist were never considered worth publication in the papers. While Al Shabaab had little success in shaping content through its Twitter handle, modest gains were made when they offered a direct rejoinder to a post from KDF describing an event. In other words, when HSM posts commented on an incident that was directly sourced from the Twitter posts of KDF, they made the news[51]. Part of the reason for their modest success emerges from the basic structures of filing news reports in which the principle of balance, the idea that accounts from all sides are weighed in to build a story, works in their favour.

CONCLUSION

In mid-April 2012, the KDF forces were integrated into the AMISOM command under the auspices of the UN and thus assumed a less aggressive role, militarily, in keeping with their new role of peacekeepers. And much to the chagrin of his Twitter 'followers', Major Chirchir announced that subsequent information on operational details in Somalia will be taken over by the AMISOM. While this did not mark an end to deliberative action in the virtual sphere, it did greatly alter the complexion of discourse in the virtual space. On its part, the HSM press had to readjust to a much more impersonal AMISOM Twitter handle that greatly limited the space for mischievous spats but one that still maintained a more legitimate status for the mainstream traditional media.

As the paper reveals, KDF exploited its official and legitimate status whose discourse easily converged with traditional media at both local and international levels. Using Twitter, KDF exploited this influence and dominated the virtual war with al-Shabaab as the war was seen more often from the KDF perspective, this is despite the fact HSM posted more tweets per day than KDF did. Not to be outdone, al Shabaab, battling obstacles of illegitimacy, with media reports labeling them militants, Islamists, jihadists or terrorists, a situation not helped with their touted merger with al-Qaida, their entry into Twitter was seen as an extension of their already delegitimized status. In fact, at one point, the U.S. government toyed with the idea of asking the US based Twitter company to shut the HSM's press account arguing that such a platform was tantamount to according terrorists legitimacy and providing them a global platform to parade jihadist ideology[52]. It was therefore not surprising that the epithet of propaganda fitly stuck on the HSM Twitter handle.

Still, while both sides made use of propaganda in their publics; it was always the case that al-Shabaab's posts became the metaphor for war propaganda. Nonetheless, their version of the war occasionally made it to the mainstream traditional media by specific rhetorical and *imageological* strategies. Firstly, the mere existence of HSM as a handle propped to answer KDF through rhetorical strategies made it gain online influence. Secondly, HSM sought to back some of their claims with pictures through Twitpic. Twitpic was used to post evidence of the death of some AMISOM soldiers and also Kenyan officials taken captive by the al-Shabaab. At the same time, the increasing focus on the civilian toll by HSM, obviously taking advantage of the lack of information given by KDF on the civilian cost of the *operation linda nchi,* occasionally ensured HSM Twitter posts were quoted, albeit with a caveat.

To sum up, the paper reveals the equalizing and liberalizing nature of the social media in Africa. The social media provides a platform for more participatory journalism and also more possibilities for user generated content. While the liberalizing attribute may send shivers down the spine of mainstream gatekeepers, this chapter shows that users were actually able to check the veracity of content, and as such heightened the possibilities for scrutiny and peer review. Still, the paper also reveals the structures and routines of the mainstream media are reproduced

in the use and consumption of the new media. It renders truth the now hackneyed phrase that new media, especially in Africa, is merely a refashioning of old media in form, consumption and content.

REFERENCES

Abel, F., Gao, Q., Houben, G.-J., & Tao, K. (2011). *Analyzing user modeling on Twitter for personalized news recommendations.* Lecture Notes in Computer Science. Retrieved from http://snurb.info/files/2012/Researching%20News%20Discussion%20on%20Twitter.pdf abgerufen

Ahmad, A. N. (2010). Is Twitter a useful tool for journalists? *Journal of Media Practice, 11*(2), 145–155. doi:10.1386/jmpr.11.2.145_1.

Bruns, A., & Burgess, J. (2012). *Researching news discussion on Twitter: New methodologies.* Retrieved November 12, 2012, from http://snurb.info/files/2012/Researching%20News%20Discussion%20on%20Twitter.pdf

Ebner, M., Lienhardt, C., Rohs, M., & Meyer, I. (2010). Microblogs in higher education-A chance to facilitate informal and process-oriented learning. *Computers & Education, 55,* 92–100. doi:10.1016/j.compedu.2009.12.006.

Entman, R. (1993). Framing: Towards clarification of a fractured paradigm. *The Journal of Communication, 43*(4), 51–58. doi:10.1111/j.1460-2466.1993.tb01304.x.

Gamson, W. A., & Modigliani, A. (1989). Media discourse and public opinion on nuclear power: A constructionist approach. *American Journal of Sociology, 95*(1), 1–37. doi:10.1086/229213.

Grant, A., & Wilkinson, J. (Eds.). (2009). *Understanding media convergence: The state of the field.* Oxford, UK: Oxford University Press.

Hamdy, N. (2009). Arab citizen journalism in action: Challenging mainstream media, authorities and media laws. *Westminster Papers in Communication and Culture*, 6(1), 92–112.

Heaivilin, N., Gerbert, B., Page, J., & Gibbs, J. (2011). Public health surveillance of dental pain via Twitter. *Journal of Dental Research*, 90(9), 1047–1051. doi:10.1177/0022034511415273 PMID:21768306.

Huberman, B., Romero, D., & Wu, F. (2009). Social networks that matter: Twitter under the microscope. *First Monday*, 14, 1–5.

Jackoway, A., Samet, H., & Sankaranarayanan, J. (2011). Identification of live news events using Twitter. In *Proceedings of the 3rd ACM SIGSPATIAL International Workshop on Location-Based Social Networks (LBSN '11)*. New York: ACM press.

Jansen, B., Zhang, M., Sobel, K., & Chowdury, A. (2009). Twitter power: Tweets as electronic word of mouth. *Journal of the American Society for Information Science and Technology*, 60(11), 2169–2188. doi:10.1002/asi.21149.

Java, A., Song, X., Finin, T., & Tseng, B. (2007). Why we Twitter: Understanding Microblogging usage and communities. In *Proceedings of the 9th WebKDD and 1st NA-KDD 2007 Workshop on Web Mining and Social Network analysis* (pp. 56-65). San Jose, CA: ACM.

Jenkins, H. (2006). *Convergence Culture: Where Old and New Media Collide*. New York: New York Uninversity Press.

Khamis, S. (2011). The transformative Egyptian media landscape: Changes, challenges and comparative perspectives. *International Journal of Communication*. Retrieved November 10, 2012, from http://ijoc.org/ojs/index.php/ijoc/article/view/813/592

Lasorsa, D. L., Lewis, S. C., & Holton, A. (2012). Normalizing Twitter: Journalism practice in an emerging communication space. *Journalism Studies*, 13(1), 19–36. doi:10.1080/1461670X.2011.571825.

London, S. (1993). *How the media frames political issues*. Retrieved November 10, 2012, from Scott's London Website: http://www.scottlondon.com/reports/frames.html

McFedries, P. (2007). Technically speaking: All A-Twitter. *IEEE Spectrum*, 44(10), 84. doi:10.1109/MSPEC.2007.4337670.

Phelan, O., McCarthy, K., & Smyth, B. (2009). Using twitter to recommend real-time topical news. *In Proceedings of the third ACM conference on Recommender systems (RecSys '09)* (pp. 385-388). New York: ACM press.

Steadman Group. (2008). *Steadman group for kenya advertising research*. Nairobi, Kenya: Steadman.

Tumasjan, A., Sprenger, T. O., Sandner, P. G., & Welpe, I. M. (2010). Predicting elections with Twitter: What 140 characters reveal about political sentiment. *Proceedings of the 4th International AAAI Conference on Weblogs and Social Media*. Washington, DC: AAAI.

Wigand, F. D. (2010). Twitter in government: Building relationships one Tweet at a time. *Proceedings of the 7th International Conference on Information Technology* (pp. 563-567). Los Alamitos, CA: IEEE.

ENDNOTES

[1]   Swahili word for operation protect the country.

2   Kenya Defense Forces Spokesperson Major Chirchir on official KDF Twitter handle, https://twitter.com/MajorEChirchir/status/145121291920347136

3   Preliminary interviews with journalists that we did indicate that most senior editors of the major media houses in Kenya raised concerns about news reports from embedded journalists whose security, food, shelter and general welfare was provided for by the military. Additionally, the same journalists had to adhere to strict guidelines set out by the military on what to relay to their bosses in Nairobi.

4   A message sent from Twitter

5   TwitPic is a website that allows users to easily post pictures to Twitter and other social media services. It is considered more of a component of Twitter although owned differently.

6   http://www.investigativeproject. org/2958/jihadi-media-joins-facebook

7   This is because local newspapers will focus more on their sources than those of the 'enemy'.

8   Bruns & Burgess. '*Researching News Discussion on Twitter*'

9   BBC-Africa's mobile phone industry 'booming' http://www.bbc.co.uk/news/world-africa-15659983

10 For details visit http://www.cck.go.ke/resc/downloads/SECTOR_STATISTICS_RE-PORT_Q4_11-12.pdf

11 http://www.sabc.co.za/news/a/c846de804cf12eecbc97fca1cd5c70fe/Kenyas-striking-doctors-turn-to-Twitter-20121003

12 For details see http://www.portland-communications.com/Twitter_in_Africa_PPT.pdf

13 Steadman Group. *Steadman Group for Kenya Advertising Research.*

14 By this term we mean those tweets that were mostly ideological and revealed an Islamist discourse.

15 https://twitter.com/MajorEChirchir/status/129518861694418944

16 The Twitter page of KDF itself contained images of the official Government of Kenya Court of Arms that clearly anchored officialdom and legitimacy. See also https://twitter.com/MajorEChirchir/status/156734736037982208

17 https://twitter.com/MajorEChirchir/status/157368656702083073

18 Daily Nation, Jan. 11, 2012.

19 http://www.globalpost.com/dispatches/globalpost-blogs/weird-wide-web/kenya-military-major-chirchir-twitter-photos-stoning-somalia

20 https://twitter.com/HSMPress/status/157209951977218048

21 https://twitter.com/MajorEChirchir/status/157368656702083073

22 https://twitter.com/MajorEChirchir/status/157376372195590144

23 See for instance https://twitter.com/HSMPress/status/144689146286440448

24 These are the troops of the internationally recognized government of the Republic of Somalia until 20 August 2012, when its tenure officially ended and the Federal Government of Somalia was inaugurated

25 See https://twitter.com/HSMPress/status/144456889898508288

26 https://twitter.com/HSMPress/status/144460227805315072

27 See, for instance http://www.bbc.co.uk/news/world-africa-15513430

28 In fact one of the tweets was only sought to clarify that one the 'civilian` was working for the militia group.

29 https://twitter.com/HSMPress/status/144784697795420161 & https://twitter.com/HSMPress/status/144757447544942594

30 This frame consists of a series of Twitter posts that were used by both handles to issue warnings of impending attacks at particular spaces and time, and also to

caution members of the public to avoid interaction with combatants or militants as they could become targets.

31 See https://twitter.com/MajorEChirchir/status/132116370056941569

32 https://twitter.com/MajorEChirchir/status/132453119589228544

33 https://twitter.com/MajorEChirchir/status/132455059236724736

34 https://twitter.com/MajorEChirchir/status/132117071919185920

35 https://twitter.com/MajorEChirchir/status/132117071919185920

36 A plant common in the Horn of Africa and chewed as a stimulant, it is an illegal drug in most western countries.

37 https://twitter.com/HSMPress/status/144460227805315072

38 https://twitter.com/HSMPress/status/145830147919056896

39 https://twitter.com/MajorEChirchir/status/145810293417717760

40 https://twitter.com/HSMPress/status/145817099980382208

41 https://twitter.com/MajorEChirchir/status/145812638260137984

42 The term POW as used by al Shabaab is deceptively used for propaganda purposes. Whilst POW are normally combatants captured in a time of war, the people it termed prisoners of war were Kenyan civil servants held hostage after militants raided an isolated Kenyan administrative office at the border between Kenya and Somalia.

43 https://twitter.com/HSMPress/status/145821019737833473

44 See details at https://twitter.com/HSMPress/status/146318025174425600; https://twitter.com/HSMPress/status/146315792261189633; https://twitter.com/HSMPress/status/146312872962695168

45 See http://m.news24.com/news24/Africa/News/Mogadishu-massacre-70-AU-troops-killed-20111020; http://www.aljazeera.com/news/africa/2011/10/2011102141422988953.html;

46 HSM preferred to call them POWs for purely propaganda purposes as they were non-combatants.

47 https://twitter.com/HSMPress/status/144871577937395712

48 See http://www.bbc.co.uk/news/world-africa-19803350; or http://www.aljazeera.com/category/person/emmanuel-chirchir.

49 *The Standard,* December *14*

50 http://blogs.aljazeera.net/africa/2011/12/13/al-shabab-starts-tweeting

51 The two frames *Our strategy, their debacle,* and *KDF War setback,* partly built by HSM directly commenting on incidents previously commented on by KDF, reveal a comparative success in making the news in Kenya's print media media than other frames.

52 See http://www.nytimes.com/2011/12/20/world/africa/us-considers-combating-shabab-militants-twitter-use.html?_r=1

Chapter 15

Use of New ICTs as "Liberation" or "Repression" Technologies in Social Movements:
The Need to Formulate Appropriate Media Policies

Brandie L. Martin
The Pennsylvania State University, USA

Anthony A. Olorunnisola
The Pennsylvania State University, USA

ABSTRACT

Participants in varying but recent citizen-led social movements in Kenya, Iran, Tunisia, and Egypt have found new voices by employing new ICTs. In some cases, new ICTs were used to mobilize citizens to join and/or to encourage use of violence against other ethnicities. In nearly all cases, the combined use of new ICTs kept the world informed of developments as ensuing protests progressed. In most cases, the use of new ICTs as alternative media motivated international actors' intervention in averting or resolving ensuing crises. Foregoing engagements have also induced state actions such as appropriation of Internet and mobile phone SMS for counter-protest message dissemination and/or termination of citizens' access. Against the background of the sociology and politics of social movements and a focus on the protests in Kenya and Egypt, this chapter broaches critical questions about recent social movements and processes: to what extent have the uses of new ICTs served as alternative platforms for positive citizens' communication? When is use of new ICTs convertible into "weapons of mass destruction"? When does state repression or take-over of ICTs constitute security measures, and when is such action censorship? In the process, the chapter appraises the roles of local and international third parties to the engagement while underscoring conceptual definitions whose usage in studies of this kind should be conscientiously employed. Authors offer suggestions for future investigations.

DOI: 10.4018/978-1-4666-4197-6.ch015

INTRODUCTION

The term alternative media had previously been employed in descriptions of non-commercial, non-mainstream and traditional or old media—that is newspapers, newsmagazines and radio (clandestine and otherwise)—whose contents were produced to challenge power structures or induce social change. Lately, usage of alternative media has witnessed an expansion in scope and horizon with the employment of platforms that now broadly include new Information and Communication Technologies (ICTs) such as the Internet and mobile telephones (Armstrong, 1981; Atton, 2002; Downing, 2003; Downing, 2008; Atkinson & Cooley, 2010).

As such, it is important to establish that research examining the intersection between social movements and the employment of alternative media in the construction and execution of resistance predate the first and second decades of the 21st century. What is also not new in the construction of 21st century social movements via new ICTs is the raison d'être; typically, participants disenchanted with actors in government either over human rights, sit-tight syndrome, reluctance to democratize or combination of all the above, seek social change. This does not exclude participants in counter-movements whose goal may be to sustain the status quo.

What is, however, of contemporary concern and our interest in this chapter are contingent issues such as: (1) the efficient employability of new ICTs; (2) the resultant procedural and communicative empowerment of citizen dissenters; (3) the procedural response and presumed communicative disempowerment of the contemporary state; and (4) the convergence and morphing of traditionally distinct concepts that raise new questions about a longstanding citizen, media and state engagements in the trajectory of social movements. In the attempt to unpack foregoing issues, we pose the following questions: (1) To what extent has the use of new ICTs served as alternative platforms for citizens' communication during protests for social change? (2) When is use of new ICTs convertible into "weapons of mass destruction"? (3) When does state repression or take-over of new ICTs constitute security measures, and when is such action censorship?

Foregoing probing questions help to drive our examination of the two cases cited in this paper. In the process, we underscore actions of local and the intervention of international actors such as new ICT providers and foreign governments who step in to mediate. New questions posed by contemporary engagements in social movements are only partly motivated by the employment of new ICTs. Some of our questions are motivated by the fluidity of social movements, which tend to delimit their ability to be organized. Hitherto (Downing, 2008) old media roles in social movements have been accorded a back seat position. We suspect that protesters' efficient or inefficient usage of new ICTs will draw differential responses from the state. By juxtaposing social movements in Kenya and Egypt, we attempted to resolve some of Downing's (2008, p. 40) concerns: First, we de-marginalized new media analysis from the "main discursive arena" of "social movement phenomena" and, by so doing, underscore the central role of old and new media in aiding social movements. Doing so enabled our exploration of ways in which the structural and operational processes of new ICTs can either serve as opportunities for social movements or pose constraints to their success. Second, studies of social movements have paid little attention to social movements in Africa and elsewhere in the third world. Yet and as Downing (2008, p. 43) informed:

Social and political movements are clearly central to contemporary political life as well as to earlier modern history. The widespread decay of inherited political institutions such as parliamentary parties and the rise of hard to check transnational corporate power are factors further intensifying the current significance of social movements on the world stage. Media research makes itself look silly if it does not foreground them.

Recently, media scholars have established positive and active ties between alternative media and user participation via the Internet. That engagement (Boyle and Schmierbach, 2009) has increased the important roles of new ICTs in mobilizations for social movement purposes. Yet, there is little cause for celebration. The classical problem of digital divide persists—limiting both the range of collective action to citizens who are connected to the Internet and the likelihood that activists can sustain collective action. But this problem is not peculiar to Africa and should not become an excuse to ignore social movement developments there.

It is notable that the Internet has empowered social movements on the African continent in ways that should arouse fresh research curiosities. Our assessment of the role of new ICTs in two social movement cases in Kenya and Egypt fills the gap that Downing (2008) underscores.[1] Through careful analysis informed by Downing's explication, we mapped the activities and communicative behaviors of actors, including local and international third parties that become directly engaged in and/or dragged into social movements. Without losing focus on counter-movements that are produced by one seemingly holistic movement, we followed the ways in which dissenting voices are expressed via traditional media and new ICTs. By so doing, we were able to weigh the comparative roles of traditional mainstream media vis-à-vis new ICTs. Shared government and private enterprise ownership of traditional media and new ICT providers led us to reassess presumed (Teer-Tomaselli, 2011) diminished power of the state to control use of new ICT outlets. This latter point informed our suggestions for consideration by actors ranging from citizens on opposing sides

of social movements through third parties such as new ICT service providers and international agencies who play mediation roles in ensuing crises.

REVIEW OF RELEVANT LITERATURE AND DEFINITION OF TERMS

Social Movements Defined

Social movements defy definition for two fundamental reasons. First, their emergence and organization are spontaneous. Though members may sustain a campaign to seek change in society's structure and/or values, their actions often are without rules and procedures. Notwithstanding, Downing (2008) suggests that social movements matter. They are sometimes constructive or dangerous and/or simply confused (p. 40).

Second, sociology and political science scholars who take the lead in studying social movements are in disparate groups with boundaries that are hard to define. Such uncoordinated efforts have yielded concepts and theories that are difficult to harness and employ with surefootedness. Following Downing's (2008) efforts, coauthors framed a study around specific stakeholders in social movements that include counter-movements, targets of action or change (which tend to be the state), the mass media (mainstream and commercialized; which typically are cast as chroniclers of social movements' events) and the publics (within and external to contexts) of social movements. Fundamentally, Downing's explication underscores existence of social change, political mobilization, framing, networks, and audiences as well as transitional movements at the confluence of any comprehensive study of social movements. He emphasizes that the extraordinary levels of mobilization now enabled by new ICTs, such as the Internet and mobile phones, merely stretch the definition and scope of media engagement in social movements "beyond broadcasting …

print ... popular music and other media of communication" (Downing, 2008, p. 44). There are, therefore, incentives for media scholars to beam searchlights into the activities of social movements. This should be familiar territory.

Use of New ICTs by Social Movements

According to the International Telecommunications Union, nearly 40% of Africans own a mobile phone and nearly 8% have access to the Internet (ITU, 2010). The uses of new ICTs, in particular the Internet and mobile phones, have been credited with providing platforms on which political, social, and economic freedoms can be expanded (Diamond, 2010). The ability of governments to censor these modes of communication has and will continue to be an area of concern in the emerging role of new ICTs as platforms of preference by citizens engaged in social movements.

The uses of new ICTs for social change and advocacy are at a relatively early stage of development (Downing, 2008; Ekine, 2010). Particularly in developing countries, the mobile phone is often the most effective means for communicating during a social crisis and can greatly aid in the efficiency of developing a *smart mob*. A *smart mob*, coined by Rheingold (2002), is a group of people who use the mobile phone to coordinate their actions. For example, smart mobs were formed in the Philippines in 2001 to oust former President Joseph Estrada; in Spain in 2004 to protest the actions of the Popular Party and to encourage, successfully, the election of the Socialist Party; as well as in Kenya during the violently contested re-election of President Mwai Kibaki, and most recently in Egypt to form nationwide protests resulting in the resignation of President Hosni Mubarak (Sharp, 2011).

The potential abilities, both positive and negative, of new ICTs to facilitate communication and mobilization of social movements deserve

research attention. As such, examples of the use of the Internet and mobile phone short message service (SMS), in Kenyan and Egyptian social movements are juxtaposed in this paper. These examples also raise questions about respective states' justification of blocking new ICTs with claims of public safety. It is important to ponder likelihood that the state acted to silence citizens engaged in social movements. The latter question is particularly necessary in contexts on the African continent where political strongholds are likely to be ethnically based and where a nation structured as a "democracy" tends to better reflect a dictatorship. Moreover, when it finds itself on the receiving end of social movements' protests, the state is often leader of the counter-movement. These contextual factors leave only a thin line between citizens' social protests for "liberation" and state actions that can be construed as "repression" of marginalized ethnic and/or disenchanted groups. The critical assessment of the case of Kenya with manifestations that may pass for SMS-induced ethnic cleansing juxtaposed with a case involving government clampdown on critical speech in Egypt provides comparative opportunity to explore the use of new ICTs for democratic expression in the "developing" world.

Adoption of the Internet and Mobile Phones

Adoption of the Internet and mobile telecommunications has grown at an exceedingly fast pace in Kenya and Egypt. From 2003 to 2008, adoption of the Internet increased from 3 to 9% in Kenya and from 4 to 17% in Egypt (World Bank, 2010). The greatest growth has been in the mobile telecommunications sector. Adoption of mobile phones increased from approximately 5 to 42% in Kenya and from 8 to 51% in Egypt (Worldbank, 2010). Particularly in developing countries, mobile phones are much more accessible to a greater socio-economic spectrum of users than the Internet. Additionally, developing countries have a higher tendency to employ Short Message Service (SMS) than voice-to-voice communication due to cost; it is more affordable and communicatively economical (as users can avoid socio-cultural pleasantries) to use SMS than to use voice-to-voice capabilities of mobile phones (Olorunnisola, 2009).

Use of New ICTs as "Liberation" or "Repression" Technologies

The term "liberation technology", coined by Diamond (2010), refers to the use of new ICT as a means "to expand political, social, and economic freedom" (p. 70). New ICTs offer, in comparison to radio and other traditional media, platforms through which citizens become recipients of information and the creators and disseminators of information. New ICTs, functioning as liberation technologies, strengthen an emergent social movement by providing a platform from which citizens can "report news, expose wrongdoings, express opinions, mobilize protests, monitor elections, scrutinize government, deepen participation, and expand the horizons of freedom" (Diamond, 2010, p. 70). The use of mobile phones to facilitate physical mobilization by sending SMS that informs individuals of the location of protests has been considered one of the most direct and powerful effects of mobile phones as liberation technologies (Diamond, 2010). Just as radio bridged the gaps of geography and illiteracy in rural Africa to inform and mobilize citizens so is the potential of mobile phones.

The use of SMS to coordinate effective, peaceful civic demonstrations or to incite fear and anger leading to violent actions calls attention to the need to be cognizant of both the positive and negative outcomes of its use (Goldstein & Rotich, 2010). It must be emphasized that technologies are inherently *tools*, which can be employed for "both

noble and nefarious purposes" (Diamond, 2010, p. 71). Just as traditional forms of mass communication such as print newspaper and radio could be employed to spread diversity of viewpoints and rational debate, they can also be employed as tools of destruction when racial and ethnic hatred incitements lead to violence (Diamond, 2010).

Through efficient mobilization of fellow citizens to participate in social movements and to spread narrative, users of the Internet and mobile phones may have the potential for unprecedented power, quite simply, at their fingertips. This caliber of power was for most of the 20th century the exclusive domain of the authoritarian state which to all intents and purposes monopolized broadcasting and stringently controlled print media forms. Because the progression of new ICTs can appropriate the power of broadcasting, this communicative power-sharing poses threats to the errant or reactionary state and, presumably, has the tendency to delimit state power of response by repression (Teer-Tomaselli, 2011).

While use of new ICTs to initiate and coordinate protests and civil disobedience may pose threat to the authoritarian and communicatively-disempowered state, their employment as "weapons of mass destruction" would appeal to a legitimate sentiment in the state; its proprietary role as custodian of power over security apparatuses. Notably, and this is where we find conceptual affinity in and expand the explication of *narrative capacity* by Atkinson & Cooley (2010): participants in social movements who employ new ICTs to disseminate violent hate speech turn mobile phones into "weapons of mass destruction" and, inadvertently, invite the state to respond by repressing access. Our review of Kenya and Egypt as recent cases where social movements employed the power of new ICTs helped appraisal of differential citizens' activities, state reactions and third-party (including providers of new ICT services and international actors) responses in crises situations.

GOVERNMENT STRUCTURE, FREE-EXPRESSION AND RESTRICTIONS

This section reviews past and current government structures in Kenya and Egypt. We unpack free-expression legislations and existent allowances for government intervention particularly in the interest of public safety or national security.

Kenya

Kenya operated a single-party government from its independence in 1963 through 1991 when it yielded to local and international pressures to become a multi-party democracy (Widner, 1992; Maxon & Ofcansky, 2000). Since independence, Kenya has ensured the rights of expression and access to information to all citizens as written in Chapter 5, Article 79(1) of its Constitution, which states as follows:

Except with his own consent, no person shall be hindered in the enjoyment of his freedom of expression, that is to say, freedom to hold opinions without interference, freedom to receive ideas and information without interference (whether the communication be to the public generally or to any person or class of persons) and freedom from interference with his correspondence (Kenyan Constitution, 2008).

However, Article 79(2) outlines limitations to freedom of speech and access to information "that is reasonably required in the interests of defense, public safety, public order, public morality or public health" (Kenyan Constitution, 2008). The Kenyan government has shown evidence in the past of restricting individual and press freedoms.[2] It increased control over the mass media after it adjudged that they were disseminating hate speech. It revised the Communications Act of 1998 in 2009 to strengthen its control over issue of broadcast licenses, production and content of traditional and online media. It also accorded itself the power to impose heavy fines and prison sentences for press offences (Freedom House, 2009; Freedom House, 2010a; RWB, 2009).

Nonetheless, the semi-independent Kenyan National Commission on Human Rights (KNCHR) and globally recognized Reporters without Boarders expressed dissatisfaction with the absence of a definition for what constitutes hate speech (KNCHR, 2008; RWB, 2009). Both consider absence of strict guidelines about hate speech a shield for government control. Though Kenya has one of the largest blogging communities in Africa (Zuckerman, 2006; 2008), there are nil cases of government censorship of online bloggers (Freedom House, 2009).

Egypt

Between independence from Britain in 1922 and 1981 when Hosni Mubarak became president and instituted superficial democratic reforms, Egypt was an authoritarian republic (Hassan, 2010). However, Mubarak's political reforms, which instituted a proportional-representation electoral system, did not eliminate public distrust and cynicism. Public and opposition party sentiments were not abated by the fact that Mubarak's party, the National Democratic Party (NDP), won majority of the votes at every election, further creating disenchantment about the validity of the democratic arrangement (Hassan, 2010). This disenchantment provided foreground for such social movements as the restiveness of the *April 6 Youth Movement* whose online activities were pivotal to the labor strikes of 2008 and 2009.

Notwithstanding the unsteadiness of the democratic structure, the Egyptian government does provide rights of expression and of the press for all citizens in Chapter 3 (Articles 47 and 48) of its 2007 Constitution as follows:

Freedom of opinion shall be guaranteed. Every individual shall have the right to express his opinion and to publicize it verbally, in writing, by photography or by other means of expression within the limits of the law. Self criticism and constructive criticism shall guarantee the safety of the national structure.

Liberty of the press, printing, publication and mass media shall be guaranteed. Censorship on newspapers shall be forbidden as well as notifying, suspending or cancelling them by administrative methods. In a state of emergency or in time of war, a limited censorship may be imposed on the newspapers, publications and mass media in matters related to public safety or for purposes of national security in accordance with the law.

Although the constitution encourages freedom of speech and of the press, the government includes the ability to censor media during matters of public safety and "for purposes of national security in accordance with the law" (Egyptian Constitution, 2007). Using broadly defined laws to restrict speech, the Egyptian government reserves right to wield great control over what citizens can say in public and what is and is not disseminated through mass media. It has also shown willingness to restrict freedoms.[3]

Egypt has a very strong blogging community that has provided platform for citizens' criticism of the government. The state has also reciprocated. In June 2010, Wael Abbas, editor of the online blog titled *Misr Digital,* was arrested and his computer confiscated at the airport. Also in 2010, three *Muslim Brotherhood* bloggers, the political party banned by Mubarak, were arrested after they wrote critical posts about the military trials of their members (Freedom House, 2010b). A Facebook activist was illegally detained and his computer confiscated after he accused a leading Egyptian advertising executive of copyright infringement (Freedom House, 2010b).

NEW ICTS IN SOCIAL MOVEMENTS: KENYA AND EGYPT

The appropriate government reaction to speech disseminated online or through mobile phone SMS is an implicit area of concern in this paper. Too much government control over new ICTs may have a negative effect on the spread of political viewpoints and healthy criticism; too little control may lead to the dissemination of hate speech, sparking violent uprisings with attendant loss of lives and properties. Identifying and analyzing the distinction between category of speech that is healthy criticism and that which qualifies as hate speech is fundamental to the formulation of appropriate government intervention and legislation. It should also drive response of international third parties.

Recent events in Kenya and Egypt provide templates for the examination of these variances for a number of reasons. First, new ICTs have become new locations for citizen-government contestations. Parsing out the factors pertinent to the progression of these contestations should clarify what qualifies as legitimate and protected speech. Doing so should enable citizen protesters and responsible government actors to avert another situation like the use of traditional media in the Rwandan genocide. Second, these sample cases should provide analytic fodder for providers of new ICTs and services (often foreign corporations) who find themselves in business terrains that present varying political cultures and are often caught in the communicative crossfire between citizen-subscribers and government issuers of operational licenses. Third, these cases serve as reference for third parties such as governmental, inter-governmental and non-governmental agencies who become engaged in conflict resolution.

Kenya

Prior to the announcement of the highly contested 2007 presidential election that gave victory to the incumbent president, the media, in particular privately owned radio stations, had been accused of fueling ethnic-targeted violence. Different stations, each with its own political slant, were either accused of airing hate speech concerning the president's tribe, the Kikuyus, or the tribes that aligned with the opposition party, the Kalenjin, Luo, and Luhya, (Chege, 2008; RWB, 2008). Following announcement of results, the government ordered the suspension of all live broadcasts including television and radio due to widespread violence among the political, ethnic-based groups (Goldstein & Rotich, 2010). Referencing the role of radio in the incitement of anger and subsequent ethnic-targeted killings in Rwanda's 1994 genocide, the Kenyan government justified banning all live broadcasts with need to weaken social tensions (RWB, 2009; Wanjiku, 2009). As the government closed traditional forms of mass communication, SMS and Internet applications such as Facebook, Twitter, Ushahidi (a website that allows users to announce and geographically map crisis situations through submitting online posts or SMS updates) and Mashada (a blogging website), became critical sources of information on the location and nature of riots throughout Kenya (Makinen & Kuira, 2008). Ushahidi and Mashada were also influential in spreading positive and negative social discourse. Kenya has a strong blogging community and these platforms were used to voice opinions concerning the contested presidential election (Goldstein & Rotich, 2010).

However, David Kobia, the administrator of Mashada[4], decided to shut down the website due to "divisive and hostile messages" targeting ethnic communities following government banning of traditional mass media (Goldstein & Rotich, 2010, p. 129). As a means to combat destructive speech, to reduce social tensions and to encourage unity, Kobia launched a new website called "I Have No Tribe" offering a platform for constructive dialogue among Kenyans (Goldstein & Rotich, 2010). Examples of constructive dialogue posted on "I Have No Tribe" include (I have No Tribe, 2008):

One of the most stable governments in Africa has fallen apart it's sad that we have become Rwanda part 2. Peace once known has disappeared and negative media portrayal of Africa at its highest on our country KENYA! We are one let's not kill each other we are one blood one people may peace be regained!!!

I pray for you Kenya, may peace return to your beautiful nation.

We look up to you Kenya. Be one, no tribe matters but being Kenyan.

Concurrently with the use of blogs, citizens began using mobile phone SMS to spread hate speech urging recipients to express their frustrations with the election results and to unleash violence on other ethnic groups (Goldstein & Rotich, 2010). The use of SMS to spread hate speech resulted in widespread violence and the killing of approximately 1,500 Kenyans (Goldstein & Rotich, 2010; BBC, 2008). An example of SMS hate-speech distributed by citizens in opposition to the incumbent government includes the following (NPR, 2008):

Fellow Kenyans, the Kikuyu's have stolen our children's future. Hope of removing them through the ballot has been stolen. We must deal with them the way they understand, violence. We must dominate them.

Supporters of the incumbent government also distributed SMS directly targeting opposing ethnically aligned political parties. An example of SMS hate-speech distributed by citizens supporting the incumbent government includes the following (NPR, 2008):

We say no more innocent Kikuyu blood will be shed. We will slaughter them right here in the capital city. For justice, compile a list of Luos and Kalus you know at work or in your estates, or elsewhere in Nairobi, plus where and how their children go to school. We will give you numbers to text this information.

Interestingly, SMS served as instruments in the hands of pro- and anti-government protesters. Both ethnically aligned political groups were guilty of distributing hate speech and using mobile phones as "weapons of mass destruction".

After identifying opposition's use of SMS to spread hate speech and mobilize citizens, the government attempted to have Kenya's largest mobile phone provider, Safaricom, disable citizens' ability to distribute SMS (Goldstein & Rotich, 2010). Justification for the ban on SMS distribution was tied to Article 79(2) of the Kenyan Constitution of 1963 which as noted earlier outlines limitations on freedom of speech "that is reasonably required in the interests of defense, public safety, public order, public morality or public health." Vodafone, a United Kingdom-owned telecommunications company, which has a 40% stake and management responsibility of Safaricom, decided to mass-disseminate SMS promoting "peace and calm" to all nine million subscribers instead of disabling citizens' use of SMS (Goldstein & Rotich, 2010, p.128; NPR, 2008). The SMS were disseminated in Swahili and English, the two dominant languages in Kenya. The SMS stated as follows:

In the interest of peace, we appeal to Kenyans to embrace each other in the spirit of patriotism and exercise strength to restore calm to our nation. Prevent trouble; choose peace (NPR, 2008).

While SMS promoting peace were being distributed, employments of SMS to spew hate speech continued. At the end of the riots the Kenyan government attempted to hold 1,700 individuals who sent hate speech messages accountable; however and as noted earlier, Kenya did not have an applicable law to prosecute SMS-distributed hate speech in 2007 (Goldstein & Rotich, 2010). We found no evidence that it does in 2011.

The Kenyan government is currently attempting to register all mobile phone users on the grounds of ensuring national security (Kadida, 2010). The potential implications of requiring all individuals to register their mobile phone Subscriber Identity Module (SIM) card and address with the government could have a chilling effect on distribution of hate speech by mobile phone but also on political critical speech.

Egypt

Following a contested parliamentary election, nationwide protests erupted in Egypt on January 25, 2011 and ended 18 days later with the resignation of President Hosni Mubarak after nearly 30 years in office (Kirkpatrick, 2011; Sharp, 2011). During the protests, the Egyptian government revoked Al Jazeera Network's license to broadcast and six of Al Jazeera's correspondents were arrested (Al Jazeera, 2011; Pompeo, 2011). The state-owned broadcasters, Nile Television and Akhbar Egypt, ran pro-Mubarak news and showcased pro-Mubarak rallies (Abouzeid, 2011).

While traditional forms of media were showcasing only pro-Mubarak content, new ICTs enabled dissemination of dissenting viewpoints. The ability for Egyptians to quickly and efficiently mobilize in Tahrir Square, Cairo and the worldwide awareness of the movement has been credited to the use of social networking websites and mobile phone SMS (Ibrahim, 2011). The *April 6 Youth Movement*, which emerged from a series of previous strikes by workers and residents in Mahalla, Egypt, strategically employed Facebook and Twitter to increase awareness of the 2011 movement nationally and globally (Dreyfuss, 2011; Radsch, 2011). By using international platforms, counter-movements were able to gain momentum by focusing the eyes of the world and, perhaps, global pressure on Mubarak and his regime. For example, a Facebook page focused on the nature and locations of the protests across Egypt amassed 56,000 followers within 24 hours of its creation

(Radsch, 2011). Approximately 15,000 Egyptians were using Twitter to send messages concerning the nature and location of protests (O'Dell, 2011). Examples of citizen-distributed SMS include the following:

Tahrir protesters are massing in 1000s, but word being passed that the BIG demo is at 3pm. (BBC, 2011a)

More protesters are back in the streets shouting: Down with Mubarak. They are on the Corniche. (BBC, 2011b)

Aware of the influence of Facebook, Twitter, and SMS to mobilize citizens, the Egyptian government shut down the Internet and SMS within the first two days of rioting (CNN, 2011). Internet access and SMS mobile phone capabilities were reinstated nearly a week later on February 2, 2011 (Gazzar, 2011). The key Internet and mobile phone service providers forced to suspend service in Egypt include Vodafone, Mobinil, and Etisalat. Justified by the emergency powers provided for in Egypt's Telecommunications Act of 2003, Vodafone, Mobinil, and Etisalat were required to comply with government's request to disable customer use and enable government access to the SMS networks (AP, 2011; RWB, 2011).

Mahmoud Salem, an Egyptian blogger known as "Sandmonkey," posted to his over 3,500 followers: "This is becoming the region's first telecommunication civil war. Our Internet & smart phones are weapons they won't allow us to have" (NPR, 2011). While the Egyptian government restricted the capability of citizens to use new ICTs to communicate, mobile phone SMS networks were conscripted by the government to intermittently send pro-Mubarak SMS. The government distributed SMS that urged the country's "honest and loyal men to confront the traitors and criminals and protect our people and honor" and identified

the location of pro-Mubarak rallies (Satter, 2011). Examples of pro-Mubarak government-distributed SMS include the following:

Egyptian youth beware of rumors and listen to the voice of reason. Egypt is above everyone so protect it (Vodafone, 2011).

Massive demonstration to start at noon this Wednesday from Mustafa Mahmoud Square, in support of President Mubarak (Presstv, 2011).

In this way the Kenyan government became arrowhead of a counter-movement. The Egyptian government also justified distribution of pro-Mubarak SMS across privately owned mobile phone networks by referencing the emergency powers provision of Article 67 of the Telecommunications Act of 2003 which states:

The State competent authorities shall have the power to subject to their administration all Telecommunication Services and networks of any Operator or Service Provider and call operation and maintenance employees of such services and networks in case of natural or environmental disasters or during declared periods of general mobilization in accordance with the provisions of Law No. 87 of 1960 or any other cases concerning National Security.

While the government thwarted citizens' use of new ICTs to mobilize, traditional landline telecommunications and mobile voice communication were still active and offered citizens innovative solutions to the blackout. Using Facebook, Twitter, and blogs, citizens disseminated techniques to circumvent the blackout. These techniques included using dial-up Internet modems, connecting to Internet service providers (ISPs) outside of Egypt, employing the "Speak 2 Tweet" Twitter function, and connecting to the ISP *Noor Group* which was still online as it serves the country's Stock Exchange and provides service to many large multinational corporations (BBC, 2011c). The "Speak 2 Tweet" service was created by Google, Twitter, and SayNow during the Egyptian blackout to enable anti-government protestors to call a specified telephone number that would record the caller's statement and post a link to the voice recording on Twitter (O'Dell, 2011).

SUMMARY AND GENERAL CONCLUSIONS

Our evaluation of citizens' protests in Kenya and Egypt uncovered activities of actors (see Downing, 2008) and multi-level activities involved as both social movements progressed. Superficially, the movements in Kenya and Egypt share the undertone of seeking increased citizens' participation in governance. Beneath the surface, however, counter-movements in Kenya collapsed around ethnic fault lines with Kikuyus in the pro-government movement and other ethnicities (Kelenjin, Luo and Luhya) in the anti-government movement. Without ethnic coloration, counter-movements in Egypt revolved around pro-Mubarak and anti-Mubarak groups. A fundamental dimension to the appreciation of the movements, particularly in Kenya, is that politics is primordial, not national. Acquisition of power is processed as ethnic winner-takes-all situation not as the overthrow of one ideology by another. This is a key factor in the evolution of party politics in Kenya as elsewhere on the African continent. As such, much of the activities of other actors engaged in both countries' social movements are better appreciated if processed, in part, as support for one segment (or ethnic enclave) of the social movement or the other.

Both social movements were covered by mainstream media within the contexts of respective countries and internationally. At the helm

of affairs were state-owned and state-controlled broadcasters who played the traditional role of supporting the extant state (ethnically controlled) as the arrowhead of the pro-government segment of the movements. In Kenya, pro-government state broadcaster became the voice of the state in its attempt to reign in the protests organized by opposition (also ethnically based) groups. Non-state controlled broadcasters–such as Aljazeera in the case of Egypt–were demobilized lending the state control over the airwaves.

Though separated by years, the social movements in Kenya and Egypt employed new ICTs as alternative platforms given non-access to mainstream media controlled by the states. Peculiarly, new ICTs became instruments in the hands of pro- and anti-government protesters who used them to mobilize, recruit participants, report progress of counter-protests and to co-disseminate hate speech. In this way, new ICTs could be termed equal-opportunity outlets to counter-dissenters who sought to manage information crucial to the progress of their respective causes. It is noteworthy that on account of the violence inducing speech disseminated by all sides to the social movements in Kenya and Egypt many citizens lost their lives.

Dissatisfied with the succor found by anti-government protesters in new ICTs, the state, especially in Egypt, appropriated control over new ICTs. Though inaccessible to citizen subscribers, the state commandeered SMS platforms for use in disseminating pro-Mubarak messages. This action doubly showcased the state as recognizing the power of new ICTs and facilitating a counter-movement campaign that branded the opposition as a band of traitors. This capability also contradicts the presumption that the state is communicatively disempowered by citizens' access to new ICTs.

The social movements in Kenya and Egypt found providers of new ICTs caught in the crossfire between citizens (subscribers) and the states (issuers of operational license). This precarious condition played out differently in Kenya and

Egypt. While providers in Kenya took the initiative to dispatch self-generated peace messages that appealed to both sides as co-ethnics bound by their Kenyan nationalities, their counterparts in Egypt acquiesced to state control. However, international social media providers such as Google, Twitter, and SayNow, who developed a technology with which to circumvent state blackouts, played a pivotal role in assisting the anti-government movement in Egypt. These contrasting behaviors may or may not have been informed by the character of the respective states. While Kenya was/is a nascent democratic state, Egypt was/is an autocratic state.

In summary, our evaluation of the social movements in Kenya and Egypt delivered evidence of the following: (1) the efficient employability of new ICTs in the progression and management of social movements; (2) the resultant procedural and communicative empowerment of citizen dissenters; (3) the procedural value of new ICTs to citizen dissenters has not converted into communicative disempowerment of the contemporary state as presumed by some (Teer-Tomaselli, 2011). In the process, we have been conscientious in clarifying conceptual overlaps between employments of old media versus new ICTs in the progression of social movements. We have also underscored the abiding power of the state in the management of access to media and communication in spite of new ICT platforms.

Given the antecedents of multiple actors involved in social movements, we uncover the need for rules of engagement. In particular, citizen dissenters need to develop both new ICTs and mainstream media strategies so as to ensure success of social movements. Strategies will have to fully appreciate the responses that hate speech will elicit from the state both in its role as arrowhead of a counter-movement and as custodian of national security apparatuses. In addition, citizen protesters will need to carefully assess non-available affordances when the state neither has nor operates democratically structured institutions. Third parties to social movements, including new ICT

providers and international governmental agencies, must carefully appraise their roles in social movements. As such, Kenya and Egypt offer ICT providers comparative scenarios driven by democratic versus non-democratic political cultures. We leave specifics to third party actors but recommend considerations of proactive rules of engagement to help the world avoid another Rwanda.

What Kenya and Egypt underscore are new questions and areas for research on how new ICTs, including the Internet and mobile phone networks, should be employed in social movements and controlled when abused. If the Internet and mobile phones are able to serve as "liberation" or "repression" technologies capable of being used for social dissent, what should be the extent of government control allowed without interfering with freedoms of speech and press? Weighing the implication of widespread blocking of the Internet and SMS must be assessed and new ICT policies developed. These issues are best resolved on a country-by-country basis when tempers are not flaring. Doing so, with the participation of all stakeholders (government, peoples' representatives, service providers, and potential conflict mediators) will provide legislative recourse when social movements become contentious.

SHORTCOMINGS AND AREAS FOR FUTURE RESEARCH

A shortcoming of this study is the absence of direct citizens' assessment of the movements in Kenya and Egypt as a way of making sense of their perspectives on the trajectories of the social movements that ensued. Future research could use interviews or the survey method or focused group discussions to explore citizen perspectives. Areas of investigation could include perceptions of media freedom in their respective home countries, their use of new ICTs as alternative platforms for political and social commentary (e.g., mobile phones, online environments.), and/or their encounters with other actors that may include the national government. Studies of this kind will benefit from collaborative research on the use of ICTs for political and social change so that scholars located in multiple contexts can bring in-depth knowledge and attendant benefits of comparative research.

REFERENCES

Abouzeid, R. (2011). Egyptian state tv: Let us tell you what's really happening. *Time*. Retrieved March 1, 2011, from http://www.time.com/time/world/article/0,8599,2046510,00.html

Al Jazeera Network (2011, January 30). Egypt shuts down Al Jazeera bureau. Retrieved March 1, 2011, from http://english.aljazeera.net/news/middleeast/2011/01/201113085252994161.html

Armstrong, D. (1981). *A trumpet to arms: Alternative media in America*. Boston, MA: South End Press.

Associated Press. (2011). *Vodafone: Egypt forced us to send pro-government messages*. Retrieved March 1, 2011, from http://www.huffingtonpost.com/2011/02/03/vodafone-egypt-text-messages_n_817952.html

Atkinson, J. D., & Cooley, L. (2010). Narrative capacity, resistance performance, and the "shape" of new social movement networks. *Communication Studies*, *61*(3), 321–338. doi:10.1080/10510971003752668.

Atton, C. (2002). *Alternative Media*. Thousand Oaks, CA: Sage Publications.

Berger, G. (2007). Media legislation in Africa: A comparative legal survey. *United Nations Educational, Scientific and Cultural Organization [UNESCO]*. Retrieved December 16, 2010, from portal.unesco.org/.../ev.php-URL_ID=25479&URL_DO=DO_TOPIC&URL_SECTION=201.html

Boyle, M. P., & Schmierbach, M. (2009). What makes a protester?: The role of mainstream and Alternative media use in predicting traditional and protest participation. *Communication Quarterly*, *57*(1), 1–17. doi:10.1080/01463370802662424.

British Broadcast Corporation [BBC]. (2011a). As it happened: Egypt unrest day five. Retrieved March 1, 2011, from http://news.bbc.co.uk/2/hi/middle_east/9380534.stm

British Broadcast Corporation [BBC]. (2011b). *As it happened: Egypt unrest on Friday*. Retrieved March 1, 2011, from http://news.bbc.co.uk/2/hi/uk_news/politics/9380441.stm

British Broadcast Corporation [BBC]. (2011c). *Old technology finds role in Egyptian protests*. Retrieved March 1, 2011, from http://www.bbc.co.uk/news/technology-12322948

Burrell, J. (2008). Livelihoods and the mobile phone in rural Uganda. *Grameen Foundation USA*. Retrieved April 6, 2009, from http://www.grameenfoundation.applab.org/section/ethnographic-research

Cable News Network [CNN]. (2011). Timeline of Egyptian protests. Retrieved March 1, 2011, from http://www.cnn.com/2011/WORLD/africa/02/03/egypt.protests.timeline/index.html

Chege, M. (2008). Kenya: Back from the brink? *Journal of Democracy*, *19*(4), 125–139. doi:10.1353/jod.0.0026.

Diamond, L. (2010). Liberation technology. *Journal of Democracy*, *21*(3), 69–83. doi:10.1353/jod.0.0190.

Downing, J. (2003). Audiences and readers of alternative media: The absent lure of the virtually unknown. *Media Culture & Society*, *25*, 625–645. doi:10.1177/01634437030255004.

Downing, J. (2008). Social movement theories and alternative media: An evaluation and critique. *Communication, Culture & Critique*, *1*, 40–50. doi:10.1111/j.1753-9137.2007.00005.x.

Dreyfuss, R. (2011). Who's behind Egypt's revolt? *The Nation.* Retrieved on March 14, 2011, from: http://www.thenation.com/blog/158159/whos-behind-egypts-revolt

Egypt. (2003). *Telecommunications Acts.* Retrieved March 17, 2011, from http://www.mcit.gov.eg/Content.aspx?Cat=3&SubCat=10

Egypt. *Constitution of Egypt, as altered 2007.* Chapter 3, Articles 47-48. Egypt's Government Services Portal. Retrieved March 17, 2011, from http://www.egypt.gov.eg/english/laws/constitution/default.aspx

Ekine, S. (2010). *SMS Uprising: Mobile phone activism in Africa.* Oxford, UK: Pambazuka Press.

Freedom House. (2009). *Special report: Kenya.* Retrieved March 16, 2011, from http://freedomhouse.org/template.cfm?page=384&key=209&parent=19&report=79

Freedom House. (2010a). *Press freedom: Kenya.* Retrieved February 24, 2010, from http://www.freedomhouse.org/template.cfm?page=251&year=2010

Freedom House. (2010b). *Press Freedom: Egypt.* Retrieved February 24, 2011, from http://www.freedomhouse.org/template.cfm?page=251&year=2010

Gazzar, S. E. (2011). Government restores internet service after a weeklong shutdown. *Wall Street Journal.* Retrieved March 1, 2011, from http://online.wsj.com/article/SB10001424052748703960804576119690514692446.html?mod=googlenews_wsj

Goldstein, J., & Rotich, J. (2010). Digitally networked technology in Kenya's 2007-08 post-election crisis. In Ekine, S. (Ed.), *SMS Uprising: Mobile phone activism in Africa.* Oxford, UK: Pambazuka Press.

Hassan, H. A. (2010). State versus society in Egypt: Consolidating democracy or upgrading autocracy. *African Journal of Political Science and International Relations, 4*(9), 319–329.

Have No Tribe, I. (2008). *Posts – All.* Retrieved March 1, 2011, from http://www.ihavenotribe.com/posts.asp?page=2&c=

Ibrahim, E. (2011). Social media blockage during Egypt protests. *Ahram Online.* Retrieved March 1, 2011, from http://english.ahram.org.eg/NewsContent/1/64/4907/Egypt/Politics-/Social-media-blockage-during-Egypt-protests.aspx

International Telecommunications Union [ITU]. (2010). Key global telecom indicators for the world telecommunication service sector. Retrieved on December 16, 2010, from http://www.itu.int/ITU-D/ict/statistics/at_glance/KeyTelecom.html

Kadida, J. (2010). Ringing in change: News can be distributed widely in Kenya, but so can hate speech. *Index on Censorship, 39,* 150–152. doi:10.1177/0306422010362319.

Kenya National Commission on Human Rights [KNCHR]. (2008). *On the brink of the precipice: A human account of Kenya's post-2007 election violence.* Retrieved March 16, 2011, from http://www.humanitarian.info/2008/09/16/kenya-national-commission-for-human-rights-makes-more-work-for-the-icc/

Kirkpatrick, D. (2011, February 11). Egypt erupts in jubilation as Mubarak steps down. *The New York Times.* Retrieved March 1, 2011, from http://www.nytimes.com/2011/02/12/world/middleeast/12egypt.html?_r=1

Makinen, M., & Kuira, M. (2008). Social media and postelection crisis in Kenya. *The International Journal of Press/Politics, 13,* 328–335. doi:10.1177/1940161208319409.

Maxon, R., & Ofcansky, T. (2000). *Historical Dictionary of Kenya.* Lanham, MD: Scarecrow Press, Inc..

National Public Radio [NPR]. (2008). *Text Messages Used to Incite Violence in Kenya.* Retrieved December 4, 2010, from http://www.npr.org/templates/story/story.php?storyId=19188853

National Public Radio [NPR]. (2011). *Foreign policy: Scramble to silence Cairo protests.* Retrieved on March 1, 2011, from: http://www.npr.org/2011/01/28/133306415/foreign-policy-scramble-to-silence-cairo-protests

O'Dell, J. (2011). How Egyptians used Twitter during the January crisis. *Mashable.* Retrieved on March 1, 2011, from: http://mashable.com/2011/02/01/egypt-Twitter-infographic/

Olorunnisola, A. (2009). GSM telephones in Nigeria's political, socio-economic and geo-cultural landscapes. In Olorunnisola, A. (Ed.), *Media and communication industries in Nigeria: Impacts of neoliberal reforms between 1999 and 2007* (pp. 103–155). Lewiston, NY: The Edwin Mellen Press.

Pompeo, J. (2011). Egypt media watch: Al Jazeera shut down; Clinton hits Sunday shows. *Yahoo News.* Retrieved March 1, 2011, from http://news.yahoo.com/s/yblog_thecutline/20110131/ts_yblog_thecutline/egypt-media-watch-al-jazeera-shut-down-clinton-hits-sunday-shows

Press, T. V. (2011). *Vodafone sent pro-Mubarak SMS.* Retrieved on March 18, 2011, from http://www.presstv.ir/detail/163417.html

Radsch, C. C. (2011). Repertoires of repression and the Egypt street: This is not a Facebook, Twitter or Wiki revolution! *The Huffington Post.* Retrieved March 1, 2011, from http://www.huffingtonpost.com/courtney-c-radsch/repertoires-of-repression_b_815714.html?ir=Media

Reporters without Borders [RWB]. (2009). President deals major blow to press freedom. Retrieved December 2, 2010, from http://en.rsf.org/kenya-president-deals-major-blow-to-02-01-2009,29657.html

Reporters without Borders [RWB]. (2011). The new media: Between revolution and repression – Net solidarity takes on censorship. Retrieved March 16, 2011, from http://en.rsf.org/the-new-media-between-revolution-11-03-2011,39764.html

Rheingold, H. (2002). *Smart mobs: The next social revolution.* Cambridge, MA: Perseus Books Group.

Satter, R. G. (2011). Vodafone: Egypt forced us to send text messages. *Yahoo News.* Retrieved March 1, 2011, from http://news.yahoo.com/s/ap/20110203/ap_on_hi_te/eu_egypt_cell_phones

Sharp, J. M. (2011). *Egypt: Background and U.S. relations.* Washington, DC: Congressional Research Service. Retrieved March 21, 2011, from fpc.state.gov/documents/organization/84928.pdf

Teer-Tomaselli, R. (2011). Transforming state-owned enterprises in the global age: Lessons from broadcasting and telecommunications in South Africa. In Olorunnisola, A., & Tomaselli, K. (Eds.), *Political economy of media transformation in South Africa* (pp. 133–166). Cresskill, NJ: Hampton Press, Inc..

The National Council for Law Reporting. (2008). The Constitution of Kenya, as altered to 2008. Chapter 5. Article 79.

Vodafone. (2011). *Statement on Egypt.* Retrieved March 1, 2011, from http://www.vodafone.com/content/index/press/press_statements/statement_on_egypt.html

Wanjiku, R. (2009). Kenya Communications Amendment Act (2009): Progressive or retrogressive? *Association for Progressive Communications.* Retrieved March 1, 2011, from www.apc.org/en/system/files/CICEWAKenya20090908_EN.pdf

Widner, J. (1992). Kenya's slow progress toward multiparty politics. *Current History (New York, N.Y.), 91*, 214–218.

World Bank. (2010). *World databank: World development indicators (WDI) & global development finance (GDF).* Retrieved March 1, 2011, from http://databank.worldbank.org/

Zuckerman, E. (2006). Citizen journalism: A look at how blogging is changing the media landscape from the Congo to Korea. *Democracy Now!* Retrieved March 16, 2011, from http://www.democracynow.org/2006/5/31/citizen_journalism_a_look_at_how

Zuckerman, E. (2008). *The Kenyan middle class... or is that the digital activist class?* [Weblog]. Retrieved March 16, 2011, from http://www.ethanzuckerman.com/blog/2008/02/13/

ENDNOTES

[1]   J. Downing (2008, p. 43) deposed that social movement studies have had "zero to say about such "Third World" phenomena as the 20th century antiapartheid movement inside and outside South Africa, or the social explosions that rocked Argentina in the first years of this decade and Indonesia in the final years of the previous one."

[2]   In 2002, Njehu Gatabaki, publisher of *Finance,* a monthly magazine, was sentenced to six months in jail for publishing a report that alleged the president was responsible for ethnic clashes (Berger, 2007). In 2005, David Ochami, of the opposition daily newspaper, *Kenya Times,* was arrested on charges of "incitement" for writing an article criticizing the actions of the president (Berger, 2007, p. 54). Also in 2005, the radio station KASS FM was forced to cease broadcasting for seven days after a program aired featuring a fierce debate between two tribally aligned political groups. The government justified its actions by stating the programming was likely to incite anger and protests among the general populous (Berger, 2007).

[3]   In 2009, Abdel Hamouda, the editor of the independent weekly newspaper *Al-Fagr,* was fined USD $1,820 for alleged defamation of a member of Mubarak's ruling party, the NDP, and at least five news publications had their licenses revoked due to publication of "defamatory" materials (Freedom House, 2010b). Also in 2009, the government blocked the satellite delivered *Hokuma Show* (Cabinet Show) after it aired a comedy sketch criticizing Egypt's Prime Minister (Freedom House, 2010b). State ownership of radio ended in 2003. The private radio stations operating in Egypt focus on providing music and entertainment content (Freedom House, 2010b).

[4]   A search of the Mashada archives did not uncover texts of hate messages that may have been disseminated during the 2007/2008 post-election violence. All blog posts within the timeframe [09/27/2007 – 02/14/2008] of the violent protests have been removed from the blog site.

Chapter 16
Social Media and Youth Interest in Politics in Kenya

Auma Churchill Moses Otieno
Nation Media Group, Kenya

Lusike Lynete Mukhongo
Moi University, Kenya

ABSTRACT

The youth in Kenya are by far the majority age-group, yet their role in politics is hampered by their inability to access mainstream political information. The objective of the study is to determine whether there is any relationship between the level of youth engagement on social media and their level of interest in politics. The study uses the post-test quasi experiment to compare political interest between a naturally occurring group of Facebook users and a naturally occurring group of non-Facebook users. The findings of the study reveal that Facebook has provided the youth with a platform where they can access political information in formats that are appealing to them. Consequently, young people have been able to mobilise themselves online and push for a political agenda. There is, therefore, need to open up online exchanges in order to create a place for young people in mainstream political discourse in Kenya.

INTRODUCTION

Kenya gained independence from Britain in 1963 and has since experienced autocratic single-party regimes, a failed coup, pluralistic democracy (multi-partism), ethnic conflicts, and a contested presidential election that left the country on the brink of civil war. Throughout this period, the Kenyan youth have been sidelined, making them gullible to the machinations of politicians (Siurala, 2002; Forbrig, 2005; Kenya National Assembly, 2007). During Kenya's post-election violence in 2007/2008, as indeed in other political theatre in the country, the youth tend to be more relevant as instruments for achieving goals defined by, and relevant to, the much older politicians, rather than using their numbers to direct political discourse and subsequently electoral outcomes. No doubt,

DOI: 10.4018/978-1-4666-4197-6.ch016

such a power arrangement often undermines youth interests, and renders the most significant Kenyan demographic largely powerless in national politics.

It has been argued that the Kenyan youth face many hurdles that often undermine their ability to fully play their role in the country's politics (Imoite, 2007), yet this was not always the case. For example, at independence, there was a significant number of youth in prominent political positions, such as, Tom Mboya, J. M. Kariuki, Martin Shikuku, Mwai Kibaki, Jean-Marie Seroney and Pio Gama Pinto. Six decades later, all of them except the demised remain fairly active and influential in national politics yet it is now even harder for the youth to rise to the stage. This is despite the fact that the youth form the single-largest voter block based on Kenya's latest census which put the national population at 38,610,097 (Kenya National Bureau of Statistics, 2009). Of these, ages 0-35 years make 79% (30,501,977), of which the youth (15-35 years) are 11,285,731, making 37% of those under 35. This shows how potentially influential the youth vote can be in Kenyan politics. The emergence of new media, and the fact that the youth drive adoption of such new information sources, may yet provide them an opportunity to play their role and exert deliberate influence in Kenya's politics. Of interest is whether political information delivered through youth-friendly channels such as social media can have implications on them truly influencing national politics.

This article, therefore, discusses the use of social media as a source of political information for the youth. It explores existing discourse in and around the general area of youth interest in politics and further reveals the extent to which social media is an effective provider of political communication to the Kenyan youth. It is fairly agreed that the use of the Internet to discover and disseminate political information seems to be growing (Borgida & Stark, 2004). However, what is of concern is the extent to which this new media platform provides true change and new practical opportunities. While no one can dispute the fact that the Internet is likely to have a significant impact on social life, there remains substantial disagreement as to the nature of the impact (Bargh & McKenna, as cited by Borgida & Stark, 2004). For example, there are questions about whether the Internet affords people who have little or no political interest a chance to develop and sustain such interest, or it merely allows those already politically interested to seek relevant information and escalate their attitudes. Consequently, the study was designed to establish the extent to which social media influences youth interest in politics in Kenya given new media's growing importance to information consumption.

THE PLACE OF THE YOUTH ON THE POLITICAL LANDSCAPE OF KENYA

The youth comprise a critical constituency in any country. In Sub-Saharan Africa, the youth are the most abundant asset because of the demographic transition in the region (Garcia & Fares, 2008). For instance, Kenya's last census data shows that 79% of the population is below 35 years of age, and the youth comprise 70% of those eligible to vote (Kenya National Bureau of Statistics, 2009). Further, among the registered voters, the youth comprise 5.9 million, but despite this, youth interests have been subordinated in decision making, policy formulation and execution (Njonjo, 2010). In the general elections held in 2007, the registered voters under the age of 40 were nearly 70% (Kanyinga, Okello, & Akech, 2010). The previous statistics reveal a trend which has been referred to as the youth bulge (Garcia & Fares, 2008; Muthee, 2010). Scholars such as Goldstone (2001) and Reno (2007) associate youth bulges in population trends with youth revolutions in the affected countries or societies. This has immense implications, given the stage of Kenya's democratic development and recent happenings in the political scene; such as the violently contested results of the presidential elections at the end of 2007 and the increasing evidence of frustration with the political leaders' management of national affairs. It, therefore, follows that because the youth population in Kenya has grown so much as to have a clear power to influence voting results, questions must be asked whether they are sufficiently prepared to play this role meaningfully and effectively.

Further, the growth in the youth population demands a politically informed youth. Given that they form an important segment of society; and that the segment comprises the largest voter block, any chance of getting the youth to make informed choices would likely prove useful for democracy and may work to improve society. However, the youth cannot be informed adequately unless they are critical consumers of media messages. As an important segment of the voting population, the youth are assuming an increasing importance in democracy, which can only be truly realised if they are aware of the various forces that come into play to influence how the media frames societal dialogue with regard to political issues. Therefore, there is need to offer the youth some effective educational platforms to help them understand the role of information in an increasingly hyper media age. This will empower them to know what to look for because media illiteracy is an impediment to the development of political systems that assures better returns when the electorate is informed and active (Mihailidis, 2009). Therefore, the study sought to answer the following three questions: (1) Can social media consistently raise Kenyan youth's political consciousness and lead them to play their civic duty responsibly? (2) What are the implications of shifts in the youth's sources of political information to their interest in politics? (3) What does social media as a platform mean for political discourse among the youth?

SOCIAL MEDIA AS A POLITICAL TOOL OF COMMUNICATION

Establishing the influence social media has on youth participation in politics offers important insights on how to get the youth involved in politics. The best illustration of the intersect between social media and politics is well captured in the United States of America presidential elections in 2008 and more recently in the Jasmine Revolution (known broadly as the Arab spring of 2011) witnessed in Tunisia and Egypt at the beginning of 2011, and to a much lesser extent in the clampdown on the 'walk to work' protests in Uganda in April 2011. Attention on the role that social media plays in influencing political action by the youth has been reinvigorated by the so called Jasmine Revolution (Arab spring) in 2011. The terms are used to refer to the political upheaval that unseated long established regimes in the Arab countries at the beginning of 2011 following daily protests by restive youths (Time, 2011). Social media was not the reason that Jasmin Revolution/Arab Spring occurred, but the youth involved in that social uprising employed their being digital natives to apply Facebook and Twitter for political mobilisation.

In Kenya, there is a rising institutional and individual utilisation of the Internet for political communication (Nyabuga, 2006). Findings from a quantitative study carried out by Auma (2010) revealed that 41.2% of students at a public university in Kenya identified Facebook.com as one of their sources for news while 29.4% identified news websites. The same study found that nearly half of students at a public university campus in Nairobi identified Facebook/Twitter as one of their key sources of information. Further, 49% of Facebook users indicated that they learnt about political events that occurred in the country the very day they happened from Facebook. It is important to note that 49% is a significant number indicating that Facebook is emerging as a significant source of political news for young people instead of television, radio and newspapers. In addition, recent evidence (Kavanaugh, Perz-Quinones, Kim and Schmitz, 2008; Raynes-Goldie and Walker, 2008) shows a trend towards increasing online participation among individuals with common political interests (Theocharis, 2010).

In a demonstration of how social media empowers its users, the Centre for International Media Assistance (2009b) found that blogs and social networking websites allow ordinary users in the United States to generate as well as consume contents and interact on webpages with people they otherwise would never have been able to communicate and interact with (Centre for International Media Assistance, 2009b). Further, users can update their status or post comments on other users' posts. For example, Newman (2010) found that one in four young people in the United Kingdom posted election related comments through social networking sites such as Facebook and Twitter. It is, therefore, clear that new media have changed the nature of citizen participation throughout the world if one considers new realities such as cell phone cameras capturing scenes of violence that would otherwise go unreported; Twitter feeds used to organise massive protests and the protests in Iran in 2009, where new media helped unite a supportive community outside the country (Faris as cited in Centre for International Media Assistance, 2009a). In Kenya, during the 2007-2008 political crisis, when the government banned live coverage of news, the youth used cell phones to send text messages to mobilise themselves in response to calls by senior, older politicians for mass action while others resorted to blogging about the political crisis. A website referred to as Ushahidi, a Swahili word that means "to witness," was established after the 2007-2008 political crisis. The now globally popular crisis mapping platform, emerged from this strife when bloggers sought for a way to crowdsource information on the Kenyan crisis. Subsequently, Ushahidi

has been used in elections in various African countries and during the Haiti earthquake crisis–it allows users to populate a map with reports of incidents in their locations.

SOCIAL MEDIA, NEW THREATS

The Internet is in many ways a paragon of democratic media, allowing anyone their say (Sutter, 2000). It has created an avenue for young people to express themselves and interact with each other from the comfort of their mobile phones, while in school, at home or in entertainment spots without fear of censorship or regulation. However, there is also literature that shows that it is not all a rosy story. A major question brought about by the popularity of social media amongst the youth is the death of the gatekeeper (Dominick, 2005, p. 19). With everybody now able to create a mass communication channel with ease and communicate to large audiences, often cases have been raised of young people posting information on the Internet with little regard to the veracity of the contents being published. As such, rumours and propaganda, and facts and truths are doled out in equal measure. Therefore, new media technologies lack the credibility and accuracy of conventional forms of media (Faris, as cited in Centre for International Media Assistance, 2009a).

In addition, the apparently significant ability of the social media to cause the youth vote faces many threats, not least the fact that by nature it presents autocratic regimes with opportunity to electronically block their use (Wu, 2010). Because of the centralised nature of social media tools such as Twitter, YouTube and Facebook, they are very susceptible to censorship, giving the example of Iran in 2009 when new media tools were used for community organising prior to and during the election, but after voting many community organising sites were blocked by the government (Faris, as cited in Centre for International Media

Assistance, 2009a). As a result, this thinking has partly contributed to the intellectual movement to develop a theory to explain the phenomenon known as the "master switch," arguing that like other game changing media platforms before it, the Internet shows pluralistic characteristics initially but eventually power ends up being concentrated in just a few hands, the proprietors (Wu, 2010). This risk of censorship by governments or economic lords/oligarchs has fed innovative spirits to develop ways of making it more difficult for repressive regimes to interfere with their subjects' Internet connectivity. One such tool is the *Tor*, which, according to its executive director Andrew Lewman, is free software and a network that is used to protect citizens' online privacy and anonymity (Centre for International Media Assistance, 2009a).

Social media tools, therefore, can present greater challenge to governments seeking to control them. For example, due to the dispersed use of tools such as Twitter and Short Message Service SMS, it is difficult for governments to find and control personalised sources of information. This makes state authorities to resort to blocking such services altogether, but even this is becoming increasingly difficult without risking a significant public opinion backlash (Faris, as cited in Centre for International Media Assistance, 2009a). However, this has not deterred state authorities and examples abound, such as authorities in Kenya unsuccessfully seeking to block gateways for mobile phone short text messages during the political turmoil in 2008; authorities in Egypt blocking Facebook and Twitter at the height of the Arab Spring protests early in 2011, an action copied by the powers in Uganda weeks later to crack down on protests over high living costs in Kampala. This then raises the question as to where the true benefit of social media as a source of political information for the youth lie, if the same social media can be more easily be blocked by state officials. The question of whether this represents a net gain or a net loss for the critical masses, is

the focus of this chapter and of more interest is the extent to which social media is replacing or supplementing conventional mass media that can no longer efficiently serve the youth.

THEORETICAL FRAMEWORK

Marshall McLuhan's media determinism theory (1960) and the Inglehart's theory of post-materialism (1988; 1990; 1997) were used to provide a framework for the arguments on whether the use of social media by the Kenyan youth influences their interest in politics. While the media determinism theory focuses on the channels through which political information reach the youth, the post-materialist theory was used to help understand information-seeking habits among the youth and what the results of such habits might be especially when political messages are involved. Marshall McLuhan's media determinism (1960) has experienced resurgence in the last 15 years following the meteoric growth of the Internet and mobile telephony globally. Even though his work was developed three decades before the Internet, McLuhan strongly believed that technological development could drive social change (Goguen, 2009).

The study used this framework to interrogate whether political information that has always been transmitted through conventional media would result in different effects if transmitted via social media (Chandler, 2009). The post-materialist theory holds that individuals and society are ever in a state of transformation and sees post-materialists as more concerned about the quality of life, the environment, democracy, and human rights (Fisher, 2011). It has also been argued that Internet users tend to be young, well educated and affluent, thus denoting a similarity to the demographic characteristics of post-materialists. Further, young people tend to display a post-materialist orientation, accompanied by a disinterest in traditional forms of political participation (Theocharis, 2010).

METHODOLOGY

The study assumed a philosophical stance more identifiable with the objective/realist ontological position and therefore took a positivist epistemological view to knowledge. It therefore sought to use quantitative techniques to understand if the use of social media influences youth interest in politics in a manner that can be said to separate facts from values. The study was designed to interrogate a relationship between the source of political information and young people's level of interest on politics. One way through which the study did this, was to generate trends over time on youth use of social media. The study, therefore, observed and measured information numerically and analysed the findings using statistical procedures. It employed a quantitative method–quasi experiment–comparing the naturally occurring control group (youths who are not on Facebook) and the naturally occurring experimental group (youths who are on Facebook). This was to help determine if the increased use of social media by the youth, which can be considered a treatment, does bring about an outcome in increased youth interest in politics. The study targeted students (18-24 age group) from one public university campus, located in Nairobi, Kenya's capital city. The sampling procedure recruited 27 male students and 22 female students into the control and the experimental groups, respectively.

The study defined political interest based on the following five factors:

1. Contributing in political debates that take place in the social media for example those provoked by shared links from Kenyan news sites.
2. Following political news at least thrice weekly, remembering political stories posted on social media in the last 24 hours.
3. Commenting, sharing or liking political links, ranks news as a theme on which they engage friends often.
4. Following activities of politicians in social media and/or interacting with politicians online.
5. Showing evidence or declaring intention to vote.

FINDINGS

Findings from the study reveal that 61% of the respondents have had a Facebook account for more than three years, while only 14% stated that they have had a Facebook account for less than a year. The quick uptake of technologies by young people in Kenya, then has significant ramifications for the development of new media (Centre for International Media Assistance, 2009b, p. 1), whose major plunk is what has come to be known as social media. While the youth may have wholly embraced the Internet and social media without fully understanding its communicative implications, it has expanded news source options for them (Mihailidis, 2009).

The development of the social media, particularly Facebook, has also provided the youth with a friendly media platform, where members in these platforms operate alternately as source and receiver in a mass communications context. In addition, it has pushed the internet deeper into the realm of mass communication; effectively offering young people a chance to become mass communicators (Dominick, 2005) with regard to political issues. While new trends show that the youth start off using these gadgets for entertainment, they then graduate to use them for more critical information seeking (Njonjo, 2010). As a result, the Internet becomes a platform that the youth can use to offer social empowerment, organise themselves to form alliances, and ultimately act as a tool for social and political change (Fenton, 2008).

While the focus of the study was on Facebook, it is important to note that there are several other social networking sites that young people in Kenya have access to. According to the findings, 71% of the Facebook users agreed that they have other social networking accounts, while 24.5% of non-Facebook users agreed that they had other social networking accounts. The study further established that the *Facebook* users also used websites such as 2go, Gmail, Google+, MySpace, My-Gamma, Blue-Space, Mixt, Netlog, Nimbuzz, Twitter, Skype, YouTube, Muicbook, Friendster, Netlog, and Winestar. This is as a result of the fact that the widespread adoption of the Internet in Kenya has been credited to falling costs, faster connectivity speeds and dynamics in mobile telephony driving the growth of the mobile Internet (Communications Commission of Kenya, 2011). For instance, as at the time of this study, it cost approximately one dollar to access unlimited Internet for the whole day on one's mobile telephone in Kenya, and one mobile telephony provider in the country offered Facebook browsing free of charge to all their subscribers. Consequently, young people in Kenya are increasingly spending a considerable amount of time on social networks. Therefore, the Internet has emerged as an influential forum in which young people in Kenya seek and acquire politically relevant information about candidates, issues, parties, and political organisations. As a result, it has impacted the society in a major way, becoming a routine feature in the lives of many people (Borgida & Stark, 2004). Consequently, what is being witnessed in Kenya is a scenario where the mainstream media houses are creating Facebook pages with formats appealing to young people. This is due to the need to reach out and disseminate news and information to young people in Kenya.

For instance, from the findings, Facebook users mainly indicated that they relied on Facebook as their source of daily news. This then explains their preference for Facebook over newspapers, because 8.1% of Facebook users indicated they read newspapers daily, while 28.6% of non-Facebook users read newspapers daily. Further, 38.8% of Facebook users read newspapers once a week while 32.7% of non-Facebook users read them more frequently, thrice weekly. This can be explained by the fact that the Facebook users can access web pages of newspapers via Facebook. Radio listeners had a positive response rate of 36.7% while majority of them, 63.3% do not listen to radio for news. However, they indicated that they listened to radio for music and not for political news. Further, a majority of Facebook users preferred radio over newspapers. This is because radio can be used as a background noise while they browse Facebook. In fact, many popular Kenyan FM radio programs have taken to urging their listeners to react to such stations through social media accounts. The reactions of listeners on the social media accounts are sometimes read on air. Of even more interest is the finding that 57.1% of Facebook users watch news on television as compared to 44.9% of non-*Facebook* users. This may be explained by the possibility that Facebook increases their interest in politics, and therefore, they are always keen to catch up with primetime news to see what else has happened. Then, often, this is what they then post on their *Facebook* pages, leading to cyclical source shifting between new media and conventional media. Ironically, because of the need to keep updating their Facebook status, they resort to television to catch up with political events happening in the country, thereby, increasing their interest in politics.

POLITICAL CONTENT IN YOUTH DISCUSSIONS IN SOCIAL MEDIA

Data from the study reveal that both the youth who are on Facebook and those who are not mostly denied discussing politics when asked directly, but seemed to admit a level of discussion when politics was unpacked into key civic governance themes such as youth empowerment, employment, and social service provision. Of those on Facebook, a significant portion, 37%, rarely commented on civic/political/governance issues, while 31% never commented. A major difference between youths on social media and those not active in that space emerged when their habits in sharing of political web links was compared. In the control group, 20.4% reported that they shared web-links related to Civic/political/governance issues very frequently. Amongst those in Facebook, 46.9% said they shared such links once a week while 16.3% said they shared them thrice a week. Yet amongst those not on Facebook, 34.7% said they shared once a week while 16.3% said they did so thrice a week. There was no difference when either group was asked to rank against other subjects in the content of their shares of Facebook. In both cases, 34% said they discussed it "least frequently." Of those on Facebook, 28.6% said they debated politics daily, 6.1% did it five times a week while 14.3% thrice weekly. However, a majority--65.3%--reported debating politics rarely or not at all.

The differences came out clearly when politics was unpacked and presented in terms such as youth empowerment, employment and access to social services. Those not on Facebook seemed comparatively more interested in youth empowerment questions, with 57.1% saying they interacted about this as compared to 51% amongst those on Facebook. It would be interesting to investigate the foundations of this revelation further, in order to establish whether those who are already on Facebook for some reason feel more empowered than those who are not on Facebook. It would also be interesting to investigate whether Facebook made Group A respondents (Facebook users) to acquire a cavalier attitude towards youth empowerment. Further, it also emerged that majority of the experimental group, that is 34.7% interacted about employment often, 18.4% did so frequently (five times a week) while 16.3% said they interacted about employment daily. Further, those on Facebook are more concerned about social services. The study established that a majority of Group A respondents, 73.5%, interacted about social

services at least three times a week, while Group B was 65.4%. This suggests that while social services are important to both cases, the experimental group's attitude to it was more pronounced. From the study, it also emerged that those on *Facebook* are more likely to have online interactions with politicians. According to the findings, 47% of those who had Facebook accounts indicated that they had interacted with politicians online through their Facebook pages. As a result, those with Facebook accounts had a stronger urge to vote at Kenya's next general election. The two cases (Group A and Group B) expressed a strong intention to vote at Kenya's next General election. However, a stronger attitude was established amongst those with Facebook accounts where 83.7% said they will vote. This compares to 76% amongst those who did not have Facebook accounts.

SIGNIFICANCE OF FACEBOOK AS A SOURCE OF POLITICAL INFORMATION FOR THE YOUTH

A significant portion of youth relies on such networks for news provision. The study found that 32.7% of Facebook users identified Facebook as their main provider of news. It was established that both the control and experimental groups rely on television and radio for news, but those in the experimental group showed a more developed appetite for news from the two platforms. The biggest portion (57.1%) depended on television as their preferred source for news followed by radio at 36.7%. The control group relied on television (44.9%), radio (28.6%) and newspapers (18.4%). The study revealed that Facebook use is associated with high reliance on offline sources of political information. Most respondents in the experimental group (Group A), that is 57.1%, claimed reliance on three platforms--newspapers, television and radio--for information on politics. Another 34.7% claimed exclusive reliance on television and 16.3% on Facebook. On the other hand, respondents in the control group (Group B) had 49% identifying television as their source of political information while only 18.4% identified newspapers/television/radio. Another 14.3% said they relied on radio.

Further, youths who are active on Facebook also reported a higher affinity for following news on newspapers and television. They reported a higher incidence of newspaper readership whereby, 71.5% said they read a newspaper at least thrice a week while the corresponding number amongst the control group respondents was 49%. However, 32.7% of the control group respondents reported reading newspapers daily, suggesting that a portion of youths who do not have Facebook accounts were avid newspaper readers. The respondents from the experimental group had a strong news seeking behaviour which remained consistent in their television viewing habits. The majority of those with Facebook accounts reported viewing news on television daily. Overall, 89.7% followed news on television at least thrice a week. Amongst those without Facebook accounts, 81.7% viewed at least once a week and 44.9% viewed daily. While radio came out as an important source of news, it was not as highly regarded as newspapers and television. This may be due to the fact that most FM stations offer a very thin volume of their repertoire to news and current affairs. Amongst those with Facebook accounts, 65.3% reported listening to news on radio at least thrice a week as opposed to 51% amongst those without Facebook accounts.

The experimental group respondents' showed a stronger appetite for news stories, with 89.7% of them reporting that they followed news on television at least thrice a week. On the other hand, the control group–revealed that 81.7% followed television news at least once a week. With regard to radio, 65.3% of those on Facebook reported listening to news at least thrice a week as opposed to 51% amongst those without Facebook accounts. Similarly, those not on Facebook are more likely not to visit news websites—49% of

them reported never having visited a news website when the comparative portion amongst those on Facebook was 22.4%. Many factors may have come into play to make news websites unattractive to the youth—one being that most Kenyan news websites carry over information packaging traditions from legacy platforms such as newspapers and therefore the youth may not feel that it serves their news needs in a timely fashion.

In addition, it was revealed that both the experimental and control group did not consider news websites an attractive source of news. For instance, amongst those with Facebook accounts, 30.6% visited news website only once and another 22.4% reported that they had never visited a news website. On the other hand, 49% of those without Facebook accounts declared that they had never visited a news website and another 24.4% had only visited once a week. Many factors may have come into play to make news websites unattractive to the youth – one being that most Kenyan news websites carry over information packaging traditions from legacy platforms such as newspapers and therefore the youth may not feel that it serves their needs. However, of importance was the fact that a majority of the experimental group could recall learning of a breaking news story through Facebook at least 24 hours prior to filling the questionnaire. This majority includes 49% who learnt of a story the same day and 21% who recalled learning of a breaking news story the previous day. The control group respondents, identified television and radio as news sources that they associated with breaking important stories. Nearly half of them, 42.9%, said they depended on television while 24.5% were dependent on radio. Newspapers came a distant third with 18.4%. This suggests a growing importance of Facebook as news channel for this demographic. It also implies that youths who are not on Facebook will need a news source to compensate for this lest they suffer from insufficient levels of news provision required to generate and sustain political interest.

TRENDS IN YOUTH RELIANCE ON SOCIAL MEDIA FOR POLITICAL INFORMATION

Findings of Auma (2010) were set as a primary benchmark for tracing trends. The study found that when respondents in the control group were asked what made them not to have a Facebook account, 26.5% pointed at lack of internet access while 49% said that they were not interested. Further, 4.5 pointed were just indifferent. It appears preference for television as a source of news is waning amongst the youth. Whilst Auma (2010) found that 78.4% of the youth identified television as an important source of news, the current study found that two years later this stood at 57.1% amongst those on Facebook and 44.9% amongst those not on Facebook. A similar trend was revealed as regards radio, which was identified by 45.1% two years ago but the figure now stands at 36.7% amongst those on Facebook and 28.6% amongst those not on Facebook.

Two years ago, the news sources were ranked by importance as television, newspapers and radio in that order. The study found that amongst those on Facebook, this ranking was television, radio and Facebook while it was television, radio and newspapers for those not on Facebook. This suggests that when Facebook is not in contention then the youth would resort to newspapers. The youth are more likely to rely on the combination of television, radio and newspapers for political information if they have Facebook accounts than if they do not. Auma (2010) found that 52% of youth rely on this combination for their political information. This number has grown amongst those on Facebook to 57.1% but it stands at 18.4% for those not on Facebook.

CONCLUSION

The general objective of the study was to determine whether there is any relationship between the level of youth engagement on social media and the level of their interest in politics. Findings indicate that the youth who are active on social media have more established interest in politics than those who are not. The study revealed that Facebook has provided the youth with a platform where they can access political information in formats that are appealing to them and interpret the information based on their needs as young people. It also emerged that Facebook use seems to intensify political information seeking behavior by the youth on other sources, such as newspapers and television news. Similarly, the data also showed that Kenyan youth who are on Facebook have post-materialist tendencies. Consequently, it has provided an avenue for young people to express their opinions, and even debate about politics. This has witnessed a trend where young people have been able to mobilise themselves online and push for a political agenda often referred to as "youth agenda" by making their voices heard through updating their status, chatting, commenting on posts and using political images on their profiles.

There is need to open up online exchanges in order to create a place for young people in mainstream political discourse in Kenya. This is because youth and social media use has significant implications for media management, youth policy, governance and national politics in Kenya. Further, the government, through social networking, should lend support to the use of economic incentives and building social connections among youth as pillars of peace building programs in Kenya and similar contexts. Social issues emerged as a key concern for the youth on social networks. These include creation of both short and longer-term employment opportunities for youth, and support to collective action among interethnic groups of youth. In addition, social networks are a responsive platform for engaging the youth in meeting civic ends. The research also points to the need to expand young people's political and civic engagement in order to significantly reduce their risk of participation in antisocial ventures.

REFERENCES

Auma, C. M. O. (2010). *Social media and young people's engagement in political discourse* [Dissertation]. Nairobi, Kenya: Moi University.

Bargh, J. A., & McKenna, K. Y. A. (2004). The Internet and social life. *Annual Review of Psychology*, *55*, 573–590. doi:10.1146/annurev.psych.55.090902.141922 PMID:14744227.

Berger, G. (2007). Looking ahead: What next for African media? In E. Baarratt & G. Berger (Eds), 50 years of journalism: Africa media since Ghana's independence (159-170) Johannesburg, South Africa: The Africa Editors' Forum, Highway Africa and Media Foundation for West Africa.

Borgida, E., & Emily, N. S. (2004). New media and politics: Some insights from social and political psychology. *The American Behavioral Scientist*, *48*(4), 467–478. doi:10.1177/0002764204270282.

Centre for International Media Assistance (CIMA). (2009a). *Special report: The role of new media in the 2009 Iranian elections*. Washington, DC: Centre for International Media Assistance.

Centre for International Media Assistance (CIMA). (2009b). *Special Report: YouthTube – Empowering Youth through Independent Media*. Washington, DC: Centre for International Media Assistance.

Chandler, D. (2009) *Technological or Media Determinism*. Retrieved October 20, 2012, from http://www.bos.org.rs/cepit/idrustvo/st/Techor-MediaDeterminism.pdf

Communications Commission of Kenya. (2011). *Quarterly Sector Statistics Report – 1ˢᵗ Quarter July-Sept 2010/2011*. Nairobi, Kenya: CCK.

Dominick, J. R. (2005). *The Dynamics of Mass Communications: Media in the Digital Age* (8th ed.). New York: McGraw Hill.

Fenton, N. (2008). New Media, Politics and Resistance. *International Journal of Cultural Studies*, *11*(2), 230–248. doi:10.1177/1367877908089266.

Fisher, S. (2011). *Modernisation, Post-Materialism, Dealignment and Party-System Change*. Oxford, UK: Oxford University.

Forbrig, J. (2005). *Revisiting Youth Political Participation: Challenges for Research and Democratic Practice in Europe*. Strasbourg, France: Council of Europe.

Garcia, M., & Fares, J. (2008). *Youth in Africa's Labour Market*. Washington, DC: The World Bank.

Goguen, J. *Against Technological Determinism*. Retrieved October 20, 2009, from http://citeseerx.ist.psu.edu/viewdoc/download?doi=10.1.1.125.2540&rep=rep1&type=pdf#page=87

Goldstone, J. A. (2001). Demography, Environment and Security. M. Weiner & S. Stanton Russel (Eds.), Demography and National Security. New York: Berghahn Books.

Imoite, J. (2007). Youth Participation in Kenya Politics: Challenges and Opportunities. In *Youth and Politics in Conflict Contexts*. Washington, DC: Woodrow Wilson International Centre for Scholars.

Kanyinga, K., Okello, D., & Akoko, A. (2010). Contradictions of Transition to Democracy in Fragmented Societies: The Kenya 2007 General Elections in Perspective. In K. Kanyinga, & D. Okello (Eds.), Tensions and Reversals in Democratic Transitions (1-28). Nairobi, Kenya: University of Nairobi.

Kavanaugh, A., Perz-Quinones, M. A., Kim, J. B., & Schmitz, J. (2008). Deliberation in Tool for Blog Discovery and Citizen-to-Citizen Participation. In *Proceedings of 9ᵗʰ Annual International Government Research* (pp. 143–152). Montreal, CA: ACM Press.

Kenya National Assembly. (2007). *The Hansard, Tuesday, 17th July, 2007*. Nairobi, Kenya: Kenya National Assembly.

Kenya National Bureau of Statistics. (2009). *Kenya National Population Census*. Nairobi, Kenya: Kenya National Bureau of Statistics.

Malouf, R., & Mullen, T. (2008). Graph-Based User Classification for Informal Online Political Discourse. *Internet Research*, *18*(2), 177–190. doi:10.1108/10662240810862239.

McLuhan, M. (1962). *The Gutenberg Galaxy: The Making of Typographic Man*. Toronto, CA: University of Toronto Press.

McLuhan, M. (1964). *Understanding the Media: The Extension's of Man*. New York: McGraw Hill.

McLuhan, M. (1967). *The Medium is the Massage: An Inventory of Effects*. New York: Random House.

Mihailidis, P. (2009). *Media Literacy: Empowering the Youth Worldwide*. Washington, DC: Centre for International Media Assistance.

Muthee, M. W. (2010). *Hitting the Target, Missing the Point: Youth Policies and Programmes in Kenya*. Washington, DC: Woodrow Wilson International Centre for Scholars.

Newman, N. (2010). *UKelection2010, Mainstream Media and the Role of the Internet: How Social and Digital Media Affected the Business of Politics and Journalism*. London: Reuters Institute for the Study of Journalism.

Njonjo, K. S. (2010). Youth Fact Book: Infinite Possibility or Definite Disaster? Nairobi, Kenya: Institute of Economic Affairs (IEA) and Friedrich-Ebert-Stiftung (FES).

Nyabuga, G. (2006). *Knowledge is Power: The Internet and the Kenyan Public Sphere*. Worcester Papers in English and Cultural Studies, 4. Retrieved March 7, 2010, from http://eprints.worc.ac.uk/310/1/Web_Knowledge_is_power_-_George_Nyabuga.pdf

Pritchard, J. L., & Sanderson, S. E. (2002). The Dynamics of Political Discourse in Seeking Sustainability. In Lance, H. G., & Holling, C. S. (Eds.), *Panarchy: Understanding Transformations in Human and Natural Systems* (pp. 147–170). Washington, DC: Island Press.

Raynes-Goldie, K., & Walker, L. (2008). Our Space: Online Civic Engagement Tools for Youth. In Bennett, L. (Ed.), *Civic Engagement: The MacArthur Series on Digital Media and Learning* (pp. 161–188). Cambridge, MA: The MIT Press.

Reno, W. (2007). The Political Economy of Order Amidst Predation in Sierra Leone. In G.B. Edna (Eds.), State of Violence: Politics, Youth, and Memory in Contemporary Africa (37-57). Charlottesville, VA: University of Virginia Press.

Siurala, L. (2002). *Can Youth Make a Difference? Youth Policy Facing Diversity and Change*. Strasbourg, France: Council of Europe.

Sutter, G. (2000). Nothing new under the Sun: Old Fears and New Media. *International Journal of Law and Information Technology*, *8*(3), 338–378. doi:10.1093/ijlit/8.3.338.

Theocharis, Y. (2010). Young People, Political Participation and Online Postmaterialism in Greece. *New Media & Society*, *13*(2), 203–223. doi:10.1177/1461444810370733.

Wu, T. (2010). *The Master Switch: The Rise and Fall of Information Empires*. New York: Knopf Doubleday Publishing Group.

Chapter 17
Twitter as Virtual Battleground:
The Case of HSM Press in Somalia

R. Bennett Furlow
Arizona State University

ABSTRACT

Somalia has been plagued by political instability and ongoing conflict for over two decades. Yet, that does not mean Somalia has been completely isolated from modern technologies and new media. The construction of cell phone towers and other means of communication is a popular and profitable business in Somalia. One of the more recent additions to Somali new media is the use of microblogging. On December 7, 2011, Somalia's al-Shabaab began a Twitter feed in both English and Arabic. In its first two months of tweeting, al-Shabaab promoted its successes on the ground, condemned what they see as unjustified acts of violence perpetrated against them, and engaged in a Twitter war with the Kenyan Defense Forces. This chapter seeks to analyze these first few months of al-Shabaab's Twitter activity. What are the main goals of al-Shabaab's use of Twitter? How effective have they been? How does their use of microblogging compare to other extremists' (such as the Taliban) use of Twitter? As Somalia is largely considered a failed state and internet penetration is not particularly dense, who is the intended audience?

INTRODUCTION

Somalia has long been the quintessential example of a failed state. The regime of Siad Barre collapsed in January 1991, and Somalia has been without an effective government ever since. Being a failed state does not mean that Somalia is without contact with the rest of the world, nor does it mean that new technologies have eluded the country. Indeed, even hardline Islamists have taken to social media sites like Twitter in an attempt to craft a public image and engage with people around the world.

DOI: 10.4018/978-1-4666-4197-6.ch017

Gabriel Weimann's *Terror on the Internet* (2006) effectively outlines the major uses of the Internet by extremist groups—communication among members, transfer of information such as instructions on bomb-making or training videos, research of potential targets, and cyber-terrorism. Since the publication of Weimann's book we have seen the rise of social media and with it, the ability to craft an image and recruit new members has become a major component of extremist Internet usage.

De Koster and Houtman's (2008) work looks at the workings of online communities focusing primarily on chat rooms. Now with new and more public ways of communication such as Facebook and Twitter we see these online communities not just talking to each other but engaging in dialogues with non-members as well. In the case of Somalia, we see this type of online communication and social media activity happening in the context of a failed state and a civil war.

On December 7, 2011, Somalia's *Harakat al-Shabaab al-Mujahideen*, better known as al-Shabaab, began using the popular microblogging site Twitter. Through the site, al-Shabaab has promoted their military successes on the ground, condemned what they see as unjustified acts of violence perpetrated against them, and engaged in a Twitter war with the Kenyan Defense Forces. This study examines the objectives and effectiveness of the first few months of al-Shabaab's Twitter campaign and compares al-Shabaab's use of microblogging to other Islamist extremists, such as the Taliban. It will also touch on the idea of technological determinism as it relates to manner in which modern extremists utilize social media.

A BRIEF LOOK AT RECENT SOMALI HISTORY

After the fall of the Siad Barre regime, Somalia fell into a state of chaos. Various warlords vied for power and were able to effectively carve out little fiefdoms across the country. A series of United Nations Security Council Resolutions led to the creation of UNOSOM I (United Nations Operation in Somalia I) (United Nations, 1992). The UNOSOM troops proved ineffective at their peacemaking mission and in December 1992, the United States began Operation Restore Hope. The U.S. mission was to protect the UN peacekeepers and create an environment in which humanitarian aid could be delivered. UNOSOM I and Operation Restore Hope were eventually replaced by UNOSOM II. This mission consisted of a much larger force and seemed better able to cope with the chaotic situation on the ground. However, in October, 1993, a U.S. attempt to apprehend Mohamed Farah Aidid, one of the most powerful warlords in Mogadishu, led to the Battle of Mogadishu. Also known as the Black Hawk Down incident, this disastrous encounter precipitated the eventual withdrawal of U.S. troops from Somalia. UNOSOM II was weakened without the U.S. support and ended, in failure, in March, 1995.

While the failed state environment has allowed warlords to prosper, it also has provided an opening for Islamist groups to shape Somalia with their particular ideological orientation. Over the ensuing years, various groups emerged and numerous islamic courts were formed. These courts developed across southern Somalia, with a large portion of them concentrated in Mogadishu.

The courts were often dominated by members of a particular clan, who would mete out harsher punishments to members of rival clans. In other words, there was an obvious clan bias in sentencing. In 2000, the various islamic courts in Mogadishu merged and formed the Islamic Courts Union (ICU) to consolidate power and rectify clan bias. Each court had a militia to enforce its rulings, and those militias merged into the ICU's own armed wing. The ICU was then able to establish a sense of limited control. It outlawed the use of *qaat*, a popular narcotic plant, and imposed order and security, as opposed to the warlords who would intentionally foment chaos. Seeking to create a more "Islamic" society, the ICU also closed down movie theaters and banned mixed-gender gatherings.

The ICU became an all-encompassing judicial and governmental system. Beyond the administration and enforcement of justice, it also ran schools and medical facilities. This kritocratic government was successful, and it was initially well received by the general populace. As the ICU grew stronger, members of warlord militias changed allegiances and joined it. By June 2006, the ICU controlled all of Mogadishu (BBC, 2006). It continued to expand beyond Mogadishu and by October controlled virtually all of southern Somalia. However, Somalia's longtime rival, Ethiopia, feared the rise of an Islamist state on its border and invaded. The ICU's fall came as quickly as its rise.

By December of 2006, Ethiopia had defeated the ICU. In defeat, the ICU splintered into several smaller groups, including al-Shabaab. Formerly the armed youth wing of the Islamic Courts, al-Shabaab was led by Aden Hashi 'Ayro, who was a protégée of Hassan Dahir Aweys, the ICU's leader. Aweys sent 'Ayro to Afghanistan in 2001, where he is believed to have trained with al-Qaeda for a few months (International Crisis Group, 2005) and brought this expertise back to Somalia.

But 'Ayro exhibited increasingly erratic and excessively violent behavior. For example, he captured a cemetery dating from the Italian colonial era and disinterred and desecrated the bodies buried there. This outraged many, including members of the ICU. This type of incident led to speculation that tension existed between Aweys and 'Ayro. When the ICU collapsed in 2006, 'Ayro managed to keep his forces together as al-Shabaab, existing as an independent group. 'Ayro was later killed in 2008 by a U.S. airstrike in Somalia.

The leadership of al-Shabaab has been less apparent since 'Ayro's death. A number of people have struggled for the top leadership position, but no one has successfully captured it. Al-Shabaab seems to have fallen prey to the one constant political obstacle in Somalia: the clan. Support for leaders has divided largely along clan lines. This has led to speculation that al-Shabaab is a fractured force. Nevertheless, al-Shabaab remains the strongest Islamist force in Somalia and the most effective at fighting the Transitional Federal Government, the government backed by the UN, U.S., and African Union.

Several other groups were formed in the aftermath of the ICU but proved too small to be effective on their own. In 2007, they joined together to form Hizbul Islam with Hassan Dahir Aweys as their leader. Over the next few years, Hizbul Islam and al-Shabaab fought each other, but Hizbul Islam was never as strong as al-Shabaab. In 2010, Hizbul Islam was finally forced to merge into al-Shabaab, making it the dominant Islamist force in the country.

The TFG, meanwhile, has received logistical and military support from neighboring Ethiopia and Kenya. With skirmishes increasing along its border, Kenya sent forces into Somalia in October 2011.

EARLY USES OF MEDIA

Extremists use the Internet for a wide variety of purposes—communication, propaganda, and fund-raising to name a few. Strictly speaking, this is not cyberterrorism or cyberwarfare, because the purpose is not to disrupt anyone else's computer systems or use of the Internet. Instead, extremists use the Internet largely for message crafting and control. Weimann (2006) points out that most extremist websites focus on issues such as "freedom of expression and political prisoners" and not on their own acts of violence. They tend to point out the undemocratic or immoral means by which their enemies attempt to oppress them. Extremists attempt to make the case on their websites and through blogs and message boards that they are the weaker, disenfranchised underdog fighting against an oppressive government. By casting themselves in the role of hero struggling against overwhelming powers they seek to justify their acts of violence.

As De Koster and Houtman (2008) point out, online sites also provide a sense of community. Web users who visit chat rooms or discussion boards have some interest in a certain subject matter but may not have people in their offline worlds who share those interests. A virtual community is, therefore, created where one can share thoughts on the area of interest, including extremist interpretations of Islam.

One use extremists make of the Internet is to frame their opponents in a certain way. They attempt to influence the user's perception of their opponents. In this case the goal is to influence members of the contested population, those who are not committed jihadis but may be leaning in that direction. If Westerners can be framed in a negative light and jihadis in a positive light, the member of the contested population may move toward the jihadist worldview. Many jihadi websites refer to Americans and Europeans as 'Crusaders' (Halverson, Goodall, & Coman, 2011). This connects current events into a widely known historical narrative in which Muslim lands are invaded by western armies who kill many innocent Muslims to occupy and exploit their resources. The invasion tragedy continues until a Muslim champion such as Saladin emerges to defeat the invaders and save Islam. By casting their enemies this way, extremists dehumanize them as an archetypal abstraction. They become immoral, aggressive infidels with a singular purpose, and therefore attacks on them become easier to justify.

These sites frequently provide sermons, photos, and videos of attacks, as well as chat rooms, discussion boards, and even manuals on tactics or bomb building. Such sites often get shut down by authorities but are typically up again within days under a new web address. They present an ongoing challenge.

Twitter, we should note, was not al-Shabaab's first foray into new media. Members of al-Shabaab have long posted on message boards and chat rooms, many of which are specialized and frequented by Islamist extremists. This is not unique to al-Shabaab but rather a typical method of using new media to communicate an ideological message to the outside world.

There is an element of soft technological determinism at work with al-Shabaab's use of technology. They have clearly embraced social media and the Internet as a means to spread their ideology, attract material support, and gather recruits. With half a billion users on Twitter it was somewhat inevitable that extremist groups would eventually embrace this technology. Al-Shabaab would most certainly exist without Twitter and without engaging on these websites, but it would look and operate in a fundamentally different way. Videos uploaded to websites, involvement in chat rooms, and an active Twitter presence are all weapons in al-Shabaab's public image arsenal. Their use of technology allows them craft an image of themselves and their opponents, respond quickly to events, and attract people to their cause.

Al-Shabaab formerly maintained a website, alkataiib.net, which has subsequently been shut down, on which it would post messages and videos in Somali, Arabic and English (Ploch, 2010). With less than two percent of the Somali population having Internet access, it is safe to conclude that website and chat room participation is intended to reach an audience outside of Somalia (CIA, 2009). Both al-Shabaab and Hizbul Islam have taken over radio stations within Somalia and used them to broadcast reports of their victories (Ibrahim, 2010). Al Shabaab has used all these media outlets to support its narrative that it is on the side of Islam, and the forces rallied against them (the U.S., Ethiopia, the TFG, etc.) are the true enemies of the Somali people.

In 2008, al-Shabaab released statements on jihadi websites expressing its commitment to global jihad, and in 2009 they released the video "Here I am at your Service, Osama" expressing its loyalty to al-Qaeda, and Osama bin Laden (Ploch, 2010). It was not until a February 2012 video release by al-Qaeda leader Ayman al-Zawahiri that a formal merger between al-Qaeda and al-Shabaab was announced (BBC, 2012). The consequences of this merger remain to be seen, but this earlier public pledge of allegiance can be interpreted in a number of ways. Prior to it, there was not much indication of a solid connection between al-Qaeda and al-Shabaab. It is believed that members of al-Qaeda such as Abdullah Ahmed Abdullah, responsible for the 1998 U.S. embassy bombings in Tanzania and Kenya, had fled to Somalia and were under the protection of Islamists within the country. And bin Laden claimed al-Qaeda involvement in the 1993 Black Hawk Down incident, although there is no evidence to support that claim. Loose ties have connected Somali Islamists to broader, globally minded Islamists like those in al-Qaeda, but in practice Somali Islamism has almost always been a local matter. Attacks very rarely have happened outside Somalia, and when they do, such as the bombing of a World Cup viewing party in Uganda in 2010, they have been in direct response to a perceived threat (Uganda provides the bulk of the African Union troops fighting in Somalia).

The public display of allegiance could be a signal to al-Qaeda and others that al-Shabaab intends to expand its goals. It could also be a means of soliciting financial and logistical support; if al-Qaeda thinks it has strong allies in Somalia, it could funnel money their direction. It could also be a way of earning, for lack of a better term, street cred. If al-Shabaab were linked to al-Qaeda, it would be perceived as a more potent force. Regardless of the motivation, these statements have been made in a public way so that people all over the world, be they Islamists or not, have become aware of al-Shabaab's dedication to the cause.

Taarnby and Hallunbaek (2010) rightly point out that as al-Shabaab has moved closer to al-Qaeda in ideology, its use of propaganda has improved. Since alkataiib.net has been taken down, Al-Shabaab-related material gets dispersed through the Global Islamic Media Front (GIMF), a popular outlet for Islamist statements. The quality of al-Shabaab's video production has also developed a sleeker look with higher production values. Al-Shabaab also gets its message out through alqimmah.net, a Swedish-based website that supports jihadi causes and has hosted online chat sessions with members of al-Shabaab.

High quality DVDs are produced by al-Shabaab and shown largely to groups of young men in Eastleigh (Taarnby, 2010), a largely Somali neighborhood in Nairobi, Kenya. Again, we see the intent to reach beyond Somalia's borders, in this case in an explicit effort to recruit fighters. As mentioned previously, Somali Islamism is largely a local affair; however, al-Shabaab has been very active in recruiting Somalis in diaspora and making an effort to get them to return to Somalia to fight. There is the well-known example of the 21 Somali-Americans from Minneapolis who were recruited and travelled to Somalia, but the more prevalent and practical recruits are displaced Somalis living in Kenya.

Omar Hammami, known as Abu Mansoor al-Amriki, a Syrian-American from Alabama, entered Somalia in 2006, after the Islamic Courts Union had taken over most of the South but just prior to the Ethiopian invasion (Putzel, 2006). He joined al-Shabaab sometime in 2007.[1] Within months he was leading al-Shabaab forces and filming his attacks. The films of him planning and executing these attacks were used for recruitment purposes, and he took an increasing role in recruitment, due in large part to his being a native English speaker and relatively young. In an obvious attempt to reach a young, Western audience, he spoke in English and Arabic and played hip-hop music over scenes of his attacks.

Given that al-Shabaab is operating in a failed state, it is tempting to presuppose limited access to new media technology. That is not the case, however. Al-Shabaab clearly is adept at using the Internet, and their video production has seen a notable rise in quality with a noticeable increase in the use of graphics, music, and subtitles. By simply being a presence on the Internet, it demonstrates that it is not backwards or anti-modern but instead very much a part of the twenty-first century. It makes sense then that al-Shabaab would move into the newest platform of new media—social networking.

@HSMPRESS

"In the name of God the Merciful." That was the initial tweet of HSMPress on December 7, 2011. That first tweet was in Arabic, but subsequently al-Shabaab has tweeted only in English on this account. On December 9 it opened @ HSMPress_arabic and on December 29 opened @HSMPress_Somali, which have been used for Arabic and Somali Language tweets respectively. The English Language site is by far the most active.

Twitter is unlike the Islamist-focused websites typically used by Islamic extremists. Twitter is a social-networking and microblogging site. A user may post mini blogs called tweets of up to 140 characters. Al-Shabaab sees Twitter as a tool to manage its image. HSMPress has four ongoing uses for Twitter. The first is to make others aware of victories in battle. Second is to use dialogue with other tweeters and retweets of news stories to shape a positive image of al-Shabaab. Third is to provide up-to-the-minute reporting on activities going on in Somalia. And fourth is to demean its opponents.

Al-Shabaab is not the only Islamist group to utilize Twitter. The Taliban has had an official Twitter account longer but is far less adept at using it. The Taliban account simply recounts what Lundry, Corman, Furlow, and Errickson (2012) refer to as victorious battle stories with links to its official website, which provides more detail on the attacks. For the Taliban, Twitter is simply a tool for disseminating information about battlefield successes.

From the inception of its Twitter program, Al-Shabaab has been much more dynamic in its tweets. While there are certainly some claims of victorious battles by al-Shabaab, the tweets go beyond that. The Taliban tweets, which appear to be written by non-native English speakers, contain very little editorializing other than the use of pejorative terms like "puppets" or "crusaders" to describe Americans and Afghans. They simply state that an attack took place and the result. For example, "6 puppet [sic] killed and wounded as convoy hits IED. KANDAHAR, Jan 25."

Al-Shabaab's approach to a victorious battle story is quite different, going beyond merely claiming victory on the ground. For example, here is a tweet from December 7 on a Kenyan-led military operation in southern Somalia known as "Operation Linda Nchi" or "Protect the Country" in Swahili:

With the rising economic burden of operation Linda Nchi, the much-hyped #Kenyan invasion has faltered quite prematurely (It began October 16, 2011).

or

#KDF retreat from the towns they'd invaded, capitulating to their fate a mere 2 months into the extravagant but wretched operation #LindaNchi.

By emphasizing the economic costs to Kenya, these tweets look beyond the specific battle to focus on the larger goal of getting Kenyan troops out of Somalia. These tweets may be far more impactful than a statement claiming some troops were killed. The English is superior to that in the Taliban tweets, indicating that the writer is most likely a native English speaker.

Kenyan Defense Forces spokesman Major Emmanuel Chirchir has been tweeting about Operation Linda Nchi since it first began. Some of his tweets follow the victorious-battle story form and merely recount KDF victories. For example, from December 6:

#OperationLindaNchi KDF bombed 2 Al Shabaab camps south of Afmadow town, killing several Al shabaab fighters &destroyed technical vehicles.

The victorious battle story tweet is a common one and it is easy to see why both the KDF and al-Shabaab utilize it. These tweets are quick-and-easy propaganda. They show success that can lead others to support the mission. People are more likely to support a winning cause than a losing one, so getting news of one's victories out quickly and often gives the impression of winning (Lundry, 2012).

Al-Shabaab has taken the victorious battle story a step further by trying to prove its claims. It is easy to claim to have killed a certain number of soldiers. Al-Shabaab, whenever possible, photographs and publishes via Twitter ID cards of fallen enemy soldiers. On December 12 they published the IDs of twelve dead Burundian soldiers who were part of the African Union mission and killed in Mogadishu. Al-Shabaab has followed this practice whenever it is able to retrieve the IDs of fallen soldiers.

The practice of showing IDs has another purpose as well. It gives HSMPress legitimacy. Anyone can open a Twitter account under someone else's name. Theoretically, whoever posts to HSMPress could be anywhere in the world. Having physical access to the IDs of recently killed soldiers shows that the writer of the tweets is probably on the ground in Somalia and indeed a member of al-Shabaab.

That al-Shabaab has a better understanding of how Twitter works than does the Taliban can be seen in its use of the # and @ symbols. The hashtag (#) is used to reference a trend on Twitter. So everyone wanting to read tweets about Operation Linda Nchi will see al-Shabaab's tweets. Inevitably this means people will respond to al-Shabaab's tweets, both positively and negatively. Unlike the Taliban, al-Shabaab seems more than willing to engage fellow Twitter users in dialogue, their

second use of Twitter. This is evident by the use of the "at" sign (@). For example, a commenter tweeted:

@HSMPress the prophet must be turning over in his grave! Your use of religions as a weapon is truly abhorrent.

Al-Shabaab responded:

@DianaNTaylorwhat's beyond abhorrent is the collective Western Crusade against Islam of which you seem quite blasé about if not supportive.

Al-Shabaab was willing to engage in a dialogue with this person, something the Taliban does not do. This use of Twitter as a tool of engagement rather than just a place to post headlines, attracts more *Twitter* followers. As of this writing, HSMPress had over 11,000 followers as opposed to the Taliban's 6,900. This is despite the fact that the Taliban has had a Twitter feed longer than al-Shabaab, has posted almost ten times as many tweets (3,570 to al-Shabaab's 399), and has greater name recognition than al-Shabaab.

It is not just the random tweeter that al-Shabaab responds to. Nazanine Moshiri, an al-Jazeera reporter, wrote a blog piece about al-Shabaab to which it responded via Twitter (Moshiri, 2011). Moshiri then had a lengthy exchange with al-Shabaab. In this Twitter-based interview, al-Shabaab claims its treatment in the media is just propaganda and it seeks to refute some commonly held beliefs, such as that it is a fragmented group. It claims to be unified, confirms that it will not negotiate or surrender, and says it wants a Somalia free from foreign invasion and ruled "according to the Laws of Shari'ah (Qur'an)."

Al-Shabaab used the Twitter interview with Moshiri as a way to clarify its message and influence her future articles. By conducting the interview in public, were Moshiri to write a piece that did not include the entire exchange or somehow made it "propaganda," al-Shabaab would have the means to refute it (Moshiri opted to reprint the entire exchange in her blog) (Moshiri, 2011).

By using Twitter to engage with non-Islamists and those who oppose al-Shabaab ideology, HSMPress is shifting the use of online media. While extremist groups have used websites to engage in conversation, it has typically been with those who are predisposed to support their views and ideology. As Twitter is public and anybody, regardless of ideology, can engage with anyone else, HSMPress is expanding beyond De Koster and Houtman's description of online communities. To read the Global Islamic Media Front, for example, one must seek out its website. Few are likely to do that unless they have an interest in Islamism. Through the use of the hashtag on Twitter, however, al-Shabaab interacts with a much wider range of people. HSMPress has not run away from this interaction with the broader public but embraced it.

Furthermore, HSMPress is not a virtual community in the same way many other websites are. As mentioned before, HSMPress has over 11,000 followers, but it follows no one. It is "asymmetric microblogging" (Gruzd et al., 2011) as opposed to the type of virtual community seen on other sites.

Al-Shabaab also can use Twitter to exploit positive articles in the popular media. It tweeted a link to an article published on the online news site *Wales Online*. The article argued that al-Shabaab might be the entity best equipped to bring stability to Somalia (Williamson, 2011). Followers of HSMPress who read the article were exposed to a somewhat positive treatment of al-Shabaab in a Western-based, legitimate news site. It also has tweeted stories that make its opponents look bad. One example is a Middle East Online story that accuses the TFG of an inability to prevent rape in camps for the internally displaced (Middle East Online, 2011). This falls in line with Weimann's argument about the role that extremists claim for

themselves. Here al-Shabaab and its followers are cast not as the evil ones but as saviors who can bring stability to a nation and protect her people.

HSMPress has as a goal the establishment of legitimacy and credibility of al-Shabaab. To that end, they tweet any accomplishment that makes al-Shabaab seem more than a violent, religiously extreme group. On January 2, 2012, for example, there were a series of tweets about the education system al-Shabaab has put into place. It claims to have opened up new universities: Plasma University (a medical school in Mogadishu) and Hiiraan University, which offers degrees in nursing, Information Technology, and Islamic Studies in South-Central Somalia. Beyond expanding higher education in Somalia, HSMPress claims that al-Shabaab had "doused the flames of enmity between warring tribes." Tribal conflict is prevalent in Somalia and is one of the factors in preventing a unified, effective government from being able to govern.

HSMPress has also from time to time been able to provide a play-by-play of events as they happen. In these instances, the writers of the tweets take on an almost war correspondent role. On December 29, there was an attack on a Medecins Sans Frontiere (Doctors without Borders) office. HSMPress sent out a series of tweets about the attack as it was happening. They tended to be straight reports of the incident with very little editorializing. As soon as the incident was over, al-Shabaab went right back to criticizing the KDF on Twitter. Similar reports were posted on December 31 regarding an Ethiopian assault on the town of Baladweyn. Tweets from this incident again were largely reporting but with a little more editorializing. They claimed that al-Shabaab forces had pushed back the Ethiopians but then admitted in the end that they were forced to retreat from the town. This up-to-the-minute reporting also confirms the idea that whoever is writing the tweets is on the ground in Somalia.

This real-time reporting can also be a danger to al-Shabaab's enemies. One fear of intelligence agencies is that the extremists Twitter could disrupt battle coordination (Weimann, 2010). If HSMPress is sending out real-time tweets of, for example, Kenyan Defense Force troop movements, followers of HSMPress can use this information to set up ambushes, roadside bombs, and so on.

Within two days of joining Twitter, al-Shabaab engaged with Major Chirchir directly. On December 9, Major Chirchir had a series of tweets regarding the ultimate goals of the KDF mission. He said there would be an increase in troops in order to achieve the ultimate goal of a "secure, stable and prosperous Somalia, at peace with its neighbors." Al-Shabaab responded with taunts such as "Far too lofty an objective don't you think? Specially from men more accustomed to pillaging &extortion," and "50,000 Ethiopian troops couldn't pacify Somalia; you think a few disillusioned & disinclined Kenyan boys are up to the task?" And "Assets are worthless without men; your inexperienced boys flee from confrontation & flinch in the face of death."

This salvo of tweets undermining and belittling the KDF illustrates al-Shabaab's fourth use of Twitter, ridicule. Ridicule becomes important especially for those facing a stronger, better equipped opponent (Goodall et al., 2012). Al-Shabaab is not as strong militarily as the Kenyan Defense Forces, so it tries to defeat the KDF in the public arena. The KDF are boys not men. They are cowards. They are less capable than the Ethiopians, and even they failed at the task. Major Chirchir had a somewhat feckless response to al-Shabaab and simply asked them to surrender. It appears as if he was not prepared for dealing with al-Shabaab in such a public forum.

Besides insinuating that the Kenyans are cowards, al-Shabaab has also played to stereotypes. One tweet discussing how the KDF runs away states, "Indeed they 'Run like a Kenyan,'" capi-

talizing on the idea that Kenyans are particularly good at track and field events and are using that talent to run away from combat.

While al-Shabaab may not be as strong militarily, it does seem to be beating the KDF in the Twitter War. Major Chirchir, in a clear attempt to portray al-Shabaab negatively, posted pictures on January 11, 2012 purporting to be of a man being stoned to death by members of al-Shabaab. He claimed the man was a Kenyan who had been killed early that week in the town of Kismayo for disagreeing with al-Shabaab. It was likely, he said, that two more men were to be killed that Friday. A few hours later, it was revealed by an independent journalist that the man in question, Mohamed Abukar Ibrahim, was Somali and was killed in 2009 by a different Islamist group, Hizbul Islam, for adultery. Hizbul Islam had subsequently merged with al-Shabaab. The photos were easy to identify as they had won second place in the World Press Photo contest in 2010.

Once the photos were revealed to have been from 2009, HSMPress jumped on Major Chirchir:

@MajorEChirchir #KDF incompetence transcends all possible limits this time & highlights amount of lies dispensed in order to hide the truth,

and

They seem unsophisticated even in their propaganda campaign. A simple Google search would have saved them such an embarrassment.

They then posted links to two different news stories with photos verifying that the incident in question was from 2009 and did not involve al-Shabaab. The al-Shabaab writers capitalized on Major Chirchir's actions by referring to his "half-witted Twitter Psyops" and calling him "Major Pinocchio."

Chirchir for his part did admit that posting the photo was a mistake (whether he knew the photo was from 2009 is unclear) but did stand by his statement that a man was executed by al-Shabaab in Kismayo earlier that week. He also maintained that the execution of two more people that Friday was still likely to occur. By January 12, HSMPress had moved on and was back to tweeting about events on the ground. Major Chirchir, however, had to do damage control via Twitter for a few days as other Twitter users jumped on him for such a blatant use of propaganda.

This incident was fantastic for al-Shabaab. This stoning that was intended to emphasize al-Shabaab's cruelty instead placed the KDF on the defensive. Major Chirchir and the KDF's use of such transparent propaganda made them look incompetent. While al-Shabaab could apparently not resist some name calling, their most effective strategy was to sit back and let other people do the fighting for them. A number of Twitter users called out Major Chirchir for attempting to deceive the public.

Al-Shabaab took a lesson from this incident—part of making yourself look good is making your enemy look bad. Starting January 15, just a few days after the photo incident, HSMPress began to tweet about civilian causalities. They mentioned five children who were killed when a KDF shell hit their home, another incident resulting in civilians being taken to a hospital, and another concerning refugees killed in a camp. All of which they blame on the KDF. The tweets are matter-of-fact and lack hyperbole, indicating a belief that the best method of damaging the KDF's image is to take a more sober approach.

GLARING OMISSIONS

It is also worth noting what is not on the HSMPress Twitter feed. Famine was declared in Somalia in July 2011, yet there is almost no mention of it in the first two months of tweets. If al-Shabaab intends to govern, then obviously a food crisis is

something it will need to solve. But al-Shabaab's only tweets on the subject did not come until January 30, 2012, and then to say that the food from the International Committee of the Red Cross could be a health hazard. Al-Shabaab subsequently banned the Red Cross from areas under its control (Chonghaile, 2012) but, as of this writing, had not mentioned the ban on Twitter.

Al-Shabaab also has been silent on major news stories from Somalia that seemingly could have been used for propaganda purposes. No mention was made of the rescue of two hostages by U.S. Navy SEALs on January 25. The two were being held by pirates, who are unrelated to al-Shabaab and Islamism in general, and were held in central Somalia in an area not controlled by al-Shabaab. Nevertheless, it was a major news event and one HSMPress could have used to discuss American imperialism and foreign intervention. But it got no mention whatsoever.

Craig Baxam, the former U.S. army soldier who had planned to join al-Shabaab (Zapotosky, 2012) but was arrested by Kenyan police in late December, also never has been mentioned. It is possible that because Baxam's plan was not particularly well thought out and that he never reached Somalia, his story was not deemed worthy of addressing. However, it seems that HSMPress could in some way capitalize on an Iraq War veteran converting to Islam and attempting to join al-Shabaab.

The other curious omission from the Twitter feed is a lack of recruitment through Twitter. In none of the tweets does HSMPress seem to be looking for new members, and there is no evidence that Twitter has played a role in recruitment. Considering that the English language feed is more active and popular than either the Arabic or Somali language feeds, it stands to reason that recruitment is not a primary objective. This is not to suggest that recruitment is not an overall objective of al-Shabaab, just to say that it is not using Twitter to accomplish that goal. The 21 Minneapolis men who were recruited to al-Shabaab were recruited prior to HSMPress coming online as were Abu

Mansoor al-Amriki and Jehad Mostafa, a Californian of Syrian descent who also joined al-Shabaab (Watson, 2012).

While recruitment may not be a prime objective of HSMPress, one of the intended audiences for extremist sites in general is their enemies, meaning the "public who is part of the opposing socio-political community in the conflict" (Weimann, 2006, p. 61). Al-Shabaab is using Twitter with this in mind. It attempts to influence the public opinion in the countries of governments that may be at odds with al-Shabaab by demonstrating that it is the moral force in the conflict and the KDF, AU, TFG, and U.S. are the violent oppressors.

As yet, the U.S. government has not attempted to shut down HSMPress as they have with other extremist sites. But if it did branch into outright recruitment, that might be the tipping point for the government. Continuing to let al-Shabaab make public statements may provide a useful tool for various intelligence agencies to learn about the group in a relatively harmless way. If al-Shabaab should move toward recruitment or encouraging attacks in areas outside of Somalia, the U.S. government might consider that more of a threat and take steps to block the site or shut it down entirely. Both sides are aware of how far they can go and are careful not to cross that threshold.

CONCLUSION

There is a curious contradiction at play here. Al-Shabaab has rejected many Western ideas and technologies yet adopted others. They have banned movies, Western music, watching sporting events, and even the wearing of bras (Routray, 2009). Yet, they have completely embraced the Internet and social media. This is a partial technological determinism. Jeffrey Gettleman points out that al-Shabaab has been technically proficient from very early on, building complex roadside and suicide bombs (2011). And as mentioned before, it has produced high-quality videos and had a presence on the Internet for years. Given that al-Shabaab

has proven adept at using technology and media in the past, it is not surprising that it has continued to develop media skills and branched out into social media. It is a fast and relative inexpensive way of disseminating a message to a larger audience. Given Twitter's popularity, it also means that people will not have to look very hard to find an al-Shabaab presence on the Internet. It is located in one of the most popular Websites in the world.

Al-Shabaab has proven adept at using Twitter for a number of purposes, most of which serve the larger goal of crafting a positive image. It describes its victories in battle, does its best to embarrass and humiliate opponents, and uses Twitter as a news outlet of sorts to provide information about ongoing current events. Al-Shabaab is effective and consistent in its use of the microblogging site, and it has only been at it for a couple of months. It is providing the model for new media warfare. It should not come as a surprise if, in the future, we see Twitter being used in a similar fashion by groups such as *Boko Haram* (Nigeria), the Lord's Resistance Army, or even other branches of al-Qaeda.

REFERENCES

BBC. (2006). *Islamists claim Mogadishu victory*. Retrieved January 20, 2012, from http://news.bbc.co.uk/2/hi/africa/5047766.stm

BBC. (2012). *Somalia's al-Shabab join al-Qaeda*. Retrieved February 15, 2012, from http://www.bbc.co.uk/news/world-africa-16979440

Central Intelligence Agency. (2012). *CIA World Fact Book*. Retrieved January 23, 2012, from https://www.cia.gov/library/publications/the-world-factbook/geos/so.html

Chonghaile, C. N. (2012, January 31). Somali Islamists ban Red Cross. *The Guardian*. Retrieved February 1, 2012, from http://www.guardian.co.uk/world/2012/jan/31/somali-islamists-ban-red-cross?newsfeed=true

De Koster, W., & Houtman, D. (2008). Stormfront is like a second home to me: On virtual community formation by right-wing extremists. *Information Communication and Society*, *11*(6), 1155–1176. doi:10.1080/13691180802266665.

Gettleman, J. (2011). Somalia's rebels Embrace Twitter as a Weapon. *New York Times*. Retrieved February 1, 2012, from http://www.nytimes.com/2011/12/15/world/africa/somalias-rebels-embrace-twitter-as-a-weapon.html?_r=3

Goodall, H. L. Jr, Cheong, P. H., Fleischer, K., & Corman, S. R. (2012). Rhetorical charms: The promise and pitfalls of humor and ridicule as strategies to counter extremist narratives. *Perspectives in Terrorism*, *6*(1), 70–79.

Gruzd, A., Wellman, B., & Takhteyev, Y. (2011, July 25). Imagining Twitter as an imagined community. *The American Behavioral Scientist*, *55*(10), 1294–1318. doi:10.1177/0002764211409378.

Halverson, J. R., Goodall, H. L. Jr, & Corman, S. R. (2011). *Master Narratives of Islamic Extremism*. New York: Palgrave Macmillan.

Ibrahim, M. (2010). Radio stations with no music may be shut in Somalia. *New York Times*. Retrieved January 23, 2012, from http://www.nytimes.com/2010/04/19/world/africa/19somalia.html

International Crisis Group. (2005). *Counterterrorism in Somalia: Losing hearts and Minds?* Retrieved from http://www.crisisgroup.org/en/regions/africa/horn-of-africa/somalia/095-counter-terrorism-in-somalia-losing-hearts-and-minds.aspx

Lundry, C., Corman, S. R., Furlow, R. B., & Errickson, K. W. (2012). Cooking the books: Strategic inflation of casualty reports by extremists in the Afghanistan conflict. *Studies in Conflict and Terrorism*. doi:10.1080/1057610X.2012.666821.

Middle East Online. (2011). Season of rape in Somalia: 'Climate of fear' sweeps IDP camps. Retrieved January 30, 2012, from http://www.middle-east-online.com/english/?id=49664

Moshiri, N. (2011). Al-Shabab starts tweeting. *Al-Jazeera*. Retrieved January 30, 2012, from http://blogs.aljazeera.net/africa/2011/12/13/al-shabab-starts-tweeting

Moshiri, N. (2011). Somalia's Shabab fighters take to Twitter. *Al-Jazeera*. Retrieved January 30, 2012, from http://www.aljazeera.com/news/africa/2011/12/20111213166218336342.html

Ploch, L. (2010, November 3). *Counterterrorism in East Africa: The U.S. Response*. Congressional Research Service Report P.13.

Putzel, C. (2010) American Jihadi [Vanguard]. Cerissa Tanner, Christof Putzel (Producers). San Francisco, CA: Current TV.

Routray, B. P. (2011). Why ban just the bra in Somalia? Ban everything. Ban food. Ban life. *Al-Arabiya News*. Retrieved February 8, 2012, from http://www.alarabiya.net/views/2011/07/29/159848.html Last accessed February 8, 2012

Taarnby, M., & Hallunbaek, L. (2010). Al Shabaab: The internationalization of militant Islamism in Somalia and the implications for radicalization processes in Europe. *Danish Ministry of Justice Report*, 13-14.

United Nations Security Council Resolutions for 1992. Retrieved January 20, 2012, from http://www.un.org/documents/sc/res/1992/scres92.htm

Watson, J. (2012). Americans rise in rank inside Somalia jihadi group. *The Guardian*. Retrieved from http://www.guardian.co.uk/world/feedarticle/10041431

Weimann, G. (2006). Terror on the Internet: The New Arena, the New Challenges (pp. 54-56, 61). Washington, DC: United States Institute of Peace Press.

Weimann, G. (2010). Terror on Facebook, Twitter and YouTube. *The Brown Journal of World Affairs*, *XVI*(II), 48.

Williamson, D. (2011). Terror group Somalia's only hope for peace and stability. *Wales Online*. Retrieved January 30, 2012, from http://www.walesonline.co.uk/news/welsh-politics/welsh-politics-news/2011/12/13/terror-group-somalia-s-only-hope-for-peace-and-stability-91466-29942080

Zapotosky, M. (2012). Craig Baxam, ex-U.S. soldier, charged with trying to aid terror group al-Shabab. *The Washington Post*. Retrieved February 1, 2012, from http://www.washingtonpost.com/local/craig-baxam-ex-us-soldier-charged-with-trying-to-aid-terror-group-al-shabab/2012/01/09/gIQAJvMbmP_story.html

ENDNOTES

[1] There are unconfirmed reports that al-Amriki was killed sometime in 2011 but he later appeared in a 2012 video. In the video he claims that he has disagreed with al-Shabaab over interpretations of sharia and his life may be in danger.

Chapter 18
Political Use of Internet During the Benin 2011 Presidential Campaign:
Fad Effect or Mid-Term Strategy?

Bellarminus Gildas Kakpovi
University Libre Bruxelles, Belgium

ABSTRACT

During the Benin presidential election of March 2011, a new communication tool (Internet) was added to the traditional tools of electoral campaign: meetings, electoral promotion gimmicks, political songs, broadcast and print media, and posters. Indeed, the three main candidates to the presidential elections integrated Internet in their comprehensive strategy, recruiting staff to take care of a Website, several user profiles on famous social networks. Meanwhile, the Internet is used by only 2.2% of the population. This chapter analyzes the Websites of the three candidates, paying particular attention to graphic design, uploaded available information, frequency of updating, and interaction with the audience. It also scrutinizes the use of various profiles on social networks. The chapter then interrogates why there was such an important investment on the Internet during this campaign, whereas data show that very few potential voters are actually connected to the Internet in Benin. This chapter identifies the role of Internet campaigning and the place that the Internet has taken in the electoral communication strategies, and tries to understand the real purpose behind this use.

INTRODUCTION

The Benin 2011 presidential election campaign was marked by an evolution as regards tools and communication practices. Indeed, the Internet became a major tool integrated into each candidate's

strategy. With the advent of this new tool—*which completes the traditional tool-kit used[1], especially the media*—candidates had a strong online presence. We can say that for the first time, the Internet was incorporated into political communication for an election in Benin. But how important was

DOI: 10.4018/978-1-4666-4197-6.ch018

this new tool in the electoral apparatus during the 2011 presidential campaign in Benin? Was it just a fad or did candidates' staff try to build a real coherent and consistent strategy? Which public was targeted?

This chapter intends to answer these questions by providing contextual elements which can aid understanding the importance of the 2011 presidential election on the one hand and the sociological and technical situation of the Internet and its users in Benin on the other hand. Then the tools used are outlined and described before analyzing how Internet strategies were built.

2011 PRESIDENTIAL ELECTIONS: THE KEY ISSUES AT STAKE

Since "La *mue politique*"[2] (Frère, 1998) that occurred in Benin through the holding of the National Conference of Vital Forces of the Nation[3], there have been several presidential elections in the country. Thus, the one held in 2011 was the fifth one. The first four elections showed "*l'habituation électorale*"[4] (Banégas, 2003) of Benin and bore out "the fact that the country was a kind of exception among West African countries" (Mayrargue, 2006, p. 157). But in 2011, to everyone's surprise, Benin coped with one of the most critical crisis the country had ever experienced under the Democratic Renewal era. The voting was held under difficult conditions. Indeed, the Independent National Electoral Commission (INEC), in charge of organizing the voting, had not been set in time and the voters' list established was strongly disputed. Moreover, the voting was postponed twice and the country faced political tensions like never before. The INEC received fourteen candidacies. But 13 candidates finally competed because Antoine Dayori, second Vice-President of the outgoing National Assembly, decided to withdraw, three days before the voting day, to support candidate Abdoulaye Bio Tchané.

Due to their political experience, their stature, or even their reputation, three candidates (Yayi Boni—*outgoing President*; Adrien Houngbédji—*single candidate, representative of the traditional opposition*; and Abdoulaye Bio Tchané—*President of the West African Development Bank until he resigned to run for presidency*) among the thirteen were seen as the main challengers by observers.

Four major facts characterized the pre-electoral period: the introduction of a computerized permanent voters' list for the first time in Benin electoral process; Yayi Boni's strong determination to stay in power; the mobilization and the gathering, for the first time, of the opposition forces around a unique candidacy; and the arrival of an outsider, Abdoulaye Bio Tchané, who reminded Candidate Yayi Boni of 2006 in many ways.

Since voters' lists were traditionally established manually, the advent of the computerized permanent voters' list really broke with habits. The setting up of this new list was a consensual decision motivated by the high number of fraud cases registered during previous elections. However this new tool had been politicized from the beginning of the process so much so that it incurred many people's wrath. This made it difficult to carry out. The opposition denounced that more than a million voters who favored them had not been counted by the census. Many associations from the "civil society" merged in the collective "Fors Elections," headed by Mr. Joseph Djogbénou. They also deplored several irregularities which harmed the computerized permanent voters' list; they then requested the postponement of the elections. The vote was initially supposed to take place on February 27th, before being postponed twice: first to March 6, and then to March 13, which was finally the election day.

The second issue was the potential second term of the outgoing President, Yayi Boni. The candidate, for his own succession, offered his people "d'aller plus loin ensemble[5]," meaning to go beyond what he had done during his five-year term. After "the Change," he was praised during his 2006 campaign—*change that was paradoxically more in line with what had already been done, and not a real break with the habits* (Mayrargue, Op.cit.). Yayi Boni then came back with a new concept: "the Restructuration," a motto that conveyed his reform program to be implemented during his possible second term, starting with the revision of the constitution. Contrary to his situation during the 2006 campaign, he then had to defend his record. His strategy consisted in pointing out the assets of his record. But he was criticized on the liabilities of the said record; and most of time, he defended himself playing on emotions instead of giving persuasive answers to questions asked. The outgoing president underlined several actions and achievements that should be a point in his government's favor. Among them, he estimated that the most important were: promoting micro-credit for women, making primary school and caesarean section free, and building several road infrastructures, notably the Godomey exchange.

After being elected in 2006, and according to his campaign promises, Yayi Boni set a zero-interest microcredit program for Beninese women. Each woman received 30,000 F CFA, that is, some US$58. The opposition claimed the amount granted was too low. In response to criticisms, supporters of the President produced reports on groups of women who had benefited from that microcredit program, showing them thanking Yayi Boni for having implemented such a project, no matter the amount they were granted. One can easily read between the lines of that populist measure (i.e., zero-interest microcredit): while satisfying women and having their support, not only do you secure their vote, but you also make sure their husband and the family circle will vote for you. Making caesarean sections free also aimed to entice women. The opposition attacked the president-candidate over this second measure he stated as one of the greatest of his term. During his meetings, candidate Houngbédji often asked his supporters: "how many of our women deliver their baby by a caesarean section? Were we sup-

posed to wait until the situation got out of hands?" The Yayi Boni camp also brandished results never achieved before in the field of road infrastructures, pointing out the Godomey exchange and several other roads built. Indeed, they put forward that during his five-year term, the president-candidate had built more roads than all the other presidents combined since the independence of the country. But when you look into the facts, there is no evidence to corroborate this theory.

The third specific aspect of this election was the gathering of the opposition parties around a single candidate. This had never happened before. Mr. Adrien Houngbédji, former Prime Minister and former President of the National Assembly, was the one chosen to represent the whole opposition merged in "l'Union fait la Nation". By gathering in the new single coalition "[…] 'l'Union fait la Nation', we want to bequeath to future generations, a more united and stronger political class to serve the whole Beninese people […]"[6]. Of course, one of the short-term goals of this alliance was to win the elections. But, "l'Union fait la Nation" was more an incidental alliance to block Yayi Boni than a real ideological union. The closer the voting day got, the more the coalition obtained other supports materialized through ceremonies for protocols signature widely broadcast in the media. Finally, this ended up in giving birth to a very heterogeneous and unholy group. As for the choice of the coalition's candidate, it had been a real brainteaser. But finally they decided to be represented by Mr. Adrien Houngbédji, who was presenting himself for the fifth time and had already been a king maker, working behind the scenes in the governments of Mathieu Kérékou and Nicéphore Soglo. In 2006 he was beaten by the "newcomer," Yayi Boni, who was then supported by the same ones who finally created "l'Union fait la Nation[7]."

The last issue at stake was the arrival of a new candidate, an outsider whose profile reminded, in many ways, the 2006 Yayi Boni. At the moment he announced his election, Bio Tchané was the President of the West African Development Bank, like Yayi Boni in 2006. Both are native of the North of the country, a region where people usually support the son of the land, because, as explained by Richard Banégas, voters' choice is generally motivated by "family or ethnics links, and vote-catching" (Banégas, 2003, p. 453). Moreover, Candidates Yayi Boni and Abdoulaye Bio Tchané are both bankers. The only main difference between the two men is that unlike Yayi Boni, Bio Tchané had already occupied a management position in the State, as Finance Minister in the Government of Kerekou, before becoming the Africa Department Director of the International Monetary Fund (IMF), from 2002 to 2008.

The candidacies of those three main challengers strengthened the regionalist feeling as well as the vote-catching-*as advocated by Richard Banégas*-during the 2011 elections. Indeed, "l'Union Fait la Nation" was described as a coalition of southern coalition while Yayi Boni was seen as the president of north people. Abdoulaye Bio Tchané was considered as the candidate of only one department of the north of the country: Borgou.

SOCIOLOGICAL AND TECHNICAL CONTEXT OF THE INTERNET

In their communication strategies, the three candidates gave a major role, in different degrees, to the new technical tool--the Internet; and yet, it only impacts a very few possible voters. Before talking about how the Internet was used during that campaign, we should look over the Internet accessibility and its use in Benin.

Like most African countries, Benin did not remain on the fringes of technological improvements and had been using the Internet since 1995. At the beginning, the Internet was seen as a luxury "product." But its access and use have been democratized over the year. Only big administrations with important financial means used the Internet in its early days in Benin. Browsing for one hour

in a cybercafé was too expensive regarding the low purchasing power in the country. In 1996, you had to pay about 5,000 F CFA (some US$10) to get one browsing hour. This price level decreased progressively. In the early 2000s, it dropped by half to 2,500 F CFA (i.e., about US$5). In spite of this reduction in the price, connecting oneself on the Internet remained too expensive for the huge part of the population. Plus, the digital divide noticed on the world scale was reinforced by a national one. "At the end of 2001, Internet users in developing countries were local elite from the wealthiest classes, and who had the highest level of education" (PNUD, 2001; Vedel, p. 207). In Benin, the figures speak for themselves shown in Table 1.

This low Internet penetration rate can be explained by five factors. First, the standard of living of the population is low. According to the United Nations Children's Fund (UNICEF)[9], in 2009, the gross national income per capita (GNI) was US$750. Not every citizen can then afford an Internet connection given the prices mentioned prior. Moreover, we should take into account the prior purchase of a computer with its accessories. The second factor is socio-cultural (Vedel, op.cit., p. 207), since using computer equipments implies some technical and linguistic predispositions.

The third reason is the lack of political will. Politicians did not earlier back the expansion of the Internet, nor did they help overcome obstacles by establishing centers where people could be taught

Table 1. Evolution of Internet Users' Number in Benin, since 2000

Year	Users	Population	%
2000	15.000	6. 419.100	0.2%
2006	100.000	7.714.766	1.3%
2009	160.000	8.791.832	1.8%
2010	200.000	9.056.010	2,2%
2011	277.040	9.598.787[8]	3%

Source: http://www.internetworldstats.com/africa.htm

the basics of computer science. Primary schools, high schools and even public administrations seriously suffered from lack of computer equipment.

Another factor is the access to electricity. Indeed, In Benin "the electrification level is still low. In 2004, 20% of Beninese households had an access to electricity compared with less than 2% in rural areas[10]."

The fifth and last factor is illiteracy that avoids a high Internet penetration. It is estimated that some 67.4% of the population is illiterate; and women constitute 78.1% of this proportion. According to the 2002 General Census of Population and Dwellings, in spite of the efforts that authorities, national and international NGOs have been making for decades, 2.3 million people aged 15 and over are still illiterate. "The literacy subsector faces institutional, quality, relevance, efficiency and access problems which have caused dysfunctions resulting in high drop-out, failure and relapse into illiteracy rates." (Ibid)

Despite all those difficulties and the digital divide mentioned previously, the situation has evolved positively thanks to local authorities who installed a submarine fibre-optic cable system, providing thus the country with a higher connection capacity. Consequently, the Internet gained in popularity and became a tool more and more used by Beninese. Over the 277.002 Internet users registered in June 30, 2012, 142.600[11] (i.e., 1.5% of the population) have one or several Facebook profile(s). We can then notice that internet penetration remains quite low. Nevertheless, the three main candidates devoted a special attention to this medium during the 2011 presidential elections. What were the specific tools they gave priority to and how did they use them?

THE MAIN INTERNET TOOLS USED TO CAMPAIGN

Americans are pioneers in online campaign practices. Most researchers (Coleman & Hall, 2001; Bimber & Davis, 2003; Chadwick, 2006; Anstead

& Chadwick, 2009; Davis et al., 2009; Foot et al., 2009; Gibson & Ward, 2012) consider that the 1992 American primary campaign has been the starting point of the use of Internet for electoral purpose. Since Bill Clinton's staff posted his biography and excerpts from his speeches on a server located at Chapel Hill—*a university of North Carolina*—specialists have been keeping on prophesying on the first online campaign. Chadwick (2006, p. 152) and Kirsten Foot et al. (2009) are both of the opinion that it was a "false start." In their diachronic study on online campaign, they define three phases. The first one is called "the discovery" and is split into two steps: experimentation and exploration. The second phase occurs during the 2000 American presidential elections and is called the "transition" one. And then came the last phase during the 2004 campaign when the Internet definitely gained respectability; it is the beginning of the "maturation" stage, mainly characterized by the commercial side of websites (Davis et al., 2009; p. 15). That campaign was "The First Real U.S. Internet Election" (Andrew Chadwick). Remember how Howard Dean, Governor of the small state of Vermont, used the Internet to lead a petition campaign to be able to stand for Democratic primary campaign.

On another side of the world, during the South Korean presidential elections in 2002, the winning candidate, Roh Moo-Hyun, fully integrated the Internet into his campaign strategy, through a social network with more than 80 000 supporters who were very active on online forums (Elledge, as cited in Chadwick, 2006, p. 163). In France, UK, Belgium and several other countries, the Internet becomes increasingly important in political communication during elections. That was what inspired Kevin Swaddle's concept called "Hi-Tech Elections" (1988, pp. 32-35).

In developed countries, the Internet is used through three main tools: websites, blogs and "online controlled communication tools" developed and administrated by the user (Davis et al., op.cit., p. 21). The latter can be divided into two different tools types: social network on one hand

and "podcast" channels like Youtube or Daily-morion, on the other hand, which host videos and whose development is astonishing. Davis et al. (Ibid) say that it is a tremendous evolution. Social networks experience an exponential growth of users and the Internet then logically evolves towards social media.

These tools play four roles: "to inform; to involve; to connect; and to mobilize" (Ibid., Foot et al., op.cit., Maarek, op.cit., Nadeau & Bastien, op.cit.). *To inform*: according to Kirsten Foot et al., the information function consists in giving information about the candidate's biography, the voting and also about the campaign itself; excerpts of the candidate speeches in various formats (audio, video or written) are posted too. *To involve*: here, the goal is to give Internet users the opportunity to join the campaign or a group of sponsors supporting the candidate. To get people involved, the staff also makes candidate's campaign materials and schedule available on the website. *To connect*: it consists in keeping Internet users posted about new supporters as well as personalities—*which are precious support*—joining the candidate's camp. *To mobilize*: by allowing visitors to download materials for the online campaign (pictures and logos) and the offline campaign (desktop wallpapers for example, in order to campaign via the computer and then directly impact all those who will use that device). Internet users can also use the "web-to-e-mail" option to email links to their friends, directly from the Candidate's website. Interactivity is one of the strengths of a mature website. But, due to many reasons and especially logistical ones, candidates have sometimes difficulties in carrying it out properly.

In the USA, France or everywhere else where "online campaigning" is developed enough, the way Internet is used to campaign during elections widely depends on the country's political culture (Foot et al., p. 40). According to Kluver (2005), Martin and Stronach (1992), and Foot et al. (op. cit.), the political culture can be defined as a symbolic environment made up of several elements: political practices, political institutions, histori-

cal and philosophical experiences, and religious orientations. It is not a great importance whether the election takes place in the USA, France, or in Benin; what matters is that candidate should always gauge if the political environment is conductive to Internet practices for election purpose.

Studying online campaigning in Benin implies taking into account specificities of the context. Although the Internet was widely used during the 2011 presidential campaign, it came in addition to traditional communication means such as giant or neighborhood (smaller) meetings, media, and propagandist songs to promote candidates (singers are usually paid for that or invited to candidate's meetings where they sing and get their artist fee). During those elections there were also big posters' campaigns all across the country as well as small posters which were handed in huge number and in several regions.

In the framework of this paper, we are going to examine with fine-tooth comb the content of the Internet tools used by the three candidates: their websites, their blogs and other social network forms. To carry out our study, we will keep the four functions of an online campaign, as described before, added to four other indicators: websites' home pages, interactivity capability, updating, graphic organization and sections of websites. These indicators will help us measure how the websites fulfill the four functions of a site designed for electoral purpose: to inform, to involve, to connect and to mobilize. Then, we will go further in the analysis thanks to discussions we had with members from the communication units of the three candidates.

The three candidates considerably used the Internet during the campaign. They mobilized different online tools. For example, for the President-candidate, Yayi Boni, "there are several tools such as websites, blogs, the official president's site, a Facebook page, a Twitter account; we tried to be present on every 'channel' and use all the resources available with Web 2.0[12]." All the communication units gave priority to the Websites.

THE THREE CANDIDATES' WEBSITES

Candidate Houngbédji had two official Web-sites[13]. The first one was his personal site, while the second was the website for the UN coalition. Maurice Tossou, a member of his communication unit stated that: "new media like the Internet has had an important dimension in our work…"[14]. Luc Vodouhè, head of that unit, described the Internet as a "hypermedia[15]." As for the outgoing president, he had only one official website whose goal was to "inform the 'general public," according to Enoch Gourou-Béra[16], one among his many communication advisors. The third candidate, Abdoulaye Bio-Tchané, also had only one official website. The head of his communication unit, Dénis Babaékpa[17], declared that his team "worked a lot with the Internet." Daniel Sossouhounto, a specialist in public communication who resigned from his position in the communication unit of Bio Tchané to finally be a mere observer of the campaign, considers that:

Only 'L'Union Fait la Nation' and Candidate Yayi Boni really used the Internet. Bio Tchané's camp did not really focused on Internet during the campaign. They did have a website but they constantly posted nonsense stuffs. And the website did not really boost the candidate. Meanwhile, the two other main challengers were using the Internet to weaken Abdoulaye Bio Tchané…[18]

The two websites of Candidate Houngbédji were: houngbedjipresident.com and adrienhoung-bedji.com. Yayi Boni's website was: boniyayi.bj. As for Abdoulaye Bio Tchané, it was: abt2011.com.

Candidates' homepages had been designed with great care. As soon as you got connected to Adrien Houngbédji's first website (Figure 1), during the pre-campaign phase, a life-sized business card displayed with this slogan: "Nous allons remettre de l'ordre dans la maison Bénin[19]." But right before the campaign began, this picture was switched and replaced with many others showing the candidate with his peers from "L'Union Fait la Nation." On his second Website (Figure 2), one could read: "Maintenant, avançons![20]," and this motto was accompanied by a family picture with young leaders from the coalition, in motion. This image was supposed to convey the dynamism proposed by the candidate to Beninese.

On the homepage of Yayi Boni's website (Figure 3), one could watch a very laudatory report. In fact, it was an advertorial directed and produced by Golfe TV channel[21] which had signed a contract with the outgoing president for his campaign. The video element, which had already been broad-casted on the TV channel, outlined the main achievements of the president-candidate during his first term. On March 13, 2011, the adverto-rial was switched and replaced with another video in which the head of state apologized to all those who had not been registered during the establishment of the computerized permanent voters' list. His statement sounded like a confes-sion, an admission of dysfunctions in the elec-toral process. Those dysfunctions had already been denounced by civil society and opponents before, in vain! Above the video player and the numerous videos available, there was a head-and-shoulders picture of the candidate with one of his campaign slogans: "Ensemble plus loin, Toujours plus loin."[22]

On the homepage of Abdoulaye Bio Tchané's Website (Figure 4), there was one of his slogans: "Avenir d'un Bénin Triomphant."[23] This slogan had not been chosen at random. Indeed, it is an acrostic with the initials "ABT" from the candi-date's name. The baobab, which was his campaign logo, was just beside the acrostic. There was also a slide show displaying pictures of the candidate with African and international personalities.

One striking thing is the similarities of the graphic charters. On the four websites (of the three candidates) the dominant colors were the same

Figure 1. First Website Homepage of candidate Adrien Houngbédji. www.houngbedjipresident.com

Figure 2. Second Website Homepage of candidate Adrien Houngbédji. www.adrienhoungbedji.com

Figure 3. Website Homepage of candidate Yayi Boni. www.boniyayi.bj

Figure 4. Website Homepage of candidate Abdoulaye Bio Tchané. www.abt2011.com

ones used during the whole campaign. The said colors were used both for traditional communication tools and on Internet. Adrien Houngbédji and his staff chose the blue color because they wanted to make Beninese dream. They tried to use the oneiric function of that color. Their strategy seemed to consist in leading the campaign and the people by the dream, a dream for better days and more wisdom. On the pictures published on the websites of the candidate, he wore blue suits. And, the blue color, synonym of youth and refreshment, was also a way to respond the attacks from the outgoing president's camp who called the 69-year-old Candidate Houngbédji and his peers: the "old school" politicians.

Yayi Boni and Abdoulaye Bio Tchané chose the green color. In the case of the outgoing president, that color reminded his 2006 winning campaign. The green was everywhere: on their official documents as well as on their websites. On boniyayi.bj, the candidate's slogan appeared on a green background. A thin yellow line passed through the background where there was a cowrie shell, logo of the candidate and symbol of money and wealth.

On the website of Bio Tchané, the slogan in form of acrostic was written in green on a-*lighter*-green background. Using this color was a way to refer to the national flag and the second verse of the national anthem: "…the green symbolizes the hope for renewal […]"[24]. These two candidates positioned themselves as the only ones that could bring hope to their compatriots. The green color also refers to "a vision for a green Benin," one of the key points in Yayi Boni's social program in 2006. At that time, the candidate promised "the revival of agriculture for a new Benin."

The interactivity, which allows candidate or their staff to launch a set of exchanges with their Website's visitors through commentaries (Greffet & Vedel, 2012, p. 42) is a fundamental aspect of an "online campaign." At the beginning of the campaign the three candidates tried to develop that interactivity on their Websites. But as the electoral campaign progressed, interactivity experienced different fates according to the camps. Even though the Websites of the candidates had been largely inspired by American, British and Occidental ones—*in spite of the different contexts*—their staffs quickly put the interactivity "option" in the back burner. They were certainly afraid that possible negative comments posted could set a self-destroying process in motion. On the Websites of Adrien Houngbédji, the interactive sections were: "The Forum," "Comments," and "Contacts." Comments were posted by Internet users from all walks of life, especially by Beninese living abroad and by expatriates living in Benin. But it seemed like comments posted had been selected with meticulous care because they were all laudatory. There is even some evidence of the filtration of comments. Indeed, in front of each comment, moderators always used verbs like: "so-and-so hammers out," "so-and-so tells," "so-and-so states." In addition, under the management of Parfait Ahoyo, head of Houngbédji's online campaign, dozens of young people were in charge of the Internet strategic watch. Mr. Ahoyo's team also put a poll online to allow people to give their opinion about themes proposed by the "New Media" section of the communication unit. Those sections encouraging interaction—*even though it was not really an interaction since the candidate never answered comments*—disappeared from one of Houngbédji's Websites in the midst of the campaign.

Interactivity experienced the same fate on the Website of outgoing President, Yayi Boni. The sections "Contact" (where one could fill a form to send a message to the candidate or his staff) or "Discussion" (where there was a kind of interactivity at the beginning of the process) disappeared in the midst of the campaign too. And yet before the section was cancelled all the comments posted were in favor of the candidate. The lack of conflicting points of view could be seen as an evidence of a possible censorship practiced by Eugène Aballo (and his team), the online campaign manager for the Yayi Boni's camp. It was then impossible to make any comment on the website but the number of people connected was displayed.

On *abt20011.com*, the interactivity existed in many ways. Indeed Internets users and especially supporters were able to comment "the commitments of the candidate," available in the section with the same name. In the "Take part in the Debate" section, visitors could make proposals about the twelve themes listed by the communication unit and put online by the "online communication unit," which were based in Paris and composed of members selected by the candidate himself.

Like on the websites of Houngbédji and Yayi, all the comments seemed to have been sweetened on abt2011.com. There was not only one comment criticizing candidates on their Websites. Nevertheless, online campaigns' managers from the three staffs never admitted this kind of practices neither confirmed our doubts.

The updating of information is one important indicator to measure whether an online campaign is consistent or not. Almost every day, the four Websites were updated with new pictures of candidates during meetings, excerpts from their speeches or even press reviews. But, if candidates and their communication advisors seemed to have planned an online strategy, they made one mistake: they did not manage to adapt their speech to the Internet, which is a specific tool. Indeed, the texts and messages used for other types of medium, such as full biographies, press conferences' speeches, declarations, and agendas, were merely copied and pasted in full on the Websites. The latter were just a kind of extension of the audiovisual and written communication; the staff did not try to find and develop an adapted communication. Neither did they make efforts to sum up information, which was drowned out in a tsunami of texts.

Consequently, the Internet user was the one who had to search for the information he needed. It didn't matter if he gave up and left the Website, mainly because of the very slow connection speed in Benin. To conclude on this section, it must be pointed out that the four Websites tried to remain true to the spirit of the four functions described before which are: "to inform, to involve, to connect and to mobilize". But finally, in spite of all the efforts they made, the staff did not manage to make websites "independent, powerful and full-fledged tools in the campaign strategy," using the words of Greffet and Thierry Vedel. Websites have proven to be mere secondary communication tools. In spite of huge financial and logistical means used to develop, run and animate them, Websites were simply an extension of other tools traditionally used during electoral campaigns.

THE BLOGGING IN THE ONLINE CAMPAIGNS (OF THE CANDIDATES)

"Blogging has been one of the strongest communication tools during our campaign," Luc Vodouhè, the head of the communication unit of candidate Houngbédji, asserted[25]. Once again, the blogs of the candidates were just extensions of their Websites. All the information published on the blogs was already available on the Websites. That clearly shows that the staff did not make any differences between Websites and blogs in their online strategies. Pictures, podcasts, articles, campaign schedules, and even biographies for some candidates like Abdoulaye Bio Tchané were posted. Apparently, unlike Websites, blogs were not judged that important by staff and that explains why the blogs were not often updated. For instance, Adrien Houngbédji's blog which was launched on January 19, 2011, just before the beginning of the campaign, was not updated until the end of elections. But it was still accessible and displayed some statistics like the number of visitors who had connected to the blog. In June 2011, three months after the elections, this figure was 1648.

The blogs of the three candidates were written in the third person and rarely in the first person. That proved that their blogs did not integrate any "personal expression dimension" (Op.cit., p. 42). Based on the way blogging was used during that campaign, it seems like candidates just wanted to follow fashion since they knew having a blog is well seen in the political blogosphere. In reality, they were far from knowing the issues at stake and the strength of a blog. Having a blog appeared to them as a luxury rather than a strategic choice. In a word, it was the bourgeoisie of blogs: what Cardon, Fouetillou, Lerondeau, and Prieur (2012, p. 85) call the "blogeoisie."

SOCIAL NETWORKS

As the Head of the communication unit of Adrien Houngbédji, Luc Vodouhè, clearly stated: all the candidates had a strong presence on social networks. Facebook has been the most used among all social networks.

We have counted more than 40 profiles on Facebook for the three candidates. But after checking, they had not been all created by candidates or their staffs. Adrien Houngbédji had two profiles administrated by the ICT section from his communication unit. Both pages were soberly named "Adrien Houngbédji." Similarly, only two profiles over the 20 or so available for Yayi Boni were directly administrated by his campaign staff. Abdoulaye Bio Tchané appeared in some 14 profiles while only one had been created by his communication unit. This overflow of non-authentic profiles raises questions about creating and administrating profiles and consequently about controlling the communication and even the image of the candidates. Many profiles were created by sympathizers, supporters or campaigners of candidates.

Most of time, the authors of those profiles had no concrete relationship with the candidates; they just tried to attract attention probably in hopes of being "congratulated" or "thanked" in return. Some profiles were also created by admirers who did not expect any reward. Nevertheless, some staff members were really anxious about all those unofficial profiles. For instance, the online staff of Candidate Yayi Boni sent a request to Facebook in October of 2010 (i.e., three months before the pre-campaign phase began), asking the closure of those profiles called "unofficial." But nothing came out of it! Therefore, the staff decided to adopt a different strategy to differ from those profiles which had more fans than the official page of Yayi Boni. Thus, "we ensured that the latest news, official pictures, and pictures from activities were immediately posted on the profiles we administrated."[26]

In reality, what the team in charge of the online campaign most feared was the management of the post-election phase, especially the management of results. Because "no one knew who was behind [these profiles] neither the kind of message the administrators would post at the decisive time of elections; would we read that elections' results are disputed and then read on a profile named 'Yayi Boni' that the candidate himself recognizes that he did not win the elections? We were constantly living with that fear."

The last attempt made by Eugène Aballo's staff consisted in contacting directly the administrators of those profiles to ask them to unite their initiatives. After that, a profile named "Friends convinced that Yayi Boni will be reelected in Benin was created in 2011," which we will discuss later. But not all the administrators joined this last initiative.

On the "official" profiles of candidates created and administrated by their staff, one could read information promoting them or arguments and counter-arguments which aimed to distance themselves from their challengers. We did not notice any filtration of comments on the "official" profiles contrary to what was done on the websites. Supporters took part in debates here and there. Supporters of so-and-so candidates were in the friend lists of so-and-so other candidates and could thus give their opinion about issues initiated by candidates' staff through messages. On the profiles of Houngbédji and Bio Tchané, Internet-using citizens often posted rough messages and comments. But they strived to attack the record of Yayi Boni's first term rather than himself directly.

On the profiles of the three candidates, the speeches took three forms: electoral self-promotion, criticism of challengers, and defense with arguments. As regards profiles created by campaigners, supporters or sympathizers, it is important to make a difference between those aimed at supporting and those aimed at attack-

ing (sometimes very violently). The first were created by supporters who wanted to bring their stone to the online campaign of their candidate. They often posted elements mainly downloaded from the websites of candidates, as we explained it before when talking about the four functions of web campaigning. Here are some examples of this kind of profile: "Youth movement for the winning of Mr. Adrien Houngbédji 2011" and "Il n'y a de richesses que d'hommes."[27] For Yayi Boni, there were, among others, "Vote Yayi Boni" and "Friends convinced that Yayi Boni will be reelected in Benin, in 2011." As for Abdoulaye Bio Tchané, we saw "A kiss for Abdoulaye Bio Tchané" and "Abdoulaye Bio Tchané's young friends." The activities were the same on all those profiles: the point was to promote one's candidate while criticizing the other candidates at the same time. Except the few times they argued, the supporters of Houngbédji and Bio Tchané joined forces against Yayi Boni, as if they had previously come to an agreement. That corroborated this popular saying: "My friends' enemies are my enemies."

However, profiles used for spreading virulent attacks raised a question: How much did candidates' staff master the Internet? Indeed, the possibility of creating a profile without revealing one's identity allows people to introduce new types of arguments in the democratic debate—while keeping their identity secret. Those kinds of arguments were very violent and enjoyed total impunity. It was an evidence of the incapacity of candidates to control and master all that was said on the Internet by their supporters. The authors found refuge in a "dissemination" tool that escapes punishment. In the Beninese media, such speeches or comments would have been strictly prohibited. The High Authority for Audiovisual and Communications, which is the media regulatory authority in Benin, supervises content especially during elections. The institution does not hesitate to convoke people and to punish every media usage that spreads regionalist, hateful or slanderous words. But the

Internet cannot be controlled by the Authority and becomes a tool that circumvents legal and deontological rules.

Nevertheless, the candidates could not be blamed for those kinds of speeches even though their supporters were responsible for the exaggeration. For example, there was a profile named "Quelqu'un d'autre, pas Adrien Houngbédji"[28] created by "Non-Violence, Oui-Paix,"[29] an organism supposed to militate for peace. The profile had about 228 subscribers and posted messages accusing Adrien Houngbédji of being a "power-hungry politician" and a "stateless man." By giving a close look to this administrator on Facebook, we realized that rather than promoting non-violence, they seemed to work for the outgoing president; they were even connected to Yayi Boni's official page on the network. But it would be premature to conclude that the administrator was a henchman working for the Yayi's camp. Another profile caught our attention: "M. Houngbédji, Dégage! Nous ne sommes pas en Côte d'Ivoire. »[30] Here, they accused Mr. Houngbédji again, asserting, in a barely veiled way, that he wanted to plunge the country in a civil war. It was not possible to react since no one knew who was the administrator to take to court for their defamatory words. That anonymity gave birth to a new violent dimension in the supporters' speeches; what could have never been possible in the Beninese media. In that climate of electoral competition, was the Internet used for new and "original" low blows? According to Enoch Gourou-Béra "disinformation was widely spread and used. So, we had to restore the truth and thus the balance in each forum."[31] Every camp could be victim of this slander's spreading campaign. And, excessive remarks were made in extension to that campaign of destabilization on the Internet.

Those Facebook pages administrated by henchmen seemed to have been created to circumvent the watch system of the High Authority for Audiovisual and Communications. But who were behind all that? The question of the identity will remain unanswered. All that means that the Internet is not only a simple place for electoral promotion, but also a network where exchanges can be made, opinions are being discussed... (Wolton, 2008). But some speeches were so rude and so rough that they made the electoral debate in 2011 so much different from the usual ones.

Twitter was also one of the social networks used by the three candidates. They used it, as they used Facebook, mainly to mobilize voters and criticize their challengers. On March 5, 2011, one could read this on the Twitter profile of the outgoing president, one could read this: "One student, One computer connected to the Internet.....but financed by what?" That message was an attack to one campaign promise made by candidate Houngbédji: "One student, one computer connected to the Internet." On April 2, 2011, the day after the results of the elections, Adrien Houngbédji posted this: "I reject the results declared by the Constitutional Court and I say NO to masquerade." Unlike those two candidates, Abt did not wait three months before the beginning of the campaign to create his Twitter account. He had been using it for months then to address his "followers." Just before 2012 began, he tweeted a message to wish a happy new year to his compatriots. But it should be mentioned that the candidates did not use Twitter the way they should. In addition to all those tools, the podcasts also played a key role in the online strategies of different candidates. Indeed, the staff put two tools at work: Youtube and Dailymotion.

YOUTUBE AND DAILYMOTION

YouTube and Dailymotion[32] are the last tools used in the online strategies of different camps. Among the three candidates, only Abdoulaye Bio Tchané really used these platforms. He created an account and set a web television channel watched by 6,027 viewers during the presidential campaign.

Several videos were put online by candidates' communication units. Said videos were related to candidates themselves, their press conferences, extracts from TV news, support marches, meeting pictures and advertising/advertorials which had already been broadcasted on TV channels. In Yayi Boni's Camp, they posted videos about his main achievements during his first term. The same images had already been widely broadcasted on television before. There were then no new elements Internet users could find while visiting those pages. Candidates' staffs wer not the only ones to post videos. Some elements were also posted by supporters, campaigners or sympathizers.

The online campaign, the strategies and choices were all led and made by online campaign teams which worked under different conditions. UN, the coalition represented by Adrien Houngbédji, had a department named "Information and Communication Technologies" working under the communication unit. The department was divided into several sections and was in charge of ensuring "the monthly and daily strategic watch on the Internet[33]." Headed by Parfait Ahoyo, a Beninese living in France who came back to his country especially for the elections, that department had about a hundred young people as members[34]. They were all members of "Adrien Houngbédji's Young Ambassadors," a group of young campaigners who were the spokesmen of the candidate to their generation. As for the outgoing president, he reappointed Eugène Aballo, a journalist who was his usual web manager and worked at the Presidency of the Republic. During the elections, he was in charge of: ensuring the strategic watch on the Internet as well as making frequent updates on the website and the different pages of his candidate. He was assisted by a dozen of persons including journalists, sociologists, lawyers, computer engineers and economists. The Web manager of Abdoulaye Bio Tchané managed the Website, the blog and the pages on social network from France, his living country.

AN INADEQUATE SPEECH FOR THE INTERNET

If the Internet allows the users to establish a different relationship with their audience, while addressing a particular segment of the population, none of the three candidates developed specific messages for their target. Indeed, the tone and the contents of the messages posted were exactly the same than those published in traditional media. Adrien Houngbédji did nothing but criticize the record of the outgoing president. The President-Candidate, in turn, defended his term and accused l'Union Fait la Nation of being a regionalist gathering. The two challengers of Yayi Boni were ready to use every means possible to win the elections; they were even ready to ruin his image. And because they wanted to bribe Internet users, who were possible voters, Abdoulaye Bio Tchané—the ABT coalition's candidate—and Adrien Houngbédji--single candidate for the coalition made of opposition's parties--constantly posted messages denigrating the outgoing government. Houngbédji chose to do it in a personal style. He generally talked in the first person, using "I." As for Abdoulaye Bio Tchané, he preferred to be more consensual at the beginning of the campaign before changing for a more criticizing style and speech towards Yayi Boni. He began using "I" instead of "He."[35] He also used "We" with two goals: to represent the authority he wants to be and also to notify he is the spokesman of Beninese. During the last week of the campaign, his supporters and he brandished "red cards" at their meetings, as a sanction against the Yayi administration and the way they had managed the country.

In response to those diatribes and denunciations, the outgoing president and its government defended their first term. Yayi Boni talked in the first person, using "I." That shows he wanted to "speak" directly to those who visited his Website. Not only did he accuse "l'Union Fait la Nation" of being a "regionalist gathering whose only goal is to harm democracy," but sometimes he chose an ironic tone, saying for example: "I am the teacher of all the candidates."

Candidates posted all the speeches they pronounced during meetings or press conferences, in full, on their websites. No particular effort was made to adapt the texts to Internet—according t its formats and usages—in order to make things easier for Internet users. The animosity between candidates was not only verbal. Indeed, Houngbédji and Yayi engaged in a hacking war.

HACKING INTO WEBSITES: ANOTHER WAR BETWEEN YAYI AND HOUNGBEDJI

A part from the venomous words exchanged on the Internet, Yayi Boni and Adrien Houngbédji also engaged themselves in a hacking war into their respective websites. Since 2010, it means one year before the elections, Internet users who connected to the candidate Yayi's Website were automatically redirected to the Website of candidate Houngbédji. All those who typed www.boniyayi.net had the website of the candidate from "l'Union fait la Nation" appearing on their screen. Supporters of Yayi Boni systematically denounced what they called "villainous acts." But the explanation was simple: a domain name (*www.boniyayi.net*) close to the official one of candidate Yayi (www.boniyayi.bj) had been bought. When we were leading our field surveys, no member from the communication unit of candidate Houngbédji admitted to be responsible for the buying of that domain name. Nevertheless, nothing excludes that it could have been a way of "self-persecution" orchestrated by the pro-Yayi themselves. Indeed, maybe Yayi's supporters organized all that themselves in order to make the adverse camp pass for cheaters.

In response to the denunciations made about that act, supporters from Houngbédji's camp just justified what happened using the maxim: "the biter bitten" in reference to another hacking

episode which had occurred previously and was beneficial to Candidate Yayi. Indeed, still during the pre-campaign phase, every Internet user who typed www.benintelecoms.com[36] was redirected to the outgoing president's Website. And yet, the real URL of the company Bénin Télécoms SA is www.benintelecoms.bj. On the side of "l'Union fait la Nation," supporters asserted that it was a "damage of a very grave nature to Benin Télécoms SA, which could lose its clients." In that case, the situation was the same: no evidence could help to know if the hacking had been orchestrated by candidate Yayi or if Houngbédji's coalition were behind and wanted to show that the outgoing president were using the state's resources to campaign, and thus unite Internet users and people against him.

Contrary to what some people thought, it was not an ethical matter; it was a strategic dynamic during the campaign which proved that Beninese politicians had really put the Internet in their strategies. But, who were targeted by this strategy and what were the results expected?

A TOOL DEVELOPED FOR THE ELITE AND BENINESE DIASPORA

The Internet was actually used during that presidential campaign in Benin. It mobilized people and required strategies. But in spite of all that, it was not the main or sole tool which could make a candidate win. Was the investment commensurate with the scope of the tool? The main goal of each candidate was to win the elections and the Internet could play a major role in that quest by informing, communicating, involving, and mobilizing voters. But which voters are we talking about, considering that only 2.2% of the population uses the Internet in the country? Communication advisors of the three candidates unanimously recognized that they were clearly targeting Beninese living abroad, young people, and elite. But, those strategies have proven to be failures, in some way.

Even though there are about 2 million Beninese living abroad, only 13,000 were registered as voters. The 2011 electoral file was based on the computerized permanent voters' list, which was supposed to be established after three essential steps: the census cartography, the census, and the enrolment of biometric data. Outside the country, the process was run in embassies. But due to the lack of coordination and poor information, only 13,000 Beninese from Diaspora were registered, which corresponds to a small proportion of voters without any electoral weight.

On the other hand, most of the time, Beninese living abroad have relatives or friends in Benin and, regularly or sporadically, they send them money and gifts. The support of those living abroad is sometimes perceived as a lifesaving act by beneficiaries. Many of the benefactors give voting advice to those living in Benin. And occasionally, family and friends are the ones who consult on how to vote, because they prefer to give their voice to the candidate who will favor opportunities and wealth to their benefactor. If the 2 million Beninese living abroad gave voting advice, they would then become a vital component for elections.

Inside the country, the online campaign targeted young people and elites in general. The final voter targeted could be indirect. Indeed, most of the time when parents, often undereducated, receive letters or have to write something, they ask their children or literate neighbors to help them. Literate persons are commonly called "akowé" since the colonial era. "Akowé" is a word used to refer to intellectuals, because "in the Latin Quarter of Africa [the nickname of Benin in the old days] accessing power [and having recognition] depends more on the level of education than on the social and community origins" (Banégas, 2003, p. 39). Most of these elites, who have a relatively high level of education, live in urban areas and their purchasing power is slightly above the national average. The elites described are thus possible

targets for candidates. But again, if we take into account the rate of illiterates in the country, elites are very few people. So, elites alone cannot sway the results of such major elections. This is where they can be important on two fronts.

Indeed, during electoral campaigns, the expertise of these elites is precious and can be determining. If candidates manage to convince these go-betweens, it means they convince thousands of illiterate Beninese with few resources; because the said go-betweens could become the "spokesmen" of candidates to populations where they probably enjoy a certain reputation, especially in their village and their ethnic group. That is the symbolism of "the child from the capital who goes back to their village" where he is expected to come with gifts and money. From this perspective, the staffs' strategies would consist in co-opting those targeted elites, first, which has not been the case. This means that all the options of the strategy were not well thought-out by the different staffs, because it is obvious that 3% of the population cannot determine the outcome of a national election. Thus, by using the Internet, the candidates showed they wanted to make it a communication tool. But, in spite of the huge investments made, no suitable strategy had been well thought-out.

CONCLUSION

Can we say that the 2011 presidential election was a starting point for an "online campaign" in Benin? Certainly, since this way of campaigning is becoming a real field for political and electoral competition, even though there were many shortcomings and weaknesses inherent in the substance and forms. The use of the Internet for electoral purpose, still at the stage of discovery and exploration, seems to develop itself at a faster pace than a normal evolution. It then goes against the national political context described previously.

So, every online campaign team did their best to develop websites including a commercial side as it is done in countries like the USA or the UK. But they did not manage to adapt the tool to the intellectual level of targeted populations. For instance, as it is done in some other contexts, a section for fundraising was available on the website of Abdoulaye Bio Tchané. Inviting the Internet users to donate for the campaign was a surprising approach because, quite the opposite, during elections, the Beninese expect politicians to give them things rather than the contrary. The "things" mentioned are often money, t-shirts, and other campaign gadgets that the candidates hand out at the end of their meetings. Therefore, asking the Beninese—who live under the poverty line for most of them—to support financially a candidate is a way of being, consciously or unconsciously, distant from local realities.

Even though, during this campaign, the way the Internet was used was almost similar to how it is put to work in the occidental context, and if it has proved to be a campaign tool, it is important to notice that it played a very limited role. Certainly, at the beginning the actors on the political stage assigned a decisive role to the Internet because of the hope it inspired. But in the facts, it was finally used in a limited way and generated insignificant–and almost non-existent--results. Nevertheless, regarding the improvements achieved in the field of the access to the Web, the Internet could become a place for "political socialization" (Norris, 2000; Bimber, 2001; Gibson & Ward, 2012, p. 110) which, in turn, could be mobilized by the candidates.

On the other hand, the roles (the four functions) of a website designed for elections were, in the main, played by the websites of the three candidates. While informing, the Websites also tried to mobilize voters, to get them involved in the campaign and to connect them; some Websites were more successful than other. The interactivity,

which is difficult to create even in countries which have been pioneers in online campaigning, was indisputably there. But as the campaign entered in its decisive phase, interactivity was sacrificed.

The Websites had another weakness which was common and characteristic during the early days of the Internet: the overflow of information; while the density of information on a Website does not render it clear and transparent (Chadwick, 2006). According to Nielsen (1999), flashy graphics do not make a website more effective or efficient. The three Websites, especially those of Adrien Houngbédji and Abdoulaye Bio Tchané, contained too much written information, what required from the Internet users an extra reading work and efforts to summarize things. Moreover, on the three Websites, they sank into flashy graphic designs as if they expected that aggressive and bright colors would make them more attractive. In a word, websites appeared to be more like "electronic brochures" (Small, cited by Greffet, 2011, p. 29) than vectors of viral marketing.

When they first began using the Internet as a campaigning tool, the USA, France and every other country where online campaigns play a major role today also experienced the early time-lapse we've noticed in Benin, during those elections. In the three communication units of the main challengers, members referred to Barack Obama's campaign in 2008, which seems to have been very inspiring to them. That explains why, in a large proportion, they replicated and tried to use the same strategies by commenting on campaign issues on their Websites, building online communities, broadcasting videos, posting pictures from the campaign, and so forth. Nevertheless, the Internet is not used yet, strictly speaking, by all the voters. Indeed, while in the USA for example, more than 60% of the population has an access to Internet from home, only some 2.5% can browse from home, in Benin. And even above this figure, we must underline that in spite of the strong will of the actors involved, the Internet has been used in a marginal way. The online campaigners copied much of what is done in other countries instead of developing adapted and well though-out strategies.

At the moment, can we say that Internet is the "fifth power" as Dick Morris, former Counselor of Bill Clinton, suggested in the USA? In the case of Benin, the answer is "No," even though the Internet is now a tool which is fully incorporated into global elections strategies. But no matter the way it will be used, the Internet will never have the same impact in Benin than in countries like the USA, because, above the Internet access rate, the political culture and thus the context which is different, the political-institutional environment is far from being the same. In Benin, radio and television will still remain the first tools for mobilizing voters for a long time to come. And politicians themselves are aware of that since they say television in itself is a medium.

WEBSITES

Internet World Stats. (2013). *World Internet Users Statistics*. Retrieved November 10, 2010, from http://www.internetworldstats.com/stats.htm

Population Data. (2013). *PopulationData.net: Toutes les populations du monde*. Retrieved December 24, 2010, from http://www.populationdata.net/index2.php

Abdoulaye Bio Tchane. (2013). *ABT, le site officiel*. Retrieved January 3, 2011, from www.abiotchane.org

Adrien Houngbedji. (2013). *Maintenant, Avancons! Un Adrien Houngbedji*. Retrieved January 2, 2011, from http://www.adrienhoungbedji.com/

Boni Yayi. (2013). *Bienvenue sur le site du President Boni Yayi*. Retrieved January 2, 2011, from http://www.boniyayi.bj/

REFERENCES

Adjovi, E. (2006). Mobilisations citoyennes et démonopolisation du travail politique au Bénin. *Perspective Afrique, 1*(3), 187–223.

Anstead, N., & Chadwick, A. (2009). Parties, Election campaigning, and the Internet: Toward a Comparative Institutional Approach. In Chadwick, A., & Howard, P. N. (Eds.), *Routledge Handbook of Internet Politics* (pp. 55–71). London: Routledge.

Banégas, R. (2003). *La démocratie à pas de caméléon. Transition et imaginaires politiques au Bénin*. Paris: Karthala.

Bimber, B. (2001). Information and Political Engagement in America. *Political Research Quarterly, 54*(1), 53–68.

Bimber, B., & Davis, R. (2003). *Campaigning Online: The Internet in US Elections*. Oxford, UK: Oxford University Press.

Bongrand, M. (1993). *Le marketing politique* (p. 128). University Presses of France.

Bradley, C. D. (1993). Access to US government information on the internet, Interpersonal Computing and Technology. *An Electronic Journal for the 21st Century*.

Cardon, D., Fouetillou, G., Lerondeau, C., & Prieur, C. (2011). Esquisse de géographie de la blogosphère politique. In Greffet, F. (Ed.), *Continuerlalutte.com. Les partis politiques sur le web* (pp. 73–94). Paris: Presses de Sciences.

Chadwick, A. (2006). *Internet Politics: States, Citizens, and New Communication Technologies*. Oxford, UK: Oxford University Press.

Coleman, S., & Hall, N. (2001). Spinning on the Web: E-campaigning and beyond. In Coleman, S. (Ed.), *Cyber Space Odyssey: The Internet in the UK Election* (pp. 7–24). London: Hansard Society.

Davis, R., Baumgartner, J., Francia, P., & Morris, J. (2009). The Internet in US. Election campaigns. In Chadwick, A., & Howard, P. N. (Eds.), *Routledge Handbook of Internet Politics* (pp. 13–24). London: Routledge.

Foot, K., Xenos, M., Schneider, S., Kluver, R., & Jankowsky, N. (2009). Electoral Web production practice in Cross-National Perspective: The Relative Influence of National Development, Political Culture, and Web Genre. In Chadwick, A., & Howard, P. N. (Eds.), *Routledge Handbook of Internet Politics* (pp. 140–155). London: Routledge.

Frère, M.-S. (1998). *Les Mots et les maux de la démocratie: Analyse du registre lexical et thématique de la transition démocratique dans la presse béninoise. Recherche en Communication* (pp. 119–146). Louvain-La-Neuve, Belgium: Université Catholique de Louvain.

Gibson, R., & Ward, S. (2011). Renouveler le parti? Les stratégies de campagne et d'organisation en ligne des partis britanniques. In Greffet, F. (Ed.), *Continuerlalutte.com. Les partis politiques sur le web* (pp. 109–123). Paris: Sciences Po. Les Presses.

Greffet, F. (2011). *L'Internet ou l'espace des possible. Les campagnes françaises en ligne depuis 2007. Continuerlalutte.com. Les partis politiques sur le web* (pp. 15–37). Paris: Sciences Po. Les Presses.

Greffet, F., & Vedel, T. (2011). L'Internet ou l'espace des possible. Les campagnes françaises en ligne depuis 2007. In *Continuerlalutte.com. Les partis politiques sur le web* (pp. 41–57). Paris: Sciences Po. Les Presses.

Klotz, R. J. (2004). *The Politics of Internet Communication*. Lanham, MD: Rowman and Littlefield.

Kluver, R., Jankowsky, N. W., Foot, K. A., & Schneider, S. M. (Eds.). (2007). *The Internet and National Elections: A Comparative Study of Web Campaigning*. New York: Routledge.

Maarek, P. (2007). Communication et marketing de l'homme politique (3rd éd., p. 466). LexisNexis Litec.

Martin, C. H., & Stronach, B. (1992). *Politics East and West: A comparison of Japanese and British political culture* (p. 360). Armonk, NY: M. E. Sharpe.

Nadeau, R., & Bastien, F. (2003). La communication électorale. In *La Communication Politique, Etat des Savoirs, Enjeux et perspectives* (pp. 159–187). Quebec: Presses Universitaires du Québec.

Norris, P. (2000). *Virtuous circle. Political Communication in Postindustrial Societies* (p. 420). Cambridge, UK: Cambridge University Press. doi:10.1017/CBO9780511609343.

PNUD. (2010). *Rapport mondial sur le développement humain 200: Mettre les nouvelles technologies au service du développement humain*. Genève, New York: De Boeck University.

Swaddle, K. (1988). Hi-Tech Elections: Technology and the Development of Electioneering since 1945. *Contemporary British History, 2*(1), 32–35.

Vedel, T. (2003). Internet et les pratiques politiques. In *La communication politique: Etat des savoirs, enjeux et perspectives* (pp. 189–214). Quebec: Presses de l'Université de Québec.

Wolton, D. (2008). *La communication politique: La construction d'un modèle*. Essentiels d'Hermès.

ENDNOTES

[1] Giant meetings, support marches, neighborhood meetings, slogans, gadgets for electoral promotion (hats, fabrics, teacups, fans, "T-shirts", lighters, playing cards, balls, plates and scarfs, all with pictures of the heads of candidates), songs to promote candidates, small and big posters, banners…

2   According to Marie-Soleil FRERE, it is a political transformation that established a multi-party system instead the single-party regime which were into force until then.

3   The conference held in February of 1990 under the leadership of Bishop Isidore De Souza. It is the starting point of the democratic process in Benin; this new era began with a transition phase.

4   The author explains that Benin was then accustomed to organize elections without major problems, what proved it became a real democracy.

5   One of the slogans he used during the campaign.

6   Read on http://www.houngbedjipresident.com/?page_id=37, on February 26th, 2011. It is important to mention that after the elections, contrary to what is said in its charter, the "UN" coalition broke up.

7   « La Renaissance du Bénin », created and led by the Soglo family, « le Parti Social Démocrate » created and led by Bruno Amoussou, « le Mouvement Africain pour le Développement et le Progrès » created and led by Séfou Fagbohoun, « Force Clé » created and led by Lazare Sèhouéto. In 2006, they all called for a vote to Yayi Boni. The same leaders, once relegated to opposition some months later, created the « l'Union Fait la Nation » coalition, in collaboration with « le Parti du Renouveau Démocratique » created and led by Mr. Houngbédji, principal opponent of the outgoing president.

8   Beninese population estimate for 2012.

9   http://www.unicef.org/french/infobycountry/benin_statistics.html.

10 According to the Beninese Ministry of Development and the one in charge of Electric Power, as they wrote it in the official document titled: « Strategies *to ensure the necessary energy supply in order to achieve the MDGs in Benin*» - *December, 2006.*

11 Read on http://www.internetworldstats.com/africa.htm, on November 10th, 2012.

12 Eugène Aballo, Head of the online campaign of the outgoing candidate - Personal interview/ Cotonou, September, 2012.

13 There was a third website designed by his communication unit but dedicated to « Adrien Houngbédji's Young Ambassadors », a group of young people devoted to his cause.

14 Maurice Tossou, personal interview/ Cotonou, March, 2011.

15 Luc Vodouhè, personal interview/Cotonou, April, 2011.

16 Enoch Gourou Béra, communication advisor of the President-Candidate-in charge of des community radio stations, personal interview/ Cotonou, April, 2011.

17 Dénis BABAEKPA, Head of the communication unit of candidate ABT, personal interview/ Cotonou, March- April, 2011.

18 Daniel Sossouhounto, personal interview/ Cotonou – April, 2011.

19 "We're going to restore order in our Home".

20 «Now, let's go forward! ».

21 That explains why they made vitriolic and cutting criticisms against the opposing camps and they sang the outgoing president praises. Many other media organizations signed contracts with a candidate or another.

22 Further, Together and Forever.

23 The future of a triumphant nation.

24 Beninese national anthem is titled « l'Aube Nouvelle » and was written and composed by Abbé Gilbert Dagnon.

25 Personal interview.

26 Eugène Aballo, Online campaign Manager of the outgoing president, Boni Yayi -personal interview/Cotonou, September, 2012.

27 It is the title of a book written by the candidate.

28 It means 'Someone else! Not Adrien Houngbédji'. In response to the title of Mr. Andoche AMEGNISSE's blog: "Tout Sauf Yayi Boni en 2011" (ie. Anyone except Yayi Boni).

29 It means «Non-Violence. Yes-Peace ».

30 It means "Mister Houngbédji, get out of here! Benin is not Ivory-Coast".

31 Personal interview.

32 Like *YouTube, Dailymotion* is a platform on which people post all types of videos. It is most used and most known in the francophone world.

33 Maurice Tossou—Personal interview.

34 According to Parfait Ahoyo.

35 "He is the answer to your concerns".

36 Bénin Télécoms SA is the Beninese telecommunications company.

Chapter 19
The Impact of Social Media on the Social, Political and Economic Environments in Africa

Oluwabukola Adelaja
University of New South Wales, Australia

ABSTRACT

The purpose of this chapter is to evaluate the effect and potentials of social media as a tool for social, political, and economic change in Africa. This chapter argues that social media has become so entrenched in various facets of society that it has become a mechanism impacting social, political, and economic life in Africa. This chapter looks at the 2011 Nigerian elections and the worldwide Kony Movement against Kony the Ugandan warlord, as tools/examples of analysis. These are some of the developments that have driven the debate about the ability of social media in bringing about social, economic, and political change and participation in the African continent. The research method adopted in this chapter involves an analysis of a growing scholarship addressing the various arguments proffered on this topic. The chapter concludes by establishing the impact of social media on social, economic, and political life in Africa as well as identifying challenges posed by this development and making recommendations for the regulatory framework required to effectively harness these potentials in Africa.

INTRODUCTION

The main focus and significance of this chapter is to evaluate the potentials of social media used as a tool for social, political, and economic change in the continent. This chapter considers the arguments for and against the ability of the use of social media to have an impact in these key areas of life in Africa. The aim here is to argue that social media has become so entrenched in various facets of society that it has become a mechanism vitally impacting social, political, and economic life in Africa. This chapter specifically focuses on the 2011 elections in Nigeria and the Kony Movement set up against Kony the Ugandan warlord. Social media played an important role

DOI: 10.4018/978-1-4666-4197-6.ch019

in the monitoring and transparency of the 2011 Nigerian elections. The movement to bring the Ugandan warlord Kony to justice is well known not only for the issue of focus of the cause, but also for the role played by social media that helped the message spread to millions globally in a matter of days[1]. These are some of the developments that have driven the debate about the potentials or possibility of the social media in bringing about social, economic, and political change and participation in the African continent (Bohler-Muller & van der Merwe, 2011).[2] The research method that is adopted in this chapter involves an analysis of a growing of scholarship addressing the various arguments in this area, while looking at the social, economic, and political climate in Africa in driving this position. This also involves an analysis of surveys conducted and reported in the body of these scholarships. In addition, this analysis will provide a better understanding of the impact of social media on the different aspects of our societies. This chapter also briefly makes recommendations for the regulatory framework needed to achieve the previously mentioned potentialities in Africa.

AN ANALYSIS OF THE IMPACT OF SOCIAL MEDIA ON SOCIETY

There is an undeniable connection between recent occurrences in the world and the social media. Since these have happened, people have become more aware of how social media can and has become a tool with which they can humanize, obscure, and abstract phenomena. This allows their voices to be heard on the global stage. Asur and Huberman (2010) postulated that the ease of use, speed and reach of social media has led to a change in the manner of societal discourse in society and has become a trend setter for topics ranging "from the environment and politics to technology and the entertainment industry."[3] Social media by nature involves the use of tools, services, and applications for social interaction.

This has become a medium where people gather and express their opinions in a simplified manner and in real time. This characteristic of social media allows people to expand their ideas and influence in many areas.

There have been critiques on the use of social media and the Internet, and concerns that that they are potentially damaging to our thinking, our culture, and our society in general. For example, Nicholas Carr (2010) in his book *The Shallows* argued that since the advent of the Internet, we are becoming ever more adept at scanning and skimming, but what we are losing is our capacity for concentration, contemplation, and reflection[4]. This position, even if it is true, does not take away from the fact that social media has changed the way in which ideas change hands and how fast those ideas spread. It has also become a valuable repository of information—statistical and otherwise—which in itself can be seen as a form of currency in its own right and a tool for change in the society.

Social media has created an avenue for the transfer, in seconds, of news and any information that would usually take days or weeks. This transfer of information in real time has never been so available to people around the world as it is now and it is still an evolving form of communication. Historically, governments have been able to control information and the spreading of ideas but since the advent of social media, there has been to some extent a shift of control from these governments to the public. This is largely due to the fact that technology is more available and affordable to people than it used to be and anyone can become a point of contact for the communication of information.

Social media has also changed the way we as a society view and use information. "The sites open up different portals through which we get information and create more diverse news outlets. Rather than reading the newspaper or hearing the news on TV, we rely on our friends on the sites to give us updates on the world around us."[5] This medium provides quick access to information and allows us to choose news that interests us without having to wait for it to become available through traditional media. Of course, the downside to this is that it becomes more challenging to verify the authenticity of information made available on social media but it does not take away from the fact that it provides access to news as it happens in real time.

A unique characteristic of social media is the provision of instant feedback to its users. According to Paun (2010), "given all the characteristics of social media, we can say that they are tools that facilitate the implementation of bilateral symmetrical communication model favouring direct communication with all audiences, instant feedback and behaviour change."[6] This of course has negative and positive aspects to it but the nature of interaction on social media creates an avenue for people to expand their social network of friends in ways that were almost unachievable before. This perhaps was why Paun[7] said that "each social media connection established on the digital landscape has the potential of adding (or reducing) meaning, understanding, to life/ humanity." We will now look as some examples of the impact of social media on the aspects of society through some recent events that have occurred.

The Arab Spring

By now most people know about the "Arab Springs". These were a series of events that proved revolutionary not because the idea of social or political uprising by the people is a new concept, but because of the unique role played by the use of social media in how the events unfolded.

The Arab Springs were a series of protests and demonstrations that took place in the Middle East starting on Saturday, December 18, 2010. These protests have led to major political upheavals and the removal from power of rulers in Tunisia, Egypt, Libya, and Yemen. There has also been a string of civil unrests in other parts of the regions such as Syria, Jordan, Bahrain, and Iraq. This phenomenon also affected other African nations such as Morocco, Algeria, Mauritania, and Sudan. The genesis of this revolution was a result of the self-immolation carried out by Mohammed Bouazizi in Tunisia on December 18, 2010. This act by one man resulted in several protests in Tunisia and quickly spread to other countries within and outside the region. In December 2010, it was through blogs and text messages that Tunisians experienced what the sociologist Doug McAdam calls "cognitive liberation."[8]

Some of the civil resistance techniques used were rallies, strikes, marches, and demonstrations. The use of social media in these uprisings was, however, the highlight of the whole process and what led to it. This is partly due to the fact that there is no precedence for such a development given that the upsurge of Internet use and social media is a relatively recent development. Social media was used mainly as a tool for communication and awareness creation despite attempts by the government authorities to suppress the use of the Internet. Social media became a tool for the expression of the power of the people. Since these occurrences, the major slogan of the demonstrators in the Arab world has been Ash-sha'b yurīd isqāṭ an-nizām ("the people want to bring down the regime").

The Role of Social Media in the Arab Spring

Instead of a typewriter or a pen ... the Internet provided a much easier way of reproducing and spreading copies of texts outside of the institutional channels.[9]

The Internet, through the use of social media, made it easier and safer to a certain extent for people involved in the movement to voice their opinions on a large scale. The uniqueness of the situation meant that the news of what was happening travelled in real time to many parts of the world. People outside the region knew what was happening and were also able to mobilise help in the form of creating more awareness of what was happening. For example, in Tunisia the level of involvement and response from people within and outside the country is seen in the following instances[10]:

- Slim Amamou, a member of the copyright-focused Pirate Party, blogged the revolution (and later briefly took a post in the national-unity government).
- Sami ben Gharbia, a Tunisian exile, monitored online censorship attempts and advertised workarounds.
- The middle-class Tunisian rapper who calls himself El Général streamed digital "soundtracks for the revolution."

The amassed uprising formed a compendium of force that led to political change in countries such as Egypt and Libya. According to Cambie (2011):

Co-creation the act of producing content by sharing voices and ideas from a wide audience is probably the most important lesson that communicators can draw from the Arab Spring.[11]

This is arguably what we can refer to as "true democracy," the government of the people, by the people and for the people. Social media has "demonopolised" issues concerning the socio-political welfare of a people from the far-fetched and often detached grip of some political leaders. Whether or not a movement of this nature leads to change in the society does not matter. The important lesson here is that people are now able to express their opinions on a worldwide platform and all it takes is the click of a mouse.

The "We Will Never Bomb You Meme"[12] Goes Viral

The "We Will Never Bomb You Meme" is currently an unfolding development. This was started by Ronny Edri, a graphic artist from Tel Aviv in Israel. He put a poster of himself holding his daughter with a slogan above their heads saying

"Iranians we love you we will never bomb your country." This started a Facebook campaign called "Israel Loves Iran." This is an effort to put a human face and lend a real voice to the people living in the disputing countries in the midst of the talk of war between the governments of Iran and Israel.

This project has opened the door for mutual expressions of love and peace to come flooding in from thousands of people. The response has been huge with messages sent also from other parts of the world such as the USA, Italy, and Canada. The importance and impact of this move on people are enormous, especially in Iran, where people are participating in this self-expressing gesture despite the risks and limitations involved in Internet use. The Iranians have been able to circumvent a ban on Facebook through finding other means to join the social media platform and post anonymously to the campaign page. These messages are from Iranians living in the diaspora and also those living within the country.

There are three Facebook pages set up for this cause, namely: "Israel loves Iran," "Love and Peace," and "Pushpin Mehina." By Friday, March 23, 2012, more than 16,000 Facebook users had clicked on "Like" for the Israel loves Iran site and more than 5,000 had showed they like Love and Peace, while Pushpin Mehina had more than 2,700 subscribers.

Whether or not this leads to a prevention of war is left to be seen. An undeniable fact is that people do have a voice and there seems to be certain boldness in them to contribute in whatever way they can to ensuring peace. Social media has offered a relatively accessible avenue for these groups of people to forge ahead in their resolve.

THEORETICAL ANALYSIS OF THE IMPACT OF SOCIAL MEDIA

But no matter how advanced the system, no matter how precise, unless we have the will to communicate, there's no connection. - Haruki Murakami

Social media has become a social way of delivering a message on a technology platform. It is becoming more accessible and easy to use, especially with the advent of mobile technology. A unique development in social media is that it not only breeds a need or capability to communicate, but also empowers users to create content. People across the globe are becoming part of a worldwide network with more sense of acceptance by the social media community.

Players in this field are no longer limited to ordinary individuals. Governments, businesses, politicians, professionals, and international organisations now realize the importance of the medium and the exchange of social, political, and economic ideas that flow within the network. Opinions expressed in this global virtual space are continuously shaping ideas and decisions made at national and international levels. Castells (1996) referred to this as the new symbolic environment.[13] This has led to the rapid development of an adaptive networking platform that promotes social interaction in a dynamically evolving technological environment.

Social Networking Theory (SNT)

Social Networking Theory (SNT) observes a society as a vastly dynamic system made up of various networks of social actors all linked through different levels of interaction and participation. "Social actors are located in these networks as nodes, and each node is said to have its position in a social network. The nature of this position is characterized by the number of connections, or ties, and thus the value, or social capital, of these connections. The relationship and exchange between nodes in turn characterizes the network."[14] SNT also involves the study of communication and technology, or in this case, social media as the communication system. The social actors in this system consist of the senders and the receivers.

The tendency was for communication to reside in the traditional forms of mass media such as newspapers, television, and radio. With the advent

of social networking and social media, "power" has to some extent been delivered to the public forum. What we are seeing now is the need for policy makers to feel the "social pulse" when looking to make social, political, and economic decisions. Concepts such as "freedom," "hope," and "democracy" now depend more on the social worldview and less institutionalized definitions or connotations of these concepts. The method of engagement based solely on military and political assets has proven unsustainable. "It's like sucking the air out of a bell jar: if there's no other way to engage us except in political terms, then we lose."[15]

In the African context, the impact of "social" power has a greater potential to impact the institutionalized decision making mechanism as we knew. For example, Africa is one of Facebook's fastest growing markets. There are currently around 32-million Facebook users in Africa. This amounts to 27% of African internet users that have Facebook profiles, compared to 18% of Internet users in Asia. Egypt by the end of 2011 had 6.5 million Facebook users; almost half joined in the first six months of 2011.[16] This impact has already begun with uprisings such as the Arab Spring, which has extended its reach to African countries such as Sudan. The upsurge in the use of social media in Africa in recent years, despite existing challenges, provides a fertile ground for building a social capital. As pointed out by Craig Newmark, founder of Craig's List, "power and influence shifts dramatically to the people and groups with the best reputations and largest networks."[17]

In a social, political, and economic environment such as Africa, the effect of the prior is that the public is more aware and able to respond quickly to developing issues. For politics, this translates into a more transparent process and an improvement of trust in how elections are conducted and the results that follow from it. In the social enclave, the participatory elements of social interaction among people become more relevant and greatly improved. Social media provides a broader view of the world and its affairs to its users and people are becoming more informed of what is going on in the global society. In Africa, the use of social media has the potential to foster the consumer economy through social media marketing. According to Evans (2011), "marketers use brands to build relationships that enhance the value of products and services for consumers."[18] This means that organisations recognise the "socio-economic" power that lies in social media and in turn it helps them to build a loyal customer base for business growth. In other words, customers are using social media to research companies and brands before deciding to patronize them. For instance, in Nigeria there is some evidence that large companies (especially the telecommunications sector) in Nigeria have a social media presence and are reasonably active in this sphere.[19] Whether this is mirrored in the small to medium (SMEs) scale business sectors in Africa is questionable. However, according to a study conducted by Mulero (2012) on a number of SMEs in South Africa, "it was discovered that with the aid of Web 2.0 technologies, social networks marketing has been widely used in promoting and improving business marketing by SMEs in South Africa"[20]. The study further found that "younger respondents (most active users of SNM) make use of SNM as a powerful marketing tool, which can be explored by many small and medium-sized enterprises."[21]

THE ROLE OF SOCIAL MEDIA IN THE 2011 NIGERIAN ELECTIONS

The April 2011 Nigerian general elections were a highly anticipated and unique one. This was due in part to the renewed confidence in the Independent National Electoral Commission (INEC) stemming from a more organized and credible voters' registration exercise organized by the Commission. The renewed confidence was also due to the perceived upright character of the chairman INEC Professor Atahiru Jega. This meant that there was an expectation of fairer representation

of the wider population being able to participate in the elections. This election process was different because INEC not only encouraged voters to participate in the elections, it also tried to foster an environment of transparency by calling on voters to stay back and monitor the counting procedures. The use of social media in the elections allowed every ordinary Nigerian citizen to participate and share the opinions in the election experiences. This led to the RECLAIMNAIJA movement in March 2011, which led to people holding up their mobile phones and chanting "The power is in our hands." It is fair to say that Nigeria had its own "Arab Spring" in this context.

One way that INEC sought to achieve this level of transparency was through the use of social media to sensitise and promote the importance of taking part in the process to Nigerian citizens. As part of this move, the then President of Nigeria, the Shehu Musa Yaradua Foundation, and a group of youth bodies organized a roundtable sponsored by the Canadian High Commission on March 4, 2011, tagged "Promoting Two Way Communication between INEC and its Stakeholders." The objective of this gathering was to identify and evaluate strategic communication issues required to better ensure transparency and encourage public participation in the election process.[22]

During the social media presentation made at the roundtable, the popularity of social media among politically active young Nigerians was shown as a trend that could no longer be ignored. This is buttressed by the fact that there is now a boom in the use of mobile devices, which are used to a large extent to access social media platforms. As of 2011, Nigeria was ranked in the top 10 [23] list of countries with the most number of Internet users, with over 43 million Nigerians accessing the Internet mostly via their mobile phones. Out of this, there were 4,369,740 Facebook users as of December 31, 2011, with a 2.8% penetration rate.[24] There is also an increase in the number of politicians, celebrities, media personalities, and opinion leaders using the social media platform to interact with the public.

From an election perspective, social media is beneficial for instant crowd sourcing, reports (incidents, results, and opinions), pictures/videos (evidence and experience), instant feedback, and many-to-many instant and direct communication. To this end, INEC was able to identify the existing and emerging social media channels and then promote the election message through these channels. It even went a step further by setting up a "Social Media Tracking Centre," which arose from a need to document the mass reaction from the public and make sense of the numbers.

Through the efforts of volunteers, the Centre was able to monitor the trends before, during and after the elections. The Centre was open from Friday afternoon preceding the Saturday elections and ran through Monday mid-day in order to capture traffic related to election results. The data collected via social media sources included reports, pictures and videos voluntarily provided by voters in order to express their opinions, present evidence and garner feedback. At a point in time, the Centre was picking up about 50 tweets per second. Twitter became the most used platform making up about 77% of the contents.[25]

It is interesting to note that traditional media houses actively utilized social media in the coverage of the Nigerian elections. Top users in this category were *Channels Television, 234Next Newspaper, Tell Magazine,* and *Daily Trust Newspaper.*

All of the traditional media houses were asked how the use of social media aided the way they provided information during the elections and they were unanimous in their belief that social media helped them to effectively get their message out there in real time. Social media offered a means for Nigerians to actually talk about the elections.[26]

The 2011 elections was the first time that social media would be used on a wide scale in Nigeria. Although some Nigerians had been on Facebook and Twitter prior to this time, it had never been used widely by political parties, government agencies, and civil society groups. Although argu-

ments have been made against the reliability and authenticity of social media data, it is safe to say that it reflects a reasonable degree of consensus of what has happened. At the very least, it serves as a corroboration of results announced by INEC.

The role that a social media play in politics has also been replicated in other parts of the world. It played a vital part in the 2009 Iran elections. "Many observers saw new media as a necessary (if not sufficient) cause of the dramatic rise of the protest movement following the election, while a subsequent backlash has sought to dismiss its significance."[27] Perhaps a very notable example in this area is the emergence of the Arab Spring. This has focused the attention of the world on the impact of social media in the political enclave and witnessed the transfer of political power from the hands of a view to the people. This has led to a few studies on the impact of social media on politics with sometimes simultaneous social and economic effect. A study[28] conducted by scholars at the George Washington University examined this impact on five levels, namely: (1) Individual Transformation; (2) Intergroup Relations; (3) Collective Action; (4) Regime Policies; and (5) External Attention.

The accessibility, anonymity and low cost of social media played an important part in the voices of millions of people being heard for the first time. It also allowed people to interact on a global level and have access to information that they might not have had access to without social media sources such as Facebook, online news, and blogs.

The Good and the Bad of the Use of Social Media in the 2011 Nigerian Elections

As it happened in other countries, social media can serve as a tool for good as well as for bad. An example for both sides is the violence[29] that erupted in northern Nigeria leading to the loss of innocent lives following the 2011 elections. This was a result of protests carried out by supports of the main opposition candidate, Muhammed Buhari, alleging rigged election results. Social media was effectively used as a means of dispatching crisis management personnel and the clarification of rumours, which in return led to the saving of so many lives[30].

Unfortunately, social media was also used to incite some of the violence that took place during this period. For example, an SMS was circulated right after the Presidential election saying:

As a consequence of the unrest in Kaduna and Zaria, Governor Yakowa has imposed a 24 hr curfew on Kaduna and Zaria while he refused to impose same in Kagoro, Kwoi, Zango and Kafanchan, Zonkwa, M/rido and Gonin Gora; thereby allowing his Christian brothers to kill Muslims as they please. This is a clear danger of voting Yakowa as Governor.[31]

Messages of the same nature were sent among Christians thereby fuelling a major unrest of tragic proportions with over 800 people killed in the riots[32].

Despite these unfortunate and avoidable occurrences, the positive impact of social media for transparency in the political process cannot be overlooked. An example of this was an incident that happened during the 2011 elections when a Nigerian @Ms.Chika411 posted a tweet on April 9 saying that senatorial candidate Kema Chikwe was fabricating the results of the elections in his favour in a private residence. The rate of response and flurry of activities from citizens and two civil society observers RECLAIMNAIJA and POLLWATCH2011 could only have been achieved on a platform such as the social media. The news spread fast and these groups sent out observers to confirm what was happening and subsequently nipped the activity in the bud. Kema Chikwe was eventually defeated by opposition candidate Chris Anyawu, marking a victory for transparency during the elections[33].

This instant technique of reporting happenings on ground meant that the traditional ways of tampering with results such as snatching or stuffing of ballot boxes were drastically reduced. The fact that INEC was willing to accept this new phenomenon allowing ordinary citizens to report happenings as they transpired ensured that people's voices could be heard in an unprecedented way. People were also able to do an on-the-spot check on the Internet via their mobile phones for the movement in the poll while they waited at the polling centers.

Social media played an important part in the efficiency in the handling of elections in Nigeria. As reported by the Global Press Institute[34], Nigerian youths were seen as "informal press observers" and they used social media platforms such as Facebook and Twitter as one of the main tools to monitor and report developments during the elections. This development has also attracted more international observers groups by having them begin to consider sending groups abroad to monitor elections in environments where they can partner with social media savvy domestic observers that have the skills and capacity to make use of social media.

THE ROLE OF SOCIAL MEDIA IN THE KONY2012 MOVEMENT

The Kony2012[35] campaign is a social movement that brought to the fore the impact of social media in spreading and promoting a cause. On March 5, 2012, a short film[36] was launched by the *Invisible Children Organisation* in a move to stop Ugandan war lord, Joseph Kony, known for creating an army of child soldiers, among other things. The main aim of this movement was to make Kony "famous" and ultimately have him arrested and tried for his crimes by December 2012.

The video was posted on the video-sharing website YouTube and went viral within a few days. The film had over 86 million views as of March 30,

2012 on YouTube and over 16.6 million views on Vimeo. It has become the most quickly and broadly shared video in Internet history. Following the storming of the Kony campaign via social media, social media experts have been formulating media strategies based on it and continue to analyse it.

Some of the reasons given by Gilad Lotan[37], VP of Research and Development for Social Flow, and media scientist Henry Jenkins[38], on why the film was able to have such a huge impact are:

- *Kony2012* as a transmedia storytelling campaign did not only utilise traditional media in conjunction with social media, it also made use of multiple points of social media platforms to get the message across as fast as it was able to travel.
- The involvement of celebrities through retweets on Twitter also played a vital role. The strategy used was to bombard celebrities with tweets with the aim of getting involved and to endorse the campaign. According to Lotan, "Once celebrities came on board, the campaign was given multiple boosts." Ellen Degeneres (@The EllenShow), for example, got mentioned 36,000 times on Twitter within the first few hours of the campaign from different users asking her to respond to Kony2012. Both Oprah and Justin Bieber chose to respond and amplify the cause, while Lady Gaga, Jay-Z, and Stephen Colbert did not.[39] An obvious tactic deployed here was to get people to ping celebrities. One should bear in mind that the unintended consequences of the level of attention and response obtained by using this tactic still remains to be analysed. It also raises the question, how would celebrities or targets of these types of campaigns make the best decisions in the circumstances? Would this same line be towed by others in their campaigns or the likes in the future?

As a result of the campaign, on March 21, 2012, the United States Senate passed a resolution[40] supporting the sending of troops by the African Union to provide assistance to African regional forces to capture Kony and other commanders of the militia group. One of the co-sponsors of the resolution, Senator Lindsey Graham, said:

This is about someone who, without the Internet and YouTube, their dastardly deeds would not resonate with politicians. When you get 100 million Americans looking at something, you will get our attention…This YouTube sensation is gonna help the Congress be more aggressive and will do more to lead to his demise than all other action combined.[41]

What does this mean for social change in Africa? We have already looked at some examples of social media activities that led to political change in the continent. This often overlaps with social and economic fields. Social media has become a way for groups to pass on their messages, interact and recruit like-minded with people. Social media has been able to mobilise people from around the world from different backgrounds and with varied interests into taking action on a united front. This has shifted the paradigm that decision making is left in the hands of few individuals or organisations, which have control over the form of the message and how it is disseminated to the public. Social media simply provides a participatory and interactive platform through which the voice of the public could be heard.

What we are seeing now is the potential for social media to redefine the social order in Africa. It demands from governments a more transparent and accountable way designing policies and actions. It also reveals a faster rate of messages relayed and response to the same. Decision makers have to think twice before taking action and releasing information to the public enclave. As an example, the Nigerian President Goodluck Jonathan has to renege on his decision to ban the

Nigerian football team Federation due to comments left on his Facebook page by football fans[42]. There is little or no room left for ill-conceived or misrepresented notions. For the first time, social media is providing a means for Africans to tell their own stories and on a broader spectrum.

Social activism has been reinvented[43] through the use of social media tools. Social media has changed the dynamics in the relationship between those in authority and those in society. We now have a platform that allows collaboration and coordination among people with similar interests and goals. According to Eltantawy (2011)[44], the impact of the use of social media during Egyptian revolution can be demonstrated by the "Resource Mobilisation Theory." This theory "is based on the notion that resources—such as time, money, organizational skills, and certain social or political opportunities—are critical to the success of social movements."[45] It is important to note at this point that in the case of the Egyptian revolution or its own version of the Arab Spring, there were other factors that determined how the events developed. These include the already delicate and volatile nature of the country's political/economic environment, the strategic location and large size of the Tahrir Square, and the closeness in timing to the occurrence of the Tunisian revolution. In addition to the previous factors, social media was an important instrumental resource that changed the dynamics of social mobilisation. It can therefore be argued that the Resource Mobilisation Theory aided in the understanding of the Egyptian revolution in a contemporary way, by looking at the impact of the use of social media at the time.

However, one must be cautious of attributing these achievements solely to the social media. The people play a large part in attaining these goals. Social media is the platform through which they are able to do so. This brings to light the issue of people control over social media looking at it from the perspective of governments. We have seen instances where the governments of China, Iran, and Syria have restricted access to the Internet.

The Internet has also been suspended in Uganda and Egypt in an effort to nip uprisings in the bud. How far are African governments willing to allow the use of internet tools considering the potential threat the tools pose to existing power frameworks?

CONCLUSION

That social media holds great potentials for the social, political and economic development of Africa is an undeniable fact. We have seen how this played out in the Nigerian election process in 2011 and how a Kentucky-based non-for-profit organization was able to capture the attention of millions of people across the globe including U.S. Senators in the *Kony2012 campaign*. The wind of economic change is also blowing across the continent in the form of major ICT developments and a rapid boom in mobile telephone use by Africans. All of the prior are definitely good for the future of the continent. However, these potentials come with challenges that flow from the dynamic nature of the social media phenomenon. A regulatory and policy framework is, therefore, essential in order to attain a sustainable level of development in Africa. It is therefore becoming more important to tour the path of cross-border and regional cooperation so as to have an enabling environment where these policies and regulations can be enforced. This nonetheless does not take away from the immense interactive and participatory tools that we have been able to take advantage of due to the emergence of social media. Social media has become part of life and is here to stay. One looks ahead to the future in positive anticipation for what new horizons lay ahead.

Social Media, in fact, is a basic human need, revealed digitally online. We want to be connected, to make a difference, to matter, to be missed. We want to belong, and yes, we want to be led. -Seth Godin (founder of Squidoo, sethgodin.typepad. com).

RECOMMENDATIONS FOR A REGULATORY FRAMEWORK

It has already been established that social media can bring about political, social, and economic change or growth in Africa. This places more emphasis on the need for a more defined regulatory framework in order to sustain such developments. Regional cooperation is also very important in this process mainly because it involves a cross-border phenomenon in the form of social media. Social media by nature raises a few issues concerning its regulation and sustenance. There is, therefore, a need to address the very foundation of social media, namely Information and Communications Technology (ICT).

The fast rate of technology growth could prove difficult to keep up with. This is coupled with the fact that predictions about technology often misses the mark and social scientists have a hard job of predicting social, political, and economic changes created by technology. As a result, regulations and policies made on technology quickly become outdated or struggle to keep up with the times. Thus, it is fundamental to form regulations and policies that are dynamic, flexible, and take the interests of parties concerned into consideration.

In terms of development, Africa has not been on the same level field with some other countries since the mid-20th century. It is, therefore, a welcome step that the field of ICT in the continent has witnessed an exponential growth in recent years and is one way of bringing a growth spurt to Africa. The following two main recommendations are made in this chapter covering some of the major issues:

- **Information and Communications Technology Reform:** This includes landlines, mobile phones and undersea broadband. This also takes the different geographical, social and political factors into consideration. How can an effective regulatory framework be formed for ICT? How will it remain flexible and dynamic to be able to keep up with advancements in technology? ICT has the potential to play an important role in various sectors including banking, agriculture, health and education.

Privatisation of the ICT sector coupled with the creation of an independent regulator is a good starting point. An obvious benefit of this is an increase in connectivity and the diffusion of pay phone. This cannot be effective without competition, which is a key factor. This should not be done at the expense of providing coverage to regional areas. There have been recent efforts by the African Telecommunications Union (ATU) to ensure that regional areas are not deprived of this important amenity in an effort to balance the economics of scale. Strong independent regulators are needed to assist policy formulation because of the weakness of regulatory bodies currently in existence in Africa. These regulators will help in the adoption of regional or continent wide policies that would lead to effective outcomes for the sector.

- **The South African Development Community:** is a model for setting up regulatory organisations on a regional level. In 1998, it created the Telecommunications Regulators Association of South Africa (TRASA) (now known as CRASA)[46], to achieve a consolidation between all national regulators within the region and to formulate regulations and policies for the benefit of its member states.

One of its focuses to help it in achieving the previous objectives is to create an independent regulatory body and conducting a restructure of the current national operator. These are also mirrored in its East and West African counterparts but they lack the essential element of enforcement. Enforcement by regulators within member states is a tool that is crucial to regional development in this area. Any existing hindrances of this nature need to be removed to foster regional and consequently continent wide growth.

- **Cybercrime Regulation:** The rapid growth in the use of social media in Africa has caused a growing concern among relevant stakeholders. Recently, there has been an increase in calls for content regulation on social networks with countries such as Nigeria and South Africa making plans to legislate social media. A major rational for these renewed calls is the consequent increase on cybercrimes. This poses a risk of cyber-attack exposure to critical economic and government sectors within Africa. Compared to other developed countries, only an average 15% of the African population uses the Internet. Even though this is low in relative terms, Africa is fast becoming a hot spot for the perpetration of cybercrime. This is largely due to the expansion of broadband internet and the absence of regulatory measures to crack down on cyber criminals.

The main challenge that is emerging is that the continent seems generally ill equipped to address the issue of cybercrimes. The U.S. and the UK are among the leading countries with a high rate of cybercrimes. However, they are able to balance this out through implementing regulatory and technologically advanced measures to curb cybercrimes. Common types of cybercrimes in Africa are: Advanced Free Fraud (popularly called "419"); phishing; and spamming. African countries, through the various regional bodies, need to work towards implement laws that are uniform coupled with a consistent approach in tackling or responding to cyber-attacks. Key areas that must form part of this law reform are the need for laws addressing identity theft and laws protecting the privacy of individuals and organizations in Africa.

Each country or region should set up or nominate an appropriate agency to develop clear and defined procedures for gathering cybercrime information and data. This should include agreements on the manner of information sharing between government agencies and relevant industry bodies. This could take the form of a Computer Emergency Response Team or a Computer Security Incidence Response Team (CERT/CSIRT).

Each country or region should establish a cybercrime reporting agency to provide a portal or system of reporting cybercrime incidents online, via the telephone or face to face. This incident reporting system should be made available free of charge to both individuals and small/medium or large scale businesses. This can also be implemented through CERT/CSIRT organization.

Also, the various law enforcement agencies should set up working groups to ensure that information is shared across borders to provide an effective means of successfully prosecuting cybercrimes.

REFERENCES

Aday, S., Farrell, H., Lynch, M., Sides, J., Kelly, J., & Zuckerman, E. (2010). United States Institute of Peace, Blogs and Bullets. *Contentious Issues in Politics*. Retrieved from http://www.usip.org/files/resources/pw65.pdf

Asuni, J., & Farris, J. (2012). *Tracking social media. The Social Media Tracking Center and the 2011 Nigerian Elections*. Retrieved from http://www.eienigeria.org/sites/default/files/files/Tracking%20Social%20Media%20and%202011%20Nigeria%20Elections.pdf

Asur, S., & Huberman, B. (2010). Predicting the future with social media. IEEE Web Intelligence. Retrieved from http://arxiv.org/pdf/1003.5699v1.pdf

Bohler-Muller, N., & Van der Merwe, C. (2011). *The Potential of Social Media to Influence Socio-Political Change on the African Continent*. Africa Institute of South Africa Policy Brief No. 46. Retrieved from http://www.ai.org.za/media/publications/Policy%20Brief/AISA%20Policy%20Brief%2046.pdf

Cambie, S. (2011). Lessons from the front line: The Arab Spring demonstrated the power of people--and social media. *Communication World.* Retrieved from http://www.iabc.com/cw/

Carr, N. (2011). *The shallows: What the Internet is doing to our brains.* New York: W.W. Norton Publishers.

Castells, M. (1996, 2000). The grand fusion: Multimedia as symbolic environment. In The Information Age: Economy, Society and Culture: The Rise of the Network Society. Doi: doi:10.1002/9781444319514.

Chidiogo, E. (2011). 800 people killed in post-election violence. Retrieved May 16, 2011, from http://dailytimes.com.ng/article/%E2%80%98800-people-killed-post-election-violence%E2%80%99

Colombo, S., Carridi, P., & Kanninmont, J. (2012). New socio-political actors in North Africa, a transatlantic perspective. Retrieved February 14, 2012, from http://www.gmfus.org/archives/new-socio-political-actors-in-north-africa-a-transatlantic-perspective

Ehidiamen, J. (2011). Nigerian youth celebrate social media as tool of successful election. Retrieved April 29, 2011, from http://www.global-pressinstitute.org/africa/nigeria/nigerian-youth-celebrate-social-media-tool-successful-election

Eltantawy, N., & Wiest, J. (2011). Social media in the Egyptian revolution: Reconsidering resource mobilization theory. *International Journal of Communication, 5,* 1207–1224. Retrieved from http://ijoc.org/ojs/index.php/ijoc.

Essoungou, A. (2011). A social media boom begins in Africa. *Africa Renewal.* Retrieved August 22, 2011, from http://www.un.org/africarenewal/magazine/december-2010/social-media-boom-begins-africa

Etzo, S., & Collender, G. *The mobile phone revolution in Africa: Rhetoric or reality?* DOI: 10.1093/afraf/adq045.

Evans, W. (2008). Social marketing campaigns and children's media use, the future of children. *Children and Electronic Media, 18*(1). Retrieved from http://futureofchildren.org/publications/journals/journal_details/index.xml?journalid=32

Freemantle, S. (2011). The five trends powering Africa's enduring allure. Retrieved from http://www.standardbank.com/Article.aspx?id=-127&src=m2011_34385466

Gladwell, M. (2002). Small change - Why the revolution will not be tweeted. *The New Yorker.* Retrieved from http://www.newyorker.com/reporting/2010/10/04/101004fa_fact_gladwell

Globacom Nigeria. (n.d.). In *Facebook.* Retrieved from https://www.facebook.com/GloWorld

Global, T. N. S. (2012). *Social skills in the classroom: Digital media use in Sub-Saharan Africa.* Retrieved from http://www.tnsglobal.com/sites/default/files/whitepaper/TNS_In_Focus_digital_media_SSA.pdf

Howard, P., & Hussein, M. (2011). The upheavals in Egypt and Tunisia: The role of the digital media. *Journal of Democracy, 22*(3), 35–48. Retrieved from http://www.journalofdemocracy.org/upheavals-egypt-and-tunisia-role-digital-media doi:10.1353/jod.2011.0041.

Human Rights Watch website, Nigeria: *Post-election violence killed 800.* Retrieved May 18, 2011, from http://www.hrw.org/news/2011/05/16/nigeria-post-election-violence-killed-800

Internet World Stats. (n.d.). *Top 20 Internet Countries.* Retrieved from http://www.internetworldstats.com/top20.htm

Israel Loves Iran. (n.d.). *Israel Loves Iran.* Retrieved from http://www.israelovesiran.com/

Jenkins, H. (2012). *Confessions of an Aca-Fan, Contextualizing #Kony2012: Invisible Children, Spreadable Media, and Transmedia Activism.* Retrieved March 12, 2012, from http://henryjenkins.org/2012/03/contextualizing_kony2012_invis.html

Kony2012 (2012). *Kony 2012.* Retrieved from http://www.kony2012.com/

Kony 2012 [Video file]. Retrieved from http://www.youtube.com/watch?v=Y4MnpzG5Sqc

Lotan, G. (2012, March 14). *KONY2012: See How Invisible Networks Helped a Campaign Capture the World's Attention.* [Web log comment]. Retrieved from http://blog.socialflow.com/post/7120244932/data-viz-kony2012-see-how-invisible-networks-helped-a-campaign-capture-the-worlds-attention. (2012, March 14).

McAdam, D. (1982). *Political Process and the Development of Black Insurgency, 1930–1970.* Chicago, IL: University of Chicago Press.

Mulero, S. (2012). *Acceptance and impact of social networks marketing using extended technology acceptance model.* Thesis. Cape Peninsula University of Technology, Cape Town, South Africa Retrieved from http://digitalknowledge.cput.ac.za:8081/jspui/bitstream/123456789/263/1/acceptance%20and%20impact%20of%20social%20networks%20marketing%20using%20extended%20technology%20acceptance%20model.pdf

Newmark, C. (2009). *A nerd's take on the future of news media.* Retrieved from http://www.huffingtonpost.com/craig-newmark/a-nerds-take-on-the-futur_b_325544.html

News, B. B. C. (2012). *Facebook influences Nigeria football team ban U-turn.* Retrieved January 14, 2013, from http://www.bbc.co.uk/news/10525699

Nigeria, M. T. N. In *Facebook.* Retrieved from https://www.facebook.com/MTNLoaded

Paun, M. (2009), Perceptions on the effectiveness of communication between public institutions and journalists through social media. *Styles of Communications, 2009*(1), 121. Retrieved from http://journals.univ-danubius.ro/index.php/communication/article/view/145

Pernisco, N. (2010). Social media impacts and implication on society. *Student Journal for Media Literacy Education, 1*(1), 11. Retrieved from http://www.understandmedia.com/pdf/SJMLE-Vol1.pdf

Shaughnessy, H. (2012). *Stop Kony/ Kony 2012 Closes on 50 Million YouTube Views: Meanwhile The Guardian Investigates.* Retrieved from http://www.forbes.com/sites/haydnshaughnessy/2012/03/09/stop-kony-kony-2012-closes-on-50-million-youtube-views-meanwhile-the-guardian-investigates /

SocialBakers. (2011). *The rise of Asia and Africa on Facebook: Statistics by continent!* Retrieved from http://www.socialbakers.com/blog/116-the-rise-of-asia-and-africa-on-facebook-statistics-by-continent/

Stepanek, M. (2013, March 15). *Occupy: The Movie.* [Web log comment]. Retrieved from http://causeglobal.blogspot.com.au/

The Communication Regulators' Association of Southern Africa (CRASA). *Welcome to CRASA.* Retrieved from http://www.crasa.org/index.php

U.S. Department of State's Report of the Advisory Committee on Cultural Diplomacy. (2005). *Cultural Diplomacy: The Linchpin of Public Diplomacy.* Retrieved from http://www.state.gov/documents/organization/54374.pdf

U.S. Senate Resolution 402. (n.d.). *A resolution condemning Joseph Kony and the Lord's Resistance Army for committing crimes against humanity and mass atrocities.* Retrieved from http://www.govtrack.us/congress/bills/112/sres402/text

Vasquez, R. (2011). *Social Networking Theory and Cultural Diplomacy*. Abridged thesis. Retrieved from http://www.eotwonline.net/2011/05/22/social-networking-and-cultural-d/

Wong, S. (2012). *Joseph Kony captures Congress' attention*. Retrieved from http://www.politico.com/news/stories/0312/74355.html

ENDNOTES

1   Essoungou A, *A social media boom begins in Africa - Using mobile phones*, Africans join the global conversation, Africa Renewal Online, 22 August 2011, available at: http://www.un.org/africarenewal/magazine/december-2010/social-media-boom-begins-africa

2   Etzo S and Collender G, The mobile phone revolution in Africa: Rhetoric or reality?, African Affairs, Volume 109, Issue 437, p. 659.

3   TNS Global Study, *Social skills in the classroom: digital media use in Sub-Saharan Africa*, available at http://www.tnsglobal.com/sites/default/files/whitepaper/TNS_In_Focus_digital_media_SSA.pdf

4   Social Bakers social media statistics website article, *The Rise of Asia and Africa on Facebook: Statistics by Continent!*, published 21 February 2011, available at: http://www.socialbakers.com/blog/116-the-rise-of-asia-and-africa-on-facebook-statistics-by-continent/

5   Shaughnessy H, *Stop Kony/ Kony 2012 Closes on 50 Million YouTube Views: Meanwhile The Guardian Investigates*, Forbes, 9 March 2012, available at: http://www.forbes.com/sites/haydnshaughnessy/2012/03/09/stop-kony-kony-2012-closes-on-50-million-youtube-views-meanwhile-the-guardian-investigates/

6   Bohler-Muller N and Van der Merwe C, *The Potential of Social Media to Influence Socio-Political Change on the African Continent*, Africa Institute of South Africa Policy Brief No 46, March 2011, available at: http://www.ai.org.za/media/publications/Policy%20Brief/AISA%20Policy%20Brief%2046.pdf

7   Asur S and Huberman B, *Predicting the Future With Social Media*, IEEE Web Intelligence, 2010, p. 492.

8   Carr N, *The Shallows: What the Internet Is Doing to Our Brains*, W.W. Norton Publishers, 2011.

9   Pernisco N, *Social Media Impacts and Implication on Society*, Student Journal for Media Literacy Education, Volume 1, Issue 1, 2010, p. 11, available at: http://www.understandmedia.com/pdf/SJMLE-Vol1.pdf

10   Paun M, *Perceptions on the Effectiveness of Communication between Public Institutions and Journalists through Social Media*, PhD Research Project, University of Bucharest Romania, p. 6.

11   Ibid p. 6.

12   McAdam D, *Political Process and the Development of Black Insurgency, 1930–1970*, University of Chicago Press, 1982.

13   Colombo S et al, *New Socio-political Actors in North Africa, a Transatlantic Perspective*, 14 February 2012, available at: http://www.gmfus.org/archives/new-socio-political-actors-in-north-africa-a-transatlantic-perspective

14   Howard P and Hussein M, *The upheavals in Egypt and Tunisia - the role of the digital media*, Journal of Democracy, Volume 22, Number 3, July 2011, p. 37.

15   Cambie S, *Lessons from the front line: the Arab Spring demonstrated the power of people--and social media*, Communication world, Vol 29 Issue 1, 2012, p. 28.

16   Iranians We Love You website, available at: http://www.israelovesiran.com/

17   Castells M, *The Grand Fusion: Multimedia as Symbolic Environment,* in The Information Age:
     Economy, Society and Culture: Volume 1: The Rise of the Network Society, Massachusetts: Blackwell
     Publishing, 1996, 2000, pp. 394-403.

18   Vasquez R, East of the West website, *Social Networking Theory and Cultural Diplomacy (abridged thesis),* available at: http://www.eotwonline.net/2011/05/22/social-networking-and-cultural-d/

19   US Department of State Advisory Committee on Cultural Diplomacy, *Cultural Diplomacy: The Linchpin of Public Diplomacy,* 15 September 2005, p. 4, available at: http://www.state.gov/documents/organization/54374.pdf

20   Standard Bank's Insight and Strategy publication, *The five trends powering Africa's enduring allure,* 23 September 2011, available at: http://www.standardbank.com/Article.aspx?id=-127&src=m2011_34385466

21   Newmark C, *A Nerd's Take On The Future Of News Media,* The Huffington Post, posted 19 October 2009, available at: http://www.huffingtonpost.com/craig-newmark/a-nerds-take-on-the-futur_b_325544.html

22   Evans W, *Social Marketing Campaigns and Children's Media Use,* The Future of Children, Volume 18, Number. 1, Children and Electronic Media (Spring, 2008), p. 182.

23   MTN Nigeria Facebook page - https://www.facebook.com/MTNLoaded, Globacom Nigeria Facebook page - https://www.facebook.com/GloWorld

24   Mulero S, Acceptance and impact of social networks marketing using extended technology acceptance model (Thesis), Cape Peninsula University of Technology, pp. 95 to 96.

25   Ibid, p. 96

26   Asuni J et al, *Tracking Social Media – The Social Media Tracking Center and the 2011 Nigerian Elections*, p. 3.

27   Internet World Stats website, available at: http://www.internetworldstats.com/top20.htm

28   Ibid at http://www.internetworldstats.com/africa.htm

29   Shehu Musa Yar'Adua Foundation and Enough is Enough Nigeria Coalition, Track-ing *Social Media - The Social Media Tracking Centre and the 2011 Nigerian Elections*, p. 4.

30   Ibid, p. 10.

31   Aday S et al, United States Institute of Peace, Blogs and Bullets, Contentious Issues in Politics, p. 13.

32   Ibid, p. 9.

33   Human Rights Watch website, *Nigeria: Post-Election Violence Killed 800*, 18 May 2011, available at: http://www.hrw.org/news/2011/05/16/nigeria-post-election-violence-killed-800

34   Tracking Social Media, op.cit, p. 16.

35   Tracking Social Media, op.cit, p. 16.

36   Chidiogo E, Daily Times article, *800 people killed in post-election violence,* 16 May 2011, available at: http://dailytimes.com.ng/article/%E2%80%98800-people-killed-post-election-violence%E2%80%99

37   Tracking Social Media, op.cit, p. 16.

38   Ehidiamen J, Global Press Institute,, *Nigerian Youth Celebrate Social Media as Tool of Successful Election,* 29 April 2011, available at: http://www.globalpressinstitute.org/africa/nigeria/nigerian-youth-celebrate-social-media-tool-successful-election

39   Kony2012 website, available at: http://www.kony2012.com/

40   Kony2012 YouTube video, available at: http://www.youtube.com/watch?v=Y4MnpzG5Sqc

41 Lotan G, Social Flow, *KONY2012: See How Invisible Networks Helped a Campaign Capture the World's Attention*, 14 March 2012, available at: http://blog.socialflow.com/post/7120244932/data-viz-kony2012-see-how-invisible-networks-helped-a-campaign-capture-the-worlds-attention

42 Jenkins H, Confessions of an Aca-Fan, *Contextualizing #Kony2012: Invisible Children, Spreadable Media, and Transmedia Activism*, 12 March 2012, available at: http://henryjenkins.org/2012/03/contextualizing_kony2012_invis.html

43 Stepanek M, Cause Global Blog, *Occupy: The Movie*, 21 March 2012, available at: http://causeglobal.blogspot.com.au/

44 Govtrack.US, S.*Res. 402: A resolution condemning Joseph Kony and the Lord's Resistance Army for committing crimes against humanity and mass atrocities, ...*, available at: http://www.govtrack.us/congress/bills/112/sres402/text

45 Wong S, Politico, *Joseph Kony captures Congress' attention*, 22 March 2012, available at: http://www.politico.com/news/stories/0312/74355.html

46 BBC News, *Facebook influences Nigeria football team ban U-turn*, 6 July 2012, available at: http://www.bbc.co.uk/news/10525699

47 Gladwell M, The New Yorker – Annals of Innovation, *Small change - why the revolution will not be tweeted*, 4 October 2012, p. 2.

48 Eltantawy N and Wiest J, *Social Media in the Egyptian Revolution: Reconsidering Resource Mobilization Theory*, International Journal of Communication Volume 5, 2011, pp. 1207–1224.

49 Ibid, p. 1209.

50 The Communication Regulators' Association of Southern Africa (CRASA) website, available at: http://www.crasa.org/index.php

Chapter 20
Public Opinion on Nigeria's Democracy:
Why the Arab Spring Stopped in the Desert

Anthony Olorunnisola
The Pennsylvania State University, USA

Ayobami Ojebode
University of Ibadan, Nigeria

ABSTRACT

As popular movements of citizens of countries in the Middle East and North African (MENA) region progressed, and in their aftermath, pundits in Nigeria and the Diaspora wondered if there would be a bandwagon effect in Africa's largest democracy. Yet, despite offline and online mobilizations, a growing national insecurity and the "Occupy Nigeria Movement" that sprang up against fuel price hikes in Nigeria, protests and revolts in Nigeria remained short-lived and aimed at piecemeal policy reforms rather than becoming a revolution to unseat the current government. Relying on a human development factors chart, the authors suggest that Nigerians' discontent appears to be motivated by yearnings for what citizens of some MENA countries already have and vice versa. As such, neither democracy nor autocracy—as systems of governance—has delivered the aspirations of African citizens.

INTRODUCTION

Periodic assessment of public opinion is a non-negotiable ingredient for the health of a democracy. It serves as a barometer for assessing the popularity of the government and of citizen input into fundamental policy choices and national direction

(Post, 2005). Yet, academic evaluations of public opinion about the progress of democracy on the African continent have been few and far between. Communication scholars have been more focused on media roles in democratic governance (Ngugi, 1995; Olorunnisola, 1997; Ansah, 1998;) and media coverage of campaigns, elections, impeach-

DOI: 10.4018/978-1-4666-4197-6.ch020

ments, and trials (Oduko, 1987; Olayiwola, 1991; Phillips, Roberts, & Benjamin, 1999; Mvendaga, 2003). Others (Leslie, 1995; Ogbondah, 1997; Jacobs, 1999; Olorunnisola, 2006; Olorunnisola & Tomaselli, 2011) prefer to examine impacts of democratization on the media either by tracking post-transition changes that media systems exhibit or roles that the mass media play in nations in transit. With the "third wave" of democracy well underway on the African continent, there is ample room for scholars to profile public appraisal of democratic governance.

Only in South Africa (Brodie, Altman, & Sinclair, 1999; *Washington Post,* Kaiser Family Foundation, & Harvard University, 2004) and in Ghana (Ansuh-Kyeremeh, 1999) have there been records of public opinion assessments focused, for instance, on the proficiency of the democratic experiments and on the viability of the several arms of government. Of recent, the NOI-Gallup polls conducted in Nigeria (2007, 2008), though quite commendable, have focused on too many variant issues thus understandably lacking depth in the specific areas of governance and democracy.

The survey of public opinion about democracy in South Africa in 1999 and 2004 (Brodie et al, 1999; *Washington Post,* Kaiser Family Foundation, & Harvard University, 2004) spurred us to craft an adapted survey with which we surveyed public opinion in Nigeria with focus on public perception of the implementation of democracy in the last twelve years. We felt the need to provide opportunity for Nigerians to appraise progress made with democratization a system of government that many Nigerians clamoured for and for which others made the supreme sacrifice. In search of contextual information, we also conducted focused group discussions in Nigeria in 2007. Our plan to conduct a second national survey after April 2011 was foreclosed by post-presidential election violence in many parts of the country. In place of a national survey, we conducted focused group discussions in 2011.

Our exploration in this chapter is part of a larger and more elaborate study. We began with multiple curiosities. Nigeria is one of the largest democracies on the African continent. Nigeria has had long years of non-democratic rule. At the time the survey and FGDs that informed the content of this chapter were administered, Nigeria had just experienced civilian-to-civilian transition; an uncommon event in its recent political history.

Our data gathering, especially the conduct of the second Focused Group Discussion, coincided with the commencement and spread in 2011 of anti-government social movements in the Middle East and North Africa (MENA) region. The bush fire of public disenchantment in the MENA region and the way in which citizens of successive countries in the region (Egypt, Libya, Tunisia, and Yemen) jumped on the bandwagon of violent protests led pundits across the African continent and in Nigeria to speculate that Nigerians may rise up against the government. We wonder in this chapter if the issues that drove social movements in the MENA region were identical to the rationale for public disenchantment in Nigeria upon which pundits based their warnings about the likelihood of a bandwagon effect. Some public commentators concluded that MENA citizens clamored for democratic ideals which ideally, open new vistas for citizen participation, an era in which the opinion and, much more than that, active participation of citizens in governance are encouraged. We were not entirely certain that western-style democracy was what MENA citizens were after. Nonetheless, why would Nigerians who have enjoyed democratic governance since 1999 join the democratization movement bandwagon in 2011? Rather than speculate, co-authors resorted to unpacking relevant public responses offered by a cross-section of Nigerians over a four-year span. Thereafter, we offer educated guesses about the consistencies or inconsistencies between the aspirations of citizens of MENA countries and experiences of Nigerians with democratic governance.

PUBLIC OPINION AS A DIMENSION OF DEMOCRACY

An increasing number of scholars are dissatisfied with the unwieldy definition of democracy and the unending stretching of the term to mean virtually anything that resembles good governance (Marcus, Mease, & Ottemoeller, 2001; Post, 2005; Maruatona, 2006). Foregoing authors find the equation of democracy with periodic elections, economic liberalism, granting of basic freedoms or with majoritarianism and popular sovereignty inadequate.

Democracy is "that form of government which aspires to realize the value of collective self-determination" (Post, 2005, p. 142). Aspiration for "self-determination" is grossly thwarted if democracy is reduced merely to regular elections or majority rule. A number of reasons account for this. Mere conduct of regular elections does not in itself make a country democratic; communist and totalitarian countries hold elections and govern on the basis of real, imagined or fabricated majorities. Secondly, democracy rests fundamentally on citizens' conviction that they are engaged in the process of self-determination. More important than the engagement is the conviction of being engaged. If, therefore, citizens' consent is coerced or influenced, that basic conviction is compromised.

Self-determination is crucial to democracy, yet it has been misinterpreted to be present once citizens duly elect representatives who make decisions on citizens' behalf. Citizens are then deemed bound by those decisions. Attempts are hardly ever made, even in advanced democracies such as Canada, to find out if the decisions are indeed the citizens' (Kornberg & Clarke, 1994). According to Post (2005, p. 144) this form of delegated decision making is an insufficient index of self-determination for it is devoid of peoples' "warranted conviction that they are engaged in the process of governing themselves." There is a fine distinction, as Post points out, between making

particular decisions and recognizing particular decisions as one's own. "Self-government is about the authorship of decisions, not about making of decisions." Applied to elections, for instance, it is not only crucial for people to recognize the outcome of elections as their own decision, but it is important that even the fundamental direction of the elections such as whether or not elections should hold at all should strongly emanate from the collective will of the people. The very process and procedure matter as much as the product. Very often, fundamental decisions are taken and citizens are asked to vote on the particulars within thickly bounded confines. This level of arm-twisting does not leave enough elbowroom for citizens to develop and express their convictions about democracy.

Scholars have observed the likely and sometimes irreconcilable disparity in citizens' views and beliefs; and between citizens' preferences and the responsibilities of the state. As Kornberg and Clarke (1994, p. 539) note, "fundamental questions such as how should a democratic political system balance liberty with equality and the rights of the individual (and more recently the group) with those of the community are long-standing and unresolved." This latter is one of the tensions inherent in democracy, reflecting the antithetic nature of the tripartite ideological cornerstones on which democracy rests: the Athenian principle that emphasizes popular sovereignty; classical liberalism that focuses on individual freedom and rights, and the principle of participatory democracy that stresses people empowerment (Kornberg & Clarke, 1994).

Post tackles this fundamental question when he argues that to citizens, it is the process, their thorough and transparent involvement in the process, which matters more than the product. When the outcome of a transparently democratic exercise is contrary to the will and preferences of certain citizens, "the decision-making is [all the same] democratic because it is experienced as self-determination": the 'winners' and the 'losers' were and still are part of the ongoing democratic engagement. But when particular 'losers' feel alienated from the "general will, or from the process by which the will is created, voting on issues is merely a mechanism for decision-making, a mechanism that can easily become oppressive and undemocratic" (Post, 2005, p. 145). Kornberg and Clarke (1994, p. 543) add that "citizens will judge governments not only in terms of their effectiveness, but also by the equity and fairness of their procedures, processes, and policy outcomes."

Further, alienation occurs when citizens do not experience the state as being responsive to their own ideals, values, and ideas. Alienation is prevented when there is a continual "mediation between the collective self-determination and the individual self-determination of particular citizens" (Post, 2005, p.145). When democracy excludes the common will of the society or the individual will of certain citizens without having given them the chance to be part of the decision-authorship process, the outcome can be mental torture as well. In essence, people are unable to call the government their own; yet they have to put up with the "aliens" in government. Citizens do not have to be 'losers' to experience alienation and they do not have to be "winners" to feel significant in the decision authorship process. "If citizens are free to participate in the formation of public opinion…if the decisions of the state are made responsive to public opinion, citizens will … experience government as their own, even if they hold diverse views and otherwise disagree" (Post, 2005, p.146).

One of the ways of forestalling alienation and mental torture of citizens is through unfettered public opinion. "A democracy without public opinion is a contradiction of terms" (Kelsen as cited by Post, 2005, p. 146). Public opinion gives a citizenry a sense of worth. It is when public opinion is freely facilitated and government decisions are made in response to people's opinion that we have citizens who can experience government as their own even if they hold diverse views. That is when citizens can be convinced that they are self-

governing. "The will of the community is always created through a running discussion between the majority and minority, through free consideration of arguments for and against a certain regulation of a subject matter" (Kelsen, cited by Post, 2005, p. 146). That discussion is about one of the dynamics of democracy (Maruatona, 2006). In sum, seeking after public opinion is panacea for public alienation from government and for avoiding citizens' mental torture about the workings of government. While procuring public opinion is necessary, it is evidently insufficient to ensure public engagement unless a government is able to frequently implement public will.

As important as scholars claim that it is, public opinion is hardly often conducted to assess the extent to which citizens regard the democratic process as theirs, or in fact, to assess what democracy means. This is as true in Africa as it is in the West (Kornberg & Clarke, 1994). This missing link in democratic governance provided further justification for our survey of public opinion about democracy in Nigeria.

DEMOCRACY IN AFRICA

Sorting through the complications surrounding democracy in Africa is quite a challenge. Marcus et al. (2001, p. 113) suggest that what exists in African "democratic" countries is neither democracy nor authoritarianism "but rather some gray area in between." This indictment of the African continent is evidently not of the people but of the executive arm of government. It is also an admission of the academic frustration that often accompanies the attempt to make sense of the installation of democracy in the African context.

As Maruatona (2006) implies, most African nations democratized as a condition for getting aids from western donors. In the ensuing game of deception, some African leaders opted for the superficial, the observable and the manifest aspects of democracy such as elections and the existence of real or ghost opposition parties. Democracy in many African countries, therefore, has minimal roots in the collective will of the people; that "gray area" (Marcus et al., 2001, p. 113) has become more conspicuous.

Evidence of the "gray area" subsists in many forms. Most authoritarian regimes in Africa conducted elections in the 1990s and in countries such as Cameroon, Togo, and Kenya, the ruling autocrat "won" the elections. Results either indicated people's preference for autocracy or underscored their helplessness. For most observers, the latter is the case (Bjorlund, Bratton, & Gibson, 1992; Adejumobi, 2000; Brown, 2001). Rather than serve as an instrument for the sustenance of democracy, elections in much of Africa have proved to be a collective weapon for truncating citizens' will. In fact, former Ugandan president, Milton Obote, it was said, defined elections as his way of controlling the people (Adejumobi, 2000). This tendency is a reversion to the old order of despotic political leadership under the guise of democratic governance.

The foregoing raises a crucial question: Is western-style democracy impracticable in the African context? As if responding to the question, Marcus et al. (2001, p. 114) say:

(A) part of the challenges facing democratic theories is that the foundation of our knowledge of democracy, and its resulting categories and variables, is based upon western definitions of democracy. Little attention has been paid to the way that people in Africa conceptualize democracy. Indeed even most empirical studies addressing the nature of African democracy look to structural elements of democracy (such as elections, national conferences, legislative makeup, etc... rather than local views or definitions of democracy. In an age in which universal suffrage elections are the sine qua non of government legitimacy, we believe that identifying what the people themselves understand by democracy may grant considerable analytical leverage both to democratic theorists and policy makers in Africa.

Marcus et al. do pose a challenging question: If democracy is terminologically western, what do we logically imply when we seek African peoples' conceptualization of the term? The underlying and unspoken assumption behind Marcus and others' proposition appears to be that cultural determinism trumps transferred terminologies and that innovations such as democracy have limitations. Where would peoples' understanding of democracy come from? We see a number of possible sources: one possibility is that citizens will draw from their participation in and observation of their representatives' implementation of democracy; another source may be citizens' knowledge of the way in which democracy works in other places in the knowable world. It is also crucial to ask: will all of peoples' assumptions about and understanding of democracy be legitimate? If so, does democracy then assume a fluidity that makes any characteristic qualify for inclusion? If not all assumptions are legitimate, then whose version and/or interpretation of democracy should serve as benchmark for assessing democratic principles? For Africans, it should be fair to argue that if systems of democratic governance are adopted, yardsticks for assessment will equally have to be borrowed and mixed with doses of local realities.

DEMOCRACY IN POST-APARTHEID SOUTH AFRICA

The surveys of public opinion of South Africans on democracy (Brodie, Altman, & Sinclair, 1999; Washington Post, Kaiser Family Foundation, & Harvard University, 2004) gave clear evidence that Africans hold certain expectations about democratic governance, about the role of political office holders, and are capable of distinguishing between democratic and autocratic regimes. The surveys report a predominant preference for democracy over apartheid among South Africans. Brodie et al. (1999) worked with a sample of 3,000 adult South Africans selected across the racial and professional strata of the country. Survey administrators conducted face-to-face interviews from November to December 1998. Data were analyzed in simple percentages.

A second South African survey was conducted in 2004 by the *Washington Post*, Kaiser Family Foundation, and Harvard University. Using a combination of stratified and random sampling techniques, the researchers conducted face-to-face interviews with 2,961 adult South Africans. As well respondents were selected across the racial and professional strata of the country. The data was collected from September to November 2003. Both South African surveys adopted only a quantitative approach.

Specific aspects of the democratic process were evaluated by the citizens. About 91% of South Africans polled preferred secret balloting; 89% counted as non-negotiable the right to vote for their party of choice; 82% regarded press freedom as indispensable in the democratic process, while 75% asked for strong opposition in order to checkmate excesses. The value attached to democracy is shown in the huge proportion (76%) of those who counted voting not to be a waste of time. As part of the evaluation, most South Africans thought things were better in democracy than in apartheid: citizens' ability to influence government was considered to be stronger (68%); the economy was better (52%); healthcare (54%); education (69%); and race relations (68%) were also seen as having improved (Brodie et al., 1999; *Washington Post*, Henry Kaiser Foundation, & Harvard University, 2004).

However, crime was seen to have remained the same by as many as 56% of the respondents; while corruption in government is seen to have worsened (50%) or stayed the same (19%). Unemployment was described by 78% to have become worse. Confidence in government and the press was not impressively high in South Africa: 54% had a lot of confidence in the mass media; 43% in the judiciary, and 56% in the legislature. The local government attracted a lot of confidence from only 44% while 48% trusted the provincial

government a lot. Though South Africans mostly preferred democracy, only 46% were certain that the nation would remain a democracy after Mandela left office, and only 30% were confident of the future under Thabo Mbeki (Brodie et al., 1999; *Washington Post*, Henry Kaiser Foundation, & Harvard University, 2004).

The South African studies cited before are instructive in that they underscore how much citizens know about democracy and how specific their assessments can get. The two South African studies spurred our attempt to conduct similar studies in Nigeria albeit more comprehensively as we added qualitative to the quantitative approaches taken by authors of the South African surveys.

THE STUDY

Following from Marcus et al. (2001) and from Post (2005), our study aimed at examining the extent to which Nigerians were convinced that they have participated in a democratic process. We also wanted to uncover Nigerians' understanding of democracy. As such, we sought responses to survey questions across the country.

In general, the following questions guided our curiosities: (1) How do Nigerians define and assess progress of democratic governance? (2) What realistic prospects does democracy (as Nigeria's experience shows) hold for Arab spring movement participants in the MENA region? (3) What experiential questions do the Arab spring movements (in spite of participating countries' better human development factors) pose for Nigeria? (4) Why did the Arab spring end in the dessert, so to speak? (5) What lessons do combined experiences offer African leaders and citizens about governance as steps are taken toward realization of Millennium Development Goals?

We adopted quantitative and qualitative approaches in our assessment of Nigerians' opinion about democracy. Our questionnaire was largely adapted from the South African surveys employed in procuring public opinion in the former apartheid enclave in 1998 and 2003. Co-authors selected questions with which to explore people's perception of democratic governance but carefully reviewed the South African questions for contextual relevance. Six hundred and twelve adult Nigerians drawn from the six geo-political zones[1] of the country were involved in the study. Field assistants[2] administered questionnaires in the form of face-to-face interviews to respondents except where respondents insisted on filling in the questionnaires on their own. Interviews were administered in the languages most preferred by the respondents.

We adopted a multistage procedure in selecting our samples. First, in each geo-political zone, using simple random sampling, we selected one out of the constituting states[3] and then stratified the selected state into rural and urban local government areas. Field assistants then selected at least 25 respondents from two rural and two urban local government areas. The selection followed further stratification along political party and employment lines. Together we had and analyzed 612 properly filled copies of the questionnaire. Final analysis revealed that supporters of the major political parties as well as those not affiliated with any party were represented in the sample; so also were fulltime employees (39%), the self-employed (20%); odd jobbers (12%); the unemployed (10%); part-time employees (6%); pensioners (6%); and those unwilling to disclose their source of income (7%).

Respondents were asked questions about structural aspects of democracy (voting, multi-partyism) and the extent to which they enjoyed freedoms. Questions also included requests for respondents to compare democratic and non-democratic governments in substantive ways (access or lack thereof to government, crime and violence, economy, education, inter-ethnic relations, corruption); to state extent of their confidence in the four estates of the realm (local government, state government, legislature, the

mass media); and to speculate about the future of democratic governance under the current/incoming administration.

The result of the analysis of the questionnaire informed another round of data collection, this time, through focus group discussions (FGDs). Discussions were organized in four of the six geo-political zones; two from the north, and two from the south; that is North Central, North West, South South, and South West. In each representative state, we conducted three discussion groups taking care to ensure that participants in the FGDs were not those earlier involved in the questionnaire administration. Together, 122 people took part in the discussions[4]. In all of these, we wanted citizens to assess democracy in Nigeria after the first 12 years. The quantitative data was gathered between March and April 2007 and the qualitative data in January 2008 and June 2011. Our use of three independently collected data sets in one combined assessment of commonalities and differences in peoples' experiences with democracy has precedence (e.g., Marcus et al.'s [2001] collation of three independent democracy studies conducted in Uganda, Madagascar, and Florida).

In the section that follows, we present only a part of the quantitative data collected in 2007 and used the qualitative data gathered in Nigeria in 2008 and 2011 to shed further insight on the quantitative data. By juxtaposing quantitative and qualitative data, we show the readers how respondents appraised each of the pertinent questions posed.

DISCUSSION OF FINDINGS

Results show what Nigerians understood democracy to mean and what their attitude to democracy was. We then show their preferences between democracy and military rule. We also show their levels of confidence in the four estates of the realm and what they felt the future held for democracy in the country.

Attitudes of Nigerians to Democracy

Twenty-five percent of Nigerian respondents disagreed with secret ballot system; 88% of Nigerians agreed respectively that the right to vote was key to democracy; 89% believed that press freedom must be guaranteed in a democracy, while 84% of Nigerians felt that democracy is not possible without a strong opposition party. Some Nigerians (16%) believed that voting was a waste of time but 86% of Nigerians agreed that a party should be allowed to campaign even in communities that predominantly support a different political party (Figure 1).

Why do Nigerians prefer the open ballot system? Nigerian discussants at the 2007 focus group discussions explained:

The open ballot system is better...in the secret ballot system, I can collect money from you and I may not vote for you; in the open ballot system it is impossible for me to collect money from you and say I want to hide. I will be in trouble...that was why there was no cheating in 1993 during Abiola's[5] election...It is (sic) open. So everyone sees who the winner is (sic).

In their words and besides the reference to the pecuniary dimension to voting, the open ballot system makes it difficult for the electorate to be dishonest with contestants and for party supporters to tamper with election results.

Another area of notable importance is the need for opposition parties: a great proportion of Nigerian respondents wanted a strong opposition party. Again, Nigerian discussants explained, stating that the ruling People's Democratic Party (PDP)[6] already had too much power and that the nonexistence of opposition parties could turn Nigeria into a one-party state. In strong and frightening words, discussants forecast that the absence of opposition would be the end of democracy:

We will be doomed because there will be no critics to checkmate the government and that will bring doom on the nation. There will be no checks and balances. The economy will be doomed, the nation will be doomed.

There will be anarchy. We are heading to destruction... and that is not democracy. Democracy thrives in the midst of opposition. There can't be democracy without opposition...

Figure 1. Respondent's attitudes to Democracy

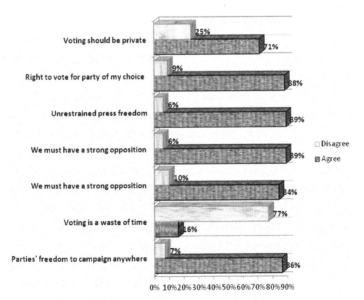

There will be killing, killing and death, war and violence everywhere, disaster for the whole country. PDP is the worst option for Nigeria. (FGD, 2007)

Nigerians' fears might, again, have been informed by their experience during the 2007 elections, after which the ruling People's Democratic Party claimed overwhelming victories in circumstances condemned as grossly unacceptable by independent and foreign observers.

As indicated, a good percentage of Nigerians (16%) felt that voting was a waste of time. Again, Nigerians spoke from experience:

One hundred percent, waste of time. This is because in Nigerian democracy...you vote but before your vote gets to the collation centre, everything is changed... What's the point? You queue up from morning. The sun beats you and yet the votes are not counted...

I was returning officer in the last elections...I went and sat down under the tree for hours without seeing any voting materials but when the results came out, the ward was represented... In some states, before the returning officers returned from the field, they had already announced the results...

The widespread irregularities that characterized the 2007 elections must have gravely influenced the feelings of the discussants.

We found it noteworthy that discussants in the 2011 FGDs reported a different disposition to the issue of voting. One respondent reported as follows:

Voting is no longer a waste of time. This (2011) election was better than the previous one (2007). In Enugu State, everyone knows that if you abuse a Reverend Father, it is a slap to them. He (the sitting governor who abused the Reverend Father) has done the worst thing. He has touched the people. As a result, they voted him out of office. The people's will prevailed through voting.

Another respondent to the 2011 FGD stated as follows:

We're not wasting our time at elections because voting is our right. Now we thank God for Atahiru Jega[7] for the election was free and fair ... most of the people protected their vote; so it is better.

Post (2005) speaks strongly about the place of experience in citizens' assessment of democracy. It is instructive that Nigerian respondents readily recall their experiences as they either indict or positively assess the process.

What are the important ingredients of democracy, as defined by Nigerians? The most important ingredients of democracy identified by Nigerians are basic necessities, right to fair and speedy trial, and freedom of religion. A great percentage of Nigerian (69%) respondents considered the existence of at least two competing political parties to be an ingredient for democracy. This is consistent with respondents' positions discussed earlier with regard to the presence or absence of opposition (See Figure 2).

It is not impossible that Nigerians are developing an aversion for elections: not only have Nigerians been involved in elections over the years but also Nigerian elections have been more often riddled by irregularities than otherwise.

Comparison of Democratic with Nondemocratic Governments

More Nigerians (63%) preferred democracy to military rule. Respondents were asked to compare specific issues under the two systems of government. The rating of democratic governance by Nigerians was gloomy: to most Nigerians, nearly everything was worse in democracy than under military rule. Seventy-four percent of Nigerian respondents say corruption in government was worse in the democratic dispensation than under the military; 67% say unemployment was worse; 61% say crime and violence was worse; 46% say education was worse, and 39% say inter-ethnic

Figure 2. Percentage of Nigerians that say the following is "very important" for a society to be called Democratic

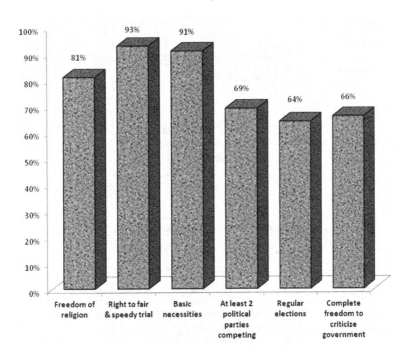

relations neither improved nor worsened. However, 49% felt that people's ability to criticize government was better with democracy, and 46% say healthcare improved while 38% felt that the economy improved (See Figure 3).

Nigerian focus group discussants were more unsparing in their comparison of the state of things under democracy with that under military. As it is with the quantitative data, the worst pounded was corruption in government:

Corruption has never been this bad in this country; ever since Nigeria got independence, from 1960.... Corruption in Nigeria has been incorporated right from the top down to the local level....

We know the military was corrupt but not as much as democrats (civilian leaders). Obasanjo was the most corrupt democratic ruler we've ever had... he's being indicted everywhere in the power sector.... (FGD, 2007)

Respondents to the 2011 FGD agreed in principle with the scourge of corruption under the democratic dispensation. One respondent deposed as follows:

Corruption has never been this bad in Nigeria. In the days of the military, there was corruption in millions (of Naira) but now it is in billions. EFCC and ICPC are losing the battle.

Another respondent to the 2011 FGD added:

Democracy would have been better than it is if there was no immunity clause. It is this immunity clause that the governors are using to steal and do things and no one can arrest them ... recklessness and power abuse (have become the order of the day).

On the rise in the wave of crime and violence in the democratic era, a discussant puts the blame squarely on politicians:

Figure 3. Were things better under the Military than under Democracy?

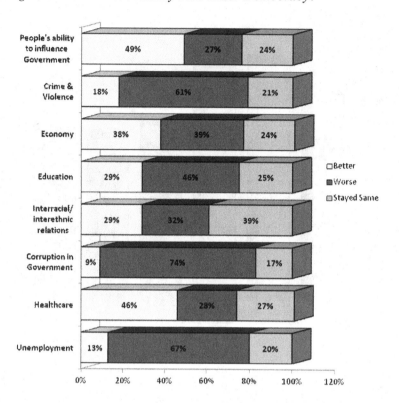

The civilians, politicians hired people who would support them in creating militias, private guards (and gave them) ammunitions to kill people. They put guns in the hands of young men to terrorize opponents in elections. At a stage, they stopped paying the young men and they (the men) are using the guns (sic) killing people on the highways. (FGD, 2007)

The military, our discussants added, were able to match criminals steel-for-steel but the democratic government could not. This was also the explanation given for the rise in inter-ethnic conflicts during the democratic era. Notably, the sentiment expressed by discussants in the 2011 FGD groups did not vary. In response to the question about level of crime and violence under the military versus the democratic government, a respondent offered:

Crime rate is more pronounced in this democratic government. Imagine all the killing and violence in the post-presidential election violence and not one culprit has been brought to book for it. Imagine all these crises here in the North. Crime is worse now. All this Boko Haram in parts of the North, military government would have finished them in one week.

Speaking of the scourge of Boko Haram attacks a second respondent deposed as follows:

This Boko Haram attacks cannot happen during the military rule. They will know how to tackle them. But under democracy ... imagine our president saying if this people can get hold of him, they would kill him. That is, he's afraid.

Addressing the problem of general insecurity in Nigeria, a third respondent deposed as follows:

Violence and deaths are more common today than they were in the past. Politicians have turned youths, unemployed youths into their warriors and they are sending them to kill others who did not support them or who belonged to other parties. The police have no power and we are all at the mercy of these thugs.

If things were this bad in democracy, why do Nigerians prefer democracy still? Our discussants explained that the most important reason is that democracy brings them freedoms hitherto not experienced:

Even though I am married to a military man, I prefer democratic or civilian regime... [because] there is freedom of speech, people contribute (their views) not really being scared what the repercussion would be, (FGD, 2007).

A respondent to the more recent (2011) FGD corroborates the latter opinion in following words:

Our democracy is 12 years old. Yes, it is better than military (government). But we have not seen the full dividends because democracy is the government of the people by the people and for the people but in Nigeria, we see government of the people for the people but I don't think it's by the people.

Other respondents anchored their preference for democracy on the absence of harassment by soldiers. Yet others noted that the media function more freely and fearlessly. All of these are illustrations of the main idea that there is more freedom in democracy.

Another reason Nigerians preferred democracy, though they claimed certain things worked better under the military, was opportunity for participation

Ideally, democracy gives room for everyone to participate; we select the government by ourselves... and we can criticize the government.

The foregoing illustrates the worth Nigerians attach to freedom—like their Ugandan, Malagasy and American counterparts (Marcus et al., 2001) and to true self-determination (Post, 2005). It also shows that Nigerian respondents prefer foregoing principles of democracy to what is practiced in Nigeria. This disconnection is one of the symptoms of alienation that Post (2005) talked about.

Confidence in the Four Estates of the Realm

We asked Nigerians to indicate the level of confidence they had in the federal government and only 14% said they had a lot of confidence in the federal government and 40% had some confidence. Among Nigerians, by far the most trusted estate is the mass media. Only 4 in 10 Nigerians had any confidence in state and local governments. Forty-eight percent of Nigerians had any confidence in the legislature; in Nigeria, 77% expressed confidence in the judiciary. Evidently, Nigerians do not have confidence in the executive and the legislative arms of government; many more (83%) had confidence in the media. It is also noteworthy that the tier of government closest to Nigerians, that is, the local government, had the worst (10%) confidence rating (See Figure 4).

Why are Nigerians so sceptical about their government? Reasons given by discussants fall under five broad headings: a track record of poor performance or non-performance, perceived insensitivity to the conditions and yearnings of the people, corruption, perceived distance maintained from the people by office holders, and the morally unacceptable ways by which many of the office holders got into power. A discussant noted: "The Federal Government is performing badly; how can we have confidence in (sic) them?"

Another observed:

Figure 4. Confidence in the 'Four Estates of the Realm'

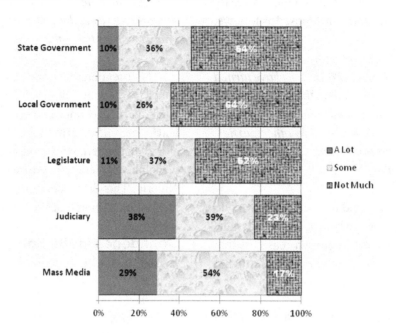

I don't have confidence in them because the ways most them got to the office was not legitimate. They just manipulated election results...the last government just imposed candidates on us... President Yar' Adua himself knows that there were anomalies in the elections...yet he is still in government. (FGD, 2007)

A respondent to the 2011 FGD had this to say about his/her confidence level in the local government:

We have no confidence level in the local govern-ment. They don't exist. I don't even know the local government name, or the name of the chairman. I don't know who he is. The local governments don't have guts; they are just there, just answer-ing the name as local government chairman. We don't even recognize their impact.

Foregoing comment is confirmation of Post's view that citizens are indeed concerned about the democratic process itself more than they are about the product. If the process is faulty, the product

will most likely be. Nigerians do not seem to experience the citizen-government affinity, that sociological level of democracy that Post (2005) alludes to. Another discussant's view of local government administration further instantiates this loss of affinity:

Where are the local governments? What are they doing? Let's look at the chairman of Ifo Local Government. He lived behind my house in Agbado Crossing in Lagos...but immediately he won the election, he left the rural area (sic) to Victoria Island[8]. We do not see them (sic) again... (FGD, 2007)

This point alone significantly explains why Nigerians are so acerbic in their assessment of their government and democracy. "Citizens do indeed have their local government's performance in mind when asked to evaluate their satisfaction with democracy" (Weitz-Shapiro, 2008).

And the legislature does not appear to be far-ing better:

We have lost confidence in the national assembly. Look at the case recently of Patricia Etteh, the number four citizen Nigeria, who is being accused of money laundering. It's a very big shame on Nigeria…the current national assembly is not doing well compared to what we had in 1979. (FGD, 2007)

Therefore, Nigerians seem to have reasons, and good reasons they claim, for not reposing any confidence in the executive and the legislature. However, about the mass media, opinions appear to be divided:

If not for the press, many of the things we know, we would not have known. When there was problem in the House, when Iyabo[9] was involved in money laundering, if the press was not there; Etteh[10] and rest, if the press was not there, there was no way we would have known. (FGD, 2007)

A respondent to the 2011 FGD made the following comments about the mass media:

I have some confidence in the mass media. But it is always the same thing: it is what the government wants them to say that they say … a press man that is to write a report on a politician who did a bad act, if the man bribes him he will change the story or may not write the full story because he received a brown envelope.

It appears that though there is no citizen-government affinity, there is a fair level of citizen-media affinity. Nigerians seem to appreciate the opportunity for "the running discussion" (Post, 2005, p. 146) that the media provide but have distaste for some of the bad eggs in the profession. In sum, discussants condemned the media for selling out and accepting bribes from government and politicians. A discussant pointed out that government media were less trustworthy than private media.

The Future of Democracy in Nigeria

Though they claimed things were bad in the democratic dispensation and confess to having no confidence in levels of the government, Nigerians maintained high hopes about the prospects of democracy. More Nigerians in 2007 (66%) were sure that their country would remain a democracy after the regime of the then outgoing president, Olusegun Obasanjo. We suspect that Nigerians did not in any way associate president Obasanjo with their nation becoming a democracy. His exit from office, therefore, could not be tantamount to the exit of democracy. See Figure 5.

Nigerians (36%) were confident of the future under President-elect Umaru Musa Yar'Adua. But many respondents (48% of Nigerians) were unsure of the future under the incoming leader; in fact, 16% of Nigerians were worried (See Figure 6).

During the focus group discussions, the voices of the worried and the unsure were overwhelming. A discussant explained his skepticism thus:

Where did Yar'Adua come from? Was he not a governor in Katsina [State]? What did he achieve? Nothing. So what do I expect now that he's president? Nothing.

Figure 5. Respondents' opinion on whether Country will remain in a Democracy after Obasanjo

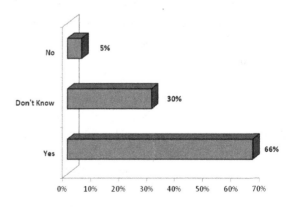

Figure 6. Nigerians' confidence in the future under Yar'Adua

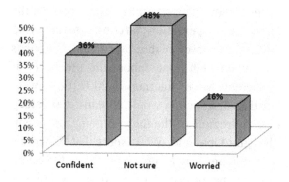

Those confident about the future were not totally silent:

Yar'Adua will lead us well because he publicly declared his assets. After the swearing in he raised up his hands and swore to stand for the truth. If a President can say that, it means that the future will be bright.

Matters of performance and transparency were regularly mentioned as respondents justified their stand on the future of Nigeria under President-elect Yar'Adua. In response to the 2011 FGD which sought respondents' opinion on the viability of Nigeria's democracy under President Jonathan, the dominant answer was the expression of hope. One respondent deposed as follows:

As a Nigerian I have been disappointed so many times but I've decided to actually give Jonathan the benefit of doubt. He's going to be different... I'm actually looking up to him to get a lot of things right. So I'm optimistic. I really hope that he doesn't mess up.

Another respondent was not that positive:

During his first term, he said if he had the opportunity to rule this country, he would declare a state of emergency on electricity. And we know

that electricity is the major source of the economic development. But he did not improve anything. If he wanted to do so well, all the things he promised, he would have started doing them one after the other. So, I can't say Goodluck Jonathan is ready to influence the economy of Nigeria.

A running theme in the latter comment and others before it underscores the extent to which our respondents were more focused on the deliverables of government–access to political leaders, resolution of perennial social problems leading to insecurities, and curbing the menace of corruption. Others including pundits and social commentators have referred, at times condescendingly, to these expectations as citizens seeking dividends of democracy less than they clamour for structural elements (voting, elections, national conferences, etc.) of democratic governance. We agree with Marcus et al. (2001) that western and local definitions of democracy do co-exist and at times conflict. While western definitions focus on those structural elements, local definitions often overlap with the structural elements but proceed beyond them to dwell on realities of developmental problems that exist in referent countries.

What realistic prospects does democracy (as Nigerians' experience shows) hold for Arab Spring movement participants in the MENA region? In the subtext of survey and FGD results, we see hints that the arrival of democratic governance–though seen erroneously as precursor of all solutions–does not necessarily lead to the provision of solutions to pre-existent socio-economic and political problems. Nigerians continue to wait for the dividends of democracy in substantive socioeconomic and political terms 12 years after the return of democratic governance. This reality sends a message to citizens of MENA countries who may conceive of democracy as the answer to all problems. Ironically, nearly all the countries in the MENA region where extant governments were dethroned post comparably positive Human Development Indicators than Nigeria. In that regard, the socio-economic dividends that Nigerians have found elusive from non-democratic and democratic governments respectively abound in the MENA countries that participated in the Arab Spring movement. Why then did the Arab Spring movement end in the desert?

WHY THE ARAB SPRING STOPPED IN THE DESERT

The widespread protests in the Middle East and North Africa (MENA) region began in December 2010 in Tunisia. Sparked off by a young man's self-immolation in protest of unemployment and corruption, the protests spread across Tunisia and beyond, eventually spilling into about twenty countries. Rationale for the protests soon expanded to include citizens' disenchantment with political leaders' sit-tight syndrome[11] and people's inability to participate in the political affairs of their respective nations. By February 2012, these sustained protests had resulted in regime changes in four countries: Tunisia, Egypt, Libya, and Yemen (Anderson, 2011; Cottle, 2011; Dunn, 2011).

What really was the force behind these protests? And why did such protest not extend to countries like Nigeria? Our examination of development indices over various years showed that the affected Arab nations did much better than Nigeria in terms of human development indices (See Table 1). For

instance, life expectancy of Nigerians was 47.7 years in 2009, much lower than Tunisians', (74.2), Egyptians', (69.9), Libyans', (74.1) and Syrians' (74.0) (World Bank, 2010).

In 2006, only 47% of Nigerians had access to an improved source of water, whereas up to 94% of Tunisians, 89% of Syrians, and 98% of Egyptians had access to improved source of water. Nigeria had by far the highest number of under-five mortality rate; the highest number of children out of primary schools, and the second lowest spending on health per capita. All these factors speak to quality of life and were comparably better in nations of the MENA region when compared to Nigeria.

Given the previous, Nigeria should have been the most likely candidate for the type of revolutionary insurgence that destabilized the Arab nations while the citizens of MENA nations should be celebrating their good fortune–living in a nation where the governments post development indicators that are favorable. It is safe to state not only that Nigerians lack many of the indicators that citizens of the MENA region have but that those amenities are not going to be available in the near future. A respondent to the 2011 FGD questions offered the following instructive comment as a reason for Nigerians' lackadaisical response to the wave of change in the MENA region:

Table 1. Human development indices

Country	Life Expectancy at Birth	% with access to improved water source	Children out of School (Primary)	Health expenditure per capita (USD)	Under-5 Mortality Rate Per 1000
Egypt	69.7	98.0	867,862.0	86.4	27.5
Libya	73.9	--	--	219.0	18.4
Nigeria	47.5	47.0	7,329,348.0	66.8	191.4
Syria	73.8	89.0	--	65.0	17.6
Tunisia	73.9	94.0	7,873.0	191.9	22.5

Source: World Bank (2010) "*World Development Indicators*" Electronic Version (Figures in this table represent performance in the year 2006)

See, it was just one angry man that started this in Tunisia. He set himself on fire out of anger about poverty and unemployment. There is more poverty in Nigeria. There is worse poverty and unemployment in Nigeria. One day, someone will set himself on fire here and it will start ... only that Nigerians will just say that person is a mad person. Let me continue with my own life ... so you can never tell (be so sure that such action will spark a revolution).

Though respondents offered the resilience of Nigerians in the face of stringent living conditions as rationale for non-participation in a movement similar to Arab Spring, we posit that the euphoria and prospects offered by democracy is recent enough that there is hope for a better future–if a good leader emerges. Knowing the likely exit date of a regime makes democratic governance more tolerable. While Nigerians groan and grumble under the imperfections and excesses of successive regimes, a focus on exit date and another wave of elections seem to sustain their endurance. Violent regime change such as through revolutionary protests are reminiscent of bloody military coup d'états of previous years which themselves were not popular movements – though some had support of some civilians. Somehow Nigerians have not seen this route as an attractive option.

Ironically, Nigerians have what the citizens of the MENA region want, that is, the disappearance of political leaders' sit-tight syndrome and the ability to participate in the process that leads to the emergence of those who control the affairs of the state. This was not the case in the MENA region where regimes were known to have lasted several decades. Absence of fundamental and democratic rights in those countries made the available good infrastructure and development to pale into insignificance.

It is evident however, that neither Nigerians nor citizens of MENA nations were experiencing a perfect system of government. The ideal government is thus one that combines provision of developmental infrastructure with meeting desire of citizens for participation in the political life of the nation.

CONCLUSION AND RECOMMENDATIONS

Quantitative and qualitative information garnered as a part of this study, only a part of which is reported here, shows that the public in Nigeria is willing to discuss democracy; is very lucid, can be conceptually informative and analytical about their responses to questions concerning democratic governance. In particular, focus group discussions held in geo-political regions of Nigeria indicated preference for governance processes that work and that people can be critical when the reverse is the case. Across the board of quantitative and qualitative data, these responses are worthy of academic attention.

Responses gathered do indicate that public feedback on the definition and assessment of democracy can be as poignant as the questions asked. We were able to uncover such experiential underpinnings of democratic experiments as Nigerian citizens' disposition to and convictions about their own engagement with the democratic process. Post (2005) was instructive when he stated that mere elections, particularly when they are manipulated, do not define legitimate democracies. Post-election actions and inactions of government continue to provide citizens with arsenal with which to rate the value of ongoing experiment with democratization. As such, the estates indicted by public opinion in this study and the sectors in which room for improvement have been identified should provide government functionaries, academics who study democratic processes and civil society organizations with agenda for monitoring governments' activities vis-à-vis citizens' participation. Persistently posing analytical questions to citizens should progressively lead to improvements in democratic governance and to departure from the "gray area" version of democracy.

Though transitional problems persist, evidence garnered from public expression of opinion in Nigeria shows that people are yearning for a responsive government, demonstrable leadership and dividends of democracy in substantive political, economic and social terms. There is desire for votes that count and choices that matter. As well, there is expressed need to feel the presence of government where it matters; in particular at the local government level.

The bastions of autocracy were fought back in Nigeria in part by the engagement of civil society organizations, the mass media and non-governmental organizations. The new atmosphere of civil liberties that the public observed in the country has not translated into the disappearance of democratic tyranny nor has it produced significant changes in the pre-existent social infrastructure. The implication should be that there is room for partnership with the public in contending with governance in the "gray area."

Though Nigeria's democratic experiment is not perfect, the rationale for the social movements that have become known as the Arab Spring did not find footing in Africa's largest democracy. As indicated earlier, citizens of countries in the MENA region sought an end to the sit-tight syndrome that characterized the rule of the Mubaraks and Ghadaffis. They desired governments that will be answerable to the people. The comparatively positive scores earned by the MENA countries on the World Development Indicators (WDIs) did not ameliorate citizens' desire for participation in their nation's governance. Hence, the ease with which the embers of disenchantment spread across the nations.

On the contrary, Nigerians enjoyed democratic governance before and at the onset of democratic governance. A social movement would have had to pull from a different set of rationales than what obtained in MENA region. We note, however, that the dividends of democracy that Nigerians asked for in our survey and in subsequent FGDs overlapped with benefits enjoyed in Egypt and Libya under Mubarak and Gadaffi. As such another way to rationalize the termination of the Arab Spring in the dessert is to state that Nigerians were unwilling to truncate a sitting government on account of dividends that may combine to inform the World Development Indicators (WDIs).

Nonetheless scholars of democratic arrangements and policy makers, particularly in developing nations, should note that the embers of public disenchantment can be motivated by one (desire for political participation as was the case in the MENA region) and by the other (desire for substantive dividends of democracy as expressed by Nigerians). In addition, while democracy is necessary it may in and of itself be insufficient, a palliative factor in the absence of dividends that citizens can gauge in their daily lives. At the same time, mere provision of services that score high on World Development Indicators by a benevolent dictator, whose stock in trade is citizens' non-participation in governance, can fall short of the desired mark. African citizens desire both; participation in government and substantive benefits of good-governance. In summation, it is crucial to speak for the value of public opinion–both as a process of information gathering and as a veritable instrument of democratic governance and policy implementation. Post (2005, p. 146) informed that when "citizens are free to participate in the formation of public opinion ... if the decisions of the state are made responsive to public opinion, citizens will ... experience government as their own, even if they hold diverse views and otherwise disagree." We agree without reservations.

REFERENCES

Adejumobi, S. (2000). Elections in Africa: A fading shadow of democracy? *International Political Science Review*, *21*(1), 59–73. doi:10.1177/0192512100211004.

Anderson, L. (2011). Demystifying the Arab Spring Parsing the Differences between Tunisia, Egypt, and Libya. *Foreign Affairs*, *90*(3), 2–7.

Ansah, P. A. V. (1998). In search of a role for the African media in the Democratic Process. *Africa Media Review*, *2*(2), 1–16.

Ansuh-Kyeremeh, K. (1999). The challenges of surveying public opinion in an emerging democracy. *International Journal of Public Opinion Research*, *11*(1), 59–74. doi:10.1093/ijpor/11.1.59.

Bjornlund, E., Bratton, M., & Gibson, C. (1992). Observing multiparty elections in Africa: Lessons from Zambia. *African Affairs*, *91*(364), 405–431.

Brodie, M., Altman, D., & Sinclair, M. (1999). *Reality check: South Africans' views of the new South Africa. A Report on the national survey of the South African people, Sponsored by the Henry J.* Kaiser Foundation and Independent Newspapers.

Brown, S. (2001). Authoritarian leaders and multiparty elections in Africa: How foreign donors help to keep Kenya's Daniel Arap Moi in Power. *Third World Quarterly*, *22*(5), 725–739. doi:10.1080/01436590120084575.

Cottle, S. (2011). Media and the Arab uprisings of 2011: Research notes. *Journalism*, *12*(5), 647–659. doi:10.1177/1464884911410017.

Dunn, A. (2011). Unplugging a nation: State media strategy during Egypt's January 25 Uprising. *World Affairs*, *35*(2), 15–24.

Jacobs, S. (1999). Tensions of a Free Press: South Africa after Apartheid. Paper presented at the Joan Shorenstein Center on the Press, Politics and Public Policy. Cambridge, MA.

Kornberg, A., & Clarke, H. D. (1994). Beliefs about democracy and satisfaction with democratic government: The Canadian Case. *Political Research Quarterly*, *47*, 537–563.

Leslie, M. (1995). Television and Capitalist Hegemony in the "New" South Africa. *The Howard Journal of Communications*, *6*(3), 164–172. doi:10.1080/10646179509361694.

Marcus, R.R., & Mease, K., & Ottemoeller. (2001). Popular Definitions of Democracy from Uganda, Madagascar, and Florida, U.S.A. *Journal of Asian and African Studies*, *36*, 113–132. doi:10.1177/002190960103600106.

Maruatona, T. (2006). Adult education, deliberative democracy and social re-engagement in Africa. *Journal of Developing Societies*, *22*(1), 11–27. doi:10.1177/0169796X06062964.

Mvendaga, J. (2003). *The Nigerian mass media and the 2003 elections*. Ibadan, Nigeria: Jodad Publishers.

Ngugi, C. M. (1995). The Mass Media and Democratization in Africa. *Media Development*, *4*, 49–52.

Oduko, S. (1987). From indigenous communication to modern television: A reflection on political development in Nigeria. *Africa Media Review*, *1*(3), 1–10.

Ogbondah, C. W. (1997). Communication and Democratization in Africa: Constitutional changes, prospects and persistent problems for the media. *Gazette*, *59*(4/5), 271–294.

Olayiwola, R. O. (1991). Political communications: Press and politics in Nigeria's second republic. *Africa Media Review*, *5*(2), 31–45.

Olorunnisola, A. A. (1997). Political ideology and news selection in local versus foreign press coverage of a domestic political event. *Ecquid Novi: Journal for Journalism in Southern Africa*, *18*(2), 247–263.

Olorunnisola, A. A. (2006). *Media in South Africa after Apartheid: A Cross-Media Assessment*. Lewiston, NY: The Edwin Mellen Press.

Olorunnisola, A. A., & Tomaselli, K. G. (Eds.). (2011). *Political economy of media transformation in South Africa*. Cresskill, NJ: Hampton Press, Inc..

Phillips, D., Roberts, N., & Benjamin, S. A. (1999). Political communication through newspaper advertisement: The case of the 1999 presidential election in Nigeria. NISER Monograph Series No 10.

Post, R. (2005). Democracy and equality. *Law, culture and the humanities. 1*, 142-153.

Post, W. Henry Kaiser Foundation, & Harvard University. (2004). *Survey of South Africans at ten years of democracy*.

Weitz-Shapiro, R. (2008). The local connection: Local government performance and satisfaction with democracy in Argentina. *Comparative Political Studies*, *41*(3), 285–308. doi:10.1177/0010414006297174.

World Bank. (2010). *World Development Indicators*. Retrieved January 14, 2013, from http://data. worldbank.org/sites/default/files/frontmatter.pdf

ENDNOTES

[1] Nigeria is officially divided into six geopolitical zones: North Central, North East, North West, South East, South-South and South-West. Unlike the states, these are not administrative units with their own political heads; rather they were created as a framework to enhance fair rotation of political elective and appointive offices across the country.

[2] We acknowledge field research assistance rendered by Mbakeren Ikeseh (North Central); Caleb Yusuf (North East); Ponchang Wuyep and his team (North West); Chibuzo Ejiogu (South East); Eyambah Mensah Offiong (South).

[3] Each geo-political zone has six states except the South East that has five, and North West that has seven.

[4] Mbakeren Ikeseh (North Central); David Ayandele (North West); Eyambah Mensah Offiong and Edidiong Umanah (South South) and Samuel Olaleye (South West) rendered field assistance at the qualitative phase of the data collection.

[5] Discussant refers to the 1993 presidential election which was adjudged the freest and the fairest in the history of Nigeria but was, for unknown reasons, annulled by the military administration of General Ibrahim Babangida.

[6] PDP has been ruling party in Nigeria since 1999; winning all three presidential elections and more seats in the national assembly than competing opposition parties. The PDP also has won more gubernatorial elections in more states of the federation, a scenario that has given the party the national presence that continues to elude opposition political parties most of which are regional players at best.

[7] Professor Atahiru Jega headed the National Electoral Commission. Though there a few hiccups at the beginning of the electoral process, many public commentators attested to the comparatively fair administration of the electoral process in 2011. Beyond com-

mentators' assessment is the reality that comparatively fewer winners of the 2011 elections have faced post-election challenges in the courts.

8   'Agbado' is a sub-urban area of Lagos that is rapidly taking on the shape of a slum; 'Victoria Island' is one of the high brow areas of Lagos harboring some of the most expensive real estates in the country.

9   Iyabo, that is, Senator Iyabo Obasanjo-Bello, is the daughter of President Olusegun Obasanjo.

10   Honourable Patricia Olubunmi Etteh was speaker, Federal House of Representatives accused of inflating the contract for the renovation of her official quarters. Mrs Etteh was forced to resign her position as speaker.

11   Ben Ali ruled Tunisia for 24 years; Mubarak ruled Egypt for 30 years; Gaddafi ruled Libya for 32 years and Saleh ruled Yemen for 33 years.

Chapter 21

New Media and the Changing Public Sphere in Uganda:
Towards Deliberative Democracy?

Kennedy Javuru
Journalist & Independent Scholar, UK

ABSTRACT

This chapter gives an exploratory overview of the emergence and growth of new media in Uganda and how the alternative nature of new media is scaffolding the notion of citizenship and deliberative democracy. The chapter also suggests that despite the new found vigour, it is too early to say whether the Ugandan new media landscape have so far become a true alternative or complementary participatory space or a genuine platform for the distribution of uncensored information. It concludes that Ugandans use new media more for social interaction and dissemination of information (in a limited way) than as an alternative political public sphere. However, there are signs that online media is emerging and the anecdotes presented in this chapter indicate the potential of this media to be a place of participation and deliberation and reducing the authoritarian control of the communicative space.

INTRODUCTION

This chapter assesses the changing media landscape in Uganda and how new media is playing an active role in pushing the agenda for recognition of the notion of citizenship and deliberative democracy. Central to the discussions are the concepts of access and participation and how the dominance of mainstream media as the sole provider of information and discursive space is being challenged. Various aspects of new media such as blogging, SMS, social media and radio talk shows are discussed to analyse the extent to which new media has opened up the deliberative space in Uganda. I assess the potential impact of new media on public debate and suggest ways in which new media fail to meet an idealized model for the public sphere in Uganda.

DOI: 10.4018/978-1-4666-4197-6.ch021

The advent of new media technology in Africa in the late 1990s was received with hysterical optimism. It was believed that Africa's impediments to development would be automatically overcome by 'leapfrogging' some of the stages of development (Banda, Okoth, & Tettey, 2009). Historically, the introduction of new technology generated widespread optimism about how the technology would affect the way humans communicated. As Kandell (1998) observes:

Each significant technological development fundamentally changes the way the world works. Just as the invention of the electric light enabled a multitude of nocturnal activities to occur and the VCR created an entire industry of video retailers, the development of the internet and the World Wide Web have spawned a revolution in communication, commerce and interpersonal behaviour (p. 110).

The excitement new media generates is based to a large extent on the disillusionment and disappointments of traditional media being overly commercialised and not inclusive. New media brings in the promise of inclusiveness and blurring the line of professionalism that old media is predicated upon. Yet almost a decade after new media technology graced the African continent, the old questions about access, inequality, inclusiveness, power and the quality of information abound (Fourie, 2001). Banda, Okoth, and Tettey (2009) note that discussions about new media technology in Africa often disregard the unusual African terrain, which defies many of the technological innovations said to be reconfiguring the structures and processes of communication globally. This includes poor telecommunication networks in most parts of Africa, resulting in low levels of Internet usage. Nevertheless, online communities are emerging across Africa and although they are mostly among the elite, they show Africans taking advantage of new technology to advance their own identities and agendas.

UGANDA'S COMMUNICATIVE SPACE

The history of the media in Uganda is closely connected to the country's political history. Since independence in 1962, subsequent governments have sought to control the economic, social, political, and cultural spheres including the mass media. The media in Uganda were harnessed for the causes of nationalism and nation-building. However, the global democratic movements of the 1990s, coupled with growing discontent over limited political participation, human rights violations, the shambolic economy, and limited communication platforms implied Uganda could not remain an 'island' in the face of sweeping changes.

The media environment in Uganda has changed dramatically in the last two decades. The liberalization of the economy in the 1990s which coincided with the global democratization movement ushered in a new period of democratization in Africa. It was also a period that witnessed many African countries adopting the multi-party political system. The spread of the 'third wave' of democratization to Africa in the early 1990s represented the most significant political change in the continent since the independence period three decades before. Throughout the continent, significant political liberalization resulted in the emergence of a free press, opposition parties, independent unions and a multitude of civic organizations autonomous from the state. In 29 African countries, the first multi-party elections in over a generation were convened between 1990 and 1994 (Bratton & Walle, 1997). In a smaller set of countries, elections were fully free and fair and resulted in the defeat and exit from power of the erstwhile authoritarian head of state. By the end of the decade, only a small minority of states were not officially multi-party electoral democracies, even if the practice of democratic politics was often far from being exemplary.

BROADCASTING

During the clamour for democracy in Africa, independent media emerged at the forefront of the campaign for democratic governments. After the liberalization of the airwaves in 1992, which seemingly challenged state monopoly of broadcasting, several players including businessmen, NGOs, churches, foreign investors, politicians, and Ugandans in the diaspora too jumped on the bandwagon to start or fund FM stations. The first private FM stations were *Sanyu FM* (October 1993) and *Capital Radio* (December 1993). The programming formats of the FM stations revolved around popular music from the United States, local pop music-punctuated by commercial advertisement and jokes from young talents picked from disco clubs (Mwesige, 1999). Today, there are more than 276 radio stations in Uganda (African Media Barometer (AMB), 2012) broadcasting in all the major languages and boasting vibrant and interactive virtual communities (Kibazo, 2007). Despite their proliferation, diversity remains a tall order for them as most stations' content remains homogenous. Some of these radio stations are privately owned by government officials or their accomplices, which sometimes limits their ability to critique the government policy view point. Although Kagadi Kibaale Community Radio; the first community radio station in the country was set up a decade ago, the growth of community radio in Uganda has been painstakingly slow. But, on a more positive note, Mwesigye (2009) argues that the advent of private radio altered the political role of radio in many parts of Sub-Saharan Africa and in particular the emergence of political call-in talk shows which creates an opportunity for ordinary citizens to question and hold those in power accountable. The private radio boom in Uganda can indeed be equated to a new form of media that is revolutionising the relationship between citizens and the media, and government and the citizens. The patchy state of online access in the country means that these radio stations represent a vital cog in the political communication space. As Peter Mwesige, a media academic, reasons in Tabaire (2003):

Talk shows have opened up new political spaces that were unimaginable only a decade ago... [it] may not be democracy in action but it is an important rehearsal for democracy (p. 193-211).

Call in talk-shows, dubbed *ekimeeza* (table talk) have become a regular, and immensely popular feature of radio broadcasting in Uganda. *Radio One, Radio Two, Simba FM, Central Broadcasting Services (CBS), Capital FM* and other stations hold live public debates once a week. The format is quiet simple; invited guests, usually government officials and opposition politicians gather at a public place outside the studio, a pub or restaurant and debate a topic selected by the moderator. Members of the public are encouraged to participate by either going to the venue or phoning in. Such talk shows appear to be oases of free speech and popular politics in a society associated with political disparity and intimidations (Nassanga, 2009). It is indeed an example of new media encouraging participation and democratic expression (Ryan, 2010). Government has been forced to find ways to contain radio talk shows' burgeoning popularity while at the same time maintaining an atmosphere of apparent liberal stances (AMB, 2010).

Television still remains an urban, elite media and according to the Uganda Media Council's figures, there are 72 licensed television stations but not all the stations are in operation. This figure is based on the number of frequencies bought (AMB, 2012). The government-owned *Uganda Broadcasting Corporation* (UBC) TV covers at least 70% of the country while the privately owned television stations remain confined to urban areas, covering less than 30% of the country (AMB, 2012). The majority of Ugandans have no access to television because of the cost of buying television sets and also because a large part of the country is not connected to the national power grid. For those who have electricity, it is very unreliable due to the rampant load shedding.

THE PRESS

Uganda's press has grown in terms of variety and quality over the past two decades.

Several private newspapers have opened and substantially improved contents. But market challenges mean a high mortality rate for even the best newspapers. For instance, in the last 20 years, 16 newspapers have closed (Kirumira, Mark, & Ajwang, 2007). This leaves only 13 newspapers on the market. The government owns five of the 13 newspapers under one company: The New Vision Printing and Publishing Corporation. Two of them; *New Vision* and *Bukedde* are dailies, while others, namely *Orumuri* (published in Runyankole), *Etop* (Iteso language), *Rupiny* (published in Luo language) are weeklies. These compete with two private daily newspapers—the *Daily Monitor*, mainly owned by the Nation Media Group, and the *Red Pepper*; a tabloid publication started in June 2001 and owned by five individuals. The *Daily Monitor*, established in 1992, prides itself as the country's first fully independent newspaper. It emerged at a time when political party activities were banned in the country and the few brave opposition politicians' voices were merely 'stray voices in the desert.' It is not by accident that the *Daily Monitor* became the defacto home of the country's opposition largely because they [opposition] could not get fair reporting in the then government controlled national daily, the *New Vision*. The *Daily Monitor* paid a heavy price for its benevolence to the county's opposition when in 1993, the government stopped advertising in the newspaper. This denied the newspaper 70% of its revenue. The Daily Monitor weathered the storm and the ban was lifted in 1998. There are five weekly newspapers; *The Weekly Observer,* started on March 25, 2004 by 10 journalists who broke away from *Daily Monitor*. The other weekly newspapers are *The East African* published by the Nation Media Group, *The Sunrise, The Weekly Message*, and *The Guardian*. The three newspapers are owned by different private individuals and published in English. There are no official figures regarding their circulation. The most recent newspaper to be launched in Uganda is *The Independent*, a biweekly newspaper founded in December 2007 by Andrew Mwenda, a journalist who previously worked with *Daily Monitor*. The newspapers that have closed in the last 20 years include *The Stream, The Vanguard, The Sun*—an English version of *Bukedde*, a Luganda paper of *New Vision*, *The Crusader* – started up by breakaway journalists from *Daily Monitor* in 1996, *Economic News, The Weekly Digest* and *The East African Procurement News*.

The birth of *The Crusader, The Weekly Observer, The Evening Mail,* and most recently, *The Independent* from *Daily Monitor* reflects conflicts that exist within Uganda's media. The break-away factions accused *Daily Monitor* management of poor remuneration of journalists and lack of editorial independence. Much as there is now a steady growth of daily, weekly and bi-monthly independent newspapers, the growth of print media has not been as explosive as it has been in the broadcast sector.

NEW MEDIA

There has also been a spectacular adoption of mobile telephony that far exceeds the uptake of the Internet. According to *Internetworldstats* (2011), Uganda had 4,178,085 Internet users as of December 31, 2011 (12.1% of the population); 346,980 Facebook users (which equates to 1% of the population). Fifty-five per cent of Internet users access the Internet from Internet cafes and only 35% of the country's population have access to mobile phones; one of the lowest levels of penetration for mobile telephony in Africa (AMB, 2012). Most people use mobile phones on a daily basis to send or receive information through phone calls, SMS, while some smart phones can be used to browse the Internet; store, play and share audio, video, images on and offline. Many media houses in Uganda, especially radio, have integrated mobile telephony as a platform for listeners to contribute news, views, stories and feedback though call in and SMS. Seventy-five per cent of Uganda's Internet users use the Internet for 'chatting with friends', with Facebook being the Internet site most accessed in the country. However, 35% of Internet users access the Internet for news and current affairs, with the on-line editions of the *Daily Monitor*, *New Vision*, and *Red Pepper* being the most popular Ugandan sites (AMB, 2012). The Internet is changing the way news is delivered in the Ugandan media. Journalists who work for established newspapers, radios, and television stations now have the opportunity to become more independent publishers of speciality blogs and hyper local news websites. The Websites can be owned and operated by the media house employing a particular journalist, or owned and operated independently by the journalist with links to or from the website of the media organizations where they work. Such Websites play an important role in the emerging news and information landscape by allowing the journalist(s) to go beyond the space, airtime and gatekeeper limitations of traditional media to publish as much and as often as they wish. Anyone with an enabled cell phone can access Web-based information from anywhere in the country. A journalist in Uganda can easily publish a personal blog or create quality online news sites using powerful and easy to use web publishing platforms like wordpress, blogger, webs, joomla, drupal, among the many others that provide complete content management systems. These new media platforms also allow for more interactivity by enabling members of the public to post comments, articles, information, or tips. However, the previous figures also clearly show that the uptake of internet usage is still very slow. While the new technologies have the potential to significantly alter the media landscape in Uganda, policy reforms lack a strategic perspective and they have not created a link between technology and efforts to improve governance.

The relationship between the government and the media in Uganda can be best described as a 'Tom and Jerry' relationship[1]. Various laws have been enacted to clip the wings of 'noisy' journalists, while at the same time the government encourages Ugandans to use their constitutional right of freedom of expression. Negotiating the media terrain in the country is akin to stepping in a minefield; you are not sure where to put your foot lest you get blown up! This begs the question about the viability of alternative media as a credible and competent channel for political discourse and deliberative democracy. The prospects look encouraging because the laws of the land are primarily designed for traditional media. However, as analyses in the later parts of this chapter will reveal, government is beginning to take interest in what goes on online and have started tracking down activities of some known online media practitioners. Never the less, new media is seen by some as an antidote to the heavy handed approach with which the government sometimes handles criticisms from the media largely because one can be anonymous and there are no premises to raid and close down. However, despite the gloomy picture, compared to previous governments, the current one under President Museveni has expanded various freedoms both in practice and by the enactment of bills of rights enshrined in the country's constitution. The liberalisation of the communications sector in the early 1990s led to an explosion of media. This upsurge in media has necessarily led to an increase in the number of critical voices that can be heard against the government. Over time, the government has sought to mute those voices. In a way, the government is scared of its own success. It is as if having let the genie out of the bottle, it wants it back in. That has proved difficult. It is now resorting, partly, to the force of legislation to achieve its aim of having a pliant population. The government is doing this well aware it can get its way because the ruling party dominates parliament. It is also important to note that while the media appears to operate in relative freedom, most media practitioners practice self-censorship (Dicklitch & Lwanga, 2003). While the government gives freedom with one hand, it takes away with the other hand through the existing libel and treason laws (Ocitti, 2006).

The growth of global digital technology powered by the Internet has triggered a trickling in of online media practices by both professional journalists and ordinary Ugandans. A number of professional journalists have their own blogs where they share information that is not governed by editorial policies stipulated by their employers, giving rise to a form of non-institutional citizen journalism. The rise in blogging and feedback has encouraged many newspapers in Uganda to set up websites with interactive features where the public is allowed to comment and raise the issues without the fear of being 'cut short' by the editor. In this context, new media can be viewed as instrumental in the democratisation of news content.

Lister, Jon, Seth, and Kieran (2003) suggest that discussions about new media force us to acknowledge, on the one hand, a rapidly changing set of formal and technological experiments and, on the other, a complex set of interactions between new technological possibilities and established media forms. As Landlow (2003) asserts, new media technologies should be seen as existing on a continuum or spectrum rather than in any fundamental opposition to one another. This perspective allows us to contextualise new media—the Internet, e-mail, cellular telephony, and so forth, in terms of the old questions posed of old media such as universal access, regulation, and content.

New media technologies have heralded a second wave of media revolution in Uganda. One of the conspicuous hallmarks of the second revolution is the realignment of relations between the news media and their audiences; the government and citizens. The relationship is shifting with the audiences who were once perceived as passive receivers of information, now performing the dual role of consumers and producers of information on the Websites of established newspapers, radio stations, social networking sites, and both personal and political blogs. While radio and new media have incorporated the public voice into their programming in the last decade (Hyden, Leslie, & Ogundimu, 2002), the print media has been slow to catch on and still uses paternalistic, top-down approach largely because in Africa, print media is still the elite's media because of the high rate of illiteracy. An attempt at studying the impact of new media on Uganda's media and political landscape is at best ambitious owing to the relative newness of the sector and the amateurish nature of the participants. The media's role in the democratization process in Uganda is still evolving. The government seems to allow an avalanche of a relatively free and privately owned independent media especially radio while using the different laws of the country to keep them [independent media] in check.

THE LEGAL FRAMEWORK AND THE FUTURE OF NEW MEDIA

In comparison to other countries in Africa, Uganda's 1995 constitution contains one of the best provisions on freedom of speech on the continent, guaranteeing 'every person the right to freedom of speech and expression, which shall include freedom of the press and other media' (Constitution of the Republic of Uganda, 1995). This promise, however, has been broken. The right to freedom of expression in the country has come under increased threats from the state machinery using the laws of the country and in some cases, outright display of state 'muscles'. Laws regulating the media have become obstacles in not only guaranteeing freedom of expression, but also handicaps in providing the platform for a coherent communicative space in the country. On August 2, 2010, Timothy Kalyegira was the first online journalist accused of sedition in Uganda. Until then, sedition charges had only been brought up against print and broadcast journalists. Mr Kalyegira's website, www.ugandarecord.co.ug, had published an article insinuating that the deadly bombings in Kampala on July 11, 2010, could have been a handiwork of state agents, not the militant Somali group, al-Shabab (Kalyegira, 2010). The most significant aspect here is that the government is getting interested in what Ugandans are writing online and it is doing something about it. The passing, in the immediate aftermath of the 7/11 bombings, of the Regulation of Interception of Communications Bill, has emboldened the government to go after online work more aggressively. It will snoop around more, hacking into people's e-mails in the name of ensuring national security (Amnesty International, 2010). Media observers in Uganda argue that the Kalyegira case is just the beginning. There will be more government interest in online contents as more Ugandans start using the World Wide Web spurred by increased access to electricity and the presence of fibre optic technology, which is speeding up internet connectivity and driving down prices. According to Mr. J. B. Mayiga, the co-ordinator of the Uganda Media Development Foundation, a Kampala based media training and advocacy body,

The government has not had a systematic way of dealing with online content. But the Kalyegira case maybe a precursor for something more concrete – a more specific law because the government is not happy with people expressing themselves freely at any forum.[2]

However, Ms Rachel Magarura, one of Uganda's foremost bloggers reckons the government clamping down on online media may not readily have any chilling effect on online users. 'I have no concerns', she said. 'There is very little political debate in the Ugandan blogosphere and there is no consistency'. She added that for many Ugandans, mostly younger urbanites, 'blogging is an escape, so it is a little frivolous'[3].

Until August 2010, free speech and expression in Uganda was muzzled by the provision on sedition from the Penal Code Act, 1950 which defined sedition as the publishing of statements aimed at bringing hatred, contempt or disaffection against the president, the government or the judiciary. The Penal Code Act provided for seven years of imprisonment on conviction. On August 25, 2010, five Ugandan judges declared the country's criminal sedition offense unconstitutional.

The constant non-expeditious trials of and attacks on journalists are causing tension among media practitioners. According to the Press Freedom Index Report of 2011, in 2011, Uganda documented 107 cases of attacks on journalists compared to 58 in 2010 and 38 in 2009. The attacks ranged from shootings, physical attacks, unlawful arrest and detention, incarceration of journalists, denying access to news scenes, confiscation of equipment, defective and tramped up charges, to verbal threats. The violations happened countrywide under different commands of mainly the police and the army (Human Rights Network for Journalists-Uganda, 2011). Newspapers deemed critical of the government have had their premises routinely raided by unknown persons and the police investigations into such raids have always yielded no arrests or prosecutions for criminal damages. Following the September 2009 riots in which several people were killed by government security forces, four radio stations, *Central Broadcasting Services* (*CBS*) belonging to Buganda Kingdom, *Radio Two* (*Akaboozi Kubiri*), *Radio Ssuubi,* and *Radio Sapienta* were closed for criticising the government's heavy handedness in quelling the riots. Government accused the radio stations of inciting violence and promoting tribalism (Human Rights House Network, 2009). *CBS* was re-opened thirteen months later after a series of closed door negotiations between the Buganda Kingdom and the government. In January 2010, a Cabinet sub-committee formed to address the *CBS* closure came up with 12 conditions for re-opening the radio station. *CBS* management was required to apologise to the government 'through the Broadcasting Council', relocate its studio from the Kabaka's[4] palace (Bulange), withdraw the court case brought by employees against the government, dismiss journalists and presenters who allegedly participated in inciting the September riots, and follow the minimum broadcasting standards. *Suubi FM, Radio Sapienta, Radio Two (Akaboozi Kubiri)* were also re-opened with stern warnings after they apologised for the misconduct of their employees. They were also forced to dismiss some presenters and journalists that the government complained against. The closure of the four radio stations is reported to have had a chilling effect on journalists from other media houses, which were reported to be exercising undue self-censorship. Others claimed receiving orders from their managers or radio station owners not to focus on the Buganda kingdom and other controversial political stories (Africa Centre for Media Excellence-ACME, 2010).

In June 2012, the government in another show of force and authority, summoned 10 journalists operating in the Busoga region for screening. The radio journalists and their managers were accused of sabotaging government programmes. The Commissioner of Police in charge of Media Crimes said he got a directive to close down two radio stations; *Basoga Baino* and *Kiira FM* after their presenters reportedly committed media crimes while on air. The presenters were accused of uttering words undermining the president and other persons in government; an act that was not acceptable. Gulumaire, a talk show host for *Ki-*

ira FM was accused of being biased by hosting mainly opposition politicians on his talk show and regulating the number of on–air callers from the ruling party, the *National Resistance Movement* (Uganda Radio Network-(URN), 2012). These are just a few of the numerous cases of government intimidation and harassment of the media. The Uganda Police now has a fully-fledged directorate in-charge of Media Crimes. In what should serve as a warning to online media, the Inspector General of Police, Gen. Kale Kayihura recently expressed the government's concern about the influence of social media and its [government's] determination to control it (Musasizi, 2012). It is believed government has become very wary of social media because the opposition politicians have been using it for mobilising protests and demonstrations that nearly brought the country to its knees in April and May 2012 (Reuters, 2011).

Uganda possesses many media laws. Most of these laws are widely understood to be intended to protect the people in power against the public's need to be informed. Few laws protect journalists and such laws are sometimes in conflict with other existing laws. The Uganda Constitution guarantees the freedom of the media in article 29 (1) (a):

Every person shall have the right to freedom of speech and expression, which include freedom of the press and other media. (Constitution of the Republic of Uganda, 1995, 29 (1) (a))

The other article that supports the media in the Constitution is 41(1) that relates to access to information thus:

Every citizen has a right of access to information in the possession of the state or any other organ or agency of state except where the release of the information is likely to prejudice the security or sovereignty of the state or interfere with the right to privacy of any other person. (Constitution of the Republic of Uganda, 1995, 41 (1))

This provision has been operationalized by the Access to Information Act (2005). But as Stapenhurst (2000) has observed, the Ugandan legislature has divided information into classes of available and non-available information, with few classes of information being deemed freely accessible. Nyamnjoh (2005) has acknowledged that an examination of most legal frameworks in Africa reveals a craving to control that leaves little doubt of law makers perceiving journalists as potential trouble makers who must be policed. The tendency is for new laws to grant freedom in principle while providing, often by administrative nexus, the curtailment of press freedom in practice. In Uganda, many subsidiary laws have been understood to contradict the media freedom enshrined in the Constitution. Some of such laws are found in the Penal Code Act, 1950 that lays down a number of penalties if one published legally prohibited information. The legal and policy frameworks regulating the media infringe on enjoyment of the freedom of expression and the press. The Press and Journalists Act, 1995 is yet another legislation that infringes on media freedom by granting powers to courts to compel journalists to reveal their sources. Section 38 that deals with protection of sources says:

A journalist shall not be compelled to disclose the source of his information except with the consent of the person who gave him the information or on an order of a court of law. (Part VIII, Section 38)

This provision is hostile to the media because in most cases, news tips particularly the ones involving corruption scandals sometimes are volunteered by junior staffs in organizations. Identifying news sources (whistle-blowers) may endanger their lives and those of their family members in addition to losing employment (ACME, 2010). Moore (2000) has correctly observed that:

As every journalist knows, sources are the lifeblood of a good story. On many occasions such sources are willing to be named; indeed it may be vital to

produce the individual as a witness to defend a defamation action. There are, however, circumstances when a source will only come forward and provide information on the understanding that their identity will not be disclosed. [...] What is clear is that any legal requirement to disclose the identity of a source acts as a severe blow to investigative journalism, undermining its ability to expose corruption and wrong-doing (pp. 142-144).

To date, there has been no notable effort from government to bring into conformity the existing media legislation with the Constitution of Uganda and International standards. Under the Electronic Media Act of 1996, the Broadcasting Council enjoys unprecedented powers of regulating media content.

THE EMERGENCE OF NEW MEDIA IN UGANDA

All the major newspapers in Uganda have Web presence and are well placed to take advantage of the growing popularity of blogging and social media among the youths and urban elite. The *Daily Monitor* has a sophisticated and successful programme of interaction encouraging readers to post emails and send SMS submissions to the newspaper but sometimes struggles to be consistent. The *New Vision* which was once owned by the government and is now a public listed company too has a web presence that appears more organised. It runs a forum which attracts significant contribution from readers every week. Crucially though, none of the Ugandan newspapers run a dedicated blog, although several journalists run active and entertaining blogs alongside their print and broadcasting work. However, a number of controversial blogs carrying political content are mushrooming mostly from the diaspora. Blogs such as *www.ugandansatheart.org* strive to emulate the earlier success enjoyed by www.radiokatwe.com, a now defunct blog that was run from outside the country by a group of Ugandan journalists in exile. *Radio Katwe*, a Ugandan speak for rumours or word of mouth, gained notoriety for reporting 'true rumours' that almost never emerged in the mainstream media but had a strong presence on the street. It encouraged reader participation and published readers' comments, letters, and thoughts at least once a day. *Radio Katwe* operated under complete anonymity and was built to resist government influence. However, in the run up to the presidential election of 2006, the government blocked access to *Radio Katwe*'s website in Uganda (IFEX, 2006). The blockade though, was short lived as *Radio Katwe* soon found other ways of circumventing the government's ban and redistributed their contents and messages on proxy servers. In fact, the site later bragged about traffic tripling in the month after the ban (Radio Katwe, 2006). It appears *Radio Katwe* has since died a natural death and its place has been taken over by the firebrand USA based website www. musevenimustgo.com that seems to find it amusing to publish stories about the private life of President Yoweri Museveni and his cronies. *Radio Katwe* is significant in the history of alternative media in Uganda because it set the bench mark for political discourse that exists in direct contrast to the current traditional media strategies.

There are plenty of blogs and microblogs focusing on Uganda. These are written by journalists and Ugandan expatriates abroad, by staff of international organizations and foreigners with a stake in Uganda. A few long-running ones include www.kalinaki.blogspot.com, www.tinywesonga. blogspot.com, www.bazanye.wordpress.com, and www.ugandacorrespondent.com.

Rosebell Kagumire's blog http://ugandajournalist.wordpress.com won a 2009 Waxal Award for Best English-language African journalist's blog. There has also been collaboration between Ugandan journalists and *The Guardian* in the UK newspaper on a blog called the Katine Chronicles (www.guardian.co.uk/katine/katine-chronicles-blog). Numerous blogs have morphed into full-fledged websites. For example, the 'pop-blog'

jackfruity (http://jackfruity.blogspot.com), originally run by American Rebekah Heacock out of Uganda, has morphed into a full-fledged website (http://jackfruity.com). Heacock now runs the blog out of New York since she became the editor and technical director of Columbia University/SIPA's 'The Morningside Post' (http://themorningside-post.com). Rebekah's blog was influential because it addressed many development issues such as climate change, digital age policy, tourism, and media. Jackfruity also reflects the heavy influence of the expatriate community on Uganda's blogosphere. Other blogs are not expat-run but are located outside Uganda, the most prominent of which are www.ugandansatheart.org and www.ugandandiasporanews.com. Some blogs are agenda driven. An example is http://gayuganda. blogspot.com, a blog that is focused on the Anti-homosexual Bill 2009 which proposed, in some instances, to impose the death penalty on gays in Uganda. The bill has attracted criticisms from human rights bodies and world leaders. However, an amended version of the bill has been presented to parliament in February 2012 with the provision on death penalty removed (Chonghaile, 2012). The development discussion in Uganda is also heavily influenced by foreign blogs such as http:// ideas4development.org and http://aidwatch.org. au. Ugandan bloggers and opinion leaders either contribute to the blogs on those websites or follow the debates on topics such as HIV/Aids and the African Growth and Opportunity ACT (AGOA), poverty alleviation, and so forth. The sites cover a wide range of issues, from development, to politics, social life, and entertainment. But how many Ugandans actually read them? Probably not many given that access to the internet is extremely limited and largely confined to the urban areas dominated by communities around universities and colleges, and in places of work. Language barriers also likely keep many people out of the blogosphere. There does not seem to be any blogs written in local languages. Regardless of the low Internet penetration levels, it is true that some new media technologies are developing at such a fast rate that there is a possibility of mass communication encapsulated in them. For example, mobile phone use has outstripped fixed land-line use in Uganda, suggesting that mobile phone is probably becoming an important part of Uganda's communication culture. There is a possibility of mobile technology becoming a seventh mass medium—the first six being print, sound recording, cinema, radio, television, and the Internet. With the possibility of the use of the Internet becoming a regular feature of mobile communication, the likelihood of the Internet itself becoming a mass medium among Ugandans is very real indeed.

SOCIAL NETWORKING STILL IN THE INFANCY STATE

If blogging has taken off, at least among those with access to the Internet, online social networks are in their infancy. Apart from Facebook and Twitter, social networks in Uganda are not well developed. The few available ones dwell on relationships--finding a lover, the perfect match, or finding a date. For example, a Muslim site www.bestmuslim.com offers dating opportunities, links and profiles of potential partners, chat rooms and a discussion forum. At Makerere University, Uganda's biggest university, www.campuser.net is a social networking site used by thousands of students free of charge, although the proprietors generate revenue through advertising. The site offers free SMS, micro-blogging, friends and dating sections, and a forum for discussions which is quite popular. Facebook is popular with the youth and the working class and Twitter is popular among the elite, especially journalists and activists.

On December 12, 2009, new media enthusiasts in Uganda demonstrated the mobilisation potential of social media when members of one Facebook network sent out word on the social networking site and on Twitter about a social gathering event. The event brought together people who chat on various social networks into one major social group (Kareire, 2009). Members of the 360° Network organized the 'Old Skool Re-union' at the main Rugby Grounds of the capital city. Attendees played childhood games such as rope skipping and dodge ball, and the crowd included top names in the country's entertainment industry. The organizers said their aim was to promote interaction and networking among members in order to exchange ideas, knowledge and to discover new business opportunities, as well as have fun. It was the second time that the group had used this organizing method. Their first was for a cocktail party two months earlier that attracted 700 attendees at a high end city bar. A renowned business management consultant gave a motivational speech there about personal finance and entrepreneurship. A casual look at Facebook shows that it provides a platform for Ugandans to share information that reports alleged government abuses and police brutalities. However, most of the information shared is skimmed off websites of newspapers, radio and television stations.

RIOTS AND PROTESTS: NEW MEDIA IN UGANDA COMES OF AGE

The riots that broke out in September 2009 gave the government the opportunity to draft draconian laws to further suppress the media particularly local radio stations in Uganda. The riot was a result of a stand-off between the central government and the Buganda Kingdom resulting in the death of 27 people. The government reacted by launching a clampdown on local radio stations accusing them of inciting violence, promoting sectarianism, campaigning against government and abusing the president. The Broadcasting Council shut down four radio stations: *Central Broadcasting Services (CBS)*, *Ssuubi FM* (a youth radio), *Sapienta* (a Christian radio) and *Akaboozi ku Bbiri*. (HRNJ Uganda, 2010). In the ensuing media blackout, Ugandans resorted to social media and mobile phone SMS to keep update of events and warn each other of places to avoid. In fact, according to residents of Kampala, most Ugandan television stations were operating under restricted broadcasting conditions, airing little or no news during the riots. 'TV Uganda is playing music videos and NTV Uganda is showing *That's so Raven*, wrote Sarah Malan, a South African ex-pat living in Kampala, in her blog (Sarah, 2009). Trisha Olsson, a development worker who tweets at *CamaraAfrica*, noted:

Wow...everyone hurry and turn to [Ugandan television station] NBS for a riveting report on...wait for it...how to play golf (Trisha, 2009).

Though newspapers were allowed to continue reporting, their news was often delayed by hours, if not an entire day. The absence of real-time coverage led many Ugandans to seek out alternative sources of information. Within 24 hours of the first violence, volunteers in Kampala, Uganda's capital city launched Uganda Witness, a crisis reporting site where Ugandans can share news of deaths, looting, presence of government forces and other riot-related information. Twitter proved an especially rich source of information. Bloggers also stepped up to fill the information void, populating Blogspirit with their personal stories, observations, and experiences during the riots. The difference in coverage can be largely attributed to the increased availability of Internet-connected mobile phones. When combined with Twitter, which is also accessible by mobile phone, new media enabled more real-time coverage, filling the gap left by mainstream media's delay in providing real time coverage and keeping both Ugandans and people in the rest of the world informed.

Following the September 2009 riots, there has been a tense atmosphere in Uganda with journalists taking extreme self-censorship and media proprietors holding individual employees responsible for legal or financial consequences arising from either critical story reporting or pro-

gramming. The Media Council officially banned open air broadcasting, *ekimeeza* (Human Rights Watch, 2010). These incidents/interventions have created a climate of uncertainty. However, some private radio stations still host guests perceived as critical of the government.

In the wake of the 'walk-to-work' protests of April 2011, the Ugandan blogosphere and social media networks went into overdrive with postings of comments and pictures of police brutality. During the protests, the mainstream media was caught up in the practice of self-censorship. The 'walk-to-work' campaigns against high fuel prices and excessive government expenditures were organised by the pressure group 'Activists for Change', who have since been outlawed. Ugandans turned to social media such as Twitter and Facebook to keep up-to-date with developments and to get a sense of what was happening from protestors, eyewitnesses, and journalists. More tellingly, The *Daily Monitor* newspaper regularly tweeted updates. That in itself was a new media breakthrough in Uganda—news being reported as it happens. There were many reports of journalists being stripped of their cameras and footage of the 'walk to work' protests. Others were beaten and injured by police. Under these conditions and with either self-censorship or political influence at play in some newsrooms and government's censorship of media coverage of the protests (Echwalu, 2009), citizen reporting on blogs, Twitter, and Facebook, was in some part filling a gap in information available to people. The challenge of course is to check facts and verify social media sources.

Recognising the danger posed by social media in mobilising and whipping public sentiments, government sought to turn off social networking sites. The Uganda Communications Commission, the media regulator, wrote to service providers asking them to 'block the use of Facebook and Twitter' and 'to eliminate the connection and sharing of information that incites the public' (Karen, 2011). In Uganda, the mobilization of organized protest is difficult and relatively well marshalled because of state regulations against social movement organizations. The Internet provides a space for speedy mobilization, while at the same time reducing the chances of personal danger. Just as Bandura (2001) suggests, new electronic technologies provide vast opportunities for people to bring their influence to bear on collective civic action. However, as technology becomes more sophisticated, and platforms for transmitting news, information, and opinion more diverse, governments of all stripes even democracies, including the United States, seek to monitor communications and obtain personal information. Usually in the name of national security, governments want access to e-mails and social networks, or to learn who is visiting which Website. This chilling development was highlighted by the United Arab Emirates' threat to ban BlackBerry e-mail unless its Canadian manufacturer, Research in Motion Ltd, allowed it to monitor encrypted messages (BBC, 2010). Soon after, India, where the Mumbai terrorists were said to have used BlackBerry devices, said it would shut down the service unless it was given access to the encrypted data (Aljazeera, 2010). Following the April 2011 'walk-to-work' protests, the Ugandan government threatened to ban Facebook and other social media networks. Alternative media in Uganda walks a fine line between reportage and advocacy and almost always against a background of government intimidation or control, ranging from the deceptively benign to the truly totalitarian.

UGANDAN NEW MEDIASCAPE: A NEW PUBLIC SPHERE OR A CASE OF NEW WINE IN OLD BOTTLES?

The concept of the public sphere, originally detailed by Habermas (1989), concerns the coming together of peoples and the discussion of ideas, often related to governance and democratic ideals. Keane (2004) describes the public sphere as:

...a particular type of spatial relationship between two or more people, usually connected by a certain means of communication (p. 366).

The linkage between people via means of communication is critical for the public sphere, and in many ways, is the only constitutive element of that space (Dahlberg, 2005a). Poor (2005) explains that the 'public' of the public sphere means that the people who participate in such discussions are acting not as private citizens, but in a public role by speaking in public and discussing issues of relevance to the wider public–those issues that have the potential to influence public opinion or public policy. The 'sphere' of the public sphere means that it is a space, often a mix of formal and informal institutions and organizations. There has been much academic discussion and increasing research on the possibility of the Internet facilitating the idea of a public sphere (Becker & Wehner, 2001; Dahlgren, 2001; Gandy, 2002; Gimmler, 2001; Noveck, 2000; Papacharissi, 2002; 2004; Sparks, 2001). Generally speaking, the public sphere is constituted by open, reasoned, and reflexive communication. More specifically, drawing upon Jürgen Habermas, whose work is the starting point for much Internet public sphere theory and research, the public sphere is based on the thematization and critique of moral, ethical, and pragmatic validity claims, accompanied by inclusive, sincere and respectful reasoning. This sphere is seen as central to strong democracy, enabling the voicing of diverse views on any issue, the constitution of publicly-oriented citizens, the scrutiny of power and ultimately, public sovereignty. In contemporary, large-scale, dispersed and complex societies, time–distance 'defying' media are required to support such communicative action. A variety of critical theorists have shown that the modern mass media (print and broadcasting) have largely failed in this role (Boggs, 2000; Curran, 2000; Gandy, 2002; Habermas, 1989; Kellner, 2004; McChesney,1999; Savigny, 2002). In contrast, the Internet has been seen as offering citizens the opportunity to encounter and engage with a huge diversity of positions, thus extending the public sphere (Blumler & Gurevitch, 2001; Gimmler, 2001; Kellner, 2004; Papacharissi, 2002).Through e-mail, discussion sites, Web publishing and Webcasting, a great variety of actors articulate and critique validity claims locally, nationally and internationally. However, those researching the possibility of the Internet expanding democratic culture also point to significant factors limiting open and reflexive debate online, including inequalities in access and participation, un-reflexive communication, corporate domination of online attention and state surveillance and censorship (Dahlberg, 2001; 2005b; Gomez, 2004; Hoar & Hope, 2002; Murdock & Golding, 2004; Wilhelm, 2000). Furthermore, a number of Internet-democracy commentators question whether the myriad of diverse views that exist online are actually intersecting, and thus the extent to which online interactions actually involve any significant problematization and contestation of positions and practices. These commentators argue that much online interaction simply involves the meeting of 'like-minded' individuals, leading to a fragmented public sphere of insulated 'deliberative enclaves' where group positions and practices are reinforced rather than openly critiqued. In contrast, other commentators argue that online participants readily seek out and deliberate with actors holding markedly different views, thus expanding the public sphere. In the aftermath of the Arab Spring, the roles of new media platforms such as Facebook, Twitter, and weblogs have become more apparent as potent tools in mobilizing mass protests against unpopular government policies around the world. Citizens have launched collective actions over single issues where government policies have affected their daily lives. The cases highlighted illustrate the general point that citizen participation within the public realm is necessarily limited. But it is also clear that Ugandan citizens are becoming increasingly empowered, while government is

acting in a conciliatory way as a result. Public spaces on the Internet, especially in social media, along with mobile phones to mobilize people, have been vital to this shift.

The Internet is especially important because it facilitates the construction of multiple alternative or counter-public spheres. This alludes to online communicative spaces in which social groups, which have no access to the conventional mass media platform, can construct shared identities and interests and coordinate public actions (Bennett, 2003; Dahlgren, 2001; Downey & Fenton, 2003). So far, these concepts have primarily been used for general reflections on the relationship between traditional mass media and public debate. However, of late, the emergence of new media and its popularity among users implies the medium has to be treated in the same light.

The Internet is seen as a perfect counterpart complement to the democratic process, encouraging conversation amongst diverse citizens and their representative groups, allowing a level of participation non-existent in traditional media, and building bottom-up support for, or dissent against, the higher-level governing bodies. Given the reality that in Uganda the government and the mainstream media enjoy a 'love hate' relationship, new media provides information and tools that may extend the role of the public in the social and political arena, and may promote more public discussions among ordinary people in contrast with traditional mass communications due to its characteristics such as high information storage capacity, easy access, communicative anonymity, and censorship difficulty. With its rapid development and penetration in Uganda through mobile telephony, new media is playing a significant role in almost every aspect of the daily life. Many Ugandans have been using new media as the most convenient and efficient way to make their voices heard on a variety of political issues. In recent years, many events have generated intensive discussions on various online forums, blogs, newspaper websites, bulletin boards, or community Websites. Many of them have either formed a kind of collective action or exerted intense political pressure on the Ugandan government to solve the problems immediately or to carry out some measures to relieve the situation. The Internet is widely understood to be a potential new public sphere, transcending geographical boundaries, and allowing for diverse citizens to converge, interact and converse (Dahlberg, 2001; Papacharissi, 2002).

Despite the voices saying that the Internet may discourage people from civic engagement and political participation as television does (Putnam, 2000), many believe that the Internet is a great communication medium for reviving the democratic process: apathetic citizens in established democratic states are provided a venue for the progressive voices that have been shut out of the corporate media outlets (Jerome & Zuniga, 2006) and disparate citizens of authoritarian regimes are united and moved towards participatory democracy (Zheng & Wu, 2005).

New media technologies can serve as an engine capable of galvanising public interest and participation in the democratic process. Popular participation is a precondition for democratic civic engagement and socio-economic development. In Uganda, there is abundant evidence to suggest that the use of new media technologies such as mobile SMS is facilitating a strategic link between the government and the citizens. In the 2011 Presidential election, the candidates engaged with the electorate by sending them personal SMS. However, for new technologies to empower citizens to participate in the political process, the citizens must have unimpeded access to the technologies. Regrettably, despite the popularity of mobile telephony in the country, the gap between those who have access to such technologies and those who do not is still massive. The public sphere described by Habermas (1989) was strictly a 'bourgeois' construct. Although it represented a new avenue for some people to speak out, it was restricted in terms of class and gender. This is because only bourgeois men could participate (Fraser, 1992). Habermas' original conception of the public sphere includes three elements: (1) it was a mediated space, often formed through discussion; (2) it gave a voice to members of the public who had previously been excluded from issues of governance; (3) all the discussions were evaluated based on their merits, not on the social status of the speaker (Poor, 2005). These three elements are important in the analysis of new media's potential as a public sphere in Uganda. The online discussions on various forums, bulletin boards, and community Websites are in mediated forms. New media does allow various people regardless of their gender, ethnicity, economic and social standing to post their opinions on a series of political, economic, and social issues. Due to online communication anonymity, people's comments on different issues are evaluated by the value and quality of their comments alone, not by their social identities. Therefore, the new media discussion forums in Uganda do satisfy Habermas' concept of public sphere.

Habermas's theory lays the groundwork for discussing the relationship between public discourse and democratic theory and practice. The media's role is crucial in these discussions. Issues of the media and public sphere revolve around the central axis of whether media enable or undermine a healthy public sphere with widespread participation. From a political economy perspective, participation in the public sphere is undermined by the concentration of media ownership and control (McChesney, 1997) and from a cultural perspective; participation in the public sphere is still possible despite unequal access to the technologies of media production and distribution (McKee, 2005). Participation takes various forms; not necessarily deliberative formats such as news reports and current affairs programming. Hence, daytime talk shows, popular music, and reality television are legitimate resources for public deliberation and debate (Lunt & Pantti, 2007).

The proliferation of media forms and outlets such as print, radio, and television broadcasting, cable and satellite distribution and the plethora of new media platforms in Uganda pose challenges for an ideal, singular or unified public sphere. Fraser's notion of subaltern counter publics, in which marginalized, oppressed, subordinate groups organize themselves to challenge their subordinate position is becoming a common scene in the media landscape around the world (Fraser, 1992). Habermas conceptualizes communicative action as a process where actors are not selfishly inclined on imposing their superiority but rather pursue their individual goals under the condition that they can harmonize their plans of action on the basis of common situation definitions (Johnson, 2006). This however, is largely missing in most of the online discourses in the Ugandan new mediascape. The discussions are not based on rationality with name calling and all sorts of tactics thrown in to win arguments. Participants indulge in asserting their superiority and righteousness of their positions and opinions. The one who 'shouts' the loudest and puts down other discussants wins! Like Nancy Fraser's (1992) critique of Habermas's assumption regarding the possibilities of equitable deliberation and debate in heterogeneous and socio-economically stratified societies, Habermas's public sphere theory ignores power differentials between various members of society in Uganda. The journalists, academics, university students, and the diaspora community who commune online carry with them a weight of authority. Participants who do not fall into those categories often feel intimidated and are made to feel less knowledgeable. Besides, the assumed model of the public sphere fails to consider fully the role of power in the process of rational deliberation and in any resulting consensus. The problem here is not that power is left untreated, but that particular aspects of power are emphasized while others are ignored. The Habermasean model focuses on difference as a force of societal disruption and on the power of rational argument in moving disputes towards consensus. However,

the model tends to overemphasize these aspects of power while largely neglecting the asymmetries in power involved in bringing about agreements and overcoming difference in deliberations. Disparities in social, cultural and economic capital influence who can speak, what can be said and how interaction is undertaken. This leads to a differentiation between the dominant discourses that achieve authoritative status and subordinate discourses that are marginalized or even silenced. This power differential between discourses is associated with the formation of social hierarchies of dominant and marginalized identities, some identities achieving advantaged social positions in relation to dominant discourse. As Fraser (1997) argues, 'hegemony points to the intersection of power, inequality and discourse' (p. 154).

Habermas's insistence on rational debate excludes expressive and affective forms of communication, publicity, and persuasion (Howley, 2010). Moreover, the popularity of new media is still urban based and the vast majority of the rural population are cut off from this supposedly 'new' public sphere. A part from participation in radio talk-shows and public debates (*ekimeeza*) rational-critical deliberations seems largely absent in the Weblogs and social media postings. In Uganda, blogs give their authors an opportunity to express views that are not being covered in the regular media. Blogs have been able to challenge government on issues such as corruption, human rights, economic policy and social justice anonymously in ways that could not have been possible without risking arrest or harassment in the past.

More recently, the growing use of new media for self-expression and the sharing of opinions have spurred the government's recognition of new media's potential to change the political landscape. The Internet is broadening the scope of civic discussion in Uganda by enabling the public to engage in issues of political and social significance in non-politicized forums. Ugandans have also begun to leverage blogs, social networking sites, forums and online videos to raise awareness and garner support for myriad causes. On the government's part, as part of its strategy to reach out to a growing population that is becoming more media savvy, members of the ruling party have also launched their own blogs to interact with Internet-savvy citizens. Reacting to the possible damage the KONY2012 video might have caused to the image of Uganda, the country's Prime Minister, Amama Mbabazi, recorded and uploaded a video on *YouTube* to reassure tourists and investors that Uganda was a safe country. The ruling party's website is awash with testimonial videos of 'ordinary' citizens who testify that life in Uganda is better under the current leadership. Access to technology has been argued to be a critical precondition to citizenry participation and democracy (Hague & Loader, 1999; Lenk, 1999). One common assumption is that the presence of the Internet backed by widespread access to both technology and networks would inadvertently lead to the creation of a vibrant civil society and greater political participation. However, in the case of Uganda, the extent to which new media has been deployed as a democratizing tool is limited. How can simple deliberation and freedom of expression be a catalyst for democracy? Some scholars hold optimistic views of the new media as a public sphere (Banda et al., 2009; Dahlberg, 2001; Dahlgren, 2001; Downey & Fenton, 2003; Ryan, 2010).They also address some contradictory issues concerning the development of the online public sphere which are synonymous with the 'Ugandan online public sphere'. The most common identified challenges facing the new media public spheres include: (1) the quality and context of discourse online due to the low levels of literacy; (2) the unequal access to the Internet typified by low newspaper circulation rate and the reliance on oral and interpersonal forms of communication; (3) the unequal participation in online discourse; (4) the possible erosion of online forums by commercialism; and (5) low levels of political participation due to the domination of the government in power (Papacharissi, 2002). All these challenges pose potential threats to the new media public sphere in Uganda.

CONCLUSION

New media offers some of the best potential for spreading and encouraging a more engaged citizen population, and also provides the most freedom and openness for promoting political discourse and democratic collective actions. In such a tricky media environment like Uganda's, in which government appears to allow freedom of expression while at the same time suppressing it through the laws of the land, various online discussion forums and bulletin boards are able to provide more diverse information than traditional media sources, and include more voices in the political discourse. No doubt these online public spheres and political participation in Uganda are still in their infancy, and there is no guarantee that they will survive in the face of government regulation and commercialization. But the enthusiasm that people have for new media serves as the most important part for the existence and development of online public spheres. Eventually, as is believed, the online public spheres will flourish in Uganda with more changes in media structure and policy, and possibly more tolerance and openness in the political system

REFERENCES

Access to Information Act. (2005). *Uganda Gazette, XCVIII*(42). Retrieved July 2, 2012, from http://www.freedominfo.org/documents/uganda_ati_act_2005.pdf

African Centre for Media Excellence-ACME. (2010). *Court dismisses Government case against closed radio station*. Retrieved August 23, 2010, from http://www.acme-ug.org/component/k2/item/29-court-dismisses-gov%E2%80%99t-caseagainst-closed-radio-station

African Media Barometer (AMB). (2010). *Uganda*. Kampala, Uganda: Friedrich-Ebert-Stiftung.

African Media Barometer (AMB). (2012). *Uganda*. Retrieved September 24, 2012, from http://www.fes-uganda.org/media/pdf/AMB%20 Uganda%202012.pdf

Aljazeera. (2010). *India threatens Black-berry ban*. Retrieved January 21, 2011, from http://www.aljazeera.com/business/2010/08/2010812143513776296.html

Allen, K. (2011). *African jitters over blogs and social media*. Retrieved November 18, 2011, from http://www.bbc.co.uk/news/world-africa-13786143

Amnesty International. (2010). Uganda. Amnesty *International Memorandum on the Regulation of interception of communications Act 2010*. London: Amnesty International Publications.

Banda, F., Mudhai, F. O., & Tettey, J. W. (2009). *African media and the digital public sphere*. New York: Palgrave Macmillan.

Bandura, A. (2001). Social cognitive theory: An agentic perspective. *Annual Review of Psychology*, *53*, 1–26. doi:10.1146/annurev.psych.52.1.1 PMID:11148297.

BBC. (2010). *Two Gulf states to ban some Black-berry functions*. Retrieved January 13, 2011, from http://www.bbc.co.uk/news/world-middle-east-10830485

Becker, B., & Wehner, J. (2001). Electronic networks and civil society: Reflections on Structural Changes in the Public Sphere. In Ess, C., & Sudweeks, F. (Eds.), *Culture, technology, communication: Towards an intercultural global village* (pp. 67–85). Albany, NY: State University of New York Press.

Bennett, L. W. (2003). New media power: The internet and global activism. In Couldry, N., & Curran, J. (Eds.), *Contesting media power: Alternative media in a networked world* (pp. 17–37). Lanham, MD: Rowman & Littlefield.

Blumler, J. G., & Gurevitch, M. (2001). The New media and our political communication discontents: Democratizing cyberspace. *Information Communication and Society*, *4*(1), 1–13.

Boggs, C. (2000). *The end of politics: Corporate power and the decline of the public sphere*. New York: Guilford Press.

Bowman, R. (2010). Rehearsing democracy: New media, political freedoms and censorship in Uganda. In Monaghan, G., & Tunney, S. (Eds.), *Web journalism: A new form of citizenship?* (pp. 248–260). Eastbourne, UK: Sussex Academic Press.

Bratton, M., & van de Nicolas, W. (1997). *Democratic experiments in Africa*. New York: Cambridge University Press.

Castells, M. (2004). An Introduction to the information age. In Webster, F. (Ed.), *The Information Society Reader* (pp. 138–149). New York: Routledge.

Chonghaile, C. N. (2012). *Uganda anti-gay bill resurrected in parliament*. Retrieved November 20, 2012, from http://www.guardian.co.uk/world/2012/feb/08/uganda-gay-death-sentence-bill

(1995). *Constitution of the Republic of Uganda*. Entebbe, Uganda: Government Printer.

Curran, J. (2000). Rethinking media and democracy. In Curran, J., & Gurevitch, M. (Eds.), *Mass Media and Society* (pp. 120–154). London: Arnold.

Dahlberg, L. (2001). Computer-mediated communication and the public sphere: A critical analysis. *Journal of Computer-Mediated Communication*, *7*(1). Retrieved April 20, 2006, from http://jcmc.indiana.edu/vol7/issue1/dahlberg.html

Dahlberg, L. (2005a). The Habermasian public sphere: Taking difference seriously? *Theory and Society*, *34*, 111–136. doi:10.1007/s11186-005-0155-z.

Dahlberg, L. (2005b). The corporate colonization of online attention and the marginalization of critical communication? *The Journal of Communication Inquiry*, *29*(2), 1–21. doi:10.1177/0196859904272745.

Dahlgren, P. (2001). The public sphere and the net: Structure, space and communication. In Bennett, L. W., & Entman, R. M. (Eds.), *Mediated politics: Communication in the future of democracy* (pp. 33–55). Cambridge, UK: Cambridge University Press.

Dicklitch, S., & Lwanga, D. (2003). The politics of being non-political: Human rights organizations and the creation of a positive human rights culture in Uganda. *Human Rights Quarterly*, *25*(2), 482–509. doi:10.1353/hrq.2003.0015.

Downey, J., & Fenton, N. (2003). New media, counter publicity and the public sphere. *New Media & Society*, *5*(2), 185–202. doi:10.1177/1461444803005002003.

Echwalu, E. (2011). *Ugandan media censored over 'walk to work' protests*. Retrieved on January 14, 2012, from http://cpj.org/blog/2011/04/ugandan-media-censored-over-walk-to-work-protests.php

Flew, T. (2005). *New media: An introduction*. Melbourne, Australia: Oxford University Press.

Fourie, P. J. (Ed.). (2001). *Media studies. Institutions, Theories and Issues (Vol. 1)*. Lansdowne, PA: Juta.

Fraser, N. (1992). Rethinking the public sphere: A contribution to the critique of actually existing democracy. In Calhoun, C. (Ed.), *Habermas and the Public Sphere* (pp. 109–142). Cambridge, MA: MIT Press.

Gandy, O. (2002). The real digital divide: Citizens versus consumers. In Lievrouw, L. A., & Livingstone, S. (Eds.), *Handbook of New Media: Social Shaping And Consequences of ICTs* (pp. 448–460). London: Sage.

Gimmler, A. (2001). Deliberative democracy, the public sphere and the internet. *Philosophy and Social Criticism*, *27*(4), 21–39. doi:10.1177/019145370102700402.

Gomez, J. (2004). Dumbing down democracy: Trends in Internet regulation, Surveillance and Control in Asia. *Pacific Journalism Review*, *10*(2), 130–150.

Goode, L. (2005). *Jürgen Habermas: Democracy and the public sphere*. London: Pluto Press.

Habermas, J. (1989). *The Structural Transformation of the Public Sphere: An Inquiry into a Category of Bourgeois Society*. Cambridge, MA: MIT Press.

Hague, B. N., & Loader, B. D. (1999). *Digital Democracy: Discourse and Decision Making in the Information Age*. London: Routledge.

Howley, K. (Ed.). (2010). *Understanding Community Media*. Thousand Oaks, CA: Sage.

Human Rights House Network. (2009). *Four radio stations closed in Uganda*. Retrieved September 11, 2009, from http://humanrightshouse.org/Articles/11722.html

Human Rights Network for Journalists-Uganda (HRNJ). (2010). *Mid-Year Press Freedom Index Report*. Retrieved January 5, 2011, from www.hrnjuganda.org

Human Rights Network for Journalists-Uganda (HRNJ). (2011). *Press Freedom Index Report 2011. Uganda. Shrinking and sinking*. Retrieved February 2, 2012, from http://www.hrnjuganda.org/reports/Press%20Freedom%20Index%20Annual%202011.pdf

Human Rights Watch. (2010). *Uganda: A media minefield. Increased threats to freedom of expression in Uganda*. New York: HRW.

Hyden, G., Leslie, M., & Ugundimu, F. F. (Eds.). (2002). *Media and Democracy in Africa*. New Brunswick, NJ: Transaction Publishers.

IFEX. (2006). *Critical website Radio Katwe blocked on eve of presidential election.* Retrieved April 13, 2012, from http://www.ifex.org/uganda/2006/02/23/critical_website_radio_katwe_blocked/

Internetworldstats. (2008). *Internet Usage and Population Statistics* Retrieved January 12, 2012, from http://www.internetworldstats.com/africa.htm

Izama, A. (2010). Journalist arrested over Kampala bomb blast story. *The Daily Monitor.* August 4, 2010.

Jerome, A., & Zuniga, M. M. (2006). *Crashing the gate: Netroots, grassroots and the rise of people-powered politics.* White River Junction, VT: Chelsea Green Publishing Company.

Johnson, P. (2006). *Habermas: Rescuing the public sphere.* London: Routledge.

Kalyegira, T. (2010). *Panic grips Ugandan government over Kampala bomb blasts.* Retrieved November 19, 2010, from www.ugandarecord.co.ug/index.php?issue=68&article=836&seo=Panicgrips Uganda government over Kampala bomb blasts

Kandell, J. J. (1998). Internet addiction on campus: The vulnerability of college students. *Cyberpsychology & Behavior, 1*(1), 11–17. doi:10.1089/cpb.1998.1.11.

Kareire, P. (2009). *Facebook 360 network meeting face to face.* Retrieved November 22, 2012, from http://www.newvision.co.ug/D/8/217/694033

Keane, J. (2004). Structural transformations of the public sphere. In Webster, F. (Ed.), *The Information Society Reader* (pp. 366–378). New York: Routledge.

Kellner, D. (2004). The Media and the crises of democracy in the age of Bush-2. *Communication and Critical. Cultural Studies, 1*(1), 29–58.

Kibazo, P., & Kanaabi, H. (2007). *FM stations in Uganda 'Quantity without Quality.* Nairobi, Kenya: Eastern Africa Media Institute.

Kirumira, M., & Ajwang, J. (2007, May 3). Uganda: The limping newspaper industry. *Daily Monitor.* Retrieved May 3, 2007, from http://allafrica.com/stories/200705020734.html

Kline, D., & Burstein, D. (2005). *Blog! How the newest media revolution is changing politics, business, and culture.* New York: CDS Books.

Landow, G. (2003). The paradigm is more important than the purchase. In Liestol, G., Morrison, A., & Rasmussen, T. (Eds.), *Digital Media Revisited: Theoretical and Conceptual Innovations in Digital Domains* (pp. 35–64). Cambridge, MA: The MIT Press.

Lenk, K. (1999). Electronic support of citizen participation in planning processes. In B. N. Hague & B. D. (Eds.), Digital Democracy: Discourse and Decision Making in the Information Age (pp. 87-95). London: Routledge.

Lister, M., Dovey, J., Giddings, S., Grant, I., & Kelly, K. (2003). *New media: A critical Introduction.* London: Routledge.

Lunt, P., & Pantti, M. (2007). Popular culture and the public sphere: Currents of feeling and social control in talk shows and reality TV. In Butch, R. (Ed.), *Media and Public Spheres* (pp. 162–174). New York: Palgrave Macmillan.

Malan, S. (2009). *Never dull moment.* Retrieved January 20, 2010, from http//www.themalans.blogspot.com/2009/09/never-dull-monet.html

McChesney, R. W. (1997). *Corporate media and the threat to democracy.* Boston, MA: Seven Stories Press.

McChesney, R. W. (1999). *Rich Media, Poor Democracy: Communication Politics in Dubious Times.* Urbana, IL: University of Illinois Press.

McKee, A. (2005). *The Public Sphere: An Introduction*. Cambridge, UK: Cambridge University Press.

McNair, B. (2006). *Cultural Chaos: Journalism, News, and Power in a Globalised World*. London: Routledge. doi:10.4324/9780203448724.

Melkote, R. S., & Steeves, H. L. (2001). *Communication for Development in the Third World*. New Delhi, India: Sage.

Moore, G. (2000). The English legal framework for investigative journalism. In de Burgh, H. (Ed.), *Investigative Journalism, Context and Practice* (pp. 123–150). London, New York: Routledge.

Murdock, G., & Golding, P. (2004). Dismantling the digital divide: Rethinking the dynamics of participation and exclusion. In Calabrese, A., & Sparks, C. (Eds.), *Towards a political economy of culture: Capitalism and communication in the twenty-first century* (pp. 244–260). Lanham, MD: Rowman & Littlefield.

Musasizi, S. (2012). Police blame 'African Spring' on social media. Retrieved October 16, 2012, from http://www.observer.ug/index. php?option=com_content&view=article&id= 21593:police-blame-african-spring-on-social-media&catid=34:news&Itemid=114

Mwesige, P. (2009). The democratic functions and dysfunctions of political talk radio: The case of Uganda. *Journal of African Media Studies*, *1*(2), 221–245. doi:10.1386/jams.1.2.221_1.

Nassanga, L. G. (2009). Participatory discussion programs as hybrid community media in Uganda. *International Journal of Media and Cultural Politics*, *5*(1/2), 119–124.

Noveck, B. S. (2000). Paradoxical partners: Electronic communication and electronic democracy. In Ferdinand, P. (Ed.), *The Internet, Democracy and Democratization* (pp. 18–35). London: Routledge. doi:10.1080/13510340008403643.

Nyamnjoh, F. B. (2004). Media ownership and control in Africa in the age of globalization. In Thomas, P. N., & Nain, Z. (Eds.), *Who Owns the Media: GLOBAL Trends and Local Resistances*. London: Zed Books.

Ocitti, J. (2006). *Press politics and public policy in Uganda: The role of journalism in democratization*. London: Edwin Mellen Press.

Olsson, T. (2009). *Trisha Olsson @CamaraAfrica*. Retrieved January 20, 2010, from http://www.twitter.com/camaraafrica

Papacharissi, Z. (2002). The self-online: The utility of personal homepages. *Journal of Broadcasting & Electronic Media*, *46*, 346–368. doi:10.1207/s15506878jobem4603_3.

Papacharissi, Z. (2004). Democracy online: Civility, politeness and the democratic potential of online political discussion groups. *New Media & Society*, *6*(2), 259–283. doi:10.1177/1461444804041444.

Poor, N. (2005). Mechanisms of an online public sphere: The website Slashdot. *Journal of Computer-Mediated Communication*, *10*(2), article 4. Retrieved April 20, 2010, from http://jcmc.indiana.edu/vol10/issue2/poor.html

Putnam, R. D. (2000). *Bowling alone: The collapse and revival of American community*. New York: Simon & Schuster. doi:10.1145/358916.361990.

Radio Katwe. (2006). How Radio Katwe has changed Uganda. Retrieved April 19, 2011, from http//www.radiokatwenews.blogspot.com/2006/03/how-rado-katwe-has-changed-uganda.html

Redpepper. (2012). Uganda threatens to block social media over protests. Retrieved May 25, 2011, from http://www.reuters.com/article/2011/04/19/us-uganda-unrest-media idUS-TRE73I3LP20110419

Salvatore, A. (2007). *The public sphere: Liberal modernity, Catholicism, Islam*. New York: Palgrave Macmillan.

Savigny, H. (2002). Public opinion, political communication and the Internet. *Politics*, 22(1), 1–8. doi:10.1111/1467-9256.00152.

Sparks, C. (2001). The Internet and the global public sphere. In Bennett, L. W., & Entman, R. M. (Eds.), *Mediated politics: Communication in the future of democracy* (pp. 75–95). Cambridge, UK: Cambridge University Press.

Stapenhurst, R. (2000). *The media's role in curbing corruption*. World Bank Institute Working Paper: Washington, DC.

Tabaire, B. (2007). The press and political repression in Uganda: Back to the future? *Journal of Eastern African Studies*, 1(2), 193–211. doi:10.1080/17531050701452408.

Uganda Radio Network-URN. (2012). Police threaten to close Jinja radio stations. Retrieved October 9, 2012, from http://ugandaradionetwork.com/a/story.php?s=43128

Wilhelm, A. G. (2000). *Democracy in the digital age: Challenges to political life in cyberspace*. London: Routledge.

Zheng, Y., & Wu, G. (2005). Information technology, public space and collective action in China. *Comparative Political Studies*, 38, 507–536. doi:10.1177/0010414004273505.

ENDNOTES

[1] Analogy is based on the cartoon series Tom and Jerry who have a love hate relationship.

[2] Interview with the author.

[3] Interview with the author.

[4] The Kabaka is the King of Buganda Kingdom.

Chapter 22
Rethinking the Democratization Role of Online Media:
The Zimbabwean Experience

Tendai Chari
University of Venda, South Africa

ABSTRACT

Online publications have become critical sites for the expression of views alternative to those of the state. This is true in Zimbabwe as in many developing states where the mainstream media operate under onerous legislative frameworks. However, the real impact of these 'new public spheres' on the country's democratization agenda is subject to contestation. This chapter examines the impact of online publications run by exiled Zimbabwean journalists on the country's democratization process. The chapter evaluates the extent to which these online publications constitute genuine alternative spaces for the mediation of national discourses. Data is elicited through focus group interviews, in-depth interviews, and textual analysis. The chapter argues that a combination of technical, social, and economic factors which limit Internet access and professional shortcomings conspire against online publications becoming genuine alternative public spheres, thus minimizing their role in the democratization of the Zimbabwean state.

INTRODUCTION

Since the turn of the millennium, Zimbabwe has witnessed a phenomenal mushrooming of online publications and news Websites. The promulgation of stringent media laws, ostensibly to tame an increasingly militant and 'unprofessional press', coupled with political instability and the worsening of the economic meltdown epitomized by hyperinflation, high unemployment rates and general social decay resulted in the closure of a number of privately owned newspapers. This triggered an exodus of journalists, who emigrated to neighboring countries, mainly South Africa and Botswana, as well as European countries, such as the United Kingdom and the United States of America. In order to earn a living, and to continue their struggle for democratization, some of the

DOI: 10.4018/978-1-4666-4197-6.ch022

journalists started online publications and news Websites that had a distinct focus on Zimbabwe. This was meant to provide an outlet for voices that were alternative to the political establishment. In a sense, most of these publications were a continuation of the closed newspapers, albeit online.

This chapter examines the role and contributions of online publications operated by Zimbabweans in the Diaspora on the country's democratization discourses and other national debates, in order to assess the extent to which they have constituted real 'alternative public spheres' in the post-colonial context. In particular, the study examines consumption habits and patterns of online publications by Zimbabwean citizens living in the country, their perceptions of online publications and the roles they ascribe to them. The chapter also examines the ethical challenges and limitations faced by these online publications which might have militated against the prosecution of their democratic mandate. In so doing, the study hopes to open pathways for theorizing the role played by online publications in democratic processes in an African context. Whether online publications are able to broaden the democratic spaces or are simply 'private spheres' to a few who are able to access them is a key question spotlighted in this chapter. Thus, the chapter addresses the following two key questions: First, what are the online publication consumption habits and patterns of Zimbabweans living in the country and what are their perceptions of these online publications in the country's democratization process? Second, what are the main ethical challenges faced by online publications and how do these undermine their role in the country's democratization process? The study utilized in-depth interviews, a focus group discussions and textual analysis. Purposive sampling was used to select subjects for the in-depth interviews. Twelve respondents were identified and asked questions relating to their consumption of online publications. Respondents were required to comment on the ethical aspects of online publications

and their role in the democratization process of the country. The use of purposive sampling was justified on the grounds that access to online news in Zimbabwe is mainly confined to urban centers and even there, not everyone has access to the Internet. The focus group comprised of fourteen (14) randomly selected part-time journalism students at a private college in the capital, Harare. Their ages ranged between 21 and 40. Data was categorized into pre-determined themes and then subjected to extensive analysis using hermeneutic interpretation (Kvale, 1996).

The chapter makes two main assumptions. The first is based on Lee's observation (cited in Nyamnjoh, 2005, p. 2) that effective democracy

...demands a system of constant interaction with all the people, accessibility at all levels, a public ethos which allows conflicting ideas to contend, and which provides for full participation in reaching consensus on socio-cultural, economic and political goals.

The second assumption is that for democracy to thrive there should not just be information, but quality information. This means that for the media to provide such information, they should be rooted in an ethical culture. As noted by Belsey and Chadwick (1992, p. 3):

The sort of alternative democratic participation and involvement that is required is impossible without information. Here, then as people of the world struggle for a worthwhile way of life within a sustainable future, is a role for the media, especially those that can still be called press, whether they are part of the print or broadcast journalism, so long as they follow the traditional role of the press as providers of information.

The remaining part of this chapter is divided into four parts. The first part gives a brief background of the media situation in Zimbabwe, starting from the country's attainment of independence in 1980 to the present. This part also discusses the information and communication technology (ICT) context of Zimbabwe, in order to understand the conditions in which online publications are consumed in the country. The second part deals with conceptual issues and literature review. The third discusses the online publication consumption habits and patterns of Zimbabwean citizens based in the country, their perceptions of online publications and the role they ascribe to them in the democratization process, as well as the ethical challenges faced by online publications and their manifestations as a way of addressing the questions identified prior. The fourth and final part makes some concluding remarks about the role of online publications in the democratization process in Zimbabwe. Suggestions for further research are also made.

THE MEDIA CONTEXT AND DEMOCRATIZATION STRUGGLES SINCE INDEPENDENCE

In 1980, Zimbabwe inherited from Rhodesia a fairly diversified media characterized by a strong state owned media and a blossoming privately-owned press which reflected the dominance of white capital in the economy. Consistent with its ambivalent media policy, which exhibited tendencies of authoritarianism and democratic impulses, the new ZANU PF government, under the leadership of Robert Mugabe, set up a trust, the Zimbabwe Mass Media Trust (ZMMT) to overlook the operations of the print media (Ronning & Kupe, 2000). ZMMT was, in principle, meant to be a buffer between the government and the public print media. However, ZMMT gradually became 'submerged in political struggles in the state and civil society' as ZANU PF sought to exert its hegemony in the political sphere, and also socio-economic and political challenges of the post-colony became more manifest (ibid, p. 160).

That the government maintained a tight grip of the state broadcaster, the Zimbabwe Broadcasting Corporation (ZBC), while media under ZMMT (i.e. the Zimbabwe Newspapers (Zimpapers), and news agencies such as the Zimbabwe Information Service (ZIS), ZIANA and the Community Newspaper Group) is illustrative of the policy ambivalence of the first two decades. While government maintained a tight grip on the state broadcaster, the Zimbabwe Broadcasting Corporation (ZBC) the print media, which fell under the ZMMT, had a modicum of independence during the first decades of independence. In relation to the privately-owned media, the government had an uneasy relationship, what Chuma (2007, p. 95) has described as 'tactical indifference', albeit punctuated by occasional but mild rebukes for lack of enough 'patriotism'.

Repressive media laws which had been used by the Ian Smith regime to muzzle the media remained on the statutes, but were rarely used in the new political dispensation. Consistent with the policy of reconciliation and to show the new government's commitment to democracy, no fundamental restructuring or nationalization of either the economy or the media was to be undertaken. Because of the relative freedom enjoyed by the media and the absence of any plans to indigenize the media, the privately owned media grew phenomenally, particularly during the first two decades of independence. Even the public media, which was heavily controlled, could occasionally criticize the government but robust debate and criticism were not tolerated. An example is the firing of Geoff Nyarota, the then editor of the state-owned *The Chronicle* after his paper exposed the corruption scandal in which top government officials abused a government car loan scheme in 1988. Nyarota was given a non-editorial job disguised as 'promotion', in order to limit his influence on the state-owned media (Chuma, 2007).

The second decade of independence (1990-1999) could be described as the golden decade of the press as it was characterized by phenomenal growth of the newspaper industry in the country. The absence of a codified media policy and a liberal economic environment occassioned by the state's adoption of the IMF and World Bank supported Economic Structural Adjustment Policy (ESAP) in 1990, the formation of a new opposition political party-the Zimbabwe Unity Movement (ZUM) fronted by former ZANU PF Secretary General, Edgar Tekere, and the growth of a civil society sector, yearning for alternative outlets to voice concerns about the harsh economic conditions occasioned by ESAP spurred the growth in the private media sector. These newspapers were very instrumental in galvanizing marginalized groups and civil society groups around issues of the economy, corruption, the land issue, the one party state debate, demands for a new constitution and issues of governance in general (Chuma, 2007; Bond & Manyanya, 2003). Government actions, such as the deployment of the national army in 1997 to help Laurent Kabila's government in the Democratic Republic of Congo to quell an insurgency by United States of America backed rebels, the awarding of unbudgeted Z$50,000 payouts to war veterans, which resulted in the sudden crash of the local currency, led to a coalescence of civil society groups to demand a new constitution.

The privately-owned media played a critical role, not only in ensuring that these issues remained on the national agenda, but also that they were articulated in a manner that sustained a robust debate. Unfortunately, due to a combination of factors, among them undercapitalization, lack of feasibility studies prior to launching, competition from government media with a longer history of establishment, high interest rates, lack of advertiser support' and mismanagement in general, some of the newspapers started after 1990 folded (Kupe, 1997). However, the appetite for alternative news remained largely because of the intensification of economic hardships in the wake of the failure of ESAP. The formation of the *Daily News* in 1999 by the Associated Newspapers of Zimbabwe, (ANZ), a group backed by a consortium of institutional

and private investors (Waldahl, 2004; Ronning & Kupe, 2000) from overseas and within the country, marked a watershed in the social and political history of the country. This also coincided with the formation of the Movement for Democratic Change (MDC), a formidable opposition party backed by society organizations, labor, students, industrialists, white commercial farmers, and Western governments. The rising dissent, partly a result of the worsening economic crisis, in the context of a controversial government led land reform program meant that the *Daily News* and editorially similar newspapers carried the mantle of venting popular discontent. Their militant journalism (and sometimes unprofessional approach), inevitably brought these media into a collision course with the increasingly beleaguered state.

In order to tame the increasingly militant and sometimes unprofessional media, the government promulgated an array of stringent media laws such as the Access to Information and Protection of Privacy Act (AIPPA, 2002), the Broadcasting Services Act (2001), the Public Order and Security Act (POSA, 2002). *The Daily News* and its sister publication, *The Daily News on Sunday* refused to comply with the requirements of AIPPA and were closed in September 2003. The *Business Tribune* and *The Weekly Tribune*, both owned by a Zanu PF aligned politician, also closed in June 2004 after failing to comply with section 71 of AIPPA. In addition, *The Weekly Times*, also a privately-owned weekly based in Bulawayo, the second city after the capital Harare, also ceased operations in February 2005 after failing to notify the Media and Information Commission (MIC) about changes in their editorial content as per the requirement of AIPPA.

Meanwhile, a tumultuous restructuring exercise in the public media, primarily at the ZBC, ZIANA and Zimpapers, saw hundreds of journalists, including senior editors, losing their jobs in retrenchments or similar shake-ups instituted by the new Minister of Information and Publicity, Jonathan Moyo, who incidentally was the architect of AIPPA. At the ZBC alone, over 400 personnel lost their jobs, many of whom left for European capitals and neighboring countries. A handful are now working for pirate radio stations such as the London based Short Wave Radio (SW Radio), and the Washington, DC based Studio 7, which is hosted on a VOA channel.

At the height of the Zimbabwean crisis, The Committee to Protect Journalists reported that Zimbabwe had the highest number of journalists (estimated to be around 90 at the time) living outside their country, making it 'one of the largest groups of exiled journalists in the world' (Nyakunu, 2005, n.p.). Apart from closures related to legal restrictions, the intensification of the economic meltdown also took a heavy toll on newspapers. A case in point was the closure in 1997, due to financial problems, of *The Sunday Mirror* and its sister publication, *The Daily Mirror*, both owned by a Zanu PF aligned intellectual and business entrepreneur, Dr Ibo Mandaza.

The closure meant further constriction of the country's media space both in terms of employment opportunities and availability of voices alternative to that of government. The only other newspapers that acted as a counterweight to the government owned media were *The Financial Gazette, The Zimbabwe Independent*, and *The Standard* (the latter two were owned by South African based Zimbabwean businessman and owner of the South African based *Mail & Guardian*), and *The Zimbabwean,* which is published in London by a former ANC executive, Wilf Mbanga.

While some former ZBC journalists found employment in pirate radio stations mentioned previously, a good number of displaced journalists from the privately-owned media started online publications and websites from their bases in different countries abroad. Examples of such publications include the *NewsZimbabwe.com, ZWNews, Zimbabwejournalists.com, ZimOnline. com, ZimDaily.com, The Zimbabwe Times.com* (now defunct) and a coterie of others. As a result, the majority of these online publications bore

resemblance, editorially, to the *Daily News* and its sister publication, the *Daily News on Sunday,* which were closed on September 11, 2003. Politically, they also shared a close ideological affinity with the MDC. Nyarota (2008a) sheds light on the ownership of these online publications:

Out of the ashes of the Daily News emerged Wilf Mbabga's The Zimbabwean, Geoffrey Nyarota's TheZimbabwean.com, Abel Mutsakani's Zimonline.com, Mduduzi Mathuthu's NewZimbabwe.com, Sandra Nyaira's Zimbabwejournalists.com, and Makusha Mugabe's Changezimbabwe.com.

Although these publications were established by people with different motives and operated from different geographical locations, the overarching vision was to continue providing an outlet for alternative views to the multitude of Zimbabweans back home, whose views were not represented in the public media. The desire to provide alternative narratives to the Zimbabwean story and to advance the democratization project is a motif recurrent in the visions, missions, and mottos of the publications. It is worth quoting one of the online publications, *ZimOnline.com,* in detail because of all the online publications it provides the most elaborate mission and vision on its web page. Having been formed in July 2004 by a group of mainly former *Daily News* journalists, *ZimOnline.com* has its mission statements as:

To provide a source of accurate, balanced and in-depth information about Zimbabwe.

To tell the other side of the Zimbabwean story that government has fought hard to prevent the world from knowing through a plethora of repressive measures which include severe restrictions on foreign media reporting from Zimbabwe and banning many foreign correspondents.

To offer an independent people-oriented news service.

To help in expanding the democratic space shrunk by the closure of mainstream newspapers in Zimbabwe.

To provide an opportunity to the ordinary masses of Zimbabwe, who bear the biggest brunt of the Zimbabwean crisis, with an opportunity to tell own stories about their plight.

To cover every other role player including the government, the opposition and civic society (http://www.zimonline.co.za/Mission.aspx).

In addition, the publication claims that 'We are more interested on issues than personalities' (ibid). *ZimDaily.com*, also founded by former *Daily News* journalists, says its mission is 'to provide you with the most independent uncensored news from Zimbabwe' (http:///zimdaily.com/news2/staticpages/index.php/about_us). Zimbabwejournalists.com states its mission as:

To play a role in expanding the shrinking democratic space in the country.

To offer an independent outlet for news for and by the people of Zimbabwe.

To tell the Zimbabwe story like it is without fear or favour.

To provide a source of balanced, authoritative, accurate and in-depth information about Zimbabwe (http://www.zinmbabwejournalists.com/about.php).

Although the number of these online publications and their influence inside and outside the country continues to grow by the day, very little is known about their real impact on the Zimbabwean body-politic and the claim that they are opening the democratic space has received scant academic scrutiny. Not much is known about consumption habits and patterns as well as the perceived role

they play in Zimbabwe's democratic struggles. The few studies available focus on production structures of online news websites and their reportage of the 'Zimbabwean crisis' (Moyo, 2007; Morgan, 2004). This study examines the way in which online media readers residing in the country interact and consume online publications. The ultimate aim is to gauge their utility as alternative public spheres and agency of democratic transformation.

INFORMATION AND COMMUNICATION TECHNOLOGY (ICT) CONTEXT

Zimbabwe has made significant strides in the development and application Information Communication Technologies (ICTs) in all sectors of the economy since independence in 1980 (Government of Zimbabwe, 2005). However, benefits derived ICTs have been sub-optimal due to lack of coordination at the policy, program, project design, and implementation levels (ibid, p. 9). The government adopted an ICT policy in 2005 whose vision is to transform Zimbabwe into a knowledge-based society by 2020. Its mission has been stated as accelerating 'the development and application of ICTs in support of economic development' (Isaacs, 2007, p. 4). In terms of infrastructure that supports ICTs, there is currently one fixed telephone network subscriber, the state-owned TelOne, three mobile subscribers, namely the state owned NetOne, Econet Wireless, owned by business mogul Strive Masiyiwa, and Telecell, which is owned by a consortium of local businessmen and some foreign investors. In addition, there are three public data service providers, one state owned broadcasting signal transmission (Transmedia), one public broadcaster (the ZBC), which runs five radio stations and over 30 Internet Service providers.

The fixed telephone network sector has experienced marginal growth, with the number of fixed telephone lines increasing from 23,650 to 287,854 between 1998 and 2002 (ibid, p.16). This sector has recently experienced stagnation (estimates put the number of fixed telephone subscribers at 390,000 (Mansfield, 2011) due to a number of problems, the main one being lack of foreign currency to revamp its archaic infrastructure. The mobile sector has, however, experienced phenomenal growth recently, with its subscriber base trebling from two million to 6.9 million by mid-2010, largely due to the relative economic stability brought about by the full dollarization of the economy (Mansfield, 2011).

The country's telecommunications regulator, the Post Telecommunications Regulatory Authority of Zimbabwe (POTRAZ), awarded 3G licenses to all the mobile operators in 2008. This would allow them to also offer Voice over Internet Protocol (VoIP services [Cellular News, 2008]). Zimbabwe ranks number 10 in Africa in terms of Internet use (Internetworldstats, 2011). The number of Internet users is about 1.481,000, which translates to 13% of the population. The Internet penetration rate is 12.2% and the number of broadband subscribers is 1,700, while the broadband penetration rate is 0.1% (Internetworldstats.com, 2010). Table 1 shows the growth of Internet users between 2000 and 2008.

Table 1 shows that the number of Internet users has increased rapidly between 2000 and 2009. This is in spite of a decade of economic regression and meltdown characterized by stratospheric in-

Table1. Internet usage and population growth: 2000-2008

YEAR	Users	Population	% Pen.	Usage Source
2000	50,000	14,712,000	0.3%	ITU
2002	500,000	13,874,610	3.6%	ITU
2005	820,000	12,247,589	6.7%	ITU
2008	1,351,000	12,382,920	10.9%	ITU
2009	1,481,000	11,392,629	13.0%	ITU

Source: http://www.internetworldstats.com/af/zw.htm

flation figures. This shows that the Internet has become a tool for citizens to stay connected with millions of relatives and friends, who left the country starting from the year 2000. It is believed that there are close to four million Zimbabweans living outside the country. Access to e-mail and Internet is mainly through cyber cafes, colleges, universities, mobile telephones, and workplaces. A few well-to-do people access Internet at home (Government of Zimbabwe, 2005; Ndlovu, 2009).

Accessibility of the Internet is hindered by, among other factors, an antiquated telecommunication infrastructure, prohibitive costs, and low electricity generation. This often results in a malfunctioning Internet system. The country's tele-density is believed to be between 2.5 and 3, meaning that there are about 2.5 and 3 telephone lines per hundred citizens (Machigere, 2008; Ndlovu, 2009). The quality of mobile networks is generally poor, forcing many people to have multiple SIM cards as backup. Electricity is erratic and generation capacity went down drastically during the period of the economic meltdown.

Load shedding can go up to 19 hours at times (The Standard, August, 23, 2010). Only 20% of households have access to electricity (UNEP Collaborating Centre on Energy and Environment, 2001) and generation capacity is very low, resulting in the country importing 41% of its electricity from neighboring countries (Davidson & Mwakasonda, 2001). Power supply shortages and load shedding do not only result in a "degraded service" but they also add to operating costs since network providers have to factor in costs of sourcing back-up facilities such as diesel generators or alternative sources of energy such as solar or wind energy (Mansfield, 2011).

Costs of accessing the Internet are very high relative to people's earnings. A visit by the author to Internet cafes in the Central Business District of the capital, Harare, in June 2011, showed that rates for accessing the internet range between USD1 and USD1.40 for 30 minutes. This is very high considering the fact that the average worker in the country takes home between USD165 and USD250, amounts which are far below the poverty datum line, which is about USD500 (*The Standard,* 2010). It could be argued that severe economic problems experienced by the country since the year 2000 constitute the biggest setback in the diffusion of new communication technologies such as the Internet.

The national ICT document identifies the following as the main challenges of confronting the ICT sector:

- Inadequate Communication Infrastructure
- Inadequate ICT Facilities
- Inadequate ICT Skills
- Limited Institutional Arrangements
- Inadequate Financial Resources
- Limited Private-Public Partnerships
- Limited Data Management Capacity
- Inadequate Horizontal and verTical Communication (Government of Zimbabwe, 2005, p. 17)

In addition, there are challenges relating to the legal and regulatory framework on ICT. These include, among others, the existence of separate and conflicting laws that regulate the ICT sector, namely, the Broadcasting Services Act (2001), the Post and Telecommunications Act (2000), the Access to Information and Protection of Services Act (2002), and the Interception of Communications Act (2007). The absence of laws that govern cyber transactions and the overlap and duplication of functions by regulatory bodies such as the Broadcasting Authority of Zimbabwe (BAZ) and POTRAZ have also been cited as stalling investment in the ICT sector (Zunguze, 2009). If government's objective of transforming the country into a knowledge-based society by 2020 is to be achieved these hurdles must be removed (Isaacs, 2007).

MEDIA AND DEMOCRACY NEXUS: A CONCEPTUAL FRAMEWORK

Although there is an outpouring of literature on the broad subject of media and democracy (Curran, 1991; Kean, 1991; Nyamnjoh, 1996; Gunther & Mugham, 2000; Ronning & Kupe, 2000; Nyamnjoh, 2005; White, 2008), literature on online media and democracy, particularly on Africa, is fragmented, if not scant.

A cross-cutting feature of literature on media and democracy is its location of the mass media in the 'public sphere', implying that the media are, in principle, open 'to all receivers and senders', since they deal with 'public matters for public purposes', and are answerable to the wider society (McQuail, 1994, p. 11). Online media lend themselves to this kind of analysis, not least because of their vast potential to facilitate many-to-many communication, but also their capacity to accommodate marginalized voices, what other scholars have described as 'alternative public spheres' (Atton, 2002; Coyer et al., 2007; Sandoval & Fuchs, 2010).

Habermas, cited by McCarthy (1989, p. xi), conceives the public sphere as the space between civil society and the state, where 'critical and robust discussion of general matters is institutionally guaranteed'. He notes that the liberal public sphere developed in specific historical circumstances of a developing market economy. In such a public sphere, state authority was monitored through informed and critical discourse by the people. This bourgeoisie 'public sphere' was exclusive of other 'classes of men'. The resultant intertwining of state and society in the 19th and 20th centuries led to the collapse of the liberal bourgeoisie public sphere, which was later replaced by the public sphere of the welfare state. It is significant to note how the expansion of the public sphere is reciprocally linked with economic progress and distribution of wealth. However, the fact remains that the 'post-liberal' era envisaged by Habermas, where the public sphere is inclusive of all and sundry is still utopian in much of the developing world.

Questions have been raised about the appropriateness of referring to newspapers and television as 'mass media' given the fact that in much of the developing world the 'mass media' remain inaccessible to the generality of the masses or are used less as organs of public information than 'technologies for managing consensus and promoting consumer culture' (McCarthy, 1989, p. xii). Without a critical mass of middle class people, how appropriate can the concept of 'public sphere' be applicable to the developing world, particularly Africa?

Some scholars argue that technological developments of the 1990s, such as the Internet, have given the concept of the public sphere new prominence (Kellner, n.d.; Dott, 1998). Kellner (n.d.) argues that in the contemporary high-tech societies, there is a significant expansion and redefinition of the public sphere which goes beyond the one conceived by Habermas. For technological optimists like Kellner, this expanded public sphere is a site of 'information, discussion, contestation, political struggle and organization that includes the old and the new "new cyberspace", as well as the interactivity of everyday life' (Kellner, n.d. p. 12). The implication for this is a reformulation of the concept of the public sphere. Kellner contends that:

My argument is that first broadcast media like radio and television and now computers have produced new public spheres and spaces for information, debate and participation to invigorate democracy and to increase the dissemination of critical and progressive ideas-as well as new possibilities for manipulation, social control and promotion of conservative positions and intensifying differences between the haves and the have- nots (p. 13).

Chae (2005) seeks to understand the culture and social conditions of the public sphere in the United States of America through an analysis of

public forums in 25 U.S. online newspapers. He describes online public forums as a 'conversational arena' in which people talk with each other in public settings about public issues (p. 3). Chae notes that the use of online forums in newspapers was shaped by the institutional relations of the companies with their mother-corporations. The present study notes that public forums are critical components of online publications with a vast potential to enhance social intercourse among citizens.

Also instructive to note is Chae's argument (following Harbermas, 1962) that the culture of the public sphere differs in accordance with the development of the social economic structure (2005, p. 26). This means that the culture of the public sphere of a country, such as the U.S., which is the most advanced information society, cannot be the same as that of a developing, socially bifurcated and economically struggling country like Zimbabwe. Even within the same state, the culture of the public sphere is bound to change over time as society transforms.

A study by Morris (2002), where he compared coverage by 'new' and traditional media of American politics observed that more than the traditional media, the new media tend to dramatize and sensationalize issues, resulting in the erosion of public trust for the new media. The observation by Morris that the presentation of political news has been changing and continues to change because new media lend themselves to dramatization and sensationalism is instructive. The present study, however, differs from Morris's in the sense that it focuses on the audience's experiences with new media, in order to understand the utility value of these media in democratization.

Scholarly work on how online media impact on democratization is growing but similar studies focusing on the African continent are far in between. The few studies available have tended to focus on how new media are impacting on journalistic practices, rather than on the broader society (Berger, 2005; Amobi, 2010; Etim, 2010;

Jones & Pitcher, 2010; Mabweazara, 2010). The few studies available (Moyo, 2007; Ofuafor, 2010) do not delve deeper into the contributions of new media in national discourses since they narrow their focus on institutional aspects of these online media. Ofuafor (2010) touches, albeit, very briefly, on how the new media have been influencing 'media reportage' in Nigeria. He argues that new media, such as the Internet, have made a significant impact on Nigerian politics by raising people's consciousness to demand 'free and fair elections' in the country and the formation of 'social communities that champion democracy, lobby for political sensitization and political campaigns' (Ofuafor, 2010, p. 6). In spite of these milestones, Ofuafor argues that a plethora of obstacles have militated against the new media's democratization role. Among these obstacles are: state control and regulation; low levels of investment in technology, resulting in low Internet access; and a low national and international bandwidth (Ofuafor, 2010, p. 7). Worth noting is that most of the obstacles that hinder use and access to new media technologies in Nigeria are applicable to the developing world, Zimbabwe included.

Moyo (2007) analyzes news Websites published by exiled Zimbabwean journalists and focuses on their production processes and practices. Moyo argues that news Websites run by Zimbabweans in the Diaspora are 'alternative media' in the sense that 'they give voice to the voiceless and articulate viewpoints that would otherwise not see the light of day under Zimbabwe's tightly controlled media environment'. One gets a sense Moyo is being overly optimistic about the capacity of online news Websites to 'empower ordinary' citizens, particularly in view of the fact that not much is known about their readership in the country, where the majority of 'ordinary' and marginalized citizens live. His claim that news Websites offer 'radical' content need further critical interrogation because media that is vigorously anti-state, but fails to question property and race relations is not necessarily radical.

ONLINE MEDIA: 'ALTERNATIVE PUBLIC SPHERES' OR PRIVATE SPHERES?

The Internet and other 'new' communication technologies have been described as 'alternative public spheres' on account of their capacity to give space to originally marginalized voices. However, there is lack of consensus on the meaning of the term 'alternative media', with some scholars defining it as non-mainstream media that are independently operated. These include community-focused media such as pirate radio stations, online discussion boards and broadcast companies, and publications owned by activists (Coyer et al., 2007). O'sullivan et al. (1983, p. 8) defines alternative media as 'Those forms of mass communication that avowedly reject or challenge established and institutionalized politics, in the sense that they all advocate change in society, or at least a critical assessment of traditional values'. For O'sullivan et al. (ibid.), alternative media (also referred to as 'radical' or 'underground media') stand in opposition to mainstream productions by representing political and social doctrines that 'lie outside the defined limits of parliamentary consensus and debate' (p. 8). Lewis (cited by Banda, 2006, p. 10) argues that alternative media serve a specific ideological purpose and identifies, among other things, access by minorities, decentralized production and interactivity as some of the key tenets of alternative media. Couldry and Curran (cited by Moyo, 2007, p. 87) conceive alternative media as media whose production challenges 'concentration of media power, whatever forms those concentrations may take in different locations'. Thus, Couldry and Curran accentuate structure rather than professional practices as the defining features of alternative media.

Sandoval and Fuchs (2010, p. 141) warn against being too optimistic about concepts like 'civil media', 'community media', 'alternative media', 'grassroots media', 'participatory media' or 'participatory culture'. They argue that in the contemporary society, which is characterized by structural inequalities, our understanding of alternative media is insufficient. They conceive 'alternative media' as 'critical media' (p. 141). The argument that democracy should not only be limited to the political realm, but also embrace other systems like an economy based on participatory ownership and decision-making, is plausible. One finds merit in the view that alternative media should be committed to pointing out the unequal, dominative and non-participatory democracy. This means that by providing 'critical content' alternative media will be able to advance social transformation and contribute towards the attainment of genuine democracy. This is because critical media expresses progressive political interests and acts as an outlet for suppressed possibilities. Sandoval and Fuchs (2010, p. 148) argue that:

...the discourse on alternative and participatory media should be situated within the context of the analysis of capitalism. Capitalism brings about structural inequalities that shape the limits and potentials of alternative media projects.

This view is corroborated by Manji (2008) who argues that there is nothing progressive or liberating about technology since we live in a divided society, where technology has a tendency of amplifying rather than ameliorating social differentiation.

Sandoval and Fuchs' conceptualization of alternative public spheres appears much broader and devoid of the sentimentalism associated with technological determinists who often view technology as 'an emancipator', which, by itself, will bring freedom, prosperity and enlightenment (Lenert cited by Mabweazara, 2010, p. 17). Such a view ignores the difficulties encountered in the use of technologies and 'their frequent failures to deliver predicted desired outcomes' (Mabweazara, 2010, p. 17).

ONLINE MEDIA CONSUMPTION HABITS AND PATTERNS

Data from the in-depth and focus group interviews indicates that the most popular online publications and Websites are *Zimsituation.com*, *NewZimbabwe.com*, *ZimOnline.com*, *Zimdaily.com*, and *TheZimbabwetimes.com* (now *Daily News*). After further probing, respondents mentioned others like *Zimgossip.com*, *The Zimbabwean*, *SW Radio* Website, *Studio 7* (VOA) Website, and *Radio VOP* Website. Levels of awareness about the existence of online publications and news Websites available in Zimbabwe are very low. This could be linked to the erratic and almost opportunistic access to the Internet reported by the respondents. Some of the respondents said they only read online news after being tipped by friends about a 'juicy' story online or if they come across an interesting story while sending an e-mail or browsing the Internet. The 'opportunistic' access to online news is reflected in the following statements by some respondents:

I only read online news publications when I go to the University of Zimbabwe where I can access the internet for free. If I do not go to the University I will not be able to read online news.

When I am researching for an assignment on the Internet, I may stumble upon an interesting story, then I end up reading it even if I had not intended to do so.

These statements suggest that the utility of online publications in the democratic transformation of the Zimbabwean society is mediated by a complex web of factors related to the economy. Limited access to the Internet and the prohibitive costs mean that online publications still have a limited impact on Zimbabweans residing in the country. The fact that some respondents merely stumble on some stories while searching for other information also suggests that online news stories do not rank that high in the priority lists of people who access the internet in Zimbabwe. This is perhaps linked to the fact that many people are unemployed (the unemployment rate is over 80%) and would be looking for jobs or trying to link up with relatives and friends in the Diaspora or they would be trying to get some other information which has an immediate impact on their socio-economic conditions.

Even those who have access to the Internet at work may not have enough time to read stories because they would be too busy to do so and would rather go on e-mail first before reading the news. A certain university where this author worked for close to ten years has a policy of blocking the Internet during working hours (8:00 AM to 4:00 PM) and unblocking it during lunch hour (1:00 PM to 2:00 PM). The author observed that immediately after the expiration of the Internet 'embargo', people would start by checking and sending e-mails before doing anything else, hoping to beat the load shedding time, which was usually around 5:00 PM. This practice is still in place and the author observed during the period this study was conducted, that a few lecturers now have laptops and 3G modems in order to circumvent this problem. What is therefore instructive is that limited access to the Internet has a strong bearing in shaping online news consumption habits. This means that economic imperatives are a key determinant on the impact of the online publications' potential to promote democratization in contemporary Zimbabwean society.

As a result of the limited access to the internet (because of cost and erratic supply, low national and international bandwidth, which results in the Internet being too slow) the downloading of news stories from online publications and Websites and reading them later is now a common phenomenon as was revealed in the focus group discussions. People with access to the Internet at work find it difficult to read news online during lunch hour since most people would be online, thus resulting in the system slowing down. Cost is not necessarily the most crucial factor in inhibiting people from reading news online. Even for those who have easy access to the Internet at work, reading news usually comes last after checking e-mail, jobs, or study opportunities. During the height of Zimbabwe's economic crisis characterized by hyperinflation, there was a popular joke that everybody, including people who were working, was looking for a job and that the Internet was the first port of call if ever the opportunity presented itself. In fact it was common for employers to deliberately limit access to the Internet for their employers as a strategy for limiting the 'brain drain'. There was speculation among workers that the Internet policy of the university mentioned previously was a strategy to limit the employees' access to job opportunities abroad. This suggests that while people would have liked to read online publications, prevailing socio-economic conditions in the country, where politics of the belly dominated disengaged the citizenry from national debates such as those championed by online publications.

In terms of content, some respondents who read online publications cited their sensational 'stuff' (i.e., 'rumor' and 'gossip' about celebrities, sports personalities, and politicians) as things that exert a strong magnetic pull on them. Other than sleazy news, online publications are able to report on controversial topics shunned by the mainstream press because of the restrictive legal environment which imposes stiff penalties for 'falsehoods', or libelous stories. One respondent talked about online publications as 'having more leverage to report on sensitive stories because they operate outside the perimeter of legal restrictions such as AIPPA and POSA'. In addition, they are also better positioned to report breaking news since they have a shorter news cycle than mainstream media, which would have to wait until the next day to report on an event. This means that their information is considered 'more up to date' than that of mainstream newspapers. A case in point is the reporting of the 2008 elections, when online publications became part of what has been described as a 'parallel market of information' (Moyo, 2010, p. 54). News Websites and cell phones moved in to fill the gaps in the reporting of the elections and the subsequent embargo imposed on presidential results. One such blogger, The Bearded Man (http://thebeardedman-blogspot.com/2008/03/Zimbabwe-election-results.2008.html), compiled the running tallies of election results before they were officially announced, thus undercutting the mainstream press. What is instructive is to note that even this 'positive' attribute of online publications was not necessarily shared by all the respondents since some cited the 'sensational nature' of online publications and their tendency towards gossip as a negative attribute. In the words of one male participant in the focus group discussion, 'these gossip stories tend to undermine the credibility of online publications'. This shows that just like mainstream newspapers, the context in which they are consumed is a complex one, and so is their readership. To understand their actual impact on democracy in Zimbabwe would require a thorough investigation of the myriad of complex social, economic, political, and ideological factors which mediate their consumption.

PARTICIPATION IN ONLINE FORUMS AND COLUMNS

Bases on the views of participants in the focus group discussions, participation in online chat forums and opinion columns among respondents is very low due, to mainly, to lack of time. The very same reasons attributable to a low readership of online news (lack of adequate access to the Internet, load shedding, high cost) were also cited as reasons for not participating in online chat forums. The following statements from some respondents shed light on the consumption habits of online publications:

I have never participated in online forums because most of the time when I am using the computer there will be several people waiting to use the same computer.

I never participate because our computers are so slow. At times I get to hear about what is online newspapers through friends who have better access to the internet.

Sometimes online publications might carry some stories which do not reflect the situation on the ground and I would want to give a proper perspective of what is happening in the country. So I sometimes participate if I feel there is need to set the record straight.

When I go to the internet cafes, I start by checking my emails. Usually the time is not even enough to reply all emails because I don't check my email every day. This means that I have no time at all to participate in online debates even if I would have wanted.

These statements show that lack of participation in online chat forums is linked to resource constraints (e.g., shortage of computers connected to the Internet, high costs, shortage of time, etc.), technical reasons (such as slow speed of the Internet as a result of a smaller bandwidth), and the actual content of online publications (i.e., stories that do not reflect the reality on the ground). The low levels of participation on online chat forums means that the range of views discussed on these forums is limited, thereby making them a medium for the privileged elite who have access to the Internet. Interactivity and the potential for a cross pollination of ideas is the hallmark of online media but when the majority of people are shut out for one reason or the other, it means that the medium becomes a preserve of the few.

A content analysis of online Websites such as *NewZimbabwe.com* shows that its opinion column is dominated by people based outside the country and a sprinkling of political heavyweights from within the country. These include the editor of the Website, Mthulisi Mathuthu; Alex Magaisa, a Zimbabwean laywer based in the UK; Lennox Mhlanga, a writer based in Botswana; UK based writers; Innocent Chofamba Sithole; Gilbert Nyambabu; Taffy Nyawanza; and Lance Mambondiani. Out of a very long list of contributors and bloggers, only a few (who are political elites) reside in the country. This shows that this vital space for social intercourse and democratic engagement is a monopoly of a few economically empowered people living in the country and in the Diaspora. Herbamas (cited by Chae, 2005, p. 26) argues that a careful study of online forums as 'public spheres' might help us to 'attain a sociological clarification of the concept from the perspective of one of its central categories'.

ONLINE PUBLICATIONS AND DEMOCRATIZATION

Opinions on the role of online publications in the democratization process of the country are rather mixed. While the majority of the respondents accentuated the limitations faced by online publications in prosecuting their democratic mandate, the minority view online publications as playing a positive role. Some respondents in the interviews said, they regard online publications as alternative spaces for different voices, and that they set the agenda for mainstream newspapers, while also acting as surveillance antennas on behalf of the citizens. The following statements are illustrative of these roles:

I would say to a certain extent they have expanded the media space in terms of being outlets for voices oppositional to the Zanu PF government. The only problem I have is that their news is generally more of the same stuff and more of the same voices. They have not made attempts to deal with various issues dogging the nation as they have tended to

restrict their news to the same handful of political protagonists. What I would have expected are well researched stories that are diverse and inclusive of the broader citizenry.

Most of these online publications carry mostly political stories while other important issues like health, development etc. are marginalized. As a result, they tend to be read by a small fraction of the society.

They have the potential to become genuine alternative platforms if only there is connectivity on nationwide scale. As it stands, connectivity and logistical problems of acquiring the computer and the cost of paying for the computer and the cost of paying for the Internet restrict online news publication to a few well to do people.

Online news publications are elitist. As a result, they have a smaller market than mainstream newspapers.

Thus, the democratic role of online publications is viewed as constrained by the lack of diversity in their content, the limited range of discourses (e.g., obsession with politics as mentioned by one of the respondents), their elite orientation, both in terms of content and target. As observed earlier, the mission and vision statements foreground the desire to fill the lacuna left by closed mainstream newspapers, which means that their content is not meant to be very different from mainstream, privately-owned newspapers. This implies that the "alternative" perspective they purport to bring relates to the state. Their ability to transcend the polarization which characterizes the public and privately-owned media is, therefore, limited.

Although they are able to publish sensitive political stories, which mainstream newspapers would hesitate to publish because of harsh media laws (e.g., stories like political scandals involving the Minister of Mines, the alleged land scandals at the City of Harare, and rumors of President

Mugabe's ill-health), their political ideologies and the manner in which they approach key national issues such as the economy, land reform, and others, is not very different from mainstream newspapers like the *Zimbabwe Independent, The Standard, and The Financial Gazette.* A few respondents mentioned the failure by these online publications to operate above political polarization as a huge inhibition to their democratic mandate. There had been an expectation that national discourses would transcend the ZANU PF-MDC dichotomy but this has not happened, resulting in views falling between the two sides (such as those of smaller political parties, like *Zanu Ndonga, Mavambo*, MDC-M (now MDC-N), and others being neglected.

However, the 'no-holds barred' approach of online publications acts as a bait for readers since they are able to publish sensational stories that 'tickle' a news starved audience. This sentiment was echoed by one respondent who said:

I like reading online publications because they tell it like it is. They do not hold back any information. We now know who among our ministers, is corrupt, who is having an extramarital affair. Even those who have HIV or Aids, we now know them. We would have never read such stories in The Herald.

This implies that, while some of the stories covered by the online publications might be interesting to the public they would not necessarily be in the public interest, because they do not enhance the informational base of the citizens, but are meant to increase ratings in a market characterized by stiff competition. Elsewhere, the ability of new media to present news in a manner that is more appealing to the reader has been noted (Morris, 2002). Morris notes how online media in the United States of America are attracting more readers because of their 'unique' packaging of the news, which borders on sensationalism, dramatization and conflict, in order to attract more audiences

and make profit (Morris, 2002, p. 7). Paletz and Entman's (cited by Morris, 2002, p. 13) observation on the tendency of online news to gravitate towards the dramatic is illuminating:

Journalists have been known to highlight, if not concoct conflict and find characters to symbolize its different sides. One reason; to attract an audience that is thought to have little patience for the abstract, the technical, the ambiguous, the controversial.

Some citizens perceive online publications as 'antennas' to alert citizens about the goings-on in the dark alleys of officialdom, particularly those stories that mainstream newspapers would not be able to report on for fear of reprisals. Such issues include allegations of human rights violations during the 2008 elections, allegations of killings in the Marange Diamond fields and other corruption scandals involving government officials. One respondent had this to say:

It is through online publications that we got to know about the killings at the Marange diamond fields. The state media was silent about the whole issue. Online websites picked the story and was broadcast the whole world

Thus, online publications were able to put the country on the international spotlight during national crises such as the 2008 cholera crisis. This resulted in an overwhelming humanitarian response by the United Nations agencies and other international donors.

Besides monitoring institutions of the state and ensuring accountability, online publications are also perceived as agenda setters on important national developments, particularly breaking news. The mainstream media take a cue from online publications, particularly on the sensational news discussed previously. A case in point is the Prime Minister, Morgan Tsvangirai's, involvement in a car accident in March 2009, in which his wife died. Online publications picked up the story before the mainstream media could publish it. In some situations, the mainstream media are forced to respond to a story that would have appeared in an online publication, either to 'set the record straight' or refute it. Examples include rumors about the alleged ill-health of President Mugabe, which appeared in some online publications in September 2010. The online publications alleged that Mugabe was 'losing the battle against cancer and had started looking for a successor'. Mugabe later dismissed the rumor when he was interviewed by Reuters (Chinaka, 2010, September 9). However, online news publications only set the news agenda on stories, seemingly that interest the public (sensational stories, gossip, and rumors) rather than on substantive stories that enhance democracy such as economic policy, governance issues, indigenization policy, the constitution-making process, the land issue, and others.

It could also be argued that there is a reciprocal agenda setting process, which takes place between the mainstream media and online publications. For serious national issues, online publications collect stories (sometimes unedited) from mainstream media and post them on their websites. Sometimes they publish opinion polls on a matter that could have been covered in the mainstream media. There is, therefore, a complex network of relationships that are created between online media and mainstream media and also among online publications themselves.

ETHICAL CHALLENGES AND IMPLICATIONS FOR DEMOCRACY

In spite of their great potential to open spaces for voices different from that of the state, there are concerns that online publications fail to adhere to basic journalistic ethics and professional standards, thus undermining their contribution to the democratization process. Respondents blamed online publications for various transgressions, the

main ones being inaccuracies, falsehoods, lack of balance, and objectivity use of anonymous sources, to mention but a few. The following statements are instructive:

Online publications do not have enough correspondents in the country to monitor what will be happening. They mostly employ freelance journalists, who are out to make quick money by publishing as many stories as they can, even if they have not cross-checked the veracity of those stories.

They seem too adversarial. They seem to write with a vengeance. They seem to think that every reader is a politician.

The internet is a jungle where anyone can write anything and get away with it. Of the online publications I have read, ethics seem to be very low on their priority list. Some of their stories are too sensational, and they seem to derive pleasure in maligning certain personalities without giving the individual concerned the right of reply, which is a fundamental aspect of ethical journalism.

Zimsituation.com just collects stories from different sources without verifying their authenticity. The problem is that they seem to target people who are outside the country mostly, who have no way of verifying the truthfulness of their reports. They are all based in the UK, America, and South Africa, among others, yet they trust someone to collect news on their behalf.

It is noteworthy that mistrust of online publications primarily emanates from perceptions about both their organizational practices, style of journalism and actual content. During the interviews some respondents claimed online publications face difficulties in cross-checking stories and sometimes rely on relatives, acquaintances and friends for news tips and information about what is happening in different parts of the country.

That online publications are viewed as detached from reality because they are domiciled abroad echoes an observation made by Lush & Kupe (2005, p. 10) that:

The further you are from the story, the more difficult it is to be objective in tune with the often complex dynamics of a story unfolding thousands of kilometers away…Distance alone makes it extremely difficult for journalists outside the country to fill the information void created by the state's propaganda machinery…

The tendency to rely on informal sources for news has been the online publication and news Website's Achilles heel on several occasions. A case in point is the publication by ZimOnline.com of a story in February 2005, alleging that three journalists working for foreign news organizations, Brian Latham, Angus Shaw, and Jaan Raath had been arrested by government police for practicing journalism without being accredited by the Media and Information Commission (MIC). The story was found to be untrue and Zimonline.com retracted and apologized, stating that:

It has been brought to our attention by Ms Mtetwa, who acts for the trio, that they were never charged or detained by the police. The police only visited the journalists' offices on Monday and questioned them about their registration status and some of the communication equipment they use at their offices. We apologize to Ms Mtetwa for attributing wrong information obtained from one of our sources to her. We apologize to the police, our colleagues, Shaw, Raath, and Latham for the inconveniences our incorrect story obviously caused. Disciplinary action is being taken against the correspondent who filed the story (Zimonline. com, 2005, February 16).

Although Zimonline.com retracted the story, millions of people had read it and most probably believed it. A retraction creates negative impressions about the news source as readers begin to question the credibility of their news sources. Thus, Arrant (2000, p. 3) notes that 'the crushing demand for fresh news items to fill up airtime twenty-four hours a day, makes accuracy and balanced reporting more difficult'. Such challenges manifested themselves during the March 29, 2008 harmonized elections when online publications were competing to be the first with the news of the results. In the process, some of them became hostages of the rumor mill that Harare, the capital city, is famous for.

An examination of some stories retrieved from some online sites shows that some Web publications published erroneous election results (e.g., that one of the Vice Presidents, Joyce Mujuru, had lost to an opposition candidate, and that the Zanu PF political commissar, Eliot Manyika had also lost his seat, resulting in him shooting and killing a Movement for Democratic Change (MDC-Tsvangirai faction) supporter in frustration (Zimonline.com, 2008)). These reports were later found to be untrue.

A content analysis of some Websites during the March 2008 election shows that some Websites misrepresented some election results. Different websites published conflicting sets of results, with one website inaccurately stating that opposition leader, Morgan Tsvangirai had received 50.3% of the vote, while the incumbent, Robert Mugabe, was reported to have garnered 42%, and independent candidate Simba Makoni, 6.8%. The House of Assembly results were also inaccurately represented as MDC-Tsvangirai (99 seats), Zanu PF (95 seats) and MDC-Mutambara and independent candidates (12 seats [Independent Election Results Centre, (http://www.zimelectionresults.com)).

That there was a prolonged delay in announcing the official results did not help matters either, thus sending the rumor mill and the 'parallel information market' on a tailspin. There was apprehension in some quarters that the rush to announce erroneous results by these online publications could trigger violence similar to that witnessed after Kenya's 2007 elections, whereby both the incumbent and the opposition leader were claiming victory. When media get implicated in such bloody events, their democratic credentials come under close scrutiny.

There is also a perception among some citizens that online publications specialize in rumor mongering and, therefore, are not sources of serious news and information. The most recent example is a rumor about the alleged death of the Reserve Bank Governor, Dr Gideon Gono. The story is believed to have originated from a 'UK based Zimbabwe online publication'. On the June 24, 2010, *ZIMEYE*, an online publication published a story on its Website headlined 'Gideon Gono dies'. The story was accompanied by Gono's photograph and a caption which read:

Harare: (ZIMEYE) Reserve bank Governor, Dr Gideon Gono died in a car accident Wednesday, which occurred along Chiredzi road. However, no other details are available as the Zimbabwean government has not declared the news official. ZIMEYE will keep readers informed of the new development'.

Another UK based website later commented about the incident saying:

The ZimDiaspora.com was also inundated with calls from across the world inquiring whether Dr Gono had actually died. This was after the UK-based Zimbabwean online publication had un-journalistically and recklessly published the false story claiming Gono was dead (The Zimbabwean, 2010, June 26).

Gono was later quoted dismissing the story as 'malicious trash' (NewZimbabwe.com, 2010, June 25). However, the story had travelled the whole world through the Internet and social networks. On an online encyclopedia, Wikipedia, Gono's profile had already been edited reflecting that he had died. The perception that online publications are purveyors of rumors engenders cynicism among

the citizens. A respondent had this to say with regard to the 'rumor mongering tag' associated with online publications:

Some of their stories are so weird that you really wonder where they get them from. The other day I read in The Zimbabwean that 60 000 people had died during a doctors' strike. More recently, there was also a story in the Zimbabwean claiming that 41 victims of the June 27 political violence had been buried at Chitungwiza cemetery disguised as paupers. One really wonders where such stories originate from. To be frank with you sometimes you really wonder whether these guys are journalists or political activists.

Sentiments like these demonstrate the extent to which online publications can engender cynicism among some readers. Some online publications have gone so far as publishing medical records of certain individuals, thus invading individual privacy. For instance, in 2006, *NewZimbabwe.com* published a story alleging that a certain government official had infected his wife with HIV. The official is alleged to have nearly killed his wife in a scuffle after the wife accused him of infecting her with the virus. Although the general approach in journalist practice is that public figures do not have an absolute right to privacy by virtue of their stature, publishing someone's medical condition without his or her consent, whatever the stature of that person is, is inexcusable in professional journalism.

Some online publications treat children of government officials as 'fair game', thus violating children's rights. For example, in February 2010 a number of online publications published the grade seven results of President Robert Mugabe's youngest son, who is a minor, claiming that he had 'dismally failed'. Some even suggested that he had 'inherited his mother's IQ' (Nehanda Radio, 2010, February 2). The story is an example of violation of children's rights. The use of pseudonyms by online journalists provides a shelter of anonymity which encourages these kinds of 'ethical atrocities'. Moyo (2007, p. 102) argues that the use of pseudonyms has to some extent eroded the credibility of online publications and Websites.

Veteran journalist, Peta Thorncroft's comments on the ethical performance of some online publications is instructive:

So I have been very disappointed with lots of external media. Zimdaily-I suppose [I] now view ZimDaily as an essential part of my life covering Zimbabwe because it makes me laugh...I have shrieked with laughter often times at some of the stories and the way they have been hounding the Chefs' children-who are in Universities and colleges overseas and some of the comments that followed on their website made me scream with laughter. So I do not take it seriously as a news outlet...

Veteran journalist and former editor of the privately owned Daily News, Geoff Nyarota, who until 2009 was operating an online publication, The Zimbabwe Times.com from the United States of America, also observes the lack of ethics in online publications when he says:

Confronted with these challenges, a number of journalists working for both the state media and the independent press have resorted to submitting refined versions of their stories to internet publications, where the ethics of online Zimbabwean journalism are ill-defined or non-existent (Lepage, 2010, p. 2).

Such statements demonstrate the practical limitations that online publications face in enhancing democratization process in Zimbabwe. This is because if these media are not accountable, they cannot enforce accountability on political institutions in the country since they themselves would be distrusted by the citizenry.

CONCLUDING REMARKS

This chapter sought to discuss the impact of online publications and news Websites on the democratization process in Zimbabwe. The main observation made is that, although online publications have to some extent opened spaces for views oppositional to the state, a host of factors, (e.g., organizational, operational, technical, and professional) undermine online publications' ability to act as genuine 'alternative public spheres'. Observations are that far fewer people read online publications in the country due to, among other factors, poor connectivity, prohibitive costs, and lack of access of the Internet and the poor infrastructure which supports it. Access to the Internet, and concomitantly online publications is opportunistic and the reading of online publications ranks very low on the priority list. In addition, online publications are generally perceived as elitist, catering for the already economically empowered and politically privileged people in society. This is a category of people who are already served by the mainstream media. In addition, online publications published by Zimbabweans in exile lack diversity in terms of political and social perspectives, primarily because of their failure to transcend the political polarization that is emblematic of the Zimbabwean society. Apart from organizational and technical factors, an unprofessional approach to journalism by these publications, such as partisan journalism, sensationalism, gossip, and rumor mongering, an obsession with issues that are interesting to the public rather than those that are in the public interest have conspired to undermine their contribution to democratization in Zimbabwe. The reception patterns of online publications in the country demonstrates the currency of a complex Web of political-economic and socio-cultural factors which act as obstacles to the widespread impact of online publications on Zimbabwe's democratization process.

There is, therefore, need to re-conceptualize and rethink the actual role that online media such as these can play in the democratization, particularly in over-regulated, socially fractured and economically bifurcated developing societies such as Zimbabwe. However, because this study is based on a limited sample one has to be nuanced about the conclusions of this study. However, more institutional studies and bigger reception studies representative of all geographical regions and social groups in the country could be conducted in order to come up with a more formidable conclusion. Also, the climate of fear prevailing in the country makes it difficult for people to speak their minds due to a history of political persecution. Be that as it may, the present study opens pathways for future studies on the role of online media on democratization in an African context.

REFERENCES

Amobi, I. (2010). *Millennial generation, new media and digital divide: Assessing global divide through ownership, literacy, access and usage of Internet and social media by young people in Nigeria*. Paper presented at the 2010 World Journalism Education Conference. Rhodes University, Grahamstown, South Africa.

Anim, E. (2010). *From mass communication to citizen journalism: New perspectives in contemporary mass communication*. Paper presented at the 2010 World Journalism Education Conference. Rhodes University, Grahamstown, South Africa.

Arant, D. (2000). *Online media ethics: A survey of US daily newspaper editors*. Paper presented at the Association for Education in Journalism and Mass Communication Convention. Phoenix, AZ.Retrieved September 5, 2008, from http://www.factstaff.elon.edu.anders/onlinesurvey.html

Atton, C. (2002). *Alternative media*. London: Sage Publications.

Banda, F. (2006). Alternative media: A viable option for Southern Africa. *Openspace, 1*(5), 80–83.

Belsey, A., & Chadwick, R. (1992). *Ethical Issues in Journalism and the Media*. London: Routledge.

Berger, G. (Ed.). (2005). *Doing Digital Journalism: How Southern African News Gatherers are Using ICT*. Grahamstown, South Africa: Rhodes University.

Blumler, J. G., & Gurevitch, M. (1995). *The Crisis of Public Communication*. London: Routledge. doi:10.4324/9780203181775.

Bond, P., & Manyanya, S. (2002). *Zimbabwe's Plunge: Exhausted Nationalism, Neoliberalism and the Search for Social Change*. Pietermaritzburg, South Africa: University of Natal Press.

Cellular News. (2008, September 9). Zimbabwe awards 3G licenses. *Cellular News*. Retrieved June 18, 2011, from http://www.cellular-news.com/story/35076.php

Chae, Y. (2005). *An aspect of the culture of the public sphere in U.S.: The Analysis of online public forums in local online newspapers*. Paper presented at the annual meeting of the International Communication Association. New York. Retrieved August 3, 2010, from http://wwwallacademic.com/meta/p13770_index.html

Chinaka, C. (2010, September 9). Mugabe dismisses rumours of poor health. *Reuters*.

Chuma, W. (2007). *Mediating the transition: The press, state and capital in a changing Zimbabwe, 1980-2004*. Unpublished doctoral thesis, University of Wiwatersrand, Johannesburg, South Africa.

Coyer, K., Dowmunt, T., & Fountain, A. (2007). *The Alternative Media*. London: Routledge.

Curran, J. (1991). Mass media and democracy: A reappraisal. In Curran, J., & Gurevitch, M. (Eds.), *Mass Media and Democracy* (pp. 267–284). London: Edward Arnold.

Davidson, O., & Mwakasonda, S. A. (2004). Electricity access for the poor: A study of South Africa and Zimbabwe. *Journal of International Energy Initiative, VIII*(4), 26–40.

Du Plooy, G. M. (Ed.). (1995). *Introduction to communication. Course Book 2. Communication Research.* Kenwyn, South Africa: Juta & Co. Ltd..

Dzamara, I. (2007). Doctors' strike: 60000 dead. *The Zimbabwean,* I, February, 2007.

Government of Zimbabwe. (2005). *E-Readiness Survey Report.* Harare, Zimbabwe: Ministry of Information and Communication Technology.

Gunther, R., & Mugham, A. (2000). *Democracy and the Media: A Comparative Perspective.* New York: Cambridge Press. doi:10.1017/CBO9781139175289.

Habermas, J. (1989). *The Structural Transformation of the Public Sphere: An Inquiry into Category of Bourgeoisie Society.* Cambridge, MA: Polity Press.

Hansen, A., Cottle, S., Negrine, R., & Newbold, C. (1998). *Mass Communication Research Methods.* London: Sage Publications.

Internet World Stats. (2010). *Internet use in Zimbabwe.* Retrieved August 25, 2010, from http://www.internetwordstats.com

Isaacs, S. (2007). *ICT in education in Zimbabwe: Survey of ICT education in Africa.* Zimbabwe Country Report. Retrieved from http://www.infodev.org

Jones, N., & Pitcher, S. (2010). Traditions, conventions and ethics: Online dilemmas in South African journalism. In Hyde-Clarke, N. (Ed.), *The Citizen and Communication: Revisiting Traditional, New and Community Media Practices in Southern Africa* (pp. 97–112). Claremont, South Africa: Juta & Co. Ltd..

Kasoma, F. (1996). The foundations of African ethics (Afriethics) and the professional practice of journalism: The case for society centered media morality. *Africa Media Review, 10*(3), 93–116.

Kean, J. (1991). *The Media and Democracy.* Cambridge, UK: Polity Press.

Kellner, D. (n.d.). *Habermas, the public sphere, and democracy: A critical intervention.* Retrieved July 15, 2010, from http://www.gseis.ucla.faculty/kellner/papers/habermas.htm

Knight, M. (2010). Blogging and citizen journalism. In Hyde-Clarke, N. (Ed.), *The Citizen and Communication: Revisiting Traditional, New and Community Media Practices in Southern Africa* (pp. 31–50). Claremont, South Africa: Juta & Co. Ltd..

Kvale, S. (1996). *Interviews: An Introduction to Qualitative Research Interviewing.* Thousand Oaks, CA: Sage Publications.

Lepage, C. (2010). *Professional journalism is not for the weak-kneed: Interview with Geoffrey Nyarota (Zimbabwe).* Retrieved June 17, 2011, from http://www.cimethics.org/newsletter/holidayissue2010/holidayissue2010_htm

Lush, D., & Kupe, T. (2005). Crisis? *What crisis? Report on International Conference on Media Support Strategies for Zimbabwe, International Media Support (IMS).* The Netherlands Institute for South Africa, (NIZA), Media Institute for Southern Africa, (MISA), Open Society Institute. Retrieved March 3, 2008, from http://www.i-m-s.dk/media/pdf/Zimbabwe

Mabweazara, H. M. (2010). New technologies and journalism practice in Africa: Towards a critical sociological approach. In Hyde-Clarke, N. (Ed.), *The Citizen and Communication: Revisiting Traditional, New and Community Media Practices in Southern Africa* (pp. 11–30). Claremont, South Africa: Juta & Co. Ltd..

Machigere, R. (2008). *The potential of harnessing the utilization of ICT in the transport sector for socio-economic development: A case for Zimbabwe*. Paper presented at the Science with Africa Conference. Addis Ababa, Ethiopia.

Manji, F. (2008). *Alternative media for social change in Africa: Myths and realities*. Paper presented at the Cape Town Book Fair. Cape Town, South Africa. Retrieved August 15, 2010, from http://www.informationforchange.org/pressentations/ctbf_firoze.pdf

Mansfield, I. (2011, May 10). Mobile broadband to ensure continued vibrancy of Zimbabwe's telecommunications market. *ITU-Cellular News*. Retrieved June 16, 2011, from htt://cellular-news.com/story/49100.php?=h

McCarthy, T. (1989). Introduction. In Habermas, J. (Ed.), *The Structural Transformation of the Public Sphere: An Inquiry into Category of Bourgeoisie Society* (pp. xi–xiv). Cambridge, MA: Polity Press.

McQuail, D. (1994). *Mass Communication Theory: An Introduction*. London: Routledge.

MMPZ. (2002). *Media under siege: Report on media coverage of the 2002 presidential and mayoral elections in Zimbabwe*. Harare, Zimbabwe: MMPZ.

Morgan, S. (2004). Online Publishing: Independent media challenge Internet in Zimbabwe. *RAPZI Newsletter*, 19.

Morris, J. J. (2002). *The new media and the dramatization of American politics*. Paper presented at the annual meeting of the American Political Science Association. Boston, MA. Retrieved on September 30, 2009, from http://www.allacademic.com.meta/p66276_index.html

Moyo, D. (2007). Alternative media, Diasporas and the media of the Zimbabwean crisis. *Ecquid Novi: African Journalism Studies*, 28(1/2), 81–105. doi:10.3368/ajs.28.1-2.81.

Moyo, D. (2010). We're all story tellers: Citizen Journalism in the age of digital 'pavement radio. In Hyde-Clarke, N. (Ed.), *The Citizen and Communication: Revisiting Traditional, New and Community Media Practices in Southern Africa* (pp. 50–74). Claremont, South Africa: Juta & Co. Ltd..

Ndlovu, R. (2009, April 16). Bridging the digital divide: Sound ITC vital. *The Zimbabwean*.

Nehanda Radio. (2010). *Mugabe's son inherits other's IQ*. Retrieved July 21, 2010, from http://nehandaradio.com/2010/02//02/mugabes-son-inherits-mothers-iq

Nyakunu, N. (2005). The working environment in Zimbabwe. In *Report on International Conference on Media Support Strategies for Zimbabwe, International Media Support (IMS), The Netherlands Institute for Southern Africa, (NIZA), Media Institute for Southern Africa, (MISA), Open Society Institute, 2005-11-30*. Retrieved March 23, 2008, from http://www.i-m-s.dk/media/pdf/Zimbabwe

Nyamnjoh, F. B. (2005). *African Media: Democracy and the Politics of Belonging*. Pretoria, South Africa: Unisa Press.

Nyamnjoh, F. B., Wete, F., & Fonchingong, T. (1996). Media and civil society in Cameroon. *Africa Media Review*, *10*(3), 37–66.

Nyarota, G. (2008). Poor health now Mugabe's worst enemy. *The Zimbabwe Times*. Retrieved June 20, 2008, from http://www.thezimbabwetimes.com

Nyarota, G. (2008a, 2 April). Charamba now targets online publications. *The Zimbabwe Times*. Retrieved from http://wwwzimbabwejournalists.com/authors

O'sullivan, T. M., Hartley, J., Saunders, D., & Fiske, J. (1983). *Key Concepts in Communication*. London: Routledge.

Ofuafor, M. (2010). *The influence of new media forms on media reportage and democracy in Nigeria*. Paper presented at the African Media and Democracy Conference. Accra, Ghana.

Ott, D. (1998). Power to the people: The role of electronic media in promoting democracy in Africa. *First Monday*. Retrieved August 15, 2010, from http://131.193.153.231/www/issues/issue3_4/ott/

Radio, S. W. (2007). Hot Seat: Foreign correspondent Peta Thornycroft on Media in Zimbabwe. [Radio programe transcript]. Retrieved February 20, 2008, from http://www.swradioafrica.com/pages/hotseat

Ronning, H. (1997). Institutions and representation. In Zhuwarara, R., Gecau, K., & Drag, M. (Eds.), *Democratization and Identity* (pp. 1–15). Harare, Zimbabwe: University of Zimbabwe.

Ronning, H., & Kupe, T. (2000). The dual legacy of democracy and authoritarianism: The media and the state in Zimbabwe. In Curran, J., & Parker, M. J. (Eds.), *De-Westernizing Media Studies* (pp. 157–177). London: Routledge.

Ronning, H., & Kupe, T. (2000). The dual legacy of democracy and authoritarianism: The media and the state in Zimbabwe. In J. Curran., & M. Jin-Park (Eds.), De-Westernizing Media Studies. London: Routledge.

Sandoval, M., & Fuchs, C. (2010). Towards a critical theory of alternative media. *Telematics and Informatics*, *27*, 171–150. doi:10.1016/j.tele.2009.06.011.

Saunders, R. (1991). Information in the interregnum: The state and Civil Society in the Struggle for hegemony in Zimbabwe, 1980-1990. Unpublished PhD thesis, Carleton University, Ottawa, Canada.

The Standard. (2010, August 23). *Urban residents decry prolonged power cuts.*

The Standard. (2010, September 5). *Power cuts give Econet connectivity nightmares.*

The Standard. (2010, August 23). *ZESA attacked for load shedding.*

The World Bank. (n.d.). *The public sphere.* Retrieved August 21, 2010, from http://www.worldbank.org/commgap blogs.worldbank.org/publicsphere

The Zimbabwean. (2010). Gono death report false. Retrieved July 10, 2011, From http://www.thezimbabwean.co.uk/news/32138/gono-death-report-false.html

Waldahl, R. (2004). *Politics and persuasion: Media coverage of Zimbabwe's 2000 election.* Harare, Zimbabwe: Weaver Press.

White, R. A. (2008). The role of the media in democratic governance. *African Communication Research*, *1*(3), 269–328.

Zimdiaspora. (2010, May 9). *Job Sikhala launches massive national party.* Retrieved August 20, 2010, from http://www.zimdiaspora.com

ZIMEYE. (2010). *Gideon Gono dies.* Retrieved August 12, 2010, from http://wwwnewzimsituation.com/5415k2/breaking-news-gideon-gono-dies-htm

Zimonline.com.ac.za. (2005, February 16). *We got it wrong.* Retrieved March 15, 2010, from http://www.zimbabwesituation.com/nov26a_2004.html

Zunguze, M. (2009). *Contextualizing ICT for Development in Zimbabwe: E-Knowledge for Women in Southern Africa.* Harare, Zimbabwe: EKONISA.

Chapter 23
Social Media, New ICTs and the Challenges Facing the Zimbabwe Democratic Process

Nhamo Anthony Mhiripiri
Midlands State University, Zimbabwe

Bruce Mutsvairo
University of Twente, The Netherlands

ABSTRACT

Social media in its various forms drew international attention to Zimbabwe during the most intense period of the Zimbabwe crisis up to 2008. It is arguable that social media activism was contributory to the current dispensation of Government of National Unity between ZANU PF and the former opposition Movement for Democratic Change. Social media induced revolution and mass rejection of the status quo of the magnitude seen in the Arab Spring might be difficult to replicate in Zimbabwe. A similar revolution with different magnitude but critical results unfolds in Zimbabwe, especially since the disputed 2008 presidential elections and the mayhem that followed. The use of new communication technologies helped publicize extra-legal activities and human rights abuses often blamed on ZANU PF affiliated militia groups and the security forces. International attention has led to diplomatic intervention.

INTRODUCTION

There is a major argument that use of social media, especially the posting of stories and footage of brutalities on-line, drew international attention to Zimbabwe and hence in a way was contributory to the current dispensation of Government of National Unity between Zimbabwe African National Union (Patriotic Front) (ZANU PF) and the former opposition Movement for Democratic Change. Social media activism remains important even though social media induced revolution and mass rejection of the status quo of the magnitude seen in the Arab Spring might be difficult to replicate in Zimbabwe. Conservative nationalists in the security sector and paramilitary groups ensure that mass demonstrations against ZANU PF are quashed. Our chapter argues a similar revolution

DOI: 10.4018/978-1-4666-4197-6.ch023

with different magnitude but critical results is unfolding in Zimbabwe, especially since the disputed 2008 presidential elections and the mayhem that followed. The use of new technologies helped publicize extra-legal activities and human rights abuses often blamed on ZANU PF affiliated militia groups, and the security forces. Websites such as www.zimbabwesituation.com, www.kubatana. net, www.sokwanele.com, www.munyori.com and www.newzimbabwe.com complemented the critical privately owned newspapers. These alternative sites of information to the state-controlled media are often criticized by ZANU PF ideologues as "Western funded agents of regime change."

E-newspapers and blogs reproduced damning empirical stories and pictures that were often picked and reproduced by the political opposition and local and international human rights groups to condemn President Robert Mugabe and ZANU PF at important international gatherings convened by regional and international bodies such as the Southern Africa Development Community (SADC), African Union (AU), and the United Nations (UN). Names of abusive security operatives were published on-line during the bloody period between the March 29, 2008 election and the June 27 presidential run-off, which MDC's Morgan Tsvangirai withdrew from, citing violence and harassment of his supporters. After the disputed June 27 election, the collapse of the Zimbabwean economy, health sector (especially the cholera outbreak that somewhat became the proverbial straw that broke the camel's back) and the diabolic state of Zimbabwe's prisons were given publicity in e-newspapers and social media sites free from state censorship (Journeymanpictures, 2008). This indirectly resulted in the old ZANU PF nationalist regime hesitating to install a unilateral government, and begrudgingly accepting the SADC and AU endorsed Global Political Agreement (GPA) with the opposition. Exposure arguably restrained the regime and operative excesses. Communica-

tion through Zimbabwean social media sites might not have resulted in popular anti-regime demonstrations but their influence in Zimbabwe-focused international opinion formulation is significant.

Recent African scholarship on ICT critique 'new' technologies and journalism practice in Africa. New ICTs are alternatively viewed as presenting African journalists with new opportunities for improved practice (Berger, 1996; Mabweazara, 2010), or as a threat to normative practices. Scholarship on Zimbabwe has focused on how ICTs have assisted in the production of alternative discursive spaces or how the Diaspora use such spaces to influence voters' opinion back home (Moyo,; 2009; 2010; Mutsvairo, 2010). How social media influence diplomatic opinion formation on the Zimbabwe situation is hardly studied and in this chapter we offer a critical analysis of the relationship between the two.

We purposively critique the contents of selected blogs, on-line newspapers that provide space for audience interactivity and popular Short Message Services (sms) dispatches by social media activists. We also studied hostile utterances and writings on new media and the regime change agenda by ZANU PF ideologues and diplomats which appear in *The Sunday Mail*. As part of our methodology, we conducted interviews with important critical civil society personalities on how their reports are constructed, the influence of social media and ICTs in the production of such reports, and how effective the reports have been in attracting international attention to Zimbabwe. We also critiqued British diplomat Philip Barclay's *Zimbabwe: Years of Hope and Despair* (2010) to ascertain for sources of information used in constructing perceptions on Zimbabwe and whether civil society activities and social media do fare in his exposé. This work and other sources involving diplomats were complementary in a situation where the diplomats were unwilling to contribute to our research.

MEDIA-INDUCED SOCIAL UNREST AND PRE-EMPTIVE CENSORSHIP

Thanks to its global ubiquity, social media engagement has become a critically important strategy for political candidates the world over. For some, social media deserves some credit for offering a helping hand in the deconstruction of authoritarian regimes thereby presenting opportunities for democratization (Gaier & Smith, 2011). Others are quite adamant social networking sites are dictating the online outlook of today (Boyd & Ellison, 2007). Given the new digital messaging landscape, it would appear as if new media tools have become the contemporary society's equivalent of samizdat, the underground network which was used by Soviet-era activists to disseminate anti-government materials.

The ZANU PF clique of the Zimbabwe government is ever wary of any mass display of public disaffection against the party and its stalwarts. The fears of a so-called "Orange Revolution" or "regime change agenda" are very real and often are met with pre-emptive actions. The fall of the Berlin Wall in 1989 saw radical changes taking place in Eastern Europe. A Mugabe communist comrade Romanian President Nicolae Ceauşescu was toppled and murdered in popular revolt in 1990. In the next decade urban-based revolutions enunciated through public protests and street demonstrations became commonly known as the Orange revolution (Mahoso, 2008, pp. 159-168). Old regimes collapsed and the most daunting was watching on international TV demonstrations against Yugoslav President Slobodan Milosevic--another ZANU PF and Mugabe's longtime ally. Tactlessly, in October 2000, opposition leader Morgan Tsvangirai, after watching the civilian coup in Yugoslavia on TV resulting in charges against Milosevic for crimes against humanity, predicted that the same fate could befall Mugabe if he did not voluntarily step down (Chan, 2010, p. 18). Tsvangirai was immediately charged for incitement to violence.

Another of Mugabe's allies, Hugo Chavez of Venezuela, survived a media orchestrated coup de tat in April 2002. It is not paranoia for ZANU PF aligned scholars like Tafataona Mahoso to say the CIA have worked with opposition leaders, the media and the military in some countries led by revolutionary groups in order to topple the latter. Christopher Reilly made similar observations in *Counterpunch* soon after Chavez was reinstated through popular will after a dramatic week in 2002.[1] Anti-Chavez demonstrations were publicized internationally, and condemnations followed when 16 people were killed by snipers and several hundred injured. The army took over, in a media orchestrated coup, and a news anchor at the private television station used to stage and announce the coup was audacious to demonstrate how they fabricated the whole thing in the "post-coup" euphoria (Bartley & O'Brian, 2003). Certainly, all this is not lost to Zimbabwean nationalists, especially when it happens to their "left-wing" allies. In their view, the broadcasting monopoly is thus justifiable as arising out of expedience to protect a revolutionary project. Zimbabwean Filmmaker Michael Raeburn (2003) frustrated with the status quo and engulfed in the regime change mood secretly made a personal documentary--*Countdown Zimbabwe*--berating Mugabe and ZANU PF, before he escaped into exile. This video did not find much distribution in Zimbabwe. Raeburn's documentary coincided with the unsuccessful MDC's "Final Push" campaigns which were expected to remove Mugabe through popular street demonstrations (Chan, 2010). Perhaps the documentary *Panorama: Secrets of the Camps* by BBC's Hillary Anderson (2004) found much publicity in the country, getting played on the state television station, mainly as a self-evident counter-propaganda project that serves to prove that material has been consistently fabricated to damn the Zimbabwe government. The documentary staged in South Africa fabricated depictions of "the insides of Zimbabwe's National Youth Training Program." Mahoso alleges similar terror tapes were forged and smuggled to the UN Human Rights Commission but were rejected as fake (Mahoso 2008, p. 164).

Mahoso has berated local journalists working for the privately owned media for creating copy that is used by international detractors at global forums that discuss Zimbabwe. Writing in his *Sunday Mail* weekly column he alleges:

For the last 15 years, the UK, U.S., and the EU have sponsored some journalists and media houses in Zimbabwe for the purpose of fabricating the very same lies which these countries then deploy against Zimbabwe at international forums. In the last two years this strategy has failed to win the majority to the side of the Western powers and their sponsored media and journalists here (Mahoso, 2011a, B13).

Rights groups can fabricate rights abuse evidence to condemn an unfavoured government. Zimbabwe has suffered its fair share of fabricated falsehoods to vilify sections of its leadership. In 2002, prominent journalist Basildon Peta wrote a fictitious story about his arrest, abuse, and harassment before he was exposed. This was after his story was already published in regional and UK leading papers. Peta fled into exile. The Zimbabwe Union of Journalists suspended Peta who was their Secretary General at the time of the fabrication[2]. Mugabe critics quickly forgave Peta for his blatant breach of ethics, preferring to regard him as a press freedom fighter. In February 2004 *BBC One* televised Hilary Anderson's fabricated video *Panorama: Secrets of the Camps* about supposed ZANU PF youth camps and the violations taking place there. The production is discredited because the accents of confessing youths are South African with Afrikaans inflections, ZANU PF slogans are chanted discordantly and untypically, and Table Mountain and Table Bay (non-Zimbabwean geomorphologic features) are visible in the background in part of the mise-

en-scene. Mahoso vigorously refutes the grisly pictures representing alleged escalation of violence in Zimbabwe in 2011. These pictures were shown to delegates at the SADC troika in Livingstone, Zambia, by ZANU PF detractors. Mahoso dismisses the pictures as file footage imported from the 1994 black-on-black violence in KwaZulu-Natal, South Africa. He again charges that between 2006-2008 similar pictures from Darfur were used in the propaganda war to represent Zimbabwe's degeneration and provoke global outrage (Mahoso, 2011b). With the vigorous inception of citizen journalism which is de-professionalized, de-capitalized and de-institutionalized, there are further possibilities of breach of journalistic ethics and professionalism (Hyde-Clarke, 2010). Outright lies, vindictiveness and malice can spur some individuals to fabricate and reproduce criminally libelous material in order to condemn a regime. Video-images can be produced and photo-shopped to create impressions of abuses and atrocities to justify international intervention.

SOCIAL MEDIA, THE FIFTH ESTATE AND THE CONTRADICTIONS OF RE-PRESENTATION

The Fifth Estate is that emergent space where ordinary people who are not necessarily media professional nor are working for specific media institutions publish their stories. Unlike the regular 'Fourth Estate', this de-institutionalized, de-capitalized and de-professionalized space of the Fifth Estate is quite often on the Internet appearing as blog sites or social media networks such as Facebook, Twitter, Badoro, and LinkedIn. Social media networking is usually a form of leisure and sustaining interpersonal communication amongst friends, relatives and colleagues. Mobile phone mass smses are another form of social media which may be mass generated using software connected to the Internet and new ICTs. Media texts posted on social media web sites are normally accompanied by a voting process or registration of hits (visits) to indicate how popular they are.

Social media is an alternative means of mass communications that employs 'new' ICTs like mobile phones and Internet to produce, store and distribute multimedia messaging, text messaging and mobile pictures. Like "citizen journalism" it simultaneously makes traditional audiences consumers and producers of content. There is interactivity in both media content production and consumption. Such citizen participation is celebrated as being the driving force behind the Arab Spring. Social media are defined as "participatory online media where news, photos, videos and podcasts are made available via social media web sites" (Evans, 2008, p. 37). Merit (2011) defines social media as Web-based tools and services that allow users to create, share, rate, and search for content and information without having to log in to any specific portal site or portal destination. Similarly, Kaplan & Haenlein (2010) believe social media is "a group of Internet-based applications that build on the ideological and technological foundations of Web 2.0, and that allow the creation and exchange of user-generated content." Other scholars prefer to place emphasis on the social network sites' ability to (1) construct a public or semi-public profile within a bounded system, (2) articulate a list of other users with whom they share a connection, and (3) view and traverse their list of connections and those made by others within the system (Boyd & Ellison, 2007).

Daughety, Eastin and Bright (2008, p. 1) alternatively view social media as "user-generated content created or produced by the general public rather than by paid professionals and primarily distributed on the Internet." Enunciating the unique features of social media, Du Plessis (2010, pp. 2-3) writes, "they are 'media rich' and empower users to share their opinions, insights, experiences, content and contacts with their friends and family through multiple content forms... such as text, audio, still images, animation, video and other

interactivity content forms." While social media technology are not a new phenomenon in military and government circles, popular social network sites such as Facebook, MySpace, and Twitter and social news sites like YouTube, made these communicative practices and technologies available to mass accessibility. To understand the emergent digital forces, we need to first accept the notion that globalization has played an important role in forcing individuals out of traditional bases of social solidarity including parties, churches, and other mass organizations (Bennett & Segerberg, 2011). Ghannam (2011) pinpoints that social networks play an active information-providing role for activists and citizens. Furthermore he claims they "mobilize, entertain, create communities, increase transparency, and seek to hold governments accountable" (Ghannam, 2011, p. 4).

However, blogging and social networking can constitute a form of public communication aspiring for "anonymous" audiences beyond those typical of the intimate sphere of friends, relatives, and colleagues. Such communicative practice on this space then becomes "citizen journalism," an important feature of the Fifth Estate (Chiumbu, 2010). Sometimes the Fifth Estate offers vibrant and incisive debate and discussion, but it can degenerate into trivialities and hate speech. Critical cyber-activism with a sense of social responsibility is existent. Many Zimbabweans pass comments on blogs in this way on the arrests of civil society activists, which information is picked up by other lobbyists, activists and the media. However, trivialities and nuisances can appear in the Fifth Estate. The hate language and obscenities prevalent on unregulated social media sites frequented by Zimbabweans–most of them using pseudonyms and resorting to indigenous languages such as Shona and Ndebele–reminds us of what Achille Mbembe (2001) calls "the aesthetics of vulgarities" when in nearly ineffectual subversive ways the subaltern throw scatological insults both at themselves and at a repressive Party-State system. Political derision and rumor function as "the perfect medium of communicating dissent and discussing the powerful in unflattering terms" (Nyamnjoh, 2005, p. 218).

Among several reasons Boyd considers are behind citizens' motivation for participation in public life include identity development, status negotiation, community maintenance, and, yes, civic engagement (Boyd, 2008, p. 112). Boyd further argues that most online activists are no longer accustomed to chat rooms or bulletin boards to chat the way forward with strangers. Instead they chose to hang out online with people they already know. In the case of Zimbabwe and Africa in general, mobile phone usage has been expanding rapidly transforming not just the economies of scale but also the way people interact socially (De Bruijn, 2011). A new study confirms rising rates of Internet penetration in Africa, singling out Kenya, Nigeria, Uganda, Tanzania and Zimbabwe (Columbus & Heacock, forthcoming). These developments have had a significant impact in spearheading online social activism continentally. Yet there is nothing new about the use of technologies to sustain activism. Shirky argues that Martin Luther adopted the new printing press to protest against the Catholic Church, and elsewhere American revolutionaries propagated their ideals using the postal service that Benjamin Franklin had designed (2011). Still, the Internet remains very much mainly an urban phenomenon in Zimbabwe, and even there accessibility is limited to a relative number of people. These people go online using their own cell phones, PCs, workplace facilities, or they patronize commercial Internet cafes. Most of the material on the Websites is published under pseudonyms as a means of concealing identity where communicators are worried about apprehension. There is the Interception of Communication Act which allows the state secret surveillance into a private individual's digital and telephonic communication. This might explain the apprehension in the social media communications. Facebook is used largely as a very apolitical social space perhaps for the same reasons.

The old guard is suspicious of the capabilities of social media tools much as the same instruments are acknowledged as offering opportunities for sustainable development. Speaking to government officials and members of the diplomatic corps at an Africa Day celebration in Harare in 2011, Acting Foreign Affairs Minister Hebert Murerwa (ZANU PF) observed that social media networks needed to be controlled because of their influence on the youth (Chikwanha, 2011, p. 19). As if to confirm the fears about adverse influences a Zimbabwean social media activist, Vikas Mavhunga, was arrested over a message he posted on Prime Minister Morgan Tsvangirai's Facebook wall, urging the prime minister to emulate the revolts in Tunisia and Egypt. The Zimbabwe Lawyers for Human Rights offered legal assistance to Mavhunga (Chikwanha, 2011, p. 19). Socialist International leader Munyaradzi Gwisai was in 2012 convicted for watching videos on the Arab Spring in a group with the intention to plot a coup in Zimbabwe. The possibility of a social media revolution similar to what happened in Egypt, Tunisia and Libya is unlikely in Zimbabwe at the moment partly due to the relatively low Internet connectivity of the country (Dutta & Mia 2010). Still, with accessibility figures set to rise thanks to the expanding mobile phone revolution, the likelihood of digital-led mass protests cannot be dismissed even though such protests will not have the same magnitude as the Arab Spring due to a number of reasons including cultural and geo-political differences. The potential of the Fifth Estate is not lost to politicians and its appeal, immediacy and informality are viewed as assets in attracting sophisticated surfers. Relatively younger politicians across the political divide are using social media networking, and prominent names that are found on Facebook are Tsvangirai (MDC), Deputy Prime Minister Arthur Mutambara (MDC), Minister Welshman Ncube (MDC), Ministers Saviour Kasukuwere and Walter Mzembi (ZANU PF). New modes of political communication using modern information and communication technology, political marketing by politicians and demographic information of their target "audiences" are potential areas of critical research.

ZANU PF IDEOLOGUES AND THE APPROPRIATION OF THE ARAB SPRING REVOLUTION

ZANU PF is ambiguous about the new ICT that makes social media possible. At their 2011 Annual Party National Conference, a resolution was called to clampdown on social media. The Party's Secretary for Legal Affairs and Zimbabwe's Minister for Defense Emmerson Mnangagwa read out the resolution blaming social networking for the devastation that had been witnessed during the year in the Arab Spring, the Occupy Wall Street demonstrations and the Riots in the UK; hence there was need to control social media activities in Zimbabwe. Ironically, the party's Department of Science and Technology was at the same conference urging "If platforms for disseminating information about the party and its policies are not in sync with modern trends, the party may not strike a chord with the majority of the electorate who are under 40 years of age. Rallies and gatherings as a source for disseminating information are now very limited and limiting the scope and geographic spread" (Muzulu, 2011). And the Central Committee Report warned the Party that if it wanted "to remain a political giant and retain competitiveness, ZANU PF has to take ICTs seriously for political mobilization" (Muzulu, 2011). ZANU PF's Jonathan Moyo already articulates party support through blogging and the Minister for Youths, Indigenization and Empowerment Saviour Kasukuwere, amongst other senior party members, is known to run a Twitter and Facebook account.

ZANU PF ideologues have taken the events of the Arab Spring and tried to appropriate them as synonymous with ZANU PF initiated economic and political programs in Zimbabwe. Mahoso (2011b) traces Zimbabwe's own Arab Spring back to 1980, when a mass vote rejected Ian Smith and Abel Muzorewa as legitimate leadership for the country. The ZANU PF organized anti-sanctions demonstrations of March 2, 2012 are similarly viewed as mass expression of the people's will against imperialists and their local agents.

The reader may wonder why we call the huge gathering which launched Zimbabwe's national anti-sanctions campaign a 'Third Chimurenga uprising'. How can it be an uprising? Who were the Zimbabweans rising against? In what way can the anti-sanctions launch be compared and contrasted with what people have been trying to do in Tunisia, Egypt, Bahrain, Jordan, Yemen and Libya? The answer is imperialism, made up of the imposition of neo-liberal corporatist polices expressed in our region as structural adjustment programmes; made up of the unilateral Nato-driven security programme called "the war on terror" in the Middle East and masquerading as Africom in the rest of Africa; made up of the global financial crisis and Western efforts to prescribe responses to the crisis for other regions of the world; made up of the myth of "change" and "democracy' which tries to substitute mere words for real work, production and livelihoods; and made up of strenuous efforts to impose and maintain the Western media template on the rest of the world. That is imperialism in practice. Fortunately or unfortunately the last imposition, that of a media template, is a double sword; it cuts those it is imposed upon and those who have fashioned, imposed and enforced it. That is why the uprisings in North Africa and in Zimbabwe could not happen according to the imperialist 'change' project and could not be predicted (Mahoso, 2011b).

Jonathan Moyo in his acetic manner attacks perceived "enemies" and agents of imperialism:

Apparently there are some U.S. and European puppets in the MDC-T and its associated elements in the foreign founded and funded NGO colony, notably the NCA (National Constitutional Assembly), ZCTU (Zimbabwe Congress of Trade Unions) and Zimbabwe Crisis Coalition—with one Philip Pasirayi being the busybody—who have spent the last few weeks imagining that they can be copycats of the turmoil in Tunisia, Egypt and Libya which they dream they can reproduce in Zimbabwe. This is what comes out of the nonsense whose distribution they intensified last week through the Internet, text messages, and pamphlets under what they think is anonymous cover when their identities are in fact known (Moyo, 2011a).

He also immediately boasts about the police's ability to squash any 'illegal' mass demonstrations against the current regime. He accuses people of adopting policies from U.S. strategists in order to "unlawfully engineer illegal public protests" in Zimbabwe.

Only God knows why these hopeless would-be copycats, whose death wish is to be arrested at the Harare Gardens and be charged with treason in accordance with the rule of law that they love preaching about, honestly think they can do an Egypt or Libya in Zimbabwe when they miserably failed to do anything near that during the height of the biting Zimbabwe dollar days of hyper-inflation. Do these failed puppets of regime change ever think? Have they forgotten how their much touted 'final push' succeeded only in pushing them further down the doldrums of their political irrelevance only yesterday (Moyo, 2011a)?

The coalition government is rubbished and Cabinet Ministers from the MDC are implicated in fueling the regime change agenda. The U.S. government is accused of clandestinely funding Zimbabwean malcontents and dissidents in order to effect regime change against the liberation movement government. The state controlled

weekly *The Sunday Mail* made allegations that a company called Casals Associates Zimbabwe (CAZ) was running a political campaign to destabilize Zimbabwe. CAZ was supposedly giving funding to NGOs hostile to Zimbabwe. Amongst the recipients of this funding was Crisis Coalition in Zimbabwe, the National Association of Non-Governmental Organizations (NANGO), ZimRights, and Kubatana Trust. Kubatana Trust in particular is accused of planning to initiate uprisings similar to those that happened in the North Africa and the Middle East. Writes Tafadzwa Chiremba (2011, p. 1) of *The Sunday Mail*, "Investigations reveal that on April 19 (2011), CAZ disbursed about US$13,960 to Kubatana Trust to "challenge undemocratic governance" by increasing its capacity to produce footage on uprisings in Egypt and Tunisia. The footage was to be distributed to Zimbabweans."

Nango was given US$24,000 to run a project called "power to the people," an initiative meant to support "efforts by progressive actors to empower citizens with an information-sharing platform." The project plans to create a central mobile phone text message platform, billboards, and advertisements for the print and electronic media. ZimRights got US$5,541 for a project called "engaging the Sadc Troika." Part of their money was allegedly used to send two officials to a human rights festival in Botswana where they presented a damning report on alleged human rights violations in Zimbabwe. They also distributed DVDs inviting international intervention into Zimbabwe (Chiremba, 2011, p.1).

THEORETICAL FRAMEWORK: DEMOCRATISING THE PUBLIC SPHERE

Public sphere as a concept is difficult to grasp, and it still lacks a clear definition, argue Adolf and Wallner (2005). Seen by others as the focal point for participatory approaches to democracy, the concept of public sphere is defined as an arena "where citizens come together, exchange opinions regarding public affairs, discuss, deliberate, and eventually form public opinion."[3] Thanks to their unrivalled democratic potential, the Internet and new media technologies have led to the emergency of cosmopolitan, reform-based movements in journalism, with the potential of creating a new public sphere avenue. The concepts of public journalism, civic journalism, citizen journalism and blogging, it can be argued, are tied to the central discourse that intends to diminish the gap between news and civic life and redefine the societal role of public sphere. The new instruments of political communication, used by agents of change and social groups through new media devices, fashion a centrepiece for political debate and action, and accordingly have become constituents of the public sphere. But while the Internet has created a new space for democratic dialogues, the real question is whether it has actually strengthened the public sphere.

Universally drawn from Jurgen Habermas' theories on the role of the public sphere in democratic discourse, the concept is defined by Gerard Hauser (1998, p. 86) as "a discursive space in which individuals and groups congregate to discuss matters of mutual interest and, where possible, to reach a common judgment." Habermas (1992) hypothesized that early modern capitalism created the conditions for the bourgeois public sphere, effectively creating an area for rational and egalitarian public debate. He defined public sphere as a "network for communicating information and points of view, the streams of communication are, in the process, filtered and synthesized in such a way that they coalesce into bundles of topically specified public opinions" (Habermas, 1992, p. 360). In attempting to define public sphere, Woodruff D. Smith (2003) suggests the first step is determining what it is not. "It does not denote vaguely defined affective features of social life such as 'public spirit,' 'patriotism,' or

even 'citizenship' unless the last is used to refer to how to act effectively in the public life of society" (Smith, 2003, p. 62).

Conditions that make it possible for the sphere to operate historically include, according Beers (2006), the rise of private property, literary influences, coffee houses and salons, and primarily the independent market-based press. Public sphere, Habermas opines, was central to creating an environment conducive for citizens to make informed decisions about what courses of action to adopt in matters related to their own affairs. Another way of looking at it is to follow Nancy Fraser's (1992, p. 110) view that it involves the establishment of a "theatre in modern societies" where "political participation is enacted through the medium of the talk." Habermas is of the view that without a functioning and democratic public sphere, government officials could not be held accountable for their actions, and citizens would be unable to claim any influence over political and government-related decisions.

He pays tribute to evolving historical circumstances, which were central to the emergence of a new civic society in the eighteenth century. He also attributes several factors for the new arrivals, arguing the need for open commercial arenas where news and matters of common concern could be freely exchanged and discussed. A new wave of intellectuals had moved into the European public sphere, augmented by a growing literacy rate, accessibility to news and books and a new form of critical journalism. The public sphere was well established in various public locations such as coffee shops and salons, evenly allowing people to freely gather and discuss matters of common interest. Habermas (1992) argues that the public sphere, thanks to the undoubted domination of mass media, developed into an arena of power struggles as practitioners jostled for influence. Fraser assumes that it was central to Habermas' account that the bourgeois public sphere was to be a discursive arena in which "private persons" deliberated about "public matters." Fraser's observation sits well with Dewey's assertion that there are two major types of humanity. These are private ones that "affect the persons directly engaged in a transaction," and public ones, "which affect others beyond those immediately concerned" (1954). Dewey was concerned that the ability to acquire or purchase a democratic institution was in itself not enough to sustain democracy. In a democratic society, the public is naturally expected to fully participate and oversee the functioning of government.

The Habemasian public paradigm has, in the wake of the Internet's rapidly increasing influence in advancing society's communication causes, extensively gone through critical debates, analyses, and discourses. Public sphere, concludes Gimmler (2001), "manipulates people, hinders the development of individuality, fragments communities, and simply creates consumers of information rather than knowledgeable and critical subjects with the capacity to make informed judgments make informed judgments." Lincoln Dahlberg refutes any suggestions the Internet has been successful in creating a public sphere, arguing "a cursory examination of the thousands of diverse conversations taking place every day online and open to anyone with Internet access seems to indicate the expansion on a global scale of the loose webs of rational-critical discourse that constitute what is known as the public sphere." (2001) Dahlberg offers a six-point criterion, which could eventually lead to the Internet's acceptance as a public sphere. These are autonomy from state and economic power; exchange and critique of criticizeable moral-practical validity claims, reflexivity, ideal role-taking, sincerity, discursive inclusion and equality (Ubayasiri, 2006).

The Internet, argues Bimber, "may be broadening the democratic base of those who express themselves to government," therefore disqualifying any notions the Internet provides the basis for "everyone" to "meet" and air their democratic view against and for the government (1992). Splichal

(2006) brings the Internet closer to the theory, arguing that the workability of public sphere is defined by the underlying principles of openness and publicity. This debate could even be drawn back to Immanuel Kant's articulation that recognizable democracy is one that is open for public scrutiny. If the Internet should thus be considered the new watershed for public sphere, it should be noted that the technological revolution has created social isolation also leading to lack of face-to-face contact, which is among the most notable characteristics of Habermas' original public sphere thesis. It is still not clear whether the democratising element of the Internet in Zimbabwe could be linked to the public sphere discourse. Certainly, citizens' ability to freely post stories on Facebook or provide comments to online stories shares the same characteristics of the traditional public sphere. Eyebrows are similarly raised when countries of the global North initiate and support social media sites and activities that are Zimbabwean focused ostensibly for the protection of human rights of ordinary Zimbabwean citizens, yet the ulterior motive might be about rapacious access to local resources preceded by removal of a "protective" and "vigilant" regime (Moyo, 2010).

PREPAREDNESS FOR SOCIAL MEDIA INDUCED MASS ACTION

A general survey will show that there is a general preparedness for at least those with access to new ICTs to be connected and possibly respond to messages and information from social media sites. Social media activities by a number of civil society organizations with regards to inventive mass communications methods are quite remarkable. The Community Radio Harare (CORAH) a civil society organization lobbying for a community radio license has been using mass sms to subscribed recipients on issues of social, cultural and health concern. The disseminating numbers are generated from South Africa, thereby circumventing the Post and Telecommunications Authority of Zimbabwe (POTRAZ) registration structures and procedures (Chipere, interviewed by Mhiripiri, 2011). The Kubatana Trust Website has provisions for mass sms-ing on its Website, besides podcasts, video archives, written text, and so forth. The National Association of Non-Governmental Organisations (NANGO) has amongst other facilities a *NangoTV*, and online television facility. The possibility of posting audio-visual material of all types and nature is likely, although at the time of our visit the "station" only showed one cryptic moving text with something that looked like handcuffs, followed by the words "Do you want to know the real garamound?" These words disintegrate into randomly scattered single letters before we see an indescript structure with a hollow at the center. Right at the end of the 3 minute long text are the words "So be it," and the ending shows "copyright 2009, undream." To a "vigilant" skeptical mind the cryptic material appears teasing but potentially subversive; the space is ready for the transmission of any kind of material, including regime change images.

The social media sites maintain a monitoring role especially over the excesses of government. They also take the opportunity to publicize government's intransigence at international meetings where the Zimbabwean government official (often from ZANU PF) might prefer to present a face of decency and credibility. For example, www.sokwanele.com writes on their blog in the Zimbabwe Inclusive Government Watch (ZIG) section

This combined issue of ZIG Watch, which focuses on breaches of the Global Political Agreement (GPA) recorded during December and January, is being released on the eve of the Zimbabwe Investment and Trade Conference taking place in South Africa on 1 and 2 March. A letter sent out to potential delegates from the Deputy Director (Bilateral Trade Relations) in Zimbabwe's Ministry of Industry and Commerce assures them that

there is "respect and protection for all private property in the country" and that the Bilateral Investment Protection and Promotion Agreement (BIPPA) signed by Zimbabwe and South Africa in 2010 is currently operational. "This means that all investments by nationals of the two countries are protected.

Such strategies to inform and influence international public opinions through using international conferences is critised by pro-ZANU PF ideologues as grandstanding and the actions of sellouts singing for their supper.

CIVIL SOCIETY AND CITIZEN MONITORING OF THE DEMOCRATIC PROCESS

Dumisani Moyo has ably shown that concerted civil society organizations and citizen monitoring of Zimbabwe's 2008 elections arguably led to ZANU PF conceding to a power-sharing scheme with the MDC (Moyo, 2010). The history of hostility, political vitriol, and violence between the two parties is well-chronicled (Sachikonye, 2011), and even in the post-2008 dispensation their co-existence in the coalition government for the most part was an uncomfortable marriage of convenience, made to last more because it was undersigned by regional and continental groups SADC and AU, who wanted to prove that there can be African solutions to African problems. Moyo shows how new ICTs enable citizen monitoring of, and citizen communication about, the state machinery, especially when elections are involved. The mobile phone and its capacity for sending sms have democratized the communication spaces. When mass sms are linked to civil society activism there arises vibrant social movement keen to scrutinize and report on the most important issues of the day. The website www.kubatana.net has facilities for mass sms and for blogging.

Typical of Zimbabwe focused civil society organizations and social media sites, *www.kubatana. net* is also variously linked to several civil society organizations such as Crisis Coalition in Zimbabwe, National Association of Non-Governmental Organizations (NANGO), Lawyers for Human Rights, and ZimRights.

The Zimbabwean Ambassador to the UN, Boniface Chidyausiku's suggestion even before the 2008 election results were announced for a government of national unity following Kenya's negotiated settlement in the previous year is attestation of the pressures of alternative social media and the circulating messages of Mugabe's defeat in the election. The free flow of mass sms messages could not have been lost on both ZANU PF nationalists, the security chiefs who are rumored to be the "real" center of power for Robert Mugabe's contemporary authority, and the regional, continental and global community. There was an avalanche of anti-Mugabe and anti-ZANU PF sms, with jokes circulated to demonstrate the demise of the old nationalist regime (Moyo 2011). In an interview with the BBC, ambassador Chidyausiku and a traditional ZANU PF man declared that, "There is no way anybody can do without the other."[4]

KUBATANA AND THE MOBILE PHONE ACTIVISM

Set up in 2001, Kubatana has proven to be a consistent, innovative and highly organized social media and activist "movement." It has won accolades with the latest being recognition from the Index on Censorship for being innovative in circumventing censorship legislation in Zimbabwe. The administrators of Kubatana Trust, who amongst other projects run the Website www.kubatana. net, claim that they are not a social media site. When asked how to define their Internet "mass" communication activities Bev Clark clarified:

I wouldn't particularly describe Kubatana as a social media site. Our primary goal has been to amplify the publishing of the civil society sector in Zimbabwe. Hence we have an online library of over 20 000 documents mostly published by NGOs, or about civic and human rights issues. We do have a blog where we try and give voice to citizens views and issues. Our text messaging/ SMS work may be considered more social media than other aspects of what we do. We have always wanted to bridge, and challenge the technological divide – therefore we use an integrated approach to publishing so that those on the margins of the access to information still get something. Social media is pretty elitist. You need access to technology and resources. Many times we use our access to technology to develop information products like newspapers and dvds. You'd probably find that more Zimbabweans have access to a dvd player than to Facebook. The "mass" in our communications has come about because we've painstakingly built a community by taking into account the fact that people's information needs are varied. People don't always want to know about politics or culture – they like a mix of information and we try to provide that. We have also always tried to be inspirational. In Zimbabwe the situation has at times appeared very dark, so we try and inject inspiration into our communication activities (E-mail interview with Mhiripiri, March 13, 2012).

Kubatana has a wide range of activities including a so-called Freedom Fone which has attracted the disapproval of the state regulator Broadcasting Authority of Zimbabwe. Kubatana uses FrontlineSMS software to create two-way dialogue between citizens in the Zimbabwe social democracy movement (Internews Europe, 2008, p. 65). High economic growth rates in many African countries have fuelled a communications revolution. Political campaigning no longer depends predominantly on rallies and government-owned media or the ability to travel physically into remote areas. Politicians and other activists can now reach voters directly and remotely via the Internet and especially the ubiquitous mobile telephone. They can expose political violence and communicate poll results instantaneously, making rigging easier to detect. Former Secretary-General to the United Nations Kofi Annan perceptively noted, "With communication and cell phones, this is where it is difficult to cheat in elections now. You are announced at the district level and cell phones go wild so by the time you go to the capital, if you have changed the figures, they will know and you will be caught out."[5]

It is also noted that during the 2011 Nigerian elections Emauwa Nelson of the Human Emancipation Lead Project, Nigeria[6] again warned would-be electoral fraudsters; "We want people to know that if they are trying to rig the election, there could be someone behind them and that person may send a text message saying what happened." In Nigeria, tens of thousands of civilian monitors recorded local electoral results and sent them via sms to a central computing system run by volunteers. Devious governments thus have to invest much more intricate ways of manipulating results or concealing any other breaches of human rights.

As often happens in the restrictive Zimbabwean media and communication spaces, civil society organizations are constantly and consistently devising innovative ways of circumventing restrictive regulations and other extra-legal forms of stifling the media (Mhiripiri, 2011). Community Radio Initiatives that have been denied licensing since 2001 have, for instance, used pre-recorded material, road shows, and publications to reach potential audiences. The same applies for the Freedom Fone project partially run under the auspices of Kubatana Trust. In this project, people could dial in to listen to pre-recorded messages in various languages or they could send in their own voice messages to the platform. In 2012, Index on Censorship recognized the project for innovation and original use of new technology to circumvent

censorship and foster debate, argument, or dissent. Zimbabwe's Broadcasting Authority has delayed issuing radio and television licenses, or where it has granted licenses, it has seen to it that ZANU PF affiliated entities or party supporters get the licenses at the detriment of other competitors. The Freedom Fone project tried to evade censorship. However, the Broadcasting Authority of Zimbabwe (BAZ) was particularly peeved with sexual health drama running on Freedom Fone, saying this was infringing on the Broadcasting Services Act (BSA). "They have asked us to stop, but we will respond since this is a telephony service rather than a broadcast one," Brenda Burrell from Freedom Fone was quoted by *The Standard* newspaper. BAZ regards the call-in programs as tantamount to illegal broadcasting. Freedom Fone was also featured an audio magazine "Inzwa" (Listen) that featured news headlines and another program where headlines in each day's newspapers were read out. Freedom Fone was also used on a constitutional project, where Constitutional Affairs minister, Eric Matinenga would respond to questions.

LIMITATIONS OF THE NEW SOCIAL MEDIA: HIGH CALL COSTS RENDERED THE PROJECT RESTRICTIVE

Kubatana does indeed relentlessly try to expand the democratic and communicative spaces in Zimbabwe. However, the cost of making telephone calls made the Freedom Fone project out of reach for many. "It limits the number of people who can access the service. But for people who are illiterate or do not have access to the Internet and newspapers, it's money worth spending," Burrell admitted (Matshazi, 2012). The newspaper coverage of the BAZ ban of Freedom Fone not quite implicitly encourages other organizations wishing to install similar mass communication technologies. Writes Matshazi in one of the newspapers

ZANU PF ideologues accuse of getting foreign funding and driving the anti-liberation movement "regime change agenda":

For organisations intending to set up their own platforms, Freedom Fone may also be costly, as some key devices are expensive, but the runners of the project said they gave free software. Freedom Fone is presently in use in Rwanda, Tanzania, Niger, Cambodia and South Africa, where Burrell says it has been more successful. The Freedom Fone project was initiated by Kubatana, a body that aims to capacitate Zimbabwean non-profit organisations to communicate and mobilise by incorporating electronic tools such as e-mail and internet into their media strategies (Matshazi, 2012).

These statements are viewed with mistrust by those who believe that there is a concerted attack putting the liberation movement under siege in order to effect regime change. All actions to "empower" civil society and allow people to communicate with ease are thus seen as never innocent, but engineered to prepare people for eventual political action to oust ZANU PF.

There is general agreement that Internet services of one form or another are going to influence national politics and future elections in Zimbabwe. Journalist Ray Ndlovu (2012) has traced which Zimbabwean politicians have adopted and adapted to new ICTs, especially Facebook. There are mobile subscriber wars between Econet Wireless Zimbabwe (EWZ), Telecel Zimbabwe, and the State-owned Net*One, which on the whole are targeting savvy and ICT compliant youths, who incidentally are the biggest potential groups of voters in the next elections. Bev Clark of Kubatana repudiates the criticism by Zimbabwean nationalists and ZANU PF who often accuse alternative media as "agents of regime change" funded by "imperialists." She says:

As I said previously, I don't think that Zanu PF (and the MDC as they grow in power) have anything to worry about in regard to alternative media having great influence in Zimbabwe. The most powerful forms of communication are radio and television. And this is why they are controlled by the state.

While her assessment might appear plausible the ubiquity of ICTs in Africa, especially the cell phone cannot be underestimated (Internews Europe, 2008).

THE SOCIAL MEDIA AND DIPLOMATIC MONITORING OF ZIMBABWE

Zimbabwe-based diplomatic missions are reluctant to disclose their specific sources of information for policy formulation in relation to the Zimbabwe state. In the past year alone attempts to conduct studies with diplomatic missions based in Zimbabwe proved futile. The first instance concerned a post-graduate student, who is also a practicing journalist, who was studying the role of the Zimbabwean press in influencing international relations (Chideme, 2011). The dissertation was completed with much inference and deductions rather than empirical data consensually collected from the respective embassies and high commissions. In the current research we sent out questionnaires to at least 15 embassies, purposively including those countries generally considered to be friendly towards the Zimbabwean government, and those that are regarded as hostile or have imposed sanctions on the country. We wanted to ascertain whether they in any way rely on ICTs and social media for data collection which eventually informs their respective countries' perceptions of Zimbabwe. None of these countries' representatives committed themselves to participating in the research. However, inferences and deductions could still be made about which civil society organizations and social media sites are sources of useful information for diplomacy.

Former diplomatic attaché to Zimbabwe, Philip Barclay, who was based in Zimbabwe and wrote a book about the most controversial period of the country around the disputed 2008 elections, makes telling evasions of confirming empirical sources of media sources (social media and civil society activist contributions) to his country Britain's policy formulations toward Zimbabwe. The following revelations from his *Zimbabwe: Years of Hope and Despair* (2010) regarding his construction of perceptions are crucial and generalizable:

Responsibility for the contents of this book is entirely mine. Its contents do not necessarily reflect the views of the (British) Foreign Office. While I worked at the British Embassy in Harare I had access to classified papers. I have made no use of that material, as it is not mine to share. There may be authors who find it profitable to betray confidence placed in them only because their diplomatic position, but I am not one of them. But this does not make my story willfully incomplete. I have felt free to use material which was readily available to any well-connected person on the ground. Zimbabweans are remarkably indiscreet and are happy to gossip and leak to just about anyone. Communications supposedly secret at 10.am, were invariably common currency on the Chitungwiza combi[7] by the evening. So this book betrays no genuine confidence, but tells what I believe to be the full story (Barclay, 2010, p. ix).

The disclaimer makes critical assumptions about reliability and methodology, using "empirical" participant observation techniques–getting *well-connected*, and participating in *gossip* and *leakage*–processes that on the whole "solidify" claims about the validity of the "true story." The social media are a known source of many breaking news, and they are (in)advertently excluded as a source of information in Barclay's methodology.

True, Websites with a social media function such as Kubatana and Sokwanele, notwithstanding their self-perpetuating claims to "legitimacy," "veracity," "impartiality," and "objectivity," are not mentioned by Barclay as sources of information for a whole spectrum of communicators, including the commuters who often use office time to surf the net and gather "latest" information. Claims to diplomatic "professionalism" pre-empt criticism about the reliance on "empirical" material derived from social sites that already contain their own inherent organizational, research and methodological problems associated with data compilation and presentation.

In spite of giving the impression that he relied on oral interviews and listening to public discussions, Barclay nonetheless hints that the British diplomatic mission was in the business of "monitoring networks":

By the start of June 2008, the MDC claimed that forty of its members had been killed. Monitoring networks were reporting collective beatings in remote villages, mass evictions and an unseen refugee crisis as thousands fled their homes. It was hard to be sure all this was true. But whatever was happening was beyond the reach of television cameras and so invisible to the world" (Barclay, 2010, p. 116) (emphasis added).

The *monitoring networks* are not conclusively named by Barclay.

Depending on their respective individual reputations, social media sites like www.kubatana.net and www.sokwanele.com function as credible sources of important information for the Zimbabwean government, Zimbabwean political parties, and international organizations interested in Zimbabwe's domestic and foreign policy such as SADC, AU, and UN. Bev Clark, an administrator of Kubatana Trust and the NGO Network Alliance, concurs that their social media site is a useful resource to critical policy makers. She notes;

I would say a site like Kubatana is vastly useful to policy makers. When we started out our primary goal was to establish a one-stop shop for human rights information on Zimbabwe. We've done this very successfully. There is immense power in the aggregation of information. It makes searching for information much more efficient. And if you've been careful, like we have, about using trustworthy sources, and been professional about how we publish, then the people forming policy and reports based on the information we carry are much more confident that they're doing a good job (13 March emailed questionnaire to Mhiripiri).

The influence of Kubatana and the work of other pro-democracy players in Zimbabwe were noted as early as 2008 by the group Internews Europe, which also acknowledged the use of social media and new ICT as a means and mode of circumventing censorship (Internews Europe, 2008, pp. 57-65). Zimbabwe is in fact described as a "closed society" where mobile phones can offer "a degree of anonymity beyond the Internet." In so-called closed societies "the mobile phone can be seen as a media platform which is less censored and under surveillance" (Internews Europe, 2008, p. 57). This comes in a publication which is in part "generously supported by the Dutch Ministry of Foreign Affairs." This implies that the European governments at least monitor the social media activities of the preferred "credible" sources of information to formulate international public and diplomatic opinion on Zimbabwe.

WHY THERE CANNOT BE NORTH AFRICA OR DID IT HAPPEN IN ZIMBABWE?

Brian Raftopoulous (2011) says a Maghreb type revolution is impossible because of the political culture of Zimbabwe where ZANU PF uses coercion and argumentation for its causes. The activities in the Arab world are either denigrated as the work of imperialists and their local stooges or alternatively, the revolutions are appropriated and given a "revolutionary" local interpretation. ZANU PF launched their "indigenization" driven and the "anti-sanctions" campaign in 2010 in anticipation of elections in 2011 or 2013 intended to unfold the Government of National Unity. The party projects itself as the logical heir of the developments in the Arab world and not the opposition parties and pro-democracy movement (Raftopolous, 2011). The uprisings in the Arab world are viewed as actions against authoritarian regimes alienated from their own mass populations because the former for many decades erroneously aligned themselves with Western imperialists. In this case ZANU PF becomes the voice of not only Zimbabweans clamoring for economic independence, but also all oppressed and economically exploited classes of the global south. Raftopoulos (2011, p. 87) gives his critical views of why Zimbabwe cannot exactly follow the Arab uprisings:

At the current time, it is highly unlikely that any such uprising will occur. The least important reason for this is the low levels of internet penetration in Zimbabwe. More fundamentally, the livelihood structure of the Zimbabwean economy has been completely deconstructed in the crisis period, with the formal working class effectively decimated. This has undercut a key constituency of the opposition movement. Moreover, there has been a movement of some 2 million Zimbabweans into the Diaspora, which has in some ways displaced the crisis at national level onto a broader regional and international plane. In addition, the land occupations of the post 2000 have not only caused displacement and economic disruption but they have created a constituency for ZANU PF through the substantive numbers of Zimbabweans who have received land. Thus the Mugabe regime has countered the challenge to its sovereignty in elections, by calling on the legitimacy and sovereignty it claims from the legacy of the liberation struggle and by taking land from the former settler community. This conflict of sovereignties, underwritten by persistent state violence and coercion, has complicated the democratic struggles in Zimbabwe and made any simple comparison with events in North Africa, which have their own enormous complexities, untenable.

However, the events in North Africa indirectly forced SADC and South Africa to shift from Thabo Mbeki's "quiet diplomacy" to a much more transparent engagement with Zimbabwe without ducking behind the rhetoric of "pan Africanism" and vigilance against imperialism. Thereafter when concern about Zimbabwe's election roadmap and human rights record has been registered by the SADC and African peers, some ZANU PF ideologues have abrasively attacked these as "regime change agents" (Raftopolous, 2011; Moyo, 2011b). However, Mugabe and the Foreign Minister were much more conciliatory sensing the folly of alienating SADC (Mugabe 2011). While Raftopolous concludes that the Arab revolutions have had some measured influences in Zimbabwe, citing cases of activists like Munyaradzi Gwisai, who have been arrested for attempting to instigate such events, and the SADC taking keen interest in Zimbabwe's domestic policies, it is still important that the transition has been slow and incremental in Zimbabwe. The ICTs were used noticeably in 2008 and that arguably was a "Zimbabwe revolution" which resulted in the Government of National Unity that a "conservative" ZANU PF still finds embarrassing and untenable. However, the scheme remains palatable and convenient where the legitimacy of ZANU PF as a party representing the majority was seriously jolted. The new ICTs and social media such as Kubatana played a critical role, more to influence international opinion, than to instigate mass uprisings. Zimbabwe's not so quiet revolution cannot be overlooked given the amount of torture, abductions, murder and beatings that were graphically posted on websites such as www.sokwanele.com, www.kubatana.net, and others.

CONCLUSION

Indeed, the increased use of social media and blogs by pro-democracy activists in Zimbabwe and in the Diaspora has forced some scholars to suggest online activists are using sites such as Facebook to voice their discontent with the government (Moyo, 2011; Mutsvairo & Kleeven, 2011). However, it is rather the significance of this active participation that has been largely ignored by scientific researchers. Empirical work is therefore lacking here. While social media sites have been credited with determining the political discourse in some parts of the world including the Middle East region, we conclude that they have largely been used for non-political campaigns in Zimbabwe. While accepting social media's role as an alternative space for political engagement, we argue that the use of Facebook among Zimbabwean youth is more of a lifestyle than a form of political activism. Politically, we observe online action, which has largely been sponsored by pro-democracy activists living abroad, has not translated into offline action on the ground.

While the civil society in Zimbabwe has embraced the social media to reach, organize and mobilize its supporters, it has notably struggled to attract meaningful political reforms even though it is too early to completely dismiss its endeavors as a failure because as shown by the works of Kubatana, the civil society is actively involved in disseminating digitally-inspired messages, which eventually will most likely have an impact in determining the country's political future. However, as things stand, owing to lack of proper coordination, differences on the best way forward among activists and accessibility problems, the social media will likely have little impact politically. Political reforms may be introduced in the due course but it is too early to talk of a Zimbabwean Spring. Diplomats will also continue to use material from civil society organizations and social media sites agonizing on their veracity and evasive on whether they actually use such civil society organizations and social media sites as sources of information.

REFERENCES

Adolf, M., & Wallner, C. (2005). *Probing the public sphere in Europe. Theoretical problems: Problems of theory and prospects for further communication research.* Paper presented at the First European Communication Conference 24. Amsterdam, The Netherlands.

Anderson, H. (2004). *Panorama: Secrets of the Camps* [Television broadcast]. London: BBC One.

Barclay, P. (2010). *Zimbabwe: Years of Hope and Despair.* London: Bloomsbury.

Beers, D. (2006). *The public sphere and online, independent journalism* (pp. 109-130). Paper presented at Canadian Society for the Study of Education. York, Canada.

Bennett, W., & Segerberg, A. (2011). Digital media and the personalization of collective action: Social technology and the organization of protests against the global economic crisis Information. *Communicatio Socialis, 14*(6), 770–799.

Bimber, B. (1999). The Internet and citizen communication with government: Does the medium matter? *Political Communication, 6*(4), 409–428. doi:10.1080/105846099198569.

Boyd, D. (2008). Can social network sites enable political action? In Fine, A., Sifry, M., Rasiej, A., & Levy, J. (Eds.), *Rebooting America* (pp. 112–116). Mountain View, CA: Creative Commons. doi:10.1386/macp.4.2.241_3.

Chan, S. (2010). *Citizen of Zimbabwe: Conversations with Morgan Tsvangirai* (2nd ed.). Harare, Zimbabwe: Weaver Press.

Chideme, M. K. (2011). The reporting of Zimbabwe-Britain bilateral relations 2008–2010. (A case of *The Herald* and *The Zimbabwe Independent*). Unpublished MA dissertation, Midlands State University, Shurugwi, Zimbabwe.

Chipere, G. Communications & Advocacy Officer (2011). Community Radio Harare, personally interviewed by Nhamo Mhiripiri in Gweru, Zimbabwe, June 2011.

Chiumbu, S. (2010). Media, alternativism and power: The political economy of community media in South Africa. In Hyde-Clarke, N. (Ed.), *The Citizen in Communication* (pp. 115–137). Claremont, South Africa: Juta.

Dahlberg, L. (2001). Extending the public sphere through cyberspace: The case of Minnesota. *E-Democracy, Peer Reviewed Journal on the Internet, 6*(3). Retrieved April 17, 2012, from http://firstmonday.org/htbin/cgiwrap/bin/ojs/index.php/fm/article/view/838/747

Daughety, T., Eastin, M, & Bright, L. (2008). Exploring consumer motivations for creating user-generated content. *Journal of Interactive advertising, 8*(2), 1-24.

Dewey, J. (1954). *The Public and its Problems.* Denver, CO: Swallow.

Dutta, S., & Mia, I. (Eds.). (2011). *The Global Information Technology Report 2010-2011* (10th ed.). Geneva, Switzerland: World Economic Forum. Retrieved June 10, 2011, from http://www.weforum.org/reports/global-information-technology-report-2010-2011-0

Evans, D. (2008). *Social Media Marketing: An Hour a Day.* London: Wiley.

Fraser, N. (1990). Rethinking the public sphere: A contribution to the critique of actually existing democracy. *Social Text, 25*(26), 56–80. doi:10.2307/466240.

Fraser, N. (1992). Rethinking the public sphere: A contribution to the critique of actually existing democracy. In Calhoun, C. (Ed.), *Habermas and the Public Sphere* (pp. 109–142). Cambridge, MA: The MIT Press.

Gaier, E., & Smith, J. (2008). Improving governance through symbiotic media structures. *Democracy and Society, 8*(2), 8–10.

Gimmler, A. (2001). Deliberative democracy, the public sphere and the internet. *Philosophy and Social Criticism, 27*(4), 21–39. doi:10.1177/019145370102700402.

Habermas, J. (1992). *Between facts and norms: Contributions to a discourse theory of law and democracy*. Cambridge, MA: Polity Press.

Hauser, G. (1998). Vernacular dialogue and the rhetoricality of public opinion. *Communication Monographs, 65*(2), 83–107. doi:10.1080/03637759809376439.

Hyde-Clarke, N. (2010). *The Citizen in Communication*. Claremont, South Africa: Juta.

Internews, E. (2008). *The promise of ubiquity: Mobile as media platform in the global South*. Retrieved March 23, 2012, from www.internews.eu

Kaplan, A. M., & Haenlein, M. (2010). Users of the world, unite! The challenges and opportunities of social media. *Business Horizons, 53*(1), 59–68. doi:10.1016/j.bushor.2009.09.003.

Mahoso, T. (2008). Reading the Tibaijuka report on Zimbabwe in a global context. In Maurice, V. (Ed.), *The Hidden Dimensions of Operation Murambatsvina in Zimbabwe* (pp. 159–168). Harare, Zimbabwe: Weaver Press.

Mahoso, T. (2011, April 24-30). Significance of anti-sanctions campaign. *The Sunday Mail*, pp. B13.

Mahoso, T. (2011, March 5). Why Zimbabwe is neither Egypt nor Tunisia. *The Sunday Mail*. Retrieved February 15, 2012, from http://www.zimpapers.co.zw/index.php?option=com_conte nt&view=article&id=2165:african-focus-with-dr-tafataona-mahoso-why-zimbabwe-is-neither-egypt-nor-tunisia&catid=48:blogs&Itemid=155

Matshazi, N. (2012, April 22). ZAB halts Freedom Fone project. *The Standard*.

Mbembe, A. (2001). *On the Post Colony*. Berkeley, CA: University of California Press.

Merit, S. (2011). Using social media for social change. Retrieved March 16, 2012 from. http://wemedia.s3.amazonaws.com/BEB93FE3-484D-49DE B95BA99EAA0CA3DB/FinalDownload/DownloadIdA7754D10A5DF0682A081F-5D79A98280 3/BEB93FE3-484D-49DE-B95B-A99EAA0CA3DB/papers/tp/ifocos_wm_social-media.pdf

Mhiripiri, N.A. (2011). Zimbabwe community radio 'initiatives': Promoting alternative media in a restrictive legislative environment. *Radio Journal: International Studies in Broadcasting and Audio Media, 9*(2/1), 107-126.

Moyo, D. (2009). Citizen journalism and the parallel market of information in Zimbabwe's 2008 elections. *Journalism Studies, 10*(4), 551–567. doi:10.1080/14616700902797291.

Moyo, D. (2010). *The new media as monitors of democracy: Mobile phones and Zimbabwe's 2008 election*. Paper presented at the Conference on Election Processes, Liberation Movements and Democratic Change in Africa. Maputo, Mozambique.

Moyo, J. (2011, February 27, 2011). Zimbabwe is not Tunisia. *The Sunday Mail*. Retrieved February 15, 2012, from http://www.zimpapers.co.zw/index.php?option=com_content&view=article&id=2109:zimb bwe -is-not-tunisia-or-egypt&cati d=39:opinion&Itemid=132

Moyo, J. (2011, April 3). Unmasking SADC Troika meeting in Zambia. *The Herald*. Retrieved February 29, 2012, from http://www.zimpapers.co.zw/index.php?option=com_content&view=article&id=2629:unmasking-sadc-troika-circus-in-zamb ia&catid=39:opinion&Itemid=132

Moyo, L. (2011). Blogging down a dictatorship: Human rights, citizen journalists and the right to communicate in Zimbabwe. *Journalism: Theory Practice and Criticism, 12*(6), 745–760. doi: doi:10.1177/1464884911405469.

Mugabe, R. (2011, April 18). President Mugabe's 31ˢᵗ Independence Address. *The Herald.* Retrieved April 30, 2012, from http://www.herald.co.zw/index.php?option=com_content&view=article&id=7997:president-mugabes-31st-independence-day-address&catid=39:opinion&Itemid=132

Mutsvairo, B. (2010). *Journalism ethics in the digital age.* Paper presented at International Conference on New Media Technologies. Bratislava, Slovakia.

Muzulu, P. (2011, December 15). ZANU PF cracks down on social media. *The Zimbabwe Independent.*

Ndlovu, R. (2012, April 20). Internet to influence next elections. *The Financial Gazette.*

Nyamnjoh, F. B. (2005). *Africa's Media: Democracy & the Politics of Belonging.* Dakar, Senegal: CODESRIA.

Power, D. (Producer), Bartley, K. (Director), & Donnacha, O.B. (Director) (2003). *The Revolution Will Not Be Televised* [Motion picture]. Ireland: Vitagraph Films. Undercover in Zimbabwe Prison [Video file]. Retrieved June 13, 2011, from http://www.youtube.com/watch?v=5UrpciPVOdk

Raeburn, M. (Director) (2003). *Zimbabwe Countdown* [Motion picture]. Zimbabwe: Journeyman Pictures. Violence a part of training police recruits in Zimbabwe [Video file]. Retrieved June 13, 2011, from http://www.youtube.com/watch?v=MiXZfwto3D8, 2.13mins.

Raftopoulos, B. (2011). Why there won't be a North African revolution in Zimbabwe. Retrieved February 15, 2012, from http://www.osisa.org/sites/default/files/sup_files/Why%20there%20won't%20be%20a%20North%20African%20revolution.pdf

Sachikonye, L. (2011). *When a state turns on its citizens: 60 years of institutionalized violence in Zimbabwe.* Ackland Park: Jacana.

Smith, W. D. (2003). Higher education, Democracy and the Public Sphere. *Thought and Action, 19*(1), 61–73.

Splichal, S. (2006). In search of a strong European public sphere: Some critical observations on conceptualizations of publicness and the (European) public sphere. *Media Culture & Society, 28*(5), 695–7147. doi:10.1177/0163443706067022.

Ubayasiri, K. (2006). The Internet and the public Sphere: A glimpse of YouTube. *Ejournalist: A Refereed Media Journal, 6*(2), 1-13

Zimbabwe Inclusive Government Watch [Video file].Retrieved April 17, 2012, from http://www.sokwanele.com/zigwatch

ENDNOTES

[1]   See, Relly, Christopher, 'The media, the CIA and the coup', *Counterpunch*, 15 April 2002, http://www.counterpunch.org/reilly0415.html, accessed 2 June 2011).

[2]   "Zim's reporter union suspends Basildon Peta," http://www.iol.co.za/news/africa/zim-s-reporter-union-suspends-basildon-peta-1.82224 (accessed 7 May 2011).

3   World Bank paper for the Communication for Governance & Accountability Program http://siteresources.worldbank.org/EXT-GOVACC/Resources/PubSphereweb.pdf (Accessed 1 June 2011).

4   BBC News (2008) 'Power-sharing call for Zimbabwe', http://news.bbc.co.uk/2/hi/africa/7372690.stm, accessed 13 March 2010.

5   Steere, M. (2008) 'Cell phones promise fairer elections in Africa': http://edition.cnn.com/2008/WORLD/europe/08/25/Cellphonedemocracy/, accessed 25 March 2010.

6   'Combi' is presented by the author as "a contraction of 'commuter omnibus'. Combis are typically minibuses packed with seated and standing passengers".

Chapter 24
Of New Media Influence on Social and Political Change in Africa:
Introspects, Retrospectives and Futuristic Challenges

Anthony A. Olorunnisola
The Pennsylvania State University, USA

ABSTRACT

This summative chapter synthesizes a few of the 26 contributors' solo and interconnected presentations and lays out the ideas and propositions therein in a way that a single author of a book would have done. To achieve these objectives the chapter draws readers' attention to the conceptual and practical evidences that scholars—whose joint efforts have helped us put this book together—employed in their treatment of a hydra-headed issue with multi-dimensional questions. The intent is to present readers with some, of many possible dimensions, from which to appraise the chapters in this book. To this end, thematic categories are employed and efforts made to underscore consistencies and inconsistencies between authors' propositions. The chapter also includes suggestions of areas needing further inquiries as those pointers may help scholars sustain an ongoing conversation about the evolving issues addressed in this volume.

INTRODUCTION

It is atypical for an edited volume to include a summative chapter. Nonetheless, there is value in such an addition to this novel collection which takes a pan-African approach to the review of the influences of 'old' (i.e., newspapers, radio, television) and 'new' (e.g., Facebook, Twitter, and blogs) media on social and political change. Previous efforts by communications, media studies and political science scholars, in particular those focused on political communication, weighed

DOI: 10.4018/978-1-4666-4197-6.ch024

the intersections between media and political (or democratic) change in Africa. Until very recently, examinations of the communications dimension to socio-political transformations had focused principally on 'old' media in single or a few assortments of African countries.

This volume comes against the background of Africa-based social and political movements, many of which, for the first time and thanks to advancements of information and communications technology (ICT), commanded simultaneously the attention of citizens of host countries at home and in the Diasporas as well as gripped the focus of observers in the international community for several weeks. Those tumultuous events, especially variants that occurred in Egypt and other North African countries, motivated academic and non-academic conversations about the clout of the contemporary African state, the fluidity of political power and the import of 'new' vis-à-vis 'old' media in the equation. Of necessity, the developments deserve thorough and ongoing scholarly examination and undoubtedly the review of strategies employed by stakeholders in host nations as well as the rationale for the interventions (or non-interference) of the committee of nations (Olorunnisola, 1996). Academic-oriented research should not dissuade but join conversations and debates held on platforms of governmental, inter-governmental, non-governmental organizations, cross-sections of the civil society and by media practitioners in and outside of the public sector. Notably, there have been multifarious attempts by many scholars and stakeholders across the globe to assess and understand these developments, so much so that no single issue—since the debate surrounding the new world information and communication order—has commanded the concentrated attention of the global academic and non-academic community as the incursion of 'new' media into social and political movements. The role of the academy in these conversations and debates should, however, be more than summative.

We are hopeful that this volume—with the many dimensions from which authors have critically appraised these developments—contributes to filling some of the noted analytical gaps.

A book that joins the conversations and debates—about an epochal issue in which Africa uncharacteristically occupies center-stage position—especially in the aftermath of Egypt's 2011 uprising should bring critical academic examination to the positive and negative claims that commentators throw up. Such a book will do well to explore the particular roles of 'new' media and the likelihood that they have supplanted 'old' media and now occupy paramount positions in the evolution of social and political movements in Africa and, possibly, elsewhere in the world. Such a book should also review the controversies and the often hyperbolic transpositions of credits, not to activists physically involved in the movements, but to the new media that they employ. This latter sentiment has become evident in descriptive coinages that include *Facebook Revolution* and *Twitter Revolution*. As such, the primary challenge that this book faces is whether or not contributors addressed foregoing phenomenon among crucial issues and posed the questions germane to such an important and timely subject at a momentous period in Africa's political life when multiple countries on the continent appear to be entering another wave—perhaps the fourth—of transformations. In addition, it is essential that such a book includes explanations for the limitations of social and political uprisings to countries in North Africa. In other words, why did the social and political movements in North African countries not have bandwagon effects on activists in countries in the Southern, Eastern and Western corners of Africa? Are Africans' desires for termination of sit-tight rulers and for installation of representative political systems limited to North Africa?

Though the lines between summation and critical analysis of this book's offer may blur in a few places in this concluding chapter, it is essential for readers to note that the goal is not to offer critical analyses—peer- and book-reviewers and scholars in search of new additions to literature on the subject matter should take on that role. Fundamentally, the goal of this chapter is to synthesize the solo and interconnected perspectives of the twenty-six contributors in a manner similar to what a single author would have done. As such this summative chapter draws readers' attention to the conceptual and practical evidences that scholars—whose joint efforts helped us put this book together—employed in their treatment of a hydra-headed issue with multi-dimensional questions. The intent is to present readers with some, of many possible dimensions, from which to appraise the chapters in the book. To this end, thematic categories are employed and efforts made to underscore consistencies and inconsistencies between authors' propositions. Where necessary, questions—many rhetorical but assessed to be germane to the subject matter—are posed to sensitize readers to the issues at hand. The chapter also includes suggestions of areas needing further inquiries as those pointers may help scholars sustain an ongoing conversation about the evolving issues addressed in this volume.

The protocols for identifying the themes that guide discussion presented in this chapter are driven by questions that are deemed pertinent to the '*post old-media*' phase of socio-political movements in Africa and by contributors' responses to factors that transcend the boundaries of individual chapters and countries. In the process, readers should uncover coherences and incoherencies that combine to tell the story of Africa's socio-political struggles with public administration in the ever-evolving process of nation-building. Readers should walk away with confirmation that African countries do share a lot of commonalities, yet, there are variations from country to country driven by factors of political history and—where the focus of this volume lies—management of media functions. The need for conscientiousness in academic assessments of African affairs is also further underscored. This chapter includes identification of futuristic and multiple research inquiries that scholars who will follow our modest effort and lead will need to ponder in order to bring clarity to issues of media ('old' and 'new') contributions to social and political changes in Africa. As noble as the intents of this chapter are, its inclusion should not preclude readers from drawing independent inferences from the solo and collective offers of contributing authors.

AFRICA IN THE THROES OF CONSTANT TRANSFORMATION

Holistically, contributors to this volume present a collage of Africa as a continent in the throes of constant transformations driven by multiple factors. Among those factors, some of which date back to the 19th century, are movements to end colonialisms, quest for leadership change, the alternation between autocracies and democracies (some managing a hybrid), dalliances with economic programs (including structural adjustment programs and neoliberalism), administrative decisions to privatize state monopolies (including media assets)—at times without careful consideration of what becomes of citizens dependent on public assets (Olorunnisola, 2009). Incidences of internecine warfare (some driven by ethnic particularisms) including those that Gettleman (2010) described as "forever wars" have plagued African countries through the decades. In more recent years, there has been a new wave of terrorism and insurgency by non-state actors, the pressures of social and political movements, and evolving media regulations. Implicitly many of the contributors to this volume question whether or not these changes—some laudable, others tumultuous—have positively influenced the lives of the citizens of respective African countries and their roles in the socio-political equation. In other words, are Africans more participatory in the management of the affairs of their respective countries now than they had been in the previous decades or centuries? Are the media ('old' and 'new') in a better position to assist the sustenance of productive dialogues between citizens and their governments? Are the governments, including the long- and near-term democratic arrangements, providing enabling environments for the mass media to play roles that will sustain public deliberations? Is there a substantial and significant difference between roles of 'old' and 'new' media when it comes to their employment and comparative impacts on social and political movements in Africa? Is there a model country—where the pangs of contestations between different stakeholders have subsided enough to enable stakeholders focus on the challenges of nation-building without rancor whether or not the models are foreign or home-grown? These among many contextual questions are pertinent to the focus of this volume.

Across the board of the chapters, contributing authors made gallant efforts to make sense of these issues. Introspection about what foregoing among many questions represent—particularly when thrown against the background of histories that date back to colonialisms for many African countries—should sensitize readers to appreciate the resilience of generations of African citizens in the face of external and internal domination. The pains of contemporary struggles to build one nation out of many disparate internal nations with conflicting interests have roots in the past. These overlays of unfinished business over several decades, coupled with arrival of new ICTs that have democratized access and enhanced social interactions among those with access, mobilized and brought some citizens to physical public squares. These developments posed many critical questions that were addressed by contributors to foregoing 23 chapters who focused directly on 15 countries and tangentially referred to another five. Similar questions and more should command the attention of the academy and help generate research and necessary policy changes in the foreseeable future.

INTRINSIC POWER OF NEW (AND SOCIAL) MEDIA TO INITIATE SOCIAL AND POLITICAL CHANGE

It is no longer trite to assume that there exists in popular culture the assumption that 'new' (and social) media initiated and completed the revolutions in Egypt among other African countries in the Middle East and North African (MENA) region. As stated earlier, editors of this book volume made a decision to chronicle foregoing events and to take on the challenge of critically examining the roles of 'new' media in the social and political movements that Africa began witnessing in 2010. Of necessity, contributors had to contend with this among many related questions: Did the revolution in Egypt succeed because of Facebook and Twitter? It is also fair to ponder the other side of the foregoing question: Would the revolution in Egypt have succeeded without Facebook and Twitter? These two interconnected questions in their variants have occupied the minds of many scholars and the pages of many journals over the past 36 or more months (see the special issues of *Journal of International Communication* and *Journal of Communication* on the Arab Spring by Allagui & Kuebler (2011) and Howard and Parks (2012) respectively). Yet, while answers diverge among scholars, pundits in the popular media appear to have settled the matter in favor of the social media (Olorunnisola & Martin, 2013). Evident in analyses and in some academic examinations of the issue is the deterministic assumption that seeps through the indication that Facebook and Twitter could carry out revolutions. Sahar Khamis (in Chapter 11) contended with this question in her examination of the Egyptian revolution. She wondered why the physical presence of multitudes of people was needed and why activists who showed up on Tahrir Square incurred injuries (many lost their lives) and risked arrests by the armed forces. While there was no doubt that many activists employed 'new' (and social) media and that some (as Aziz Douai and Mohamed Ben

Moussa competently showed in Chapter 12) played 'influential' roles in such domain, the outstanding challenge is how to place activists' and new (and social) media roles in proper perspective so that the supreme sacrifices of citizens whose lives were lost are not minimized.

While Facebook and Twitter may not have carried out actual revolutions, credit should be accorded to their respective roles in enabling activists to build and sustain solidarity networks within and beyond the countries that played hosts to the social movements. Such extension of networks enabled citizens in the Diasporas, media consumers around the world, observers in governmental and inter-governmental organizations to stay informed–via text messages and audio-visuals captured on citizen-reporters' phone-cameras and beamed via television. A variant of this case was efficiently made with the experience of Zimbabweans in Diaspora by Nhamo Mhiripiri and Bruce Mutsvairo (Chapter 23). Though new media have not succeeded in changing the political status quo in Zimbabwe, they have assisted in broadening the horizon of citizens' response to government, helped draw attention to the shenanigans of government and focus international attention on human rights abuses. The co-authors did not hesitate to credit social media activism engaged in by Zimbabweans for the eventual creation of a Government of National Unity between ruling Zimbabwe African National Union–Patriotic Front (ZANU-PF) and its former nemesis, Movement for Democratic Change (MDC).

Readers who are convinced of the intrinsic power of 'new' (and social) media to initiate and successfully carry out social movements will have to contend with two among many externally-validated evidences. First, not all social movements that employ 'new' media have succeeded. For example, the April 6 Youth Movement in Egypt—which called for an April 6, 2008 strike—used Facebook but was nonetheless unsuccessful

(Faris, 2009). Second, the testimonials of activists in the Egyptian movement placed the role of 'new' media in the movement in perspective; one such interviewee (Aouragh & Alexander, 2011, p. 1,351) deposed as follows:

What we call a social network is not actually a social network; these are social tools. Twitter and Facebook are not the social networks; we are the social network. And we have personal relations with each other. And to prove that, when the social networks were gone, they were filtered or blocked, during the high days of the revolution in Egypt a couple of weeks ago, we still operated .... The social network is us. We use whatever tools we have. They may be Internet tools, they may be phone lines, (and) they may be paper-based communications. Turning off the technology doesn't turn off the social network, because it is about people, not about technology.

The blunt assertion of the demarcation between human and technology-based networks by this activist is simply instructive. Such testimony offers external validity to the caution inserted by many contributors to this volume when they signaled that assessors should not be too hasty to allocate all the credits for a successful movement to the tools employed by activists before they thoroughly understand the stack-up of factors that inform success or failure of campaigns. The lesson for academics is to exercise caution in the appraisal of these issues and to be painstaking in analyses. In the near future, contributions of scholars who have been conscientious enough to pose unasked questions and to question popular assumptions will be useful as scholars continue to process these evolving relationships.

IDENTITY OF EMPLOYERS OF 'NEW' (AND SOCIAL) MEDIA IN SOCIAL MOVEMENTS

Questions about the identity of those who employed 'new' (and social) media in the process of social movements in African countries are crucial and present valid corollary to this examination of the intrinsic power of 'new' media to initiate social movements and revolutions. Who actually was on Facebook and Twitter? Auma Otieno and Lusike Mukhongo (in Chapter 16) and Bennett Furlow (in Chapter 17) pointedly pondered this question. Their contributions add to the arsenal of readers interested in parsing out who did what, with what tools and what impacts on the outcome of the social movements in reference in this volume and elsewhere in the public domain. In Otieno and Mukhongo's contribution, readers are notified of the generational divide indicating that the youth were more prolific in the use of 'new' and social media for engagement in political activism than the older generation who were not 'connected'. The co-authors, however, foregrounded this impression with a couple of important clarifications. In the first instance, youth in Kenya between the 15-35 age brackets make up 37% of the population and were found to be increasingly participatory in political party affairs. In the second instance, 'social media was not the reason that Jasmin Revolution/ Arab Spring occurred, but the youth involved … employed their being digital natives to apply Facebook and Twitter for political mobilization'. This latter clarification finds resonance in the testimony of the young Egyptian activist whose testimony (Aouragh & Alexander, 2011, p. 1,351) was shared in fair detail earlier in this chapter.

Bennett Furlow (Chapter 17) added evidence that militant groups such as al-Shabaab (more often including young recruits) preferred to use 'new' media technology such as Twitter, though the group positioned itself against perceived representatives of the West—including the Transitional Federal Government of Somalia that is backed by the United Nations—and implored its members to abstain from other artifacts of western culture. These exposés become instructive when we add externally-validated data presented by others curious enough about the role of 'new' and social media in social movements to investigate the actual location of users and the languages employed. Olorunnisola & Martin (2013) found evidence that the majority of those who disseminated messages through Twitter were not physical participants in the Egyptian movement but people (mostly young and urbane) who were outside of the locations occupied by the movements; some but not all were Egyptian citizens in the Diaspora. In addition, these 'cyberactivists' used English, and not Egyptian Arabic in their messages and tweets, typifying a combination of Western education and/or generational preferences for new technologies. While the activities of this group brought a new and unusual dimension to social movements, there ought to be a line that demarcates their participation from that of activists who marched, were confronted by the armed forces and in many instances killed.

Further, employers of new and social media were not just individuals who were activists and members of groups engaged in social movements. Contributors to this volume provided evidence that stakeholders in government also used 'old' and 'new' (and social) media in counter-insurgency (see Martin & Olorunnisola, Chapter 15) and in the prosecution of electioneering campaigns (see Kakpovi, Chapter 18). In the former instance, the Kenyan and Egyptian governments were able to match the power of media ('old' and 'new') deployment with insurgents while retaining monopoly control over other state apparatuses to which insurgents had no access. This raises a crucial question about the current status of the African state. We will suggest later in this summation that the African state is not yet a victim – in spite of the loss of power by some longstanding heads of states

In the instance of political campaigns, and as Kakpovi showed, contestants for the Beninese presidency in 2011 added the use of the Internet (specifically Websites, blogs, Facebook, Twitter, YouTube, and Dailymotion) to traditional media that included political songs, print and broadcast media and posters. This was notwithstanding low penetration into the popular culture (about 3% of the population in 2011) of the Internet and such other pre-requisites of new information and communication technologies such as electricity (which was available to about 20% of the population) and literacy (32.6%). Not only does this scenario underscore the digital divide between technology haves and have-nots, it poses questions about the notion that 'old' media are no longer relevant and that 'new' media could have so greatly impacted the direction of social movements in referent African countries. Here again, we see locational and access variances between Africans resident on the continent and those in the Diasporas. In the case of Benin and as Kakpovi carefully showed, candidates' investments in new media apparatuses were not commensurate with the possible reaches of new media in Benin nor did it appear that the attempt was to lure voters based in the country:

But which voters are we talking about, considering that only 2.2% of the population uses the Internet in the country? Communication advisors of the three candidates unanimously recognized that they were clearly targeting Beninese living abroad, young people and elite... Even though there are about 2 million Beninese living abroad, only 13 000 were registered as voters... On the other hand, most of time Beninese living abroad have relatives or friends in Benin and, regularly or sporadically, they send them money and gifts. The support of those living abroad is sometimes perceived as a lifesaving act by beneficiaries. Many of the benefactors give voting advice to those living in Benin. And occasionally, family and friends are the ones who consult on how to vote, because they prefer to give their voice to the *candidate who will favor opportunities and wealth to their benefactor. If the 2 million Beninese living abroad gave voting advices, they would then become a vital component for elections*

The Benin example (corroborated by the example of 2 million Zimbabweans in the Diaspora; see Mhiripiri & Mutsvairo, chapter 23) serves as a pointer to the growing profile of African citizens in the Diasporas where issues of importance to the home country–such as national politics and elections–are concerned. They (Diaspora citizens) are also partly responsible for migration of some 'old' media to 'new' media spaces. Many are themselves operators of online publications (see Tendai Chari's Chapter 22) and carry out the kinds of investigative journalism that were instrumental in fighting autocrats but have eluded their respective countries since the end of autocracies (see Douai & Olorunnisola, Chapter 1). Though the adoption of enabling policies remain controversial even in larger African countries like Nigeria, it is remarkable that a relatively small African country like Benin Republic has enacted policy that enables Beninese in the Diaspora to vote in national elections. Undoubtedly, the issue of the ability of citizens in African Diasporas to vote in national elections will remain on the burner of many national assemblies in the foreseeable future. There is opportunity for scholars with focus on African politics, especially those whose foci latch into political communication (and emerging technologies that have added dimensions to the process) to track this issue and the factors that support and militate against enabling policies by many African governments. For now and as typified by the cases of Benin, Egypt, and Zimbabwe among others, the expansion of the 'electorate' and 'cyberactivists' beyond the shores of African countries will continue to give 'new' media an edge as preferred media—this would include cases where dissemination and usages overlap when 'old' media establish online presence.

HAVE 'NEW' (AND SOCIAL) MEDIA REPLACED THE 'ALTERNATIVE' AND 'OLD' MEDIA?

Kennedy Javuru (Chapter 21) posed, implicitly, the question that is on top of the minds of many academics who have sought additional ways of making sense of the advancement and place of 'new' (and social) media in contemporary African social and political affairs. Are 'new' media to all intents and purposes the contemporary 'alternative media'? What do these 'new' media forms have in common with traditional alternative media? Who were the operators of alternative media and have they migrated online?

In his presentation of the case of Uganda, Javuru more or less answered all foregoing three questions as represented by the following statement:

The riot was a result of a stand-off between the central government and the Buganda Kingdom resulting in the death of 27 people. The government reacted by launching a clampdown on local radio stations accusing them of inciting violence, promoting sectarianism, campaigning against government and abusing the president. The Broadcasting Council shut down four radio stations: Central Broadcasting Services (CBS), Ssuubi FM (a youth radio), Sapienta (a Christian radio) and Akaboozi ku Bbiri, (HRNJ Uganda, 2010). In the ensuing media blackout, Ugandans resorted to social media and mobile phone SMS to keep update of events and warn each other of places to avoid.

Asking whether or not new media are the contemporary 'alternative' media provides subtext, discussed further in another thematic domain, for the examination of whether or not 'new' media are uniquely different from their traditional media cousins. The issue of 'new' media as alternative outlets, though pointedly raised to a lesser extent in this volume, has to occupy the attention of those in the varying disciplines, from communications through political science to sociology. Especially scholars focus on the location of power and whether or not the center has created margins necessitating the erection of alternative ways for those who occupy the periphery to voice their opinions.

Notably as well, the word 'alternative' has taken many dimensions in the trajectory of communications within African nations. We also see the notion of 'alternative' in the contestation between Africa, the developing world, and advanced nations. Expression of support for the creation of alternative outlets, which found footing in the debates such as that surrounding the new world and information order, led to the creation of such an entity as the Pan-African News Agency (PANA). In these various domestic and international iterations of ways in which alternative media ('old' and 'new') gained prominence and relevance, focus has typically been centered on the availability of counter-mainstream outlets that provide the opportunity for the less-powerful (individuals and nations) to challenge the powers that be (Switzer & Adhikari, 2000; Couldry & Curran, 2003; Dare, 2007). Given the demise of 'old' alternative media soon after transition to democracy in South Africa as Wasserman (2010) noted, a void was created in the public sphere. It is safe to suggest that 'new' media's operational mechanisms may be unique in their ability to provide alternative outlets for voices seeking new spaces for the expression of their opinions. A little over a decade ago, Anton Harber (2002; cited in Wasserman, 2010) provided a template for the role of 'new alternative journalisms in democratic society' (p. 28) when he elaborated as follows:

So where are our alternative voices of today? Let me hasten to say that we would not be looking for the same voice as before. Great journalism would [no] longer, I believe, be defined by defiance and bravery – as it had to be during the years of repression, when getting something said was often more important than how one said it; courage will be required, yes, the courage to swim against the tide, to probe uncomfortable wounds; it is now about telling stories which get under the skin of this complex and difficult country; it is about material which – through careful research and thoughtful compilation – leads us to understandings which are not apparent on the surface; it is about writing which makes us think more carefully about this country and its people.

Though Harber's commentary was focused on South Africa, his prognosis can apply to any African country. Qualifying factors will be the overthrow of autocracies, the disappearance of donor support, and disillusionment of journalists who worked in alternative media outlets about what their roles should be in the new dispensation. These factors have combined to diminish or eliminate the ranks of practitioners who work in traditional alternative media outlets. As all new solutions do, the democracies that replaced entrenched autocracies came with new or renewed problems in social and political domains. With a message of agitation to propagate and the relatively inexpensive access to new information and communications technologies, could 'new' media—with the capability to aggregate all cadres of users across strata of societies and in the global community—become the domain of alternative media? Couldry & Curran (2003) speaking of media power as "the emergent theme of social conflict in late modernity" (p. 4-5), made such a bold prediction when they deposed as follows:

This is not the first time in history that media power has been explicitly contested; it was crucial to the French Revolution, to the slow social and cultural revolutions against Soviet rule in Eastern Europe in the 1970s and 1980s (Downing 2001) and to the Iranian Revolution of the 1970s (Sreberny-Mohammadi & Mohammadi, 1994). What was missing from those major conflicts was access by all sides to global means of self-representation, which could change the scale on which those con-

flicts were played out. The Internet, particularly through its linkages into traditional media, now gives any local actor the potential to reach global audiences (Hardt & Negri, 2000). As the scale-effects of media transform specific conflicts, it is possible that social actors may start to compete explicitly for influence over those scale-effects (that is, over media power)

Similar questions–about the possibilities inherent in 'access by all sides to global means of self-representation'—could be asked of all social and political movements in Africa, especially those that occurred during the 'old' media era when the state controlled all mainstream media and communications apparatuses. However, and given recent social movements in Africa, that future that Couldry and Curran were slightly hesitant to predict is here and the competition over media power has begun. Nonetheless, the outstanding question that scholars should ponder as they work to appraise trajectories of the activities of stakeholders in the civil society is whether the scenario is as realistic yet in the African situation as it is in the West.

OLD AND NEW MEDIA CAN BE TOOLS OF SOCIAL INCOHESION

One positive outcome of any social movement is when the dictator is overthrown; but are there more dimensions to the employment of media ('old' and 'new') in the ensuing process? Predictions of normative theorists (see Siebert, Peterson, & Schramm, 1956) and texts on national development about the role of media in developing nations are often deterministic and focused on positive outcomes given the establishment of certain parameters (Schramm, 1964). It was, therefore, nearly impossible to anticipate that the mass media will not function in ways that lead respective societies toward possible and demonstrable socio-economic and political change. Events in varying African countries appear to have challenged foregoing notion, bringing to fore the limitations of theories when transported beyond the confines of their origin. In Chapter 2 and speaking of the Arab world, Bouziane Zaid warns that the anticipation that the 'interplay among mass media, politics and society' will lead to political change has been unrealistic. Citing Ayish (2003) he clarifies:

Rather, mass media functioned as a support system for the authoritarian regimes. Arab regimes used mass media mostly for propaganda and entertainment purposes at the expense of other functions and services. The effects of mass media on democracy, politics, and society were at best minimal.

It is safe to assume that foregoing scenario contributed to the groundswell of anti-authoritarian sentiment that the world witnessed during prosecution (ongoing in Syria where an uprising has turned into a full scale civil war) of 'Arab Spring' and the way in which 'new' (and social) media became preferred methods of short-circuiting mainstream media while spreading the embers of citizens' discontent.

But 'old' media have remained potent in the process of social movements until they are shut down by governments (Martin & Olorunnisola, Chapter 15; Olorunnisola & Martin, 2013). Readers should also note in Timothy Kituri's Chapter 5 the extent to which radio, that ubiquitous medium that is present in virtually every African homestead, can be employed to incite ethnic violence in the aftermath of a controversial election. As Kituri testified,

The local language radio stations played a big role in the violence following the 2007 general elections. They acted as catalyst by allowing, through incompetent journalism, messages of tribal hatred which evoked fears based on historic events to fill the airwaves. In an atmosphere of economic desperation and a general distrust for the government, Kenyans were looking for changes

and were emotionally invested in the election process. As a fairly young democratic country, Kenya needs media which will act as watchdogs and ensure that the government and all elected officials are held accountable.

The same absence of professionalism and ethics that Kituri noted laid at the core of the 1994 genocide in Rwanda (see Gilberds in Chapter 4) where international donor agencies—including IREX, USAID and UNESCO—have committed funds and training programs to ameliorate the problem so as to increase public confidence in and credibility of the media. Though the problems associated with professionalism persist and deserve to be confronted, Gilberds doubted that reform projects which 'rely on normative theories of the media's role in society and emphasize the professionalization of journalists as the foundation of ... a vibrant democracy ...' can work. She suggested that the prospects are weakened by

(D)emocratic deficits of Western media, notably "the structural inequality of media access and political power characteristic of highly marketized and commercialized systems" (Hackett, 2003). Other related themes that are likewise absent are the continued dominance of international communication flows by Northern-based transnational media corporations; the integration of media with the political project of global corporatization; and the possibility that global media, marketized economies, and authoritarian regimes actively reinforce each other.

These issues—of ethical and interventionists' dilemmas–are fundamental and go beyond the humanitarian and philanthropic desires of donor agencies, noble as those are, to assist nations in transit and in varying post-conflict stages that need a professional cadre of media practitioners. They address the theoretical and philosophical orientations that underpin content of the interventionists' media training programs. There is ample heuristic room in the critical postulation of Gilberds' commentary for scholars to identify ways in which the mere acknowledgement of cited hypocrisy can inform contextually-relevant content development and motivate pedagogical designs of training programs that locales can implement. This would especially be the case when those training modules are exported to nations in transit; where democratic cultures may be in infancy and professionals in the media sectors are indeed steeped in the quagmire of ethnic particularisms.

Readers should note that the problem of ethnocentrism is not peculiar to practitioners employed by 'old' media establishments. Brandie Martin & Anthony Olorunnisola add in Chapter 15 that 'new' (and social) media can take off from where 'old' media stop when citizens locked out of 'old' (or traditional) media forms resort to the use of short message service (SMS) applications on their cellular phones to also perpetuate hate messages.

Peculiarly, new ICTs became instruments in the hands of pro- and anti-government protesters who used them to mobilize, recruit participants, report progress of counter-protests and to co-disseminate hate speech. In this way, new ICTs could be termed equal-opportunity outlets to counter-dissenters who sought to manage information crucial to the progress of their respective causes. It is noteworthy that on account of the violence inducing speech disseminated by all sides to the social movements in Kenya and Egypt many citizens lost their lives.

Evidently the use and value of new media also have dualistic purposes that go beyond their more advertised employment by downtrodden citizens for liberation purposes. While many examples cited by contributing authors across different forms of citizens' and governments' employment of media for positive and nefarious activities properly locate 'old' and 'new' media as tools, readers should not miss one dimension to the raging debate about the differential values of 'new' versus 'old' media. Cellular phones in the

hands of citizens could be potent weapons of mass destruction as radio was in Kenya and Rwanda; though the debacle in Kenya in 2007 pales when compared to the genocide in Rwanda in 1994. Yet, Rwanda has to remain a reference point in the efforts–including policy-making, construction of legal structures and design of training modules— of those attempting to make sense of reasonable intervention measures. The outstanding question for readers interested in this issue is this: if 'old' and 'new' media can co-equally be employed as tools of development and social incohesion, in what ways are they substantially different?

THE AFRICAN STATE IN THE ERA OF 'NEW' MEDIA

How potent are the powers of the African state during an era when activists who lead social and political movements employ 'new' (and social) media? This question is useful to ponder across the African continent especially in the aftermath of social movements in Tunisia, Egypt and Libya which saw the removal of of President Zine El Abidine Ben Ali (January 14, 2011), of Hosni Mubarak (February 11, 2011), and the assassination of Muammar Gaddafi (October 20, 2011) respectively. The three were long-serving autocrats at the outset of the movements against their administrations. Can African leaders sustain power when faced by the slingshot of 'new' and social media wielded by citizen-activists? Contributors to this volume appear to suggest that the fates of Ben Ali, Mubarak and Gaddafi do not necessarily signal a death knell for the ability of the state to control the deployment of information via 'old' or 'new' media by citizens, especially those with subversive agenda. As Terje Skjerdal suggested in Chapter 3, the Ethiopian government has home-groomed and perfected the art of *selective liberalization*; readers should find his identification of strategies employed by government an interesting read. On the one hand:

Liberalization is found to occur in formal regulation (where it is easily observed by outsiders), and in areas where the risk of losing control with the flow of information is less for the government.... Ethiopian media reform ensures that the state media remain a dominant voice while opening up for limited competition in the private media market. Importantly, however, the move towards liberalization is challenged by a strong undercurrent of unofficial policy which may represent a return to informal coercion towards the media industry.... For example, strategic appointments in both the state media and regulatory units such as EBA are mainly of political nature. Broadcasting licenses are similarly assumed to be awarded merely to groups close to the government; at least not to groups that directly oppose the ruling interests (Amare, 2009).

On the other hand:

Legislation adjacent to media regulation has a controlling effect on media activity, as in the example of the anti-terrorism proclamation. The official news agency has been drawn closer to the government, possibly with the intention of controlling the flow of information. Websites and radio channels run by Ethiopians in the diaspora are readily blocked by Ethiopian authorities. In-depth interviews with journalists show that they operate with lesser or larger degree of fear for reactions from outsiders and public officials, causing both private and state media outlets to execute self-censorship and shun critical reporting (Skjerdal, 2008; 2010a).

As Skjerdal pointed out, this dualistic approach to management of media capabilities is not unique to Ethiopia (Ogbondah, 1997; 2004). One implication is that government is evolving and that sitting heads of states will find ways of responding to perceived social crises. Another implication, useful for scholars of African media to note, is that an approach to studying media

regulation which isolates contiguous regulations and clauses that stifle media freedom can miss the mark by creating the impression that media have wider margins of freedom than are realistic. Yet another implication is that the African state is as vibrant—and perhaps as paranoid—in the 'post old-media' era as it was in the years before.

Other authors (see, for example, Ufuoma Akpojivi in Chapter 6; Twange Kasoma in Chapter 7, and Ullajama Kivikuru in Chapter 8) provide examples of ways in which the African State—as represented in examples drawn from Nigeria, Ghana, Zambia, Namibia and Tanzania respectively— has continued to unleash letters of the law on the activities of 'errant' media.

Though employment of 'new' (and social) media by activists is relatively recent, the African State has practice in dealing with alternative and clandestine or guerilla (Dare, 2007) media. The case of Kenya--detailed in Chapter 15 by Brandie Martin and Anthony Olorunnisola—underscores the ability of the State to quickly deploy its powers when events can be categorized as dangerous to national security. In the case of Kenya and though the state was a party with interest in the contested election results, the resort to control first of traditional and then of 'new' (and social) media apparatuses stacks the odds against activists. The alternating roles of the state which enabled movement from contestant in a manipulated election to custodian of national security should confound third parties in the international community who must also take cognizance of and balance sympathetic considerations for activists with the rights of the government to maintain peace. These dual positions of the state should also inform the strategies of activists in social movements. How then should this dilemma be resolved?

In Chapter 19, Oluwabukola Adelaja draws readers' attention to the existence of a regulatory vacuum where crimes committed with the use of 'new' (and social) media—cybercrime—are concerned. In anticipated response to readers who may on the basis of low penetration of Internet access in Africa question this recommendation, Adelaja stated as follows: 'Compared to other developed countries, only an average 15% of the African population uses the Internet. Even though this is low in relative terms, Africa is fast becoming a hot spot for the perpetration of cybercrime'. The larger and abiding issue—given the often biased location of the state—remains whether or not regulations crafted to fight cybercrime and such other infractions that may be disguised to handicap practitioners in 'old' and 'new' media domains should be nation-specific or enshrined in regional and/or international edicts to which member states append their signatures. Until such a time when these issues are resolved and in spite of the overthrow of some African heads of states, it may be too early to discount the African government.

WHY DID THE ARAB SPRING TERMINATE IN THE DESERT?

It is reasonable to suggest that the origination and spread of the social movement now known as the Arab Spring sent shivers down the spine of many African heads of states. It is equally reasonable to state that many citizens of African countries wished for their own version of the movements that toppled Ben Ali, Hosni Mubarak and Muammar Gaddafi. Why then have there been fewer attempts and nearly non-existent success stories in other regions of Africa?

Olorunnisola & Ojebode (see Chapter 20) pointedly addressed this issue—basing evidence on the opinions of Nigerians across six geopolitical regions. In sum and on the one hand, the co-authors found that Nigerians continue to savor the re-installed (suspended in 1983, fully reinstated in 1999) democratic governance in spite of its many problems. One area of satisfaction is that respective administrations, compared to the era of military governance, have shorter shelf-lives. Another is the recent ability of citizens to

verify that their votes in elections—ranging from state levels to the presidential–counted. On the other hand, a cursory review of a recent Human Development factors chart showed that Nigerians do not enjoy the quality of life attributed to citizens of the MENA countries. In sum, what Nigerians had in participation in the political process, though flawed, was elusive in countries that participated in the Arab Spring.

While it will be an incomplete assessment to state categorically that the social movements in the MENA region were all about political disenchantments, it should also be analytically-dishonest to state that Nigerians and/or other African citizens who did not initiate social movements or occupy public squares are completely satisfied with their respective governments and conditions of living. It may rather be near-accurate to suggest that neither autocracies nor democracies have fulfilled the aspiration of African citizens. Scholars in media and communication as well as those in political communication, psychology and sociology have ample opportunities to explore the level of content and/or discontent of Africans with their respective socio-political locations.

It is far easier—and other contributors to this volume have directly and indirectly alluded to this notion—to find explanations for non-participation in the repression of free opinion and of association, in the narrowing of spaces and installation of statutory regulations that limit individual—and institutional-freedoms in African countries (e.g., Zaid, Chapter 2; Skjerdal, Chapter 3; Akpojivi, Chapter 6; Kasoma, Chapter 7; Kivikuru, Chapter 8; and Turner, Chapter 10). This notion is consistent with suggestion elsewhere in this summative chapter that the African State remains in control of the affairs of respective nations, holds allocative powers with which to purchase loyalties, and has more than equal opportunities to deploy media ('old' and 'new') as do activists in civil society. In addition, the State holds monopoly control over the armed forces and has shown willingness to deploy when occasions arise to suppress insurgents.

Foregoing factors may explain why the successes of social movements in Tunisia, Egypt and Libya have not spread to or taken firm holds even in the MENA region. Seth Jones (2013) underscored these factors in his elaborate essay on the Arab Spring when he offered the following assessment of progress so far:

The initial results of the tumult were indeed inspiring. Broad-based uprisings removed Tunisia's Zine el-Abidine Ben Ali, Egypt's Hosni Mubarak, and Libya's Muammar al Qaddafi from power. Since the toppling of these dictators, all three countries have conducted elections …. The prospects for further democratization, however, have dimmed. Most countries in the Arab world have not jumped political tracks, and those that did begin to liberalize are now struggling to maintain order, lock in their gains, and continue moving forward … even after all the changes, the region … remains the least free in the world with Freedom House estimating that 72 percent of the countries and 85 percent of the people there still lack basic political rights and civil liberties … Syria has descended into a bloody civil war along sectarian lines … in Egypt, the poster child for regional political reform, the Muslim Brotherhood-led government has attempted to solidify its control and silence the media using tactics reminiscent of the Mubarak era.

These evidences of continued uncertainties further indicate that the realities of change go beyond the initial successes of movements and the employment of (new) media in the process. As Jones further clarified, it is 'common but false assumption … that doing away with a dictatorship necessarily leads to freedom'. Evidently, the journey toward freedom has to be processed at the threshing machines of social dialogue as democracy is further entrenched.

IS THIS VOLUME THE FINAL ANSWER?

This book headed to press against the background of the return on January 25, 2013 of Egyptians to Tahrir Square on the second anniversary of the toppling of Hosni Mubarak and, among others, to protest against President Mohamed Morsi's policies and 'to rekindle the demands of a revolution they say has been hijacked by Islamists who have betrayed its goals', (el-Shemi & Perry, 2013). At about the same time, the world's media attention returned to Mali where ongoing crisis forced the European Union and the U.N. to increase support for the Africa-led counter-insurgency against Islamists who had turned 'the once peaceful democracy into a haven for international terrorists' (Bittermann, 2013). This is evidence that this volume is not going to provide the final answer to the question of socio-political uncertainties on the African continent.

Contributors have also not completely resolved the overriding and presumably ongoing question of the extent to which 'new' media may have completely overtaken 'old' media in their contributions to the success of social movements in Africa, or elsewhere. Activists in social movements continue to employ and deploy the overlapping capabilities of all forms of media in the execution of their agenda. Stakeholders in government also do the same; underscoring the uniqueness of the democratization of access to variegated media that have accompanied and changed the dynamics of 21st century movements. When authors in this volume extolled the power of 'new' media, they did so in circumstances where 'old' media were under lock down and 'new' media provided alternatives or when 'new' media abilities defied geography and got the global community involved in the progression of social movements. Authors also provided evidence that 'new' media had assisted activists in winning some but not all social mobilizations.

Like their counterparts in the 'old' media, African governments have attempted to limit the reach of 'new' media with measured success.

One issue that the book's contributors do not, however, equivocate about is that information is power. Africa's ongoing saga with political reforms is deeply embedded in the struggle to strategically use and manipulate the new information communication landscape in the political process. Citizens are astute enough to understand that communication technologies do not a revolution make, but they are nevertheless acutely aware that contemporary social movements cannot be effective without being social media savvy (Howard, Agarwal, & Hussain, 2011) or by discounting the clout of the state. We anticipate that as access to new media continues to expand in Africa; their employment will materially be linked to citizens' aspirations for increased stake in the political future of their respective countries.

With direct and indirect focus on more than 20 countries (the UN membership roster contains 54 African countries; African Union lists 53) this volume covers more issues and more regions than is typically found in books of its kind. Notwithstanding its broad scope, the book's geographical coverage falls short in representation of African countries. We are, therefore, unable to claim that the chapters cover all of the diversities of social and political changes that are underway on the African continent today. As such, readers should not make the assumption that the contents of chapters represented in this volume speak for the entire continent. However, we can modestly take credit for opening a substantial amount of issues across a significant number of African countries for critical examination.

As earlier indicated, the themes identified and employed in this summative task represent only one sketch or dimension from which readers should assess authors' contributions. As well, the 24 chapters contained in this volume may not end up answering all of the questions that may

be posed by those contending with the roles and functions of media ('old' and 'new') in contemporary Africa. There is, undoubtedly, additional work to be done in the attempt to understand the ever-dynamic role of all media in the evolution of social and political change in Africa. Our attempt in this collection, though valiant, should be considered foundational with ample gaps for other scholars to fill.

REFERENCES

Adelaja, B. (2013). The impact of social media on the social, political, and economic environments in Africa. In Olorunnisola, A., & Douai, A. (Eds.), *New Media Influence on Social and Political Change in Africa (319-335)*. Hershey, PA: IGI-Global.

Akpojivi, U. (2013). Looking beyond elections: An examination of Media Freedom in the Re: Democratization of Nigeria. In Olorunnisola, A., & Douai, A. (Eds.), *New Media Influence on Social and Political Change in Africa (84-100)*. Hershey, PA: IGI-Global.

Allagui, I., & Kuebler, J. (2011). The Arab Spring and the role of ICTs: Editorial introduction. *International Journal of Communication, 5*, 1435–1442.

Amare, A. (2009). Democracy and press freedom. In Müller-Schöll, U. (Ed.), *Democracy and the Social Question: Some Contributions to a Dialogue in Ethiopia* (pp. 26–34). Addis Ababa, Ethiopia: Falcon Printing Enterprise.

Aouragh, M., & Alexander, A. (2011). The Egyptian experience: Sense and nonsense of the Internet revolution. *International Journal of Communication, 5*, 1344–1358.

Ayish, M. (2003). *Arab World Television in the World of Globalization*. Hamburg, Germany: Ubersee Institute.

Bittermann, J. (2013). French President on Military Offensive: 'We are winning in Mali'. Retrieved January 29, 2013 from http://www.cnn.com/2013/01/29/world/africa/mali-military-offensive/index.html

Chari, T. (2013). Rethinking the democratization role of online media: The Zimbabwean Experience. In Olorunnisola, A., & Douai, A. (Eds.), *New Media Influence on Social and Political Change in Africa (379-401)*. Hershey, PA: IGI-Global.

Couldry, N., & Curran, J. (Eds.). (2003). *Contesting Media Power: Alternative Media in a Networked World*. Lanham, MD: Rowman & Littlefield Publishers.

Dare, S. (2007). *Guerrilla Journalism: Dispatches from the Underground*. Ibadan, Nigeria: Kraft Books Limited.

Douai, A., & Moussa, M. B. (2013). Twitter frames: Finding social media's "influentials"' during the "Arab Spring.". In Olorunnisola, A., & Douai, A. (Eds.), *New Media Influence on Social and Political Change in Africa*. Hershey, PA: IGI-Global.

Douai, A., & Olorunnisola, A. A. (2013). New Media and the Question of African Democracy. In Olorunnisola, A., & Douai, A. (Eds.), *New Media Influence on Social and Political Change in Africa*. (1-14) Hershey, PA: IGI-Global.

el-Shemi, A., & Perry, T. (2013). Violence, protesters return to Tahrir Square, Suez as Egypt marks Revolution. Retrieved January 29, 2013, from http://worldnews.nbcnews.com/_news/2013/01/25/16692054-violence-protesters-return-to-tahir-square-suez-as-egypt-marks-revolution?lite

Faris, D. (2009). The end of the beginning: The failure of April 6th and the future of electronic activism in Egypt. *Arab Media & Society, 9*(Fall). Retrieved January 28, 2013, from http://www.arabmediasociety.com/?article=723

Gettleman, J. (2010). Africa's forever wars: Why the continent's conflicts never end. *Foreign Policy*, March/April. Retrieved January 28, 2013, from http://www.foreignpolicy.com/articles/2010/02/22/africas_forever_wars

Gilberds, H. (2013). Articulations and rearticulations: Antagonisms of media reform in Africa. In Olorunnisola, A., & Douai, A. (Eds.), *New Media Influence on Social and Political Change in AFRICA (51-66)*. Hershey, PA: IGI-Global.

Hackett, R. (2003) *Media reform: Democratizing the media, democratizing the state* [Review of the book]. *Canadian Journal of Communication, 28*(3). Retrieved April 19, 2011, from http://www.cjconline.ca/index.php/journal/article/view/1380/1457 HRNJ Uganda

Howard, P. N., Agarwal, S. D., & Hussain, M. M. (2011). When do States disconnect their digital networks? Regime responses to the political uses of social media. *Communication Review, 14*(3), 216–232. doi:10.1080/10714421.2011.597254.

Howard, P. N., & Parks, M. R. (2012). Social media and political change: Capacity, constraint, and consequence. *The Journal of Communication, 62*(2), 359–358. doi:10.1111/j.1460-2466.2012.01626.x.

Javuru, K. (2013). New media and the changing public sphere in Uganda. In Olorunnisola, A., & Douai, A. (Eds.), *New Media Influence on Social and Political Change in Africa (357-378)*. Hershey, PA: IGI-Global.

Jones, S. G. (2013). The mirage of the Arab Spring: Deal with the region you have not the region you want. *Foreign Policy*, January/February. Retrieved January 29, 2013, from http://www.foreignaffairs.com/articles/138478/seth-g-jones/the-mirage-of-the-arab- spring

Kasoma, T. (2013). Media regulation and journalists' perceptions of their role in society: A case of Zambia and Ghana. In Olorunnisola, A., & Douai, A. (Eds.), *New Media Influence on Social and Political Change in Africa (101-117)*. Hershey, PA: IGI-Global.

Kituri, T. (2013). Fanning the flames of fear: A critical analysis of local language radio as a catalyst to the post-election violence in Kenya. In Olorunnisola, A., & Douai, A. (Eds.), *New Media Influence on Social and Political Change in Africa*. (67-83) Hershey, PA: IGI-Global.

Martin, B. L., & Olorunnisola, A. A. (2013). Use of new ICTs as "liberation" or "repression" technologies in social movements: The need to formulate appropriate media policies. In Olorunnisola, A., & Douai, A. (Eds.), *New Media Influence on Social and Political Change in Africa (257-272)*. Hershey, PA: IGI-Global.

Mhiripiri, N., & Mutsvairo, B. (2013). Social media, new ICTs and the challenges facing Zimbabwe democratic process. In Olorunnisola, A., & Douai, A. (Eds.), *New Media Influence on Social and Political Change in Africa (402-422)*. Hershey, PA: IGI-Global.

Moussa, M. B. (2013). A grassroots approach to the democratic role of the Internet in developing countries: The case of Morocco. In Olorunnisola, A., & Douai, A. (Eds.), *New Media Influence on Social and Political Change in Africa (218-240)*. Hershey, PA: IGI-Global.

Ogbondah, C. W. (1997). Communication and democratization in Africa: Constitutional changes, prospects and persistent problems for the media. *International Communication Gazette*, *59*(4-5), 271–294. doi:10.1177/0016549297059004003.

Ogbondah, C. W. (2004). Democratization and the media in West Africa: An analysis of recent constitutional and legislative reforms for press freedom in Ghana and Nigeria. *West Africa Review*, *6*. Retrieved January 24, 2013, from http://www.westafricareview.com/issue6/ogbondah.html

Olorunnisola, A. A. (1996). When tribal wars are mass mediated: Re-evaluating the policy of "non-interference.". *International Communication Gazette*, *56*, 123–138. doi:10.1177/001654929605600203.

Olorunnisola, A. A. (Ed.). (2009). *Media and communications industries in Nigeria: Impacts of neoliberal reforms between 1999 and 2007*. Lewiston, NJ: The Edwin Mellen Press.

Olorunnisola, A. A., & Martin, B. L. (2013). Influences of media in social movements: Problematizing hyperbolic inferences about impacts. *Telematics and Informatics*, *30*, 275–288. doi:10.1016/j.tele.2012.02.005.

Olorunnisola, A. A., & Ojebode, A. A. (2013). Public opinion on Nigeria's democracy: Why the Arab Spring stopped in the Desert. In Olorunnisola, A., & Douai, A. (Eds.), *New Media Influence on Social and Political Change in AFRICA (336-356)*. Hershey, PA: IGI-Global.

Schramm, W. (1964). *Mass Media and National Development: The Role of Information in the Developing Countries*. Stanford, CA: Stanford University Press. doi:10.1177/000276426400800305.

Siebert, F. S., Peterson, T., & Schramm, W. (1956). *Four Theories of the Press: The Authoritarian, Libertarian, Social Responsibility and Soviet Communist Concepts of What the Press Should Be and Do*. Champaign, IL: University of Illinois Press.

Skjerdal, T. S. (2008). Self-censorship among news journalists in the Ethiopian state media. *African Communication Research*, *1*(2), 185–206.

Skjerdal, T. S. (2010). Justifying self-censorship: A perspective from Ethiopia. *Westminster Papers in Communication and Culture*, *7*(2), 98–121.

Skjerdal, T. S. (2013). Selective liberalization: An analysis of media reform in a semi-democratic society. In Olorunnisola, A., & Douai, A. (Eds.), *New Media Influence on Social and Political Change in Africa (32-50)*. Hershey, PA: IGI-Global.

Switzer, L., & Adhikari, M. (Eds.). (2000). *South Africa's Resistance Press: Alternative Voices in the Last Generation Under Apartheid*. Athens, OH: Ohio University Press.

Turner, I. (2013). The changing state of the South African Nation: Political proximity to business from a linguistic perspective. In Olorunnisola, A., & Douai, A. (Eds.), *New Media Influence on Social and Political Change in AFRICA (168-186)*. Hershey, PA: IGI-Global.

Wasserman, H. (2010). *Tabloid Journalism in South Africa: True story!* Bloomington, IN: Indiana University Press.

Zaid, B. (2013). Moroccan media in democratic transition. In *A*. Olorunnisola & A. Douai (Eds.), *New Media Influence on Social and Political Change in Africa* (15-31). Hershey, PA: IGI-Global.

Compilation of References

Abdel Kouddous, S. (2012). Egypt's new war of information. *Jadaliyya*. Retrieved January 12, 2013, from http://www.jadaliyya.com/pages/index/3960/egypts-new-war-of-information.

Abdel Rahman, A. (2002). *Issues of the Arab press in the twenty-first century*. Cairo, Egypt: Al-Arabi lilnashr Wal Tawzi'.

Abdel Rahman, A. (1985). *Studies in the contemporary Egyptian press*. Cairo, Egypt: Dar Al Fikr Al-Arabi.

Abdi, J., & Deane, J. (2008). *The Kenyan 2007 elections and their aftermath: The role of media and communication*. London: BBC World Service Trust.

Abdulai, A. (2009). *Political context study-Ghana*. Retrieved from http://www.polis.leeds.ac.uk/assets/files/research/research-projects/abdulai-ghana-political-context-study-jan09.pdf

Abdulla, R. A. (2006). An overview of media developments in Egypt: Does the Internet make a difference?[GMJ]. *Global Media Journal*, *1*, 88–100.

Abel, F., Gao, Q., Houben, G.-J., & Tao, K. (2011). *Analyzing user modeling on Twitter for personalized news recommendations*. Lecture Notes in Computer Science. Retrieved from http://snurb.info/files/2012/Researching%20News%20Discussion%20on%20Twitter.pdf abgerufen

Abouzeid, R. (2011). Egyptian state tv: Let us tell you what's really happening. *Time*. Retrieved March 1, 2011, from http://www.time.com/time/world/article/0,8599,2046510,00.html

Access to Information Act. (2005). *Uganda Gazette, XCVIII*(42). Retrieved July 2, 2012, from http://www.freedominfo.org/documents/uganda_ati_act_2005.pdf

Adam, H., Van Zyl Slabbert, F., & Moodley, K. (1998). *Comrades in Business – Post-liberation politics in South Africa*. Cape Town, South Africa: Tafelberg Publishers.

Aday, S., Farrell, H., Lynch, M., Sides, J., Kelly, J., & Zuckerman, E. (2010). United States Institute of Peace, Blogs and Bullets. *Contentious Issues in Politics*. Retrieved from http://www.usip.org/files/resources/pw65.pdf

Adejumobi, S. (2000). Elections in Africa: A fading shadow of democracy? *International Political Science Review*, *21*(1), 59–73. doi:10.1177/0192512100211004.

Adelaja, B. (2013). The impact of social media on the social, political, and economic environments in Africa. In Olorunnisola, A., & Douai, A. (Eds.), *New Media Influence on Social and Political Change in Africa (319-335)*. Hershey, PA: IGI-Global.

Adjovi, E. (2006). Mobilisations citoyennes et démonopolisation du travail politique au Bénin. *Perspective Afrique*, *1*(3), 187–223.

Adolf, M., & Wallner, C. (2005). *Probing the public sphere in Europe. Theoretical problems: Problems of theory and prospects for further communication research*. Paper presented at the First European Communication Conference 24. Amsterdam, The Netherlands.

African Centre for Media Excellence-ACME. (2010). *Court dismisses Government case against closed radio station*. Retrieved August 23, 2010, from http://www.acme-ug.org/component/k2/item/29-court-dismisses-gov%E2%80%99t-caseagainst-closed-radio-station

African Charter on Broadcasting. (2001). *Final Report Ten Years On: Assessment, Challenges and Prospects*. Retrieved January, 12, 2001, from http://portal.unesco.org/ci/en

African Media Barometer (AMB). (2010). *Uganda.* Kampala, Uganda: Friedrich-Ebert-Stiftung.

African Media Barometer (AMB). (2012). *Uganda.* Retrieved September 24, 2012, from http://www.fes-uganda.org/media/pdf/AMB%20Uganda%202012.pdf

African Media Barometer. (2009). *Ghana.* Windhoek, Namibia: Media Institute of Southern Africa.

African Media Barometer. (2009). *Zambia.* Windhoek, Namibia: Media Institute of Southern Africa.

Agence National de Réglementation des Télécommunications. (2010). *Tableau de bord trimestriel du marché Internet.* Retrieved June 2, 2010, from http://www.anrt.ma/fr/admin/download/upload/file_fr1874.pdf

Ahmad, A. N. (2010). Is Twitter a useful tool for journalists? *Journal of Media Practice, 11*(2), 145–155. doi:10.1386/jmpr.11.2.145_1.

Ake, C. (1991). Rethinking African Democracy. *Journal of Democracy, 2*(1), 32–44. doi:10.1353/jod.1991.0003.

Akinfeleye, R. (2003). *Fourth estate of the realm or fourth estate of the wreck: Imperative of social responsibility of the press.* Lagos, Nigeria: University of Lagos Press.

Akpojivi, U. (2011, June 27). The FOI Act: Beyond the euphoria. *Guardian Newspaper.* Retrieved from http://www.ngrguardiannews.com/index.php?option

Akpojivi, U. (2012). *Media freedom and media policy in new democracies: An analysis of the nexus between policy formation and normative conceptions in Ghana and Nigeria.* PhD Thesis. Leeds, UK: University of Leeds.

Akpojivi, U. (2013). Looking beyond elections: An examination of Media Freedom in the Re: Democratization of Nigeria. In Olorunnisola, A., & Douai, A. (Eds.), *New Media Influence on Social and Political Change in Africa (84-100).* Hershey, PA: IGI-Global.

Al Jazeera Network (2011, January 30). Egypt shuts down Al Jazeera bureau. Retrieved March 1, 2011, from http://english.aljazeera.net/news/middleeast/2011/01/201113085252994161.html

Alemayehu G. M. (2003). A discourse on the draft Ethiopian press law. *International Journal of Ethiopian Studies, 1*(1), 103–120.

Alhassan, A. (2004). *Development Communication Policy and Economic Fundamentalism in Ghana.* Tampere, Finland: Acta Universitatis Tamperensis.

Aljazeera. (2010). *India threatens Blackberry ban.* Retrieved January 21, 2011, from http://www.aljazeera.com/business/2010/08/2010812143513776296.html

Al-Kallab, S. (2003). The Arab satellites: The pros and cons. *Transnational Broadcasting Studies Journal (TBS), 10.* Retrieved January 21, 2013, from http://www.tbsjournal.com/Archives/Fall03/Salih_Kallab.html

Allagui, I., & Kuebler, J. (2011). The Arab Spring and the role of ICTs: Editorial introduction. *International Journal of Communication, 5*, 1435–1442.

Allen, K. (2011). *African jitters over blogs and social media.* Retrieved November 18, 2011, from http://www.bbc.co.uk/news/world-africa-13786143

Aluoka, O. (2008.). Kenya's Post-Election Violence. Retrieved November 21, 2008, from http://www.tokyofoundation.org/en/sylff/voices-from-the-sylff-community/kenya2019s-post-election-violence

Alzouma, G. (2005). Myths of digital technology in Africa Leapfrogging development? *Global Media and Communication, 1*(3), 339–356. doi:10.1177/1742766505058128.

AMARC. (2003). *The Kathmandu declaration.* Kathmandu, Nepal: AMARC. Retrieved from http://www.amarc.org/index.php?p=The_Kathmandu_Declaration

Amare A. (2009). Democracy and press freedom. In Müller-Schöll, U. (Ed.), *Democracy and the Social Question: Some Contributions to a Dialogue in Ethiopia* (pp. 26–34). Addis Ababa, Ethiopia: Falcon Printing Enterprise.

Ambrose, B. (1995). *Democratization and the protection of human rights in Africa: Problems and prospects.* London: Praeger.

Amnesty International. (2010). Uganda. Amnesty *International Memorandum on the Regulation of interception of communications Act 2010.* London: Amnesty International Publications.

Amobi, I. (2010). *Millennial generation, new media and digital divide: Assessing global divide through ownership, literacy, access and usage of Internet and social media by young people in Nigeria.* Paper presented at the 2010 World Journalism Education Conference. Rhodes University, Grahamstown, South Africa.

Amupala, J. (1989). Developmental *Radio Broadcasting in Namibia and Tanzania: A Comparative Study*. University of Tampere, Department of Journalism and Mass Communication. Report No 27.

Anderson, D. M. (2005). Yours in struggle for Majimbo: Nationalism and the Party Politics of Decolonization in Kenya, 1955-64. *Journal of Contemporary History, 3*(40), 547–564. doi:10.1177/0022009405054571.

Anderson, H. (2004). *Panorama: Secrets of the Camps* [Television broadcast]. London: BBC One.

Anderson, L. (2011). Demystifying the Arab Spring Parsing the Differences between Tunisia, Egypt, and Libya. *Foreign Affairs, 90*(3), 2–7.

Andsager, J., Wyatt, R., & Martin, E. (2004). *Free expression and five democratic publics support for individual and media rights*. Cresskill, NJ: Hampton Press Inc..

Anim, E. (2010). *From mass communication to citizen journalism: New perspectives in contemporary mass communication*. Paper presented at the 2010 World Journalism Education Conference. Rhodes University, Grahamstown, South Africa.

Ansah, P. A. V. (1998). In search of a role for the African media in the Democratic Process. *Africa Media Review, 2*(2), 1–16.

Anstead, N., & Chadwick, A. (2009). Parties, Election campaigning, and the Internet: Toward a Comparative Institutional Approach. In Chadwick, A., & Howard, P. N. (Eds.), *Routledge Handbook of Internet Politics* (pp. 55–71). London: Routledge.

Ansuh-Kyeremeh, K. (1999). The challenges of surveying public opinion in an emerging democracy. *International Journal of Public Opinion Research, 11*(1), 59–74. doi:10.1093/ijpor/11.1.59.

Anyanwu, J. (1992). President Babangida's structural adjustment programme and inflation in Nigeria. *Journal of Social Development in Africa, 7*(1), 5–24.

Aouragh, M., & Alexander, A. (2011). The Egyptian experience: Sense and nonsense of the Internet revolution. *International Journal of Communication, 5*, 1344–1358.

Appadurai, A. (1996). *Modernity at Large: Cultural Dimensions of Globalization*. Minneapolis, MN: University of Minnesota Press.

Arant, D. (2000). *Online media ethics: A survey of US daily newspaper editors*. Paper presented at the Association for Education in Journalism and Mass Communication Convention. Phoenix, AZ. Retrieved September 5, 2008, from http://www.factstaff.elon.edu.anders/onlinesurvey.html

Arendt, H. (1998). *Between Past and Future: Eight Exercises in Political Thought*. New York: Penguin.

Arkosah-Sarpong, K. (2008). *The corruption of Jerry Rawlings*. Retrieved from http://www.ghanaweb.com/GhanaHomePage/features/artikel.php?ID=150169

Armijo, E. (2009). Building open societies: Freedom of the press in Jordan and Rwanda. *International Journal of Communications Law and Policy, 13*, 26–48.

Armstrong, D. (1981). *A trumpet to arms: Alternative media in America*. Boston, MA: South End Press.

Arntsen, H. (2009). *Drawings for Change? A view of the Zimbabwean 2008 General Elections as Interpreted by News Cartoons. Paper presented in the NordMedia09 Conference*. Sweden: Karlstad.

Article 19 (June 7, 2011). Nigeria: Freedom of Information Act - A ray of hope for democracy. Retrieved from http://www.typepad.com/services/trackback/6a00d83451e0be69e201538f04b3c8970b

Article 19. (2007). Nigeria's 2007 elections and media coverage January 2007. Retrieved May 12, 2008, from http://www.article19.org

Article 19. (2010, March). Comment on anti-terrorism proclamation, 2009, of Ethiopia. Report.

Asante, C. E. (1996). *The Press in Ghana: Problems and Prospects*. Lanham, MD: University Press of America, Inc..

Asante, C. E. (1997). *Press freedom and development: A research guide and selected bibliography*. Westport, CT: Greenwood Press.

Associated Press. (2011). *Vodafone: Egypt forced us to send pro-government messages*. Retrieved March 1, 2011, from http://www.huffingtonpost.com/2011/02/03/vodafone-egypt-text-messages_n_817952.html

Asuni, J., & Farris, J. (2012). *Tracking social media. The Social Media Tracking Center and the 2011 Nigerian Elections.* Retrieved from http://www.eienigeria.org/sites/default/files/files/Tracking%20Social%20Media%20and%202011%20Nigeria%20Elections.pdf

Asur, S., & Huberman, B. (2010). Predicting the future with social media. IEEE Web Intelligence. Retrieved from http://arxiv.org/pdf/1003.5699v1.pdf

Atia, T. (2006, July). Paradox of the free press in Egypt. USEF Expert Panel Discussion. Washington, DC.

Atkinson, J. D., & Cooley, L. (2010). Narrative capacity, resistance performance, and the "shape" of new social movement networks. *Communication Studies, 61*(3), 321–338. doi:10.1080/10510971003752668.

Atton, C. (2002). *Alternative media.* London: Sage Publications.

Auma, C. M. O. (2010). *Social media and young people's engagement in political discourse* [Dissertation]. Nairobi, Kenya: Moi University.

Avgerou, C. (2007). *Information Systems in Developing Countries: A Critical Research Review.* Working paper series. London: London School of Economics and Political Science.

Ayish, M. (2003). *Arab World Television in the World of Globalization.* Hamburg, Germany: Ubersee Institute.

Ayodele, L. (2009). *Court restrains NBC from shutting Adaba FM-PM News Lagos.* Retrieved May 12, 2009, from http://www.saharareporters.com

Bailey, F. G. (2001). *Stratagems and spoils: A social anthropology of politics.* Oxford, UK: Westview Press.

Baker, E. (2007). *Media concentration and democracy: Why ownership matters.* Cambridge, UK: Cambridge University Press.

Balancing Act. (2008). *African broadcast and film markets.*

Banda, F. (2006). Alternative media: A viable option for Southern Africa. *Openspace, 1*(5), 80–83.

Banda, F. (2009). *Towards an Africana agenda for journalism education. Introductory address at WJEC Africa-Regional preparatory colloquium.* Grahamstown, South Africa: Rhodes University.

Banda, F., Mudhai, F. O., & Tettey, J. W. (2009). *African media and the digital public sphere.* New York: Palgrave Macmillan.

Bandura, A. (2001). Social cognitive theory: An agentic perspective. *Annual Review of Psychology, 53,* 1–26. doi:10.1146/annurev.psych.52.1.1 PMID:11148297.

Banégas, R. (2003). *La démocratie à pas de caméléon. Transition et imaginaires politiques au Bénin.* Paris: Karthala.

Barclay, P. (2010). *Zimbabwe: Years of Hope and Despair.* London: Bloomsbury.

Barendt, E. (1985). *Freedom of speech.* Oxford, UK: Clarendon Press.

Bargh, J. A., & McKenna, K. Y. A. (2004). The Internet and social life. *Annual Review of Psychology, 55,* 573–590. doi:10.1146/annurev.psych.55.090902.141922 PMID:14744227.

Barker, J., & Mendel, T. (2003). *The legal framework for freedom of expression in Ethiopia.* Retrieved January 9, 2012, from www.article19.org/pdfs/publications/ethiopia-legal-framework-for-foe.pdf

Barrie, A. (2008). The "bring me my machine gun" campaign. *FoxNews.* Retrieved April 30, 2012, from http://www.foxnews.com/story/0,2933,321785,00.html

Barth, F. (1969). *Ethnic groups and boundaries.* London: George Allen and Unwin.

BBC. (2006). *Islamists claim Mogadishu victory.* Retrieved January 20, 2012, from http://news.bbc.co.uk/2/hi/africa/5047766.stm

BBC. (2010). *Two Gulf states to ban some Blackberry functions.* Retrieved January 13, 2011, from http://www.bbc.co.uk/news/world-middle-east-10830485

BBC. (2012). *Somalia's al-Shabab join al-Qaeda.* Retrieved February 15, 2012, from http://www.bbc.co.uk/news/world-africa-16979440

Beaumont, P. (2012). Egypt: one year on, the young heroes of Tahrir Square feel a chill wind. *The Observer.* Retrieved January 12, 2013, from http://www.guardian.co.uk/world/2012/jan/15/tahrir-square-elbaradei-protesters

Becker, B., & Wehner, J. (2001). Electronic networks and civil society: Reflections on Structural Changes in the Public Sphere. In Ess, C., & Sudweeks, F. (Eds.), *Culture, technology, communication: Towards an intercultural global village* (pp. 67–85). Albany, NY: State University of New York Press.

Becker, L. B., & Tudor, V. (2005). *Non-U.S. funders of media assistance projects. Report, James M.* Cox Center for International Mass Communication Training and Research.

Beers, D. (2006). *The public sphere and online, independent journalism* (pp. 109-130). Paper presented at Canadian Society for the Study of Education. York, Canada.

Belsey, A., & Chadwick, R. (1992). *Ethical Issues in Journalism and the Media.* London: Routledge.

Ben Ashour, A. (1992). *Mass media in Morocco.* Unpublished Master's thesis. Institut Supérieur de Journalisme.

Ben Moussa, M. (2011). *The use of the Internet by social movements in Morocco: Implications collective action and political change.* Unpublished PhD thesis, Concordia University, Portland, Oregon.

Bendourou, O. (1996). Power and opposition in Morocco. *Journal of Democracy*, 7(3), 108–122. doi:10.1353/jod.1996.0041.

Bennett, L. W. (2003). New media power: The internet and global activism. In Couldry, N., & Curran, J. (Eds.), *Contesting media power: Alternative media in a networked world* (pp. 17–37). Lanham, MD: Rowman & Littlefield.

Bennett, W., & Segerberg, A. (2011). Digital media and the personalization of collective action: Social technology and the organization of protests against the global economic crisis Information. *Communicatio Socialis*, 14(6), 770–799.

Bentivegna, S. (2006). Rethinking politics in the world of ICTs. *European Journal of Communication*, 21(3), 331–343. doi:10.1177/0267323106066638.

Berger, (2009). How to improve standards of journalism education. *African Communication Research, 2*(2), 271–90.

Berger, G. (2007). Looking ahead: What next for African media? In E. Baarratt & G. Berger (Eds), 50 years of journalism: Africa media since Ghana's independence (159-170) Johannesburg, South Africa: The Africa Editors' Forum, Highway Africa and Media Foundation for West Africa.

Berger, G. (2002). Theorizing the media-democracy relationship in South Africa. *International Communication Gazette*, 64(1), 21–45. doi:10.1177/1748048502064001 0201.

Berger, G. (2007). *Media Legislation in Africa: A Comparative Legal Survey.* Grahamstown, South Africa: Unesco & Rhodes University.

Berger, G. (2007). In search of journalism education excellence in Africa: Summary of the 2006 Unesco project. *Ecquid Novi: African Journalism Studies, 28*(1–2), 149–155. doi:10.3368/ajs.28.1-2.149.

Berger, G. (2010). The struggle for press self-regulation in contemporary South Africa: Charting a course between an industry charade and a government doormat. *Communicatio, 36*(3), 289–308. doi:10.1080/02500167.2010.518783.

Berger, G. (Ed.). (2005). *Doing Digital Journalism: How Southern African News Gatherers are Using ICT.* Grahamstown, South Africa: Rhodes University.

Bhabha, H. K. (1994, 2002). The location of culture. London: Routledge.

Bimber, B. (1999). The Internet and citizen communication with government: Does the medium matter? *Political Communication*, 6(4), 409–428. doi:10.1080/105846099198569.

Bimber, B. (2001). Information and Political Engagement in America. *Political Research Quarterly, 54*(1), 53–68.

Bimber, B., & Davis, R. (2003). *Campaigning Online: The Internet in US Elections.* Oxford, UK: Oxford University Press.

Bittermann, J. (2013). French President on Military Offensive: 'We are winning in Mali'. Retrieved January 29, 2013 from http://www.cnn.com/2013/01/29/world/africa/mali- military-offensive/index.html

Bjornlund, E., Bratton, M., & Gibson, C. (1992). Observing multiparty elections in Africa: Lessons from Zambia. *African Affairs, 91*(364), 405–431.

Blackledge, A. (2005). Discourse and power in a multilingual world. *Journal of Language and Politics*, 1-263.

Blankson, I. A. (2002). Re-examining civil society in emerging Sub-Sahara African democracies: The state, the media, and the public in Ghana. *Global Media Journal, 1*(1), Fall. Retrieved from http://lass.purduecal.edu/cca/gmj/fa02/gmj-fa02-blankson.htmgmj-fa02-blankson.htm

Blankson, I. A. (2007). Media independence and pluralism in Africa. Opportunities of democratization and liberalization. In Blankson, I. A., & Murphy, P. D. (Eds.), *Negotiating democracy. Media transformations in emerging democracies* (pp. 15–34). Albany, NY: State University of New York Press.

Blankson, I. A., & Murphy, P. (Eds.). (2007). *Negotiating democracy: Media transformations in emerging democracies*. Albany, NY: State University of New York Press.

Blee, K., & Taylor, V. (2002). The uses of semi-structured interviews in social movement research. In Klandermans, B., & Staggenborg, S. (Eds.), *Methods of Social Movement Research* (pp. 92–117). Minneapolis, MN: University of Minnesota Press.

Blommaert, J. (2006). *Discourse: A critical introduction. Key topics in sociolinguistics*. Cambridge, UK: Cambridge University Press.

Blommaert, J., & Bulcaen, C. (2000). Critical discourse analysis. *Annual Review of Anthropology*, 447–466. doi:10.1146/annurev.anthro.29.1.447.

Blumler, J. G., & Gurevitch, M. (1995). *The Crisis of Public Communication*. London: Routledge. doi:10.4324/9780203181775.

Blumler, J. G., & Gurevitch, M. (2001). The New media and our political communication discontents: Democratizing cyberspace. *Information Communication and Society, 4*(1), 1–13.

Boadi, G. (2004). Africa: The Quality of Political Reform. In Boadi, G. (Ed.), *Democratic Reform in Africa the Quality of Progress* (pp. 5–28). Boulder, CO: Lynne Rienner Publishers Inc..

Boafo, K. (1985). Utilizing development communication strategies in African societies: A critical perspective. *Gazette, 35*, 83–92.

Boggs, C. (2000). *The end of politics: Corporate power and the decline of the public sphere*. New York: Guilford Press.

Bohler-Muller, N., & Van der Merwe, C. (2011). *The Potential of Social Media to Influence Socio-Political Change on the African Continent*. Africa Institute of South Africa Policy Brief No. 46. Retrieved from http://www.ai.org.za/media/publications/Policy%20Brief/AISA%20Policy%20Brief%2046.pdf

Bond, S. (1997). *Neocolonialism and the Ghanaian media: An in-depth look at international news coverage in Ghanaian newspapers, television and radio*. Retrieved from http://digitalcollections.sit.edu/cgi/viewcontent.cgi?article=1058&context=african_diaspora_isp

Bond, P., & Manyanya, S. (2002). *Zimbabwe's Plunge: Exhausted Nationalism, Neoliberalism and the Search for Social Change*. Pietermaritzburg, South Africa: University of Natal Press.

Bongrand, M. (1993). *Le marketing politique* (p. 128). University Presses of France.

Borgida, E., & Emily, N. S. (2004). New media and politics: Some insights from social and political psychology. *The American Behavioral Scientist, 48*(4), 467–478. doi:10.1177/0002764204270282.

Bourgault, L. M. (1995). *Mass media in Sub-Saharan Africa*. Bloomington, IN: Indiana University Press.

Bowman, R. (2010). Rehearsing democracy: New media, political freedoms and censorship in Uganda. In Monaghan, G., & Tunney, S. (Eds.), *Web journalism: A new form of citizenship?* (pp. 248–260). Eastbourne, UK: Sussex Academic Press.

BOYD. D. M., Golder, S., & Lotan, G. (2010). Tweet, Tweet, Retweet: Conversational aspects of retweeting on Twitter. *HICSS43* (Vol. 0, pp. 1-10). Manoa, HI. IEEE. Retrieved January 13, 2013, from http://www.computer.org/portal/web/csdl/doi/10.1109/HICSS.2010.412

Boyd-Barrett, O. (1977). Media Imperialism: Towards an International Framework for the Analysis of Media Systems. In Curran, J., Gurewitch, M., & Woollacott, J. (Eds.), *Mass Communication and Society* (pp. 116–135). London: Arnold & Open University Press.

Boyd-Barrett, O. (2002). More research needed on changing nature of journalism re 'commercial' and 'public' spheres. *Ecquid Novi, 23*(1), 94–95.

Boyd, D. (1977). Egyptian radio: Tool of political and national development. *Journalism Monographs (Austin, Tex.), 55*, 501–507, 539.

Boyd, D. (1999). *Broadcasting in the Arab world: A survey of the electronic media in the Middle East* (3rd ed.). Ames, IA: Iowa State University Press.

Boyd, D. (2008). Can social network sites enable political action? In Fine, A., Sifry, M., Rasiej, A., & Levy, J. (Eds.), *Rebooting America* (pp. 112–116). Mountain View, CA: Creative Commons. doi:10.1386/macp.4.2.241_3.

Boyle, M. P., & Schmierbach, M. (2009). What makes a protester?: The role of mainstream and Alternative media use in predicting traditional and protest participation. *Communication Quarterly, 57*(1), 1–17. doi:10.1080/01463370802662424.

Bradley, C. D. (1993). Access to US government information on the internet, Interpersonal Computing and Technology. *An Electronic Journal for the 21st Century.*

Bratton, M., Mattes, R., & Gyimah-Boadi, E. (2005). *Public opinion, democracy, and market reform in Africa.* Cambridge, UK: Cambridge University Press.

Bratton, M., & van de Nicolas, W. (1997). *Democratic experiments in Africa.* New York: Cambridge University Press.

British Broadcast Corporation [BBC]. (2011). As it happened: Egypt unrest day five. Retrieved March 1, 2011, from http://news.bbc.co.uk/2/hi/middle_east/9380534.stm

British Broadcast Corporation [BBC]. (2011). *As it happened: Egypt unrest on Friday.* Retrieved March 1, 2011, from http://news.bbc.co.uk/2/hi/uk_news/politics/9380441.stm

British Broadcast Corporation [BBC]. (2011). *Old technology finds role in Egyptian protests.* Retrieved March 1, 2011, from http://www.bbc.co.uk/news/technology-12322948

British Broadcasting Corporation [BBC] News. (2011). Profile: Egypt's Wael Ghonim. BBC News-Middle East. February 8, 2011. Retrieved January 13 2013 from http://www.bbc.co.uk/news/world-middle-east-12400529

Brodie, M., Altman, D., & Sinclair, M. (1999). *Reality check: South Africans' views of the new South Africa. A Report on the national survey of the South African people, Sponsored by the Henry J*. Kaiser Foundation and Independent Newspapers.

Brown, K. (2010, February 12). Zuma sticks to state's five top priorities. *Business Day.* Retrieved April 30, 2012, from http://www.businessday.co.za/Articles/Content.aspx?id=93571

Brown, S. (2001). Authoritarian leaders and multiparty elections in Africa: How foreign donors help to keep Kenya's Daniel Arap Moi in Power. *Third World Quarterly, 22*(5), 725–739. doi:10.1080/01436590120084575.

Bruns, A., & Burgess, J. (2012). *Researching news discussion on Twitter: New methodologies.* Retrieved November 12, 2012, from http://snurb.info/files/2012/Researching%20News%20Discussion%20on%20Twitter.pdf

Buhlungu, S., & Adler, G. (Eds.). (1997). Labour and liberalisation in Zambia. *South African Labour Bulletin, 21*(2), 48–64.

Burke, K. (1969). *A rhetoric of motives.* Berkeley, CA: University of California Press.

Burrell, J. (2008). Livelihoods and the mobile phone in rural Uganda. *Grameen Foundation USA.* Retrieved April 6, 2009, from http://www.grameenfoundation.applab.org/section/ethnographic-research

Butler, A. (2000). Is South Africa heading towards authoritarian rule? Instability myths and expectations traps in a new democracy. *Politikon: South African Journal of Political Studies, 27*(2), 189–205. doi:10.1080/713692335.

Cable News Network [CNN]. (2011). Timeline of Egyptian protests. Retrieved March 1, 2011, from http://www.cnn.com/2011/WORLD/africa/02/03/egypt.protests.timeline/index.html

Cabral, A. (1974). National liberation and culture. *Transition, 45*, 12–17. doi:10.2307/2935020.

Calhoun, C. (1992). Introduction: Habermas and the public sphere. *Habermas and the Public Sphere*, 1-48.

Calingaert, D. (2006). Election Rigging and How to Fight it. *Journal of Democracy, 17*, 138–151. doi:10.1353/jod.2006.0043.

Callamard, A. (2010). Accountability, transparency, and freedom of expression in Africa. *Social Research, 77*(4), 1211–1240.

Cambie, S. (2011). Lessons from the front line: The Arab Spring demonstrated the power of people--and social media. *Communication World*. Retrieved from http://www.iabc.com/cw/

Cammaerts, B., Audenhove, L. V., Nulens, G., & Pauwels, C. (2003). *Beyond the digital divide: Reducing exclusion, fostering inclusion*. Brussels, Belgium: VUB Brussels University Press.

Carbone, G. (2009). *Does democratisation deliver social welfare? Political regimes and health policy in Ghana and Cameroon*. Retrieved from www.sisp.it/files/papers/2009/giovanni-carbone-425.pdf

Cardon, D., Fouetillou, G., Lerondeau, C., & Prieur, C. (2011). Esquisse de géographie de la blogosphère politique. In Greffet, F. (Ed.), *Continuerlalutte.com. Les partis politiques sur le web* (pp. 73–94). Paris: Presses de Sciences.

Carpentier, N., Lie, R., & Servaes, J. (2001). *Community media: Muting the democratic media discourse?* Paper presented at Social theory and Discourse: The International Social Theory Consortium Second Annual conference. Brighton, UK.

Carpentier, N. (2005). Identity, contingency and rigidity: The (counter-) hegemonic constructions of the identity of the media professional. *Journalism, 6*(2), 199–219. doi:10.1177/1464884905051008.

Carr, N. (2011). *The shallows: What the Internet is doing to our brains*. New York: W.W. Norton Publishers.

Carroll, W. K., & Hackett, R. A. (2006). Democratic media activism through the lens of social movement theory. *Media Culture & Society, 28*(1), 83–104. doi:10.1177/0163443706059289.

Castells, M. (1996, 2000). The grand fusion: Multimedia as symbolic environment. In The Information Age: Economy, Society and Culture: The Rise of the Network Society. Doi: doi:10.1002/9781444319514.

Castells, M. (2001). *The Internet galaxy: Reflections on the Internet, business, and society*. Oxford, UK: Oxford University Press.

Castells, M. (2004). An Introduction to the information age. In Webster, F. (Ed.), *The Information Society Reader* (pp. 138–149). New York: Routledge.

Cavatorta, F. (2005). The international context of Morocco's stalled democratization. *Democratization, 12*(4), 548–566. doi:10.1080/13510340500226101.

Cavatorta, F. (2006). Civil society, Islamism, and democratisation: The case of Morocco. *Modern African Studies, 44*(2), 203–222. doi:10.1017/S0022278X06001601.

Cborra, C., & Navarra, D. (2005). Good governance, development theory and aid policy: Risks and challenges of E-government in Jordan. *Journal of Information Technology for Development, 11*(2), 141–159. doi:10.1002/itdj.20008.

Cellular News. (2008, September 9). Zimbabwe awards 3G licenses. *Cellular News*. Retrieved June 18, 2011, from http://www.cellular-news.com/story/35076.php

Central Intelligence Agency. (2012). *CIA World Fact Book*. Retrieved January 23, 2012, from https://www.cia.gov/library/publications/the-world-factbook/geos/so.html

Centre for International Media Assistance (CIMA). (2009). *Special report: The role of new media in the 2009 Iranian elections*. Washington, DC: Centre for International Media Assistance.

Centre for International Media Assistance (CIMA). (2009). *Special Report: YouthTube – Empowering Youth through Independent Media*. Washington, DC: Centre for International Media Assistance.

Chabal, P. (2009). *Africa: The politics of suffering and smiling*. London: Zed Books.

Chadwick, A. (2006). *Internet Politics: States, Citizens, and New Communication Technologies*. Oxford, UK: Oxford University Press.

Chae, Y. (2005). *An aspect of the culture of the public sphere in U.S.: The Analysis of online public forums in local online newspapers*. Paper presented at the annual meeting of the International Communication Association. New York. Retrieved August 3, 2010, from http://wwwallacademic.com/meta/p13770_index.html

Chanda, E. (2010, May 3). Statutory media regulation not an option for Zambia. *The Post*. Retrieved from http://www.postzambia.com

Chandler, D. (2009) *Technological or Media Determinism*. Retrieved October 20, 2012, from http://www.bos.org.rs/cepit/idrustvo/st/TechorMediaDeterminism.pdf

Chan, S. (2010). *Citizen of Zimbabwe: Conversations with Morgan Tsvangirai* (2nd ed.). Harare, Zimbabwe: Weaver Press.

Chari, T. (2013). Rethinking the democratization role of online media: The Zimbabwean Experience. In Olorunnisola, A., & Douai, A. (Eds.), *New Media Influence on Social and Political Change in Africa (379-401)*. Hershey, PA: IGI-Global.

Chatfield, A. T., & Alhujran, O. (2009). *A cross-country comparative analysis of e-government service delivery among Arab countries. Information Technology for Development, 15(3)*. Indianapolis, IN: Wiley Periodicals.

Chege, M. (2008). Kenya: Back from the brink? *Journal of Democracy, 19*(4), 125–139. doi:10.1353/jod.0.0026.

Chideme, M. K. (2011). The reporting of Zimbabwe-Britain bilateral relations 2008–2010. (A case of *The Herald* and *The Zimbabwe Independent*). Unpublished MA dissertation, Midlands State University, Gweru, Zimbabwe.

Chidiogo, E. (2011). 800 people killed in post-election violence. Retrieved May 16, 2011, from http://dailytimes.com.ng/article/%E2%80%98800-people-killed-post-election-violence%E2%80%99

Chilton, P., & Schäffner, C. (2002). Introduction: Themes and principles in the analysis of political discourse. In Chilton, P., & Schäffner, C. (Eds.), *Politics as Text and Talk. Analytic Approaches to Political Discourses* (pp. 1–44). Amsterdam, The Netherlands: John Benjamins Publishing.

Chinaka, C. (2010, September 9). Mugabe dismisses rumours of poor health. *Reuters*.

Chipere, G. Communications & Advocacy Officer (2011). Community Radio Harare, personally interviewed by Nhamo Mhiripiri in Gweru, Zimbabwe, June 2011.

Chiumbu, S. (2010). Media, alternativism and power: The political economy of community media in South Africa. In Hyde-Clarke, N. (Ed.), *The Citizen in Communication* (pp. 115–137). Claremont, South Africa: Juta.

Chiumbu, S., & Moyo, D. (2009). Media, politics and power: Re-gearing policy and propaganda in crisis Zimbabwe. In Skare Orgeret, K., & Rønning, H. (Eds.), *The power of communication. Changes and challenges in African media* (pp. 177–214). Oslo, Norway: Unipub.

Cho, J., De Zuniga, H. G., Rojas, H., & Shah, D. V. (2003). Beyond access: The digital divide and Internet uses and gratifications. *IT & Society, 1*(4), 46–72.

Chonghaile, C. N. (2012). *Uganda anti-gay bill resurrected in parliament*. Retrieved November 20, 2012, from http://www.guardian.co.uk/world/2012/feb/08/uganda-gay-death-sentence-bill

Chonghaile, C. N. (2012, January 31). Somali Islamists ban Red Cross. *The Guardian*. Retrieved February 1, 2012, from http://www.guardian.co.uk/world/2012/jan/31/somali-islamists-ban-red-cross?newsfeed=true

Christians, C. G., Glasser, T. L., McQuail, D., Nordenstreng, K., & White, R. A. (2009). *Normative theories of the media: Journalism in democratic societies*. Urbana, IL: University of Illinois Press.

Chuma, W. (2007). *Mediating the transition: The press, state and capital in a changing Zimbabwe, 1980-2004*. Unpublished doctoral thesis, University of Wiwatersrand, Johannesburg, South Africa.

Chuma, W. (2010). Reforming the media in Zimbabwe: Critical reflections. In Moyo, D., & Chuma, W. (Eds.), *Media policy in a changing Southern Africa. Critical reflections on media reforms in the global age* (pp. 90–109). Pretoria, South Africa: Unisa Press.

Ciborra, C. (2003). Unveiling e-government and development: Governing at a distance in the new war. Working Paper Series. London: London School of Economics and Political Science.

Ciborra, C. (2005). Interpreting e-government and development: Efficiency, transparency or governance at a distance? *Information Technology & People, 18*(3), 260–279. doi:10.1108/09593840510615879.

CIPEV. (2008). *Report of the Commission of Inquiry into Post-Election Violence*. Nairobi, Kenya: Commission of Inquiry into Post-Election Violence.

Cohen, T. (1995, February 17). Visible shift required without a radical break – Mandela. *Business Day, 0*.

Coleman, S., & Hall, N. (2001). Spinning on the Web: E-campaigning and beyond. In Coleman, S. (Ed.), *Cyber Space Odyssey: The Internet in the UK Election* (pp. 7–24). London: Hansard Society.

Colombo, S., Carridi, P., & Kanninmont, J. (2012). New socio-political actors in North Africa, a transatlantic perspective. Retrieved February 14, 2012, from http://www.gmfus.org/archives/new-socio-political-actors-in-north-africa-a-transatlantic-perspective

Comaroff, J. L. (1997). Of totemism and ethnicity: Consciousness, practice and the signs of inequality. In Grinker, R. R., & Steiner, C. B. (Eds.), *Perspectives on Africa: A reader in culture, history, and representation* (pp. 69–85). London: Blackwell Publishers.

Comaroff, J. L., & Comaroff, J. (2009). *Ethnicity.Inc.* Chicago: The University of Chicago Press. doi:10.7208/chicago/9780226114736.001.0001.

Communications Commission of Kenya. (2011). *Quarterly Sector Statistics Report – 1ˢᵗ Quarter July-Sept 2010/2011*. Nairobi, Kenya: CCK.

Corbin, J., & Strauss, A. L. (1990). Grounded theory research: Procedures, canons, and evaluative criteria. *Qualitative Sociology, 13*(1), 3–21. doi:10.1007/BF00988593.

Cottle, S. (2011). Media and the Arab uprisings of 2011: Research notes. *Journalism, 12*(5), 647–659. doi:10.1177/1464884911410017.

Couldry, N. (2010). *Why Voice Matters: Culture and Politics after Neoliberalism*. London: Sage.

Couldry, N., & Curran, J. (Eds.). (2003). *Contesting Media Power: Alternative Media in a Networked World*. Lanham, MD: Rowman & Littlefield Publishers.

Couldry, N., Livingstone, S., & Markham, T. (2007). *Media Consumption and Public Engagement. Beyond the Presumption of Attention*. Basingdale, UK: Palgrave. doi:10.1057/9780230800823.

Coyer, K., Dowmunt, T., & Fountain, A. (2007). *The Alternative Media*. London: Routledge.

Curran, J. (1979). Press Freedom as a Property Right: The Crisis of Press Legitimacy. *Media Culture & Society, 1*, 59–82. doi:10.1177/016344377900100106.

Curran, J. (1991). Mass media and democracy: A reappraisal. In Curran, J., & Gurevitch, M. (Eds.), *Mass Media and Democracy* (pp. 267–284). London: Edward Arnold.

Curran, J. (2000). Rethinking media and democracy. In Curran, J., & Gurevitch, M. (Eds.), *Mass Media and Society* (pp. 120–154). London: Arnold.

Dahlberg, L. (2001). Computer-mediated communication and the public sphere: A critical analysis. *Journal of Computer-Mediated Communication, 7*(1). Retrieved April 20, 2006, from http://jcmc.indiana.edu/vol7/issue1/dahlberg.html

Dahlberg, L. (2001). Extending the public sphere through cyberspace: The case of Minnesota. *E-Democracy, Peer Reviewed Journal on the Internet, 6*(3). Retrieved April 17, 2012, from http://firstmonday.org/htbin/cgiwrap/bin/ojs/index.php/fm/article/view/838/747

Dahlberg, L. (2005). The Habermasian public sphere: Taking difference seriously? *Theory and Society, 34*, 111–136. doi:10.1007/s11186-005-0155-z.

Dahlberg, L. (2005). The corporate colonization of online attention and the marginalization of critical communication? *The Journal of Communication Inquiry, 29*(2), 1–21. doi:10.1177/0196859904272745.

Dahlgren, P. (2001). The public sphere and the net: Structure, space and communication. In Bennett, L. W., & Entman, R. M. (Eds.), *Mediated politics: Communication in the future of democracy* (pp. 33–55). Cambridge, UK: Cambridge University Press.

Dahlgren, P. (2001). The Transformation of Democracy? In Axford, B., & Huggins, R. (Eds.), *New Media and Politics* (pp. 64–68). London: Sage. doi:10.4135/9781446218846.n3.

Dahlgren, P. (2005). The Internet, public spheres, and political communication: Dispersion and deliberation. *Political Communication, 22*, 147–162. doi:10.1080/10584600590933160.

Dare, S. (2007). *Guerrilla Journalism: Dispatches from the Underground*. Ibadan, Nigeria: Kraft Books Limited.

Daughety, T., Eastin, M, & Bright, L. (2008). Exploring consumer motivations for creating user-generated content. *Journal of Interactive advertising, 8*(2), 1-24.

Davidson, O., & Mwakasonda, S. A. (2004). Electricity access for the poor: A study of South Africa and Zimbabwe. *Journal of International Energy Initiative, VIII*(4), 26–40.

Davies, M. M., & Mosdell, N. (2006). *Practical Research Methods for Media and Cultural Studies: Making People Count.* Edinburgh, UK: Edinburgh University Press.

Davis, G. (2010, February 12). Zuma promises year of action. *Cape Times.* Retrieved April 30, 2012, from http://www.iol.co.za/index.php?set_id=1&click_id=13&art_id=vn20100212042130569C413199

Davis, R., Baumgartner, J., Francia, P., & Morris, J. (2009). The Internet in US. Election campaigns. In Chadwick, A., & Howard, P. N. (Eds.), *Routledge Handbook of Internet Politics* (pp. 13–24). London: Routledge.

De Beer, A. (1997). *The state of journalism education in Africa – East, West and South: An overview for the World Conference on Journalism Education.* Institute for Media Analysis in South Africa.

De Koster, W., & Houtman, D. (2008). Stormfront is like a second home to me: On virtual community formation by right-wing extremists. *Information Communication and Society, 11*(6), 1155–1176. doi:10.1080/13691180802266665.

Della Porta, D., & Diani, M. (2006). *Social Movements: An Introduction.* Malden, MA: Blackwell Publishing.

Desrues, T., & Moyano, E. (2001). Social Change and Political Transition in Morocco. *Mediterranean Politics, 6*(1), 21–47. doi:10.1080/713604490.

Deuze, M. (2002). Global journalism education and Sanef audit: major issues to be taken seriously. *Ecquid Novi, 23*(1), 89–93.

Dewey, J. (1996). The Collected Works of John Dewey, 1882-1953. Charlottesville, VA: Intel ex. Corporation.

Dewey, J. (1954). *The Public and its Problems.* Denver, CO: Swallow.

Diamond, L. (2002). Elections Without Democracy Thinking about Hybrid Regimes. *Journal of Democracy, 13*, 21–35. doi:10.1353/jod.2002.0025.

Diamond, L. (2008). Consolidating Democracy. In Leduc, L., Norris, P., & Niemi, R. (Eds.), *Comparing Democracies 2 New Challenges in the Study of Elections and Voting* (pp. 210–227). London: Sage Publications.

Diamond, L. (2008). Progress and Retreat in Africa the Rule of Law vs. the Big man. *Journal of Democracy, 19*, 138–149. doi:10.1353/jod.2008.0029.

Diamond, L. (2010). Liberation technology. *Journal of Democracy, 21*(3), 69–83. doi:10.1353/jod.0.0190.

Diamond, L. J. (1996). Is the third wave over? *Journal of Democracy, 7*(3), 20–37. doi:10.1353/jod.1996.0047.

Diani, M. (2000). The Concept of Social Movement. In Nash, K. (Ed.), *Readings in Contemporary Political Sociology* (pp. 155–176). Malden, MA: Blackwell.

Dicklitch, S., & Lwanga, D. (2003). The politics of being non-political: Human rights organizations and the creation of a positive human rights culture in Uganda. *Human Rights Quarterly, 25*(2), 482–509. doi:10.1353/hrq.2003.0015.

DiMaggio, P., Hagittai, W., & Neuman, R. (2001). Social Implications of the Internet. *Annual Review of Sociology, 27*, 307–336. doi:10.1146/annurev.soc.27.1.307.

Dominick, J. R. (2005). *The Dynamics of Mass Communications: Media in the Digital Age* (8th ed.). New York: McGraw Hill.

Douai, A. (2009). In democracy's shadow: The 'new' independent press and the limits of media reform in Morocco. *Westminster Papers in Communication and Culture, 6*(1), 7–26.

Douai, A., & Moussa, M. B. (2013). Twitter frames: Finding social media's "influentials'" during the "Arab Spring.". In Olorunnisola, A., & Douai, A. (Eds.), *New Media Influence on Social and Political Change in Africa.* (202-217) Hershey, PA: IGI-Global.

Douai, A., & Olorunnisola, A. A. (2013). New Media and the Question of African Democracy. In Olorunnisola, A., & Douai, A. (Eds.), *New Media Influence on Social and Political Change in Africa.* (1-14) Hershey, PA: IGI-Global.

Downey, J., & Fenton, N. (2003). New media, counter publicity and the public sphere. *New Media & Society*, *5*(2), 185–202. doi:10.1177/1461444803005002003.

Downing, J. (2001). *Radical media: Rebellious communication and social movements*. London: Sage.

Downing, J. (2003). Audiences and readers of alternative media: The absent lure of the virtually unknown. *Media Culture & Society*, *25*, 625–645. doi:10.1177/01634437030255004.

Downing, J. (2008). Social movement theories and alternative media: An evaluation and critique. *Communication, Culture & Critique*, *1*, 40–50. doi:10.1111/j.1753-9137.2007.00005.x.

Downing, J. D. H. (1992). The alternative public realm: The organisation of the 1980s anti-nuclear press in West Germany and Britain. In Scannell, P., Schlesinger, P., & Sparks, C. (Eds.), *Culture and power: A media, culture and society reader* (pp. 259–277). London: Sage.

Dralega, C. A. (2008). *ICT Based Development of Marginal Communities: Participatory Approaches to Communication, Empowerment and Engagement in Rural Uganda*. Oslo, Norway: Faculty of Humanities.

Dreyfuss, R. (2011). Who's behind Egypt's revolt? *The Nation*. Retrieved on March 14, 2011, from: http://www.thenation.com/blog/158159/whos-behind-egypts-revolt

Du Plooy, G. M. (Ed.). (1995). *Introduction to communication. Course Book 2. Communication Research*. Kenwyn, South Africa: Juta & Co. Ltd..

Dunn, A. (2011). Unplugging a nation: State media strategy during Egypt's January 25 Uprising. *World Affairs*, *35*(2), 15–24.

Dutta, S., & Mia, I. (Eds.). (2011). *The Global Information Technology Report 2010-2011* (10th ed.). Geneva, Switzerland: World Economic Forum. Retrieved June 10, 2011, from http://www.weforum.org/reports/global-information-technology-report-2010-2011-0

Dutton, W. H., Shepherd, A., & di Gennaro, C. (2007). Digital divides and choices reconfiguring access: National and cross-national patterns of Internet diffusion and use. In Anderson, B., Brynin, M., Gershuny, J., & Raban, Y. (Eds.), *Information and Communication Technologies in Society: E-living in a Digital Europe* (pp. 31–45). London: Routledge.

Dzamara, I. (2007). Doctors' strike: 60000 dead. *The Zimbabwean*, I, February, 2007.

Ebner, M., Lienhardt, C., Rohs, M., & Meyer, I. (2010). Microblogs in higher education-A chance to facilitate informal and process-oriented learning. *Computers & Education*, *55*, 92–100. doi:10.1016/j.compedu.2009.12.006.

Echwalu, E. (2011). *Ugandan media censored over 'walk to work' protests*. Retrieved on January 14, 2012, from http://cpj.org/blog/2011/04/ugandanmedia-censored-over-walk-to-work-protests.php

Economist. (2008, February 7). *Ethnic cleansing in Luoland*. Retrieved November 21, 2008, from http://www.economist.com/world/mideast-africa/displaystory.cfm?story_id=10653938

Economy. *Online Etymology Dictionary*. Retrieved July 30, 2010, from http://etymonline.com/index.php?term=economy&allowed_in_frame=0

Eddouada, S. (2001). Feminism and Politics in Moroccan Feminist Non-Governmental Organisations. Retrieved January 13, 2013, from http://www.postcolonialweb.org/poldiscourse/casablanca/eddouada2.html

Edström, Y. (2010). *"We are like Chameleons!" Changing mediascapes, Cultural Identities and City Sisters in Dar es Salaam*. Uppsala, Sweden: Acta Universitatis Upsaliensis.

Egypt. (2003). *Telecommunications Acts*. Retrieved March 17, 2011, from http://www.mcit.gov.eg/Content.aspx?Cat=3&SubCat=10

Ehidiamen, J. (2011). Nigerian youth celebrate social media as tool of successful election. Retrieved April 29, 2011, from http://www.globalpressinstitute.org/africa/nigeria/nigerian-youth-celebrate-social-media-tool-successful-election

Ekine, S. (2010). *SMS Uprising: Mobile phone activism in Africa*. Oxford, UK: Pambazuka Press.

Ekpu, R. (1990). Nigeria's Embattled Fourth Estate. *Journal of Democracy*, *1*, 107–116. doi:10.1353/jod.1990.0025.

El Badry, Y. (2012). Military to form committee to provide 'true information' to the media (trans. from Al-Masry Al-Youm). *Egypt Independent*. Retrieved January 12, 2013, from http://www.almasryalyoum.com/en/node/604766

El Gundy, Z. (2012). Revolutionary activists take fight into cyberspace. *Ahram Online*. Retrieved January 12, 2013, from, http://english.ahram.org.eg/NewsContent/1/64/31488/Egypt/Politics-/Revolutionary-activists-take-fight-into-cyberspace.aspx

El Kobbi, M. (1992). *L'Etat et la Presse au Maroc*. Paris: L'auteur.

El-Hennawy, N. (2011). Looking to consolidate its influence, Brotherhood takes to the media. *Egypt Independent*. Retrieved January 12, 2013, from http://www.almasryalyoum.com/en/node/572181

Ellis, S., & Kessel, I. (Eds.). (2009). Introduction: African social movements or social movements in Africa? In S. Ellis & I. van Kessel (Eds.), Movers and Shakers: Social Movements in Africa (pp. 1–16). Leiden, Netherlands: Brill.

el-Shemi, A., & Perry, T. (2013). Violence, protesters return to Tahrir Square, Suez as Egypt marks Revolution. Retrieved January 29, 2013, from http://worldnews.nbcnews.com/_news/2013/01/25/16692054-violence-protesters-return-to-tahir-square-suez-as-egypt-marks-revolution?lite

Eltantawy, N., & Wiest, J. (2011). Social media in the Egyptian revolution: Reconsidering resource mobilization theory. *International Journal of Communication*, *5*, 1207–1224. Retrieved from http://ijoc.org/ojs/index.php/ijoc.

Emerson, T. (1982). The First Amendment in the Year 2000. In Halpern, S. (Ed.), *The Future of our Liberties: Perspectives on the Bill of Rights* (pp. 57–73). Westport, CT: Greenwood.

Entman, R. (1993). Framing: Towards clarification of a fractured paradigm. *The Journal of Communication*, *43*(4), 51–58. doi:10.1111/j.1460-2466.1993.tb01304.x.

Eriksen, T. H. (1993, 2002). ethnicity and nationalism: Anthropological perspectives (2nd ed). London: Pluto Press.

Eskandar, A. (2007, May 7). Lines in the sand: Problematizing Arab media in the post-taxonomic era. *Arab Media & Society*. Retrieved from http://www.arabmediasociety.com/index.php?article=226&p=4

Essoungou, A. (2011). A social media boom begins in Africa. *Africa Renewal*. Retrieved August 22, 2011, from http://www.un.org/africarenewal/magazine/december-2010/social-media-boom-begins-africa

Ethiopian Press Agency. (2008). Basis and directives for a developmental and democratic philosophy of our media operation. Draft policy document.

Etzo, S., & Collender, G. *The mobile phone revolution in Africa: Rhetoric or reality?* DOI: 10.1093/afraf/adq045.

Eur, A. C. (2009). *Report 2009 on press freedom: Rwanda*. Retrieved April 19, 2011, from http://www.eurac-network.org/web/

Evans, W. (2008). Social marketing campaigns and children's media use, the future of children. *Children and Electronic Media*, *18*(1). Retrieved from http://futureofchildren.org/publications/journals/journal_details/index.xml?journalid=32

Evans, D. (2008). *Social Media Marketing: An Hour a Day*. London: Wiley.

Eyes on Kenya. (2008, February 7). *Eyes on the media in Kenya: Kenya's wolf in sheep skin or her redemption?* Retrieved December 21, 2008, from http://eyesonkenya.org/blog/?p=55

Fairclough, N. (1989). *Language and power*. London: Logman.

Fairclough, N. (1992). *Discourse and social change*. Cambridge, UK: Polity Press.

Fairclough, N. (2002). *Media Discourse (reprint)*. London: Arnold.

Fairclough, N., & Wodak, R. (1997). Critical discourse analysis. In van Dijk, T. A. (Ed.), *Discourse as social interaction. Discourse studies: A multidiciplinary introduction* (pp. 258–284). London: Sage.

Faquihi, F. (23 April 2010). 2M Capte plus de téléspectateur qu'Al Oula. *L'Economiste*, p. 12.

Fardon, R., & Furniss, G. (2000). African broadcast cultures. In Fardon, R., & Furniss, G. (Eds.), *African broadcast cultures: Radio in transition* (pp. 1–20). Oxford, UK: James Currey.

Faris, D. (2009). The end of the beginning: The failure of April 6th and the future of electronic activism in Egypt. *Arab Media & Society, 9*(Fall). Retrieved January 28, 2013, from http://www.arabmediasociety.com/?article=723

Fastenberg, D. (2010, October 20). Why is Twitter so popular in Brazil? *Time Magazine*. Retrieved January 13, 2013, from http://www.time.com/time/world/article/0,8599,2026442,00.html

Federal Government of Nigeria. (1987). *Nigeria Mass Communication Policy*. Lagos, Nigeria: Federal Government Press.

Federal Government of Nigeria. (1990). *Official Secret Act*. Lagos, Nigeria: Federal Government Press.

Federal Government of Nigeria. (1992). *National Broadcasting Commission Act No. 38*. Lagos, Nigeria: Federal Government Press.

Federal Government of Nigeria. (1999). *National Broadcasting Commission Act No. 55*. Lagos, Nigeria: Federal Government Press.

Federal Government of Nigeria. (1999). *Nigeria Criminal Code*. Lagos, Nigeria: Federal Government Press.

Federal Government of Nigeria. (2011). *Freedom of Information Act*. Lagos, Nigeria: Federal Government Press.

Federal Republic of Nigeria. (1999). *1999 Constitution of the Federal Republic of Nigeria*. Lagos, Nigeria: Federal Government Press.

Feintuck, M. (1999). *Media Regulation, Public Interest and the Law*. Edinburgh, Scotland: Edinburgh University Press.

Fenton, N. (2008). New Media, Politics and Resistance. *International Journal of Cultural Studies, 11*(2), 230–248. doi:10.1177/1367877908089266.

Ferguson, J. (2006). *Global Shadows. Africa in the Neoliberal World Order*. Durham, NC: Duke University Press.

Findahl, O. (1999). Public Service Broadcasting–A fragile, yet durable Construction. *Nordicom Review, 20*, 13–19.

Fisher, S. (2011). *Modernisation, Post-Materialism, Dealignment and Party-System Change*. Oxford, UK: Oxford University.

Fitch Ratings. (2012). South Africa mine violence highlights structural challenges. Retrieved on August 24, 2012, from www.fitchratings.com

Flanagan, J. (2010, February 27). Jacob Zuma prepares for tea at Buckingham Palace. *Telegraph*. Retrieved April 30, 2012, from http://www.telegraph.co.uk/news/worldnews/africaandindianocean/southafrica/7333017/Jacob-Zuma-prepares-for-tea-at-Buckingham-Palace.html

Flew, T. (2005). *New media: An introduction*. Melbourne, Australia: Oxford University Press.

Foot, K., Xenos, M., Schneider, S., Kluver, R., & Jankowsky, N. (2009). Electoral Web production practice in Cross-National Perspective: The Relative Influence of National Development, Political Culture, and Web Genre. In Chadwick, A., & Howard, P. N. (Eds.), *Routledge Handbook of Internet Politics* (pp. 140–155). London: Routledge.

Forbrig, J. (2005). *Revisiting Youth Political Participation: Challenges for Research and Democratic Practice in Europe*. Strasbourg, France: Council of Europe.

Foucault, M. (1970). *The order of things: An archaeology of the human sciences*. New York: Pantheon Books.

Foundation for Democratic Process. (FODEP, 1996). Zambia's 18 November 1996 Presidential and Parliamentary Elections: Final Election Monitoring Report. Lusaka, Zambia.

Foundation for Democratic Process. (FODEP, 2002). Zambia's 27 December 2001 Presidential and Parliamentary Elections: Final Election Monitoring Report. Lusaka, Zambia.

Fourie, P. J. (Ed.). (2001). *Media studies. Institutions, Theories and Issues (Vol. 1)*. Lansdowne, PA: Juta.

Fraser, N. (1990). Rethinking the public sphere: A contribution to the critique of actually existing democracy. *Social Text*, (25/26): 56–80. doi:10.2307/466240.

Fraser, N. (1995). From Redistribution to Recognition: Dilemmas of Justice in a 'Post-Socialist' Age. *New Left Review, 212*, 68–93.

Freedman, E., & Shafer, R. (2008). *Ambitious in theory but unlikely in practice: A critique of UNESCO's Model Curricula for Journalism Education for Developing Countries and Emerging Democracies.* Paper presented at the International Association for Media and Communication Research. Stockholm, Sweden.

Freedom House. (2009). *Special report: Kenya.* Retrieved March 16, 2011, from http://freedomhouse.org/template.cfm?page=384&key=209&parent=19&report=79

Freedom House. (2010). *Freedom of the Press.* Retrieved from http://www.freedomhouse.org/

Freedom House. (2010). *Press freedom: Kenya.* Retrieved February 24, 2010, from http://www.freedomhouse.org/template.cfm?page=251&year=2010

Freedom House. (2010). *Press Freedom: Egypt.* Retrieved February 24, 2011, from http://www.freedomhouse.org/template.cfm?page=251&year=2010

Freeland, C. (2011). The Middle East and the groupon effect. *AFP.* Retrieved January 12, 2013, from http://blogs.reuters.com/chrystia-freeland/2011/02/18/the-middle-east-and-the-groupon-effect/

Freemantle, S. (2011). The five trends powering Africa's enduring allure. Retrieved from http://www.standardbank.com/Article.aspx?id=-127&src=m2011_34385466

Frère, M.-S. (1998). *Les Mots et les maux de la démocratie: Analyse du registre lexical et thématique de la transition démocratique dans la presse béninoise. Recherche en Communication* (pp. 119–146). Louvain-La-Neuve, Belgium: Université Catholique de Louvain.

Frère, M.-S. (2009). After the hate media: Regulation in the DRC, Burundi and Rwanda. *Global Media and Communication, 5*(3), 327–352. doi:10.1177/1742766509348675.

Fürsich, E., & Shrikhande, S. (2007). Development Broadcasting in India and Beyond: Redefining on Old Mandate in the Age of Media Globalization. *Journal of Broadcasting & Electronic Media, 51*(1), 110–128. doi:10.1080/08838150701308101.

Gadzekpo, A. (2005). *Ghana: Country Assessment Paper.* Legon, Ghana: University of Ghana.

Gadzekpo, A. (2006). *Guardians of Democracy: The Media and Good Governance. School of Communication Studies.* Legon, Ghana: University of Ghana.

Gaffney, D. (2010). iranElection: Quantifying online activism. In *Proceedings of the WebSci10: Extending the Frontiers of Society On-Line.* Raleigh, NC. Retrieved January 13, 2013, from http://journal.webscience.org/295/2/websci10_submission_6.pdf

Gaier, E., & Smith, J. (2008). Improving governance through symbiotic media structures. *Democracy and Society, 8*(2), 8–10.

Gamson, W. A., & Modigliani, A. (1989). Media discourse and public opinion on nuclear power: A constructionist approach. *American Journal of Sociology, 95*(1), 1–37. doi:10.1086/229213.

Gandy, O. (2002). The real digital divide: Citizens versus consumers. In Lievrouw, L. A., & Livingstone, S. (Eds.), *Handbook of New Media: Social Shaping And Consequences of ICTs* (pp. 448–460). London: Sage.

Gans, H. J. (1980). *Deciding What's News: A Study of CBS Evening News, NBC Nightly News, Newsweek, and Time.* New York: Vintage Books.

Garcia, M., & Fares, J. (2008). *Youth in Africa's Labour Market.* Washington, DC: The World Bank.

Gathara, P., & Wanjau, M. K. (2009). Bringing change through laughter: Cartooning in Kenya. In N.J. Kimani & J.J. Middleton (Eds.), Media and Identity in Africa (275-286). Edinburgh, UK: Edinburgh University Press.

Gazzar, S. E. (2011). Government restores internet service after a weeklong shutdown. *Wall Street Journal.* Retrieved March 1, 2011, from http://online.wsj.com/article/SB10001424052748703960804576119690514692446.html?mod=googlenews_wsj

Gettleman, J. (2010). Africa's forever wars: Why the continent's conflicts never end. *Foreign Policy,* March/April. Retrieved January 28, 2013, from http://www.foreignpolicy.com/articles/2010/02/22/africas_forever_wars

Gettleman, J. (2011). Somalia's rebels Embrace Twitter as a Weapon. *New York Times.* Retrieved February 1, 2012, from http://www.nytimes.com/2011/12/15/world/africa/somalias-rebels-embrace-twitter-as-a-weapon.html?_r=3

Ghannam, J. (2011). Social *media in the Arab world: Leading up to the uprisings of 2011. A report to the Center for International Media Assistance.* Retrieved January 12, 2013, from http://cima.ned.org/publications/social-media-arab-world-leading-uprisings-2011-0

Gibson, R., & Ward, S. (2011). Renouveler le parti? Les stratégies de campagne et d'organisation en ligne des partis britanniques. In Greffet, F. (Ed.), *Continuerlalutte. com. Les partis politiques sur le web* (pp. 109–123). Paris: Sciences Po. Les Presses.

Giglio, M. (2011, February 21). The Facebook freedom fighter. *Newsweek*.

Gilberds, H. (2013). Articulations and rearticulations: Antagonisms of media reform in Africa. In Olorunnisola, A., & Douai, A. (Eds.), *New Media Influence on Social and Political Change in Africa (51-66)*. Hershey, PA: IGI-Global.

Gimmler, A. (2001). Deliberative democracy, the public sphere and the internet. *Philosophy and Social Criticism, 27*(4), 21–39. doi:10.1177/019145370102700402.

Girard, B. (1992). *A passion for radio: Radio waves and community*. Montreal, Canada: Black Rose Books.

Gladwell, M. (2002). Small change - Why the revolution will not be tweeted. *The New Yorker*. Retrieved from http://www.newyorker.com/reporting/2010/10/04/101004fa_fact_gladwell

Gladwell, M. (2000). *The tipping point: How little things can make a big difference*. Boston, MA: Back Bay Books.

Globacom Nigeria. (n.d.). In *Facebook*. Retrieved from https://www.facebook.com/GloWorld

Global, T. N. S. (2012). *Social skills in the classroom: Digital media use in Sub-Saharan Africa*. Retrieved from http://www.tnsglobal.com/sites/default/files/whitepaper/TNS_In_Focus_digital_media_SSA.pdf

Goguen, J. *Against Technological Determinism*. Retrieved October 20, 2009, from http://citeseerx.ist.psu.edu/viewdoc/download?doi=10.1.1.125.2540&rep=rep1&type=pdf#page=87

Golding, P. (1977). Media Professionalism in the Third World: The transfer of ideology. In Curran, J., Gurewitch, M., & Woollacott, J. (Eds.), *Mass Communication and Society* (pp. 291–308). London: Arnold & Open University Press.

Goldsmith, J., & Wu, T. (2006). *Who Controls the Internet?: Illusions of a Borderless World*. New York: Oxford University Press.

Goldstein, J., & Rotich, J. (2010). Digitally networked technology in Kenya's 2007-08 post-election crisis. In Ekine, S. (Ed.), *SMS Uprising: Mobile phone activism in Africa*. Oxford, UK: Pambazuka Press.

Goldstone, J. A. (2001). Demography, Environment and Security. M. Weiner & S. Stanton Russel (Eds.), Demography and National Security. New York: Berghahn Books.

Gomez, J. (2004). Dumbing down democracy: Trends in Internet regulation, Surveillance and Control in Asia. *Pacific Journalism Review, 10*(2), 130–150.

Goodall, H. L. Jr, Cheong, P. H., Fleischer, K., & Corman, S. R. (2012). Rhetorical charms: The promise and pitfalls of humor and ridicule as strategies to counter extremist narratives. *Perspectives in Terrorism, 6*(1), 70–79.

Goode, L. (2005). *Jürgen Habermas: Democracy and the public sphere*. London: Pluto Press.

Government of Zimbabwe. (2005). *E-Readiness Survey Report*. Harare, Zimbabwe: Ministry of Information and Communication Technology.

Graft, P. V., & Svenson, J. (2006). Explaining eDemocracy development: A quantitative empirical study. *Information Polity, 11*, 123–134.

Gramsci, A. (1971). *Selections from prison notebooks*. London: Lawrence and Wishart.

Grant, A., & Wilkinson, J. (Eds.). (2009). *Understanding media convergence: The state of the field*. Oxford, UK: Oxford University Press.

Greffet, F. (2011). *L'Internet ou l'espace des possible. Les campagnes françaises en ligne depuis 2007. Continuerlalutte.com. Les partis politiques sur le web* (pp. 15–37). Paris: Sciences Po. Les Presses.

Grossman, L. (2009, June 17). Iran's protests: Why Twitter is the medium of the movement. *Time Magazine*. Retrieved January 13, 2013, from http://www.time.com/time/world/article/0,8599,1905125,00.html

Gruzd, A., Wellman, B., & Takhteyev, Y. (2011). Imagining Twitter as an Imagined Community. *American Behavioral Scientist Special issue on Imagined Communities*. Retrieved January 13, 2013, from http://homes.chass.utoronto.ca/~wellman/publications/imagining_twitter/Imagining%20Twitter_AG_Sep1_2010_final.pdf

Gruzd, A., Wellman, B., & Takhteyev, Y. (2011, July 25). Imagining Twitter as an imagined community. *The American Behavioral Scientist, 55*(10), 1294–1318. doi:10.1177/0002764211409378.

Gunther, R., & Mugham, A. (2000). *Democracy and the Media: A Comparative Perspective.* New York: Cambridge Press. doi:10.1017/CBO9781139175289.

Gyimah-Boadi, E. (1997). Civil Society in Africa: The Good, the Bad, the Ugly. *Journal for a Civil Society, 1*(1). Retrieved from http://civnet.org/journal/issue1/egboadi.htm.

Gyimah-Boadi, E. (2004). *Democratic reform in Africa: The quality of progress.* Boulder, CO: Lynne Rienner.

Habermas, D. (1996). *Between Facts and Norms: Contributions to a Discourse of Law and Democracy.* Cambridge, UK: Polity Press.

Habermas, J. (1989). *The structural transformation of the public sphere: An inquiry into a category of bourgeois society.* Cambridge, MA: MIT Press.

Habermas, J. (1992). *Between facts and norms: Contributions to a discourse theory of law and democracy.* Cambridge, MA: Polity Press.

HACA. (2009). *Rapport sur l'Attribution de Nouvelles Licences.* Retrieved June 9, 2010, from http://www.haca.ma/pdf/Rapport%20G2%20MEP.pdf

Hachten, W. A. (1971). *Muffled drums: The news media in Africa.* Ames, IA: Iowa University Press.

Hachten, W. A. (1981). *The World News Prism: Changing Media of International Communication* (3rd ed.). Ames, IA: Iowa State University Press.

Hackett, R. (2003) *Media reform: Democratizing the media, democratizing the state* [Review of the book]. *Canadian Journal of Communication, 28*(3). Retrieved April 19, 2011, from http://www.cjconline.ca/index.php/journal/article/view/1380/1457 HRNJ Uganda

Hackett, R., & Zhao, Y. (1998). *Sustaining democracy? Journalism and the Politics of Objectivity.* Toronto: Garamond Press.

Haggarty, L., Shirley, M. M., & Wallsten, S. (2002). *Telecommunication Reform in Ghana.* Retrieved from http://citeseerx.ist.psu.edu/viewdoc/download?doi=10.1.1.13.47&rep=rep1&type=pdf

Hague, B. N., & Loader, B. D. (1999). *Digital Democracy: Discourse and Decision Making in the Information Age.* London: Routledge.

Hallin, D. C., & Mancini, P. (2004). *Comparing media systems: Three models of media and politics.* New York: Cambridge University Press. doi:10.1017/CBO9780511790867.

Halverson, J. R., Goodall, H. L. Jr, & Corman, S. R. (2011). *Master Narratives of Islamic Extremism.* New York: Palgrave Macmillan.

Hamdy, N. (2009). Arab citizen journalism in action: Challenging mainstream media, authorities and media laws. *Westminster Papers in Communication and Culture, 6*(1), 92–112.

Hamelink, C. (1983). *Cultural Autonomy in Global Communications. Planning National Information Policy.* New York, London: Longman.

Hamroush, A. (1989). *The story of journalism in Egypt.* Cairo, Egypt: Al Mostaqbal.

Hansen, D. Shneiderman, B., & Smith, M. (2011). Analyzing social media networks with NodeXL: Insights from a connected world. Burlington, MA: Morgan Kaufmann.

Hansen, A., Cottle, S., Negrine, R., & Newbold, C. (1998). *Mass Communication Research Methods.* London: Sage Publications.

Harper, D. (2001). Commodification. *Online Etymology Dictionary.* Retrieved July 30, 2010, from: http://etymonline.com/index.php?term=commodification&allowed_in_frame=0Politics. *Online Etymology Dictionary.* Retrieved July 30, 2010, from: http://etymonline.com/index.php?term=politics&allowed_in_frame=0

Harro-Loit, H. (2005). The Baltic and Norwegian journalism market. In Bærug, R. (Ed.), *The Baltic media world* (pp. 90–120). Riga, Latvia: Flera Printing House.

Hartley, W. (1995, February 18). It's time to get tough – Mandela. *The Natal Witness,* 1

Hassan, H. A. (2010). State versus society in Egypt: Consolidating democracy or upgrading autocracy. *African Journal of Political Science and International Relations*, *4*(9), 319–329.

Hasty, J. (2005). Sympathetic Magic/Contagious Corruption: Sociality, Democracy, and the Press. *Public Culture*, *17*, 339–370. doi:10.1215/08992363-17-3-339.

Hatchen, W. (1993). *The growth of media in the Third World*. Ames, IA: Iowa State University Press.

Hauser, G. (1998). Vernacular dialogue and the rhetoricality of public opinion. *Communication Monographs*, *65*(2), 83–107. doi:10.1080/03637759809376439.

Haut Autorité de la Communication Audiovisuelle. (2004). *Loi Relative à la Communication Audiovisuelle*. Retrieved April 15, 2010, from http://www.haca.ma/pdf/commaudiovisuelle.pdf

Haut Commissariat au Plan. (2004). *Recensement Général de la Population et de l'Habitat*. Retrieved May 20, 2010, from http://www.hcp.ma/pubData/Demographie/RGPH/RGPH_Rapport_National.pdf

Have No Tribe, I. (2008). *Posts – All*. Retrieved March 1, 2011, from http://www.ihavenotribe.com/posts.asp?page=2&c=

Hay, C. (2002). *Political analysis: A critical introduction*. New York: Palgrave.

Heaivilin, N., Gerbert, B., Page, J., & Gibbs, J. (2011). Public health surveillance of dental pain via Twitter. *Journal of Dental Research*, *90*(9), 1047–1051. doi:10.1177/0022034511415273 PMID:21768306.

Heath, C. W. (1988). Private sector partcipation in public service broadcasting: The case of Kenya. *The Journal of Communication*, *3*, 96–108. doi:10.1111/j.1460-2466.1988.tb02062.x.

Heeks, R. (2002). E-Government in Africa: Promise and practice. *Information Polity*, *7*, 97–114.

Heeks, R. (2007). Theorizing ICT4D research. *Information Technologies and International Development*, *3*(3), 4. doi:10.1162/itid.2007.3.3.1.

Heeks, R. (2010). Development 2.0: The IT-enabled Transformation of International Development. *Communications of the ACM*, *53*(4), 22–24. doi:10.1145/1721654.1721665.

Heeks, R. (2010). Do information and communication technologies (ICTs) contribute to development? *Journal of International Development*, *22*(5), 625–640. doi:10.1002/jid.1716.

Hegel (1896). *Hegel's Philosophy of Right*. Translated by S. W. Dyde. London: George Bell and Sons.

Hellyer, H. A. (2012). Violence and the Egyptian military. *Foreign Policy*. Retrieved January 12, 2013, from http://mideast.foreignpolicy.com/posts/2012/01/13/violence_and_the_egyptian_military

Henze, P. B. (1998). A political success story. *Journal of Democracy*, *9*(4), 40–54. doi:10.1353/jod.1998.0062.

Herbst, J. (2000). Understanding Ambiguity during Democratization in Africa. In Hollified, J., & Jillson, C. (Eds.), *Pathways to Democracy: The Political Economy of Democratic Transition* (pp. 275–289). London: Routledge.

Herskovitz, J., & Govender, P. (2012). *South Africa is not falling apart: Zuma*. Retrieved from http://www.msnbc.msn.com/id/50215912/ns/world_news-africa/t/south-africa-not-falling-apart-zuma/

Hidass, A. (1992). *Liberté et Communication au Maroc. L'Information au Maghreb*. Tunis, Tunisia: Ceres Production.

Hilbert, M. (2009). The Maturing Concept of E-Democracy: From E-Voting and Online Consultations to Democratic Value Out of Jumbled Online Chatter. *Journal of Information Technology & Politics*, *6*, 87–110. doi:10.1080/19331680802715242.

Hlongwane, S. (2012). *South Africa: ANC backtracks on key clauses, but the secrecy bill battle is far from won*. Retrieved from http://allafrica.com/stories/201208300390.html

Höhne, M. V. (2008). Newspapers in Hargeysa: Freedom of speech in post-conflict Somaliland. *Afrika Spectrum*, *43*(1), 91–113.

Holmes, S. (1990). Liberal Constraints on Private Power?: Reflections on the Origins and Rationale of Access Regulation. In Lichtenberg, J. (Ed.), *Democracy and the Mass Media* (pp. 21–65). Cambridge, UK: Cambridge University Press. doi:10.1017/CBO9781139172271.003.

Holtzhausen, D. (2002). A Postmodern Critique of Public Relations Theory and Practice. *Communicatio, 28*(1), 29–38. doi:10.1080/02500160208537955.

Honeycutt, C., & Herring, S. C. (2009). Beyond Microblogging: Conversation and Collaboration via Twitter. In Proceedings of *HICSS 2009* (pp. 1-10). Manoa, HI: IEEE Press. Retrieved January 13, 2013, from http://doi.ieeecomputersociety.org/10.1109/HICSS.2009.89

Howard, P. N. (2011). *The digital origins of dictatorship and democracy: Information technology and political Islam.* Oxford, UK: Oxford University Press. doi:10.1017/S1537592711004853.

Howard, P. N., Agarwal, S. D., & Hussain, M. M. (2011). When do States disconnect their digital networks? Regime responses to the political uses of social media. *Communication Review, 14*(3), 216–232. doi:10.1080/10714421.2011.597254.

Howard, P. N., & Parks, M. R. (2012). Social media and political change: Capacity, constraint, and consequence. *The Journal of Communication, 62*(2), 359–358. doi:10.1111/j.1460-2466.2012.01626.x.

Howard, P., & Hussein, M. (2011). The upheavals in Egypt and Tunisia: The role of the digital media. *Journal of Democracy, 22*(3), 35–48. Retrieved from http://www.journalofdemocracy.org/upheavals-egypt-and-tunisia-role-digital-media doi:10.1353/jod.2011.0041.

Howarth, D. R. (2000). *Discourse.* Philadelphia, PA: Open University Press.

Howley, K. (2003). *Community Media. People, Places, and Communication Technologies.* Cambridge, UK: Cambridge University Press.

Howley, K. (2009). *Understanding community media.* Thousand Oaks, CA: Sage.

Huberman, B. A., Romero, D. M., & Wu, F. (2008). Social networks that matter: Twitter under the microscope. *First Monday, 14*(1), 1-9. SSRN. Retrieved from http://arxiv.org/abs/0812.1045

Huberman, B., Romero, D., & Wu, F. (2009). Social networks that matter: Twitter under the microscope. *First Monday, 14*, 1–5.

Human Development Reports. (2005). *Fifty Years of Human Development & Perspectives to 2025.* Retrieved January 10, 2008, from http://hdr.undp.org/en/reports/nationalreports/arabstates/morocco/name,3380,en.html

Human Rights House Network. (2009). *Four radio stations closed in Uganda.* Retrieved September 11, 2009, from http://humanrightshouse.org/Articles/11722.html

Human Rights Network for Journalists-Uganda (HRNJ). (2010). *Mid-Year Press Freedom Index Report.* Retrieved January 5, 2011, from www.hrnjuganda.org

Human Rights Network for Journalists-Uganda (HRNJ). (2011). *Press Freedom Index Report 2011. Uganda. Shrinking and sinking.* Retrieved February 2, 2012, from http://www.hrnjuganda.org/reports/Press%20Freedom%20Index%20Annual%202011.pdf

Human Rights Watch. (2009, June 30). *An analysis of Ethiopia's draft anti-terrorism law. Report.*

Human Rights Watch. (2010). *Uganda: A media minefield. Increased threats to freedom of expression in Uganda.* New York: HRW.

Humphreys, P. (1996). *Mass Media and Media Policy in Western Europe.* Manchester, UK: Manchester University Press.

Hundt, M. (1995). *Modellbildung in der Wirtschaftssprache: Zur Geschichte der Institutionen- und Theoriefachsprachen der Wirtschaft.* Tübingen, Germany: Niemeyer. doi:10.1515/9783110954685.

Huntington, S. P. (1991). Democracy's third wave. *Journal of Democracy, 2*(2), 12–34. doi:10.1353/jod.1991.0016.

Husband, C. (2000). Media and the public sphere in multi-ethnic societies. In Cottle, S. (Ed.), *Issues in cultural and media studies: Ethnic minorities and the media.* Buckingham, UK: Open University Press.

Hyde-Clarke, N. (2010). *The Citizen in Communication.* Claremont, South Africa: Juta.

Hydén, G., & Okigbo, C. (2002). The media and the two waves of democracy. In Hydén, G., Leslie, M., & Ogundimu, F. F. (Eds.), *Media and democracy in Africa* (pp. 29–54). New Brunswick, NJ: Transaction Publishers.

Ibahrine, M. (2007). *The Internet and politics in Morocco: The political use of the Internet by Islam oriented political movements*. Berlin, Germany: VDM Verlag.

Ibrahim, E. (2011). Social media blockage during Egypt protests. *Ahram Online*. Retrieved March 1, 2011, from http://english.ahram.org.eg/NewsContent/1/64/4907/Egypt/Politics-/Social-media-blockage-during-Egypt-protests.aspx

Ibrahim, M. (2010). Radio stations with no music may be shut in Somalia. *New York Times*. Retrieved January 23, 2012, from http://www.nytimes.com/2010/04/19/world/africa/19somalia.html

IFEX. (2006). *Critical website Radio Katwe blocked on eve of presidential election*. Retrieved April 13, 2012, from http://www.ifex.org/uganda/2006/02/23/critical_website_radio_katwe_blocked/

Ifidon, E. (2003). Transitions from Democracy in Nigeria: Toward a Pre-emptive Analysis. *American Journal of Political Science, 7*(1), 109–128.

IMF/World Bank. (2001). How the International Monetary Fund and the World Bank undermine democracy and erode human rights: Five case studies. *Global Exchange*, 1-16.

Imoite, J. (2007). Youth Participation in Kenya Politics: Challenges and Opportunities. In *Youth and Politics in Conflict Contexts*. Washington, DC: Woodrow Wilson International Centre for Scholars.

Independent Online. (1999). *About IOL and Independent Newspapers*. Retrieved January 17, 2013, from: http://www.iol.co.za/about-iol-1.458#id.d2yhp2g99e8

International Crisis Group. (2005). *Counter-terrorism in Somalia: Losing hearts and Minds?* Retrieved from http://www.crisisgroup.org/en/regions/africa/horn-of-africa/somalia/095-counter-terrorism-in-somalia-losing-hearts-and-minds.aspx

International Research and Exchange Board (IREX). (2009). *Media strengthening in Rwanda program: Co-operative agreement and work plan narrative for July 2009-June 2011*. Washington, DC: IREX.

International Telecommunications Union [ITU]. (2010). Key global telecom indicators for the world telecommunication service sector. Retrieved on December 16, 2010, from http://www.itu.int/ITU-D/ict/statistics/at_glance/KeyTelecom.html

Internet World Stats. (2010). *Internet use in Zimbabwe*. Retrieved August 25, 2010, from http://www.internet-wordstats.com

Internet World Stats. (2010). Internet users and population statistics for Africa. Retrieved January 13, 2013, from http://www.internetworldstats.com/stats1.htm#africa

Internet World Stats. (n.d.). *Top 20 Internet Countries*. Retrieved from http://www.internetworldstats.com/top20.htm

Internetworldstats. (2008). *Internet Usage and Population Statistics* Retrieved January 12, 2012, from http://www.internetworldstats.com/africa.htm

Internews, E. (2008). *The promise of ubiquity: Mobile as media platform in the global South*. Retrieved March 23, 2012, from www.internews.eu

IRIN. (2008, January 22). *Kenya: Spreading the word of hate*. Retrieved November 12, 2008, from http://www.irinnews.org/printreport.aspx?reportid=76346

Isaacs, S. (2007). *ICT in education in Zimbabwe: Survey of ICT education in Africa*. Zimbabwe Country Report. Retrieved from http://www.infodev.org

Iskandar, A. (2006, July). *Paradox of the free press in Egypt*. USEF Expert Panel Discussion Notes. Washington, DC.

Iskandar, A. (2011, April 24). *Personal interview*. Washington, DC.

Iskandar, A. (2012). Egypt media flourish amid fears. *Huffington Post*. Retrieved January 12, 2013, from http://www.huffingtonpost.com/adel-iskandar/egypt-television_b_1195958.html

Iskander, E. (2011). Connecting the national and the virtual: Can Facebook activism remain relevant after Egypt's January 25 uprising? *International Journal of Communication, 5*, 1225–1237.

Ismail, J. A., & Deane, J. (2008). The 2007 General election in Kenya and its aftermath: The role of local language media. *The International Journal of Press/Politics, 3*(13), 319–327. doi:10.1177/1940161208319510.

Israel Loves Iran. (n.d.). *Israel Loves Iran*. Retrieved from http://www.israelovesiran.com/

Izama, A. (2010). Journalist arrested over Kampala bomb blast story. *The Daily Monitor*. August 4, 2010.

Jackoway, A., Samet, H., & Sankaranarayanan, J. (2011). Identification of live news events using Twitter. In *Proceedings of the 3rd ACM SIGSPATIAL International Workshop on Location-Based Social Networks (LBSN '11)*. New York: ACM press.

Jacobs, S. (1999). Tensions of a Free Press: South Africa after Apartheid. Paper presented at the Joan Shorenstein Center on the Press, Politics and Public Policy. Cambridge, MA.

Jacobs, S. (2003). Reading Politics, Reading Media. In Jacobs, S., & Wassermann, H. (Eds.), *Shifting Selves-Post-Apartheid Essays on Mass Media, Culture and Identity* (pp. 29–53). Cape Town, South Africa: Kwela Books.

Jallov, B. (2011). How Can the Internet and Social Media Contribute to Development Communication for Empowerment. In Braskov, R. S. (Ed.), *Social Media in Development Communication*. Roskilde, Denmark: Roskilde Universitets Trykkeri.

Janas, J. (1991). *History of the mass media in Ethiopia*. Warsaw, Poland: Warsaw University Press.

Jansen, B., Zhang, M., Sobel, K., & Chowdury, A. (2009). Twitter power: Tweets as electronic word of mouth. *Journal of the American Society for Information Science and Technology, 60*(11), 2169–2188. doi:10.1002/asi.21149.

Java, A., Song, X., Finin, T., & Tseng, B. (2007). Why we Twitter: Understanding Microblogging usage and communities. In *Proceedings of the 9th WebKDD and 1st NA-KDD 2007 Workshop on Web Mining and Social Network analysis* (pp. 56-65). San Jose, CA: ACM.

Javuru, K. (2013). New media and the changing public sphere in Uganda. In Olorunnisola, A., & Douai, A. (Eds.), *New Media Influence on Social and Political Change in Africa (357-378)*. Hershey, PA: IGI-Global.

Jeffrey, H. (2000). Understanding Ambiguity during Democratization in Africa. In Hollified, J., & Jillson, C. (Eds.), *Pathways to Democracy: The Political Economy of Democratic Transition* (pp. 245–258). London: Routledge.

Jenkins, H. (2012). *Confessions of an Aca-Fan, Contextualizing #Kony2012: Invisible Children, Spreadable Media, and Transmedia Activism*. Retrieved March 12, 2012, from http://henryjenkins.org/2012/03/contextualizing_kony2012_invis.html

Jenkins, G. (2008). Resource Mobilisation Theory and the Study of Social Movements. In Ruggiero, V., & Montagna, N. (Eds.), *Social Movements: A reader* (pp. 118–127). London: Routledge.

Jenkins, H. (2004). The cultural logic of media convergence. *International Journal of Cultural Studies, 7*(1), 33–43. doi:10.1177/1367877904040603.

Jenkins, H. (2006). *Convergence Culture: Where Old and New Media Collide*. New York: New York Uninversity Press.

Jerome, A., & Zuniga, M. M. (2006). *Crashing the gate: Netroots, grassroots and the rise of people-powered politics*. White River Junction, VT: Chelsea Green Publishing Company.

Jibo, M., & Okoosi, A. (2003). The Nigerian Media: An Assessment of its Role in Achieving Transparent and Accountable Government in the Fourth Republic. *Nordic Journal of African Studies, 12*(2), 180–195.

Johnson, J. (2002). In-depth interviewing. In Gubrium, J., & Holstein, J. (Eds.), *Handbook of Interview Research: Context and Method* (pp. 83–103). Thousands Oaks, CA: Sage Publications.

Johnson, P. (2006). *Habermas: Rescuing the public sphere*. London: Routledge.

Johnstone, J. W. C., Slawski, E. J., & Bowman, W. W. (1976). *The news people: A sociological portrait of American journalist and their work*. Urbana, IL: University of Illinois Press.

Jones, S. G. (2013). The mirage of the Arab Spring: Deal with the region you have not the region you want. *Foreign Policy*, January/February. Retrieved January 29, 2013, from http://www.foreignaffairs.com/articles/138478/seth-g-jones/the-mirage-of-the-arab- spring

Jones, N., & Pitcher, S. (2010). Traditions, conventions and ethics: Online dilemmas in South African journalism. In Hyde-Clarke, N. (Ed.), *The Citizen and Communication: Revisiting Traditional, New and Community Media Practices in Southern Africa* (pp. 97–112). Claremont, South Africa: Juta & Co. Ltd..

Joseph, R. (1991). Africa: The Rebirth of Political Freedom. *Journal of Democracy*, 2, 20–24. doi:10.1353/jod.1991.0055.

Joseph, R. (2008). Progress and Retreat in Africa Challenges of a Frontier Region. *Journal of Democracy*, 19, 94–108. doi:10.1353/jod.2008.0028.

Kadida, J. (2010). Ringing in change: News can be distributed widely in Kenya, but so can hate speech. *Index on Censorship*, 39, 150–152. doi:10.1177/0306422010362319.

Kalyango, Y. Jr, & Eckler, P. (2010). Media performance, agenda building, and democratization in East Africa. In Salmon, C. T. (Ed.), *Communication Yearbook, 34*, 354–89. New York: Routledge.

Kalyegira, T. (2010). *Panic grips Ugandan government over Kampala bomb blasts*. Retrieved November 19, 2010, from www.ugandarecord.co.ug/index.php?issue=68&article=836&seo=Panicgrips Uganda government over Kampala bomb blasts

Kamwangamalu, N. K. (2003). Social change and language shift: South Africa. *Annual Review of Applied Linguistics*, 23, 225–242. doi:10.1017/S0267190503000291.

Kandell, J. J. (1998). Internet addiction on campus: The vulnerability of college students. *Cyberpsychology & Behavior*, 1(1), 11–17. doi:10.1089/cpb.1998.1.11.

Kanyinga, K., Okello, D., & Akoko, A. (2010). Contradictions of Transition to Democracy in Fragmented Societies: The Kenya 2007 General Elections in Perspective. In K. Kanyinga, & D. Okello (Eds.), Tensions and Reversals in Democratic Transitions (1-28). Nairobi, Kenya: University of Nairobi.

Kaplan, A. M., & Haenlein, M. (2010). Users of the world, unite! The challenges and opportunities of social media. *Business Horizons*, 53(1), 59–68. doi:10.1016/j.bushor.2009.09.003.

Kareire, P. (2009). *Facebook 360 network meeting face to face*. Retrieved November 22, 2012, from http://www.newvision.co.ug/D/8/217/694033

Karikari, K. (2010, August). African media breaks 'culture of silence'. *Africa Renewal*, pp. 23–25.

Kasoma, T. (2007). *Brown envelope journalism and professionalism in development reporting: A comparison of Zambia and Ghana*. Unpublished PhD dissertation, University of Oregon, Oregon, USA.

Kasoma, F. (1997). Communication and press freedom in Zambia. In Eribo, F., & Jong-Ebot, W. (Eds.), *Press Freedom and Communication in Africa* (pp. 135–156). Asmara, Eritrea: Africa World Press.

Kasoma, F. P. (1995). The role of the independent media in Africa's change to democracy. *Media Culture & Society*, 537–555. doi:10.1177/016344395017004002.

Kasoma, F. P. (1996). The foundations of African ethics (Afriethics) and the professional practice of journalism: The case of society-centered media morality. *Africa Media Review*, 10(3), 93–116.

Kasoma, F. P. (1997). The independent press and politics in Africa. *International Communication Gazette*, 59, 295–310. doi:10.1177/0016549297059004004.

Kasoma, T. (2013). Media regulation and journalists' perceptions of their role in society: A case of Zambia and Ghana. In Olorunnisola, A., & Douai, A. (Eds.), *New Media Influence on Social and Political Change in Africa (101-117)*. Hershey, PA: IGI-Global.

Katulis, B. (2004). *Women's freedom in focus: Morocco*. Retrieved June 6, 2010, from http://www.freedomhouse.org/uploads/special_report/32.pdf

Katz, E., & Lazarsfeld, P. F. (1955). *Personal Influence*. Glencoe, IL: Free Press.

Kausch, K. (2008). Morocco: Negotiating change with the Makhzen: Project on freedom of association in the Middle East and North Africa. *Fundación para las Relaciones Internacionales y el Diálogo Exterior* (FRIDE) (pp. 1-27). Retrieved January 13, 2013, from http://www.fride.org/publication/391/morocco:-negotiating-change-with-the-makhzen

Kavanaugh, A., Perz-Quinones, M. A., Kim, J. B., & Schmitz, J. (2008). Deliberation in Tool for Blog Discovery and Citizen-to-Citizen Participation. In *Proceedings of 9th Annual International Government Research* (pp. 143–152). Montreal, CA: ACM Press.

Kayumba, C., & Kimonyo, J. P. (2006). Media assistance to post-genocide Rwanda. In Zeeuw, J., & Kumar, K. (Eds.), *Promoting democracy in post-conflict societies* (pp. 211–236). Boulder, CO: Lynne Reinner Publishers.

Keane, J. (2004). Structural transformations of the public sphere. In Webster, F. (Ed.), *The Information Society Reader* (pp. 366–378). New York: Routledge.

Kean, J. (1991). *The Media and Democracy*. Cambridge, UK: Polity Press.

Kegley, C. W. (2007). *World politics: Trend and transformation*. Toronto: Thomson Nelson.

Kellner, D. (2000). Habermas, the public sphere, and democracy: A critical intervention. In Hahn, L. E. (Ed.), *Perspectives on Habermas* (pp. 259–288). IL, Peru: Open Court.

Kellner, D. (2004). The Media and the crises of democracy in the age of Bush-2. *Communication and Critical. Cultural Studies*, *1*(1), 29–58.

Kenya National Assembly. (2007). *The Hansard, Tuesday, 17th July, 2007*. Nairobi, Kenya: Kenya National Assembly.

Kenya National Bureau of Statistics. (2009). *Kenya National Population Census*. Nairobi, Kenya: Kenya National Bureau of Statistics.

Kenya National Commission on Human Rights [KNCHR]. (2008). *On the brink of the precipice: A human account of Kenya's post-2007 election violence*. Retrieved March 16, 2011, from http://www.humanitarian.info/2008/09/16/kenya-national-commission-for-human-rights-makes-more-work-for-the-icc/

Khamis, S. (2011). The transformative Egyptian media landscape: Changes, challenges and comparative perspectives. *International Journal of Communication*. Retrieved November 10, 2012, from http://ijoc.org/ojs/index.php/ijoc/article/view/813/592

Khamis, S., & Vaughn, K. (2011). Cyberactivism in the Egyptian revolution: How civic engagement and citizen journalism tilted the balance. *Arab Media & Society*, *13*(Summer), 2011. Retrieved January 12, 2013, from http://www.arabmediasociety.com/?article=769

Khamis, S. (2007). The role of new Arab satellite channels in fostering intercultural dialogue: Can Al-Jazeera English bridge the gap? In Seib, P. (Ed.), *New Media and the New Middle East* (pp. 39–52). New York: Palgrave Macmillan.

Khamis, S. (2008). Modern Egyptian media: Transformations, paradoxes, debates and comparative perspectives. *Journal of Arab and Muslim Media Research*, *1*(3), 259–277. doi:10.1386/jammr.1.3.259_1.

Khamis, S., & Sisler, V. (2010). The new Arab 'cyberscape': Redefining boundaries and reconstructing public spheres. *Communication Yearbook*, *34*, 277–316.

Khamis, S., & Vaughn, K. (2011). 'We Are All Khaled Said': The potentials and limitations of cyberactivism in triggering public mobilization and promoting political change. *Journal of Arab & Muslim Media Research*, *4*(2/3), 139–157.

Kibazo, P., & Kanaabi, H. (2007). *FM stations in Uganda 'Quantity without Quality*. Nairobi, Kenya: Eastern Africa Media Institute.

Kibnesh C. (2006). Use of Internet as a medium of disseminating information by Ethiopian newspapers. Unpublished MA thesis, Addis Ababa University, Addis Ababa, Ethiopia.

Kirkpatrick, D. (2011). Egyptian premier, warning of economic dangers, pleads for peace. *New York Times*. Retrieved January 12, 2013, from http://www.nytimes.com/2011/12/23/world/middleeast/egypts-prime-minister-adds-more-blame-on-protesters.html

Kirkpatrick, D. (2011, February 11). Egypt erupts in jubilation as Mubarak steps down. *The New York Times*. Retrieved March 1, 2011, from http://www.nytimes.com/2011/02/12/world/middleeast/12egypt.html?_r=1

Kirkpatrick, D. (2011). Tahrir Square, walled in. *The Lede. New York Times.* Retrieved January 12, 2013, from http://thelede.blogs.nytimes.com/2011/12/23/tahrir-square-walled-in/#more-150307

Kirumira, M., & Ajwang, J. (2007, May 3). Uganda: The limping newspaper industry. *Daily Monitor.* Retrieved May 3, 2007, from http://allafrica.com/stories/200705020734.html

Kituri, T. (2013). Fanning the flames of fear: A critical analysis of local language radio as a catalyst to the post-election violence in Kenya. In Olorunnisola, A., & Douai, A. (Eds.), *New Media Influence on Social and Political Change in Africa.* (67-83) Hershey, PA: IGI-Global.

Kivikuru, U. (2000). *An Arm of Democracy for Promoting Human Rights or Simple Rhetoric? SSKH Medelanden 54.* Helsinki, Finland: University of Helsinki.

Kivikuru, U. (2006). Top-Down or Bottom-Up? Radio in the Service of Democracy: Experiences from South Africa and Namibia. *Gazette, 68*(1), 5–31.

Kline, D., & Burstein, D. (2005). *Blog! How the newest media revolution is changing politics, business, and culture.* New York: CDS Books.

Klotz, R. J. (2004). *The Politics of Internet Communication.* Lanham, MD: Rowman and Littlefield.

Kluver, R., Jankowsky, N. W., Foot, K. A., & Schneider, S. M. (Eds.). (2007). *The Internet and National Elections: A Comparative Study of Web Campaigning.* New York: Routledge.

KNCHR. (2007). *Still Behaving Badly.* Nairobi, Kenya: Kenya National Commission on Human Rights.

Knight, M. (2010). Blogging and citizen journalism. In Hyde-Clarke, N. (Ed.), *The Citizen and Communication: Revisiting Traditional, New and Community Media Practices in Southern Africa* (pp. 31–50). Claremont, South Africa: Juta & Co. Ltd..

Konde, H. (1984). *Press Freedom in Tanzania.* Arusha, Tanzania: East African Publications.

Kony2012 (2012). *Kony 2012.* Retrieved from http://www.kony2012.com/

Kornberg, A., & Clarke, H. D. (1994). Beliefs about democracy and satisfaction with democratic government: The Canadian Case. *Political Research Quarterly, 47,* 537–563.

Koyugi, J. (2008, January 20). *Kenya will never be the same.* Retrieved January 1, 2009, from http://kenyaburning.wordpress.com/2008/01/20/kenya-will-never-be-the-same/

Kperogi, F. A. (2012). The evolution and challenges of online journalism in Nigeria. In Siapera, E., & Veglis, A. (Eds.), *The handbook of global online journalism.* Malden, MA: Wiley-Blackwell. doi:10.1002/9781118313978.ch24.

Kruger, F. (2009). *Media Courts of Honour: Self-Regulation Councils in Southern Africa and Elsewhere.* Windhoek, Namibia: Friedrich Ebert Stiftung.

Kunle, A. (2010). *Focus Nigeria.* [Television series].

Kuper, A., & Kuper, J. (2001). Serving a New Democracy: Must the Media Speak Softly? Learning from South Africa. *International Journal of Public Opinion Research, 13*(4), 355–376. doi:10.1093/ijpor/13.4.355.

Kvale, S. (1996). *Interviews: An Introduction to Qualitative Research Interviewing.* Thousand Oaks, CA: Sage Publications.

Laclau, E., & Mouffe, C. (1985). *Hegemony and socialist strategy: Towards a radical democratic politics.* London: Verso.

Lakoff, G., & Johnson, M. (1985). *Metaphors we live by.* Chicago, IL: University of Chicago Press. Retrieved April 30, 2012, from http://www.gbv.de/dms/bowker/toc/9780226468006.pdf

Lamnadi, A. (1999). *Communication policy making and electronic media in Morocco: The introduction of private television.* Unpublished Dissertation, Ohio University, OH.

Landow, G. (2003). The paradigm is more important than the purchase. In Liestol, G., Morrison, A., & Rasmussen, T. (Eds.), *Digital Media Revisited: Theoretical and Conceptual Innovations in Digital Domains* (pp. 35–64). Cambridge, MA: The MIT Press.

Lasorsa, D. L., Lewis, S. C., & Holton, A. (2012). Normalizing Twitter: Journalism practice in an emerging communication space. *Journalism Studies, 13*(1), 19–36. doi:10.1080/1461670X.2011.571825.

Latour, B. (2005). Reassembling the social: An introduction to actor network theory. New York: Oxford.

LeDuc, L., Niemi, R. G., & Norris, P. (2008). Introduction: Comparing Democratic Elections. In Leduc, L., Niemi, R., & Norris, P. (Eds.), *Comparing Democracies 2 New Challenges in the Study of Elections and Voting* (pp. 1–39). London: Sage Publications.

Lekgoathi, S. P. (2009). You are listening to Radio Lebowa of the South African Broadcasting Corporation: Vernacular Radio, Bantustan Identity and Listenership, 1960 – 1994. *Journal of Southern African Studies, 35*(3), 575–594. doi:10.1080/03057070903101821.

Lenk, K. (1999). Electronic support of citizen participation in planning processes. In B. N. Hague & B. D. (Eds.), Digital Democracy: Discourse and Decision Making in the Information Age (pp. 87-95). London: Routledge.

Leon, T. (1998). *Hope and fear: Reflections of a Democrat.* Johannesburg, South Africa: Jonathan Ball Publishers.

Lepage, C. (2010). *Professional journalism is not for the weak-kneed: Interview with Geoffrey Nyarota (Zimbabwe).* Retrieved June 17, 2011, from http://www.cimethics.org/newsletter/holidayissue2010/holidayissue2010_htm

Leslie, M. (1995). Television and Capitalist Hegemony in the "New" South Africa. *The Howard Journal of Communications, 6*(3), 164–172. doi:10.1080/10646179509361694.

Leveau, R. (1985). *Le Fellah Marocain Défenseur du Trône.* Paris: Presses de Sciences Po.

Leveau, R. (1997). Morocco at the crossroads. *Mediterranean Politics, 2*(2), 95–113. doi:10.1080/13629399708414621.

Levi, A. (1966). The Value of Freedom: Mill's Liberty (1859-1959). In Radcliff, P. (Ed.), *Limits of Liberty: Studies of Mill's On Liberty* (pp. 6–17). Belmont, CA: Wadsworth Publishing.

Levingstone, S. (1999, April 14). Does territoriallity drive human aggression? *International Herald Tribune.*

Levitsky, S., & Way, A. (2010). Why Democracy needs a Level Playing Field. *Journal of Democracy, 21,* 55–68.

Lichtenberg, J. (1990). Foundations and Limits of Freedom of the Press. In Lichtenberg, J. (Ed.), *Democracy and the Mass Media* (pp. 102–135). Cambridge, UK: Cambridge University Press. doi:10.1017/CBO9781139172271.005.

Lichtenberg, J. (1990). Introduction. In Lichtenberg, J. (Ed.), *Democracy and the Mass Media* (pp. 1–20). Cambridge, UK: Cambridge University Press. doi:10.1017/CBO9781139172271.002.

Lievrouw, L., & Livingstone, S. (2006) Introduction to the updated student Ed. In L. Lievrouw, & S. Livingstone (Eds.), *Handbook of new media: Social shaping and social consequences* (pp. 1-14). London: Sage. Retrieved from http://eprints.lse.ac.uk/21502/1/Introduction_to_the_updated_student_Ed._(LSERO).pdf

Lindberg, S. (2006). The Surprising Significance of African Elections. *Journal of Democracy, 17,* 139–151. doi:10.1353/jod.2006.0011.

Linz, J., & Stepan, A. (1996). *Problems of Democratic Transition and Consolidation.* Baltimore, MD: The Johns Hopkins University Press.

Lister, M., Dovey, J., Giddings, S., Grant, I., & Kelly, K. (2003). *New media: A critical Introduction.* London: Routledge.

London, S. (1993). *How the media frames political issues.* Retrieved November 10, 2012, from Scott's London Website: http://www.scottlondon.com/reports/frames.html

Lotan, G. (2012, March 14). *KONY2012: See How Invisible Networks Helped a Campaign Capture the World's Attention.* [Web log comment]. Retrieved from http://blog.socialflow.com/post/7120244932/data-viz-kony2012-see-how-invisible-networks-helped-a-campaign-capture-the-worlds-attention. (2012, March 14).

Loxton, L. (2000, February 5). Mbeki puts SA on course. *Business Report.* Retrieved from April 20, 2012, from http://www.busrep.co.za/index.php?fSectionId=561&fArticleId=74876

Lundry, C., Corman, S. R., Furlow, R. B., & Errickson, K. W. (2012). Cooking the books: Strategic inflation of casualty reports by extremists in the Afghanistan conflict. *Studies in Conflict and Terrorism*. doi:10.1080/1057610X.2012.666821.

Lunt, P., & Pantti, M. (2007). Popular culture and the public sphere: Currents of feeling and social control in talk shows and reality TV. In Butch, R. (Ed.), *Media and Public Spheres* (pp. 162–174). New York: Palgrave Macmillan.

Lush, D., & Kupe, T. (2005). Crisis? *What crisis? Report on International Conference on Media Support Strategies for Zimbabwe, International Media Support (IMS)*. The Netherlands Institute for South Africa, (NIZA), Media Institute for Southern Africa, (MISA), Open Society Institute. Retrieved March 3, 2008, from http://www.i-m-s.dk/media/pdf/Zimbabwe

Maarek, P. (2007). Communication et marketing de l'homme politique (3rd éd., p. 466). LexisNexis Litec.

Mabweazara, H. M. (2010). New technologies and journalism practice in Africa: Towards a critical sociological approach. In Hyde-Clarke, N. (Ed.), *The Citizen and Communication: Revisiting Traditional, New and Community Media Practices in Southern Africa* (pp. 11–30). Claremont, South Africa: Juta & Co. Ltd..

Machigere, R. (2008). *The potential of harnessing the utilization of ICT in the transport sector for socio-economic development: A case for Zimbabwe*. Paper presented at the Science with Africa Conference. Addis Ababa, Ethiopia.

Mackey, R. (2011). Egyptian military adviser calls attack on woman justified. *The Lede. New York Times*. Retrieved January 12, 2013, from http://thelede.blogs.nytimes.com/2011/12/22/egyptian-military-adviser-calls-attack-on-woman-justified/

Mackey, R. (2011, February 5). Updates on day 12 of Egypt protests. The Lede News Blog. *The New York Times*. Retrieved from http://thelede.blogs.nytimes.com/2011/02/05/latest-updates-on-day-12-of-egypt protests

Mackey, R. (2011). Observers confronted with anger, gunshots and a dead child in Syria. *The Lede. New York Times*. Retrieved January 12, 2013, from http://thelede.blogs.nytimes.com/

Maghraoui, A. (2001). Morocco in transition: Political authority in crisis. *Middle East Report*. Retrieved June 15, 2007, from http://www.merip.org/mer/mer218/218_mghraoui.html

Mahoso, T. (2011, April 24-30). Significance of anti-sanctions campaign. *The Sunday Mail*, pp. B13.

Mahoso, T. (2011, March 5). Why Zimbabwe is neither Egypt nor Tunisia. *The Sunday Mail*. Retrieved February 15, 2012, from http://www.zimpapers.co.zw/index.php?option=com_content&view=article&id=2165:african-focus-with-dr-tafataona-mahoso-why-zimbabwe-is-neither-egypt-nor-tunisia&catid=48:blogs&Itemid=155

Mahoso, T. (2008). Reading the Tibaijuka report on Zimbabwe in a global context. In Maurice, V. (Ed.), *The Hidden Dimensions of Operation Murambatsvina in Zimbabwe* (pp. 159–168). Harare, Zimbabwe: Weaver Press.

Mail & Guardian Online. (n.d.). *About Us*. Retrieved January 17, 2013, from http://mg.co.za/page/about-us/

Maina, L. W. (2006). *African media development initiative: Kenya research findings and conclusion*. London: BBC World Service Trust.

Makinen, M., & Kuira, M. (2008). Social media and post-election crisis in Kenya. *The International Journal of Press/Politics*, *13*, 328–335. doi:10.1177/1940161208319409.

Makoe, A. (2000, February 5). What we need are jobs, Mr. President! *The Sunday Independent*. Retrieved April 30, 2012, from http://www.iol.co.za/index.php?set_id=1&click_id=13&art_id=ct20000205175221108M126696

Malan, S. (2009). *Never dull moment*. Retrieved January 20, 2010, from http//www.themalans.blogspot.com/2009/09/never-dull-monet.html

Malešević, S. (2004). *The sociology of ethnicity*. London: Sage Publications.

Malouf, R., & Mullen, T. (2008). Graph-Based User Classification for Informal Online Political Discourse. *Internet Research*, *18*(2), 177–190. doi:10.1108/10662240810862239.

Mamdani, M. (1996). *Citizen and subject: Contemporary Africa and the legacy of late colonialism*. Princeton, NJ: Princeton University Press.

Mandela, N. (1995, February 18). Address of President Nelson Mandela on the occasion of the opening of the second session of the democratic parliament: Cape Town, South Africa. Retrieved April 30, 2012, from http://www.info.gov.za/speeches/1995/170595001.htm

Manji, F. (2008). *Alternative media for social change in Africa: Myths and realities.* Paper presented at the Cape Town Book Fair. Cape Town, South Africa. Retrieved August 15, 2010, from http://www.informationforchange.org/pressentations/ctbf_firoze.pdf

Mansell, R. (2012). ICTs, discourse and knowledge societies: Implications for policy and practice. In D. Frau-Meigs J. Nicey, M. Palmer, & P. Tupper (Eds.), NWICO to WSIS: 30 years of communication geopolitics: actors and flows, structures and divides. Bristol, UK: ECREA series.

Mansfield, I. (2011, May 10). Mobile broadband to ensure continued vibrancy of Zimbabwe's telecommunications market. *ITU-Cellular News.* Retrieved June 16, 2011, from htt://cellular-news.com/story/49100.php?=h

Marcuse, H. (1969). Repressive Tolerance. In Wolff, R., & Marcuse, H. (Eds.), *A Critique of Pure Tolerance* (pp. 95–137). London: Beacon Press.

Marcus, R.R., & Mease, K., & Ottemoeller. (2001). Popular Definitions of Democracy from Uganda, Madagascar, and Florida, U.S.A. *Journal of Asian and African Studies, 36,* 113–132. doi:10.1177/002190960103600106.

Martin, B. L., & Olorunnisola, A. A. (2013). Use of new ICTs as "liberation" or "repression" technologies in social movements: The need to formulate appropriate media policies. In Olorunnisola, A., & Douai, A. (Eds.), *New Media Influence on Social and Political Change in Africa (257-272).* Hershey, PA: IGI-Global.

Mártin-Barbero, J. (1997). Cultural decentring and palimpsests of identity. *Media Development, 44*(1), 18–22.

Martin, C. H., & Stronach, B. (1992). *Politics East and West: A comparison of Japanese and British political culture* (p. 360). Armonk, NY: M. E. Sharpe.

Maruatona, T. (2006). Adult education, deliberative democracy and social re-engagement in Africa. *Journal of Developing Societies, 22*(1), 11–27. doi:10.1177/0169796X06062964.

Marwell, G., & Oliver, V. (2008). Resource Mobilisation Theory and the Study of Social Movements. In Ruggiero, V., & Montagna, N. (Eds.), *Social Movements: A Reader* (pp. 128–143). London: Routledge.

Masenyama, K. (2006). The South African Broadcasting Corporation and Dilemmas of National Identity. In Alexander, P., Dawson, M. C., & Icharam, M. (Eds.), *Globalisation and New Identites- A View from the Middle* (pp. 157–171). Johannesburg, South Africa: Jacana Media.

Matibini, P. (2006). *The Struggle for Media Law Reforms in Zambia.* Lusaka, Zambia: Media Institute of Southern Africa – Zambia Chapter.

Matshazi, N. (2012, April 22). ZAB halts Freedom Fone project. *The Standard.*

Maxon, R., & Ofcansky, T. (2000). *Historical Dictionary of Kenya.* Lanham, MD: Scarecrow Press, Inc..

Mazrui, A. A., & Mazrui, A. M. (1998). *The power of babel: Language and governance in the African experience.* Oxford, UK: James Currey.

Mbaine, A. E. (2010). *Concurrent state and self regulation: A unique challenge for journalism practice in Uganda.* Paper presented at World Journalism Education Congress. Grahamstown, South Africa.

Mbeki, T. (2000, February 4). *State of the Nation address of the president of South Africa, Thabo Mbeki, National Assembly Chamber.* Cape Town, South Africa. Retrieved April 30, 2012, from http://www.info.gov.za/speeches/2000/000204451p1001.htm

Mbembe, A. (2001). *On the Post Colony.* Berkeley, CA: University of California Press.

Mbembe, A. (2003). Necropolitics. *Public Culture, 15*(1), 11–40. doi:10.1215/08992363-15-1-11.

McAdam, D. (1982). *Political Process and the Development of Black Insurgency, 1930–1970.* Chicago, IL: University of Chicago Press.

McAdam, D., McCarthy, J. D., & Zald, M. (1996). *Comparative Perspectives on Social Movements: Political Opportunities, Mobilizing Structures, and Cultural Framings.* New York: Cambridge University Press. doi:10.1017/CBO9780511803987.

McCarthy, J., & Zald, M. N. (2003). *Social movement in an organizational society: Collected essays*. New Brunswick, NJ: Transaction Publishers.

McCarthy, T. (1989). Introduction. In Habermas, J. (Ed.), *The Structural Transformation of the Public Sphere: An Inquiry into Category of Bourgeoisie Society* (pp. xi–xiv). Cambridge, MA: Polity Press.

McChesney, R. W. (1997). *Corporate media and the threat to democracy*. Boston, MA: Seven Stories Press.

McChesney, R. W. (1999). *Rich Media, Poor Democracy: Communication Politics in Dubious Times*. Urbana, IL: University of Illinois Press.

McFedries, P. (2007). Technically speaking: All A-Twitter. *IEEE Spectrum*, *44*(10), 84. doi:10.1109/MSPEC.2007.4337670.

McGreal, C. (2008, February 7). *'Who's to blame? It depends where you begin the story'*. Retrieved December 10, 2008, from http://www.guardian.co.uk/world/2008/feb/07/kenya.chrismcgreal

McKee, A. (2005). *The Public Sphere: An Introduction*. Cambridge, UK: Cambridge University Press.

McKenzie, R. (2006). *Comparing Media from around the World*. Boston, MA: Allyn & Bacon.

McKinley, D. T. (2000, March 1). The evolution of the ANC. *Daily Mail & Guardian*. Retrieved April 30, 2012, from www.hartford-hwp.com/37a/171.html

McLuhan, M. (1962). *The Gutenberg Galaxy: The Making of Typographic Man*. Toronto, CA: University of Toronto Press.

McLuhan, M. (1964). *Understanding the Media: The Extension's of Man*. New York: McGraw Hill.

McLuhan, M. (1967). *The Medium is the Massage: An Inventory of Effects*. New York: Random House.

McLure, J. (2008, April 10). Stuck in Somalia. *Newsweek*. Retrieved January 9, 2012, from http://www.newsweek.com/2008/04/10/stuck-in-somalia.html

McLure, J. (2010, May 14). Ethiopian rights groups forced to reduce work before elections. *Bloomberg Businessweek*. Retrieved April 19, 2011, from http://www.businessweek.com/news/2010-05-14/ethiopian-rights-groups-forced-to-reduce-work-before-elections.html

McNair, B. (1998). *The sociology of journalism*. London, New York, Sydney, Auckland: Arnold.

McNair, B. (2006). *Cultural Chaos: Journalism, News, and Power in a Globalised World*. London: Routledge. doi:10.4324/9780203448724.

McNamara, L. (2009). Counter-terrorism laws: How they affect media freedom and news reporting. *Westminster Papers in Communication and Culture*, *6*(1), 27–44.

McQuail, D. (1992). *Media Performance Mass Communication and the Public Interest*. London: Sage Publication.

McQuail, D. (1994). *Mass Communication Theory: An Introduction*. London: Routledge.

McQuail, D. (2000). *McQuail's Mass Communication Theory* (4th ed.). London: Sage Publications Ltd..

McQuail, D. (2003). *Media Accountability and Freedom of Publication*. Oxford, UK: Oxford University Press.

MDDA. (2009). Trends of ownership and control of media in South Africa. Version 3.3.[Research Report]. Media Development and Diversity Agency. Retrieved January 17, 2013, from http://www.mdda.org.za/trends of ownership and control of media in south Africa ver 3.3. final 20-june 202009.pdf

Media Foundation for West Africa. (2008). *Media Alert West Africa 2008: Annual State of the Media Report*. Ghana: MFWA.

Media Foundation for West Africa. (2010). *Ghana Freedom of Information coalition raises red flag over lack of transparency in the passage of the FOI*. Retrieved from http://www.mediafound.org/index.php?option=com_content&task=view&id=489&Itemid=45

Media Institute of Southern Africa. (2009). *So This is Democracy? State of media freedom in Southern Africa 2009*. Windhoek, Namibia: MISA.

Media Rights Agenda. (2002). *Airwaves Monitor Report 2002*. Nigeria: Lagos.

Media sustainability Index. *Africa 2006-2007 Nigeria*. Lagos, Nigeria.

Mekuria M. (2005). *The Ethiopian media landscape*. Ethiopian Mass Media Training Institute.

Melkote, R. S., & Steeves, H. L. (2001). *Communication for Development in the Third World*. New Delhi, India: Sage.

Melone, S., Terzis, G., & Beleli, O. (2002). *Using the media for conflict transformation: A common ground experience*. Berlin: Berghof Research Center for Constructive Conflict Management. Retrieved from http://www.radiopeaceafrica.org/assets/texts/pdf/Common_Ground_Experience_en.pdf

Melucci, A. (1989). *Nomads of the Present: Social Movements and Individual Needs in Contemporary Society*. Philadelphia, PA: Temple University Press.

Melucci, A. (1996). *Challenging codes: Collective action in the information age*. Cambridge, UK: Cambridge University Press. doi:10.1017/CBO9780511520891.

Merit, S. (2011). Using social media for social change. Retrieved March 16, 2012 from. http://we-media.s3.amazonaws.com/BEB93FE3-484D-49DE B95BA99EAA0CA3DB/FinalDownload/DownloadIdA-7754D10A5DF0682A081F5D79A982803/BEB93FE3-484D-49DE-B95B-A99EAA0CA3DB/papers/ tp/ifocos_wm_socialmedia.pdf

Mesfin N. (2010). Welcome to Addis. What it means being a journalist in Ethiopia. In F. Mdlongwa & M. Letlhaku (Eds.), *Harnessing Africa's digital future* (pp. 64–73). Johannesburg, South Africa: Konrad Adenauer Stiftung. Retrieved from http://www.spiml.co.za/uploads/1285226894.pdf

Mhiripiri, N.A. (2011). Zimbabwe community radio 'initiatives': Promoting alternative media in a restrictive legislative environment. *Radio Journal: International Studies in Broadcasting and Audio Media, 9*(2/1), 107-126.

Mhiripiri, N., & Mutsvairo, B. (2013). Social media, new ICTs and the challenges facing Zimbabwe democratic process. In Olorunnisola, A., & Douai, A. (Eds.), *New Media Influence on Social and Political Change in Africa (402-422)*. Hershey, PA: IGI-Global.

Mhlanga, B. (2006). *Community Radio as Dialogic and Participatory: A Critical Analysis of Governance, Control and Community Participation, A Case Study of XK FM Radio Station*. Unpublished Master's thesis.

Mhlanga, B. (2009). The community in community radio: A case study of XK FM, Interrogating Issues of Community Participation, Governance, and Control. *Ecquid Novi African Journalism Studies, 30*(1), 58–72. doi:10.3368/ajs.30.1.58.

Mhlanga, B. (2010). The ethnic imperative: Community radio as dialogic and participatory and the case study of XK FM. In Hyde-Clarke, N. (Ed.), *The citizen in communication: Revisiting traditional, new and community media practices in South Africa* (pp. 155–178). Claremont, CA: JUTA.

Middle East Online. (2011). Season of rape in Somalia: 'Climate of fear' sweeps IDP camps. Retrieved January 30, 2012, from http://www.middle-east-online.com/english/?id=49664

Mihailidis, P. (2009). *Media Literacy: Empowering the Youth Worldwide*. Washington, DC: Centre for International Media Assistance.

Mill, S. J. (1974). *On Liberty*. London: Penguin Group.

Mindshare. (2008). *Media scene in Morocco*. Unpublished Document.

Ministry of Communication. (2003). *Le Domaine de la Communication au Maroc*. Rabat, Morocco: Al Anbaa.

Ministry of Communication. (2006). *Rapport Annuel sur l'Etat de la Presse Ecrite et la Communication Audiovisuelle Publique*. Retrieved May 15, 2010, from http://www.mincom.gov.ma/NR/rdonlyres/319E32BD 570D-4490-834D-319FB5344BE5/0/RapportdelapresseVF2006.pdf

MMPZ. (2002). *Media under siege: Report on media coverage of the 2002 presidential and mayoral elections in Zimbabwe*. Harare, Zimbabwe: MMPZ.

Moore, G. (2000). The English legal framework for investigative journalism. In de Burgh, H. (Ed.), *Investigative Journalism, Context and Practice* (pp. 123–150). London, New York: Routledge.

Morgan, S. (2004). Online Publishing: Independent media challenge Internet in Zimbabwe. *RAPZI Newsletter, 19*.

Moriarty, T. A. (2003). *Finding the words: a rhetorical history of South Africa's transition from apartheid to democracy*. Westport, CT: Praeger Publishers.

Morris, J. J. (2002). *The new media and the dramatization of American politics*. Paper presented at the annual meeting of the American Political Science Association. Boston, MA. Retrieved on September 30, 2009, from http://www.allacademic.com.meta/p66276_index.html

Moshiri, N. (2011). Al-Shabab starts tweeting. *Al-Jazeera*. Retrieved January 30, 2012, from http://blogs.aljazeera.net/africa/2011/12/13/al-shabab-starts-tweeting

Moshiri, N. (2011). Somalia's Shabab fighters take to Twitter. *Al-Jazeera*. Retrieved January 30, 2012, from http://www.aljazeera.com/news/africa/2011/12/2011121316621833642.html

Motsa, M. (2009). *African Media Barometer 2009 – Swaziland*. Windhoek, Namibia: Media Institute of Southern Africa & Friedrich-Ebert-Stiftung.

Mouffe, C. (2000). Politics and passions: The stakes of democracy. *Ethical Perspectives*, *17*, 143–150.

Moussa, M. B. (2013). A grassroots approach to the democratic role of the Internet in developing countries: The case of Morocco. In Olorunnisola, A., & Douai, A. (Eds.), *New Media Influence on Social and Political Change in Africa (218-240)*. Hershey, PA: IGI-Global.

Moyer, B. (2008). Is the Fourth Estate a Fifth Column?: Corporate Media Colludes with Democracy's Demise. Retrieved on September 10, 2008, from.http://www.inthesetimes.com/article/3790/is_the_fourth_estate_a_fifth_column/

Moyo, D. (2010). *The new media as monitors of democracy: Mobile phones and Zimbabwe's 2008 election*. Paper presented at the Conference on Election Processes, Liberation Movements and Democratic Change in Africa. Maputo, Mozambique.

Moyo, J. (2011, April 3). Unmasking SADC Troika meeting in Zambia. *The Herald*. Retrieved February 29, 2012, from http://www.zimpapers.co.zw/index.php?option=com_content&view=article&id=2629:unmasking-sadc-troika-circus-in-zambia&catid=39:opinion&Itemid=132

Moyo, J. (2011, February 27, 2011). Zimbabwe is not Tunisia. *The Sunday Mail*. Retrieved February 15, 2012, from http://www.zimpapers.co.zw/index.php?option=com_content&view=article&id=2109:zimbbwe -is-not-tunisia-or-egypt&catid=39:opinion&Itemid=132

Moyo, L. (2010). Language, cultural and communication rights of ethnic minorities in South Africa: A human rights approach. *The International Communication Gazette, 1748-0485, 72*(4-5), 425-440.

Moyo, D. (2007). Alternative media, Diasporas and the media of the Zimbabwean crisis. *Ecquid Novi: African Journalism Studies*, *28*(1/2), 81–105. doi:10.3368/ajs.28.1-2.81.

Moyo, D. (2009). Citizen journalism and the parallel market of information in Zimbabwe's 2008 elections. *Journalism Studies*, *10*(4), 551–567. doi:10.1080/14616700902797291.

Moyo, D. (2010). We're all story tellers: Citizen Journalism in the age of digital 'pavement radio. In Hyde-Clarke, N. (Ed.), *The Citizen and Communication: Revisiting Traditional, New and Community Media Practices in Southern Africa* (pp. 50–74). Claremont, South Africa: Juta & Co. Ltd..

Moyo, D. (2010). Zimbabwe and Zambia: Musical chairs and reluctant liberalisation. In Moyo, D., & Chuma, W. (Eds.), *Media policy in a changing Southern Africa. Critical reflections on media reforms in the global age* (pp. 169–200). Pretoria, South Africa: Unisa Press.

Moyo, L. (2011). Blogging down a dictatorship: Human rights, citizen journalists and the right to communicate in Zimbabwe. *Journalism: Theory Practice and Criticism*, *12*(6), 745–760. doi: doi:10.1177/1464884911405469.

Mrutu, E. (2008). *Community radio in Africa. Case study: Tanzania*. Unpublished Licentiate Thesis, University of Tampere, Tampere, Sweden.

Mudhai, O. F., Tettey, W. J., & Banda, F. (Eds.). (2009). *African media and the digital public sphere*. Basingstoke, UK: Palgrave Macmillan. doi:10.1057/9780230621756.

Mueller, D. C. (2003). *Capitalism and democracy: Challenges and responses in an increasingly interdependent world*. Northampton, MA: Edward Elgar Publishing.

Mufwene, S. (2002). Colonisation, globalisation and the future of languages in the twenty-first Century. *International Journal of Multilingual Societies*, *4*(2), 162–193.

Mugabe, R. (2011, April 18). President Mugabe's 31st Independence Address. *The Herald*. Retrieved April 30, 2012, from http://www.herald.co.zw/index.php?option=com_content&view=article&id=7997:president-mugabes-31st-independence-day-address&catid=39:opinion&Itemid=132

Muganwa, G. (2007). *The enigma of press freedom in Rwanda*. Kigali, Rwanda: The Tizianoproject. Retrieved April 19, 2011, from http://tizianoproject.org/features/the_enigma_of_press_frededom_i/

Mukwasa, R. (2011, April 27). Ronnie threatens to close several radio stations. *The Post*. Retrieved from http://www.postzambia.com

Mulero, S. (2012). *Acceptance and impact of social networks marketing using extended technology acceptance model*. Thesis. Cape Peninsula University of Technology, Cape Town, South Africa Retrieved from http://digitalknowledge.cput.ac.za:8081/jspui/bitstream/123456789/263/1/acceptance%20and%20impact%20of%20social%20networks%20marketing%20using%20extended%20technology%20acceptance%20model.pdf

Mungiu-Pippidi, A., & Munteanu, I. (2009). Moldova's 'Twitter revolution. *Journal of Democracy*, *20*(3), 136–142. doi:10.1353/jod.0.0102.

Murdock, G., & Golding, P. (2004). Dismantling the digital divide: Rethinking the dynamics of participation and exclusion. In Calabrese, A., & Sparks, C. (Eds.), *Towards a political economy of culture: Capitalism and communication in the twenty-first century* (pp. 244–260). Lanham, MD: Rowman & Littlefield.

Murphy, C. (2003). *Violence in Kenya*. Denver, CO: University of Denver.

Murphy, S. M., & Scotton, J. F. (1987). Dependency and Journalism Education in Africa: Are There Alternative Models? *Africa Media Review*, *1*(3), 11–35.

Musasizi, S. (2012). Police blame 'African Spring' on social media. Retrieved October 16, 2012, from http://www.observer.ug/index.php?option=com_content&view=article&id=21593:police-blame-african-spring-on-social-media&catid=34:news&Itemid=114

Muthee, M. W. (2010). *Hitting the Target, Missing the Point: Youth Policies and Programmes in Kenya*. Washington, DC: Woodrow Wilson International Centre for Scholars.

Mutsvairo, B. (2010). *Journalism ethics in the digital age*. Paper presented at International Conference on New Media Technologies. Bratislava, Slovakia.

Muzulu, P. (2011, December 15). ZANU PF cracks down on social media. *The Zimbabwe Independent*.

Mvendaga, J. (2003). *The Nigerian mass media and the 2003 elections*. Ibadan, Nigeria: Jodad Publishers.

Mwenda, A. M. (2007). Personalizing power in Uganda. *Journal of Democracy*, *18*(3), 23–37. doi:10.1353/jod.2007.0048.

Mwesige, P. (2009). The democratic functions and dysfunctions of political talk radio: The case of Uganda. *Journal of African Media Studies*, *1*(2), 221–245. doi:10.1386/jams.1.2.221_1.

n.a. (1995), February 18). Address greeted by warm applause. *The Citizen*, 11

n.a. (1995b, February 18). Corruption to be fought. *The Citizen*, 11

n.a. (1995c, February 18). Govt 'doesn't have money to meet demands'. *The Citizen*, 11

n.a. (1995d, February 18). War on crime. *The Citizen*, 6

n a. (2000, February 4). An ABC guide to Mbeki's speech. *IOL Online*. Retrieved January 17, 2013, from http://www.iol.co.za/news/politics/an-abc-guide-to-mbeki-s-speech-1.27209#.UPfQN6wx_9o

n a. (2010, December 14). Zuma sues Zapiro, Avusa for R5m. *Mail & Guardian Online*. Retrieved January 17, 2013, from http://mg.co.za/article/2010-12-14-zuma-sues-zapiro-avusa-for-r5m

Nadeau, R., & Bastien, F. (2003). La communication électorale. In *La Communication Politique, Etat des Savoirs, Enjeux et perspectives* (pp. 159–187). Quebec: Presses Universitaires du Québec.

Naguib, R. (2011). A year in review: the SCAF rules in 93 letters. *Egypt Independent*. Retrieved January 12, 2013, from http://www.almasryalyoum.com/en/node/575366

Nassanga, L. G. (2009). Participatory discussion programs as hybrid community media in Uganda. *International Journal of Media and Cultural Politics, 5*(1/2), 119–124.

National Broadcasting Commission. (2006). *Nigeria Broadcasting Code* (4th ed.). Lagos, Nigeria: Regent.

National Broadcasting Commission. (2006). *Quick News Update*. Retrieved January 12, 2010, from http://www.nbc.gov.ng

National Broadcasting Commission. (2009). *NBC Suspends Radio Adaba Licence*. Retrieved December 23, 2008, from http://www.nbc.gov.ng

National Public Radio [NPR]. (2008). *Text Messages Used to Incite Violence in Kenya*. Retrieved December 4, 2010, from http://www.npr.org/templates/story/story.php?storyId=19188853

National Public Radio [NPR]. (2011). *Foreign policy: Scramble to silence Cairo protests*. Retrieved on March 1, 2011, from: http://www.npr.org/2011/01/28/133306415/foreign-policy-scramble-to-silence-cairo-protests

Navarra, D. (2010). The Architecture of Global ICT Programs: A Case Study of E-Governance in Jordan. *Information Technology for Development, 16*(2), 128–140. doi:10.1080/02681101003741681.

Nderitu, T. (2008). When radio spreads violence: Free speech questioned in Kenya. Retrieved January 5, 2009, from http://towardfreedom.com/home/content/view/1268/63/

Ndlela, N. (2007). Broadcasting Reforms in Southern Africa: Continuity and Change in the Era of Glocalisation. *Westminster Papers in Communication and Culture, 4*(3), 67–87.

Ndlovu, R. (2009, April 16). Bridging the digital divide: Sound ITC vital. *The Zimbabwean.*

Ndlovu, R. (2012, April 20). Internet to influence next elections. *The Financial Gazette.*

Ndlovu-Gatsheni, S. , J. (2009). Africa for Africans or Africa for natives only? new nationalism and nativism in Zimbabwe and South Africa. *Africa Spectrum, 1*, 61–78.

Negm, N. (2011, August 20). *Personal interview* Cairo, Egypt.

Nehanda Radio. (2010). *Mugabe's son inherits other's IQ*. Retrieved July 21, 2010, from http://nehandaradio.com/2010/02//02/mugabes-son-inherits-mothers-iq

Nelson, A. (2008). The web 2.0 revolution - extended version. *Carnegie Reporter*. Retrieved January 12, 2013, from http://carnegie.org/publications/carnegie-reporter/single/view/article/item/71/

Nelson, A. (2011). *Funding free expression: Perceptions and reality in a changing landscape*. Center for International Media Assistance. Retrieved April 19, 2011, from http://cima.ned.org/sites/default/files/CIMA-Funding_Free_Expression_06-01-11.pdf

Network Information Centre. (2010). *Statistiques, nic. ma*. Retrieved June 4, 2010, from http://www.nic.ma/statistiques.asp

Newman, N. (2010). *UKelection2010, Mainstream Media and the Role of the Internet: How Social and Digital Media Affected the Business of Politics and Journalism*. London: Reuters Institute for the Study of Journalism.

Newmark, C. (2009). *A nerd's take on the future of news media*. Retrieved from http://www.huffingtonpost.com/craig-newmark/a-nerds-take-on-the-futur_b_325544.html

News, B. B. C. (2012). *Facebook influences Nigeria football team ban U-turn*. Retrieved January 14, 2013, from http://www.bbc.co.uk/news/10525699

Ngugi, C. M. (1995). The Mass Media and Democratization in Africa. *Media Development, 4*, 49–52.

Ngwanakilala, N. (1981). *Mass Communication and Development of Socialism in Tanzania*. Dar es Salaam, Tanzania: Tanzania Publishing House.

Nielsen, P. E. (2009). Media in post-communist Mongolia. Challenges and opportunities in the democratization process. *Nordicom Review, 30*(2), 19–33.

Nigeria, M. T. N. In *Facebook*. Retrieved from https://www.facebook.com/MTNLoaded

Njonjo, K. S. (2010). Youth Fact Book: Infinite Possibility or Definite Disaster? Nairobi, Kenya: Institute of Economic Affairs (IEA) and Friedrich-Ebert-Stiftung (FES).

Nkrumah, K. (1965). *The African journalist*. Dar es Salaam, Tanzania: Tanzanian Publishers.

Nordenstreng, K., & Ngwanakilala, N. (1987). *Tanzania and the New Information Order. A Case Study of Africa's Second Struggle*. Dar es Salaam, Tanzania: Tanzania Publishing House.

Norris, P. (2000). *Virtuous circle. Political Communication in Postindustrial Societies* (p. 420). Cambridge, UK: Cambridge University Press. doi:10.1017/CBO9780511609343.

Norris, P. (2001). *Digital divide: Civic engagement, information poverty, and the Internet worldwide*. Cambridge, UK: Cambridge University Press. doi:10.1017/CBO9781139164887.

Norris, P. (2002). *Democratic phoenix: Political activism worldwide*. Cambridge, MA: Cambridge University Press. doi:10.1017/CBO9780511610073.

Noveck, B. S. (2000). Paradoxical partners: Electronic communication and electronic democracy. In Ferdinand, P. (Ed.), *The Internet, Democracy and Democratization* (pp. 18–35). London: Routledge. doi:10.1080/13510340008403643.

Nowrogee, B., & Manby, B. (1993). *Divide and rule: State-sponsored ethnic violence in Kenya*. New York: Human Rights Watch.

Nurudeen, N. A. (2012, 16 January). Nigeria: Facebook users hit 4.3 million – Report. *Daily Trust*. Retrieved January 21, 2013, from http://allafrica.com/stories/201201161269.html

Nyabuga, G. (2006). *Knowledge is Power: The Internet and the Kenyan Public Sphere*. Worcester Papers in English and Cultural Studies, 4. Retrieved March 7, 2010, from http://eprints.worc.ac.uk/310/1/Web_Knowledge_is_power_-_George_Nyabuga.pdf

Nyagudi, L. (2008, January 24). *Kenya: Spreading the words of hate*. Retrieved November 4, 2008, from http://mfoa.africanews.com/site/list_messages/15067

Nyakunu, N. (2005). The working environment in Zimbabwe. In *Report on International Conference on Media Support Strategies for Zimbabwe, International Media Support (IMS), The Netherlands Institute for Southern Africa, (NIZA), Media Institute for Southern Africa, (MISA), Open Society Institute, 2005-11-30*. Retrieved March 23, 2008, from http://www.i-m-s.dk/media/pdf/Zimbabwe

Nyamnjoh, F. (2005). *Africa's Media Democracy and the Politics of Belonging*. London: Zed Books.

Nyamnjoh, F. (2005). *Africa's Media, Democracy and the Politics of Belonging*. London: Zed Books.

Nyamnjoh, F. B. (2004). Media ownership and control in Africa in the age of globalization. In Thomas, P. N., & Nain, Z. (Eds.), *Who Owns the Media: GLOBAL Trends and Local Resistances*. London: Zed Books.

Nyamnjoh, F. B. (2005). *African Media: Democracy and the Politics of Belonging*. Pretoria, South Africa: Unisa Press.

Nyamnjoh, F. B., Wete, F., & Fonchingong, T. (1996). Media and civil society in Cameroon. *Africa Media Review*, *10*(3), 37–66.

Nyarota, G. (2008). Poor health now Mugabe's worst enemy. *The Zimbabwe Times*. Retrieved June 20, 2008, from http://www.thezimbabwetimes.com

Nyarota, G. (2008a, 2 April). Charamba now targets online publications. *The Zimbabwe Times*. Retrieved from http://wwwzimbabwejournalists.com/authors

O'Dell, J. (2011). How Egyptians used Twitter during the January crisis. *Mashable*. Retrieved on March 1, 2011, from: http://mashable.com/2011/02/01/egypt-Twitter-infographic/

O'sullivan, T. M., Hartley, J., Saunders, D., & Fiske, J. (1983). *Key Concepts in Communication*. London: Routledge.

Ocitti, J. (1999). *Media and democracy in Africa. Mutual political bedfellows or implacable arch-foes?* Cambridge, MA: Harvard University Retrieved from www.wcfia.harvard.edu/fellows/papers/1998-99/ocitti.pdf

Ocitti, J. (2006). *Press politics and public policy in Uganda: The role of journalism in democratization*. London: Edwin Mellen Press.

Odhiambo, L. O. (2002). The media environment in Kenya Since 1990. *African Studies*, *61*(2), 295–318. doi:10.1080/0002018022000032965.

Oduko, S. (1987). From indigenous communication to modern television: A reflection on political development in Nigeria. *Africa Media Review*, *1*(3), 1–10.

Ofuafor, M. (2010). *The influence of new media forms on media reportage and democracy in Nigeria.* Paper presented at the African Media and Democracy Conference. Accra, Ghana.

Ogbondah, C. W. (2004). Democratization and the media in West Africa: An analysis of recent constitutional and legislative reforms for press freedom in Ghana and Nigeria. *West Africa Review, 6.* Retrieved January 24, 2013, from http://www.westafricareview.com/issue6/ogbondah.html

Ogbondah, C. W. (1997). Communication and Democratization in Africa: Constitutional changes, prospects and persistent problems for the media. *Gazette, 59*(4/5), 271–294.

Ogbondah, C. W. (2002). Media laws in political transition. In Hydén, G., Leslie, M., & Ogundimu, F. F. (Eds.), *Media and democracy in Africa* (pp. 55–80). New Brunswick, NJ: Transaction Publishers.

Ojo, E. (2003). The Mass Media and the Challenges of Sustainable Democratic Values in Nigeria: Possibilities and Limitations. *Media Culture & Society, 25,* 821–840. doi:10.1177/0163443703256006.

Okumu, W. (2007). Gaps and challenges in preventing and combating terrorism in East Africa. In Okumu, W., & Botha, A. (Eds.), *Understanding terrorism in Africa: Building bridges and overcoming gaps* (pp. 60–70). Pretoria, South Africa: Institute for Security Studies.

Olayiwola, R. O. (1991). Political communications: Press and politics in Nigeria's second republic. *Africa Media Review, 5*(2), 31–45.

Olorunnisola, A. (2009). GSM telephones in Nigeria's political, socio-economic and geo-cultural landscapes. In Olorunnisola, A. (Ed.), *Media and communication industries in Nigeria: Impacts of neoliberal reforms between 1999 and 2007* (pp. 103–155). Lewiston, NY: The Edwin Mellen Press.

Olorunnisola, A. A. (1996). When tribal wars are mass mediated: Re-evaluating the policy of "non-interference.". *International Communication Gazette, 56,* 123–138. doi:10.1177/001654929605600203.

Olorunnisola, A. A. (1997). political ideology and news selection in local versus foreign press coverage of a domestic political event. *Ecquid Novi: Journal for Journalism in Southern Africa, 18*(2), 247–263.

Olorunnisola, A. A. (2006). *Media in South Africa after Apartheid: A Cross-Media Assessment.* Lewiston, NY: The Edwin Mellen Press.

Olorunnisola, A. A. (Ed.). (2009). *Media and communications industries in Nigeria: Impacts of neoliberal reforms between 1999 and 2007.* Lewiston, NJ: The Edwin Mellen Press.

Olorunnisola, A. A., & Martin, B. L. (2013). Influences of media in social movements: Problematizing hyperbolic inferences about impacts. *Telematics and Informatics, 30,* 275–288. doi:10.1016/j.tele.2012.02.005.

Olorunnisola, A. A., & Ojebode, A. A. (2013). Public opinion on Nigeria's democracy: Why the Arab Spring stopped in the Desert. In Olorunnisola, A., & Douai, A. (Eds.), *New Media Influence on Social and Political Change in AFRICA (336-356).* Hershey, PA: IGI-Global.

Olorunnisola, A. A., & Tomaselli, K. G. (Eds.). (2011). *Political economy of media transformation in South Africa.* Cresskill, NJ: Hampton Press, Inc..

Olsson, T. (2009). *Trisha Olsson @CamaraAfrica.* Retrieved January 20, 2010, from http://www.twitter.com/camaraafrica

Onyango-Obbo, C. (2010, March 17). The death has occurred of Mrs Africa Media Freedom. *Daily Nation.* Retrieved January 9, 2012, from http://www.nation.co.ke/blogs/The%20death%20has%20occurred%20of%20Mrs%20Africa%20Media%20Freedom%20/-/445642/881294/-/view/asBlogPost/-/6pgorcz/-/index.html

Open Net Initiative. (2009). *Internet filtering in Morocco.* Retrieved June 10, 2010, from http://opennet.net/sites/opennet.net/files/ONI_Morocco_2009.pdf

Organization of African Unity (OAU). (1981, June 27). *African Charter on Human and Peoples' Rights.* Retrieved January 9, 2012, from http://www1.umn.edu/humanrts/instree/z1afchar.htm

Ott, D. (1998). Power to the people: The role of electronic media in promoting democracy in Africa. *First Monday*. Retrieved August 15, 2010, from http://131.193.153.231/www/issues/issue3_4/ott/

Oyeleye, A. (2004). The Mediation of Politicians and the Political Process in Nigeria. *Parliamentary Affairs*, *57*, 157–168. doi:10.1093/pa/gsh013.

Papacharissi, Z. (2002). The self-online: The utility of personal homepages. *Journal of Broadcasting & Electronic Media*, *46*, 346–368. doi:10.1207/s15506878jobem4603_3.

Papacharissi, Z. (2002). The virtual sphere: The Internet as a public sphere. *New Media & Society*, *4*(1), 9–27. doi:10.1177/14614440222226244.

Papacharissi, Z. (2004). Democracy online: Civility, politeness and the democratic potential of online political discussion groups. *New Media & Society*, *6*(2), 259–283. doi:10.1177/1461444804041444.

Parliament of the Republic of South Africa. (2004). *National Assembly Guide to Procedure*. Creda, Cape Town. Retrieved April 30, 2012, from http://www.parliament.gov.za/content/GUIDE.pdf

Paun, M. (2009), Perceptions on the effectiveness of communication between public institutions and journalists through social media. *Styles of Communications, 2009*(1), 121. Retrieved from http://journals.univ-danubius.ro/index.php/communication/article/view/145

Pernisco, N. (2010). Social media impacts and implication on society. *Student Journal for Media Literacy Education*, *1*(1), 11. Retrieved from http://www.understandmedia.com/pdf/SJMLE-Vol1.pdf

Perry, A., & Blue, L. (2008). The Demons That Still Haunt Africa. *Time*, 32–35.

Peters, H. (2005). Rede: England. In Ueding, G. (Ed.), *Historisches Wörterbuch der Rhetorik* (pp. 751–756). Tübingen, Germany: Niemeyer.

Phelan, O., McCarthy, K., & Smyth, B. (2009). Using twitter to recommend real-time topical news. *In Proceedings of the third ACM conference on Recommender systems (RecSys '09)* (pp. 385-388). New York: ACM press.

Phillips, D., Roberts, N., & Benjamin, S. A. (1999). Political communication through newspaper advertisement: The case of the 1999 presidential election in Nigeria. NISER Monograph Series No 10.

Pitts, G. (2000). Democracy and press freedom in Zambia: Attitudes of members of parliament towards media and media regulations. *Communication Law and Policy*, *5*(2), 269–294. doi:10.1207/S15326926CLP0502_5.

Ploch, L. (2010, November 3). *Counterterrorism in East Africa: The U.S. Response*. Congressional Research Service Report P.13.

PNUD. (2010). *Rapport mondial sur le développement humain 200: Mettre les nouvelles technologies au service du développement humain*. Genève, New York: De Boeck University.

Pompeo, J. (2011). Egypt media watch: Al Jazeera shut down; Clinton hits Sunday shows. *Yahoo News*. Retrieved March 1, 2011, from http://news.yahoo.com/s/yblog_thecutline/20110131/ts_yblog_thecutline/egypt-media-watch-al-jazeera-shut-down-clinton-hits-sunday-shows

Poor, N. (2006). Mechanisms of an online public sphere: The website Slashdot. *Journal of Computer-Mediated Communication*, *10*(2), 00-00.

Post, R. (2005). Democracy and equality. *Law, culture and the humanities*. *1*, 142-153.

Post, W. Henry Kaiser Foundation, & Harvard University. (2004). *Survey of South Africans at ten years of democracy*.

Power, D. (Producer), Bartley, K. (Director), & Donnacha, O.B. (Director) (2003). *The Revolution Will Not Be Televised* [Motion picture]. Ireland: Vitagraph Films. Undercover in Zimbabwe Prison [Video file]. Retrieved June 13, 2011, from http://www.youtube.com/watch?v=5UrpciPVOdk

Press Reference. (n.d.). *Ghana*. Retrieved from http://www.pressreference.com/Fa-Gu/Ghana.html

Press, T. V. (2011). *Vodafone sent pro-Mubarak SMS*. Retrieved on March 18, 2011, from http://www.presstv.ir/detail/163417.html

Pritchard, J. L., & Sanderson, S. E. (2002). The Dynamics of Political Discourse in Seeking Sustainability. In Lance, H. G., & Holling, C. S. (Eds.), *Panarchy: Understanding Transformations in Human and Natural Systems* (pp. 147–170). Washington, DC: Island Press.

Przeworski, A. (n.d.). Democracy and economic development. *Political Science and Public Interest*, 1-27.

Puppis, M. (2010). Media governance: A new concept for the analysis of media policy and regulation. *Communication, Culture & Critique, 3*(2), 134–149. doi:10.1111/j.1753-9137.2010.01063.x.

Putnam, R. D. (2000). *Bowling alone: The collapse and revival of American community*. New York: Simon & Schuster. doi:10.1145/358916.361990.

Putzel, C. (2010) American Jihadi [Vanguard]. Cerissa Tanner, Christof Putzel (Producers). San Francisco, CA: Current TV.

Pye, L. (1963). *Communications and Political Development*. Princeton, NJ: Princeton University Press.

Qadir, S., Clapham, C., & Gill, B. (1993). Sustainable Democracy: Formalism vs. Substance. *Third World Quarterly, 14*(3), 415–422. doi:10.1080/01436599308420334.

QFM. (2012, November 23). *IBA to be operational in Jan 2013 – Sakeni*. Retrieved from http://www.qfmzambia.com/blog_details.php?idx=10450

Radio Katwe. (2006). How Radio Katwe has changed Uganda. Retrieved April 19, 2011, from http//www.radiokatwenews.blogspot.com/2006/03/how-rado-katwe-has-changed-uganda.html

Radio, S. W. (2007). Hot Seat: Foreign correspondent Peta Thornycroft on Media in Zimbabwe. [Radio programe transcript]. Retrieved February 20, 2008, from http://www.swradioafrica.com/pages/hotseat

Radsch, C. (2012). *The revolution will be blogged: Cyberactivism in Egypt*. Unpublished doctoral dissertation. American University, Washington DC.

Radsch, C. C. (2011). Repertoires of repression and the Egypt street: This is not a Facebook, Twitter or Wiki revolution! *The Huffington Post*. Retrieved March 1, 2011, from http://www.huffingtonpost.com/courtney-c-radsch/repertoires-of-repression_b_815714.html?ir=Media

Raeburn, M. (Director) (2003). *Zimbabwe Countdown* [Motion picture]. Zimbabwe: Journeyman Pictures. Violence a part of training police recruits in Zimbabwe [Video file]. Retrieved June 13, 2011, from http://www.youtube.com/watch?v=MiXZfwto3D8, 2.13mins.

Raftopoulos, B. (2011). Why there won't be a North African revolution in Zimbabwe. Retrieved February 15, 2012, from http://www.osisa.org/sites/default/files/sup_files/Why%20there%20won't%20be%20a%20North%20African%20revolution.pdf

Rakner, L. (2003). *Political and Economic Liberalisation in Zambia 1991–2001. The Nordic Africa Institute*. Sweden: Elanders Gotab.

Ralphs, G. (2007). The Contribution of Achille Mbembe to the Multi-disciplinary Study of Africa. *Postamble, 3*(2), 18–29.

Ram, N. (2007). A response to the journalism education curricula. A Speech at the World Journalism Education Congress. Singapore.

Ramaprasand, J. (2002). Tanzanian Journalist Profile: Demographics, Work Background, Choice of Profession, and Assessment of Press Freedom. *International Communication Bulletin, 37*(1-2), 2–17.

Raynes-Goldie, K., & Walker, L. (2008). Our Space: Online Civic Engagement Tools for Youth. In Bennett, L. (Ed.), *Civic Engagement: The MacArthur Series on Digital Media and Learning* (pp. 161–188). Cambridge, MA: The MIT Press.

Redpepper. (2012). Uganda threatens to block social media over protests. Retrieved May 25, 2011, from http://www.reuters.com/article/2011/04/19/us-uganda-unrest-media idUSTRE73I3LP20110419

Reisigl, M. (2008). Rhetoric of political speeches. In Wodak, R., & Koller, V. (Eds.), *Handbook of Communication in the Public Sphere* (pp. 243–269). Berlin, New York: Mouton de Gruyer.

Relief Web. (2008). *Kenya: Spreading the Word of Hate*. Retrieved November 9, 2008, from http://www.reliefweb.int/rw/RWB.NSF/db900SID/AMMF-7B4DL3?OpenDocument

Reno, W. (2007). The Political Economy of Order Amidst Predation in Sierra Leone. In G.B. Edna (Eds.), State of Violence: Politics, Youth, and Memory in Contemporary Africa (37-57). Charlottesville, VA: University of Virginia Press.

Reporters without Borders [RWB]. (2009). President deals major blow to press freedom. Retrieved December 2, 2010, from http://en.rsf.org/kenya-president-deals-major-blow-to-02-01-2009,29657.html

Reporters without Borders [RWB]. (2011). The new media: Between revolution and repression – Net solidarity takes on censorship. Retrieved March 16, 2011, from http://en.rsf.org/the-new-media-between-revolution-11-03-2011,39764.html

Reporters Without Frontiers. (2009). *2009 Country Report*. Retrieved June 8, 2010, from http://en.rsf.org/report-morocco,160.html

Republic of Ghana. (1992). *The 1992 Constitution of the Federal Republic of Ghana*. Accra, Ghana: Government Printers.

Reuters. (2010). Reactions to the State of the Nation Address. *Business Report*. Retrieved April 30, 2012, from http://www.busrep.co.za/index.php?fSectionId=552&fArticleId=5349000

Rheingold, H. (2002). *Smart mobs: The next social revolution*. Cambridge, MA: Perseus Books Group.

Richards, D. (1999). *Free Speech and the Politics of Identity*. Oxford, UK: Oxford University Press.

Rifaat, Y. (2008). Blogging the body: The case of Egypt. *Surfacing: An Interdisciplinary Journal for Gender in the Global South, 1*(1). Retrieved January 13, 2013, from http://www.aucegypt.edu/GAPP/IGWS/GradCent/Documents/FrontPages.pdf

Righter, R. (1978). *Whose News? Politics, the Press and the Third World*. New York: Times Books.

Riley, J. (1998). *Routledge Philosophy Guidebook to Mill On Liberty*. London: Routledge.

Rioba, A. (2009). *Media in Tanzania's Transition to Multiparty Democracy. An Assessment of Policy and Ethical Issues*. Unpublished Licentiate thesis, University of Tampere, Tampere, Sweden.

Rodriguez, C. (2001). *Fissures in the Mediascape. An International Study of Citizens' Media*. Cresskill, NJ: Hampton Press.

Ronning, H., & Kupe, T. (2000). The dual legacy of democracy and authoritarianism: The media and the state in Zimbabwe. In J. Curran., & M. Jin-Park (Eds.), De-Westernizing Media Studies. London: Routledge.

Ronning, H. (1997). Institutions and representation. In Zhuwarara, R., Gecau, K., & Drag, M. (Eds.), *Democratization and Identity* (pp. 1–15). Harare, Zimbabwe: University of Zimbabwe.

Roodt, D. (2009, April 14). South Africa: Skins And Velskoene -- Why Zuma is Befriending Afrikaners. *Business Day*, 14. Retrieved August 30, 2010, from http://allafrica.com/stories/200904140038.html

Rossouw, M. (2010, February 12). In Madiba's shadow: Zuma stresses reconciliation but makes it clear there's little in state's kitty. Mail & Guardian, 4

Ross, T. J. (2010). A test of democracy: Ethiopia's Mass Media and Freedom of Information Proclamation. *Penn State Law Review, 114*(3), 1047–1066.

Routray, B. P. (2011). Why ban just the bra in Somalia? Ban everything. Ban food. Ban life. *Al-Arabiya News*. Retrieved February 8, 2012, from http://www.alarabiya.net/views/2011/07/29/159848.html Last accessed February 8, 2012

Rozumilowicz, B. (2002). Democratic Change: A Theoretical Perspective. In Price, M., Rozumilowicz, B., & Verhulst, S. (Eds.), *Media Reform Democratising the Media, Democratising the State* (pp. 9–26). London: Routledge.

Ruggiero, V., & Montagna, N. (Eds.). (2008). *Social Movements: A Reader*. London: Routledge.

Rugh, W. (1979). *The Arab press: News media and political process in the Arab World*. Syracuse, NY: Syracuse University Press.

Rugh, W. (2004). *Arab mass media: Newspapers, radio, and television in Arab politics*. Westport, CT: Praeger.

Rummel, R. J. (1996). Democratization. In Vogele, W., & Powers, R. (Eds.), *Protest, power, and change: An encyclopedia of nonviolence action from act-up to women's suffrage*. Hamden, CT: Garland Publishing. Retrieved from http://www.hawaii.edu/powerkills/DEMOC.HTM#

Ryu, A. (2008, January 30). *Radio broadcasts incite Kenya's ethnic violence*. Retrieved September 4, 2008, from http://www.voanews.com/english/archive/2008-01/2008-01-30-voa38.cfm

Ryu, A. (2008, March 19). Despite power-sharing accord, ethnic division in Kenya runs deep. Retrieved December 20, 2008, from http://www.voanews.com/english/archive/2008-03/2008-03-19-kenyaland.cfm

Sachikonye, L. (2011). *When a state turns on its citizens: 60 years of institutionalized violence in Zimbabwe*. Ackland Park: Jacana.

Saco, D. (2002). *Cyber Democracy: Public Space and the Internet*. Minneapolis, MN: University of Minnesota.

Sakr, N. (2001). *Satellite realms: Transnational television, globalization and the Middle East*. London: I.B. Tauris.

Salawu, A. (2006). Indigenous language media: A veritable tool for African language learning. *Journal of Multicultural Discourses, 1*(1), 86–95. doi:10.1080/10382040608668533.

Salazar-Ferro, M. (2010, June 17). *Journalists in exile 2010. An exodus from Iran, East Africa. CPJ special report*. Retrieved January 9, 2012, from http://cpj.org/reports/2010/06/journalists-exile-2010-iran-africa-exodus.php

Salazar, P. (2000). Press Freedom and Citizen Agency in South Africa: A Rhetorical Approach. *The Public, 7*(4), 55–68.

Salazar, P. J. (2002). *An African Athens: Rhetoric and the shaping of democracy in South Africa. Rhetoric, knowledge and society*. Mahwah, NJ: Erlbaum.

Salvatore, A. (2007). *The public sphere: Liberal modernity, Catholicism, Islam*. New York: Palgrave Macmillan.

Sandoval, M., & Fuchs, C. (2010). Towards a critical theory of alternative media. *Telematics and Informatics, 27*, 171–150. doi:10.1016/j.tele.2009.06.011.

Sangaparee, C. (2011, May 25). *Who Caused The Crisis In The NDC?* Retrieved from http://www.ghanaweb.com/GhanaHomePage/NewsArchive/artikel.php?ID=208870

Sangwa, J. (n.d.). Press freedom in Zambia. *Southern African Media Law Briefing*. Retrieved from http://www.fxi.org.za/pages/Publications/Medialaw/zambia.htm

Sapa. (1995, February 18): Errors 'part of learning'. *The Citizen*, 11

Sapa. (2010, February 11). Disappointment follows Zuma's address. *Business Report*. Retrieved April 30, 2012, from http://www.busrep.co.za/index.php?fSectionId=552&fArticleId=5348999

Sapa. (2010, February 11). Opposition critical of Zuma's speech. *IOL online*. Retrieved April 30, 2012, from http://www.iol.co.za/index.php?set_id=1&click_id=13&art_id=nw20100211211607751C657048

Sapa. (2010, February 18). Historic evening opening for Parliament. *Mail & Guardian Online*. Retrieved April 30, 2012, from

Sassen, S. (2004). Towards a technology of Information technology. In C. Avgerou, C. Ciborra., & F. Land (Eds.), The Social Study of Information and Communication Technology: Innovation, Actors and Contexts (pp. 77–103). Oxford, UK: Oxford University Press.

Sater, J. (2007). *Civil Society and Political Change in Morocco*. London: Routledge.

Satter, R. G. (2011). Vodafone: Egypt forced us to send text messages. *Yahoo News*. Retrieved March 1, 2011, from http://news.yahoo.com/s/ap/20110203/ap_on_hi_te/eu_egypt_cell_phones

Saul, J. S. (2008). *Decolonization and Empire. Contesting the Rhetoric and Rerality of Resubordination in Southern Africa and Beyond*. Johannesburgh, South Africa: Wits University Press.

Saunders, R. (1991). Information in the interregnum: The state and Civil Society in the Struggle for hegemony in Zimbabwe, 1980-1990. Unpublished PhD thesis, Carleton University, Ottawa, Canada.

Savigny, H. (2002). Public opinion, political communication and the Internet. *Politics, 22*(1), 1–8. doi:10.1111/1467-9256.00152.

SBWire. (2012). *Internet users in Egypt to get double by 2012*. Retrieved January 12, 2013, from http://www.sbwire.com/press-releases/sbwire-75087.htm

Scanlon, T. (1990). Content Regulation Reconsidered. In Lichtenberg, J. (Ed.), *Democracy and the Mass Media* (pp. 331–354). Cambridge, UK: Cambridge University Press. doi:10.1017/CBO9781139172271.013.

Scannell, P. (1992). Public service broadcasting and modern public life. In Scannell, P., Schlesinger, P., & Sparks, C. (Eds.), *Culture and power: A media, culture and society reader* (pp. 317–348). London: Sage.

Scannell, P. (2007). *Media and communication*. London: Sage.

Schedler, A. (2002). Elections without Democracy the Manipulation. *Journal of Democracy, 13*, 36–50. doi:10.1353/jod.2002.0031.

Scheufele, B. T. (2004). Framing-effects approach: A theoretical and methodological critique. *Communications, 29*, 401–428. doi:10.1515/comm.2004.29.4.401.

Scheufele, D. (2000). Agenda-Setting, Priming, and Framing Revisited: Another Look at Cognitive Effects of Political Communication. *Mass Communication & Society, 3*(2/3), 297–316. doi:10.1207/S15327825MCS0323_07.

Schramm, W. (1964). *Mass Media and National Development: The Role of Information in the Developing Countries*. Stanford, CA: Stanford University Press. doi:10.1177/000276426400800305.

Schubert, K., & Klein, M. (2001). *Das Politiklexikon*. Bonn, Germany: J.H.W. Dietz. Retrieved April 30, 2012, from http://kunstbewegung.info/cde/rlp-definitionen-lexika/4891-politik-definition.html.

Seaton, J. (2003). Broadcasting history. In Curran, J., & Seaton, J. (Eds.), *Power without responsibility: The press, broadcasting and new media in Britain* (pp. 109–236). London: Routledge.

Seib, P. (2007). New media and prospects for democratization. In Seib, P. (Ed.), *New Media and the New Middle East* (pp. 1–18). New York: Palgrave Macmillan. doi:10.1057/9780230605602.

Senghaas, D. (1977). *Weltwirtschaftsordnung und Entwicklundspolitik*. Frankfurt, Germany: Plädoyer für Dissoziation.

Shade, L. R. (2002). *Gender and Community in the Social Construction of the Internet*. New York: P. Lang.

Shah, H. (1996). Modernization, marginalization, and emancipation: Toward a normative model of journalism and national development. *Communication Theory, 6*(2), 143–166. doi:10.1111/j.1468-2885.1996.tb00124.x.

Sharp, J. M. (2011). *Egypt: Background and U.S. relations*. Washington, DC: Congressional Research Service. Retrieved March 21, 2011, from fpc.state.gov/documents/organization/84928.pdf

Shaughnessy, H. (2012). *Stop Kony/ Kony 2012 Closes on 50 Million YouTube Views: Meanwhile The Guardian Investigates*. Retrieved from http://www.forbes.com/sites/haydnshaughnessy/2012/03/09/stop-kony-kony-2012-closes-on-50-million-youtube-views-meanwhile-the-guardian-investigates/

Shaw, A. (2010, August 9). SA journalists fight proposed media laws. *Mail & Guardian Online*. Retrieved January 17, 2013, from http://www.mg.co.za/article/2010-08-09-sa-journalists-fight-proposed-media-laws

Shelley, F. M. (2011). Orientalism, idealism, and realism: The United States and the Arab Spring. *The Arab World Geographer, 14*(2), 169–173.

Shigetomi, S. (2009). Rethinking theories on social movements and development. In Shigetomi, S., & Makino, K. (Eds.), *Protest and Social Movements in the Developing World* (pp. 1–16). Cheltenham, UK: Edward Elgar Publishing.

Shilgba, L. K. (2010). On President Jonathan and His Political Party. Retrieved June 19, 2010, from http://www.saharareporters.com

Shimelis B. (2002). The state of the press in Ethiopia. In Bahru Z., & Pausewang, S. (Eds.), *Ethiopia: The challenge from below* (pp. 184–200). Stockholm, Sweden: Nordiska Afrikainstitutet.

Sibeko, S. (2010, January 4). South Africa's President Zuma marries for fifth time. Retrieved July 24, 2010, from http://www.reuters.com/article/idUS-TRE60325E20100104

Sidi Hida, B. (2007). *Social movements and stakeholder. Development NGOs face of globalization and the state in Morocco*. Unpublished doctoral dissertation. Catholic University of Louvain. Université catholique de Louvain, Belgium.

Siebert, F. S., Peterson, T., & Schramm, W. (1956). *Four Theories of the Press: The Authoritarian, Libertarian, Social Responsibility and Soviet Communist Concepts of What the Press Should Be and Do*. Champaign, IL: University of Illinois Press.

Simberg, N. (2011). *African News Flow in Africa – New Patterns or Old Habits? African News Coverage in two Namibian and two Tanzanian Newspapers.* Unpublished Master's thesis. University of Helsinki, Helsinki, Finland.

Simutanyi, N. (2002). *Challenges To Democratic Consolidation In Zambia: Public Attitudes To Democracy and the Economy.* Afrobarometer Paper No. 17. Retrieved from www.afrobarometer.org/index.php?option=com_docman&task

Singh, J. P. (1999). *Leapfrogging development: The political economy of telecommunications restructuring.* Albany, NY: SUNY.

Siurala, L. (2002). *Can Youth Make a Difference? Youth Policy Facing Diversity and Change.* Strasbourg, France: Council of Europe.

Skjerdal, T. S. (2011). Teaching journalism or teaching African journalism? Experiences from foreign involvement in a journalism programme in Ethiopia. *Global Media Journal: African Edition, 5*(1), 24-51.

Skjerdal, T. S. (2008). Self-censorship among news journalists in the Ethiopian state media. *African Communication Research, 1*(2), 185–206.

Skjerdal, T. S. (2010). Justifying self-censorship: A perspective from Ethiopia. *Westminster Papers in Communication and Culture, 7*(2), 98–121.

Skjerdal, T. S. (2010). Research on brown envelope journalism in the African media. *African Communication Research, 3*(3), 367–406.

Skjerdal, T. S. (2013). Selective liberalization: An analysis of media reform in a semi-democratic society. In Olorunnisola, A., & Douai, A. (Eds.), *New Media Influence on Social and Political Change in Africa (32-50).* Hershey, PA: IGI-Global.

Skjerdal, T. S., & Lule, H. (2009). Uneven performances by the private press in Ethiopia: An analysis of 18 years of press freedom. *Journal of Communication and Language Arts, 3*(1), 44–59.

Skjerdal, T. S., & Ngugi, C. M. (2007). Institutional and governmental challenges for journalism education in East Africa. *Ecquid Novi – African. Journalism Studies, 28*(1–2), 176–190.

Smith, A. D. (1986). *The ethnic origins of nations.* Oxford, UK: Blackwell.

Smith, W. D. (2003). Higher education, Democracy and the Public Sphere. *Thought and Action, 19*(1), 61–73.

SocialBakers. (2011). *The rise of Asia and Africa on Facebook: Statistics by continent!* Retrieved from http://www.socialbakers.com/blog/116-the-rise-of-asia-and-africa-on-facebook-statistics-by-continent/

Sparks, A. (2003). *Beyond the miracle.* Johannesburg, South Africa: Jonathan Ball.

Sparks, C. (2001). The Internet and the global public sphere. In Bennett, L. W., & Entman, R. M. (Eds.), *Mediated politics: Communication in the future of democracy* (pp. 75–95). Cambridge, UK: Cambridge University Press.

Splichal, S. (2006). In search of a strong European public sphere: Some critical observations on conceptualizations of publicness and the (European) public sphere. *Media Culture & Society, 28*(5), 695–7147. doi:10.1177/0163443706067022.

Stapenhurst, R. (2000). *The media's role in curbing corruption.* World Bank Institute Working Paper: Washington, DC.

Steadman Group. (2008). *Steadman group for kenya advertising research.* Nairobi, Kenya: Steadman.

Stekelenburg, S., & Klandermans, M. (Eds.). (2009). *Protest and Social Movement in the Developing World.* Cheltenham, UK: Edward Elgar Publishing.

Stepanek, M. (2013, March 15). *Occupy: The Movie.* [Web log comment]. Retrieved from http://causeglobal.blogspot.com.au/

Stepanova, E. (2011). The role of information communication technologies in the Arab Spring. *Implications beyond the region.* PONARS Eurasia Policy Memo no. 159. Washington, DC: George Washington University.

Straus, S. (2007). What is the relationship between hate radio and violence? Rethinking Rwanda's "Radio Machete". *Politics & Society, 35*, 609–637. doi:10.1177/0032329207308181.

Sutherland, E. (2007). Unbundling local loops: global experiences. Learning Information Networking and Knowledge Centre (LINK). Retrieved January 13, 2013, from http://link.wits.ac.za/papers/LINK.pdf

Sutter, G. (2000). Nothing new under the Sun: Old Fears and New Media. *International Journal of Law and Information Technology*, *8*(3), 338–378. doi:10.1093/ijlit/8.3.338.

Swaddle, K. (1988). Hi-Tech Elections: Technology and the Development of Electioneering since 1945. *Contemporary British History*, *2*(1), 32–35.

Swain, J. (2008, February 3). Kenya violence: 'We waited, now we'll chop them to bits'. Retrieved November 21, 2008, from http://www.timesonline.co.uk/tol/news/world/africa/article3295501.ece

Switzer, L., & Adhikari, M. (Eds.). (2000). *South Africa's Resistance Press: Alternative Voices in the Last Generation Under Apartheid*. Athens, OH: Ohio University Press.

Taarnby, M., & Hallunbaek, L. (2010). Al Shabaab: The internationalization of militant Islamism in Somalia and the implications for radicalization processes in Europe. *Danish Ministry of Justice Report*, 13-14.

Tabaire, B. (2007). The press and political repression in Uganda: Back to the future? *Journal of Eastern African Studies*, *1*(2), 193–211. doi:10.1080/17531050701452408.

Tarrow, S. (1998). *Power in movement: Social movements and contentious politics*. Cambridge, MA: Cambridge University Press. doi:10.1017/CBO9780511813245.

Taylor, S. (2009). *African Media Barometer 2009 – Botswana*. Windhoek, Namibia: Media Institute of Southern Africa & Friedrich-Ebert-Stiftung.

Teer-Tomaselli, R. (2011). Transforming state-owned enterprises in the global age: Lessons from broadcasting and telecommunications in South Africa. In Olorunnisola, A., & Tomaselli, K. (Eds.), *Political economy of media transformation in South Africa* (pp. 133–166). Cresskill, NJ: Hampton Press, Inc..

Teer-Tomaselli, R., & Mjwacu, T. (2003). Developing the Communicative Competence: the Potentials and Limitations of Community Radio. In Malmelin, N. (Ed.), *The science of caring/transmitting. Communication perspectives to society, culture and citizenship* (pp. 24–43). Helsinki, Finland: University of Helsinki.

Tettey, W. (2001). The Media and Democratization in Africa: Contributions, Constraints and Concerns of the Private Press. *Media Culture & Society*, *23*(1), 5–31. doi:10.1177/016344301023001001.

Tettey, W. (2006). The Politics of Media Accountability in Africa: An Examination of Mechanisms and Institutions. *International Communication Gazette*, *68*, 229–248. doi:10.1177/1748048506063763.

Tettey, W. J. (2001). The media and democratization in Africa: Contributions, constraints and concerns of the private press. *Media Culture & Society*, *23*, 5–31. doi:10.1177/016344301023001001.

The Communication Regulators' Association of Southern Africa (CRASA). *Welcome to CRASA*. Retrieved from http://www.crasa.org/index.php

The Initiative for an Open Arab Internet. (2009). *The second report of the Arabic Network for Human Rights Information (HR info)*. Morocco. Retrieved January 13, 2013, from http://www.openarab.net/en/node/364

The National Council for Law Reporting. (2008). The Constitution of Kenya, as altered to 2008. Chapter 5. Article 79.

The Press freedom Committee of The Post (2010, May 20). Al Cross Zambia FOI Speech. *The Post*. Retrieved from http://www.postzambia.com

The Proudly South African Campaign. (n.d.). *About Us*. Retrieved January 17, 2013, from http://www.proudlysa.co.za/consumer-site

The Standard. (2010, August 23). *Urban residents decry prolonged power cuts*.

The Standard. (2010, August 23). *ZESA attacked for load shedding*.

The Standard. (2010, September 5). *Power cuts give Econet connectivity nightmares*.

The World Bank. (n.d.). *The public sphere*. Retrieved August 21, 2010, from http://www.worldbank.org/commgap blogs.worldbank.org/publicsphere

The Zimbabwean. (2010). Gono death report false. Retrieved July 10, 2011, From http://www.thezimbabwean.co.uk/news/32138/gono-death-report-false.html

Theocharis, Y. (2010). Young People, Political Participation and Online Postmaterialism in Greece. *New Media & Society, 13*(2), 203–223. doi:10.1177/1461444810370733.

Therborn, G. (1980). *The ideology of power and the power of ideology*. London: Verso.

Thomas, J. (1997). Discourse in the Marketplace: The Making of Meaning in Annual Reports. *Journal of Business Communication*, (34): 47–66. doi:10.1177/002194 369703400103.

Thompson, A. (n.d.). *Journalism training and media freedom in Rwanda*. Retrieved April 19, 2011, from http://www.waccglobal.org/en/20074-communicating-peace/476-Journalism-training-%09and-media-freedom-in-Rwanda.html

Thompson, M. (2008). ICT and development studies: Towards development 2.0. *Journal of International Development, 20*(6), 821–835. doi:10.1002/jid.1498.

Thomspon, M., & Walsham, G. (2010). ICT research in Africa: Need for a strategic developmental focus. *Information Technology for Development, 16*(2), 112–127. doi:10.1080/02681101003737390.

Thussu, D. K. (2006). International Communication: Continuity and change (2ndEd). London. Arnold.

Thussu, D. K. (2007). The 'Murdochization' of news? The case of Star TV in India. *Media Culture & Society, 29*(4), 592–611. doi:10.1177/0163443707076191.

Thussu, D. K. (Ed.). (2009). *Internationalising media studies*. London: Routledge.

Tilly, C. (1984). *Big Structures, Large Processes, Huge Comparisons*. New York: Russell Sage Foundation.

Tilly, C., & Tarrow, S. (2007). *Contentious Politics*. Boulder, CO: Paradigm Publishers.

Times Media Group Limited. (n.d.). *Media Group Division*. Retrieved January 17, 2013, from http://www.timesmedia.co.za/businesses/media/

Times of Zambia. (2010, August 12). *State opposed to ZAMEC launch*. Retrieved from http://www.times.co.zm/

Tleane, C., & Duncan, J. (2003). *Public broadcasting in the era of cost recovery: A critique of the South African Broadcasting Corporation's crisis of accountability.* Johannesburg, South Africa: Freedom of Expression Institute.

Tomaselli, K., & Teer-Tomaselli, R. (2008). Exogenous and Endogenous Democracy: South African Politics and Media. *The International Journal of Press/Politics,* (13), pp. 171–180. Retrieved April 30, 2012, from http://hij.sagepub.com/content/13/2/171

Tom, D. (2004). The Watchdog inside a Cage: The Nigerian Press and Censorship Laws. *Ethiope Research Abraka Journal of the Arts. Law and Social Science, 1*, 91–118.

Touraine, A. (1981). *The Voice and the Eye: An Analysis of Social Movements*. Cambridge, MA: Cambridge University Press.

Touraine, A. (1985). An introduction to the study of social movements. *Social Research, 52*, 749–788.

Tumasjan, A., Sprenger, T. O., Sandner, P. G., & Welpe, I. M. (2010). Predicting elections with Twitter: What 140 characters reveal about political sentiment. *Proceedings of the 4th International AAAI Conference on Weblogs and Social Media*. Washington, DC: AAAI.

Tunstall, J. (1977). *The media are American*. New York: Columbia University Press.

Turner, I. (2013). The changing state of the South African Nation: Political proximity to business from a linguistic perspective. In Olorunnisola, A., & Douai, A. (Eds.), *New Media Influence on Social and Political Change in AFRICA (168-186)*. Hershey, PA: IGI-Global.

Tynes, R. (2007). Nation-building and the diaspora on Leonenet: A case of Sierra Leone in cyberspace. *New Media & Society, 9*(3), 407–518. doi:10.1177/1461444807076980.

U.S. Department of State's Report of the Advisory Committee on Cultural Diplomacy. (2005). *Cultural Diplomacy: The Linchpin of Public Diplomacy*. Retrieved from http://www.state.gov/documents/organization/54374.pdf

U.S. Senate Resolution 402. (n.d.). *A resolution condemning Joseph Kony and the Lord's Resistance Army for committing crimes against humanity and mass atrocities.* Retrieved from http://www.govtrack.us/congress/bills/112/sres402/text

Ubayasiri, K. (2006). The Internet and the public Sphere: A glimpse of YouTube. *Ejournalist: A Refereed Media Journal, 6*(2), 1-13

Uganda Radio Network-URN. (2012). Police threaten to close Jinja radio stations. Retrieved October 9, 2012, from http://ugandaradionetwork.com/a/story.php?s=43128

Ugboajah, F. O. (1985). Media habits of rural and semi-rural (slum) Kenya. *International Communication Gazette, 36,* 155–174. doi:10.1177/001654928503600301.

Uko, N. (2004). *Romancing the Gun: The Press as a Promoter of Military Rule.* Trenton, NJ: Africa World Press Inc..

UN Department of Economic and Social Affairs. (2010). *UN e-government 2010 survey.* Retrieved January 13, 2013, from http://kz.mofcom.gov.cn/accessory/201009/1284225105383.pdf

UN Human Development Programme [UNDP]. (2009). *Human Development Report: Morocco.* Retrieved January 13, 2013, from http://hdrstats.undp.org/en/countries/country_fact_sheets/cty_fs_MAR.html

UN ICT Task Force. (2005). Measuring ICT: The global status of ICT indicators. Retrieved from https://www.itu.int/ITU-D/ict/partnership/material/05-42742%20GLOBAL%20ICT.pdf

UNESCO Institute for Statistics. (2003). Retrieved July 8, from http://www.uis.unesco.org/ev.php?URL_ID=3754&URL_DO=DO_TOPIC&URL_SECTION=201

UNESCO. (1991). *Final Report: Seminar on promoting an independent and pluralistic African Press.* Windhoek, Namibia: UNESCO.

UNESCO. (1991, May 3). *Windhoek declaration on promoting idependent and pluralistic media.* Retrieved from www.cpu.org.uk/userfiles/WINDHOEK%20DECLARATION.pdf

UNESCO. (2001, May 3). *African Charter on Broadcasting.* Retrieved from www.misa.org/broadcasting/brochure.pdf

United Nations Educational, Scientific, and Cultural Organization. (2007). *Model Curricula for Journalism Education for Developing Countries & Emerging Democracies.* Retrieved April 19, 2011, from http://unesdoc.unesco.org/images/0015/001512/151209E.pdf.United Nations

United Nations Educational, Social, and Cultural Organization. (1980). *Many Voices, One World.* Paris: UNESCO.

United Nations Educational, Social, and Cultural Organization. (2002). *Communications Training in Africa: Model Curricula.* Retrieved April 19, 2011, from http://portal.unesco.org/ci/en/files/24219/11731978671com_training_en.pdf/com _25 training_en.pdf

United Nations Security Council Resolutions for 1992. Retrieved January 20, 2012, from http://www.un.org/documents/sc/res/1992/scres92.htm

USAID. (2008). *Rwanda media strengthening program: Request for applications.* Washington, DC: USAID.

van der Graft, P., & Sevensson, J. (2006). Explaining eDemocracy development: A quantitative empirical study. *Information Polity, 11,* 123–134.

Van der Veur, P. R. (2002). Broadcasting and political reform. In Hydén, G., Leslie, M., & Ogundimu, F. F. (Eds.), *Media and democracy in Africa* (pp. 81–106). New Brunswick, NJ: Transaction Publishers.

Van Dijk, T. A. (1998). *Critical discourse analysis.* Retrieved April 19, 2011, from http://www.hum.uva.nl/teun/cda.htm

Van Dijk, J. A. G. M. (2005). *The Deepening Divide: Inequality in the Information Society.* Thousand Oaks, CA: Sage Publications.

Van Dijk, J. A. G. M. (2006). *The Network Society: Social Aspects of New Media.* Thousand Oaks, CA: Sage Publications.

van Dijk, T. A. (1993). Principles of critical discourse analysis. *Discourse & Society, 4*(2), 249–283. doi:10.1177/0957926593004002006.

van Dijk, T. A. (1997). Discourse as interaction in society. In van Dijk, T. A. (Ed.), *Discourse as Social Interaction: Discourse Studies: A Multidiciplinary Indtoruction* (Vol. 2, pp. 1–37). London: Sage. doi:10.4135/9781446221884.n1.

van Noppen, J.-P. (2004). CDA: A discipline come of age. *Journal of Sociolinguistics*, 8(1), 107–126. doi:10.1111/j.1467-9841.2004.00253.x.

Van Staden, G. (2000, February 6). The Long View. *Business Report*. Retrieved April 30, 2012, from http://www.busrep.co.za/index.php?fSectionId=561&fArticleId=74876

Vasquez, R. (2011). *Social Networking Theory and Cultural Diplomacy*. Abridged thesis. Retrieved from http://www.eotwonline.net/2011/05/22/social-networking-and-cultural-d/

Vedel, T. (2003). Internet et les pratiques politiques. In *La communication politique: Etat des savoirs, enjeux et perspectives* (pp. 189–214). Quebec: Presses de l'Université de Québec.

Vernacular Radio Fuelled Ethnic Clashes. (2008). *The Nairobi Chronicle*. Retrieved November 22, 2008, from http://nairobichronicle.wordpress.com/2008/08/04/vernacular-radio-fuelled-ethnic-clashes/

Vodafone. (2011). *Statement on Egypt*. Retrieved March 1, 2011, from http://www.vodafone.com/content/index/press/press_statements/statement_on_egypt.html

Voltmer, K. (2008). *Government performance, collective accountability, and the news media*. Paper presented at the Harvard-World Bank workshop The Role of the News Media in the Governance Reform. Cambridge, MA.

von Nahmen, C. (2001). *Deutschsprähige Medien in Namibia. Vom Windhoeker Anzeiger zum Deutschen Hörfunkprogramm der Namibian Broadcasting Corporation. Geschichte, Bedeutung und Funktion der deutschsprachigen Medien in Namibia 1898-1998*. Windhoek, Namibia: Namibia Wissenschaftliche Gesellschaft.

Wadhmas, N. (2008). World Spotlignt: Kenya in Crisis. *Time*, 7.

Wafula, E. (2008, May 6). *Africa Brief*. Retrieved November 9, 2008, from http://africabrief.blogspot.com/2008_05_04_archive.html

Waldahl, R. (2004). *Politics and persuasion: Media coverage of Zimbabwe's 2000 election*. Harare, Zimbabwe: Weaver Press.

Wallerstein, I. (1960). *Africa: The politics of independence, interpretation modern history*. New York: Vintage.

Wallerstein, I. (2001). *Unthinking social science: The limits of nineteenth-century paradigms* (2nd ed.). Philadelphia, PA: Temple University Press.

Walsham, G., Robey, F., & Sahay, S. (2007). Foreword: Special issue on information systems in developing countries. *Management Information Systems Quarterly*, 31(2), 317–326.

Walsham, G., & Sahay, S. (2006). Research on information systems in developing countries: Current landscape and future prospects. *Information Technology for Development*, 12(1), 7–24. doi:10.1002/itdj.20020.

Wanjiku, R. (2009). Kenya Communications Amendment Act (2009): Progressive or retrogressive? *Association for Progressive Communications*. Retrieved March 1, 2011, from www.apc.org/en/system/files/CICEWAKenya20090908_EN.pdf

Warschauer, M. (2003). Dissecting the Digital Divide: A Case Study in Egypt. *The Information Society*, 19(4), 297–304. doi:10.1080/01972240309490.

Wasserman, H. (2010). *Tabloid Journalism in South Africa: True story!* Bloomington, IN: Indiana University Press.

Wasserman, H., & Boloka, M. (2004). Privacy, the Press and the Public Interest in Post-Apartheid South Africa. *Parliamentary Affairs*, 57, 185–195. doi:10.1093/pa/gsh015.

Waterbury, J. (1970). *The commander of the Faithful: The Moroccan political elite: A study of segmented politics*. New York: Columbia University Press.

Watson, J. (2012). Americans rise in rank inside Somalia jihadi group. *The Guardian*. Retrieved from http://www.guardian.co.uk/world/feedarticle/10041431

Weaver, D. H., & Wilhoit, G. C. (1991). *The American journalist: A portrait of U.S. news people and their work*. Bloomington, IN: Indiana University Press.

Weimann, G. (2006). Terror on the Internet: The New Arena, the New Challenges (pp. 54-56, 61). Washington, DC: United States Institute of Peace Press.

Weimann, G. (2010). Terror on Facebook, Twitter and YouTube. *The Brown Journal of World Affairs*, XVI(II), 48.

Weitz-Shapiro, R. (2008). The local connection: Local government performance and satisfaction with democracy in Argentina. *Comparative Political Studies*, *41*(3), 285–308. doi:10.1177/0010414006297174.

Wesemüller, E. (2005). *African nationalism from Apartheid to post-Apartheid South Africa: A critical analysis of ANC Party political discourse.* Stuttgart, Germany: Ibidem-Verlag.

White, R. A. (2008). The Role of the Media in Democratic Governance. *African Communication Research*, *1*(3), 269–328.

Widner, J. (1992). Kenya's slow progress toward multiparty politics. *Current History (New York, N.Y.)*, *91*, 214–218.

Wigand, F. D. (2010). Twitter in government: Building relationships one Tweet at a time. *Proceedings of the 7th International Conference on Information Technology* (pp. 563-567). Los Alamitos, CA: IEEE.

Wilcox, D. (1975). *Mass Media in Black Africa.* New York: Praeger.

Wilhelm, A. G. (2000). *Democracy in the digital age: Challenges to political life in cyberspace.* London: Routledge.

Wilkes, A. (1986). Freedom of Information. In Curran, J., Ecclestone, J., Oakley, G., & Richardson, A. (Eds.), *Bending Reality the State of the Media* (pp. 229–235). London: Pluto Press.

Williams, K. (2003). *Understanding media theory.* New York: Oxford University Press.

Williamson, D. (2011). Terror group Somalia's only hope for peace and stability. *Wales Online.* Retrieved January 30, 2012, from http://www.walesonline.co.uk/news/welsh-politics/welsh-politics-news/2011/12/13/terror-group-somalia-s-only-hope-for-peace-and-stability-91466-29942080

Williams, R. (1979). Institutions of the Technology. In Mattelart, A., & Siegelaub, S. (Eds.), *Communication and Class Struggle: Capitalism, Imperialism* (pp. 265–268). New York: International General.

Wilson, E. (2004). *The information revolution and developing countries.* Cambridge, MA: MIT Press.

Wiuff Moe, L. (2010). *Addressing state fragility in Africa. A need to challenge the established 'wisdom'?* The Finnish Institute of International Affairs Report No 22.

Wodak, R. (2004). Critical discourse analysis. *Qualitative Research Practice*, 185-201.

Wodak, R. (1999). Critical discourse analysis at the end of the 20th century. *Research on Language and Social Interaction*, *32*(1&3), 185–193.

Wolton, D. (2008). *La communication politique: La construction d'un modèle.* Essentiels d'Hermès.

Wonacott, P. (2010, February 8). Zuma Apologizes for Fathering Child Out of Wedlock. *The Wall Street Journal.* Retrieved January 17, 2013, from http://online.wsj.com/article/SB1000142405274870419710457505101385217470.html#

Wong, S. (2012). *Joseph Kony captures Congress' attention.* Retrieved from http://www.politico.com/news/stories/0312/74355.html

World Association of Newspapers. (2007). Declaration of Table Mountain. Retrieved from www.declarationoftablemountain.org

World Association of Newspapers. (2007). Press Freedom in Africa: the Key to Good Governance and Development 2007. Retrieved February 24, 2009, from http://www.wanpress.org/print.php3?id_article

World Bank. (2006). *Annual Report.* Retrieved January 8, 2006, from http://treasury.worldbank.org/web/AnnualReport 2006.pdf

World Bank. (2010). *World databank: World development indicators (WDI) & global development finance (GDF).* Retrieved March 1, 2011, from http://databank.worldbank.org/

World Bank. (2010). *World Development Indicators.* Retrieved January 14, 2013, from http://data.worldbank.org/sites/default/files/frontmatter.pdf

Wu, T. (2010). *The Master Switch: The Rise and Fall of Information Empires.* New York: Knopf Doubleday Publishing Group.

Young, C. (1996). Africa: An interim balance sheet. *Journal of Democracy*, *7*(3), 53–68. doi:10.1353/jod.1996.0053.

Young, C. (1997). Democracy and the ethnic question in Africa. *Africa Insight*, 27(1), 4–14.

Zaid, B. (2010). *Public service television policy and national development in Morocco: Contents, production, and audiences.* Saarbrück, Germany: VDM Verlag.

Zaid, B. (2013). Moroccan media in democratic transition. In *A.* Olorunnisola & A. Douai (Eds.), *New Media Influence on Social and Political Change in Africa* (15-31). Hershey, PA: IGI-Global.

Zambia National Broadcasting Corporation. (2011, June 3). *FOI to be presented when ready.* Retrieved from http://www.znbc.co.zm/

Zapotosky, M. (2012). Craig Baxam, ex-U.S. soldier, charged with trying to aid terror group al-Shabab. *The Washington Post.* Retrieved February 1, 2012, from http://www.washingtonpost.com/local/craig-baxam-ex-us-soldier-charged-with-trying-to-aid-terror-group-al-shabab/2012/01/09/gIQAJvMbmP_story.html

Zayani, M. (2008). The challenges and limits of universalist concepts: Problematizing public opinion and a mediated Arab public sphere. *Middle East Journal of Culture and Communication*, *1*, 60–79. doi:10.1163/187398608X317423.

Zegeye, A., & Harris, R. L. (Eds.). (2003). *Media, identity and the public sphere in post-Apartheid South Africa.* Leiden, The Netherlands: Brill Publishers.

Zembylas, M. (2009). ICT for education, development, and social justice: Some theoretical issues. In Vrasidas, C., Zembylas, M., & Glass, G. V. (Eds.), *ICT for Education, Development, and Social Justice* (pp. 17–29). Charlotte, NC: Information Age.

Zetter, K. (2011, March 5). TED 2011: Wael Ghonim — Voice of Egypt's revolution. *Wired.* Retrieved January 13, 2013, from http://www.wired.com/epicenter/2011/03/wael-ghonim-at-ted/

Zhao, D., & Rosson, M. B. (2009). How and why people Twitter: The role that micro-blogging plays in informal communication at work. *Human Factors*, 243-252. ACM. Retrieved January 13, 2013, from http://portal.acm.org/citation.cfm?id=1531710

Zheng, Y., & Wu, G. (2005). Information technology, public space and collective action in China. *Comparative Political Studies*, *38*, 507–536. doi:10.1177/0010414004273505.

Ziegler, D., & Asante, M. (1992). *Thunder and Silence the Mass Media in Africa.* Trenton, NJ: Africa World Press Inc..

Zimbabwe Inclusive Government Watch [Video file]. Retrieved April 17, 2012, from http://www.sokwanele.com/zigwatch

Zimdiaspora. (2010, May 9). *Job Sikhala launches massive national party.* Retrieved August 20, 2010, from http://www.zimdiaspora.com

ZIMEYE. (2010). *Gideon Gono dies.* Retrieved August 12, 2010, from http://wwwnewzimsituation.com/5415k2/breaking-news-gideon-gono-dies-htm

Zimonline.com.ac.za. (2005, February 16). *We got it wrong.* Retrieved March 15, 2010, from http://www.zimbabwesituation.com/nov26a_2004.html

Žižek, S. (2008). *The plague of fantasies.* London: Verso.

Zuckerman, E. (2006). Citizen journalism: A look at how blogging is changing the media landscape from the Congo to Korea. *Democracy Now!* Retrieved March 16, 2011, from http://www.democracynow.org/2006/5/31/citizen_journalism_a_look_at_how

Zuckerman, E. (2008). *The Kenyan middle class... or is that the digital activist class?* [Weblog]. Retrieved March 16, 2011, from http://www.ethanzuckerman.com/blog/2008/02/13/

Zuma, J. (2010). *State of the Nation Address by his Excellency JG Zuma, President of the Republic of South Africa, at the Joint Sitting of Parliament.* Cape Town, South Africa. Retrieved April 30, 2012, from http://www.info.gov.za/speeches/2010/10021119051001.htm

Zunguze, M. (2009). *Contextualizing ICT for Development in Zimbabwe: E-Knowledge for Women in Southern Africa.* Harare, Zimbabwe: EKONISA.

About the Contributors

Anthony A. Olorunnisola is Professor of Communications and head of the Department of Film/ Video & Media Studies at the College of Communications, Pennsylvania State University at University Park, USA. He teaches undergraduate and graduate courses that include World Media Systems and Comparative Theories of Press Systems and has published severally on media in African transitional societies. His numerous publications include *Media in South Africa after Apartheid* (2006); *Media and Communications Industries in Nigeria: Impacts of Neoliberal Reforms between 1999 and 2007* (2009); *Political Economy of Media Transformation in South Africa* (2011), co-edited with Keyan Tomaselli. He serves on the editorial boards of seven academic journals and has been guest-editor of special issues of the *Journal of Communication and Language Arts* and the *International Journal of Social and Management Science* --both issues focused on aspects of media and political culture in Africa. He was a William J. Fulbright fellow in Nigeria (2005-2006) and had been visiting professor at the Lagos State University and the University of Ibadan, Nigeria respectively. Email: axo8@psu.edu.

Aziz Douai is an Assistant Professor of Communication at the University of Ontario Institute of Technology, Canada. His research focuses on new media and activism, Arab media and democracy, global media and international conflict, among other areas of international communications. Dr. Douai's publications have appeared in *The Journal of International Communication, The Global Media Journal, First Monday, The Journal of Arab & Muslim Media Research, Arab Reform Bulletin, International Communication Research Journal,* and *The Westminster Papers in Communication and Culture.* His most recent article, "Commenting in the online Arab public sphere: Debating the Swiss minaret ban and the 'Ground Zero' mosque online," was recently published in *The Journal of Computer Mediated Communication.* Email: Aziz.Douai@uoit.ca.

* * *

Oluwabukola Adelaja is a Nigerian and Australian lawyer with a background in legal research and media/technology law. Oluwabukola currently works for the law firm King & Wood Mallesons as a Knowledge Consultant focusing on legal research/training in various fields of dispute resolution, holds a Master's degree in Media and Technology Law from the University of New South Wales in Australia and is currently working towards a PhD in the area of social media regulation in Africa. Email: bukolaadelaja@yahoo.com.au.

Ufuoma Akpojivi is a Postdoctoral Fellow at the North West University, South Africa. He is currently looking at attitudes and perceptions of Generation Y students toward information privacy using loyalty cards, and mobile advertisement. His research interests cut across but are not limited to media policy, new media and political participation, citizens empowerment and disempowerment, democratization processes in emerging democracies, public relations, and advertising. He has presented papers at both national and international conferences and has numerous publications to his credit. Email: fuoteg@yahoo.com.

Tendai Chari is a lecturer in the Media Studies Department at the University of Venda, South Africa. He is studying for a doctorate in Media Studies at the University of Witwatersrand in South Africa. Previously, he lectured at the University of Zimbabwe where he coordinated the Media Programme, the Zimbabwe Open University, the National University of Science and Technology, (Zimbabwe) and Fort Hare University (South Africa). His research interests are online media, political communication, media representation, and media ethics. His other publications have appeared in the *Journal of African Media Studies*, *African Identities*, *Global Media Journal*, and *Ecquid-Novi: Journal of African Media Studies*. Email: tendai.chari@yahoo.com.

Pamela Chepngetich-Omanga is a Junior Fellow at the Bayreuth International Graduate School of African Studies, at the University of Bayreuth in Germany. Her research interests are in the general scope of representation, Gender and Race studies in the Media. Her current project reflects on the dynamics of self representations of Refugees with a specific focus on photographic representations of refugees in Kenya's Daadab Camp.

R. Bennett Furlow is a doctoral candidate in Religious Studies at Arizona State University and a research associate at the Center for Strategic Communication. His work is primarily focused on religious extremist groups and the relationship between religion and politics. His doctoral dissertation deals with the development of Islamism in Somalia from the colonial period to the present. Email: Bennett. Furlow@asu.edu.

Heather Gilberds is a doctoral candidate in the School of Journalism and Communication at Carleton University. Heather's research aims to understand the nature of activists' engagement with development institutions, and takes a critical look at the production and dissemination of knowledge in the context of media and communication for development. Her doctoral research explores issues related to community media activism, appropriate technology, and North-South partnerships in development initiatives. Email: heathergilberds@gmail.com.

Kennedy Javuru is a Ugandan born UK-based journalist and academic. He has extensive experience in both mainstream and community media. He has produced television documentary programs for Channel4 and BBC televisions. His research interests are in the areas of alternative journalism, new media, community media, and ICTs for development. He has consulted for UNESCO, UNICEF, DFID, Development Media International (DMI), and various civil society organizations around the world. Email: javken@hotmail.com.

Bellarminus Gildas Kakpovi is a PhD Student from the Department of Information and Communication Sciences at Université Libre de Bruxelles. His areas of research are hybrid, from political science to information and communication science. His PhD research is about political communication in Benin. He earned his first Master's in Media Management at Université Senghor d'Alexandrie (Egypt), and his second one in Political Science at Université Catholique de Louvain (UCL) in Belgium. He previously worked as a journalist at Radio Tokpa and Office de Radiodiffusion et Télévision du Bénin (ORTB). Email: Bellarminus.Kakpovi@ulb.ac.be.

Twange Kasoma has a PhD in Media and Society with emphasis in International and Development Communication from the University of Oregon. She is an Assistant Professor of Mass Communications at Emory & Henry College, Virginia. Classes she teaches include: International Communication, Media and Society, Mass Media Research Methods, and Reporting, Writing and Editing. She also offers a study abroad course to her native country Zambia, where students learn through hands-on experience about journalistic practice in Africa. Her research has focused on journalistic professionalism and ethics, development reporting, media regulation, and the role of the media in African society. Email: tkasoma@ehc.edu.

Sahar Khamis is an Assistant Professor in the Department of Communication at the University of Maryland, College Park. She is an expert on Arab and Muslim media and the former Head of the Mass Communication and Information Science Department in Qatar University. Dr. Khamis holds a PhD in Mass Media and Cultural Studies from the University of Manchester in England. She is the co-author of the book: *Islam Dot Com: Contemporary Islamic Discourses in Cyberspace*, Palgrave Macmillan, New York, 2009. Email: skhamis@umd.edu.

Timothy Kituri was born in Kenya where he completed his first degree, a Bachelor of Arts in Communication specializing in Public Relations from Daystar University. After a short stint as a Public Relations Officer at Pan Africa Insurance, Tim left Kenya and moved to Canada. Tim completed his second degree, a Bachelor of Commerce in Marketing at Saint Mary's University in Halifax, Nova Scotia. After seven years in Nova Scotia, Tim moved to Victoria, B.C., where he completed his Master's in Professional Communication with a Specialization in International and Intercultural Communication from Royal Roads University in Victoria, B.C. Tim is currently working at Royal Roads University in the Marketing Department as an Education Advisor and he is also working on a Graduate Certificate in Executive Coaching. Email: Timothy.Kituri@gmail.com.

Ullamaija Kivikuru is Emerita Professor of Journalism from the University of Helsinki, Finland. Her main research interests have been in media and democracy and development communication. She has worked as a professional journalist for more than a dozen years. After returning to the university, she has taught at the University of Helsinki and Tanzania School of Journalism (now School of Journalism and Mass Communication, University of Dar es Salaam), plus visited several eastern and southern African university departments where she was responsible for teaching journalism and media studies courses. Email: ullamaija.kivikuru@helsinki.fi.

Brandie Martin is a Doctoral Fellow in the College of Communications at The Pennsylvania State University. Her research interests include the areas of telecommunications policy, Internet governance, and the role of information and communication technologies in global development. Brandie has published articles in *Telecommunications Policy, Information Technologies & International Development, Communications & Strategies,* and *Telematics and Informatics.* Brandie graduated from Iowa State University in 2010 with an M.S. in Journalism and Mass Communication with a minor in Technology and Social Change. She will graduate with a PhD in Mass Communications from The Pennsylvania State University in 2013. Email: ms.brandiemartin@gmail.com.

Nhamo Anthony Mhiripiri is a Senior Lecturer in Media and Society Studies at the Midlands State University in Zimbabwe. He attained his M.A. in Communication and Media Studies from the University of Zimbabwe, and a PhD in Cultural and Media Studies from the University of KwaZulu-Natal, where he also did his Post-Doctoral Fellowship. He has a wide range of interests, including critical political economy of the media, film and video studies, visual anthropology, and critical media theory. He is also a published poet and short story writer. Email: nhamoanthony@yahoo.com.

Brilliant Mhlanga holds a PhD from the University of Westminster. He is currently a member of the Mass Media and Communications Group & a Lecturer in Media Cultures at the University of Hertfordshire, and remains affiliated to the National University of Science & Technology (NUST), Zimbabwe. He is currently working on a number of topics, among them a book titled: *Bondage of Boundaries & the 'Toxic Other' in Postcolonial Africa: The Northern Problem & Identity Politics Today,* and another project provisionally titled: *On the Banality of Evil: Cultural Particularities & Genocide in Africa.* His research interests include: media and development communication, community radio, ethnic minority media, ethnicity, nationalism and postcolonial studies, media policies & political economy of the media. Email: bsigabadem@gmail.com.

Mohamed Ben Moussa is a Post-Doctoral Fellow at McGill University in Montreal, Canada. He received a PhD in Communication from Concordia University, Montreal. He also holds an M.A. in Communication from The University of Leeds, UK. His research interests include new media and social movements, social media and political change, international communication, and media and development. His work appeared or is forthcoming in *Westminster Papers in Communication and Culture, Arab Media and Society, Canadian Journal of Communication,* among others. Email: mohamed.benmoussa@mail.mcgill.ca.

Lusike Lynete Mukhongo has a PhD in Communication Studies (Moi University, 2010). She is a Lecturer of Media and Politics in Moi University, Kenya. Her research interests include media and governance; human rights; and gender and armed conflicts. She is widely published in media, ethnic conflicts, and political mobilization in Africa. Her most recent publication: *Human Rights Violation of the Internally Displaced Persons (IDPs),* published in *African Ecclesial Review* (AFER). Email: Lusikem@gmail.com.

Bruce Mutsvairo won a Netherlands Institute of Southern Africa scholarship to study at the Cardiff School of Journalism (Cardiff University) in the UK, where he completed a Master of Arts (M.A.) in International Journalism in 2005. He worked as a professional journalist for the Associated Press en route to earning another postgraduate fellowship to pursue a Master of Philosophy (MPhil) in International Politics at the University of Hull, UK, before taking up his PhD studies at Leiden University. He has taught Journalism and Academic Writing in English at various Universities, including Webster University, Emerson College, University of Mississippi's Meek School of Journalism, and New Media and Amsterdam University College. He currently conducts research on the impact of citizen journalism on the democratization of sub-Saharan African countries at the University of Twente, The Netherlands. Email: B.Mutsvairo@auc.nl.

Ayobami Ojebode holds a PhD in Development Communication from the University of Ibadan, Nigeria. His research interest is in media, democracy, and development. He has published in numerous reputable outlets. Currently the Head of the Department of Communication and Language Arts at the University of Ibadan, Dr. Ojebode has enjoyed several visiting/research scholarships in leading universities in Europe and the United States. Email: ayo.ojebode@gmail.com.

Duncan Omanga is a Junior Fellow at the Bayreuth International Graduate School of Graduate Studies (BIGSAS). He is also a PhD candidate at the Bayreuth University Media Studies Department. His research interests are mainly on the media in Africa with a bias towards how both new and old media relate to terrorism, gender, political change, and popular culture. Email: ankodani@yahoo.com.

Auma Churchill Moses Otieno is a pioneer online journalist in Kenya. Otieno is the Managing Editor for Digital at Nation Media Group, Eastern Africa's largest media house. He has over 10 years experience in content production for digital platforms and has led newsroom change for new media. He holds a Master of Philosophy degree in Communication Studies and a Bachelor of Science degree in Communications and Public Relations, both from Moi University. He also has a diploma in Journalism from the St Augustine's University of Tanzania and was a Fellow in Online Journalism at the New York University. Email: cotieno@gmail.com.

Terje S. Skjerdal (PhD) is Associate Professor at NLA University College, Kristiansand, Norway. He has previously served as Academic Coordinator for the M.A. programme in Journalism at Addis Ababa University, Ethiopia. His research has lately dealt with the phenomenon of competing loyalties among journalists in the Ethiopian state media. He has published various articles on African media research, and serves on the advisory boards of *African Communication Research*, *Ecquid Novi: African Journalism Studies*, and *Journal of African Media Studies*. Email: terje.skjerdal@nla.no.

Irina Turner is a qualified Arts Manager (Potsdam University of Applied Sciences, Germany) and holds a M.A. degree in Media Theory and Practice from the University of Cape Town, South Africa. She is currently completing her PhD project at the Bayreuth International Graduate School of African Studies (BIGSAS) at Bayreuth University, Germany. As an affiliate to SACOMM, South African Communication Association, Irina's research interest lies in interdisciplinary approaches combining aspects of Cultural and Media Studies with Linguistics to study society, culture, and language in post-apartheid South Africa. Her focus is on questions of politics, gender, and language change. Since 2005, Irina has been working as an administrator with a focus on Human Resources and Development in the academic, NGO, and private sectors in South Africa and Germany. She is also an experienced tutor for Media Studies and currently lectures as the chair of African Language Studies at Bayreuth University. Email: turner.irina@gmail.com.

Bouziane Zaid was born in Casablanca, Morocco. He obtained his PhD (2009) in Communication from the University of South Florida. His research interests are in the areas of media law and policy, public service broadcasting, development communication, and critical media studies. He is author of *Public Service Television Policy and National Development in Morocco: Contents, Production, and Audiences*, and co-author of *Mapping Digital Media: Morocco*. Zaid now works as an Assistant Professor and Chair of the Communication Studies Program and serves as the Undergraduate Program Coordinator at the School of Humanities and Social Sciences at Al Akhawayn University in Ifrane, Morocco. Email: B.Zaid@aui.ma.

Index

A

Africa Independent Television (AIT) 95
African Media Barometer (AMB) 359, 373-374
African National Congress (ANC) 121
African Renaissance 172, 185
African Telecommunications Union (ATU) 329
Agence France-Presse (AFP) 132
Al-Qaeda 12, 285, 287, 289, 295
Al-Shabaab 11-12, 241-242, 246-253, 285-295, 297, 428
Alternative Media 51-53, 58, 61-63, 191, 232, 257-259, 269, 361, 366, 369, 374, 379, 388-389, 398, 400-401, 415, 420, 430-431, 438
alternative public sphere 379
Arab spring 1-2, 11-12, 14, 28, 202, 222, 235, 241-242, 244, 275, 277, 319, 321-325, 328, 331, 333, 336, 341, 350-354, 370, 402, 406-408, 426, 428, 432, 435-439
assimilationism 162
Associated Press (AP) 132
autocentric development 119

B

Bantu Radio Station 147
British Broadcasting Corporation (BBC) 41, 150
businification 168-169, 171-172, 175, 177, 179-181

C

Central African Republic 7, 34
citizen journalism 188-189, 192-193, 200, 254, 272, 357, 362, 398-400, 405-406, 410, 420
citizen monitoring 412
civic engagement 12, 188-189, 192, 200, 239, 282, 284, 371, 407

civil liberty 2, 4, 15-16, 69-70, 72, 353, 436
collective action 205-206, 212-215, 218-219, 221-236, 238, 259, 282, 325, 371, 378, 419
Commission of Inquiry into the Post-Election Violence (CIPEV) 73
Committee to Protect Journalists (CPJ) 36
communication landscape 188, 437
communicative empowerment 258, 268
community owned 161-162
confrontational strategy 51-53, 58
Congress of South African Trade Unions (CO-SATU) 7
consumption habits 379-381, 384, 389-391
corporate values 181
crime rate 346
Critical discourse analysis (CDA) 68
cultural media 150
cultural pluralism 8, 147-149, 160, 163
cyberactivism 11, 26, 188, 192, 198, 200-201
cyber activists 203, 210-212
Cybercrime 319, 330, 434-435
cyberterrorism 287
cyberwarfare 287

D

Deliberative Democracy 354, 357, 361, 375, 420
democracy analysts 3
Democratic Association of Moroccan Women (ADFM) 234
democratic consolidation 8, 87-89, 95, 117
Democratic governance 1-2, 4-6, 9, 11, 117, 336-337, 339-342, 344, 350, 352-353, 401, 435
democratic journalism 57
Democratic Republic of Congo 34, 382
democratic transition 5, 15-16, 24-25, 28, 98-99, 222, 440